Data-Centric Systems and Applications

For further volumes:
http://www.springer.com/series/5258

Roberto De Virgilio • Francesco Guerra
Yannis Velegrakis

Editors

Semantic Search over the Web

 Springer

Editors

Roberto De Virgilio
Department of informatics and Automation
University Roma Tre
Rome
Italy

Francesco Guerra
University of Modena and Reggio Emilia
Modena
Italy

Yannis Velegrakis
University of Trento
Trento
Italy

ISBN 978-3-642-25007-1   ISBN 978-3-642-25008-8 (eBook)
DOI 10.1007/978-3-642-25008-8
Springer Heidelberg New York Dordrecht London

Library of Congress Control Number: 2012943692

ACM Computing Classification: H.3, I.2

Printed on acid-free paper

Springer is part of Springer Science+Business Media (www.springer.com)

Introduction

The Web has become the world's largest database with search being the main tool that enables organization and individuals to exploit its huge amounts of information that is freely offering. Thus, having a successful mechanism for finding and retrieving the most relevant information to a task at hand is of major importance. Traditionally, Web search has been based on textual and structural similarity. Given the set of keywords that comprise a query, the goal is to identify the documents containing all these keywords (or as many as possible). Additional information such as information from logs, references from authorities, popularity, and personalization has been extensively used to further improve the accuracy. However, one of the dimensions that has not been captured to its full extent is that of *semantics*, that is, fully understanding the meaning of the words in a query and in a document. Combining search and semantics gives birth to the idea of the *semantic search*. Semantic search can be described in a sentence as the effort of improving the accuracy of the search process by understanding the context and limiting the ambiguity.

The idea of the semantic Web is based on this goal and aims at making the semantics of the Web content machine understandable. To do so, a number of different technologies that allowed for richer modeling of the Web resources, alongside annotations describing their semantics, have been introduced. Furthermore, the semantic Web went on to create associations between different representations of the same real-world entity. These associations are either explicitly specified or derived off-line and then remain static. They allow data from many different sources to be interlinked, giving birth to the so-called linked open data cloud. Nevertheless, semantics have yet to fully penetrate existing data management solutions and become an integral part in information retrieval, analysis, integration, and data exchange techniques.

Unfortunately, the generic idea of semantic search has remained in its infancy. Existing solutions are either search engines that simply index the semantic Web data, like Sindice, or the traditional search engines enhanced with some basic form of synonym exploitation, as supported by Google and Bing. Semantic search is about using the semantics of the query terms instead of the terms themselves. This means using synonyms and related terms, providing additional materials in the answer that may be related to elements already in the result, searching not only in the content but also in the semantic annotations of the data, exploiting ontological knowledge through advanced reasoning techniques, treating the query as a natural language expression, clustering the results, offering faced browsing, etc.

All the above mean that there are currently numerous opportunities to exploit in the area of semantic search on the Web. In this work, we try to give a generic overview of the works that have been done in the field and in other related areas. However, the work should definitely not be considered as a survey. It is simply intended to provide the reader with a taste of the many different aspects of the problem and go deep in some specific technologies and solutions.

The book is divided into three parts. The first part introduces the notion of the Web of Data. It describes the different types of data that exist, their topology, and their storing and indexing techniques. It also shows how semantic links between the data can be automatically derived.

The second part is dedicated specifically to Web search. It presents different kinds of search, such as the exploratory or the path-oriented, alongside methods for efficiently implementing them. It talks about the problem of interactive query construction and also about the understanding of the keyword query semantics. Other topics include the use of uncertainty in query answering or the exploitation of ontologies. The second part concludes with some reference to Mashup technologies and the way they are affected by the semantics.

The theme of the third part of the book is Linked Data and, more specifically, how recommender system ideas can be used in the case of linked data management alongside techniques for efficient query answering.

Rome, Italy   *Roberto De Virgilio*
Modena, Italy   *Francesco Guerra*
Trento, Italy   *Yannis Velegrakis*

Contents

Part I   Introduction to Web of Data

1   **Topology of the Web of Data**   3
Christian Bizer, Pablo N. Mendes, and Anja Jentzsch

2   **Storing and Indexing Massive RDF Datasets**   31
Yongming Luo, François Picalausa, George H.L. Fletcher,
Jan Hidders, and Stijn Vansummeren

3   **Designing Exploratory Search Applications upon Web
Data Sources**   61
Marco Brambilla and Stefano Ceri

Part II   Search over the Web

4   **Path-Oriented Keyword Search Query over RDF**   81
Roberto De Virgilio, Paolo Cappellari, Antonio Maccioni,
and Riccardo Torlone

5   **Interactive Query Construction for Keyword Search on
the Semantic Web**   109
Gideon Zenz, Xuan Zhou, Enrico Minack, Wolf Siberski,
and Wolfgang Nejdl

6   **Understanding the Semantics of Keyword Queries on
Relational Data Without Accessing the Instance**   131
Sonia Bergamaschi, Elton Domnori, Francesco Guerra, Silvia
Rota, Raquel Trillo Lado, and Yannis Velegrakis

7   **Keyword-Based Search over Semantic Data**   159
Klara Weiand, Andreas Hartl, Steffen Hausmann,
Tim Furche, and François Bry

8   **Semantic Link Discovery over Relational Data** 193
     Oktie Hassanzadeh, Anastasios Kementsietsidis,
     Lipyeow Lim, Renée J. Miller, and Min Wang

9   **Embracing Uncertainty in Entity Linking** 225
     Ekaterini Ioannou, Wolfgang Nejdl, Claudia Niederée,
     and Yannis Velegrakis

10   **The Return of the Entity-Relationship Model: Ontological**
     Query Answering 255
     Andrea Calì, Georg Gottlob, and Andreas Pieris

11   **Linked Data Services and Semantics-Enabled Mashup** 283
     Devis Bianchini and Valeria De Antonellis

Part III   Linked Data Search Engines

12   **A Recommender System for Linked Data** 311
     Roberto Mirizzi, Azzurra Ragone, Tommaso Di Noia,
     and Eugenio Di Sciascio

13   **Flint: From Web Pages to Probabilistic Semantic Data** 333
     Lorenzo Blanco, Mirko Bronzi, Valter Crescenzi,
     Paolo Merialdo, and Paolo Papotti

14   **Searching and Browsing Linked Data with SWSE*** 361
     Andreas Harth, Aidan Hogan, Jürgen Umbrich,
     Sheila Kinsella, Axel Polleres, and Stefan Decker

Index 415

Contributors

Sonia Bergamaschi Dipartimento di Ingegneria dell'Informazione, Università di Modena e Reggio Emilia, Modena, Italy

Devis Bianchini Department of Electronics for Automation, University of Brescia, Brescia, Italy

Christian Bizer Web-based Systems Group, Freie Universität Berlin, Berlin, Germany

Lorenzo Blanco Dipartimento di Informatica e Automazione, Università degli Studi Roma Tre, Rome, Italy

Marco Brambilla Dipartimento di Elettronica e Informazione, Politecnico di Milano, Milano, Italy

Mirko Bronzi Dipartimento di Informatica e Automazione, Università degli Studi Roma Tre, Rome, Italy

François Bry Institute for Informatics, University of Munich, München, Germany

Andrea Calì Department of Computer Science and Information Systems, Birkbeck University of London, London, UK

Paolo Cappellari Interoperable System Group, Dublin City University, Dublin, Ireland

Stefano Ceri Dipartimento di Elettronica e Informazione, Politecnico di Milano, Milano, Italy

Valter Crescenzi Dipartimento di Informatica e Automazione, Università degli Studi Roma Tre, Rome, Italy

Valeria De Antonellis Department of Electronics for Automation, University of Brescia, Brescia, Italy

Roberto De Virgilio University Roma Tre, Rome, Italy

Tommaso Di Noia Dipartimento di Elettrotecnica ed Elettronica, Politecnico di Bari, Bari, Italy

Eugenio Di Sciascio Dipartimento di Elettrotecnica ed Elettronica, Politecnico di Bari, Bari, Italy

Stefan Decker Digital Enterprise Research Institute, National University of Ireland, Galway, Ireland

Elton Domnori Dipartimento di Ingegneria dell'Informazione, Università di Modena e Reggio Emilia, Modena, Italy

George H.L. Fletcher Department of Mathematics and Computer Science, Eindhoven University of Technology, Eindhoven, The Netherlands

Tim Furche Department of Computer Science and Institute for the Future of Computing, Oxford University, Oxford, UK

Georg Gottlob Computing Laboratory, University of Oxford, Oxford, UK

Oxford-Man Institute of Quantitative Finance, University of Oxford, Oxford, UK

Francesco Guerra Dipartimento di Economia Aziendale, Università di Modena e Reggio Emilia, Modena, Italy

Andreas Harth Karlsruhe Institute of Technology, Institute AIFB, Karlsruhe, Germany

Andreas Hartl Institute for Informatics, University of Munich, München, Germany

Oktie Hassanzadeh University of Toronto, Toronto, Ontario, Canada

Steffen Hausmann Institute for Informatics, University of Munich, München, Germany

Jan Hidders Faculty of Electrical Engineering Mathematics and Computer Science, Delft University of Technology, Delft, The Netherlands

Aidan Hogan Digital Enterprise Research Institute, National University of Ireland, Galway, Ireland

Ekaterini Ioannou University Campus – Kounoupidiana, Technical University of Crete, Chania, Greece

Anja Jentzsch Web-based Systems Group, Freie Universität Berlin, Berlin, Germany

Anastasios Kementsietsidis IBM T.J. Watson Research Center, Hawthorne, NY, USA

Sheila Kinsella Digital Enterprise Research Institute, National University of Ireland, Galway, Ireland

Lipyeow Lim University of Hawaii at Manoa, Honolulu, HI, USA

Yongming Luo Department of Mathematics and Computer Science, Eindhoven University of Technology, Eindhoven, The Netherlands

Antonio Maccioni University Roma Tre, Rome, Italy

Pablo N. Mendes Web-based Systems Group, Freie Universität Berlin, Berlin, Germany

Paolo Merialdo Dipartimento di Informatica e Automazione, Università degli Studi Roma Tre, Rome, Italy

Renée J. Miller University of Toronto, Toronto, Ontario, Canada

Enrico Minack L3S Research Center, Hannover, Germany

Roberto Mirizzi Dipartimento di Elettrotecnica ed Elettronica, Politecnico di Bari, Bari, Italy

Wolfgang Nejdl L3S Research Center, Hannover, Germany

Claudia Niederée L3S Research Center, Hannover, Germany

Paolo Papotti Dipartimento di Informatica e Automazione, Università degli Studi Roma Tre, Rome, Italy

François Picalausa Université Libre de Bruxelles, Brussels, Belgium

Andreas Pieris Department of Computer Science, University of Oxford, Oxford, UK

Axel Polleres Siemens AG Österreich, Vienna, Austria

Digital Enterprise Research Institute, National University of Ireland, Galway, Ireland

Azzurra Ragone Dipartimento di Elettrotecnica ed Elettronica, Politecnico di Bari, Bari, Italy

Exprivia S.p.A., Molfetta, BA, Italy

Silvia Rota Dipartimento di Ingegneria dell'Informazione, Università di Modena e Reggio Emilia, Modena, Italy

Wolf Siberski L3S Research Center, Hannover, Germany

Riccardo Torlone University Roma Tre, Rome, Italy

Raquel Trillo Informatica e Ing. Sistemas, Zaragoza, Spain

Jürgen Umbrich Digital Enterprise Research Institute, National University of Ireland, Galway, Ireland

Stijn Vansummeren Université Libre de Bruxelles, Brussels, Belgium

Yannis Velegrakis University of Trento, Trento, Italy

Min Wang HP Labs China, Beijing, China

Klara Weiand Institute for Informatics, University of Munich, München, Germany

Gideon Zenz L3S Research Center, Hannover, Germany

Xuan Zhou Renmin University of China, Beijing, China

Part I
Introduction to Web of Data

Chapter 1
Topology of the Web of Data

Christian Bizer, Pablo N. Mendes, and Anja Jentzsch

1.1 Introduction

The degree of structure of Web content is the determining factor for the types of functionality that search engines can provide. The more well structured the Web content is, the easier it is for search engines to understand Web content and provide advanced functionality, such as faceted filtering or the aggregation of content from multiple Web sites, based on this understanding.

Today, most Web sites are generated from structured data that is stored in relational databases. Thus, it does not require too much extra effort for Web sites to publish this structured data directly on the Web in addition to HTML pages, and thus help search engines to understand Web content and provide improved functionality.

An early approach to realize this idea and help search engines to understand Web content is Microformats,[1] a technique for marking up structured data about specific types on entities—such as tags, blog posts, people, or reviews—within HTML pages. As Microformats are focused on a few entity types, the World Wide Web Consortium (W3C) started in 2004 to standardize RDFa [1] as an alternative, more generic language for embedding any type of data into HTML pages.

Today, major search engines such as Google, Yahoo, and Bing extract Microformat and RDFa data describing products, reviews, persons, events, and recipes from Web pages and use the extracted data to improve the user's search experience. The search engines have started to aggregate structured data from different Web sites and augment their search results with these aggregated information units in the form of rich snippets which combine, for instance, data

---

[1] http://microformats.org/

C. Bizer (✉) · P.N. Mendes · A. Jentzsch
Web-based Systems Group, Freie Universität Berlin, Garystr. 21-14195 Berlin, Germany
e-mail: christian.bizer@fu-berlin.de; pablo.mendes@fu-berlin.de; anja.jentzsch@fu-berlin.de

R. De Virgilio et al. (eds.), *Semantic Search over the Web*,
Data-Centric Systems and Applications, DOI 10.1007/978-3-642-25008-8_1,
© Springer-Verlag Berlin Heidelberg 2012

describing a product with reviews of the product from different sites.[2] Another major consumer of RDFa data is Facebook which imports structured data from external Web sites once a user clicks a Facebook *Like*-button on one of these sites.[3]

The support of Microformats and RDFa by major data consumers, such as Google, Yahoo! Microsoft, and Facebook, has led to a sharp increase in the number of Web sites that embed structured data into HTML pages. According to statistics presented by Yahoo!, the number of Web pages containing RDFa data has increased by 510% between 2009 and 2010. As of October 2010, 430 million Web pages contained RDFa markup, while over 300 million of pages contained microformat data [34]. In a recent move, Google, Yahoo!, and Microsoft have jointly agreed on a set of vocabularies for describing over 200 different types of entities. Entity descriptions that are expressed using these vocabularies and are embedded into HTML pages using the Microdata or RDFa Lite syntax[4] will be equally understood by all three search engines. This move toward standardization is likely to further increase the amount of structured data being published on the Web.

Parallel to the different techniques to embed structured data into HTML pages, a set of best practices for publishing structured data directly on the Web has gotten considerable traction: Linked Data [4, 10]. The Linked Data best practices are implemented today by hundreds of data providers including the UK and US governments, media companies like the BBC and the New York Times, various national libraries, and a worldwide community of research institutions. While microformats, RDFa, and microdata focus on publishing descriptions of single, isolated entities on the Web, Linked Data focuses on making the relationships between entities explicit. Data describing relationships is published in the form of *RDF links*. RDF links can span different Web servers and connect all data that is published as Linked Data into a single global data graph [5]. As of September 2011, this data graph consists of over 31 billion edges (RDF triples) [12].

This chapter gives an overview of the topology of the Web of Data that has been created by publishing data on the Web using the Microformats, RDFa, Microdata, and Linked Data publishing techniques. Section 1.2 discusses Microformats and provides statistics about the Microformats deployment on the Web. Sections 1.3 and 1.4 cover RDFa and Microdata. Section 1.5 discusses Linked Data and gives an overview of the Linked Data deployment on the Web. For each of the four techniques, we:

1. Summarize the main features and give an overview of the history of the technique
2. Provide a syntax example which shows how data describing a person is published on the Web using the technique
3. Present deployment statistics showing the amounts and types of data currently published using the specific technique

---

[2]http://www.google.com/support/webmasters/bin/answer.py?answer=1095551

[3]http://developers.facebook.com/docs/opengraph/

[4]http://www.whatwg.org/specs/web-apps/current-work/multipage/microdata.html

The syntax examples highlight how the different techniques handle (1) the identification of entities; (2) the representation of type information—e.g., that an entity is a person; (3) the representation of literal property values, such as the name of the person; and (4) the representation of relationships between entities, such as that Peter Smith knows Paula Jones.

In order to provide an entry point for experimentation as well as for the evaluation of search engines that facilitate Web data, Sect. 1.6 gives an overview of large-scale datasets that have been crawled from the Web of Data and are publicly available for download.

1.2 Microformats

Microformats[5] (also referred to as μF) are community-driven vocabulary agreements for providing semantic markup on Web pages. The motto of the Microformats community is "designed for humans first, machines second." Each Microformat defines a vocabulary and a syntax for applying the vocabulary to describe the content on Web pages. A Microformat's syntax commonly specifies which properties are required or optional and which classes should be nested under one another.

Microformats emerged as a community effort, in contrast to other semantic markup technologies which sought the route of a standardization body. Early contributors to Microformats include Kevin Marks, Tantek Çelik, and Mark Pilgrim, among others. The first implementations of Microformats date back to 2003,[6] when they were mostly found in the blogosphere. One early microformat, the XHTML Friends Network (XFN),[7] allowed one to represent human relationships between blog owners through the use of marked-up hyperlinks between blogs. In 2004 followed *XOXO* for representing outlines in XHTML; *VoteLinks* for specifying endorsement and disagreement links; *rel-license* for embedding links to licenses; *hCard* for representing people, companies, and organizations; and *hCalendar* for representing calendars and events. The year of 2005 saw the introduction of *hReview*, for embedding reviews (e.g., of products or services) in Web documents. Many other microformats have been introduced since then, amounting to more than 25 drafts and specifications available from http://microformats.org.

It is argued that the simplistic approach offered by Microformats eases the learning curve and therefore lowers the entry barrier for newcomers. On the other hand, due to the lack of a unified syntax for all microformats, consuming structured data from Microformats requires the development of specialized parsers for each format. This is a reflection of the Microformats approach to address specific use

---

[5]http://microformats.org/

[6]http://microformats.org/wiki/history-of-microformats

[7]http://gmpg.org/xfn/

```
<head  profile ="http ://gmpg. org / xfn /11" >
<head  profile ="http :// microformats . org / profile / hcard">
...
<div  class ="vcard">
 <a  class ="url  fn"  href ="http :// example .com/ Peter . html">
    Peter  Smith </a>
 <a  rel ="met  acquaintance "
        href ="http :// example .com/ Paula . html">Paula  Jones </a>.
 </ div >
```

Fig. 1.1 Microformats representation of the example entity description

cases, in contrast to RDFa and Microdata (presented in the following sections) which support the representation of any kind of data.[8]

1.2.1   Microformats Syntax

Microformats consist of a definition of a vocabulary (names for classes and properties), as well as a set of rules (e.g., required properties, correct nesting of elements). These rules largely rely on existing HTML/XHTML attributes for inserting markup. One example is the HTML attribute `class`, commonly used as a style sheet selector, which is reused in microformats for describing properties and types of entities.

Figure 1.1 shows an HTML snippet containing the Microformat representation of our example data describing Peter Smith. The `vcard` added in line 4 is a root class name indicating the presence of an hCard. Since hCards are used for representing contact information about people, organizations, etc., one could assume that an entity of one of those types is present in that page. The properties of an hCard are represented by class names added to HTML elements inside the hCard. The example in Fig. 1.1 shows the properties `url` (Peter's home page) and `fn` (Peter's full name). The markup also states that Peter knows Paula through the use of the properties `met` and `acquaintance` defined in the XFN microformat. An hCard parser should be aware that the `url` property refers to the value of the `href` attribute, while `fn` refers to the value of the child text of the HTML element. Such parsing instructions are described within each microformat specification.

The microformats community encourages mixing microformats and reusing existing formats when creating new ones. Naming conflicts between formats are not handled through the microformats technology, but rather through a social process[9] of creating microformat specifications.

---

[8]http://microformats.org/2011/02/11/whats-next-for-microformats
[9]http://microformats.org/wiki/process

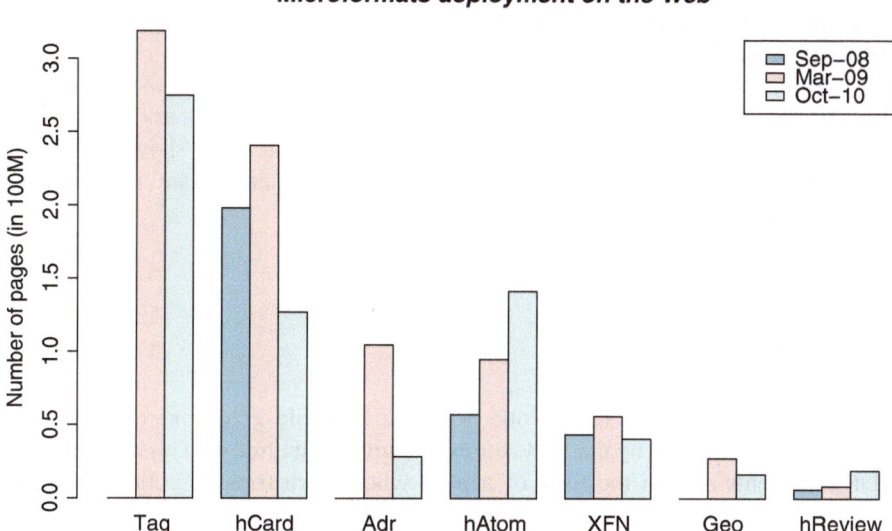

Fig. 1.2 Microformats deployment on the Web, according to [34]

1.2.2 Microformats Deployment on the Web

In June 2006, Yahoo! Local announced the deployment of hCalendar, hCard, and hReview microformats on almost all business listings, search results, events, and reviews [16]. Yahoo! Europe followed in 2008 with a deployment of approximately 26 million more annotated pages describing merchants in classified listings, resulting on the largest deployment of the hListing format at that time.

These developments were followed with the adoption from the data consuming side. In March 2008, Yahoo! Search announced that it was indexing semantic markup including hCard, hCalendar, hReview, hAtom, and XFN [17]. In May 2009, Google also announced that they would be parsing the hCard, hReview, and hProduct microformats and using them to populate search result pages [20].

Since then, a number of major Web sites have started to support microformats. For instance, Facebook publishes approximately 39 million event pages annotated with hCalendar, Yelp.com adds hReview and hCard to all of their listings (about 56 million businesses), and Wikipedia templates are able to automatically generate microformats such as geo, hCard, and hCalendar markup.[10]

The most recent publicly available statistics about the deployment of Microformats on the Web were produced by Yahoo! Research [34] and presented in January 2011. Figure 1.2 shows the deployment of some of the most common microformats

---

[10]http://en.wikipedia.org/wiki/Category:Templates_generating_microformats

on the Web. The results are based on an analysis of a sample of 12 billion Web pages indexed by Yahoo! Search. Results are displayed for samples obtained in 2008, 2009, and 2010.

Microformats commonly associated with blogs are prevalent in this sample (hAtom, tag, hCard). Besides hAtom and hReview, the numbers do not show a trend of stable increase and, in some cases (e.g., hCard, adr, xfn, geo), show a reduction on the number of deployments since 2008. The microformats tag, adr, and geo were not counted in 2008 and therefore are missing.

1.3 RDFa

The resource description framework (RDF) is a simple graph-based data model which is recommended by the W3C for exchanging structured data on the Web [31]. RDF represents data in the form of triples, where each triple is composed by an entity identifier, a property, and a value for this property.

The RDFa [1] serialization format for embedding RDF data into HTML pages was proposed in 2004 by Mark Birbeck as a way to "make more of the information that is contained within HTML-family documents available to RDF tools." The initial note was presented to the Semantic Web Interest Group in 2004 and developed jointly with the XHTML 2 Working Group into a W3C Recommendation published in October 2008.

RDFa allows one to embed RDF triples within the HTML *document object model (DOM)*. A detailed introduction to RDFa is given in the W3C RDFa Primer [1]. In contrast to the Microformats approach, where each Microformat defines its syntax and vocabulary, RDFa provides a single syntax which can be used together with any vocabulary or mixture of terms from multiple vocabularies.

1.3.1 RDFa Syntax

The RDFa syntax specifies how HTML elements may be annotated with entity identifiers, entity types, string properties, and relationship properties. Figure 1.3 shows the RDFa representation of the example data about Peter Smith. The HTML attribute @about indicates that the current HTML element describes the entity identified by the URI reference http://example.com/Peter. The HTML attribute @rel specifies a relationship property between the anchor HTML element and the target URL. In the example, it uses the property foaf:knows to state that Peter knows Paula. For string properties, the attribute @property is introduced, as shown by usage of foaf:name to express Peter's name.

A central idea of RDFa is the support for multiple, decentralized, independent, extensible vocabularies, in contrast to the community-driven centralized management of microformats.

```
<html xmlns="http://www.w3.org/1999/xhtml"
       xmlns:rdf="http://www.w3.org/1999/02/22-rdf-syntax-ns#"
       xmlns:foaf="http://xmlns.com/foaf/0.1/">
 ...
   <div about="http://example.com/Peter" typeof="foaf:Person">
   <span property="foaf:name">Peter Smith</span> knows
   <a rel="foaf:knows" href="http://example.com/Paula">
       Paula Jones </a>.
   </div>
 ...
```

Fig. 1.3 RDFa representation of the example entity description

RDFa annotations are encouraged to directly reuse existing RDF vocabularies. However, for cases where no suitable vocabulary exists, data providers can define their own vocabularies, which in turn can be reused by third parties. Since anybody can define their own vocabularies, the possibility of naming conflicts raises an important concern as vocabularies get deployed on Web scale. This issue is handled in RDFa through the use of URI references for uniquely identifying vocabulary terms. Each vocabulary is identified by a URI that represents a namespace, and classes and properties within this vocabulary are prefixed with the vocabulary's namespace. For example, the Friend-of-a-Friend (FOAF) vocabulary is identified by the namespace http://xmlns.com/foaf/0.1/, and the property "homepage" is identified by http://xmlns.com/foaf/0.1/homepage. If somebody else has another property called "homepage" whose definition is incompatible with FOAF, they can place it in their own namespace (e.g., http://example.com/homepage).

As we have seen in the example, RDFa also supports the usage of URI references to identify real-world entities, such as Peter Smith, and provides for representing relationships between URI-identified entities (Peter and Paula). As URI references are globally unique, it is also possible to represent cross-server references and thus represent RDF links (see Sect. 1.5 on Linked Data) using RDFa.

1.3.2 RDFa Deployment on the Web

In March 2010, one of the major electronics retailers in the USA, BestBuy, started to publish 450,000 item descriptions using RDFa and the Good Relations vocabulary [27] for representing product data [36].

In April 2010, Facebook announced[11] the Open Graph Protocol (http://ogp. me/), an RDFa-based markup for embedding structured data about people, places, organizations, products, films, as well as other entity types into HTML pages. Whenever a Facebook user clicks the *Like* button on a page that is marked up using

---

[11]http://developers.facebook.com/blog/post/377/

Table 1.1 Number of sites (second-level domains) publishing RDFa data divided by vocabulary

Vocabulary	Number of sites
Dublin Core (dc)	344,545
Open Graph Protocol (ogp)	177,761
Creative Commons (cc)	37,890
Google's Rich Snippets Vocabulary (rich)	6,083
Friend-of-a-Friend (foaf)	2,545
Semantically-Interlinked Online Communities (sioc)	1,633
Electronic Business Cards (vcard)	1,349
Good Relations (goodrel)	488
Reviews (rev)	369
CommonTag (tag)	272
iCalendar Schema (ical)	62

the Open Graph Protocol, Facebook imports the structured data from this page and uses it to describe the entity within other internal Facebook pages. Initial publishers using Open Graph Protocol included IMDB, Microsoft, NHL, Posterous, Rotten Tomatoes, TIME, and Yelp.[12]

In October 2010, another major online retailer, Overstock.com, announced the addition of RDFa to nearly one million pages.[13] Other prominent publishers of RDF include MySpace, BBC music, and Newsweek.

The RDFa usage statistics published by Yahoo! Research show that the usage of RDFa has increased between March 2009 and October 2010 from 72 to 430 million Web pages (a 510% increase) [34].

In June 2011, the W3C collected data[14] about the most used RDFa vocabularies in order to develop a default profile for RDFa 1.1.[15] Table 1.1 shows the number of sites (second-level domains) using each vocabulary. The numbers are again based on a crawl from Yahoo!.

The Dublin Core vocabulary is generally used on the Web to describe authorship of Web pages, and therefore is the most commonly used vocabulary. Facebook's Open Graph Protocol has appeared in the second position, confirming that the company's endorsement of RDFa has been one of the factors in the rise of adoption. Licensing information through Creative Commons markup is the third most common use of RDFa, according to these statistics. Product information, reviews, and offers are other prominent types of information in this sample and are represented using the Google's Rich Snippets, Good Relations, and Reviews vocabularies. Social networking information is also well represented in the sample through SIOC and FOAF.

---

[12]http://rdfa.info/2010/04/22/facebook-adopts-rdfa/

[13]http://rdfa.info/2010/10/07/overstock-com-adds-rdfa-to-nearly-one-million-pages/

[14]http://www.w3.org/2010/02/rdfa/profile/data/

[15]http://www.w3.org/profile/rdfa-1.1

1.4   Microdata

Microdata[16] is an alternative proposal for embedding structured data into Web pages which was initially presented as part of the HTML 5 standardization effort in 2009. The development of HTML5 has been led by the WHATWG, a community of individuals from corporations such as Apple, Opera Software, and Mozilla Foundation whose interest is to evolve HTML and related technologies. Since May 2007, the W3C HTML Working Group decided to take WHATWG's HTML5 specification as a starting point for the next major version of HTML. Microdata is an attempt to provide a simpler alternative to RDFa and Microformats. It defines five new HTML attributes (as compared to zero for Microformats and eight for RDFa), provides a unified syntax (in contrast to Microformats), and allows for the usage of any vocabularies (similarly to RDFa).

The proposal has gained substantial attention since the announcement by Google, Microsoft, and Yahoo! that they are collaborating on *Schema.org*, a collection of vocabularies for marking up content on Web pages [15]. Although the *Schema.org* vocabularies can be used in either RDFa or microdata markup, the initiative has chosen microdata as its preferred serialization syntax.[17]

Concerns were raised about the fact that the W3C currently has two draft specifications (Microdata and RDFa) with the same objective, which prompted a decision from the W3C to separate the Microdata from the HTML5 specification.[18]

1.4.1   Microdata Syntax

Figure 1.4 shows how our example data about Peter Smith is represented using *Schema.org* vocabulary terms and encoded using the microdata syntax.

Microdata consists of a group of name–value pairs. The groups are called items, and each name–value pair is a property. In order to mark up an item, the `itemscope` attribute is applied to an HTML element (line 1). The `itemid` attribute allows a Microdata item to be associated with a unique identifier (line 1). To add a property to an item, the `itemprop` attribute is used on one of the item's descendants (lines 2–3).

Microdata items can also be described with an entity type—e.g., on line 1 `http://schema.org/Person`—which helps consumers to make sense and properly display information. Types are identified using URI references. The item type is given as the value of an `itemtype` attribute on the same element as the `itemscope` attribute.

---

[16]http://www.whatwg.org/specs/web-apps/current-work/multipage/microdata.html

[17]http://schema.org/docs/gs.html

[18]http://lists.w3.org/Archives/Public/public-html/2010Jan/att-0218/issue-76-decision.html

```
<div  itemscope  itemtype ="http :// schema . org / Person "
                      itemid ="http :// example .com/ Peter">
    <span  itemprop ="name"> Peter  Smith </span>
    <a  href ="http :// example .com/ Paula "
                      itemprop ="knows"> Paula  Jones </a>
</div>
```

Fig. 1.4 Microdata representation of the example entity description

The value of an item property can itself be another item with its own set of properties. For example, Peter Smith knows a Paula Jones, who is also of type Person (line 3). In order to specify that the value of a property is another item, a new `itemscope` has to begin immediately after the corresponding `itemprop`.

Items can use nondescendant properties via the attribute `itemref`. This attribute is a list of the `ids` of properties or nested items elsewhere on the page.

Tool support for Microdata is currently not yet widespread. No major release of a Web browser[19] supports the Microdata DOM API. However, the MicrodataJS Javascript library can be used to emulate its behavior. Nevertheless, the support for Microdata is expected to rise quickly. The upcoming Opera 12 browser has announced support for Microdata. Moreover, Google provides a Rich Snippets testing tool which can be used for validating Microdata markup.

1.4.2 *Microdata Deployment on the Web*

One of the major drivers in Microdata deployment on the Web is the Schema.org initiative. The *Schema.org* vocabularies cover over 220 different types of entities including creative works, events, organizations, persons, places, products, offers, and reviews.

For now, *Schema.org* is not aimed at covering the whole variety and richness of structured data on the Web. Therefore, it offers an extension mechanism that lets Web developers extend the existing vocabularies. By extending *Schema.org* schemas and using extensions to mark up data, search applications can at least partially understand the markup and use the data appropriately. Also, if the extended schema gains adoption and proves useful to search applications, search engines have announced that they may start using this data. Extensions that gain significant adoption on the Web may be moved into the core *Schema.org* vocabulary.

As Microdata is still in its early days, it is difficult to get solid statistics about Microdata deployment. One source of statistics is the Sindice search engine which has crawled 329.13 million documents and thus operates on a much smaller corpus than the 12 billion page corpus used for generating the Yahoo! statistics. As of July 2011, Sindice has crawled 2,085,050 documents containing Microdata and using

---

[19]As of the time of writing Opera 11.60 is the only stable release that supports the Microdata DOM API.

Table 1.2 Schema.org type usage according to Sindice

Vocabulary term	Number of documents
http://schema.org/Product	1,253,153
http://schema.org/Book	264,918
http://schema.org/Place	201,622
http://schema.org/Person	191,078
http://schema.org/Offer	136,630
http://schema.org/Organization	17,980
http://schema.org/LocalBusiness	13,300
http://schema.org/Recipe	4,815
http://schema.org/Review	3,519
http://schema.org/Event	442

terms from the *Schema.org* vocabularies. The pages originate from around 100 Web sites. Table 1.2 shows the amount of entities for the ten most popular *Schema.org* entity types as currently indexed by Sindice. Due to the recent interest in microdata following the announcement of *Schema.org*, these numbers are expected to rise significantly.

1.5   Linked Data

In contrast to Microformats, RDFa, and Microdata, which provide for embedding structured data into HTML pages, the term *Linked Data* refers to a set of best practices for publishing structured data directly on the Web [10, 25]. These best practices were introduced by Tim Berners-Lee in his Web architecture note *Linked Data* [4] and have become known as the *Linked Data principles*. These principles are the following:

1. Use URIs as names for things.
2. Use HTTP URIs, so that people can look up those names.
3. When someone looks up a URI, provide useful information, using recommended standards (RDF, SPARQL).
4. Include links to other URIs, so that they can discover more things.

The first Linked Data principle advocates using URI references to identify not just Web documents and digital content but also real-world objects and abstract concepts. These may include tangible things, such as people, places, and cars, or those that are more abstract, such as the relationship type of *knowing somebody*, the set of all green cars in the world, or the color green itself. This principle can be seen as extending the scope of the Web from online resources to encompass any object or concept in the world.

The HTTP protocol is the Web's universal access mechanism. In the classic Web, HTTP URIs are used to combine globally unique identification with a simple, well-understood retrieval mechanism. Thus, the second Linked Data principle advocates the use of HTTP URIs to identify objects and abstract concepts, enabling these URIs to be *dereferenced* (i.e., looked up) over the HTTP protocol into a description of the identified object or concept.

In order to enable a wide range of different applications to process Web content, it is important to agree on standardized content formats. The agreement on HTML as a dominant document format was an important factor that allowed the Web to scale. The third Linked Data principle therefore advocates the use of a single data model for publishing structured data on the Web—the resource description framework (RDF), a simple graph-based data model that has been designed for use in the context of the Web [31]. For serializing RDF data, the RDF/XML syntax [2] is widely used in the Linked Data context.

The fourth Linked Data principle advocates the use of hyperlinks to connect not only Web documents but also any type of thing. For example, a hyperlink may be set between a person and a place or between a place and a company. In contrast to the classic Web where hyperlinks are largely untyped, hyperlinks that connect things in a Linked Data context have types which describe the relationship between the things. For example, a hyperlink of the type *friend of* may be set between two people, or a hyperlink of the type *based near* may be set between a person and a place. Hyperlinks in the Linked Data context are called *RDF links* in order to distinguish them from hyperlinks between classic Web documents.

Across the Web, many different servers are responsible for answering requests attempting to dereference HTTP URIs in many different namespaces and (in a Linked Data context) returning RDF descriptions of the resources identified by these URIs. Therefore, in a Linked Data context, if an RDF link connects URIs in different namespaces, it ultimately connects resources in different datasets.

Just as hyperlinks in the classic Web connect documents into a single global information space, Linked Data uses hyperlinks to connect disparate data into a single global dataspace. These links, in turn, enable applications to navigate the dataspace. For example, a Linked Data application that has looked up a URI and retrieved RDF data describing a person may follow links from this data to data on different Web servers, describing, for instance, the place where the person lives or the company for which the person works.

The Linked Data principles enable the implementation of generic applications that operate over the complete dataspace, since the resulting Web of Linked Data is based on standards for the identification of entities, the retrieval of entity descriptions, and the parsing of descriptions into RDF as common data model. Examples of such applications include Linked Data browsers which enable the user to view data from one data source and then follow RDF links within the data to other data sources. Other examples are Linked Data search engines, such as *Sig.ma*[20] [41], *Falcons*[21] [21], *SWSE*[22] [24], and *VisiNav*[23] [22], which crawl the Web of Linked Data and provide advanced query capabilities on top of the dataspace.

---

[20]http://sig.ma/

[21]http://iws.seu.edu.cn/services/falcons/documentsearch/

[22]http://www.swse.org/

[23]http://sw.deri.org/2009/01/visinav/

Linked Data builds directly on the Web architecture [29] and applies this architecture to the task of publishing and interconnecting data on global scale. Linked Data thus strongly advocates the usage of URIs for the globally unique identification of real-world entities. This practice distinguishes Linked Data from Microformats, RDFa, and Microdata which also provide language features for the globally unique identification of entities but where these features are less widely used in practice. Another difference between Linked Data and the other formats is the strong focus of Linked Data on setting RDF links that connect data between different servers. Setting links between entities is also possible using the RDFa and Microdata syntaxes, but the focus of the deployment of these technologies has been until today to describe entities within one Web page, rather than interconnecting disparate sources.

1.5.1 RDF/XML Syntax

Whenever a Linked Data client looks up an HTTP URI over the HTTP protocol and asks for the content type `application/rdf+xml`, the corresponding Web server returns an RDF description of the identified object using the RDF/XML syntax [2].

Figure 1.5 shows how our example description of Peter Smith is serialized using the RDF/XML syntax. Lines 2 and 3 define the namespaces of the vocabularies used within the description. It is interesting to note that it is common practice in the Linked Data context to mix terms from different widely used vocabularies to cover different aspects of the description. In our case, we use the RDF base vocabulary as well as FOAF, a vocabulary for describing people. Lines 6 and 7 state that there is a thing, identified by the URI `http://example.com/Peter` (line 6) of type `foaf:Person` (line 7). Line 8 states that this thing has the name Peter Smith. Line 9 states that Peter Smith knows Paula Jones, which is identified by the URI reference `http://example.com/People/Paula`.

```
<?xml version ="1.0" encoding ="UTF−8"?>
<rdf :RDF
   xmlns:rdf ="http ://www.w3. org/1999/02/22 − rdf −syntax−ns#"
   xmlns:foaf ="http :// xmlns .com/ foaf /0.1/" >

   <rdf : Description  rdf :about="http :// example .com/ Peter">
      <rdf :type  rdf :resource ="http :// xmlns .com/ foaf /0.1/ Person"/>
      <foaf :name>Peter  Smith </foaf :name>
      <foaf :knows  rdf :resource ="http :// example .com/ Paula"/>
   </rdf : Description >
</rdf :RDF>
```

Fig. 1.5 RDF/XML representation of the example entity description about Peter Smith

1.5.2 Linked Data Deployment on the Web

The deployment of Linked Data on the Web was initialized by the W3C *Linking Open Data (LOD) project*,[24] a grassroots community effort founded in January 2007. The founding aim of the project was to identify existing datasets that are available under open licenses, convert them to RDF according to the Linked Data principles, and publish them on the Web.

Figure 1.6 illustrates the September 2011 scale of the *Linked Data cloud* originating from the W3C Linking Open Data project and classifies the datasets by topical domain, highlighting the diversity of datasets present in the cloud. Each node in the diagram represents a distinct dataset published as Linked Data. The arcs indicate that RDF links exist between items in the two connected datasets. Heavier edges roughly correspond to a greater number of links between two datasets, and bidirectional arcs indicate the existence of outward links to one another.

The LOD community maintains a catalog of all known Linked Data sources, the *LOD Cloud Data Catalog*.[25] Table 1.3 gives an overview of the data sources that are cataloged as of July 2011. For each topical domain, the table lists the number of data sources, the number of RDF triples served by these data sources, as well as the number of RDF links that are set between data sources. The numbers are taken from the *State of the LOD Cloud* document[26] which on a regular basis compiles summary statistics about the datasets that are cataloged within the LOD Cloud Data Catalog.

Altogether, the 295 data sources that are currently cataloged serve over 31 billion RDF triples to the Web. A total of 504 million of these triples are RDF links that connect entity descriptions from different data sources.

In the following sections we will give a short overview of major datasets from each topical domain and highlight the wide variety of the available data.

1.5.2.1 Cross-Domain Data

Some of the first datasets that appeared in the Web of Linked Data are not specific to one topic, but span multiple domains. This cross-domain coverage is crucial for helping to connect domain-specific datasets into a single, interconnected dataspace, thereby avoiding fragmentation of the Web of Data into isolated, topical data islands. Cross-domain datasets often serve as linkage hubs on the Web of Data.

The prototypical example of cross-domain Linked Data is *DBpedia*[27] [13], a Linked Data version of Wikipedia. Things that are the subject of a Wikipedia article are automatically assigned a DBpedia URI, based on the URI of that

---

[24]http://esw.w3.org/topic/SweoIG/TaskForces/CommunityProjects/LinkingOpenData

[25]http://thedatahub.org/group/lodcloud

[26]http://lod-cloud.net/state/

[27]http://dbpedia.org/

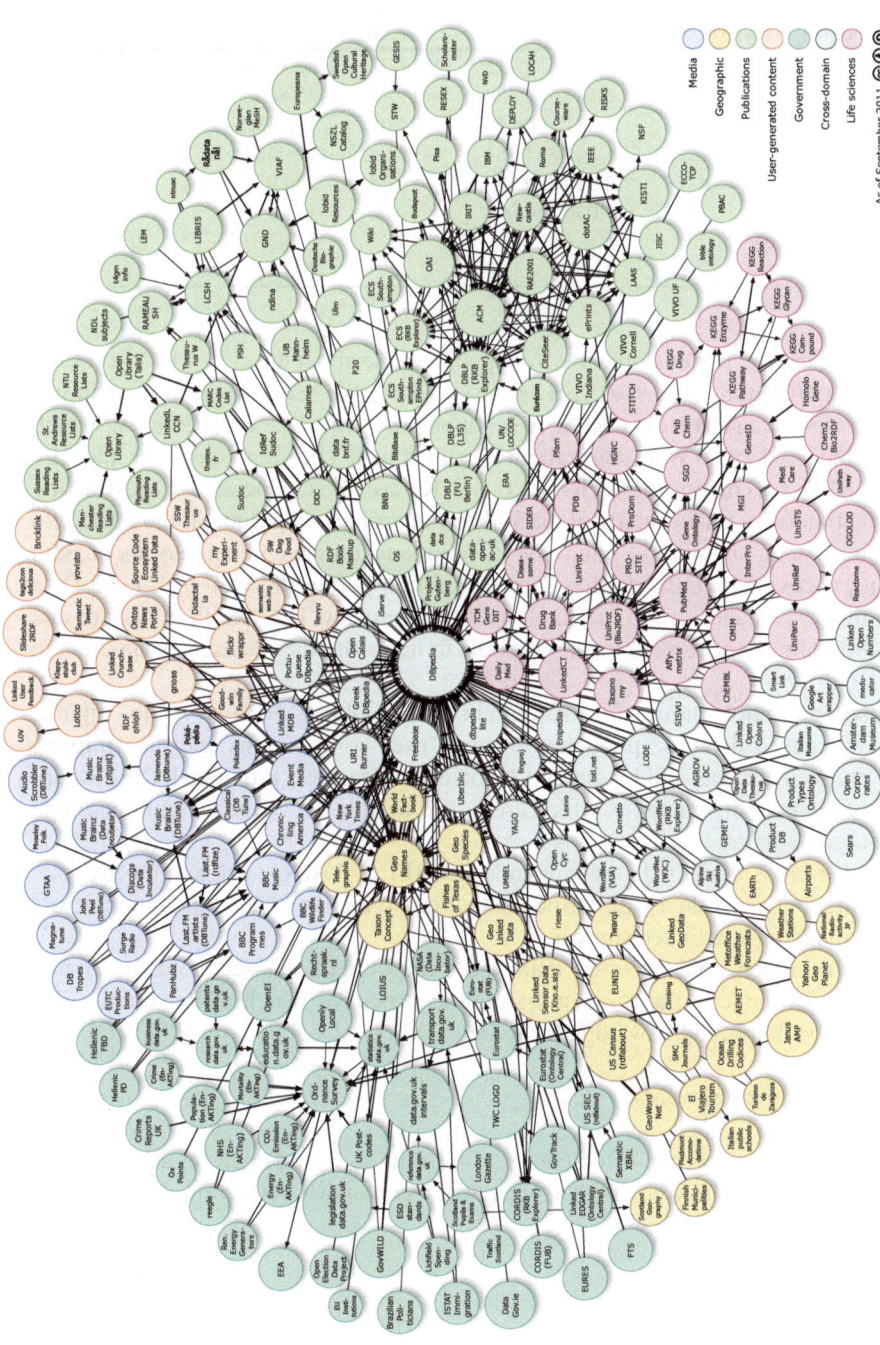

Fig. 1.6 Linking Open Data cloud as of September 2011. The colors classify datasets by topical domain

Table 1.3 Number of datasets, amount of triples, and amount of RDF links per topical domain

Domain *Datasets*		Triples	Percent	RDF links	Percent
Cross-domain	41	4,184,635,715	13.23	63,183,065	12.54
Geographic	31	6,145,532,484	19.43	35,812,328	7.11
Government	49	13,315,009,400	42.09	19,343,519	3.84
Media	25	1,841,852,061	5.82	50,440,705	10.01
Libraries	87	2,950,720,693	9.33	139,925,218	27.76
Life sciences	41	3,036,336,004	9.60	191,844,090	38.06
User Content	20	134,127,413	0.42	3,449,143	0.68
	295	31,634,213,770		503,998,829	

Wikipedia article. For example, the Wikipedia article about the city of Berlin has the following URI http://en.wikipedia.org/wiki/Berlin. Therefore, Berlin has the corresponding DBpedia URI http://dbpedia.org/resource/Berlin, which is not the URI of a Web page about Berlin, but a URI that identifies the city itself. RDF statements that refer to this URI are then generated by extracting information from various parts of the Wikipedia articles, in particular the infoboxes commonly seen on the right-hand side of Wikipedia articles. Because of its breadth of topical coverage, DBpedia has served as a hub within the Web of Linked Data from the early stages of the Linking Open Data project. The wealth of inward and outward links connecting items in DBpedia to items in other datasets is apparent in Fig. 1.6.

A second major source of cross-domain Linked Data is *Freebase*,[28] an editable, openly licensed database populated through user contributions and data imports from sources such as Wikipedia and Geonames. Freebase provides RDF descriptions of items in the database, which are linked to items in DBpedia with incoming and outgoing links.

Further cross-domain datasets include UMBEL,[29] YAGO [40], and OpenCyc.[30] These are, in turn, linked with DBpedia, helping to facilitate data integration across a wide range of interlinked sources.

Besides a rich pool of entity data, the cross-domain datasets contain a lot of domain knowledge in the form of taxonomic structures which makes them a rich source of background knowledge for search applications.

1.5.2.2 Geographic Data

Geographical datasets can often connect information from varied topical domains. This is apparent in the Web of Data, where the *Geonames*[31] dataset frequently serves

---

[28]http://www.freebase.com

[29]http://umbel.org/

[30]http://sw.opencyc.org/

[31]http://www.geonames.org/

as a hub for other datasets that cover geographical data, also only partly. Geonames is an open-license geographical database that publishes Linked Data about 8 million locations.

A second significant dataset in this area is *LinkedGeoData* [39], a Linked Data conversion of data from the *OpenStreetMap* project, which provides information about more than 350 million spatial features. Wherever possible, locations in Geonames and LinkedGeoData are interlinked with corresponding locations in DBpedia, ensuring there is a core of interlinked data about geographical locations.

Linked Data versions of the EuroStat,[32] World Factbook,[33] and US Census[34] datasets begin to bridge the worlds of statistics, politics, and social geography, while *Ordnance Survey* (the national mapping agency of Great Britain) has begun to publish Linked Data describing the administrative areas within Great Britain,[35] in efforts related to the *data.gov.uk* initiative described in Sect. 1.5.2.4.

1.5.2.3   Media Data

One of the first large organizations to recognize the potential of Linked Data and to adopt the principles and technologies into their publishing and content management workflows has been the British Broadcasting Corporation (BBC). Following earlier experiments with publishing their catalogue of programs as RDF, the BBC released in 2008 two large sites that combine publication of Linked Data and conventional Web pages. The first of these, */programmes*,[36] provides a URI for and a RDF description of every episode of the TV or radio program broadcast across the BBC's various channels [32].

The second of these sites, */music*,[37] publishes Linked Data about every artist whose music has been played on BBC radio stations. This type of music data is interlinked with DBpedia, and it receives incoming links from a range of music-related Linked Data sources. These cross dataset links allow applications to consume data from all these sources and integrate it to provide rich artist profiles, while the playlist data can be mined to find similarities between artists that may be used to generate recommendations.

A second major publisher of Linked Data in the media industry is the New York Times. The New York Times has published a significant proportion of its internal subject headings as Linked Data[38] under a *Creative Commons Attribution* license, interlinking these topics with DBpedia, Freebase, and Geonames. The intention is

---

[32]http://ckan.net/package?q=eurostat&groups=lodcloud

[33]http://www4.wiwiss.fu-berlin.de/factbook/

[34]http://www.rdfabout.com/demo/census/

[35]http://data.ordnancesurvey.co.uk/

[36]http://www.bbc.co.uk/programmes

[37]http://www.bbc.co.uk/music

[38]http://data.nytimes.com/

to use these liberally licensed data as a map to lead people to the rich archive of content maintained by the New York Times.

1.5.2.4   Government Data

Governmental bodies and public-sector organizations produce a wealth of data, ranging from economic statistics, to registers of companies and land ownership, reports on the performance of schools, crime statistics, and the voting records of elected representatives.

The potential of Linked Data for easing the access to government data is increasingly understood, with both the *data.gov.uk*[39] and *data.gov*[40] initiatives publishing significant volumes of data on the Web according to the Linked Data principles. The approach taken in the two countries differs slightly: to date, the latter has converted very large volumes of data, while the former has focused on the creation of core data-level infrastructure for publishing Linked Data, such as stable URIs to which increasing amounts of data can be connected [38].

A very interesting initiative is being pursued by the *UK Civil Service*,[41] which has started to mark up job vacancies using RDFa. By providing information about open positions in a structured form, it becomes easier for external job portals to incorporate civil service jobs [8]. If more organizations would follow this example, the transparency in the labor market could be significantly increased [11].

In order to provide a forum for coordinating the work on using Linked Data and other Web standards to improve access to government data and increase government transparency, W3C has formed an eGovernment Interest Group.[42]

1.5.2.5   Libraries and Education

With an imperative to support novel means of discovery and a wealth of experience in producing high-quality structured data, libraries are natural complementors to Linked Data. This field has seen some significant early developments which aim at integrating library catalogs on a global scale; interlinking the content of multiple library catalogs, for instance, by topic, location, or historical period; interlinking library catalogs with third-party information (picture and video archives, or knowledge bases like DBpedia); and at making library data more easily accessible by relying on Web standards.

Examples include the American Library of Congress and the German National Library of Economics which publish their subject heading taxonomies as Linked

---

[39]http://data.gov.uk/linked-data

[40]http://www.data.gov/semantic

[41]http://www.civilservice.gov.uk/

[42]http://www.w3.org/egov/wiki/Main_Page

Data (see Note[43] and [37], respectively), while the complete content of *LIBRIS* and the Swedish National Union Catalogue is available as Linked Data.[44] Similarly, the *OpenLibrary*, a collaborative effort to create "one Web page for every book ever published,"[45] publishes its catalogue in RDF.

Scholarly articles from journals and conferences are also well represented in the Web of Data through community publishing efforts such as DBLP as Linked Data,[46] RKBexplorer,[47] and the Semantic Web Dog Food Server[48] [35].

High levels of ongoing activity in the library community will no doubt lead to further significant Linked Data deployments in this area. Of particular note in this area is the new *Object Reuse and Exchange (OAI-ORE)* standard from the *Open Archives Initiative* [42], which is based on the Linked Data principles. The OAI-ORE, Dublin Core, SKOS, and FOAF vocabularies form the foundation of the new Europeana Data Model.[49] The adoption of this model by libraries, museums, and cultural institutions that participate in Europeana will further accelerate the availability of Linked Data related to publications and cultural heritage artifacts.

In order to provide a forum and to coordinate the efforts to increase the global interoperability of library data, the W3C has started a Library Linked Data Incubator Group.[50]

1.5.2.6   Life Sciences Data

Linked Data has gained significant uptake in the life sciences as a technology to connect the various datasets that are used by researchers in this field. In particular, the Bio2RDF project [3] has interlinked more than 30 widely used datasets, including UniProt (the Universal Protein Resource), KEGG (the Kyoto Encyclopedia of Genes and Genomes), CAS (the Chemical Abstracts Service), PubMed, and the Gene Ontology. The W3C *Linking Open Drug Data* effort [51] has brought together the pharmaceutical companies Eli Lilly, AstraZeneca, and Johnson & Johnson, in a cooperative effort to interlink openly licensed data about drugs and clinical trials, in order to aid drug discovery [30].

---

[43] http://id.loc.gov/authorities/about.html

[44] http://blog.libris.kb.se/semweb/?p=7

[45] http://openlibrary.org/

[46] http://dblp.l3s.de/; http://www4.wiwiss.fu-berlin.de/dblp/; http://dblp.rkbexplorer.com/

[47] http://www.rkbexplorer.com/data/

[48] http://data.semanticweb.org/

[49] http://version1.europeana.eu/c/document_library/get_file?uuid=9783319c-9049-436c-bdf9-25f72e85e34c&groupId=10602

[50] http://www.w3.org/2005/Incubator/lld/

[51] http://esw.w3.org/HCLSIG/LODD

1.5.2.7   User-Generated Content and Social Media

Some of the earliest datasets in the Web of Linked Data were based on conversions of, or wrappers around, *Web 2.0* sites with large volumes of *user-generated content.* This has produced datasets and services such as the *FlickrWrappr*,[52] a Linked Data wrapper around the Flickr photo-sharing service. These were complemented by user-generated content sites that were built with native support for Linked Data, such as *Revyu.com* [26] for reviews and ratings, and Faviki[53] for annotating Web content with Linked Data URIs.

Initially, the Linked Data best practices were adopted mainly by research projects and Web enthusiasts. These third parties took existing datasets, converted them into RDF, and served them on the Web. Alternatively, they implemented Linked Data wrappers around existing Web APIs. Today, Linked Data technologies are increasingly adopted by the primary data producers themselves and are used by them to provide access to their datasets. As of September 2011, out of the 295 datasets in the LOD cloud, 113 (38.57%) are published by the data producers themselves, while 180 (61.43%) are published by third parties.

1.5.2.8   Vocabulary Usage by Linked Data Sources

A common practice in the Linked Data community is to reuse terms from widely deployed vocabularies, whenever possible, in order to increase homogeneity of descriptions and, consequently, ease the understanding of these descriptions. As Linked Data sources cover a wide variety of topics, widely deployed vocabularies that cover all aspects of these topics may not exist yet. Therefore, publishers commonly also define proprietary terms and mix these terms with the widely used ones in order to cover the more specific aspects and to publish the complete content of a dataset on the Web.

Nearly all data sources in the LOD cloud use terms from the W3C base vocabularies RDF, RDF Schema, and OWL. In addition, 191 (64.75%) of the 295 data sources in the LOD cloud catalog use terms from other widely deployed vocabularies. Table 1.4 shows the distribution of the most widely used vocabularies in the Linked Data context.

It is interesting to note that these widely used vocabularies cover generic types of entities (such as the Friend-of-a-Friend (FOAF) vocabulary [54] being used to describe people or the Basic Geo Vocabulary (geo) [55] being used to describe locations)

---

[52]http://www4.wiwiss.fu-berlin.de/flickrwrappr/

[53]http://www.faviki.com/

[54]http://xmlns.com/foaf/0.1/

[55]http://www.w3.org/2003/01/geo/wgs84_pos

but that domain-specific vocabularies such as the Music Ontology (mo) [56] or the Bibliographic Ontology (bibo) [57] are also starting to gain traction.

A total of 190 (64.4%) out of the 295 data sources in the LOD cloud use proprietary vocabulary terms in addition to widely used terms, while 102 (34.58%) do not use proprietary vocabulary terms. In order to enable applications to automatically retrieve the definition of vocabulary terms from the Web, URIs identifying vocabulary terms should be made dereferenceable. Guidelines for doing this are given in the W3C Note Best Practice Recipes for Publishing RDF Vocabularies.[58] This best practice is currently implemented by 159 (83.68%) out of these 190 data sources that use proprietary terms, while 31 (16.31%) do not make proprietary term URIs dereferenceable.

A central idea of Linked Data is to set RDF links between entities on the Web. This does not only apply to instance data but can also be applied to publish correspondences between vocabulary terms on the Web and thus provide integration hints that enable Linked Data applications to translate data between different vocabularies. The W3C recommendations define the following terms for representing such correspondences (mappings): `owl:equivalentClass`, `owl:equivalentProperty`, or if a looser mapping is desired: `rdfs:subClassOf`, `rdfs:subPropertyOf`, and `skos:broadMatch`, `skos:narrowMatch`.

The Web site Linked Open Vocabularies[59] tracks the RDF links that are set between terms from 127 nonproprietary vocabularies that are used in the Linked Data context. According to TheDataHub.org data set catalog, 15 (7.89%) out of the 190 data sources that use proprietary terms provide mappings to other vocabularies for their terms.

Table 1.4 Number of linked data sources using specific vocabularies

Vocabulary	Number of data sources
Dublin Core (dc)	92 (31.19%)
Friend-of-a-Friend (foaf)	81 (27.46%)
Simple Knowledge Organization System (skos)	58 (19.66%)
Basic Geo Vocabulary (geo)	25 (8.47%)
AKTive Portal (akt)	17 (5.76%)
Bibliographic Ontology (bibo)	14 (4.75%)
Music Ontology (mo)	13 (4.41%)
Electronic Business Cards (vcard)	10 (3.39%)
Semantically-Interlinked Online Communities (sioc)	10 (3.39%)
Creative Commons (cc)	8 (2.71%)

---

[56]http://purl.org/ontology/mo/

[57]http://bibliontology.com/

[58]http://www.w3.org/TR/2008/NOTE-swbp-vocab-pub-20080828/

[59]http://labs.mondeca.com/dataset/lov/index.html

1.6   Evaluation Data

As the deployment of structured data on the Web rises, the opportunities for semantic search applications increase, and the need for evaluation datasets to test and compare these applications becomes evident. One approach to obtain Web data is to use publicly available software for crawling the Web, such as Nutch[60] for crawling Web pages and LDSpider [28] for crawling Linked Data. However, there exist already a number of publicly available evaluation datasets that have been crawled from the Web and can be promptly used for evaluating semantic search applications.

- *ClueWeb09.* The ClueWeb09 corpus is a collection of approximately 1 billion Web pages (25TB) in ten languages[18]. The corpus has been crawled in January and February 2009 and contains microdata as well as RDFa data. The corpus has been extensively used in the Text Retrieval Conference (TREC) for evaluating information retrieval and other related human language technologies.
- *TREC Entity.* One of the extensions of the ClueWeb09 corpus, which is of particular interest to semantic search applications, was developed for the TREC Entity Retrieval track. This conference track aims at evaluating the ability of systems to find related entities on Web pages. The TREC Entity dataset defines topics, which consist of information needs and acceptable answers. One example information need is "recording companies selling the Kingston Trio's songs." Acceptable answers for that information need would include home pages of the companies sought after—e.g., http://www.capitolrecords.com/ and http://www. deccarecords-us.com/—retrieved from the ClueWeb09 collection. The 2010 edition of TREC Entity developed 50 of such topics, which were extended by other 50 topics in its 2011 edition.
- *CommonCrawl.* The CommonCrawl corpus consists of 2.8 billion Web pages which have been crawled in November 2010. CommonCrawl is currently working on a new 2012 edition of their corpus which is likely to be available in Spring 2012.
- *WebDataCommons.* The WebDataCommons project extract all Microformat, Microdata and RDFa data from the CommonCrawl corpus and provides the extracted data for download. The dataset that has been extracted from the 2010 CommonCrawl corpus consists of 5.2 billion RDF triples out of which approximately 80% are Microformat data.
- *Sindice 2011.* The Sindice 2011 dataset has been crawled from the Web by the Sindice search engine [19]. The dataset consists of 11 billion RDF triples which have been extracted from 230 million Web documents containing RDF, RDFa, and Microformats and have been crawled from the Web of Linked Data. The documents originate from 270,000 second-level domains. The dataset contains descriptions of about 1.7 billion entities. Detailed statistics are provided on

---

[60]http://nutch.apache.org/

the dataset page.[61] The Sindice 2011 dataset is used in the TREC Entity 2011 evaluation campaign, which introduced an LOD variant, where the retrieved entity identifiers are Linked Open Data URIs instead of homepages URLs, e.g., `dbpedia:Sony_BMG` and `dbpedia:Universal_Music_Group`.

- *Billion Triple Challenge*. The Billion Triple Challenge (BTC) data sets are precrawled collections of Linked Data from 2009, 2010 and 2011. Precrawled datasets that consists exclusively Linked Data are the Billion Triple Challenge (BTC) datasets dating from 2009, 2010, and 2011 [23]. The latest version, BTC2011, has been crawled in May/June 2011 and consists of 2 billion RDF triples from Linked Data sources. The BTC data is employed in the Semantic Web Challenge, an academic competition that happens as part of the International Semantic Web Conference. The central idea of this competition is to apply Semantic Web techniques for the construction of Web applications that integrate, combine, and create information needed to perform user-driven tasks.
- *SemSearch 2011*. Yet another prominent example use of the BTC datasets is the Semantic Search Challenge in the World Wide Web Conference. The Semantic Search Challenge establishes an academic competition for the best systems that can answer a number of queries that are focused on the task of entity search. Two sets of queries are provided. For the entity search track, the queries are a subset from the Yahoo! Search Query Tiny Sample, available from the Yahoo! Webscope.[62] For the list search track, the queries have been handwritten by the organizing committee. The evaluation of the results was performed through a crowdsourcing process[14] that used Amazon's Mechanical Turk.[63]

1.7 Conclusion

This chapter gave an overview of the different techniques that are currently used to publish structured data on the Web as well as about the types and amounts of data that is currently published on the Web using each technique. The chapter has shown that the Web of Data is not a vision anymore, but it is actually there. For search engines, this means that they can draw on a large corpus of structured data that is embedded into HTML pages and helps them to understand the content of these pages. The Web of Data also contains many datasets which are directly published on the Web according to the Linked Data principles. These datasets provide a rich pool of detailed domain-specific entity data as well as taxonomic classifications which can both be used as background knowledge to improve search applications.

Looking at the types of data that are currently published on the Web, we can conclude that Microformats, RDFa, and Mircodata are mostly used to publish data that is directly relevant for end-user queries—such as data describing products,

---

[61]http://data.sindice.com/trec2011/statistics.html

[62]http://webscope.sandbox.yahoo.com/

[63]http://mturk.com

reviews, people, organizations, news, and events. The range of data that is published as Linked Data is wider and includes many very specific entity types such as statistical data, government data, research data, library data, as well as cross-domain datasets like DBpedia and Freebase. Another distinguishing factor between Microformats, RDFa, and Linked Data is the emphasis on setting links between entity descriptions. While Microformats and RDFa data mostly remain isolated and existing language features to connect entries between data sources are not widely used, the focus of the Linked Data community lies clearly on interconnecting data between different sources and thus on easing data discovery as well as data integration.

Applications that want to exploit the Web of Data are facing two main challenges today:

- *Semantic Heterogeneity.* The different techniques that are used to publish data on the Web lead to a certain degree of syntax heterogeneity. But as current search engines like Google, Yahoo!, Bing, and Sindice show, this syntax heterogeneity can easily be bridged by using multiple parsers in parallel. What is harder to overcome is the semantic heterogeneity that results from different data sources using different vocabularies to represent data about the same types of entities. The semantic heterogeneity is further increased by the fact that, in an open environment like the Web, different data sources also use the same vocabulary in different ways, for instance, squeezing different types of values into the same property. A coarse-grained starting point to handle semantic heterogeneity is the increased adoption of common vocabularies by many data sources [6] as well as the practice to set equivalence and subclass/subproperty links between terms from different vocabularies that has emerged in the Linked Data community [25]. Advanced techniques to tackle semantic heterogeneity in the context of the Web include schema clustering [33] as well as machine-learning-based techniques that derive correspondences by looking at both—the vocabulary and the instance level [7]. Such methods are likely to produce good results in the context of the Web of Data as large amounts of instance data are readily available on the Web for training. Besides these potentials, high-quality data integration will always still requires human intervention. The current challenge for search applications is to find the appropriate mix of both.
- *Data Quality.* The Web is an open medium and everybody can publish data on the Web. Thus, the Web will always contain data that is outdated, conflicting, or intentionally wrong (spam). As search applications start to aggregate data from growing numbers of Web data sources, the task of assessing the quality of Web data and deciding which data to trust becomes increasingly challenging. Groundwork for tracking the provenance of Web data is currently done by the W3C Provenance Working Group.[64] The range of data quality assessment methods that are potentially applicable in the Web context is very wide, and

---

[64]http://www.w3.org/2011/prov/wiki/Main_Page

the right mixture of these methods will depend on the application context. Data quality assessment is likely to again involve human intervention, at least in the form of manually assessing explanations provided by a system about its trust decisions [9].

Handling semantic heterogeneity and data quality in the Web context poses interesting research challenges. But as current search engines like Google, Bing, Sig.ma, Falcons show, pragmatic approaches already suffice go a long way.

The better we learn to handle these challenges, the more sophisticated the functionality of search engines can get. The development of applications that exploit the Web of Data is just starting, and we are likely to see a wide range of innovative applications emerge around the topics of Web-scale data integration and aggregation as well as Web-scale data mining.

References

1. Adida, B., Birbeck, M.: RDFa primer—bridging the human and data webs—W3C recommendation. http://www.w3.org/TR/xhtml-rdfa-primer/ (2008). Accessed 1 February 2012, URL http://www.w3.org/TR/xhtml-rdfa-primer/
2. Beckett, D.: RDF/XML Syntax Specification (Revised)—W3C Recommendation. http://www.w3.org/TR/rdf-syntax-grammar/ (2004). Accessed 1 February 2012
3. Belleau, F., Nolin, M., Tourigny, N., Rigault, P., Morissette, J.: Bio2rdf: Towards a mashup to build bioinformatics knowledge systems. J. Biomed. Inform. **41**(5), 706–716 (2008)
4. BernersLee, T.: Linked data design issues. http://www.w3.org/DesignIssues/LinkedData.html (2006). Accessed 1 February 2012
5. Berners-Lee, T.: Giant global graph. http://dig.csail.mit.edu/breadcrumbs/node/215 (2007). Accessed 1 February 2012, URL http://dig.csail.mit.edu/breadcrumbs/node/215
6. Berners-Lee, T., Kagal, L.: The fractal nature of the semantic web. AI Magazine **29**(3) (2008)
7. Bilke, A., Naumann, F.: Schema matching using duplicates. Proceedings of the International Conference on Data Engineering, 05–08 April 2005
8. Birbeck, M.: Rdfa and linked data in uk government web-sites. Nodalities Magazine **7** (2009)
9. Bizer, C., Cyganiak, R.: Quality-driven information filtering using the WIQA policy framework. J. Web Semant. Sci. Serv. Agents World Wide Web **7**(1), 1–10 (2009)
10. Bizer, C., Heath, T., Berners-Lee, T.: Linked data - the story so far. Int. J. Semant. Web Inf. Syst. **5**(3), 1–22 (2009)
11. Bizer, C., Heese, R., Mochol, M., Oldakowski, R., Tolksdorf, R., Eckstein, R.: The impact of semantic web technologies on job recruitment processes. Proceedings of the 7th Internationale Tagung Wirtschaftsinformatik (WI2005), 2005
12. Bizer, C., Jentzsch, A., Cyganiak, R.: State of the LOD cloud. http://www4.wiwiss.fu-berlin.de/lodcloud/state/ (2011). Accessed 1 February 2012, URL http://www4.wiwiss.fu-berlin.de/lodcloud/state/
13. Bizer, C., Lehmann, J., Kobilarov, G., Auer, S., Becker, C., Cyganiak, R., Hellmann, S.: Dbpedia – a crystallization point for the web of data. J. Web Semant. Sci. Serv. Agents World Wide Web **7**(3), 154–165 (2009)
14. Blanco, R., Halpin, H., Herzig, D.M., Mika, P., Pound, J., Thompson, H.S., Tran Duc, T.: Repeatable and reliable search system evaluation using crowdsourcing. Proceedings of the 34th International ACM SIGIR Conference on Research and Development in Information, SIGIR '11, ACM, New York, NY, USA, 2011, pp. 923–932 DOI http://doi.acm.org/10.1145/2009916.2010039 URL http://doi.acm.org/10.1145/2009916.2010039

15. Blog, G.: Introducing schema.org: search engines come together for a richer web. http://googleblog.blogspot.com/2011/06/introducing-schemaorg-search-engines.html (2011). Accessed 1 February 2012

16. Blog, Y.S.: We now support microformats. http://www.ysearchblog.com/2006/06/21/we-now-support-microformats/ (2006). Accessed 1 February 2012

17. Blog, Y.S.: The Yahoo! search open ecosystem. http://www.ysearchblog.com/archives/000527.html (2008). Accessed 1 February 2012

18. Callan, J.: The Sapphire Web Crawler – crawl statistics. http://boston.lti.cs.cmu.edu/crawler/crawlerstats.html (2009). Accessed 1 February 2012

19. Campinas, S., Ceccarelli, D., Perry, T.E., Delbru, R., Balog, K., Tummarello, G.: The Sindice-2011 dataset for entity-oriented search in the web of data. 1st international workshop on entity-oriented search (EOS) 2011

20. Central, G.W.: Introducing rich snippets. http://googlewebmastercentral.blogspot.com/2009/05/introducing-rich-snippets.html (2011). Accessed 1 February 2012

21. Cheng, G., Qu, Y.: Searching linked objects with falcons: approach, implementation and evaluation. Int. J. Semant. Web Inform. Syst. (IJSWIS) 5(3), 49–70 (2009)

22. Harth, A.: Visinav: a system for visual search and navigation on web data. Web Semant. Sci. Serv. Agents World Wide Web 8(4), 348–354 (2010). DOI DOI:10.1016/j.websem.2010.08.001. URL http://www.sciencedirect.com/science/article/B758F-50THXFH-1/2/84c276a928b5889c9870f9e57eda2658

23. Harth, A.: The billion triple challenge datasets. http://km.aifb.kit.edu/projects/btc-2011/ (2011). Accessed 1 February 2012

24. Harth, A., Hogan, A., Umbrich, J., Decker, S.: SWSE: objects before documents! Proceedings of the Semantic Web Challenge 2008, 2008

25. Heath, T., Bizer, C.: Linked Data – Evolving the Web into a Global Data Space. Morgan and Claypool Publishers, Seattle, WA USA (2011). URL http://linkeddatabook.com/

26. Heath, T., Motta, E.: Revyu: linking reviews and ratings into the web of data. J. Web Semant. Sci. Serv. Agents World Wide Web 6(4) (2008)

27. Hepp, M.: Goodrelations: an ontology for describing products and services offers on the web. Proceedings of the 16th International Conference on Knowledge Engineering and Knowledge Management, Acitrezza, Italy, 2008

28. Isele, R., Harth, A., Umbrich, J., Bizer, C.: LDSpider: an open-source crawling framework for the web of linked data. ISWC 2010 posters and demonstrations track: collected abstracts vol. 658, 2010

29. Jacobs, I., Walsh, N.: Architecture of the World Wide Web, Volume One (2004). http://www.w3.org/TR/webarch/, Accessed 1 February 2012

30. Jentzsch, A., Hassanzadeh, O., Bizer, C., Andersson, B., Stephens, S.: Enabling tailored therapeutics with linked data. Proceedings of the WWW2009 Workshop on Linked Data on the Web, 2009. URL http://events.linkeddata.org/ldow2009/papers/ldow2009_paper9.pdf

31. Klyne, G., Carroll, J.J.: Resource description framework (RDF): concepts and abstract syntax – W3C recommendation (2004). Accessed 1 February 2012, Http://www.w3.org/TR/rdf-concepts/

32. Kobilarov, G., Scott, T., Raimond, Y., Oliver, S., Sizemore, C., Smethurst, M., Bizer, C., Lee, R.: Media meets semantic web – how the bbc uses dbpedia and linked data to make connections. The semantic web: research and applications, 6th European semantic web conference, 2009, pp. 723–737

33. Madhavan, J., Shawn, J.R., Cohen, S., Dong, X., Ko, D., Yu, C., Halevy, A.: Web-scale data integration: you can only afford to pay as you go. Proceedings of the Conference on Innovative Data Systems Research, 2007

34. Mika, P.: Microformats and RDFa deployment across the Web. http://tripletalk.wordpress.com/2011/01/25/rdfa-deployment-across-the-web/ (2011). Accessed 1 February 2012

35. Möller, K., Heath, T., Handschuh, S., Domingue, J.: Recipes for semantic web dog food – the eswc and iswc metadata projects. Proceedings of the 6th International Semantic Web Conference and 2nd Asian Semantic Web Conference, Busan, Korea, 2007

36. Myers, J.: Creating local visibility to open box products with front-end semantic web. http://
    jay.beweep.com/2010/03/30/creating-local-visibility-to-open-box -products-with-front-end-
    semantic-web/ (2010). Accessed 1 February 2012
37. Neubert, J.: Bringing the "thesaurus for economics" on to the web of linked data. Proceedings
    of the WWW2009 Workshop on Linked Data on the Web, 2009
38. Sheridan, J., Tennison, J.: Linking uk government data. Proceedings of the WWW2010
    Workshop on Linked Data on the Web, 2010. URL http://ceur-ws.org/Vol-628/ldow2010_
    paper14.pdf
39. Søren, A., Jens, L., Sebastian, H.: Linkedgeodata – adding a spatial dimension to the web of
    data. Proceedings of the International Semantic Web Conference, 2009
40. Suchanek, F.M., Kasneci, G., Weikum, G.: Yago: a core of semantic knowledge. In: Williamson
    C.L., Zurko M.E., Patel-Schneider P.F., Shenoy P.J. (eds.) Proceedings of the 16th International
    Conference on World Wide Web, ACM, Banff, Alberta, Canada, 8–12 May 2007, pp. 697–706,
    URL http://doi.acm.org/10.1145/1242572.1242667
41. Tummarello, G., Cyganiak, R., Catasta, M., Danielczyk, S., Delbru, R., Decker, S.: Sig.ma:
    live views on the web of data. Web Semant. Sci. Serv. Agents World Wide Web 8(4), 355–
    364 (2010). DOI DOI:10.1016/j.websem.2010.08.003. URL http://www.sciencedirect.com/
    science/article/B758F-50THXFH-3/2/50a61206ad3a34d5541aebf5a465484a
42. Van de Sompel, H., Lagoze, C., Nelson, M., Warner, S., Sanderson, R., Johnston, P.: Adding
    escience assets to the data web. Proceedings of the 2nd Workshop on Linked Data on the Web
    (LDOW2009), 2009

Chapter 2
Storing and Indexing Massive RDF Datasets

Yongming Luo, François Picalausa, George H.L. Fletcher, Jan Hidders,
and Stijn Vansummeren

2.1 Introduction: Different Perspectives on RDF Storage

The resource description framework (RDF for short) provides a flexible method for modeling information on the Web [34,40]. All data items in RDF are uniformly represented as triples of the form *(subject, predicate, object)*, sometimes also referred to as *(subject, property, value)* triples. As a running example for this chapter, a small fragment of an RDF dataset concerning music and music fans is given in Fig. 2.1.

Spurred by efforts like the Linking Open Data project [35,75], increasingly large volumes of data are being published in RDF. Notable contributors in this respect include areas as diverse as the government [11], the life sciences [9], Web 2.0 communities, and so on.

To give an idea of the volumes of RDF data concerned, as of September 2012, there are 31,634,213,770 triples in total published by data sources participating in the Linking Open Data project [5]. Many individual data sources (like, e.g., PubMed, DBpedia, MusicBrainz) contain hundreds of millions of triples (797, 672, and 179 millions, respectively). These large volumes of RDF data motivate the need for scalable native RDF data management solutions capable of efficiently storing, indexing, and querying RDF data.

In this chapter, we present a general and up-to-date survey of the current state of the art in RDF storage and indexing.

It is important to note that RDF data management has been studied in a variety of contexts. This variety is actually reflected in a richness of the perspectives and approaches to storage and indexing of RDF datasets, typically driven by particular classes of query patterns and inspired by techniques developed in various research

Y. Luo (✉) · F. Picalausa · G.H.L. Fletcher · J. Hidders · S. Vansummeren
Department of Mathematics and Computer Science, Eindhoven University of Technology,
P.O. Box 513, 5600 MB Eindhoven, The Netherlands
e-mail: y.luo@tue.nl; fpicalau@ulb.ac.be; g.h.l.fletcher@tue.nl; a.j.h.hidders@tudelft.nl;
stijn.vansummeren@ulb.ac.be

R. De Virgilio et al. (eds.), *Semantic Search over the Web*,
Data-Centric Systems and Applications, DOI 10.1007/978-3-642-25008-8_2,
© Springer-Verlag Berlin Heidelberg 2012

```
{⟨work5678,    FileType,    MP3 ⟩,
 ⟨work5678,    Composer,    Schoenberg ⟩,
 ⟨work1234,    MediaType,   LP ⟩,
 ⟨work1234,    Composer,    Debussy ⟩,
 ⟨work1234,    Title,       La Mer ⟩,
 ⟨user8604,    likes,       work5678 ⟩,
 ⟨user8604,    likes,       work1234 ⟩,
 ⟨user3789,    name,        Umi ⟩,
 ⟨user3789,    birthdate,   1980 ⟩,
 ⟨user3789,    likes,       work1234⟩,
 ⟨user8604,    name,        Teppei ⟩,
 ⟨user8604,    birthdate,   1975 ⟩,
 ⟨user8604,    phone,       2223334444 ⟩,
 ⟨user8604,    phone,       5556667777 ⟩,
 ⟨user8604,    friendOf,    user3789 ⟩,
 ⟨Debussy,     style,       impressionist⟩,
 ⟨Schoenberg,  style,       expressionist⟩, . . . }
```

Fig. 2.1 A small fragment of an RDF dataset concerning music fans

communities. In the literature, we can identify three basic perspectives underlying this variety.

2.1.1   The Relational Perspective

The first basic perspective, put forward by the database community, is that an RDF graph is just a particular type of relational data, and that techniques developed for storing, indexing, and answering queries on relational data can hence be reused and specialized for storing and indexing RDF graphs. In particular, techniques developed under this perspective typically aim to support the full SPARQL language. The most naive approach in this respect is simply to store all RDF triples in a single table over the relation schema *(subject, predicate, object)*. An important issue in this approach is that, due to the large size of the RDF graphs and the potentially large number of self-joins required to answer queries, care must be taken to devise an efficient physical layout with suitable indexes to support query answering. In addition to this simple *vertical representation*, there also exists a *horizontal representation* where the triple predicate values are interpreted as column names in a collection of relation schemas. For example, we can divide the music fan dataset of Fig. 2.1 into five relations: Works, Users, Composers, Likes, and FriendOf; the Users relation would have columns Name, BirthDate, and Phone. Major issues here are dealing with missing values (e.g., subject work5678 does not have a title) and multivalued attributes (e.g., user8604 has two phone numbers). In Sect. 2.2, we give an up-to-date survey of the literature on the relational perspective, thereby complementing earlier surveys focusing on this perspective [36, 50, 62, 64–66, 69].

2.1.2   The Entity Perspective

The second basic perspective, originating from the information retrieval community, is resource centric. Under this *entity perspective*, resources in the RDF graph are interpreted as "objects," or "entities." Similarly to the way in which text documents are determined by a set of keyword terms in the classical information retrieval setting, each entity is determined by a set of attribute–value pairs in the entity perspective [18, 78]. In particular, a resource r in RDF graph G is viewed as an entity with the following set of (attribute, value) pairs:

$$\text{entity}(r) = \{(p, o) \mid (r, p, o) \in G\} \cup \{(p^{-1}, o) \mid (o, p, r) \in G\}.$$

Figure 2.2 illustrates this idea for the RDF graph in Fig. 2.1. Techniques from the information retrieval literature can then be specialized to support query patterns that retrieve entities based on particular attributes and/or values [18]. For example, we have in Fig. 2.2 that user8604 is retrieved when searching for entities born in 1975 (i.e., have 1975 as a value on attribute birthdate) as well as when searching for entities with friends who like Impressionist music. Note that entity user3789 is not retrieved by either of these queries. Further discussion and a survey of the literature on this perspective are given in Sect. 2.3.

2.1.3   The Graph-Based Perspective

The third basic perspective, originating from research in semistructured and graph databases, relaxes the entity-centric interpretation of resources in the entity

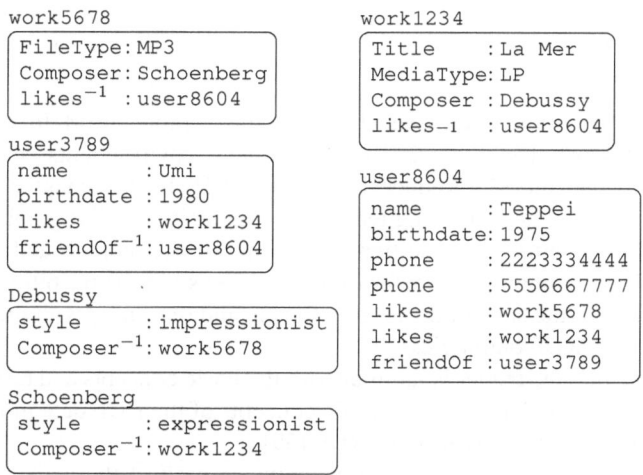

Fig. 2.2 The entity view of the music dataset in Fig. 2.1

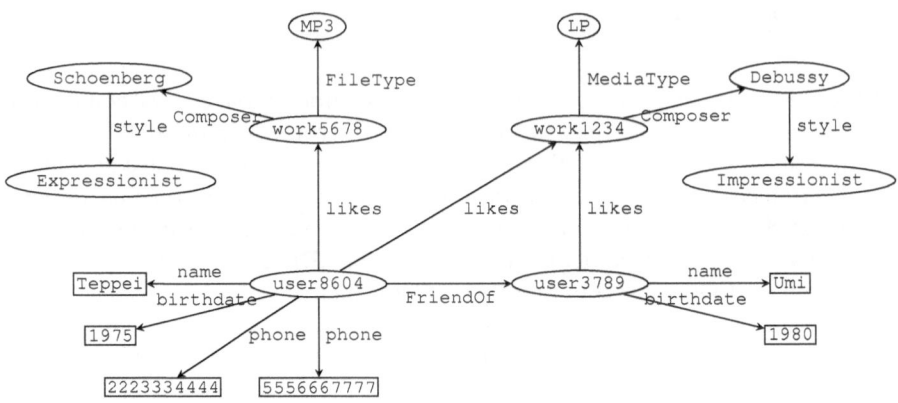

Fig. 2.3 The graph view of the music dataset in Fig. 2.1

view, focusing instead on the structure of the RDF data. Under this *graph-based perspective*, the focus is on supporting navigation in the RDF graph when viewed as a classical graph in which subjects and objects form the nodes, and triples specify directed, labeled edges. Under this perspective, the RDF graph of Fig. 2.1 is hence viewed as the classical graph depicted in Fig. 2.3. Typical query patterns supported in this perspective are graph-theoretic queries such as reachability between nodes. For example, in the graph of Fig. 2.3, we might be interested to find those users which have a fan of Debussy somewhere in their social network (i.e., in the friendOf subgraph). The major issue under this perspective is how to explicitly and efficiently store and index the implicit graph structure. Further details and a survey of the literature on the graph-based perspective are given in Sect. 2.4.

2.1.4 Proviso

We note that recent research has devoted considerable effort to the study of managing massive RDF graphs in distributed environments such as P2P networks [58] and the MapReduce framework [63]. In this chapter, in contrast, we focus on storage and indexing techniques for a single RDF graph instance in a non-distributed setting. In addition, we focus on the storage and indexing of *extensional* RDF data only, and refer to other surveys [43, 50, 62, 69] and Chap. 10 for an overview of the state of the art in inferring and reasoning with the *intentional* data specified by RDF ontologies.

We assume that the reader is familiar with the basic concepts and terminology of the relational data model, as well as basic concepts of the RDF data model [34, 40], and the SPARQL query language for RDF [59].

There are obviously tight connections between each of the above perspectives since they are interpretations of the same underlying data model. It is therefore sometimes difficult to clearly identify to which perspective a particular storage or indexing approach has the most affinity. Where appropriate, we indicate such "hybrids" in our detailed survey of the literature, to which we turn next.

2.2 Storing and Indexing Under the Relational Perspective

Conceptually, we can discern two different approaches for storing RDF data in relational databases. The *vertical representation* approach stores all triples in an RDF graph as a single table over the relation schema *(subject, predicate, object)*. The *horizontal representation* approach, in contrast, interprets triple predicate values as column names, and stores RDF graphs in one or more wide tables. Additional indexes can be built on top of these representations to improve performance. We survey both representations next, and conclude with indexing.

2.2.1 A Note on the Storage of IRIs and Literal Values

Before we dive into the details of the vertical and horizontal representations, it is important to note that both approaches generally make special provisions for storing RDF resources efficiently. Indeed, rather than storing each IRI or literal value directly as a string, implementations usually associate a unique numerical identifier to each resource and store this identifier instead. There are two motivations for this strategy. First, since there is no a priori bound on the length of the IRIs or literal values that can occur in RDF graphs, it is necessary to support variable-length records when storing resources directly as strings. By storing the numerical identifiers instead, fixed-length records can be used. Second, and more importantly, RDF graphs typically contain very long IRI strings and literal values that, in addition, are frequently repeated in the same RDF graph. The latter is illustrated in Fig. 2.1, for example, where `user8604` is repeated eight times. Since this resource would be represented by an IRI like `http://www.example.org/users/user8604` in a real-world RDF graph, storing the short numerical identifiers hence results in large space savings.

Unique identifiers can be computed in two general ways:

- Hash-based approaches obtain a unique identifier by applying a hash function to the resource string [30, 31, 64], where the hash function used for IRIs may differ from the hash function used for literal values. This is the approach taken by 3-Store [31], for example, where the hash functions are chosen in such a way that it is possible to distinguish between hash values that originate from IRIs and literal values. Of course, care must be taken to deal with possible hash collisions. In the extreme, the system may reject addition of new RDF triples when a collision is detected [31].

  To translate hash values back into the corresponding IRI or literal value when answering queries, a distinguished *dictionary* table is constructed.

- Counter-based approaches obtain a unique identifier by simply maintaining a counter that is incremented whenever a new resource is added. To answer queries, dictionary tables that map from identifiers to resources and vice versa are constructed [7, 32, 33, 56, 57]. Typically, these dictionary tables are stored as BTrees for efficient retrieval.

  A variant on this technique that is applicable when the RDF graph is static is to first sort the resource strings in lexicographic order, and to assign the identifier n to the nth resource in this order. In such a case, a single dictionary table suffices to perform the mapping from identifiers to resources and vice versa [77].

Various optimizations can be devised to further improve storage space. For example, when literal values are small enough to serve directly as unique identifiers (e.g., literal integer values), there is no need to assign unique identifiers, provided that the storage medium can distinguish between the system-generated identifiers and the small literal values [15, 16]. Also, it is frequent that many IRIs in an RDF graph share the same namespace prefix. By separately encoding this namespace prefix, one can further reduce the storage requirements [15, 16, 49].

2.2.2 Vertical Representation

In the vertical representation (sometimes also called *triple store*), triples are conceptually stored in a single table over the relation schema *(subject, predicate, object)* [7, 10, 30, 31, 80]. Some implementations include an additional *context* column in order to store RDF *datasets* rather than single RDF graphs. In this case, the *context* column specifies the IRI of the named graph in which the RDF triple occurs.

An important issue in the vertical representation is that, due to the large size of the RDF graphs and the potentially large number of self-joins required to answer queries, care must be taken to devise an efficient physical layout with suitable indexes to support query answering [15, 32, 33, 41, 49, 56, 57, 67, 79].

2.2.2.1 Unclustered Indexes

One of the first proposals for addressing this scalability issue compared the impact of adding the following four different sets of BTree indexes on the triple table [49]:

1. The first set of unclustered indexes consists of an index on the subject column (s) alone, an index on the property (p) column alone, and index on the object column (o) alone.
2. The second set of unclustered indexes consists of a combined index on subject and property (sp), as well as an index on the object column (o) alone.

3. The third set of unclustered indexes consists of a combined index on property and object (*po*).
4. The final set has a combined clustered index on all columns together (*spo*).

The authors note that, for an ad hoc set of queries and on a specific RDF graph, the first set of indexes drastically improves the SQL-based query processing performance, whereas the other index sets achieve less performance.

More recently, Kolas et al. extend the idea of indexing each of the subject, predicate, and object columns separately [41]. In their Parliament database system, each RDF resource r (IRI or literal) is mapped, by means of a BTree, to a triple of pointers (p_1, p_2, p_3). Here, p_1 points to the first record in the triple table in which r occurs as a subject, p_2 points to the first record in which r occurs as a predicate, and similarly p_3 points to the first record in which r occurs as an object. In addition, each record in the triple table is extended with three additional pointers that point to the next triple in the table containing the same subject, predicate, and object, respectively. In this way, a linked list is constructed. While this layout consumes very little storage space, traversing large linked lists may incur a nonnegligible disk I/O cost.

2.2.2.2   Clustered BTree Indexes

Whereas the above indexes are *unclustered* and hence simply store pointers into the triple table (avoiding storing multiple copies of the RDF triples), there are many triple stores that aggressively store the vertical representation table in multiple sorted orders according to various permutations of the sequence *(context, subject, predicate, object)* and its subsequences [10, 15, 56, 57, 79]. Usually, a *clustered* BTree is constructed for each of the selected permutations for efficient retrieval; the desired triple ordering is then available in the leaves of the BTree. While these approaches are more demanding in terms of storage space, they support efficient query answering since the availability of the various sorted versions of the triple table enables fast merge joins.

- Weiss et al. [79] consider this approach in their HexaStore engine by creating six different clustered BTree indexes: spo, sop, pso, pos, osp, and ops. Additionally, common payload spaces are shared between indexes. For example, the spo and pso indexes share a common materialized set of associated o values. In this way, some storage redundancy is eliminated. Due to the remaining redundancy in the indexes, efficient retrieval of both fully and partially specified triples is supported. For example, it suffices to consult the sop index to retrieve all triples with subject User8604 and object user3789. Recently, Wang et al. proposed to implement these indexes by means of a column-oriented database instead of using BTrees [77].
- Neumann and Weikum [56, 57] take this approach further in their RDF-3X engine by adding, to the six indexes above, the so-called *projection indexes* for each strict subset of {*subject, predicate, object*}, again in every order. This adds

additional nine indexes: s, p, o, sp, ps, so, os, op, and po. Instead of storing triples, the projection indexes conceptually map search keys to the number of triples that satisfy the search key. For example, the projection index on subject alone maps each subject s to the cardinality of the multiset

$$\{|\ (p,o)\ |\ (s,p,o)\ \text{occurs in the RDF Graph}\ |\}.$$

The projection indexes are used to answer aggregate queries, to avoid computing some intermediate join results, and to provide statistics that can be used by the RDF-3X cost-based query optimizer. RDF-3X also includes advanced algorithms for estimating join cardinalities to facilitate query processing.

To reduce the storage space required, RDF-3X in addition uses a compression scheme at the BTree leaf block level. The idea behind this compression scheme is simple: in a given index sort order, say spo, it is likely that subsequent triples share a common subject or subject–predicate prefix. In this case, these repetitions are not stored.

- The widely used Virtuoso DBMS and RDF engine also stores different permutations of $spoc$ [15, 16] (where c indicates the context column). By default, however, only clustered BTree indexes on $cspo$ and $ocps$ are materialized, although other indexes can be enabled by the database administrator. The storage cost for these indexes is reduced by introducing compression schemes at the data level, as well as at the page level.

  In addition, Erling and Mikhailov [16] report that in practical RDF graphs, many triples share the same predicate and object. To take advantage of this property, Virtuoso builds bitmap indexes for each opc prefix by default, storing the various subjects. McGlothlin et al. build on this idea and use bitmap indexes instead of BTrees as the main storage structure [53].

  Furthermore, Atre et al. [4] build a virtual 3D bitmap upon an RDF graph, with each dimension representing the subjects, predicates, and objects, respectively. Each cell of this 3D bitmap hence states the existence of one combination of the coordinates, i.e., a triple. By slicing the bitmap from different dimensions, several 2D bit matrices (BitMats) are generated, essentially indicating various permutations of the triples. These so-called *BitMats* are compressed and stored on disk, along with a metafile maintaining summary and location information. Bit operations on this metafile are used to filter out BitMats during join evaluation, thereby accelerating query evaluation.

- Finally, Fletcher and Beck [17] propose a hybrid of the unclustered and clustered approaches, wherein a single BTree index is built over the set of all resources appearing in the dataset. The payload for a resource r consists of three sorted lists, namely op where r appears as a subject, so where r appears as a predicate, and sp where r appears as an object. The advantage of this so-called TripleT approach is simplicity of design and maintenance, as well as increased locality of data, in the sense that all information pertaining to a resource is available in a single local data structure. The TripleT index was shown to be competitive with the previous approaches, in terms of both storage and query evaluation costs.

2.2.2.3   Variations on the Clustered Index Approach

Predating the above approaches, Harth et al. [32, 33] considered clustered BTree indexing of *spoc* quads in their YARS system. Since they were not interested in answering queries involving joins, only 6 of the 16 subsets of *spoc* are materialized: *spoc*, *poc*, *ocs*, *csp*, *cp*, *os*. In a more recent work, Harth et al. alternatively consider the use of extensible hash tables and in-memory sparse indexes instead of BTrees [33]. They observe that while disk I/O decreases from $O(\log(n))$ to $O(1)$ to answer queries on n quads by using extensible hash tables rather than BTrees, 16 hash tables are required to mimic the behavior of the six BTrees. As an alternative to hash tables, Harth et al. note that a similar decrease in disk I/O can be obtained by constructing an in-memory sparse index for each of the six subsets of *spoc*. Each entry in a sparse index points to the first record of a sorted block on disk. Evidently, there is a trade-off between main memory occupation and performance: to accommodate larger RDF graphs or to reduce main-memory consumption, the index can be made sparser by making the sorted blocks larger, at the expense of more disk I/O.

Wood et al. [82] build on this idea by representing the six sparse indexes on *spoc* using AVL trees [82]. For performance reasons, nodes of the AVL tree point to separate pages of 256 ordered triples. Each node of the AVL tree stores the first and the last triples of the page it represents to enable traversal of the tree without accessing the pages.

2.2.3   Horizontal Representation

Under the horizontal representation, RDF data are conceptually stored in a single table of the following format: the table has one column for each predicate value that occurs in the RDF graph and one row for each subject value. For each (s, p, o) triple, the object o is placed in the p column of row s. The music fan data from Fig. 2.1 would hence be represented by the following table.

subject	FileType	Composer	...	phone	friendOf	style
work5678	MP3	Schoenberg				
work1234		Debussy				
...						
user8604				{2223334444, 5556667777}	user3789	
Debussy						impressionist
Schoenberg						expressionist

As can be seen from this example, it is rare that a subject occurs with all possible predicate values, leading to sparse tables with many empty cells. Care must hence be taken in the physical layout of the table to avoid storing the empty cells. Also, since it is possible that a subject has multiple objects for the same predicate (e.g., user8604 has multiple phone numbers), each cell of the table represents in principle a *set* of objects, which again must be taken into account in the physical layout.

2.2.3.1 Property Tables

To minimize the storage overhead caused by empty cells, the so-called *property-table approach* concentrates on dividing the wide table in multiple smaller tables containing related predicates [46, 68, 80]. For example, in the music fan RDF graph, a different table could be introduced for Works, Fans, and Artists. In this scenario, the Works table would have columns for Composer, FileType, MediaType, and Title, but would not contain the unrelated phone or friendOf columns. The following strategies have been proposed to identify related predicates:

- In the popular Jena RDF, the grouping of predicates is defined by applications [80]. In particular, the application programmer must specify which predicates are multivalued. For each such multivalued predicate p, a new table with schema (*subject*, p) is created, thereby avoiding replicating other values. Jena also supports so-called *property-class* tables, where a new table is created for each value of the rdf:type predicate. Again, the actual layout of each property-class table is application defined. The remaining predicates that are not in any defined group are stored independently.
- In RDFBroker, Sintek et al. [68] identify related predicates by computing, for every subject x in the RDF graph G, the set of predicates $P_x = \{p \mid \exists o, ((x, p, o) \in G)\}$. For each such set P_x, a corresponding predicate table over the relational schema {*subject*} $\cup P_x$ is created. Queries can be answered by first identifying the property tables that have all of the predicate values specified in the query, answering the query on these tables, and then taking the union of the results.

  Sintek et al. note that this approach actually creates many small tables, which is harmful for query evaluation performance. To counter this, they propose various criteria for merging small tables into larger ones, introducing NULL values when a predicate is absent.
- Levandoski et al. [46] leverage previous work on association rule mining to automatically determine the predicates that often occur together, through a methodology they call data-centric storage. The methodology aims at maximizing the size of each group of predicates, while minimizing the number of NULL values that will occur in the tables. The remaining predicates that are not in any group are stored independently.

2.2.3.2   Vertical Partitioning

The so-called *vertically partitioned database approach* (not to be confused with
the vertical representation approach of Sect. 2.2.2) takes the decomposition of the
horizontal representation to its extreme [1]: each predicate column p of the
horizontal table is materialized as a binary table over the schema (*subject, p*). Each
row of each binary table essentially corresponds to a triple. Note that, hence, both
the empty cell issue and the multiple object issue are solved at the same time. Abadi
et al. [1] and Sidirourgos [67] note that the performance of this approach is best
when sorting the binary tables lexicographically according to (*subject, p*) to allow
fast joins; and that this approach is naturally implemented by a column-oriented
database.

2.2.3.3   Disadvantages and Advantages

It has been observed that, in both approaches, the distinction between predicate
values (which are elevated to the status of column names) and subject and object
values (which are stored as normal values) is a weakness when answering queries
that do not specify the predicate value. For such queries, the whole horizontal table
(or all of its partitions) must be analyzed. This hinders performance, especially in
the presence of many predicates values. Moreover, the relational schema must be
changed whenever a new predicate value is added to the RDF graph. This is not
well supported in relational database management systems, where relation schemas
are traditionally considered to be static.

   On the positive side, the horizontal representation makes it easy to support
typing of object values (e.g., it becomes possible to declare that object values of
predicate age are integers, whereas object values of predicate birthdate are
dates). Moreover, it is easy to integrate existing relational data with RDF data: it
suffices to consider the key of a relational table as the subject and the remaining
columns as predicates. As such, the existing table essentially becomes a new RDF
graph [80].

2.2.4   More on Indexing

While some of the storage strategies presented in Sects. 2.2.2 and 2.2.3 already
provide storage strategy-dependent indexes, additional indexes may be desired to
speed up query processing even further.

2.2.4.1   Literal-Specific Indexes

A first line of work in this respect targets the indexation of the *literals* occurring in an
RDF graph. To support full-text search, for example, one can add inverted indexes

on string literals [15, 32], or N-grams indexes [45] to support regular expression search. Similarly, if it is known that particular literals hold geographical information (e.g., latitude and longitude), specialized spatial indexes such as kd- and quad-trees can be added [42].

2.2.4.2   Join Indexes

A second line of work extends the classical idea of join indexes [74] to the RDF setting. In particular, Chong et al. [10] propose the construction of six binary join indexes to speed up self-joins in the vertical representation storage approach: there is an index for the self-join on subject–subject, on subject–predicate, on subject–object, on predicate–predicate, on predicate–object, and on object–object. In this way, a SPARQL query that expresses a join between two triple patterns, like

```
SELECT ?work
WHERE {
  ?user <likes>     ?work      .
  ?work <Composer> "Debussy" .
}
```

can be answered using the object–subject join index.

Groppe et al. [25] extend this idea further. They remark in particular that triple patterns in SPARQL queries rarely consist of variables only but also contain IRIs or literals (as in the example above). In order to find the joining triples that satisfy the mentioned IRI/literal requirements, Groppe et al. extend the notion of a join index and store, for each of the possible self-joins listed above (subject–subject, subject–predicate,...): 16 different indexes. Conceptually, each of the latter indexes map sequences of IRIs and literals that do not occur in the join position to the pair of joining triples.

To illustrate, consider the join index on subject–object which is meant to aid in answering joins of two triple patterns, say $(?x, p_1, o_1)$ and $(s_2, p_2, ?x)$ like in the example query above. Groppe et al. construct the 16 indexes that map all subsets of p_1, o_1, s_2, p_2 to the joining triples. So, in an RDF graph consisting of the triples

tid	subject	predicate	object
t_1	a	b	c
t_2	d	e	a
t_3	f	g	d

the 16 indexes would be constructed as follows:

p_1	o_1	s_2	p_2	
b	c	d	e	(t_1, t_2)
b	a	f	g	(t_2, t_3)

...

p_1	s_2	p_2	
b	d	e	(t_1, t_2)
b	f	g	(t_2, t_3)

...

p_1	
b	(t_1, t_2)
b	(t_2, t_3)

This approach can be further extended to handle joins between more than two triple patterns.

2.2.4.3 Materialized Views

Finally, a third line of work applies the classical notion of answering queries using views [28] to the RDF setting, thereby also extending the work on join indexes discussed above.

In a nutshell, when answering queries using views, we are given a query Q over an RDF graph G, as well as a set of materialized (relational) views $V_1, \ldots, V_n$ over G, and we want to find the cheapest query execution plan for Q that can use both G and the views $V_1, \ldots, V_n$. Of course, a critical difficulty in this respect is the selection of the views $V_1, \ldots, V_n$ to materialize.

In the RDF_MATCH approach, Chong et al. [10] propose to materialize so-called *subject–property tables* in addition to the (vertically represented) RDF graph. A subject–property table is similar to the property tables from the horizontal representation storage approach: for a set of subject values and a group of related single-valued predicates, a table is constructed where each predicate occurs as a column name. Each row contains one subject value, along with the object value of each predicate. Contrary to property tables of the horizontal store approach, however, the proposed view here is not the primary way of storage.

In the RDFMatView system, Castillo et al. [8] offer the users the possibility to identify and materialize SPARQL basic graph pattern. They note that basic graph patterns can be viewed as conjunctive queries, for which query containment is known to be decidable. When processing a new query, materialized views that can be used to answer the query are selected based on a query containment test. Subsequently, the selected views are assembled to help in the processing. A corresponding cost model to compare alternate rewritings is also proposed. A similar approach uses expression trees of the input expression as the basis for caching intermediate query results [85].

The authors of RDFViewS [22] take the complementary approach of identifying important conjunctive queries in a given weighted workload. An RDF Schema is used to guide the process of selecting the appropriate conjunctive queries.

2.3 Storing and Indexing Under the Entity Perspective

As mentioned earlier in Sect. 2.1, a major alternative way to view an RDF graph is to treat it as a collection of entity descriptions [18, 78]. Similarly to the way in which text documents are viewed as sets of keyword terms in the classical information retrieval setting, each entity is determined by a set of attribute–value and relationship–entity pairs in the entity perspective. Approaches under the entity perspective make heavy use of the inverted index data structure [81]. The reason for this is twofold. First and foremost, inverted indexes have proven to scale to very large real-world systems. Moreover, many of the aspects of inverted indexes have been thoroughly studied (e.g., encoding and compression techniques), from which the new approaches for RDF storage and indexing can benefit.

A large part of the work under the entity perspective investigates how to map the RDF model to traditional information retrieval (IR) systems. Typically, the following two general types of queries are to be supported:

- *Simple keyword queries.* A keyword query returns all entities that contain an attribute, relationship, and/or value relevant to a given keyword. To illustrate, in Fig. 2.2, if the keyword query is "work5678," query evaluation returns the set of all entities having work5678 somewhere in their description, namely, the entities work5678, Debussy, and user8604.
- *Conditional entity-centric queries.* A conditional entity-centric query returns all known entities that satisfy some given conditions on a combination of attribute, relationships, and values at the same time. For Fig. 2.2, the query "retrieve all entities with the value work5678 on the Composer^{-1} attribute" is such a conditional entity-centric query. This query returns the set of entities having value work5678 on the Composer^{-1} attribute, namely, the entity Debussy.

Note that, in contrast to relational approaches, query results under the entity perspective return a subset of the known entities, rather than relational tables. In this respect, the relational queries are more powerful since they allow the restructuring and combination of data (e.g., by performing joins, etc.), whereas the entity-centric queries only return data in their existing form. It should be noted, however, that set operations (intersection, union, etc.) are usually supported in the entity perspective to further manipulate the returned set of entities [18]. A nice comparison of index maintenance costs between relational and entity perspective systems is presented in [12].

In the rest of this section, we will introduce some of the representative works in the literature. Note that this is not an exhaustive survey of this rapidly advancing research area, but rather a selection of recent systems that illustrate the basic concepts of storage and indexing RDF data under the entity perspective.

2.3.1 Dataspaces

Dong and Halevy [13] were the first to consider inverted indexes for answering entity-centric queries over RDF graphs, in the context of the so-called *dataspace support system paradigm*. First proposed by Franklin et al. [20, 29], the dataspaces paradigm constitute a gradual, pay-as-you-go, approach to the integration of information from across diverse, interrelated, but heterogeneous data sources. In this setting, dataspaces should also provide query support in a pay-as-you-go setting, depending on the querying capabilities of the data sources themselves. For example, if a data source is plain text, maybe only keyword search is enabled. If it is semistructured data, a corresponding structured query language (comparable to XQUERY or SPARQL) could be supported. This also requires the underlying index structure to be flexible enough to accommodate the query language.

While Dong and Halevy [13] do not explicitly use the terms *RDF data model* and *RDF graphs*, the data model that they use is equivalent to RDF. Specifically, in their paper, data from different sources are unified in triples of the form (*entity, attribute, value*) or (*entity, association, entity*). These triples are then passed to the indexer for further processing. The proposed system supports both simple keyword queries and conditional entity-centric queries, and always returns a collection of entities. The system also provides support for synonyms and hierarchies, which support the discovery of more relevant results than plain querying. Referring to Fig. 2.2, for example, if the (static) system-defined hierarchy indicates that MediaType is a superclass of FileType, then the evaluation of the conditional entity-centric query "retrieves all entities with value MP3 on the MediaType attribute" with hierarchy expansion containing the entity work1234.

The basic indexing structure of Dong and Halevy is an inverted index. Each *term* in this index points to an inverted list that contains all the identifiers of all entities that *match* the term. There are three kinds of terms:

- To start with, every value v is considered a term. An entity e matches the term v if there exists a triple (*entity e, attribute a, value v*), for some attribute a. This is the same as the traditional IR approaches, to provide answering keyword query capability.
- To support conditional entity-centric queries, concatenations of a value v and attribute a (denoted $v//a//$) are also considered to be terms. An entity matches such a term if the triple (*entity e, attribute a, value v*) is present.
- Moreover, concatenations of value v and association a_1 ($v//a_1//$) are also considered terms. An entity e_1 matches this term if there exists a pair of triples (*entity e_1, association a_1, entity e_2*) and (*entity e_2, attribute a_2, value v*) for some entity id e_2 and some attribute a_2. These kinds of terms are designed to boost a specialized conditional entity-centric query, called the *one-step keyword query*. Such queries are meant to return all entities in which a given keyword appears, as well as entities that are related to entities in which the keyword appears.

For example, when indexing the example dataset in Fig. 2.2, the values (MP3), (Schoenberg), and (user8604) will be treated as terms (among others). The concatenations of values and attributes (MP3//FileType//) and (Schoenberg//Composer//) will also be considered as terms (among others). Then entity work5678 matches both of these terms, and will hence appear in the inverted list of both terms. Furthermore, because of the triple (user8604, likes, work5678), two associations (user8604, likes, work5678) and (work5678, likes^{-1}, user8604) will be generated. For the first association, we will treat (MP3//likes//) and (Schoenberg//likes//) as terms pointing to user8604. For the latter association, we let the terms (Teppei//likes^{-1}), (1975//likes^{-1}), (2223334444//likes^{-1}), and (5556667777//likes⁻¹) have the entity work5678 in their inverted lists.

Hierarchies are supported using three methods: duplication, hierarchy path, and a hybrid of these two. The idea is to materialize some of the queries as terms beforehand, so that query answering will be accelerated. The system has a built-in synonym table. By using this table, synonymous attributes are transformed to a canonical one in the index, and thereby, related results are naturally returned.

Updates are quite expensive on this index, because one entity is distributed over several inverted lists. The authors suggest to group updates together and do batch update operations to ease I/O cost. An open issue from this approach is that the result highly relies on how well the information is extracted and matched with each other from the data sources, and how well the hierarchy and synonym information are maintained. These are also open problems in information retrieval research in general.

2.3.2 SIREn

SIREn is part of the Sindice search engine project from DERI, where the objective is to index the entire "Web of Data" as a dataspace [12]. In SIREn, data are unified to a set of quadruples of the form of (*dataset, entity, attribute, value*), upon which a tree model is built. In this tree, the dataset is the root, then the entity, attribute, and value are the children of the previous element, respectively. Each node in the tree is encoded with some encoding scheme (Dewey Order for instance [24]), so that the relationship between two nodes in a tree can be determined by only looking at the encoding value. SIREn has a clear definition of logical operators on this tree model. All query answering is then done by translating these logical operators into physical operations on a representation of this tree.

SIREn extends traditional inverted indexes for physically representing these trees. This is done mainly by extending the inverted list component of the index. For indexing in SIREn, the search term could be the identifier of the dataset, the entity, the attribute, or the value. The corresponding inverted list consists of five different streams of integers: a list of entity identifiers, of term frequencies, of attribute identifiers, of value identifiers, and of term positions. Further refinement is done for each term to reduce the index size. Notice that each step of query answering does not return a collection of entities, but rather a collection of nodes in the tree model. Intermediate results can then be used as an input for subsequent operations.

To answer a keyword query, the system performs a lookup of the search term, then returns related terms with their inverted lists. The keyword query could come with a specified type, and then only the given type of inverted lists is returned. Partial matching is supported by the keyword search, such as prefix matching and regular expression, depending on the organization of the terms. To answer conditional entity-centric queries, the system first performs a keyword search with a specific type, then a join of two inverted lists is performed. Results can be further refined by other logical operations, such as projections.

Compression techniques are also incorporated in SIREn. Five inverted files are created complying with the five types of inverted lists discussed above. Each inverted file is constructed in a block-based fashion, and then various compression techniques are studied on these files. One limitation of SIREn is that join operations between data from different data sources are not efficiently supported.

2.3.3 Semplore

Semplore [76] is another representative approach of the entity perspective approach, also using inverted indexes as the storage back end. Semplore works on RDF datasets, and supports hybrid query combing of a subset of SPARQL and full-text search.

Semplore has three indexes: an ontology index, an entity index, and a textual index. The ontology index stores the ontology graph of the dataset, including super-/subconcepts and super-/subrelations. The entity index stores the relationships between the entities. The textual index handles all triples with the "text" predicate, enabling the system to do keyword search. The highlight of Semplore is to type RDF resources as Document, Field, and/or Term concepts in the inverted indexes. Moreover, the system uses a position list in inverted lists as another dimension of the inverted index. In particular, for each triple (s, p, o),

- For the ontology index, (p, o) is treated as a term and s is treated as a document. Here $p \in \{subConOf, superConOf, subRelOf, superRelOf, type\}$.
- For the entity index, two permutations (p, s, o) and (p^{-1}, o, s) are stored. Here p/p^{-1} is treated as a term and s/o is treated as a document. o/p is stored in the position list. For example in Fig. 2.2, for entity work5678, the following mapping is done:

Term	Document	Position list
FileType	work5678	MP3
FileType^{-1}	MP3	work5678
Composer	work5678	Schoenberg
Composer^{-1}	Schoenberg	work5678
likes	user8604	work5678
likes^{-1}	work5678	user8604

- For the textual index, (p, k) is treated as a term, where p is "text," and k is a token appearing in o. s is treated as the document. Following the previous example, if one more triple (work5678, text, "wonderful description") is added for entity work5678, then the words wonderful and description will both be treated as terms, having work5678 in their inverted lists.

Semplore has three basic operators: basic retrieval, merge-sort, and mass union. An input query is translated into these operations and performed on the index. The main idea is to traverse the query parse tree in a depth first way, combining intermediate results.

To be able to handle incremental updates, Semplore proposes a block-based index structure, splitting inverted lists into blocks. The Landmark technique [48] is used to locate a document in one inverted list. When blocks are full, they can split as nodes split in a BTree. Single update and batch update are both supported in this case.

Semplore supports a richer query expressiveness than the dataspace and SIREn approaches. It can answer queries concerning entity relations. However, this also involves more I/O cost, where the join operation becomes the dominant operation in the system. Also due to the incompleteness of the permutations, it is not possible to answer queries when predicates are missing (e.g., queries like (a,?,b)).

2.3.4 More on Information Retrieval Techniques

Information retrieval techniques are also widely used in other RDF systems. Here we mention some of them.

The most common use of IR techniques is using an inverted index to provide full-text search functionality. In YARS2 [33], similar to the dataspace approach, for each triple (s, p, o), the index uses the literals appearing in object position (o) as terms, pointing to a list of subjects as the inverted list. Some systems also benefit from wildcard/prefix search functionality from inverted indexes, for example, [55, 82]. Natural language processing techniques may also be used for identifying keywords in the literal strings or URIs.

Another common use is object consolidation [72, 78], which is the merging of resources from different datasets as the same entity. Several techniques such as word cleaning and synonym merging are applied in this case.

Finally, we note that several systems (e.g., [14, 44, 71]) take a hybrid approach of supporting an entity perspective on the underlying RDF dataset, while translating search queries into structured queries on the data, typically organized under the graph-based perspective, which we discuss in the next section.

2.4 Storing and Indexing Under the Graph-Based Perspective

As the name *RDF graph* already hints at, the RDF data model can be seen as essentially a graph-based data model, albeit with special features such as nodes that can act as edge labels and no fundamental distinction between schemas and instances, which can be represented in one and the same graph. This graph-based nature implies that both the types of queries and updates that need to be supported as well as the types of data structures that can be used to optimize these will be similar to those for graph databases [2]. Typical queries would, for example, be pattern matching, for example, find an embedding of a certain graph, and path expressions, such as check if there is a certain type of path between two nodes. Graph databases, in turn, are similarly closely related to object-oriented and semistructured databases. Indeed, many ideas and techniques developed earlier for those databases have already been adapted to the RDF setting. For example, Bönström et al. show in [6] that RDF can be straightforwardly and effectively stored in an object-oriented database by mapping both triples and resources to objects.

One of the key ideas that has been at the center of much research for graph-based and semistructured data is the notion of *structural index*. This section is therefore organized as follows. We first discuss the application of general graph-based indexing techniques to RDF databases. This is followed by a section on structural indexes where we first present their historical development for graph-based and semistructured databases, and then their application to RDF databases.

2.4.1 General Graph-Based Indexing Methods

2.4.1.1 Suffix Arrays

The problem of matching simple path expressions in a labeled graph can be seen as a generalization of locating the occurrences of a string as a substring in a larger target string. A well-known indexing structure for the latter setting is that of the *suffix array*, which can be described as follows. Assuming that the lexicographically sorted list of all suffixes of the target string is $[s_1, \ldots, s_n]$, then a suffix array is an array $a[1..n]$ such that $a[i] = (s_i, j_i)$ with j_i the starting position of s_i in the target string. Given a search string s, we can quickly find in the array all entries $1 \leq i \leq n$ where s is a prefix of s_i, and therefore, j_i is a position where s occurs. This idea can be generalized to node and edge-labeled directed acyclic graphs as follows. The suffixes are here defined as alternating lists of node and edge labels that occur on paths that end in a leaf, i.e., a node with no outgoing edges. With each suffix, the suffix array then associates, instead of j_i, a set of nodes in the graph. This approach is adapted and applied to RDF by Matono et al. in [51] where classes are interpreted as node labels and predicates as edge labels. The authors justify their approach by claiming that in practical RDF graphs, cycles are rare, but propose nonetheless an extension that can deal with cycles by marking in suffixes the labels that represent repeating nodes.

2.4.1.2 Tree Labeling Schemes

A common technique for optimizing path queries in trees is to label the nodes in the trees in such a way that the topological relationship between the nodes can be determined by an easy comparison of the labels only. For example, for XML, a common labeling scheme was introduced by Li and Moon [47]. They label each node with a tuple $(pre, post, level)$, where pre is an integer denoting the position of the node in a preorder tree walk, $post$ is an integer denoting the position of the node in a postorder tree walk, and $level$ is the level of the node in the tree where the root is the lowest level. Two nodes with labels (pr_1, po_1, l_1) and (pr_2, po_2, l_2) will have an ancestor–descendant relationship iff $pr_1 < pr_2$ and $po_1 < po_2$. They have a parent–child relationship iff in addition $l_2 = l_1 + 1$. We refer to Gou and Chirkova [24] for an overview of such labeling schemes for XML. In principle, this technique can be also applied to directed acyclic graphs if we transform them into a tree by (1) adding a single new root node above the old root nodes and (2) duplicating nodes that have multiple incoming edges. Clearly this can lead to a very redundant representation, but it can still speed up certain path queries. This approach is investigated by Matono et al. in [52] where, like in [51], it is assumed that RDF graphs are mostly acyclic. Note that for some parts of the RDF graph such as the Class hierarchy and the Predicate hierarchy described by an RDF Schema ontology, this assumption is always correct. As such, these hierarchies are stored separately by Matono et al. [51, 52]. Further study of interval-based labeling schemes for RDF graphs with and without cycles has been undertaken by Furche et al. [21].

2.4.1.3 Distance-Based Indexing

In [73], Udrea et al. propose a tree-shaped indexing structure called GRIN index where each node in the tree identifies a subgraph of the indexed RDF graph. This is done by associating with each node a pair (r, d) with a resource r and a distance d, defined as minimal path length and denoted here as $\delta_G(r, s)$ for the distance between r and s in graph G, which then refers to the subgraph that is spanned by the resources that are within distance d of r. The index tree is binary and built such that (1) the root is associated with all resources in the indexed graph, (2) the sets of indexed graph nodes associated with sibling nodes in the tree do not overlap, and (3) the set of nodes associated with a parent is the union of those of its two children. As is shown in [73], such indexes can be built using fairly efficient clustering algorithms similar to partitioning around medoids.

Given a query like a basic graph pattern, we can try to identify the lowest candidate nodes in the tree that refer to subgraphs into which the pattern might match. There are two rules used for this, where we check for query q and an index node with pair (r, d):

1. If q mentions resource s and $\delta_G(r, s) > d$, then the index node is not a candidate, and neither are all of its descendants.
2. If q contains also a variable v and $\delta_G(r, s) + \delta_q(s, v) > d$, then the index node is not a candidate and neither are any of its descendants. Note that this rule eliminates viable candidates because it is not necessarily true that if v is mapped to r_v by a matching of the query then $\delta_G(r, s) + \delta_q(s, v) = \delta_G(r, r_v)$. However, this rule was found to work well in practice in [73].

The query is then executed with standard main-memory-based pattern matching algorithms on the subgraphs associated with the lowest remaining candidates, i.e., those that have no parent in the index tree which is a candidate. The restriction to the lowest is correct if we assume that the basic graph pattern is connected and mentions at least one resource.

2.4.1.4 System Π

Several graph-based indexing techniques were investigated by Wu et al. in the context of System Π, a hypergraph-based RDF store. In [83], which preceded system Π, Wu et al. propose to use an index based on Prüfer sequences. These sequences had already been suggested for indexing XML by Rao and Moon in [61] and can encode node-labeled trees into sequences such that the problem of finding embeddings of tree patterns is reduced to finding subsequences. However, since RDF graphs may contain cycles and have labeled edges, this method needs to be adapted considerably and loses much of its elegance and efficiency, which is perhaps why it was not used in System Π as presented by Wu and Li in [83]. A technique mentioned in both papers is the encoding of the partial orderings defined by the Class and Property hierarchies in RDF Schema ontologies using a labeling technique based on prime numbers. First, each node n in the partial order is assigned a unique prime number $p(n)$. Then, we define $c(n) = \Pi_{m \preceq n} p(m)$ where $\preceq$ denotes the partial order. It then holds that $n \preceq n'$ iff $c(n')$ is a multiple of $c(n)$.

2.4.2 Structural Indexes

An often recurring and important notion for indexing semistructured data is the *structural index* (or *structure index* or *structural summary*, as it is also known). They can be explained straightforwardly if we assume that the data instance is represented by a directed edge-labeled graph. An example of a structural index is then a reduced version of this graph where certain nodes have been merged while maintaining all edges. In the resulting graph, we store with each node m the set $M(m)$ of nodes, also called the *payload* of m, which were merged into it. The crucial property of such an index is that for many graph queries, such as path expressions and graph patterns, it holds that they can be executed over the structural index and then give us a set of candidate results that contain the correct results as a subset. For example, consider the query that returns all pairs of nodes (n_1, n_2) such that there is a directed path from n_1 to n_2 that satisfies a certain regular expression. If, when executed over a structural index, the pair of merged nodes (m_1, m_2) is returned, then all pairs in $M(m_1) \times M(m_2)$ can be considered as candidate results. In fact, for certain types of queries and merging criteria, it can be shown that the set of candidate results is always *exactly* the correct result, in which case the index is said to be *precise*. However, even if this is not the case, in which case the index is called *approximate*, the structural index can provide a quick way of obtaining a relatively small set of candidate solutions, especially if the original graph has to be stored on disk but the index fits in main memory.

2.4.2.1 Dataguides, 1-Indexes, 2-Indexes, and T-Indexes

The first work that introduced structural indexes was that by Goldman and Widom [23] which introduced a special kind of structural index called the *dataguide*. In their setting, both the data instance and the structural index are rooted graphs. The dataguides have the restriction that each node has for each label at most one outgoing edge with that label. The focus is on queries defined by path expressions that are evaluated starting from the root. For certain path expressions and a particular type of dataguide called *strong dataguide*, it is shown that the dataguide is precise. This work was extended by Milo and Suciu in [54] where three types of structural indexes were introduced: the *1-index*, the *2-index*, and the *T-index*. The 1-index focuses on the same queries as dataguides, but the merging of nodes is based on an equivalence relation based on bisimulation that follows the edges in reverse, which can be relatively efficiently computed, but still produces a precise index. The 2-index focuses on queries of the form $* x_1 P x_2$ where $*$ is the wildcard path expression that matches any path and P is an arbitrary path expression. The variables x_1 and x_2 indicate the positions in the path that are returned as a result, so the result is a set of pairs of nodes. A T-index focuses on an even wider class of queries, viz., those of the form $T_1 x_1 T_2 x_2 \cdots T_n x_n$ where each T_i is either a path expression or a formula expressing a local condition. A different T-index is defined for each query template, where a query template is defined by choosing for certain T_i a particular path expression, and specifying for others only if they are a path expression or a formula. The 2-index and T-indexes are not based on merging on single nodes, as in dataguides and 1-indexes, but rather on tuples of n nodes or less, but also here, there is an accompanying notion of equivalence and a result that says that these indexes are precise for the queries they are defined for.

2.4.2.2 Localized Notions of (Bi)similarity

This work was applied and extended in an XML setting by Kaushik et al. in [39]. Here data instances are modeled as a node-labeled tree with additional idref edges that may introduce cycles. The authors observe that 1-indexes can become very large in practice and that they can be reduced in size if we redefine the equivalence relation for merging by basing it on k bisimulation which essentially considers only the local environment of a node within distance k. This causes the equivalence relation to be coarser, therefore more nodes to be merged, and so produces a smaller index, called an A(k)-index. However, it also causes the resulting index to be only approximate and no longer precise for the considered query language (namely, regular path expressions). It is shown that this approximation is relatively rare in practice, and that it often can be detected that the result is precise without considering the original data instance graph.

This work was subsequently extended by Kaushik et al. in [37] for the subset of XPath known as BPQ, the *Branching Path Queries*. These queries allow the use of the forward axes `child` and `descendant`, the backward axes `parent` and `ancestor`, and navigating using the `idref` attributes both forward and backward. They also allow filtering conditions for intermediate nodes that consist of path expressions combined with the `and`, `or`, and `not` operators. The basic trick here is to extend the instance graph with all the reverse edges, i.e., for a `child` edge, we add a reverse `parent` edge, and for every `idref` edge, we add a reverse $idref^{-1}$ edge. We then can again define a notion of equivalence based on forward and backward bisimulation, which now looks in both directions, and results in a precise index. Moreover, we can again reduce the size of the index by considering only the local environment of a node up to distance k and sacrificing precision.

2.4.2.3   Connections with Query Language Fragments

Since for structural indexes there is a trade-off between size and precision, that is a smaller index is probably less precise, and because efficiency requires that indexes are as small as possible, it is interesting to determine what the smallest index is that is still precise for a certain query language. It was, for example, shown by Kaushik et al. in [37] that for XML and the XPath subset BPQ, the smallest precise structural index is defined based on forward and backward bisimulation. Similar results were obtained by Ramanan in [60] where it was shown that for the positive fragment of BPQ, i.e, without negation, and for TPQ (Tree Pattern Queries), not bisimulation but simulation defines the smallest precise structural index. Similar results for other fragments of XPath were obtained by Gyssens et al. in [26] and by Wu et al. in [84]. The usefulness of such analysis is shown by Fletcher et al. in [19] where an improved version version of A(k) indexes is proposed, called P(k) indexes, which for each k is shown to be minimal and precise for a certain well-defined practical XPath fragment.

2.4.2.4   Structural Indexes Combined with Other Indexing Techniques

Structural indexes can be combined and extended with other indexing techniques. For example, Kaushik et al. present in [38] an information retrieval system that retrieves XML documents based on path expression that may contain some position keywords. In order to efficiently match the keywords, the structural index is extended with an inverted list that not only maps keywords to element and text nodes, but also provides a pointer to the index node whose payload contains that element or text node. This can be seen as an extension to the indexing mechanism of SIREn, as discussed in Sect. 2.3.2, but now the small trees that represent entities are generalized to XML documents.

Another combination is presented by Arion et al. in [3] where XML documents are indexed with a structural index that is essentially a 1-index as presented in Sect. 2.4.2 except that it is required to be a tree. Although this may make the index larger than necessary, this is compensated by the fact that it allows the use of the (*pre, post, level*) labeling scheme on the index itself, which allows faster execution of path expressions over this tree structure.

2.4.2.5 Parameterizable Index Graphs

One of the first instances where structural indexes were explicitly used for RDF graphs is by Tran and Ladwig [70]. In their work, it is assumed that the RDF graph is essentially an edge-labeled graph with the edge labels explicitly distinct from the graph nodes. Consequently, in basic graph patterns, it is not allowed to have variables in the predicate position of a triple pattern. Although this excludes certain typical RDF use cases where data and metadata are queried together, it makes the indexing and query optimization problem more similar to that in classical graph databases.

The fundamental notion is that of *parameterizable index graph*, or PIG, which is a structural index based on forward and backward bisimulation, as was introduced by Kaushik et al. in [37]. For a certain index, the types of edges that are considered for this bisimilarity can be restricted as specified by two sets: one containing the edges labels, i.e., predicate names, that are considered for the forward direction and the other set those for the backward direction. These sets can be used to tune the index for certain workloads.

Based on the PIG, three concrete indexing structures are defined: (1) An index *PIGidx* that represents the PIG itself and maps predicate names to a sorted list of pairs that represent the edges in the PIG associated with that predicate name. (2) An index we will call *VPSOidx* over keyspace (v, p, s, o) with v a node in PIG, which allow prefix matching, i.e., we can do lookups for v, vp or vps, and returns sorted results. A tuple (v, p, s, o) is indexed if (s, p, o) is in the RDF graph and s is in the payload of v. (3) A similar index we will call *VPOSidx* over keyspace (v, p, o, s).

Given these indexes, the result of a query that is a basic graph pattern can then be computed as follows. First we apply the query to the PIG and obtain answers in terms of PIG nodes. This can be done by iterating over the triple patterns in the basic graph pattern, and for each extend the intermediate result, by equijoining it appropriately with the pairs associated by PIGidx with the mentioned predicate name. For a query with n triple patterns, the result is a set of tuples of the form $T = (v_1, \ldots, v_{2n})$ where for $1 \leq i \leq n$, each pair (v_{2i-1}, v_{2i}) is a local matching for the ith triple pattern. For such pairs (v_{2i-1}, v_{2i}), we can define an associated set L_i of pairs at the RDF graph level such that L_i contains (r_{2i}, r_{2i-1}) iff r_{2i} and r_{2i-1} are in the payload of $(v_{2i-1}$ and $v_{2i})$, respectively, and (r_{2i}, p_i, r_{2i-1}) is in the RDF graph, where p_i the predicate in triple pattern i. For each such T, we can then construct a set of corresponding tuples of $2n$ resources in the RDF graph by equijoining these L_i using appropriate equality conditions. Depending on the equality conditions and the join order, we can compute each additional join step using either VPSOidx or VPOSidx plus some selections. Finally, we take the union of all these sets, and project the result such that we have only one column for each variable in the query.

There are several ways in which these proposed indexes and the query executing procedure can be optimized. The PIG can, for example, be made smaller by restricting the bisimulation to depth k as in A(k) and P(k) indexes. The query execution can be optimized by considering different join orders, and since for certain tree-shaped queries PIGidx is in fact a precise index, these can sometimes be pruned from a query after the first step of query execution over PIGidx.

2.4.2.6   gStore

Another RDF datastore that features indexing structures that can be thought of as a structural index is gStore, presented by Zou et al. in [86]. In this system, the focus is on answering queries with wildcards over disk-based data, and supporting this with an index that is easy to maintain. Also here, as for parameterized index graphs, the assumption is made that the RDF graph is treated as essentially an edge-labeled graph.

The key idea of gStore is to assign to each resource not only an integer identifier but also a *signature*. The signature is a bit-string that contains some information about the triples in which the resource occurs as the subject. It is determined as follows. First, we define for each of these relevant triples a bit-string of $M + N$ bits, where M bits are used to encode the predicate and N bits are used to encode the object. The predicate is encoded in M bits by applying some appropriate hash function. If the object is a resource, then it is also mapped by means of a hash function to an N bits number. If the object is a literal, however, then we determine the N bits as follows: first determine the set of 3-grams of the literal, and then apply a hash function h that maps each 3-gram to a number in $[1...N]$. We set the ith bit to 1 iff there is a 3-gram in the set that is mapped by h to i. Given these encodings of each triple in $M + N$ bits, we then combine all these bit-strings into a single bit-string of $M + N$ bits by taking their bitwise OR (remember that all of the triples have the same subject s). The key insight is if we do the same for variables in a basic graph pattern, while mapping variables in the object to $M + N$ zeros, this gives us a quick way to filter out certain impossible matches by checking if the bit-string of the variable is subsumed by the bit-string of the resource.

The indexing structure built over the signatures of resources is called a VS-tree, a vertex signature tree. This is a balanced tree such that each of its leaves corresponds to a signature of a resource and the internal nodes correspond to signatures obtained by taking the bitwise OR of the children's signatures. The tree is optimized to efficiently locate a certain signature of a resource when starting from the root. At each level in the tree, we also add edges between tree nodes at the same level. Such an edge indicates the existence of at least one triple between resources associated with the leaves of the subtrees rooted at these tree nodes. More precisely, between index tree nodes m_1 and m_2 at level l, there will be an edge iff there is a leaf node m_1' below m_1 and a leaf node m_2' below m_2 such that these correspond to signatures of the resources r_1 and r_2, respectively, and there is a triple of the form (r_1, p, r_2). Moreover, this edge between m_1 and m_2 in the index is labeled with a bit-string of M bits which is the bitwise OR of the signatures of all predicates that hold among all such r_1 and r_2. Note that at each higher level of this index, we therefore find a smaller, more abstract, and summarized structural index of the original RDF graph. This allows us to determine all matchings of a basic graph pattern, by starting from the root and moving one level down each time, each step eliminating more impossible matchings and refining those that remain, until we have matchings on the leaves. In the final step, we can translate these to matchings on the actual resources which we can check against the actual RDF graph.

2.5 Conclusion and Future Work

In this chapter, we have provided an up-to-date survey of the rich variety of approaches to storing and indexing very large RDF datasets. As we have seen, this is a very active area of research, with sophisticated contributions from several fields. The survey has been organized by the three main perspectives which unify the many efforts across these fields: relational, entity, and graph-based views on RDF data.

We conclude with brief indications for further research. Across all perspectives, a major open issue is the incorporation of schema and ontology reasoning (e.g., RDFS and OWL) in storage and indexing. In particular, there has been relatively little work on the impact of reasoning on disk-based data structures (e.g., see [27, 69]). Furthermore, efficient maintenance of storage and indexing structures as datasets evolve is a challenge for all approaches where many research questions remain open. Possible directions for additional future work in the entity perspective are the investigation of support for richer query languages and integration of entity-centric storage and indexing with techniques from the other two perspectives. Finally, it is clear from the survey that graph-based storage and indexing is currently the least developed perspective. A major additional direction for research here is the development and study of richer structural indexing techniques and related query processing strategies, following the success of such approaches for semistructured data.

Acknowledgements The research of FP is supported by an FNRS/FRIA scholarship. The research of SV is supported by the OSCB project funded by the Brussels Capital Region. The research of GF, JH, and YL is supported by the Netherlands Organisation for Scientific Research (NWO).

References

1. Abadi, D., Marcus, A., Madden, S., Hollenbach, K.: SW-Store: a vertically partitioned DBMS for semantic web data management. VLDB J. **18**, 385–406 (2009)
2. Angles, R., Gutierrez, C.: Survey of graph database models. ACM Comput. Surv. **40**, 1:1–1:39 (2008)
3. Arion, A., Bonifati, A., Manolescu, I., Pugliese, A.: Path summaries and path partitioning in modern XML databases. World Wide Web **11**, 117–151 (2008)
4. Atre, M., Chaoji, V., Zaki, M.J., Hendler, J.A.: Matrix "bit" loaded: a scalable lightweight join query processor for RDF data. Proceedings of the 19th International Conference on World Wide Web, WWW '10, pp. 41–50. ACM, New York, NY, USA (2010)
5. Bizer, C., Jentzsch, A., Cyganiak, R.: State of the LOD cloud. http://www4.wiwiss.fu-berlin.de/lodcloud/state/. Retrieved July 5, 2011
6. Bönström, V., Hinze, A., Schweppe, H.: Storing RDF as a graph. Proceedings of the First Conference on Latin American Web Congress, pp. 27–36. IEEE Computer Society, Washington, DC, USA (2003)
7. Broekstra, J., Kampman, A., van Harmelen, F.: Sesame: a generic architecture for storing and querying RDF and RDF schema. International semantic web conference, pp. 54–68. Sardinia, Italy (2002)
8. Castillo, R.: RDFMatView: indexing RDF data for SPARQL queries. 9th international semantic web conference (ISWC2010), 2010
9. Center, Q.G.: Bio2RDF. http://bio2rdf.org/, 10 March 2012
10. Chong, E.I., Das, S., Eadon, G., Srinivasan, J.: An efficient SQL-based RDF qeurying scheme. VLDB, pp. 1216–1227. Trondheim, Norway (2005)
11. Data.gov. http://www.data.gov, 10 March 2012
12. Delbru, R., Campinas, S., Tummarello, G.: Searching web data: an entity retrieval and high-performance indexing model. Web Semant. Sci. Serv. Agents World Wide Web **10**, 33–58 (2012)
13. Dong, X., Halevy, A.Y.: Indexing dataspaces. ACM SIGMOD, Beijing, 2007, pp. 43–54
14. Elbassuoni, S., Ramanath, M., Schenkel, R., Weikum, G.: Searching RDF graphs with SPARQL and keywords. IEEE Data Eng. Bull. **33**(1), 16–24 (2010)
15. Erling, O.: Towards web scale RDF. SSWS. Karlsruhe, Germany (2008)
16. Erling, O., Mikhailov, I.: RDF support in the virtuoso DBMS. In: Auer S., Bizer C., Müller C., Zhdanova A.V. (eds.) CSSW, *LNI*, vol. 113, pp. 59–68. GI (2007)
17. Fletcher, G.H.L., Beck, P.W.: Scalable indexing of RDF graphs for efficient join processing. CIKM, pp. 1513–1516, Hong Kong, 2009
18. Fletcher, G.H.L., Van Den Bussche, J., Van Gucht, D., Vansummeren, S.: Towards a theory of search queries. ACM Trans. Database Syst. **35**, 28:1–28:33 (2010)
19. Fletcher, G.H.L., Van Gucht, D., Wu, Y., Gyssens, M., Brenes, S., Paredaens, J.: A methodology for coupling fragments of XPath with structural indexes for XML documents. Inform. Syst. **34**(7), 657–670 (2009)
20. Franklin, M., Halevy, A., Maier, D.: From databases to dataspaces: a new abstraction for information management. SIGMOD Rec. **34**, 27–33 (2005)
21. Furche, T., Weinzierl, A., Bry, F.: Labeling RDF graphs for linear time and space querying. In: De Virgilio, R., Giunchiglia, F., Tanca, L. (eds.) Semantic Web Information Management, pp. 309–339. Springer, Berlin, Heidelberg, New York (2009)
22. Goasdoué, F., Karanasos, K., Leblay, J., Manolescu, I.: Rdfviews: a storage tuning wizard for rdf applications. In: Huang, J., Koudas, N., Jones, G.J.F., Wu, X., Collins-Thompson, K., An, A. (eds.) CIKM, pp. 1947–1948. ACM, New York (2010)
23. Goldman, R., Widom, J.: DataGuides: enabling query formulation and optimization in semistructured databases. VLDB, pp. 436–445, Athens, Greece, 1997
24. Gou, G., Chirkova, R.: Efficiently querying large XML data repositories: a survey. IEEE Trans. Knowl. Data Eng. **19**(10), 1381–1403 (2007)

25. Groppe, S., Groppe, J., Linnemann, V.: Using an index of precomputed joins in order to speed up SPARQL processing. ICEIS, pp. 13–20, Funchal, Madeira, Portugal, 2007
26. Gyssens, M., Paredaens, J., Van Gucht, D., Fletcher, G.H.L.: Structural characterizations of the semantics of XPath as navigation tool on a document. ACM PODS, pp. 318–327, Chicago, 2006
27. Haffmans, W.J., Fletcher, G.H.L.: Efficient RDFS entailment in external memory. In: SWWS, pp. 464–473. Hersonissos, Crete, Greece (2011)
28. Halevy, A.Y.: Answering queries using views: a survey. VLDB J. **10**(4), 270–294 (2001)
29. Halevy, A.Y., Franklin, M.J., Maier, D.: Principles of dataspace systems. PODS, pp. 1–9, Chicago, 2006
30. Harris, S.: SPARQL query processing with conventional relational database systems. Web Inform. Syst. Eng. WISE 2005 Workshops **3807**, 235–244 (2005)
31. Harris, S., Gibbins, N.: 3store: efficient bulk RDF storage. PSSS1, Proceedings of the First International Workshop on Practical and Scalable Semantic Systems, pp. 1–15, Sanibel Island, Florida, 2003
32. Harth, A., Decker, S.: Optimized index structures for querying RDF from the web. IEEE LA-WEB, pp. 71–80, Buenos Aires, Argentina (2005)
33. Harth, A., Umbrich, J., Hogan, A., Decker, S.: YARS2: a federated repository for querying graph structured data from the web. ISWC. Busan, Korea (2007)
34. Hayes, P.: RDF Semantics. W3C Recommendation (2004)
35. Heath, T., Bizer, C.: Linked Data: Evolving the Web into a Global Data Space. Morgan and Claypool, San Francisco (2011)
36. Hertel, A., Broekstra, J., Stuckenschmidt, H.: RDF storage and retrieval systems. In: Staab, S., Rudi Studer, D. (eds.) Handbook on Ontologies, International Handbooks on Information Systems, pp. 489–508. Springer, Berlin, Heidelberg (2009)
37. Kaushik, R., Bohannon, P., Naughton, J.F., Korth, H.F.: Covering indexes for branching path queries. ACM SIGMOD, pp. 133–144. Madison, WI (2002)
38. Kaushik, R., Krishnamurthy, R., Naughton, J.F., Ramakrishnan, R.: On the integration of structure indexes and inverted lists. ACM SIGMOD, pp. 779–790. Paris (2004)
39. Kaushik, R., Shenoy, P., Bohannon, P., Gudes, E.: Exploiting local similarity for indexing paths in graph-structured data. IEEE ICDE, pp. 129–140. San Jose, CA (2002)
40. Klyne, G., Carroll, J.J.: Resource description framework (RDF): concepts and abstract syntax. W3C Recommendation (2004)
41. Kolas, D., Emmons, I., Dean, M.: Efficient linked-list RDF indexing in parliament. In: Fokoue A., Guo Y., Liebig T. (eds.) Proceedings of the 5th International Workshop on Scalable Semantic Web Knowledge Base Systems (SSWS2009), *CEUR*, vol. 517, pp. 17–32. Washington DC, USA (2009)
42. Kolas, D., Self, T.: Spatially-augmented knowledgebase. In: Aberer, K., Choi, K.S., Noy, N.F., Allemang, D., Lee, K.I., Nixon, L.J.B., Golbeck, J., Mika, P., Maynard, D., Mizoguchi, R., Schreiber, G., Cudré-Mauroux. P. (eds.) ISWC/ASWC, Lecture Notes in Computer Science, vol. 4825, pp. 792–801. Springer, Berlin Heidelberg (2007)
43. Konstantinou, N., Spanos, D.E., Mitrou, N.: Ontology and database mapping: a survey of current implementations and future directions. J. Web Eng. **7**(1), 1–24 (2008)
44. Ladwig, G., Tran, T.: Combining query translation with query answering for efficient keyword search. ESWC, pp. 288–303. Crete (2010)
45. Lee, J., Pham, M.D., Lee, J., Han, W.S., Cho, H., Yu, H., Lee, J.H.: Processing SPARQL queries with regular expressions in RDF databases. Proceedings of the ACM Fourth International Workshop on Data and Text Mining in Biomedical Informatics, DTMBIO '10, pp. 23–30. ACM, New York, NY, USA (2010)
46. Levandoski, J.J., Mokbel, M.F.: RDF data-centric storage. ICWS, pp. 911–918. IEEE (2009)
47. Li, Q., Moon, B.: Indexing and querying xml data for regular path expressions. Proceedings of the 27th International Conference on very Large data bases, VLDB '01, pp. 361–370. Morgan Kaufmann Publishers Inc., San Francisco, CA, USA (2001)

48. Lim, L., Wang, M., Padmanabhan, S., Vitter, J.S., Agarwal, R.: Dynamic maintenance of web indexes using landmarks. Proceedings of the 12th International Conference on World Wide Web, WWW '03, pp. 102–111. ACM, New York, NY, USA (2003)
49. Ma, L., Su, Z., Pan, Y., Zhang, L., Liu, T.: RStar: an RDF storage and query system for enterprise resource management. ACM CIKM, pp. 484–491. Washington, D.C. (2004)
50. del Mar Roldán García, M., Montes, J.F.A.: A survey on disk oriented querying and reasoning on the semantic web. IEEE ICDE workshop SWDB. Atlanta (2006)
51. Matono, A., Amagasa, T., Yoshikawa, M., Uemura, S.: An indexing scheme for RDF and RDF schema based on suffix arrays. SWDB, pp. 151–168. Berlin (2003)
52. Matono, A., Amagasa, T., Yoshikawa, M., Uemura, S.: A path-based relational RDF database. ADC, pp. 95–103. Newcastle, Australia (2005)
53. McGlothlin, J.P., Khan, L.R.: Rdfkb: efficient support for rdf inference queries and knowledge management. In: Desai B.C., Saccà D., Greco S. (eds.) IDEAS, ACM international conference proceeding series, pp. 259–266. ACM (2009)
54. Milo, T., Suciu, D.: Index structures for path expressions. ICDT, pp. 277–295. Jerusalem (1999)
55. Minack, E., Sauermann, L., Grimnes, G., Fluit, C.: The sesame lucenesail: Rdf queries with full-text search. Techinical report, NEPOMUK Consortium, (2008)
56. Neumann, T., Weikum, G.: RDF-3X: a RISC-style engine for RDF. VLDB. Auckland, New Zealand (2008)
57. Neumann, T., Weikum, G.: x-RDF-3X: fast querying, high update rates, and consistency for RDF databases. Proc. VLDB Endow. 3, 256–263 (2010)
58. Oren, E., Kotoulas, S., Anadiotis, G., Siebes, R., ten Teije, A., van Harmelen, F.: Marvin: distributed reasoning over large-scale semantic web data. J. Web Semant. 7(4), 305–316 (2009)
59. Prud'hommeaux, E., Seaborne, A.: SPARQL query language for RDF. W3C Recommendation (2008)
60. Ramanan, P.: Covering indexes for XML queries: bisimulation – simulation – negation. Proceedings of the 29th International Conference on very Large Data Bases – Volume 29, VLDB '2003, pp. 165–176. VLDB Endowment (2003)
61. Rao, P., Moon, B.: Sequencing XML data and query twigs for fast pattern matching. ACM Trans. Database Syst. 31, 299–345 (2006)
62. Rohloff, K., Dean, M., Emmons, I., Ryder, D., Sumner, J.: An evaluation of triple-store technologies for large data stores. OTM 2007 Workshop SSWS, pp. 1105–1114. Vilamoura, Portugal (2007)
63. Rohloff, K., Schantz, R.E.: Clause-iteration with mapreduce to scalably query datagraphs in the shard graph-store. Proceedings of the Fourth International Workshop on Data-Intensive Distributed Computing, DIDC '11, pp. 35–44. ACM, New York, NY, USA (2011)
64. Sakr, S., Al-Naymat, G.: Relational processing of RDF queries: a survey. ACM SIGMOD Record 38, 23–28 (2009). URL http://www.sigmod.org/publications/sigmod-record/0912
65. Schmidt, M., Hornung, T., Küchlin, N., Lausen, G., Pinkel, C.: An experimental comparison of RDF data management approaches in a SPARQL benchmark scenario. ISWC, pp. 82–97. Karlsruhe (2008)
66. Schmidt, M., Hornung, T., Lausen, G., Pinkel, C.: SP^{2}Bench: a SPARQL performance benchmark. IEEE ICDE. Shanghai (2009)
67. Sidirourgos, L., Goncalves, R., Kersten, M., Nes, N., Manegold, S.: Column-store support for RDF data management: not all swans are white. Proc. VLDB Endow. 1, 1553–1563 (2008)
68. Sintek, M., Kiesel, M.: RDFBroker: a signature-based high-performance RDF store. ESWC, pp. 363–377. Budva, Montenegro (2006)
69. Theoharis, Y., Christophides, V., Karvounarakis, G.: Benchmarking database representations of RDF/S stores. In: Gil Y., Motta E., Benjamins V.R., Musen M.A. (eds.) International semantic web conference. Lecture Notes in Computer Science, vol. 3729, pp. 685–701. Springer, Berlin, Heidelberg, New York (2005)
70. Tran, T., Ladwig, G.: Structure index for RDF data. Workshop on Semantic Data Management (SemData@ VLDB) (2010)

71. Tran, T., Wang, H., Rudolph, S., Cimiano, P.: Top-k exploration of query candidates for efficient keyword search on graph-shaped (RDF) data. ICDE, pp. 405–416. Shanghai (2009)
72. Tummarello, G., Cyganiak, R., Catasta, M., Danielczyk, S., Delbru, R., Decker, S.: Sig.ma: live views on the web of data. Web Semant. Sci. Serv. Agents World Wide Web **8**(4), 355–364 (2010). DOI 10.1016/j.websem.2010.08.003
73. Udrea, O., Pugliese, A., Subrahmanian, V.S.: GRIN: a graph based RDF index. AAAI, pp. 1465–1470. Vancouver, B.C. (2007)
74. Valduriez, P.: Join indices. ACM Trans. Database Syst. **12**, 218–246 (1987)
75. W3C SWEO Community Project: Linking open data. http://www.w3.org/wiki/SweoIG/TaskForces/CommunityProjects/LinkingOpenData, 10 March 2012
76. Wang, H., Liu, Q., Penin, T., Fu, L., Zhang, L., Tran, T., Yu, Y., Pan, Y.: Semplore: a scalable IR approach to search the web of data. Web Semant. Sci. Serv. Agents World Wide Web **7**(3), 177–188 (2009)
77. Wang, X., Wang, S., Pufeng, D., Zhiyong, F.: Path summaries and path partitioning in modern XML databases. Int. J. Modern Edu. Comput. Sci. **3**, 55–61 (2011)
78. Weikum, G., Theobald, M.: From information to knowledge: harvesting entities and relationships from web sources. PODS, pp. 65–76. Indianapolis (2010)
79. Weiss, C., Karras, P., Bernstein, A.: Hexastore: sextuple indexing for semantic web data management. VLDB, Auckland, New Zealand (2008)
80. Wilkinson, K.: Jena property table implementation. SSWS, pp. 35–46. Athens, Georgia, USA (2006)
81. Witten, I., Moffat, A., Bell, T.: Managing Gigabytes: Compressing and Indexing Documents and Images. Morgan Kaufmann, Los Altos, CA (1999)
82. Wood, D., Gearon, P., Adams, T.: Kowari: a platform for semantic web storage and analysis. XTech. Amsterdam (2005)
83. Wu, G., Li, J.: Managing large scale native RDF semantic repository from the graph model perspective. ACM SIGMOD Workshop IDAR, pp. 85–86. Beijing (2007)
84. Wu, Y., Gucht, D.V., Gyssens, M., Paredaens, J.: A study of a positive fragment of path queries: Expressiveness, normal form and minimization. Comput. J. **54**(7), 1091–1118 (2011)
85. Yang, M., Wu, G.: Caching intermediate result of sparql queries. In: Srinivasan, S., Ramamritham, K., Kumar, A., Ravindra, M.P., Bertino, E., Kumar, R. (eds.) WWW (Companion Volume), pp. 159–160. ACM, New York (Los Angeles, CA) (2011)
86. Zou, L., Mo, J., Chen, L., Özsu, M.T., Zhao, D.: gStore: answering SPARQL queries via subgraph matching. Proc. VLDB Endowment **4**(8), 482–493 (2011)

Chapter 3
Designing Exploratory Search Applications upon Web Data Sources

Marco Brambilla and Stefano Ceri

3.1 Introduction

Search is the preferred method to access information in today's computing systems. The Web, accessed through search engines, is universally recognized as the source for answering users' information needs. However, offering a link to a Web page does not cover all information needs. Even simple problems, such as "Which theater offers an at least three-stars action movie in London close to a good Italian restaurant," can only be solved by searching the Web multiple times, e.g., by extracting a list of the recent action movies filtered by ranking, then looking for movie theaters, then looking for Italian restaurants close to them. While search engines hint to useful information, the user's brain is the fundamental platform for information integration.

An important trend is the availability of new, specialized data sources—the so-called "long tail" of the Web of data. Such carefully collected and curated data sources can be much more valuable than information currently available in Web pages; however, many sources remain hidden or insulated, in the lack of software solutions for bringing them to surface and making them usable in the search context. A new class of tailor-made systems, designed to satisfy the needs of users with specific aims, will support the publishing and integration of data sources for vertical domains; the user will be able to select sources based on individual or collective trust, and systems will be able to route queries to such sources and to provide easy-to-use interfaces for combining them within search strategies, at the same time, rewarding the data source owners for each contribution to effective search. Efforts such as Google's Fusion Tables show that the technology for bringing hidden data sources to surface is feasible.

M. Brambilla (✉) · S. Ceri
Dipartimento di Elettronica e Informazione, Politecnico di Milano, P.za L. Da Vinci, 32. I-20133 Milano, Italy
e-mail: marco.brambilla@polimi.it; stefano.ceri@polimi.it

R. De Virgilio et al. (eds.), *Semantic Search over the Web*,
Data-Centric Systems and Applications, DOI 10.1007/978-3-642-25008-8_3,
© Springer-Verlag Berlin Heidelberg 2012

In this chapter, we focus on building complex search applications upon structured Web data, by providing a set of software engineering guidelines and tools to the designer. We assume that the search services available on the Web have been identified and registered within a search service integration platform, and based on that, we allow for the definition of vertical applications through conceptual definition of the domains of interest. In particular, we define a pattern-based approach for defining the structure of Web entities, for defining their integration, and for specifying information seeking strategies upon them. We focus on *exploratory queries*, that is, queries where, given the current context of interaction, the user is able to follow links to connected concepts, thus adding a new query fragment or rolling back to a previous result combination. Exploratory queries are by nature incremental. Our proposal for addressing exploratory search upon multidomain, structured Web data sources, is presented in the Liquid Query paradigm [5], which allows users to interact with the search computing result by asking the system to produce "more result combinations," or "more results from a specific service," or "performing an expansion of the result" by adding a subquery which was already planned while configuring the query.

The technological support for our work is provided by the search computing (SeCo) framework [14, 15], which provides a general purpose Web integration platform and search engine upon distinct sources. The main purpose of our framework is lowering the complexity of building search applications. The impact of this work can be potentially high: when the complexity threshold of building structured entity search applications will be lowered, a variety of new market sectors will become more profitable and accessible. In several scenarios, search-enabled Web access will grow in interest and value when SMEs or local businesses will see the opportunity of building search applications tailored to their market niche or sale region.

The chapter is organized as follows: Sect. 3.2 discusses the related work; Sect. 3.3 defines the basic concepts for describing entities and their connections on the Web; Sect. 3.4 defines the design patterns for building Web applications, presenting several examples; Sect. 3.5 shows how some examples have been already deployed as Web applications within SeCo; Sect. 3.6 presents the tool platform for allowing query execution, service registration, and application deployment; and Sect. 3.7 concludes.

3.2 State of the Art

The design of novel search systems and interfaces is backed by several studies aimed at understanding users' search behavior on the Web. After the seminal work by Broder [13], other studies have investigated search behaviors and effectiveness of result page composition [16] by analyzing search engine logs. A review of approaches to search log data mining and Web search investigation is in [2].

A specific class of studies is devoted to exploratory search, where the user's intent is primarily to learn more on a topic of interest [20, 25]. Such information seeking behavior challenges the search engine interface, because it requires support to all the stages of information acquisition, from the initial formulation of the area of interest, to the discovery of the most relevant and authoritative sources, to the establishment of relationships among the relevant information elements. A number of techniques have been proposed to support exploratory search, and user studies have been conducted to understand the effectiveness of the various approaches (e.g., [19]), including analyses of the involvement of the user in the information extraction process [21].

Linked Data (LD) and other open or proprietary data are made available through Web APIs (e.g., see Google Places API and Google Fusion Tables [17]) and/or search-specific languages (e.g., see the Yahoo query language (YQL) framework [26]). Methods, models, and tools are being devised for efficiently designing and deploying applications upon such new data services and data access APIs. An important aspect of LD is their use of universal references for data linking; this aspect raises the hopes of solving the data-matching problem, which has so far limited the practical applicability of data integration methods.

However, data access and linking so far has not been concerned with data search. The efficient support of such data services requires mastering both data and control dependencies, and strategy optimization must consider rank aggregation, optimal result paging, and so on [9]. When data sources must be joined, the join operation must take into account ranking [8]; join can either be based on exact methods, according to the rank-join theory, or on approximate methods, that favor the speed of result production [18]. Data integration strategies should aim at obtaining a suitable number of results (e.g., neither too few, nor too many). Normally, a computation should not be set up so as to exhaust a searchable data source, as the user is rarely interested to inspect all of them [10]. The ultimate controller is the user, who sees service results or their compositions and can halt their production.

The search system Kosmix [23] already uses such an approach for describing data sources that is sufficient for selecting relevant sources and driving simple queries to them, but it currently does not support the combination of data sources through operations.

3.3 Structured Entity Registration and Integration on the Web

An increasing number of data sets are becoming available on the Web as (semi)structured data instead of user-consumable pages. Linked Data plays a central role in this, thanks to initiatives such as W3C Linked Open Data (LOD) community project, which are fostering LD best practice adoption [4]. However, several other kinds of (nonlinked) data sources can be available on the Web.

Fig. 3.1 Overview of the
description levels for a search
service

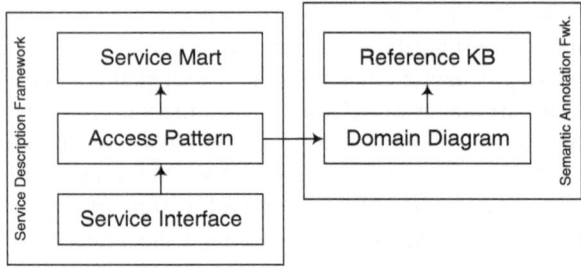

We envision the integration and search upon generic Web data sources through
their registration and semiautomatic tagging. Tags can be extracted from general
ontologies (such as YAGO) so as to build an abstract view of the sources that can be
helpful in routing queries to them [24].

The feasibility of the approach is demonstrated by the search computing
framework (http://www.search-computing.org). In this framework, services are
registered and modeled according to the different layers described in Fig. 3.1.
During registration, each data service becomes known in terms of: the entities that it
describes (conceptual view), its access pattern (logical view), and the call interface,
with a variety of QoS parameters (physical view); these three views compose the
service description framework (SDF) at different levels of abstractions [22]. Access
pattern information from all the services is used to create the domain diagram (DD),
referring in turn to one or more knowledge bases (KB); these views describe the
semantic annotation framework (SAF).

At the conceptual level, the definition of a service mart includes the object's name
and the collection of the object's attributes. All attributes are typed; attributes can be
atomic (single valued) or part of a repeating group (multivalued). Service marts are
specific data patterns; their regular organization helps structuring search computing
applications, in a way very similar to the so-called "data marts" used in the context
of data warehouses. Service marts are instrumental in supporting the notion of "Web
of objects" [1] that is gaining popularity as a new way to think of the Web, going
beyond the unstructured organization of Web pages.

At the logical level, service marts are associated with one or more access patterns
representing the signatures of service calls. Access patterns contain a subset of the
service mart's attributes tagged with I (input), O (output), or R (ranking). Ranking
attributes are essential to characterize the nature of the service, as we expect most
services to respond to search queries by producing itemized result lists in rank order;
moreover, when rank attributes are explicitly presented, they are used by the search
computing system to associate a global ranking to query results, and then present
them to users in global rank order.

At the physical level, each access pattern may be mapped to several service
implementations, called service interfaces. Service interfaces are registered by
providing a service identifier and the names of physical parameters, which are
mapped to the access pattern's attributes. Additional descriptions include details

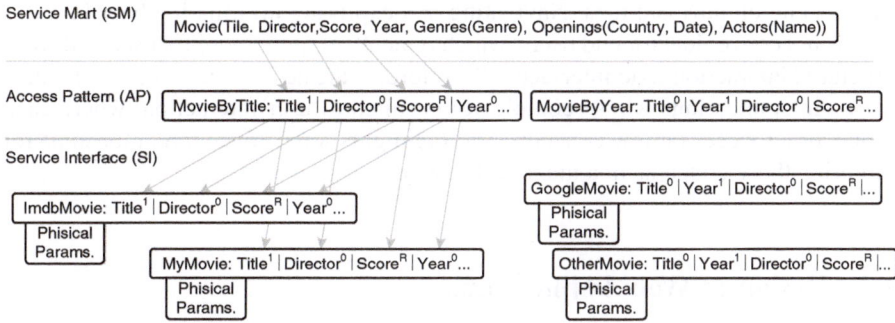

Fig. 3.2 Example of descriptions for accessing movie information through the service mart, access pattern, and service inteface layers

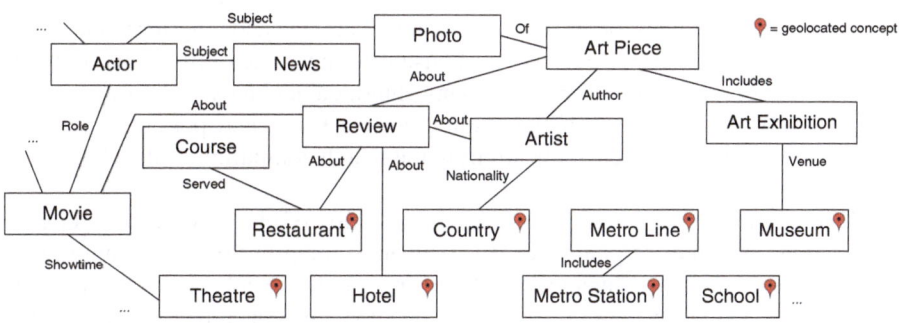

Fig. 3.3 Example of service mart diagram with connected concepts

about the Web service endpoint and the protocol to be used for its invocation, together with basic statistics on the service behavior describing the quality of service (QoS).

Figure 3.2 provides a concrete example of some registered services, all referring to the concept of movie. Movie is registered as a service mart, together with two associated access patterns and service interfaces, with the respective attribute mappings (mappings are shown only for the first access pattern for brevity).

Figure 3.3 is a representation at the service mart level of a set of registered concepts, covering information from different fields. Figure 3.3 also shows some of the relationships between concepts, which are drawn when the concepts share parameters, enabling navigation from one of them (in output) to another (in input). Indeed, more navigations are possible, e.g. when they share output parameters that can be compared (joined), or when outputs from two or more concepts enable filling the input for a third concept. Moreover, concepts which are labeled by a localization symbol may be connected by geographic proximity. Thus, the representation of Fig. 3.3 only hints to the complexity of interconnecting services, which is indeed fully captured by the data dictionary mentioned in Fig. 3.1; data dictionary connections, called connection patterns, are drawn at the logical level as they depend on attribute tags. Navigating and exploring information based on this view is not convenient for end users, which typically require more focused and well-structured interactions and interfaces. Therefore, in the next section, we discuss how to design applications whose complexity is suited to user interaction, where each application focuses on few concepts, and highlights some concept relationships for exploring those concepts in a manageable way.

3.4   Design of Web Applications

A Web application is built around a specific search process that a user wants to perform. Examples of processes range from very simple ones, such as deciding where to spend an evening in a city by choosing restaurants and other amenities, such as concerts, movies, or art festivals, to more complex and long-term ones, such as exploring options for job offers and house offerings. Such tasks may complete in one interaction or instead require many intermediate steps, where a user can progressively select subsets of the results, browse them, and possibly backtrack decisions. Examples of such applications in the search computing context have been demonstrated [5].

Designing a Web application requires the selection of one specific *goal* for each application; examples of goals are "planning an evening in SF," or "planning long weekend options from Chicago," or "selecting candidate job offers for software programmers in the bay area," or "browsing postdoc offers in cloud computing." The *processes* for achieving such goals may be classified as either *short-term* (serviced by a session whose span is accounted in seconds or at most minutes) or *long-lived* (spanning over days, in which case a search session should be suspended and then resumed—and partial results may be subject to a verification by repeating queries).

Processes are divided into smaller *tasks*; as design method, we associate each task with exactly one interaction with the search computing system. Each task consists of getting input parameters, issuing a query over services, presenting results to the user, allowing them to browse the instance and perform operations upon them (e.g., selecting the most interesting ones), and then decide the next task or exit/save the session—therefore, in each task execution, we expect an interaction with one or more services. While short-term processes may require few task interactions (possibly just one), long-lived processes may require many tasks.

Tasks are chosen according to a *workflow*, which presents legal sequences of tasks or choices of tasks; search computing natively supports search histories, and therefore, a possible user's choice of next task is always backtracking an arbitrary number of tasks in the history. This allows workflows to be quite simple, consisting either of free choices among tasks, or of hierarchies where the execution of one task opens up the possibility of executing lower-level tasks; a hierarchy often degenerates to a simple sequence when one task is followed by just one task.

After every task execution, the search computing system builds the "new" *task result* by joining the "old" result with the results produced by the task's query; therefore, the sequential execution of two tasks in the workflow requires the existence of a connection pattern between the corresponding services. This is obviously a strong constraint in building applications, but it yields many advantages, such as giving a precise semantics to the "current query" and its results throughout a session, allowing results to be globally ordered according to a "current goal function" (typically a weighted function or ranks produced by services), and thus allowing the presentation of the top items and/or the use of diversification for producing interesting items. Such computations are supported by Panta Rhei, the search computing query execution engine [11].

The method presented above consists in choosing among well-identified *patterns* for task composition, and then verifying that such patterns are supported by access and connection patterns of tasks. Such patterns are: the fully connected network, the hierarchy (either forming a single star or a snowflake), and the sequence, where tasks can either be simple (mapped to one service) or composite (mapped to many services). In the following, we present several designs of Web applications based on the above patterns.

3.4.1 Night Planner

A night planner is a short-term Web application presenting several geolocalized services, describing restaurants, shows, movies, family events, music concerts, and the like. The workflow is free; therefore, any service can be chosen after any other service, using the fully connected pattern; a *night plan* is just the combination of several such services, representing a dinner option, then a music concert, and so on. Selected restaurants are ranked by distance from the user and possibly by their score; when the concert service is queried, it produces combinations of restaurants and shows, and their ranking is based on the new distance between the restaurant and the concert hall, the previous distance from the user location, and the scores of restaurants and concerts; diversification allows seeing appropriately chosen combinations of restaurants and concerts. The planner may be augmented hierarchically with services showing reviews of each plan ingredient, and/or some options for public transportation from home or the closest parking; these selections only make sense in the context of few specific alternatives of the current solution. The resulting application design is shown in Fig. 3.4.

3.4.2 Weekend Browser

A weekend browser is a short-term Web application presenting to users the events which are occurring in one or more selected cities of interest. The application is sequential, because the user enters the application by browsing events; but once he is considering a particular location, he is offered additional services for

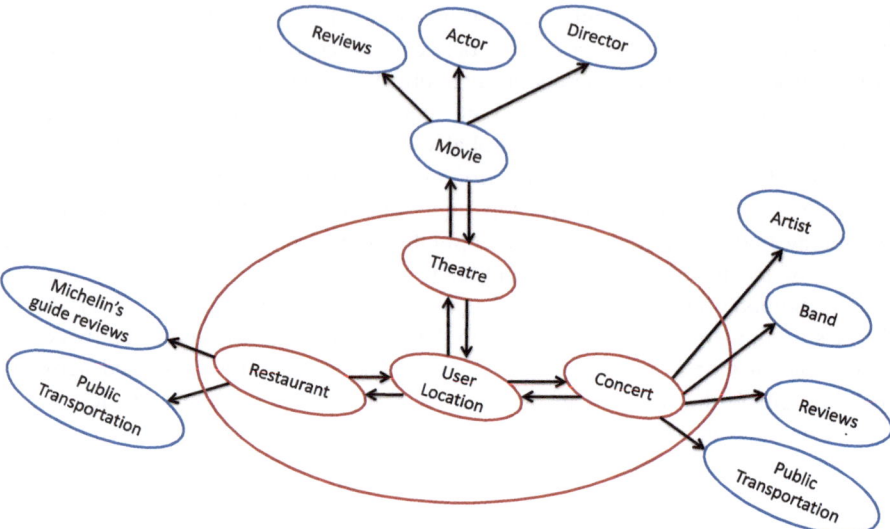

Fig. 3.4 Night Planner application design

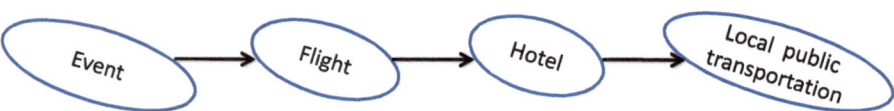

Fig. 3.5 Weekend browser

completing the weekend plan by adding transportation to the location (flights), then hotels in the location, then transportation from the airport to the hotel and to the chosen events. The sequence is defined by the application designer, who establishes that attending the event is the primary motivation for using this application, then checking the existence of a suitable transportation, and finally completing the plan by adding the hotel choice and local transports to it. Several instances of this application can be further specialized by event types (e.g., be associated with a sport team allowing fans to follow road games of the team, or be specialized on classic concerts within Europe). The resulting application design is shown in Fig. 3.5.

3.4.3 Real-Estate Browser

A real-estate browser is a long-lived, hierarchical application. It is centered around a real-estate service or service integrator presenting offers (for buy or rent) of various houses, and in addition, it has services which describe the house district or proximity in terms of: distance from work; availability of public transport from work; vicinity to schools of given grade, to supermarkets, to green and parks, and to hospitals and specialist doctor's clinics; and the like. These services are ancillary to the primary service, as each user may be interested in a subset of them. In a typical interaction, a user may select some house offers (e.g., based on their area, cost, and bedrooms) and evaluate them according to some search dimensions (e.g., distance from work, distance from doctor's clinics for some disease). The designer may simplify the interaction by combining several services into one query (e.g., walkability and vicinity to markets and parks). The two variants of the application are shown in Fig. 3.6a, b.

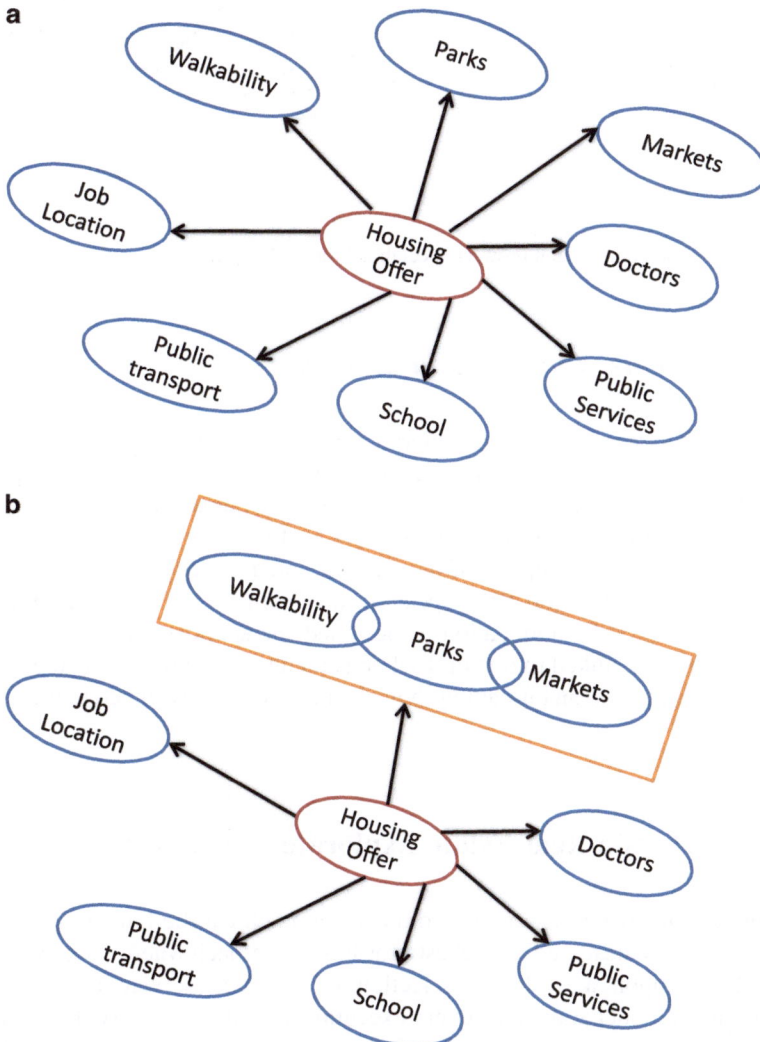

Fig. 3.6 (**a**) Real-estate offer browser, with (**b**) a variant showing several services explored as a single task (and a single query to several data sources)

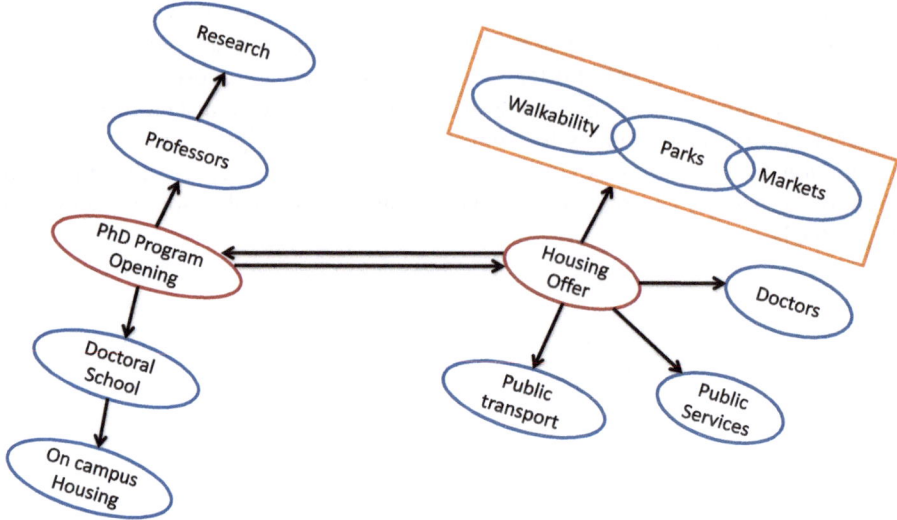

Fig. 3.7 Job-house combination browser specialized for PhD applications

3.4.4 Job-House Combination Browser

A work-job browser is a long-lived, hierarchical application where two hierarchical roots, one centered on work offers and one on house offers, are present; depending on the choice of the designer, this may be considered as a hierarchy (work offers come first) or a simple free interaction (work and house offers equally relevant). While the house star is a replica of the one presented in Sect. 3.4.3, the job star is centered on the notion of job offer. Specialized versions of such a service may exist, e.g., Fig. 3.7 shows the application as designed for applicants to PhD programs, where openings are linked to doctoral schools, then to their professors, then to their research programs, and an on-campus housing may be directly linked to the doctoral school.

3.5 Aspects of a Real-Estate Exploratory Browser

Web applications which use an exploratory approach can be built in a variety of ways; in SeCo, we designed an orchestrator-based approach where each exploratory step is based upon a cycle of: selection of the next service to be invoked, provisioning of input parameters, query execution, data display, and data processing. Data processing, in turn, may consist of the request for more data, or the selection of some results for further investigations, or of projection/aggregation/reordering of current results, before entering the next step. The orchestrator allows recovering

Fig. 3.8 Service selection form

previous steps, and in particular, this may result in backtracking one or more steps, which is typical of explorations.

We also developed generic UIs which depend on the specific data type results. Generic data are represented through "tabular" or "atom" views; geolocalized data are placed on maps—together with all Linked data which can be associated to geolocations through direct mappings; quantitative data can be plotted on XY diagrams, histograms, timelines, and so on. In [3], we demonstrated aspects of the job-house combination browser, by showing how the generic orchestrator and UIs adapt to that particular application; here we focus on the real-estate part.

Figure 3.8 shows a form-based UI for selecting services at the beginning of one step, based upon the specific available information (a ZIP code, city and state, coordinates, nearness to coordinates.)

The user chooses the third option based on his current location (Stagg Street in Brooklyn, NY; coordinates are automatically obtained from mobile devices), and is offered a number of alternative house offerings, displayed in Fig. 3.9. Each offer is associated with a ranking which depends on the distance and also from the closeness of the offer with specified search criteria; based on the selected service and API, the user is prompted with an additional form for specifying alternatives between buy and rent, number of bedrooms, price range, etc., to better focus the search (in this particular example, we used zillow, www.zillow.com.)

Next, several other services can be inspected which give information about nearby services, e.g. schools, walk score, hotels, doctors, theaters, events, car rentals, census, news, job offers in proximity, restaurants; these alternatives are shown in the form of Fig. 3.10. Note that the richness of options here is the novelty, compared to a fixed set of options that is typically provided by a real-estate integrator. Some may be available due to choices of specific users, who made previous use of such services and tagged them to be always available whenever they search is "by coordinate," as in the current situation.

In the continuation of the session, we assume the user to check for medical specialists, and specifically for cardiologists, in the neighborhood of two house offers that were selected at the previous step; the result is then a list of combinations

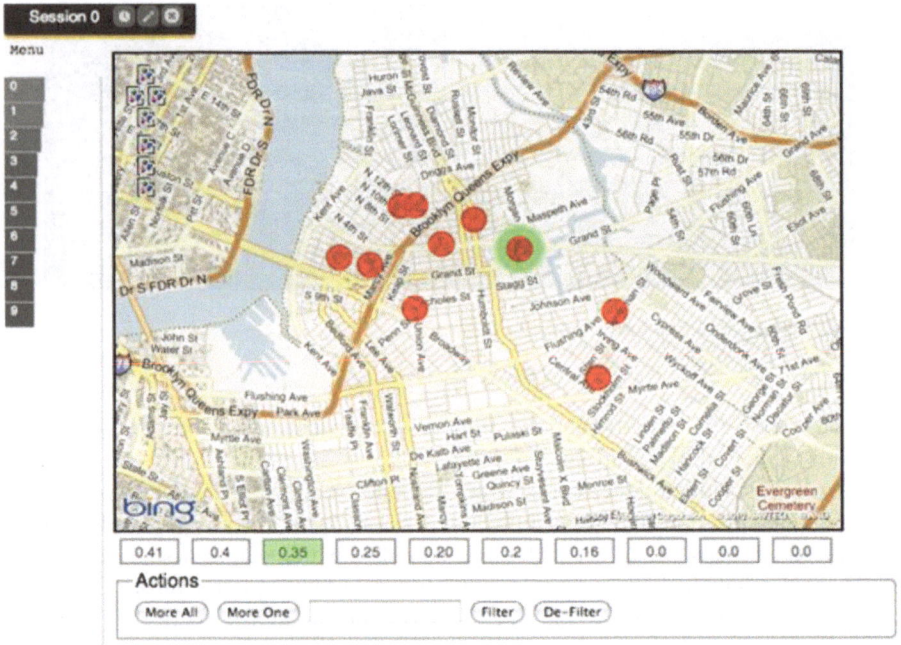

Fig. 3.9 House offers in proximity of a given location

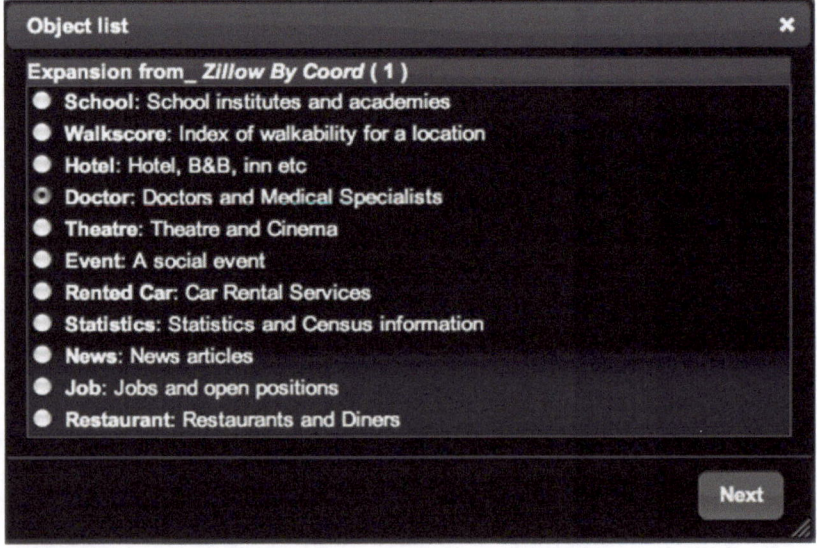

Fig. 3.10 Service exploration in "proximity" of house offer locations

of interconnected pairs, where each pair represents housing (red) and doctor's offices (green), and certain pairs are ranked better than others by taking into account the geographic distance between locations, the doctor's office reputation, and the original ranking of the two house offers. Figure 3.11a, b show the display of offers on the map and in the atom view, which is selectively displaying house offers' usecode, price and bedrooms, and doctors' name, specialty, street, and city.

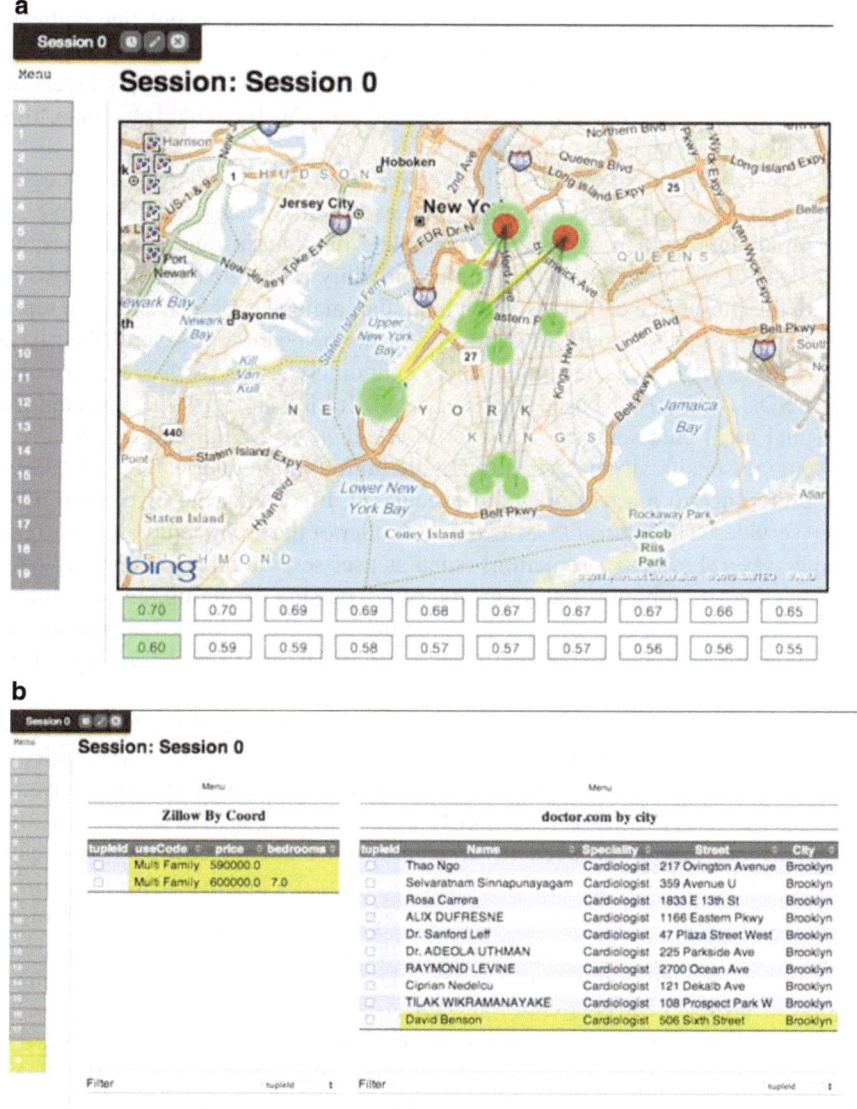

Fig. 3.11 Joint house offer/doctor exploration on the map (**a**) and atom view (**b**)

3.6   Deployment Architecture

The deployment of exploratory Web applications integrating data sources requires a number of software components and quite sophisticated interactions between them; in this section, we present the architecture currently under development within the search computing system. The software modules in Fig. 3.12 are horizontally divided into processing modules, repositories, and design tools, and vertically organized as a two-tier, three-layer infrastructure, with the client tier dedicated to user interaction and the server tier further divided into a control layer and execution layer; the client–server separation occurs between processing layers and repositories, and communications are performed using Web-enabled channels. Tools address the various phases of interaction.

The *processing modules* include the *service invocation framework*, in charge of invoking services that query the data sources. Such services typically have few input parameters (which are used to complete parametric queries) and produce results constituted by a "chunk" of tuples, possibly ranked, each equipped with a tuple-id; thus, a service call maps given input parameters to a given chunk of tuples. The framework includes built-in wrappers for the invocation of several Web-based infrastructures (e.g., YQL, GBASE), query endpoint (e.g., SPARQL), and resources (e.g., WSDL- and REST-based Web services). It also supports the invocation of legacy and local data sources. The *execution engine* is a data- and control-driven query engine specifically designed to handle multidomain queries [11]. It takes as input a reference to a query plan and executes it, by driving the invocation of the needed services. The *control layer* is the controller of the architecture; it is designed to handle several system interactions (such as user session management and query planning), and it embodies the *query analyzer* (parsing, planning, and optimizing the queries) and the *query orchestrator* (acting as a proxy toward all the internal components of the platform through a set of APIs). The *user interaction layer* is the front end of the SeCo system.

The *repository* contains the set of components and data storages used by the system to persist the artifacts required for its functioning. On the server side, the *Service mart repository* contains the description of the search services consumed by the system, represented at different levels of abstraction. The *query repository* and *results repository* are used in order to persist query definitions and query results which are heavily used, while the *user repository* and *application repository* store, respectively, a description of users accessing an application and of the configuration files (query configuration, result configuration, etc.) required by the user interface for an application. On the client side, three persistent repositories have been designed, respectively, the *query descriptions*, which are used by the high-level query processor as reference definitions of the query models; the *service mart descriptions* and the *application descriptions*, managed by the user interface on the user's browser to persistently cache application's configuration files and service descriptions.

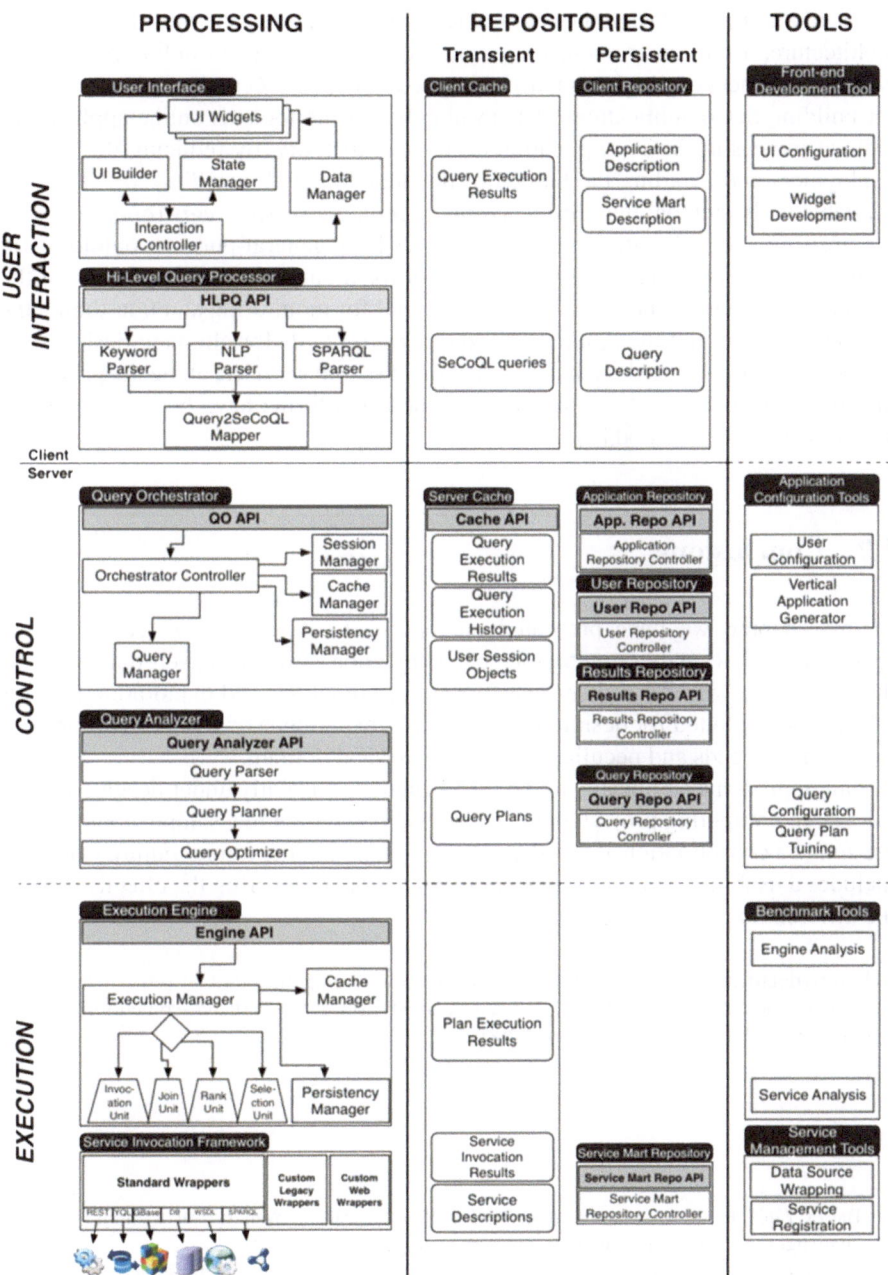

Fig. 3.12 The architecture of the search computing platform

To configure and design the set of objects and components involved in the SeCo architecture, a *tool suite* is currently under development as an online platform in which developers can login and, according to their role, access the right set of tools for building SeCo applications. The availability of the tools as online applications aims at increasing SeCo application design productivity, by reducing the time to deployment and avoiding the burden of downloading and installing software. The available tools include: the *service wrapping tool*, the *service registration tool* [12] (comprising the integration with the YAGO [23] general-purpose ontology for definition of terms), the *service analysis tool* for monitoring and evaluation of the service performance, the *execution analysis* tool for monitoring and fine-tuning the engine behavior, and the *application configuration tools* for allowing designers to define applications based on the composition of search services, along the principles discussed in Sect. 3.4. Several demos of these platforms have been presented at WWW [6], ACM-Sigmod [7], and ICWE [3].

3.7 Conclusions

In this chapter, we have presented our approach for designing vertical search applications that enable exploratory behavior upon structured Web data sources; the approach is general and consists of a set of guidelines and exploration patterns that can be exploited for designing a better user experience on the data exploration, based on the needs and peculiarities of each vertical domain.

Our approach is applicable to the infrastructures currently under development in the search computing project and has been validated on a few sample applications; we aim at a consolidation and wider experimentation in the future. Future work also includes a usability and user satisfaction evaluation, comparing the effectiveness of the different exploration strategies.

Acknowledgements This research is part of the search computing (SeCo) project, funded by ERC, under the 2008 Call for "IDEAS Advanced Grants" (http://www.search-computing.org). We wish to thank all the contributors to the project.

References

1. Baeza-Yates, R., Broder, A., Maarek, Y.: The New Frontier of Web Search Technology: seven challenges. SeCO Workshop 2010, pp. 3–9. Springer LNCS (2010)
2. Baeza-Yates, R.: Applications of web query mining. ECIR: European Conference on Information Retrieval, 2005, pp. 7–22. Springer LNCS 3408 (2005)
3. Barbieri, D., Bozzon, A., Brambilla, M., Ceri, S., Pasini, C., Tettamanti, L., Vadacca, S., Volonterio, R., Zagorac, S.: Exploratory multi-domain search on web data sources with liquid queries. ICWE 2011 Conference, Demo session, June 2011, Paphos, Cyprus, 2011
4. Bizer, C., Heath, T., Idehen, K., Berners-Lee, T.: Linked data on the web. WWW 2008, ACM, Beijing, China, 2008

5. Bozzon, A., Brambilla, M., Ceri, S., Fraternali, P.: Liquid query: multi-domain exploratory search on the web. WWW '10, Raleigh, NC, ACM, New York, NY, USA, pp. 161–170, April 2010

6. Bozzon, A., Brambilla, M., Ceri, S., Fraternali, P., Vadacca, S.: Exploratory search in multi-domain information spaces with Liquid Query. WWW 2011 Conference, Demo session, March 2011

7. Bozzon, A., Brambilla, M., Ceri, S., Corcoglioniti, F., Fraternali, P., Vadacca, S.: Search computing: multi-domain search on ranked data. ACM-Sigmod 2011 Conference, Demo session, June 2011

8. Braga, D., Campi, A., Ceri, S., Raffio, A.: Joining the results of heterogeneous search engines. Inf. Syst. **33**(7–8), 658–680 (2008)

9. Braga, D., Ceri, S., Daniel, F., Martinenghi, D.: Optimization of multi-domain queries on the web. VLDB '08, Auckland, NZ, 2008

10. Braga, D., Ceri, S., Daniel, F., Martinenghi, D.: Mashing up search services. IEEE Inter. Comput. **12**(5), 16–23 (2008)

11. Braga, D., Grossniklaus, M., Corcoglioniti, F., Vadacca, S.: Efficient computation of search computing queries. In: Ceri, S., Brambilla, M. (eds.) Search Computing Trends and Development. Springer LNCS vol. 6585, pp. 148–164 (2011)

12. Brambilla, M., Tettamanti, L.: Tools supporting search computing application development. In: Ceri, S., Brambilla, M. (eds.) Search Computing Trends and Development. Springer LNCS vol. 6585, pp. 169–181 (2011)

13. Broder, A.: A taxonomy of web search. SIGIR Forum **36**(2), 3, 10 (2002)

14. Ceri, S., Brambilla, M. (eds.): Search Computing Trends and Development. Springer LNCS 6585 (2011)

15. Ceri, S., Brambilla, M. (eds.): Search Computing Challenges and Directions. Springer LNCS 5950, ISBN 978-3-642-12309-2 (2010)

16. Danescu-Niculescu-Mizil, C., Broder, A.Z., Gabrilovich, E., Josifovski, V., Pang, B.: Competing for users' attention: on the interplay between organic and sponsored search results. WWW 2010, Raleigh, NC, ACM, USA, pp. 291–300, April 2010

17. Google: Fusion tables. http://tables.googlelabs.com/ (2009). Accessed June 12, 2009

18. Ilyas, I., Beskales, G., Soliman, M.: A survey of top-k query processing techniques in relational database systems. ACM Comput. Surv. **40**(4) (2008)

19. Kules, B., Capra, R., Banta, M., Sierra, T.: What do exploratory searchers look at in a faceted search interface? JCDL, Joint Conference on Digital Libraries, pp. 313–322 (2009)

20. Marchionini, G.: Exploratory search: from finding to understanding. Commun. ACM **49**(4), 41–46 (2006)

21. Parameswaran, A., Das Sarma, A., Polyzotis, N., Widom, J., Garcia-Molina, H.: Human-assisted graph search: it's okay to ask questions. PVLDB **4**(5), 267–278 (2011)

22. Quarteroni, S.: Question answering, semantic search and data service querying. In: St-Dizier P. (ed.) 6th Workshop on Knowledge and Reasoning for Answering Questions (KRAQ'11), Chiang Mai, Thailand, November 2011

23. Rajaraman, A.: Kosmix: high performance topic exploration using the deep web. P-VLDB **2**(2) (2009). Lyon, France

24. Suchanek, F., Bozzon, A., Della Valle, E., Campi, A.: Towards an ontological representation of services in search computing. In: Ceri, S., Brambilla, M. (eds.) Search Computing Trends and Development. Springer LNCS 6585, pp. 101–112 (2011)

25. White, R.W., Roth, R.A.: Exploratory search. Beyond the Query, Response Paradigm. In: Marchionini, G. (ed.) Synthesis Lectures on Information Concepts, Retrieval, and Services Series, vol. 3. Morgan and Claypool, San Francisco (2009)

26. Yahoo!. YQL. http://developer.yahoo.com/yql/ (2009). Accessed December 1, 2011

Part II
Search over the Web

Chapter 4
Path-Oriented Keyword Search Query over RDF

Roberto De Virgilio, Paolo Cappellari, Antonio Maccioni,
and Riccardo Torlone

4.1 Introduction

We are witnessing a smooth evolution of the Web from a worldwide information space of linked documents to a global knowledge base, where resources are identified by means of uniform resource identifiers (URIs, essentially string identifiers) and are semantically described and correlated through resource description framework (RDF, a metadata data model) statements.

With the size and availability of data constantly increasing (currently around 7 billion RDF triples and 150 million RDF links), a fundamental problem lies in the difficulty users face to find and retrieve the information they are interested in. In general, to access semantic data, users need to know the organization of data and the syntax of a specific query language (e.g., SPARQL or variants thereof). Clearly, this represents an obstacle to information access for nonexpert users. For this reason, keyword search-based systems are increasingly capturing the attention of researchers. Recently, many approaches to keyword-based search over structured and semistructured data have been proposed [1, 11–14, 16, 18]. These approaches usually implement IR strategies [21, 22] on top of traditional database management systems with the goal of freeing the users from having to know data organization and query languages.

Typically, keyword-based search systems address the following key steps: identifying (substructures holding) data matching input keywords, linking identified data (substructures) into solutions (since data is usually scattered across multiple

R. De Virgilio (✉) · A. Maccioni · R. Torlone
Department of Informatics and Automation, University Rome Tre, Rome, Italy
e-mail: dvr@dia.uniroma3.it; maccioni@dia.uniroma3.it; torlone@dia.uniroma3.it

P. Cappellari
Interoperable System Group, Dublin City, University, Dublin, Ireland
e-mail: pcappellari@computing.dcu.ie

R. De Virgilio et al. (eds.), *Semantic Search over the Web*,
Data-Centric Systems and Applications, DOI 10.1007/978-3-642-25008-8_4,
© Springer-Verlag Berlin Heidelberg 2012

places, e.g., in different tables or XML elements), and ranking solutions according to a relevant criterion (i.e., a suitable scoring function). Eventually, only the top-k solutions, i.e., those k solutions with highest score, are returned to the users as query answers.

For instance, let us consider the example in Fig. 4.1. It is inspired by the RDF version of the DBLP dataset (a database about scientific publications). Vertices in ovals represent an entity, such as *aut1* and *aut2*, or a concept, such as *Conference* and *Publication*. Vertices in rectangles are literal values, such as *Bernstein* and *Buneman*. Edges describe connections between vertices. For instance, the entity *aut1* is a *Researcher* whose name is *Bernstein*. In this example, given the query $Q_1 = \{\texttt{Bernstein, SIGMOD, 2008}\}$, two answers (i.e., the top 2) are S_1 and S_2, in order, as depicted in Fig. 4.1. The vertices matching Q_1 are emphasized in gray.

Given a query and a dataset, in order to obtain an exact answer, a process should first produce the candidate solutions, then filter and rank such solutions to return the final, exact, result. Referring to Fig. 4.1, the search task shall produce candidate solutions, S_1 and S_2 (and others, possibly), then the rank task orders and filters the these solutions to return S_1 before S_2 (S_1 has higher score than S_2). A limit of the current approaches is that they compute the best answers only in an approximate way (e.g., [1, 13]).

In this framework, search is a complex task that could produce many irrelevant candidates impacting on the quality of the final result. Recently, three measures have been proposed to evaluate this aspect [19]: *exhaustivity*, *specificity*, and *overlap*. Exhaustivity measures the relevance of a solution in terms of the number of keywords it contains. Specificity measures the precision of a solution in terms of the number of keywords it contains with respect to other irrelevant terms

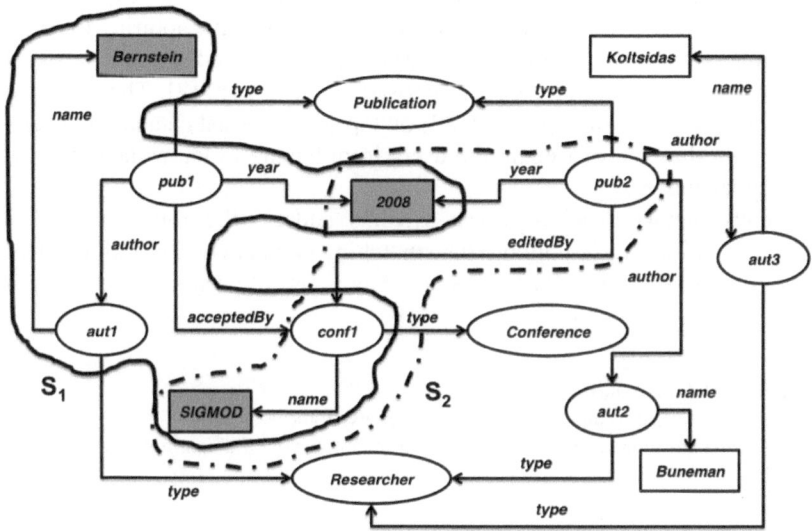

Fig. 4.1 An RDF graph from DBLP

occurring in the solution. Overlap measures the information content of a solution in terms of its intersection with other solutions. Clearly, the best ranking strategy balances exhaustivity and specificity while reducing overlap. In this respect, current approaches mainly focus on finding the most exhaustive solutions at the cost of a high level of overlapping. It turns out, however, that the quality of result is highly dependent on both the construction of candidate solutions and their ranking. For this reason, the problems of searching and ranking are strongly correlated.

Building on the above considerations, in this chapter, we present a novel keyword-based search technique over RDF graph-shaped data. We use a previous work [24] as starting point. That work focuses exclusively on computing qualitative results in an approximate order, ignoring efficiency and scalability issues. In this chapter, we merge a solution building strategy with a ranking method with the goal of generating the best k results in the first k produced answers, greatly reducing the complexity of the overall process. Referring to our example, in case of top-2 exploration, our proposal is able to produce in order S_1 and S_2 in the first two scans of the retrieval process.

Our search process proceeds as follows. The RDF graph is indexed off-line in order to efficiently retrieve the portions of interest for a query. The first task in evaluating a query consists of identifying the nodes (or edges) matching the query keywords. From the data graph point of view (i.e., RDF), we have sink nodes (i.e., classes and data values), intermediate and source nodes (i.e., URIs), and edges. As in [23], we can assume users enter keywords corresponding to attribute values (e.g., a name) rather than verbose URI; thus keywords refer principally to properties (i.e., edges) and literals (i.e., sinks). Under this assumption, we do not search URIs: this is not a limitation because nodes labeled by URIs are usually linked to literals which represent verbose descriptions of such URIs.

In our approach, we index all paths starting from a source and ending into a sink that we say represent the main flow of information in the graph. From a knowledge base paradigm point of view, these paths correspond to ontological assertions (i.e., A-Box) on an ontology vocabulary (i.e., T-Box). We cluster all assertions sharing the same portion of the vocabulary. Therefore, paths are clustered according to their *structure* (i.e., if they share edges) and, within each cluster, ranked according to their score. Solutions are generated by combining the most promising paths from each cluster. To combine such paths, we propose two different strategies: the first has a linear computational cost, whereas the second guarantees that at each step, the produced solution is the best possible (in the sense that the following solutions cannot have a higher rank). The first strategy enables the search to scale seamlessly with the size of the input, and the result shifts more to be exhaustive rather than specific. The second, inspired from the threshold algorithm proposed by Fagin et al. [5], guarantees the monotonicity of the output as we show that the first k solutions generated are indeed the top-k: the result is optimally balanced between exhaustivity and specificity. In addition, we propose a variant of the second strategy that is both linear and monotonic. In this case, the result shifts more to be specific rather than exhaustive. Finally, all the strategies we propose avoid the generation of overlapping solutions.

To validate our approach, we have developed a system for keyword-based search over RDF data that implement the techniques described in this chapter. Experiments over widely used benchmarks have shown very good results with respect to other approaches, in terms of both effectiveness and efficiency.

In sum, the contributions of our work are the following:

- A novel approach to keyword-based search over RDF data that combine an exploration technique with a ranking mechanism to find best solutions first
- Two strategies for the construction of the query answers: one generating good results quickly, the other generating best results first
- The development of a system for keyword-based search showing the improvements that can be achieved compared to earlier approaches

The rest of the chapter is organized as follows. In Sect. 4.2, we introduce some preliminary issues. In Sects. 4.3 and 4.4, we illustrate our strategies for keyword-based search over RDF data. In Sect. 4.5, we discuss the related research, and in Sect. 4.6, we present the experimental results. Finally, in Sect. 4.7, we draw our conclusions and sketch future works.

4.2 Preliminary Issues

This section states the problem we address and introduces some preliminary notions and terminology used during the presentation of our solution.

Informally, given a query as a list of keywords, we address the problem of exploring a graph-shaped dataset to find subgraphs holding information relevant to the query.

Definition 4.1. A labeled directed graph G is a five-element tuple $G = \{V, E, \Sigma_V, \Sigma_E, L_G\}$ where V is a set of vertices and $E \subseteq V \times V$ is a set of ordered pairs of vertices, called edges. Σ_V and Σ_E are the sets of vertices and edge labels, respectively. The labeling function L_G defines the mappings $V \to \Sigma_V$ and $E \to \Sigma_E$.

Problem Statement. Given a labeled directed graph G and a keyword search-based query $Q = \{z_1, z_2, \ldots, z_n\}$, where each z_i is a keyword, we aim at finding the top-k ranked answers $S_1, S_2, \ldots, S_k$ to Q.

An answer S_i to a query Q is composed of connected subgraphs in G containing at least one vertex matching a keyword z_i. Many proposals (e.g., [1, 13]) provide an exact matching between keywords and labels of data elements. In our framework, we adopt an IR approach to support an imprecise matching that involves syntactic and semantic similarities. As a result, the user does not need to know the exact labels of the data elements when doing keyword search. We say that a vertex v matches a keyword when the label associated with a vertex (i.e., $L_G(v)$) contains the keyword or a semantic expansion of the keyword.

Definition 4.2 (Match). Given a labeled directed graph $G = \{V, E, \Sigma_V, \Sigma_E, L_G\}$ and a keyword search query Q, a vertex $v \in V$ matches Q if there occurs one of the following:

- There exists some keyword $z_i \in Q$ whose value is equal to or contained in $L_G(v)$, either lexically or on semantic query expansion.
- There exists some keyword $z_i \in Q$ whose value is equal to or contained in the label of an edge e (i.e., $L_G(e)$) directly connected with v, either lexically or according to a semantic query expansion.[1]

Figure 4.1 depicts an example inspired by the RDF version of the DBLP dataset. Vertices in ovals represent an entity, such as *aut1* and *aut2*, or a concept, such as *Conference* and *Publication*. Vertices in rectangles are literal values, such as *Bernstein* and *Buneman*. Edges describe connections between vertices. For instance, the entity *aut1* is a *Researcher* whose name is *Bernstein*.

In this example, given the query $Q_1 = \{$Bernstein, SIGMOD, 2008$\}$, two answers are S_1 and S_2 as depicted in Fig. 4.1. The vertices matching Q_1 are emphasized in gray.

The *sources* of a graph are those vertices v_{so} with no ingoing edges, that is, there is no pair $(v_i, v_{so}) \in E$ with $v_i, v_{so} \in V$. The *sinks* are the vertices v_{si} with no outgoing edges, that is, there is not a pair $(v_{si}, v_j) \in E$ with $v_{si}, v_j \in V$. Vertices in V that are not sources neither sinks are referred to as *intermediary vertices*.

Data Structures. In our approach, as explained in detail later, we avoid graph traversal at query execution time by indexing information on the reachability of vertices in terms of paths. In particular, we define a path as the sequence of vertices and edges from a source to another vertex.

Definition 4.3 (Full-Path). Given a graph $G = \{V, E, \Sigma_V, \Sigma_E, L_G\}$, a full-path is a sequence $pt = l_{v_1} - l_{e_1} - l_{v_2} - l_{e_2} - \cdots - l_{e_{n-1}} - l_{v_f}$ where $v_i \in V$, $e_i \in E$, $l_{v_i} = L_G(v_i)$, $l_{e_i} = L_G(e_i)$ and v_1 is a source. Each l_{v_i} and l_{e_i} are tokens in pt.

Each vertex $v \in V$ is reachable by at least one full-path. Sources are special vertices because they allow to reach any part of the (directed) graph. If a source is not present, a fictitious one can be added. For instance, the graph in Fig. 4.1 has two sources: *pub1* and *pub2*. An example of full-path is $pt_k =$ pub1-author-aut1-name-Bernstein, having tokens pub1, author, aut1, name, Bernstein. The length of a path is the number of vertices occurring in the path, while the position of a vertex corresponds to the position into the presentation order of all vertices. For instance, pt_k has length 3 and the vertex aut1 has position 2.

Answers to a query are built by assembling paths containing vertices matching at least one keyword. Such paths represent our primary source of information, and we refer to them as *sound paths*.

---

[1]We do not explore further the notion of semantic query expansion and refer here to standard IR techniques.

Definition 4.4 (Sound Path). Given a graph G and a query $Q = \{z_1, \ldots, z_n\}$, a sound path is a full-path $pt = l_{v_1} - l_{e_1} - l_{v_2} - l_{e_2} - \cdots - l_{e_{n-1}} - l_{v_f}$ where at least v_f matches a keyword $z_i \in Q$ (i.e., others v_i can match one or more keywords in case). We denote $pt \models z_i$.

For instance, with respect to the query Q_1 and the graph depicted in Fig. 4.1, we have the following sound paths:

p_1 : publ-year-2008
p_2 : publ-author-autl-name-Bernstein
p_3 : publ-acceptedBy-confl-name-SIGMOD
p_4 : pub2-year-2008
p_5 : pub2-editedBy-confl-name-SIGMOD

In a path, the sequence of the edge labels describes the corresponding structure. To some extent, such a structure describes a schema for the category of data (values on vertices) sharing the same connection types. While we cannot advocate the presence of a schema, we can say that such a sequence is a *template* for the path. Therefore, given a path pt, its template t_{pt} is the path itself where each vertex label in pt is replaced with the wildcard #. In the example of reference, Fig. 4.1, the template t_{p_2} associated to p_2 is #-author-#-name-#. We say that p_2 *satisfies* t_{p_2}, denoted with $p_2 \approx t_{p_2}$. Multiple paths can share the same template. Data belonging to paths sharing the same template can be considered as homogeneous. Therefore, we group paths into *clusters* with respect to the template they share: clusters partition the graph. For instance, we can group the sound paths from the graph of Fig. 4.1 as follows:

cl_1 : #-year-# $\{p_1, p_4\}$
cl_2 : #-author-#-name-# $\{p_2\}$
cl_3 : #-acceptedBy-#-name-# $\{p_3\}$
cl_4 : #-editedBy-#-name-# $\{p_5\}$

The answer to a query is a combination of sound paths. When possible, each path belongs to a different cluster. Since we would correlate all the keywords, any pair of paths in a solution must intersect in a vertex at least. We define and denote the intersection between two paths as follows:

Definition 4.5 (Intersection). Given two paths pt_1 and pt_2, there is an intersection between pt_1 and pt_2, denoted by $pt_1 \leftrightarrow pt_2$, if $\exists v_i \in pt_1$ and $\exists v_j \in pt_2$ such that $v_i = v_j$.

For instance, the paths p_3 and p_5 have an intersection in confl and SIGMOD. Finally, a solution S is a directed labeled graph built on a set of sound paths presenting pairwise intersections, as defined below.

Definition 4.6 (Solution). A solution S is a set of sound paths $pt_1, pt_2, \ldots, pt_n$ where $\forall pt_a, pt_b \in S$, there exists a sequence $[pt_a, pt_{w_1}, \ldots, pt_{w_m}, pt_b]$, with

$m < n$, such that $pt_{w_i} \in S$, $pt_a \leftrightarrow pt_{w_1}$, $pt_b \leftrightarrow pt_{w_m}$, and $\forall i \in [1, m-1]$: $pt_{w_i} \leftrightarrow pt_{w_{i+1}}$.

Given a set of sound paths $P = \{pt_1, pt_2, \ldots, pt_n\}$, we denote with $S(\{pt_1, pt_2, \ldots, pt_n\})$ (or $S(P)$) to say that $pt_1, pt_2, \ldots, pt_n$ (or P) represent a solution S. As for a sound path, if a solution S contains a vertex that matches a keyword z_i, then we denote $S \models z_i$.

On the graph illustrated in Fig. 4.1, given the query Q_1, the answers are represented by the solutions $S_1(\{p_1, p_2, p_3\})$ and $S_2(\{p_4, p_5\})$.

Scoring Function. A fundamental feature of search systems is the ability to return the solutions to a query in order of relevance. To this end, we use a scoring function to rank the candidate paths. Solutions are ranked according to a scoring function as well. Note that, as will be clarified during the discussion, our approach is scoring function independent. We here define a scoring function for completeness of presentation and evaluation, as this function is later needed to run our experiments. In literature, several metrics have been proposed [10, 21–23]. We define a single scoring function to assess the relevance of a subgraph with respect to the query of reference. In fact, while a solution is a proper subgraph, a sound path can be seen as the simplest possible subgraph. We assess a subgraph on two key factors: its topology and the relevance of the information carried from its vertices and edges. The topology is evaluated in terms of the length of its paths. This is a basic metric for ranking answer widely used in recent approaches to keyword search (e.g., [11]). The relevance of the information carried from its vertices is evaluated through an implementation of TF/IDF (term frequency and inverse document frequency).

Definition 4.7. Given a query $Q = \{z_1, \ldots, z_n\}$, a graph G, and a subgraph sg in G, the score of sg with respect to Q is

$$score(sg, Q) = \frac{\alpha(sg)}{\omega_{str}(sg)} \cdot \sum_{z \in Q} (\rho(z) \cdot \omega_{ct}(sg, z))$$

where:

- $\alpha(sg)$ is the relative relevance of sg within G
- $\rho(z)$ is the weight associated to each keyword z with respect to the query Q
- $\omega_{ct}(sg, z)$ is the *content* weight of z considering sg
- $\omega_{str}(sg)$ is the *structural* weight of sg

The relevance of sg is measured as follows:

$$\alpha(sg) = \left(\prod_{v_i \in sg} \left(\frac{\deg^-(v_i) + 1}{\deg^+(v_i) + 1} \right) \right)^{\frac{1}{|V(sg)|}}$$

Inspired by link analysis algorithms (e.g., PageRank [2]), we consider the relevance of each vertex $v_i \in V$ as the ratio between the in-degree ($\deg^-$) and the out-degree ($\deg^{+}$) of v_i. The relevance of sg is the geometric mean[2] of the relevance of each vertex $v_i \in sg$. In $\alpha(sg)$, we indicate the number of vertices in sg as $|V(sg)|$.

The scoring supports the specification of weights on the input keywords, i.e., $\rho(z)$. For instance, we can imagine that the order of the keywords in the query represents the relevance of each keyword. While our system supports the specification of such relevant information, in the remaining of the discussion, we assume the input keywords have all the same relevance, meaning that for a hypothetical user, all the keywords have the same relevance (i.e., $\rho(z) = 1, \forall z$).

In the scoring function, ω_{ct} aims to capture the *commonness* of a keyword z in sg. The commonness measures the relative number of graph elements which it actually represents. The higher the commonness, the lower its contribution should be. This function has been inspired by the pivoted normalization weighting method [21, 22], one of the most used metric in IR. Formally, it is defined as follows:

$$
\omega_{ct}(sg, z) = \begin{cases} \left(1 + \dfrac{tf}{\mathrm{d}f_{sg}(z)}\right) \cdot \left(1 + \frac{|\mathcal{PT}|}{DF(z)+1}\right), & \text{if } sg \models z \\ 0, & \text{otherwise} \end{cases}
$$

where:

- tf is the number of times a keyword z matches a vertex or an edge in sg, and $\mathrm{d}f_{sg}(z)$ is the number of paths of sg where z has a match (i.e., if sg is a path then $\mathrm{d}f_{sg}(z) = 1$)
- $|\mathcal{PT}|$ and $DF(z)$ are the number of all sound paths $\mathcal{PT}$ matching Q and the number of paths in $\mathcal{PT}$ having a match with z, respectively

Factor ω_{str} exploits the structural features of sg, evaluating the *proximity* (distance) of the keywords in sg. The higher the structural weight, the lower the proximity and its contribution should be. In other terms, a shorter path between two keyword elements should be preferred. We define

$$
\omega_{str}(sg) = |V(sg)|
$$

where $|V(sg)|$ is the number of vertices in sg. The structural weight normalizes the content weight. In this way, we have a score balanced between content and structural features, i.e., between specificity and exhaustivity.

For instance, let us consider the score of p_1 in our running example with respect to the query Q_1. The vertices publ and 2008 present the relative relevances (i.e., $\frac{\deg^{-}(v_i)+1}{\deg^{+}(v_i)+1}$) 0.2 and 3, respectively. The path p_1 has $\alpha(p_1) = \sqrt{0.2 \cdot 3} = 0.77$ and $\omega_{str}(p_1) = 2$, having two vertices. Since we assume all keywords in Q_1 have the same relevance, $\rho(z_i) = 1, \forall z_i \in Q_1$. Finally, we have to calculate ω_{ct}. Given $|\mathcal{PT}| = 5$ and $DF(2008) = 2$, we have

---

[2]The geometric mean of a dataset $\{a_1, a_2, \ldots, a_n\}$ is given by $\sqrt[n]{a_1 \cdot a_2 \cdots a_n}$.

$\omega_{ct}(p_1, \text{Bernstein}) = \omega_{ct}(pt_1, \text{SIGMOD}) = 0$ and $\omega_{ct}(pt_1, 2008) = (1+1) \cdot (1 + \frac{5}{1+2}) = 5.33$. At the end, we have $score(p_1, Q_1) = 2.05$.

4.3 Linear Strategy for Solution Building

The approach is composed of two main phases: an *off-line indexing*, where the graph G is indexed in order to have immediate access to the information of interest, and the *keyword processing* (on the fly), where the query evaluation takes place. The first task is efficiently performed by implementing an index structure, as we will describe in Sect. 4.6. In the second task, given the query Q our framework retrieves all sound paths $\mathcal{PT}$ by using the index and explores the best solutions from $\mathcal{PT}$ through a strategy that guarantees a linear time complexity with respect to the size of the input $\mathcal{PT}$, that is, $I = |\mathcal{PT}|$. Before computing solutions, we organize the paths of $\mathcal{PT}$ into clusters.

4.3.1 Clustering

Given the list $\mathcal{PT}$, we group the paths into clusters according to their template, and we return the set $\mathcal{CL}$ of all the clusters. Therefore, $\mathcal{CL}$ is computed as shown in Algorithm 1.

The set of clusters is implemented as a map where the key is a template and the value is a cluster with such template associated. Each cluster is implemented as a priority queue of paths, where the priority is based on the score (descending) associated to each path. For each $\text{pt} \in \mathcal{PT}$ (line [2]), we search the cluster cl having associated the same template t_{cl} corresponding to the schema of pt (line [3]). If there does not exist such cluster, we create a new one (line [4]). At the end, we will insert pt in cl (line [5]) and we update the map $\mathcal{CL}$ with the new cl with the template of pt (t_{pt}) as key (line [6]). Referring to the example of Fig. 4.1, we have the set of clusters $\mathcal{CL} = \{cl_1, cl_2, cl_3, cl_4\}$. In particular in cl_1, we have p_1 more relevant than p_2 (i.e., $score(p_1, Q_1) > score(p_2, Q_1)$). It is

---

Algorithm 1: Clustering of paths

Input : A list of sound paths $\mathcal{PT}$.
Output: The map $\mathcal{CL}$ of the clusters.

$\mathcal{CL} \leftarrow \emptyset$;
foreach $\text{pt} \in \mathcal{PT}$ **do**
  if $\nexists(t_{cl}, \text{cl}) \in \mathcal{CL} : \text{pt} \approx t_{cl}$ **then**
    $\lfloor$ $\text{cl} \leftarrow \emptyset$;
  $\text{cl}.\text{Enqueue}(\text{pt})$;
  $\mathcal{CL}.\text{put}(t_{pt}, \text{cl})$;
return $\mathcal{CL}$;

Algorithm 2: Building solutions in linear time

Input : The map $\mathcal{CL}$, a number k.
Output: A list $\mathcal{S}$ of k solutions.

$\mathcal{S} \leftarrow \emptyset$;
while $|\mathcal{S}| < $ k *and* $\mathcal{CL}$ *is not empty* **do**
    First $\leftarrow \emptyset$;
    CC $\leftarrow \emptyset$;
    foreach cl $\in \mathcal{CL}$ **do**
        First $\leftarrow$ First $\cup$ cl.DequeueTop() ;
    CC $\leftarrow$ FindCC(First) ;
    ccSols $\leftarrow \emptyset$;
    foreach $cc \in$ CC **do**
        sol $\leftarrow$ newSolution(cc) ;
        ccSols.Enqueue(sol) ;
    $\mathcal{S}$.InsertAll(ccSols.DequeueTop(k- $|\mathcal{S}|$)) ;
return $\mathcal{S}$;

---

straightforward to demonstrate that the time complexity of the clustering is $O(I)$: we have to execute I insertions into $\mathcal{CL}$ at most.

4.3.2   Linear Building

Given the set of clusters $\mathcal{CL}$, the building of solutions is performed by generating the connected components CC from the most promising paths in $\mathcal{CL}$. Algorithm 2 illustrates the main steps of the process.

The algorithm iterates k times at most to produce the best k solutions (i.e., a list $\mathcal{S}$). At the beginning of each iteration, we initialize the set First containing the most relevant paths from each cluster, that is, the paths with the highest score (lines [3–6]). The task is supported by the function DequeueTop that extracts from the cluster cl the top score path (i.e., multiple paths if they have the same score). Then we compute CC from First (line [7]), supported by the function FindCC, and for each component, we generate a new solution (lines [8–11]) by using the function newSolution. The resulting set of solutions ccSols is implemented as a priority queue with respect to the score of a solution. From ccSols, we insert the top n elements into S, where n results from the difference between k and the actual size of S (i.e., $|S|$). In this case, we use a variant of DequeueTop, giving n as input to extract the top-n elements, and InsertAll to insert the solutions into S (line [12]). The execution concludes when we produced k solutions (i.e., $|S| < k$) or $\mathcal{CL}$ became empty.

Algorithm 3 describes the function FindCC. It iterates on the set First: a path pt is extracted and a supporting recursive function FindCC_AUX computes the connected component between pt and the updated First (lines [3–4]). As shown in Algorithm 4, FindCC_AUX searches all paths $pt_i \in$ First such that pt_i and

---

Algorithm 3: Find CC from a set of paths

Input : A set First of paths.
Output: A set CC of connected components in First.

CC $\leftarrow \emptyset$;
while First *is not empty* **do**
　| First $\leftarrow$ First $\smallsetminus$ {pt};
　| CC $\cup$ FindCC_AUX (pt, First)
return CC;

Algorithm 4: FindCC__AUX: a recursive function supporting FindCC

Input : A path pt, a set of paths First.
Output: The connected component built from pt.

PQ $\leftarrow \emptyset$;
PQ $\leftarrow$ PQ $\cup$ {pt};
foreach $pt_i \in$ First*:* $pt_i \leftrightarrow$ pt **do**
　| First $\leftarrow$ First $- pt_i$;
　| PQ $\leftarrow$ PQ $\cup$ FindCC_AUX (pt_i, First) ;
return PQ ;

---

pt present an intersection (i.e., $pt_i \leftrightarrow$ pt). Until there are paths pt_i having an intersection with pt, we extract pt_i from First, insert them into the final result PQ, and we call the recursion (lines [4–5]).

Algorithm 2 produces the best-k solutions in linear time with respect to the number I of sound paths matching the input query Q: it is in $O(k \times I) \in O(I)$. In the worst case, the algorithm iterates k times. The execution in lines [4–5] is $O(|(CL)|) \in O(I)$. Then we have to evaluate the execution of FindCC: since such function calls FindCC_AUX for each connected component (i.e., at most for each path within First), the complexity of the task is $O(I)$. Finally, both the executions in lines [9–11] and line [12] are in $O(I)$ (i.e., at most we have to make I insertions). Therefore, the entire sequence of operations in the Algorithm 2 is in $O(k \times I) \in O(I)$.

Referring again to the example of Fig. 4.1, in the first iteration of the algorithm, the most promising paths from each cluster are First $= \{p_1, p_2, p_3, p_5\}$. FindCC extracts from First the connected component cc_1 containing all the paths (i.e., they have pairwise intersections). Therefore, cc_1 will be returned as the first solution $S_1(\{p_1, p_2, p_3, p_5\})$. At the second iteration, First $= \{p_4\}$: the second solution will be $S_2(\{p_4\})$. Since $\mathcal{CL}$ is empty, the algorithm ends at the second iteration. In this example, we do not have overlap, and in particular, we obtain a solution S_1 exhaustive but not optimally specific (i.e., p_5 is excess). This suggests that such strategy tends to shift more to be exhaustive rather than specific. Moreover, it cannot assure the monotonicity of the solutions: it may happen the generation of a sequence of two solutions S_i and S_{i+1} where $score(S_{i+1}, Q) > score(S_i, Q)$. Let us suppose to generate a first solution S_1 containing more than one path and in particular containing the path pt'_1 with the highest score. Then at the second iteration, we have a path pt'_2 with the second most high score that does not present an intersection with any other extracted paths. Therefore, we will have a second solution $S_2(\{pt'_2\})$. In this case, if the scores of pt'_1 and pt'_2 are comparable, then it may happen that $score(S_2, Q) = score(pt'_2, Q) > score(S_1, Q)$ due to the more complex structural weight of S_1. Of course the scores of the two solutions could be comparable, but the monotonicity is violated.

Since monotonicity is our most important target, in the next section we provide a variant of our algorithm to explore top-k solution that guarantees such property. In this way, our framework will be able to allow the exploration of top-k solution in both linear and monotonic ways. A strong point of this algorithm is the independence from ad hoc scoring functions: it requires very general properties on the way to rank solutions.

4.4 Monotonic Strategy for Solution Building

Monotonicity of the building is a relevant challenge in keyword search systems. This means to return the optimal solution at each generation step instead of waiting the processing of blocks of candidate solutions and then selecting the optima. In this section, we provide a second strategy allowing such capability. An important point of this algorithm is a joint use of the scoring function at the generation time of a solution. It introduces a method to establish if the solution we are generating is the optimum. Moreover, an optimization allows to guarantee the execution in linear time also.

4.4.1 Scoring Properties

For our purposes, we make some assumptions on the scoring function. Such assumptions represent general properties to guarantee the monotonicity.

Property 1 *Given a query Q and a path pt, we have*

$$score(pt, Q) = score(S(\{pt\}), Q)$$

It means that every path has to be evaluated as well as the solution containing exactly that path. The property allows us to avoid the case in which $score(pt_1, Q) > score(pt_2, Q)$ and $score(S(\{pt_1\}), Q) < score(S(\{pt_2\}), Q)$.

Moreover, let us consider a set of paths $P = \{pt_1, pt_2, \ldots, pt_n\}$ and P^* the power set of P. We provide a second property as follows:

Property 2 *Given a query Q, a set of path P, and the path $pt_\beta \in P$, such that $\forall pt_j \in P : score(pt_\beta, Q) \geqslant score(pt_j, Q)$, with $pt_\beta \neq pt_j$, we have*

$$score(S(P_i), Q) \leq score(S(\{pt_\beta\}), Q) \ \forall P_i \subseteq P^*$$

In other words, given the set P containing the candidate paths to be involved into a solution, the scores of all the possible resulting solutions generated from P (i.e., P^*) are bounded by the score of the most relevant path pt_β of P. Such property is supported by the threshold algorithm (TA) [5]. TA computes the top-k objects with the highest scores from a list of candidates: the score of each object is computed by an aggregation function, assumed monotone, on top of the individual scores obtained for each of the object's attributes. Iteratively, the process includes objects into the result until the score of the k-ranked object is higher than the upper bound score of all remaining objects. Compared to TA, here the object is a subgraph resulting by the best composition of sound paths that are the attributes. However, we do not use an aggregation function, nor do we assume the aggregation to be monotone. TA introduces a mechanism to optimize the number of steps n to compute the best k objects (where it could be $n > k$), while our framework tries to produce k optimal solutions in k steps.

Although the above properties refer to the data structures used in our framework, they are very general. For instance, we can demonstrate that the two properties are fulfilled by the most common IR-based approaches. To this aim, we refer to the pivoted normalization weighting method (SIM) [22], which inspired most of the IR scoring functions. Let us consider a collection of documents $D = \{D_1, \ldots, D_m\}$ to evaluate with SIM against a query Q'. PROPERTY 1 is trivial: the score of any document $D_i \in D$ is the same as a document included into an answer to Q' as a complete answer. Now let $D^* = \{D'_1, D'_2, \ldots, D'_n\}$ the power set of D and D_β the most relevant document in D with respect to Q'. Each document can be considered as a set of terms possibly matching a keyword of Q', while each $D'_i \in D^*$ results from the concatenation of two or more documents in D. We remind that SIM weights a keyword z of Q' into a document D_i as $weight(z, D_i) = \frac{ntf(D_i)}{ndl(D_i)} \cdot idf$. In such weight, ntf evaluates the number of occurrences of z into D_i, ndl measures the length of the document D_i (i.e., number of terms), and idf quantifies the document frequency, that is, the number of documents in which z occurs. All of these measures are normalized: ntf by applying the log function twice, ndl by the ratio with the average document length in the collection D, and idf by applying the log function on the ratio between the total number of documents (i.e., $|D|$) and the document frequency. To verify PROPERTY 2, we have to show that $weight(z, D_\beta) \geq weight(z, D'_i)$, $\forall D'_i \in D^*$. Since idf is the same in both the terms, we can consider just ntf and ndl. If D_β has the highest score, then $weight(z, D_\beta)$ presents the best percentage of occurrences of z on top of the number of terms in the document. So given $D'_i \in D^*$, if $ntf(D_\beta)$ and $ntf(D'_i)$ are often comparable (i.e., due by applying the log function twice), $ndl(D_\beta)$ is less than $ndl(D'_i)$ (i.e., relevantly through the normalization): at the end, we have $\frac{ntf(D_\beta)}{ndl(D_\beta)} \geq \frac{ntf(D'_i)}{ndl(D'_i)}$, that is, $weight(z, D_\beta) \geq weight(z, D'_i)$. Therefore, SIM satisfies the PROPERTY CH05:PROP02. Similarly, we can demonstrate that also our scoring function satisfies the two properties.

4.4.2 Checking the Monotonicity

To check the monotonicity, we introduce a *threshold* τ. Such threshold is functional to define the so-called τ-*test*. As in Algorithm 2, we start computing the connected components from a set containing the most important paths of each cluster. Then, differently from the previous strategy, we do not verify only the intersection between paths but in particular if and how much it is opportune to insert a path into a partially generated solution. This task is supported by τ-*test*.

First of all, we have to introduce some notations as follows:

- cc represents a connected component containing candidate paths to be inserted into a solution.
- $s_{cc} \subset cc$ is the set of paths just inserted into the optimal solution (i.e., the set of paths that satisfied τ-*test* so far).
- pt_s is the path, not yet extracted from the set of clusters $\mathcal{CL}$, with the highest score in $\mathcal{CL}$.
- pt_x is a path in $\{cc \smallsetminus s_{cc}\}$ (i.e., a candidate path to insert into s_{cc}).
- pt_y is the path in $\{cc \smallsetminus s_{cc}\}$ with the highest score.

Then we define the threshold τ as

$$\tau = \max\{score(pt_s, Q), score(pt_y, Q)\}$$

τ can be considered as the upper bound score for the potential solutions to generate in the next iterations of the algorithm.

Now, we provide the following theorem:

Theorem 4.1. *Given a query* Q, *a scoring function satisfying the properties* PROPERTY 1 *and* PROPERTY 2, *a connected component* cc, *a subset* $s_{cc} \subset cc$ *representing an optimal solution, and a path* $pt_x \in \{cc \smallsetminus s_{cc}\}$, $S(s_{cc} \cup \{pt_x\})$ *is still optimum iff*

$$score(S(s_{cc} \cup \{pt_x\}), Q) \geq \tau$$

The condition provided by Theorem 4.1 is the τ-*test*.

Proof. **[Necessary Condition].** Let us assume that $S(s_{cc} \cup \{pt_x\})$ is an optimal solution. We have to verify if the score of such solution is still greater than τ. Reminding to the definition of τ, we can have two cases:

- $\tau = score(pt_s, Q) > score(pt_y, Q)$.
  In this case, $score(pt_s, Q)$ represents the upper bound for the scoring of the possible solutions to generate in the next steps. Recalling PROPERTY 1, we have $score(pt_s, Q) = score(S(\{pt_s\}), Q)$. Referring to PROPERTY 2, the possible solutions to generate will present a score less than $score(S(\{pt_s\}), Q)$: $S(s_{cc} \cup \{pt_x\})$ is optimum. Therefore, $score(S(s_{cc} \cup \{pt_x\})) \geq \tau$.

- $\tau = score(pt_y, Q) > score(pt_s, Q)$.
  In a similar way, $score(S(s_{cc} \cup \{pt_x\}), Q) \geq \tau$.

[Sufficient Condition]. Let us consider $score(S(s_{cc} \cup \{pt_x\}), Q) \geq \tau$. We have to verify if $S(s_{cc} \cup \{pt_x\})$ is an optimal solution. From the assumption, $score(S(s_{cc} \cup \{pt_x\}), Q)$ is greater than both $score(pt_s, Q)$ and $score(pt_y, Q)$. Recalling again the properties of the scoring function, the possible solutions to generate will present a score less than both $score(S(pt_s), Q)$ and $score(S(\{pt_y\}), Q)$. Therefore, $S(s_{cc} \cup \{pt_x\})$ is an optimal solution.   □

4.4.3 Monotonic Building

As in Sect. 4.3, we start from a set of clusters $\mathcal{CL}$, grouping all informative paths matching the input query Q with respect to the shared template. To generate the top-k solutions guaranteeing the monotonicity, in the building algorithm of Sect. 4.3, we introduce an exploration procedure employing the $\tau\text{-}test$ to check if the solution we are generating is (still) optimum. Algorithm 5 illustrates the new building process. As in Algorithm 2, the process starts computing the connected components from the top paths of each cluster (lines [2–6]). Once extracted such paths, if the set of clusters $\mathcal{CL}$ is not empty, we can activate the $\tau\text{-}test$ (lines [7–10]); otherwise, since we have all possible paths in the connected components, we proceed as in Algorithm 2 (lines [12–15]).

Algorithm 5: Monotonic building of top-k solutions

Input : A list $\mathcal{CL}$ of clusters, a number k.
Output: A list S of k solutions.

while $|S| < $ k **do**
    First $\leftarrow \emptyset$;
    CC $\leftarrow \emptyset$;
    foreach cl $\in \mathcal{CL}$ **do**
        First $\leftarrow$ First $\cup$ cl.DequeueTop() ;
    CC $\leftarrow$ FindCC(First) ;
    if $\mathcal{CL}$ *is not empty* **then**
        $pt_s \leftarrow$ getTopPath($\mathcal{CL}$);
        BSols $\leftarrow$ MonotonicityExploration(CC, $\mathcal{CL}$, pt_s);
        S.InsertAll(BSols) ;
    else
        foreach $cc \in$ CC **do**
            sol $\leftarrow$ newSolution(cc);
            ccSols.Enqueue(sol) ;
        S.InsertAll(ccSols.DequeueTop(k- $|S|$)) ;
return S;

Algorithm 6: Monotonicity exploration

Input : A set CC of connected components, a list $\mathcal{CL}$ of clusters, a path pt_s.
Output: A list of solutions BSols.

CCOpt ← ∅;
foreach cc ∈ CC **do**
    $\lfloor$ CCOpt.Enqueue(MonotonicityAnalysis(cc, ∅, pt_s));
BSols.InsertAll(CCOpt.DequeueTop());
InsertPathsInClusters(CCOpt, $\mathcal{CL}$);
return BSols ;

In the τ-$test$, we calculate the top path pt_s from $\mathcal{CL}$ and we activate the exploration to find the optimal solutions. The process is supported by the function getTopPath to extract pt_s from $\mathcal{CL}$ and by the function Monotonicity Exploration to find the best solutions to insert into S. The function MonotonicityExploration is described in Algorithm 6. It takes as input the set of connected components CC, the set of clusters $\mathcal{CL}$, and the path pt_s. This function has to extract from each connected component cc the optimal subset of paths (i.e., representing the optimal solution). Such subsets are collected into a priority queue CCOpt (lines [2–3]). Therefore, the top elements of CCOpt will correspond to the optimal solutions: we implement a list BSols of such solutions (line [4]). At the end, all excluded paths in CCOpt will be reinserted into $\mathcal{CL}$ by using the function InsertPathsInClusters (line [5]).

The queue CCOpt is computed by the analysis of monotonicity through the τ-$test$. The analysis is performed by the recursive function MonotonicityAnalysis, as shown in Algorithm 7. It takes as input the connected component cc, the current optimal solution OptS, and the top path pt_s contained in $\mathcal{CL}$. The idea is to generate OptSols, that is, the set of all solutions (candidate to be optimal) by combining OptS with the paths of cc. If cc is empty, we return OptS as it is (i.e., we cannot explore more). Otherwise, we analyze all paths pt_x ∈ cc that present an intersection with a path pt_i of OptS. If there is not any intersection, then OptS is the final optimal solution (lines [6–7]). Otherwise, for each pt_x, we calculate τ (line [9]), through the function getTau, and we execute the τ-$test$ on each new solution tryOptS, that is, OptS ∪ $\{pt_x\}$. If tryOptS satisfies the τ-$test$, then it represents the new optimal solution: we insert it into OptSols and we invoke the recursion on tryOptS (lines [9–12]). Otherwise, we keep OptS as optimal solution and skip pt_x (line [14]). At the end, we take the best OptS from OptSols by using TakeMaximal (line [15]) described in Algorithm 8. Such function selects the solution from OptimSols that contains more sound paths firstly (line [4]) and then presents the highest score (line [6]). Let us consider our running example. As for the linear strategy, in the first iteration of the algorithm, we start from First = $\{p_1, p_2, p_3, p_5\}$. The paths of First have scores 2.05, 1.63, 1.6, and 1.49, respectively. Now the exploration will consider all possible combinations of such paths to find the optimal solution(s). Therefore, at the beginning, we have OptS = $\{p_1\}$, since p_1 has the highest score, and pt_s

---

Algorithm 7: Monotonicity analysis

Input : A set of paths cc, a solution OptS, a path pt_s.
Output: The new (in case) optimal solution OptS.

if cc *is empty* **then**
  └ **return** OptS;
else
  │ OptSols ← ∅;
  │ **foreach** $pt_x \in cc$ **do**
  │   │ **if** $(\nexists pt_i \in$ OptS $: pt_x \leftrightarrow pt_i)$ *and* OptS *is not empty* **then**
  │   │   └ OptSols ← OptSols ∪ OptS ;
  │   │ **else**
  │   │   │ tryOptS ← OptS ∪ $\{pt_x\}$;
  │   │   │ τ ← getTau $(cc$ - $\{pt_x\}$, pt_s);
  │   │   │ **if** score (tryOptS, Q) $\geq \tau$ **then**
  │   │   │   │ OptSols ← OptSols ∪ MonotonicityAnalysis $(cc$ - $\{pt_x\}$,
  │   │   │   └ tryOptS, pt_s);
  │   │   │ **else**
  │   │   │   └ OptSols ← OptSols ∪ OptS ;
  │ OptS ← TakeMaximal (OptSols) ;
  └ **return** OptS;

Algorithm 8: Take maximal

Input : A list OptimSols of solutions.
Output: A solution best.

maxScore ← 0;
maxCardinality ← 0;
foreach sol ∈ OptimSols **do**
  │ **if** | sol |≥ maxCardinality **then**
  │   │ maxCardinality ←| sol |;
  │   │ **if** score (sol, Q) > maxScore **then**
  │   │   └ maxScore ← score (sol);
  │   └ best ← sol;
return best;

---

is p_4. The value of τ is 1.86. Then the algorithm will retrieve the following admissible optimal solutions: $S_1'(\{p_1, p_2, p_3\})$, $S_2'(\{p_1, p_3\})$, and $S_3'(\{p_1, p_2, p_5\})$. Such solutions are admissible because they satisfy the τ-test and corresponding paths present pairwise intersections. During the computation, the analysis skips the solutions $S_4'(\{p_1, p_2, p_3, p_5\})$ and $S_5'(\{p_1, p_3, p_5\})$ because they do not satisfy the τ-test: the scores of S_4' and S_5' are 1.55 and 1.26, respectively, which are both less than τ. Finally, the function TakeMaximal will select S_1' as the final first optimal solution S_1 since it has more sound paths and the highest score. Following a similar process, at the second iteration, the algorithm will return $S_2(\{p_4, p_5\})$ with a lesser score than S_1. Exhaustivity and specificity are optimally balanced (i.e., we have all the keywords and strictly correlated).

Although such analysis reaches our target, the computational complexity of the building is in $O(I^2)$. As for Algorithm 2, in the worst case, the computation iterates k times. In lines [2–6], we follow the same strategy of Algorithm 2. Therefore, the executions in lines [4–5] and line [6] are in $O(|\mathcal{CL}|) \in O(I)$ and $O(I)$, respectively. Then we have a conditional instruction: if the condition is true, we execute the monotonicity exploration (lines [8–10]); otherwise, we consider each connected component $cc \in CC$ as a solution to insert into $\mathcal{S}$ (lines [12–15]). As in Algorithm 2, the execution in lines [12–15] is in $O(I)$. In lines [8–10], we call the function `MonotonicityExploration` that executes the analysis of monotonicity at most I times. Such analysis is performed by the recursive function `MonotonicityAnalysis`: in Algorithm 7, the main executions are in lines [9–12] and line [15]. In both the execution is in $O(I)$, since we have I elements to analyze at the most. Since in Algorithm 6 both the operations in line [4] and in line [5] are in $O(I)$, the complexity of the monotonicity exploration is $O(I^2)$. Therefore, we conclude that the monotonic strategy to build top-k solutions is in $O(I^2)$.

To reduce the complexity of the monotonic strategy, we provide a variant of the monotonicity analysis, as shown in Algorithm 9. It allows to reach a linear time complexity of the overall process, that is, $O(I)$. Instead of computing all possible combinations between `OptS` and the paths $pt_x \in cc$, we select the top pt_x (one or more if equal score) having an intersection with a path of `OptS` (lines [4–7]). The task is performed by the function `DequeueWithIntersection`. The analysis will return `tryOptS` if it satisfies the τ-$test$, `OptS` otherwise (lines [10–13]). The study of complexity is straightforward: in the worst case, in Algorithm 6, we have a unique connected component cc containing all input sound paths (i.e., $|cc| = I$). Therefore, the function `MonotonicityAnalysis` (the linear version) is invoked

---

Algorithm 9: Linear monotonicity analysis

Input   : A priority queue cc, a solution OptS, a path pt_s.
Output: A solution OptS.

if cc *is empty* **then**
  | **return** OptS;
else
  | **if** OptS *is empty* **then**
  | | $pt_x \leftarrow cc$.Dequeue ();
  | **else**
  | | $pt_x \leftarrow cc$.DequeueWithIntersection (OptS);
  | tryOptS $\leftarrow$ OptS $\cup \{pt_x\}$;
  | $\tau \leftarrow$ getTau (cc, pt_s);
  | **if** score (tryOptS, Q) $\geq \tau$ **then**
  | | **return** MonotonicityAnalysis (cc, tryOptS, pt_s);
  | **else**
  | | $cc \leftarrow cc \cup \{pt_x\}$;
  | | **return** OptS ;

Table 4.1 Top-k solutions building

Strategy	Complexity	Solution quality
$\mathcal{L}$	$O(I)$	More $\mathcal{EX}$ rather than $\mathcal{SP}$
$\mathcal{M}$	$O(I^2)$	Optimality between $\mathcal{EX}$ and $\mathcal{SP}$
$\mathcal{LM}$	$O(I)$	More $\mathcal{SP}$ rather than $\mathcal{EX}$

once: `MonotonicityAnalysis` recurses at most I times. The complexity of `MonotonicityExploration` is in $O(I)$, and then also the entire building by using the linear version of the monotonicity analysis is in $O(I)$. Recalling again our running example, we start from `First` $= \{p_1, p_2, p_3, p_5\}$. The optimal solution `OptS` starts from pt_1 having the highest score. Then we try to insert the second most relevant path, that is, p_2. `OptS` $= \{p_1, p_2\}$ satisfies the τ-$test$. Similarly, we can insert p_3 into `OptS`, while we have to discard p_5 since the τ-$test$ is not satisfied. Finally, we have the solution $S_1(\{p_1, p_2, p_3\})$ and, at the second iteration, $S_2(\{p_4, p_5\})$. In this case, we obtain the same result but in linear time. Nevertheless, with respect to the building using Algorithm 7, we could generate solutions more specific and (possibly) less exhaustive, since we compose each solution starting from the most relevant sound path (i.e., we privilege strict connections between keywords).

Table 4.1 summarizes all discussed results. Given the size I of the input, that is, the number of sound paths, the linear strategy ($\mathcal{L}$) shows a linear time complexity $O(I)$ in the worst case, where the result shifts more to be exhaustive ($\mathcal{EX}$) rather than specific ($\mathcal{SP}$). The monotonic strategy ($\mathcal{M}$) provides an optimal balance between $\mathcal{EX}$ and $\mathcal{SP}$, with quadratic time complexity in the worst case, that is, $O(I^2)$. The variant of the monotonic strategy ($\mathcal{LM}$) shows again a linear time complexity $O(I)$, where the result shifts more to be specific rather than exhaustive.

4.5 Related Work

This chapter is an evolution of a previous work [24] by the same authors. In that work, authors provided a path-based keyword search process to build top-k solutions in an approximate way: the focus was exclusively on the quality of the result, without addressing efficiency. In this chapter, we introduced the two strategies and, consequently, new algorithms to reach scalability and a formal checking of the monotonicity.

The most prominent proposals to keyword search can be classified in a *schema-based* or *schema-free* approach. Schema-based approaches [11, 17, 20] are common on relational databases. In such works, (top-k) answers are trees composed of joined tuples, so-called *joined tuples trees* (JTTs). The work in [11] is the first to incorporate an IR-style technique to build JTTs. The score of a solution results from the aggregation of the scores of the involved tuples, normalized by the size of the tree (i.e., number of tuples). The authors introduce an upper bound function that bounds the score of potential answers to halt the top-k solution building as soon as possible. However, because evaluating such function is expensive, authors resort to an over-approximation of the upper bound, taking from accuracy. The work in [17] is similar to [11], but candidate answers are seen as monolithic virtual documents assessed by a standard IR function. Such technique avoids the need to design a mechanism to merge the contributions from the several tuples and attributes in the candidate answer. In [20], the authors provide three strategies to interconnect tuples into JTTs: (1) all connected trees up to a certain size, (2) all sets of tuples that are reachable from a root tuple within a radius, and (3) all sets of multicenter subgraphs within a radius. A common drawback of these approaches is that when executing a search, the keyword query is converted into a set of SQL statements that should generate candidate answers. All the queries have to be executed, but some (could) return empty results, leading to inefficiency, which is likely to worsen with the size of the dataset. The approach in [25], still schema aware but working on graphs, partially avoids this problem. Here the authors rely on an RDFS domain knowledge to convert keywords in query guides that help users to incrementally build the desired semantic query. While unnecessary queries are not built (thus not executed), there is a strict dependency on the users' feedback. A second drawback is the need to implement optimizations, in order to halt the process from computing all possible answers before returning the top-k, which introduce approximations on the top-k computation. Our approach overcomes all these limits. In the linear strategy, while trading off accuracy in the top-k computation, we guarantee a system that scales extremely well with the size of the input. In the monotonic strategy, top-k solutions are computed in exact ranked order in the first k steps.

Schema-free approaches [1, 8, 10, 13–15, 23] are more general as they work on arbitrary graph-shaped data. A general approach searches for the top-k connected trees, each representing a *(minimal) Steiner tree* [7]. In [1, 13], the authors propose backward and bidirectional graph exploration techniques, allowing polynomial data complexity. In [14], assuming the size of the query bounded, authors prove that top-k answers in an approximate order can be computed linearly to k and polynomially in the size of the input. Inspired by [14], authors in [8] propose a practical implementation of an engine returning answers in ranked order in polynomial time. Specifically, answers are first generated in an approximate order, then ranked more precisely in a second analysis. Another approximate approach is provided in [15]. It precomputes and indexes all the maximal *r-radius* subgraphs on disk. Then, extending the Steiner tree problem, *r-radius Steiner graphs* can be computed by pruning undesired parts from the maximal r-radius subgraphs. In all of these approaches, a relevant drawback is that finding a (minimal) Steiner tree is known as an NP-hard problem [7]. Therefore, the algorithms rely on (rather) complex sub-routines or heuristics to calculate approximations of Steiner trees. In the best case, such proposals have polynomial complexity in time. A relevant result of our framework is to present a polynomial time complexity (i.e., linear or quadratic) in the worst case: the upper bound complexity of our approach is a lower bound for the others. Moreover, while we can guarantee to build the top-k solutions in the first k steps of the execution, these works can only provide approximate solutions or have to compute all the solutions up front and then rank. In [10], authors present a bilevel index to expedite the discovery of connections between nodes matching keywords, in order to efficiently build the answer trees. A slightly different approach is the work in [23]. It proposes a system that interprets the keyword query into a set of candidate conjunctive queries. The user can refine the search by selecting which of the computed candidate queries best represent their information need. Candidate queries are computed exploring the top-k subgraphs matching the keywords. This is a semiautomatic system, opposed to ours that is completely automatic.

4.6 Experimental Results

We implemented our approach in a Java system. In our experiments, we used a widely accepted benchmark on DBLP[3] for keyword search evaluation. It is a dataset containing 26M triples about computer science publications. We used the same set of queries as in [10, 13, 23], and we compared our results with these works. Moreover, other two datasets were employed: IMDB[4] (a portion of 6M triples) and LUBM [9] (generating 50 universities corresponding to 8M triples). Experiments were conducted on a dual core 2.66GHz Intel Xeon, running Linux RedHat, with 4 GB of memory, 6 MB cache, and a 2-disk 1Tbyte striped RAID array, and we used Oracle 11g v2 as relational DBMS to build our index, as described below.

4.6.1 Index

To build solutions efficiently, we index the following information: vertices' labels (for keyword-to-element mapping) and the full-paths ending into sinks, since they bring information that might match the query. The first information enables to locate vertices matching the keywords, the second allows us to skip the expensive graph traversal at runtime. The indexing process is composed of three steps: (1) hashing of all vertices' labels, (2) identification of sources and sinks, and (3) computation of the full-paths. The first and the second steps are relatively easy. The third step requires to traverse the graph starting from the sources and following the routes to the sinks. To compute full-paths, we have implemented an optimized version of the breadth-first-search (BFS) paradigm, where independently concurrent traversals are started from each source. Similarly to [4], and differently from the majority of related works (e.g., [10]), we assume that the graph cannot fit in memory and that can only be stored on disk. Specifically, we store the index in Oracle, a relational DBMS.

Figure 4.2 shows the schema of our index, populated with the information from the graph of Fig. 4.1. Such schema is described in detail in [3]. Briefly, the table

---

[3]http://knoesis.wright.edu/library/ontologies/swetodblp/
[4]http://www.linkedmdb.org/

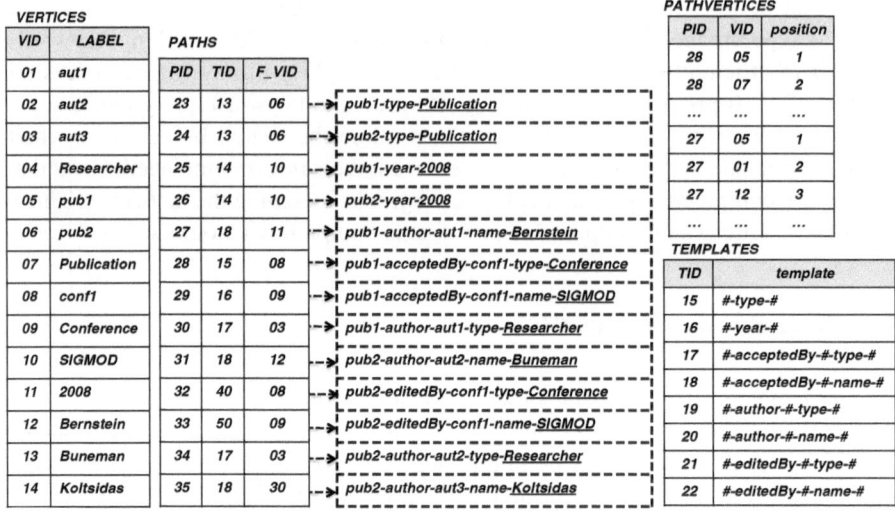

Fig. 4.2 An example of logical modeling of the index

VERTICES describes information about vertices identified by an oid (i.e., *VID* that is the key of the table) corresponding to the hashing of the *label* (i.e., URI or literal values) and the relevance *rel*. The table PATHS contains the full-paths resulting from the BFS traversal: each path is identified by the oid *PID* and the corresponding sink *F_VID* (an external reference to VERTICES) and presents the *length*, the relative relevance *rel*, and the associated template *TID*, as a reference to the table TEMPLATES containing information about templates of all occurring full-paths. Finally, PATHVERTICES has information of contained vertices for each path (e.g., necessary to test the intersection between paths). In particular, the table associates the *PID* of each path to the *VID* of the occurring vertices and the corresponding position of such vertices in the path (*PID* and *VID* represent the key). Because the index can be very large, in order to maintain a high level of performance, we fine-tune the relational DBMS at the physical level. Specifically, we employ the Oracle index-organized tables (IOTs) that are a special style of table structure stored in a BTree index frame. Along with primary key values, in the IOTs, we also store the nonkey column values. IOTs provide faster access to table rows by the primary key or any key that is a valid prefix of the primary key. Because the nonkey columns of a row are present in the BTree leaf block itself, there is no additional block access for index blocks. In our case, PATHS and PATHVERTICES are organized as IOTs. The matching is supported by standard IR engines (cf. Lucene domain index (LDi)[5]) embedded into Oracle as a type of index. In particular, we define an LDi index on the attributes *label* and *template* of tables VERTICES and TEMPLATES,

---

[5] http://docs.google.com/View?id=ddgw7sjp_54fgj9kg

respectively. Further, semantically similar entries such as synonyms, hyponyms, and hypernyms are extracted from WordNet [6], supported by LDi. In this way, from each input keyword, we provide a query on such tables, we extract the matching tuples, and following the references, we return the corresponding entries of PATHS. On top of this index organization, we implemented several procedures in PL/SQL, exploiting the native optimizations of Oracle, to support the maintenance: insertion, deletion, and update of new vertices or edges. The efficiency of such operations is documented in [3].

4.6.2 Query Execution

For query execution evaluation, we compared the different strategies of our system (i.e., linear $\mathcal{L}$, monotonic $\mathcal{M}$, and the variant linear/monotonic $\mathcal{LM}$), with the most related approaches: SEARCHWEBDB ($\mathcal{SWDB}$) [23], EASE ($\mathcal{EASE}$) [15], and the best performing techniques based on graph indexing, that is, 1,000 $\mathcal{BFS}$ and 300 $\mathcal{BFS}$ that are two configurations of BLINKS (see details in [10]). Table 4.2 shows the query set in detail. The table lists ten queries: for each one, we provide the list of keywords, and for each keyword, the number of matching and the corresponding number of retrieved sound paths to compose. For instance in Q_1, the keyword *algorithm* matches 1,299 nodes and retrieves about 31,590 sound paths.

We ran the queries ten times and measured the average response time. Precisely, the total time of each query is the time for computing the top ten answers. We performed *cold-cache* experiments (i.e., by dropping all file-system caches before restarting the various systems and running the queries): the query runtimes are shown in Fig. 4.3 (in ms and logarithmic scale).

In general, $\mathcal{EASE}$ and $\mathcal{SWDB}$ are comparable with $\mathcal{BFS}$. Our system performs consistently better (in any strategy) for most of the queries, significantly

Table 4.2 DBLP query dataset

Query	Input keywords	# of keyword nodes	# of sound paths
Q_1	Algorithm 1999	(1299, 941)	(31590, 1071617)
Q_2	Michael database	(744, 3294)	(44248, 15859)
Q_3	Kevin statistical	(98, 335)	(5807, 4725)
Q_4	Jagadish optimization	(1, 694)	(219, 11750)
Q_5	Carrie carrier	(6, 6)	(174, 551)
Q_6	Cachera cached	(1, 6)	(16, 69)
Q_7	Jeff dynamic optimal	(45, 770, 579)	(2764, 16869, 10649)
Q_8	Abiteboul adaptive algorithm	(1, 450, 1299)	(217, 14655, 31590)
Q_9	Hector jagadish performance improving	(6, 1, 1349, 173)	(865, 219, 25631,4816)
Q_{10}	Kazutsugu johanna software performance	(1, 3, 993, 1349)	(4, 282, 43949, 25631)

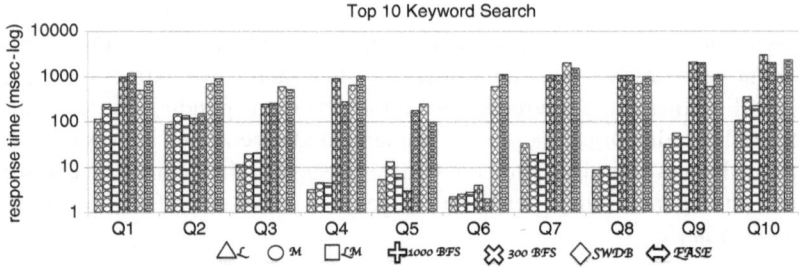

Fig. 4.3 Response times on DBLP

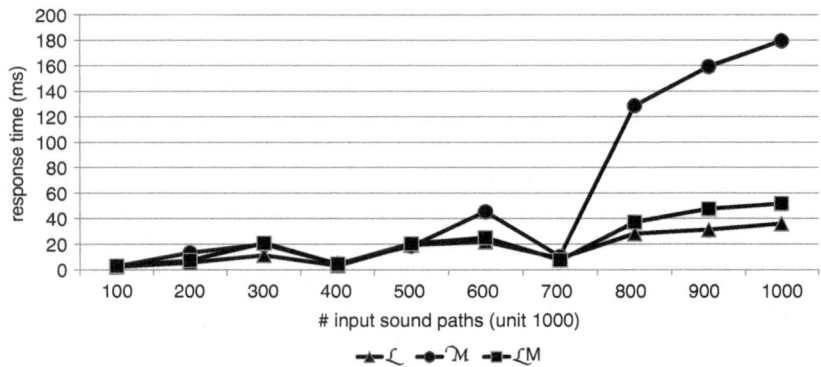

Fig. 4.4 Scalability with respect to #paths on DBLP

outperforming the others in some cases (e.g., Q_4 or Q_8). This is due to the greatly reduced (time) complexity of the overall process with respect to the others that spend much time traversing the graph and computing candidates to be (in case) solutions. An evaluation of the scalability of our system is reported in Fig. 4.4. The figure shows the scalability with respect to the size of the input, that is, the number I of sound paths. It shows the search time (ms) for all ten queries with respect to the corresponding number of matching sound paths. The diagram proves the studies of complexity summarized in Table 4.1. Both $\mathcal{L}$ and $\mathcal{LM}$ follow a similar linear trend while $\mathcal{M}$ shows a quadratic trend. We performed similar experiments on IMDB and LUBM. We formulated five queries for both datasets. Figure 4.5 shows the response times for our approach (in any strategy), $\mathcal{EASE}$ and $\mathcal{SWDB}$. The queries Q1 to Q5 were executed on IMDB while queries Q6 to Q10 on LUBM. Q1 and Q5 contain two keywords, Q2, Q3, Q7, Q8 three keywords, while the others four keywords. The results confirm the significant speedup of our approach with respect to the others.

We have also evaluated the effectiveness of results. The first measure we used is the reciprocal rank (RR). For a query, RR is the ratio between 1 and the rank at which the first correct answer is returned or 0 if no correct answer is returned. In DBLP, for all ten queries, we obtained RR $= 1$ in $\mathcal{M}$ and $\mathcal{LM}$. In this case, the

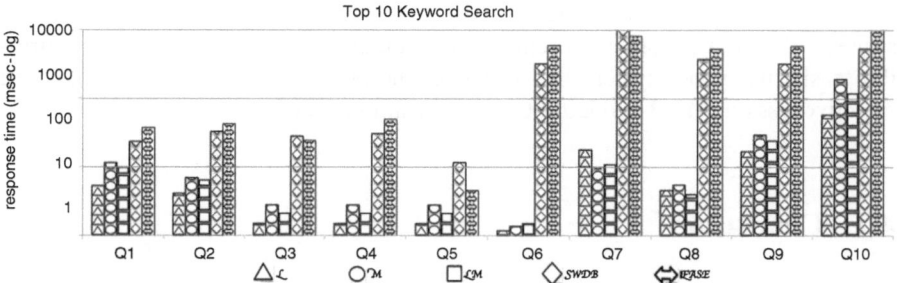

Fig. 4.5 Response times on IMDB and LUBM

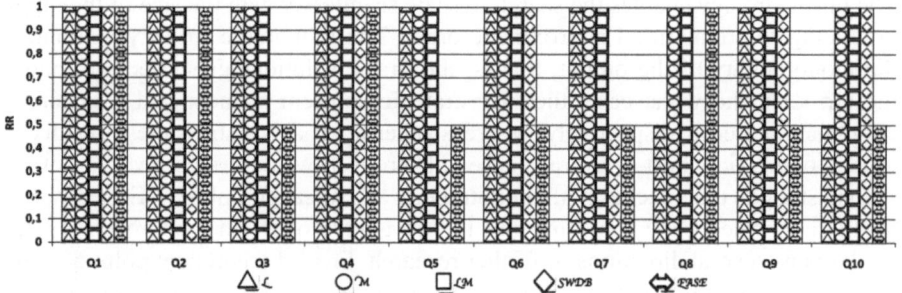

Fig. 4.6 RR measures for all frameworks in DBLP

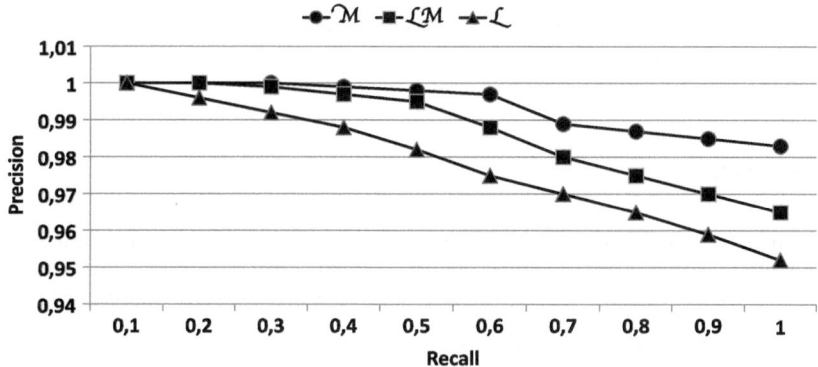

Fig. 4.7 Effectiveness of YAANII

monotonicity is never violated. In $\mathcal{L}$, we have an overall RR $= 1$, but RR $= 0.5$ for Q_8 and Q_{10} due to the violated monotonicity. As documented in Fig. 4.6, we compared our RR values, in any strategy, with that of $\mathcal{EASE}$ and $\mathcal{SWDB}$.

Then, we measured the interpolation between precision and recall that for each strategy on the DBLP dataset, that is, for each standard level r_j of recall (i.e., 0.1, ..., 1.0), we calculate the average max precision of queries in $[r_j, r_{j+1}]$, i.e., $P(r_j) = max_{r_j \le r \le r_{j+1}} P(r)$. We repeated this procedure for each strategy: Fig. 4.7 shows the results. As to be expected, the monotonic strategy $\mathcal{M}$ presents the highest quality (i.e., a precision in the range [0.98,1]). Then the variant $\mathcal{LM}$ and the linear strategy $\mathcal{L}$ follow in order presenting good quality though. Such result confirms the feasibility of our system that produces the best solutions in linear time. The effectiveness on IMDB and LUBM follows a similar trend.

4.7 Conclusion

In this chapter, we have presented a novel approach to keyword search query over large RDF datasets. We have provided two strategies for top-k query answering. The linear strategy enables the search to scale seamlessly with the size of the input, producing solutions in an approximate order. The monotonic strategy guarantees the monotonicity of the output, that is, the first k solutions generated are indeed the top-k. In the worst case, the two strategies present a linear and a quadratic computational cost, respectively, whereas other approaches show these results as lower bounds (i.e., best or average cases). Moreover, we described a variant of the second strategy that reaches both monotonicity and linear complexity. Experimental results confirmed our algorithms and the advantage over other approaches. This work opens several directions of further research. From a theoretical point of view, we are investigating a unique strategy that allows to reach both monotonicity and a linear time complexity, producing solutions that optimally balance exhaustivity and specificity. From a practical point of view, we are widening a more synthetic catalogue to index information, optimization techniques to speed up the index creation and update (mainly DBMS independent), and compression mechanisms.

References

1. Bhalotia, G., Hulgeri, A., Nakhe, C., Chakrabarti, S., Sudarshan, S.: Keyword searching and browsing in databases using banks. ICDE, pp. 431–440 (2002)
2. Brin, S., Page, L.: The anatomy of a large-scale hypertextual web search engine. Comput. Networks **30**(1–7), 107–117 (1998)
3. Cappellari, P., Virgilio, R.D., Miscione, M., Roantree, M.: A path-oriented rdf index for keyword search query processing. DEXA (2011)
4. Dalvi, B.B., Kshirsagar, M., Sudarshan, S.: Keyword search on external memory data graphs. Proc. VLDB **1**(1), 1189–1204 (2008)
5. Fagin, R., Lotem, A., Naor, M.: Optimal aggregation algorithms for middleware. PODS, pp. 102–113 (2001)
6. Fellbaum, C. (ed.): WordNet an Electronic Lexical Database. MIT, Cambridge, MA (1998)
7. Garey, M.R., Graham, R.L., Johnson, D.S.: The complexity of computing Steiner minimal trees. SIAM J. Appl. Math. **32**(4), 835–859 (1977)
8. Golenberg, K., Kimelfeld, B., Sagiv, Y.: Keyword proximity search in complex data graphs. SIGMOD, pp. 927–940 (2008)
9. Guo, Y., Pan, Z., Heflin, J.: Lubm: a benchmark for owl knowledge base systems. J. Web Sem. **3**(2-3), 158–182 (2005)

10. He, H., Wang, H., Yang, J., Yu, P.S.: Blinks: ranked keyword searches on graphs. SIGMOD (2007)
11. Hristidis, V., Gravano, L., Papakonstantinou, Y.: Efficient ir-style keyword search over relational databases. VLDB, pp. 850–861 (2003)
12. Hristidis, V., Koudas, N., Papakonstantinou, Y., Srivastava, D.: Keyword proximity search in xml trees. IEEE Trans. Knowl. Data Eng. **18**(4), 525–539 (2006)
13. Kacholia, V., Pandit, S., Chakrabarti, S., Sudarshan, S., Desai, R., Karambelkar, H.: Bidirectional expansion for keyword search on graph databases. VLDB (2005)
14. Kimelfeld, B., Sagiv, Y.: Finding and approximating top-k answers in keyword proximity search. PODS, pp. 173–182 (2006)
15. Li, G., Ooi, B.C., Feng, J., Wang, J., Zhou, L.: Ease: an effective 3-in-1 keyword search method for unstructured, semi-structured and structured data. SIGMOD (2008)
16. Liu, F., Yu, C.T., Meng, W., Chowdhury, A.: Effective keyword search in relational databases. SIGMOD (2006)
17. Luo, Y., Lin, X., Wang, W., Zhou, X.: Spark: top-k keyword query in relational databases. SIGMOD (2007)
18. Luo, Y., Wang, W., Lin, X., Zhou, X., Member, S., Wang, I.J., Li, K.: Spark2: Top-k keyword query in relational databases. IEEE Trans. Knowl. Data Eng. **99**, 1 (2011)
19. Piwowarski, B., Dupret, G.: Evaluation in (xml) information retrieval: expected precision-recall with user modelling (eprum). SIGIR, pp. 260–267 (2006)
20. Qin, L., Yu, J.X., Chang, L.: Keyword search in databases: the power of rdbms. SIGMOD (2009)
21. Singhal, A.: Modern information retrieval: a brief overview. Data(base) Eng. Bull. **24**(4), 35–43 (2001)
22. Singhal, A., Buckley, C., Mitra, M.: Pivoted document length normalization. SIGIR, pp. 21–29 (1996)
23. Tran, T., Wang, H., Rudolph, S., Cimiano, P.: Top-k exploration of query candidates for efficient keyword search on graph-shaped (rdf) data. ICDE, pp. 405–416 (2009)
24. Virgilio, R.D., Cappellari, P., Miscione, M.: Cluster-based exploration for effective keyword search over semantic datasets. ER, pp. 205–218 (2009)
25. Zenz, G., Zhou, X., Minack, E., Siberski, W., Nejdl, W.: From keywords to semantic queries – incremental query construction on the semantic web. J. Web Semant. **7**(3), 166–176 (2009)

Chapter 5
Interactive Query Construction for Keyword Search on the Semantic Web

Gideon Zenz, Xuan Zhou, Enrico Minack, Wolf Siberski, and Wolfgang Nejdl

5.1 Introduction

With the advance of the semantic Web, increasing amounts of data are available in a structured and machine-understandable form. This opens opportunities for users to employ semantic queries instead of simple keyword-based ones to accurately express the information need. However, constructing semantic queries is a demanding task for human users [11]. To compose a valid semantic query, a user has to (1) master a query language (e.g., SPARQL) and (2) acquire sufficient knowledge about the ontology or the schema of the data source. While there are systems which support this task with visual tools [21, 26] or natural language interfaces [3, 13, 14, 18], the process of query construction can still be complex and time consuming. According to [24], users prefer keyword search, and struggle with the construction of semantic queries although being supported with a natural language interface.

Several keyword search approaches have already been proposed to ease information seeking on semantic data [16, 32, 35] or databases [1, 31]. However, keyword queries lack the expressivity to precisely describe the user's intent. As a result, ranking can at best put query intentions of the majority on top, making it impossible to take the intentions of all users into consideration.

G. Zenz (✉) · E. Minack · W. Siberski · W. Nejdl
L3S Research Center, Appelstr. 9a, 30167 Hannover, Germany
e-mail: zenz@l3s.de; minack@l3s.de; siberski@l3s.de; nejdl@l3s.de

X. Zhou
Renmin University of China, 500 Information BLD, Beijing 100872, China
e-mail: xuan.zhou.mail@gmail.com

R. De Virgilio et al. (eds.), *Semantic Search over the Web*,
Data-Centric Systems and Applications, DOI 10.1007/978-3-642-25008-8_5,
© Springer-Verlag Berlin Heidelberg 2012

In this chapter, we describe QUICK,[1] a system for querying semantic data. QUICK internally works on predefined domain-specific ontologies. A user starts by entering a keyword query, QUICK then guides the user through an incremental construction process, which quickly leads to the desired semantic query. Users are assumed to have basic domain knowledge, but do not need specific details of the ontology, or proficiency in a query language. In that way, QUICK combines the convenience of keyword search with the expressivity of semantic queries. This system has also been presented in [34].

The chapter is organized as follows. Section 5.2 shows an introductory example to provide an overview on how to use QUICK. After introducing some preliminary notions in Sect. 5.3, Sect. 5.4 presents our framework for incremental query construction. In Sect. 5.6, we describe the algorithms for generating near-optimal query guides. Section 5.7 introduces optimization techniques to improve query execution performance. In Sect. 5.8, we present the results of our experimental evaluation. Section 5.9 reviews the related work. We close with conclusions in Sect. 5.10.

5.2   Motivating Example

Suppose a user looks for a movie set in *London* and directed by *Egdar Wright*.[2] The user starts by entering a keyword query, for instance *"wright london."* Of course, these keywords can imply a lot of other semantic queries than the intended one. For example, one possible query is about an actor called *London Wright*. Another one could search for a character *Wright*, who was performed by an actor *London*. QUICK computes all possible semantic queries and presents selected ones in its interface (see right-hand side of the prototype interface shown in Fig. 5.1).

More importantly, it also generates a set of query construction options and presents them in the construction pane (left-hand side of the user interface). If the intended query is not yet offered, the user can incrementally construct this query by selecting an option in the construction pane. Whenever the user makes a selection, the query pane changes accordingly, zooming into the subset of semantic queries that conform to the chosen options. At the same time, a new set of construction options is generated and presented in the construction pane. We call this series of construction options *query guide*, because it offers the user a path to the intended query. In the screenshot, the user has already selected that *"london"* should occur in the movie plot, and is now presented alternate construction options for *"wright."* When the user selects the desired query, QUICK executes it and shows the results.

The generated construction options ensure that the space of semantic interpretations is reduced rapidly with each selection. For instance, by specifying that

---

[1]QUery Intent Constructor for Keywords.

[2]Throughout this paper, we use the IMDB movie dataset as an example to illustrate our approach.

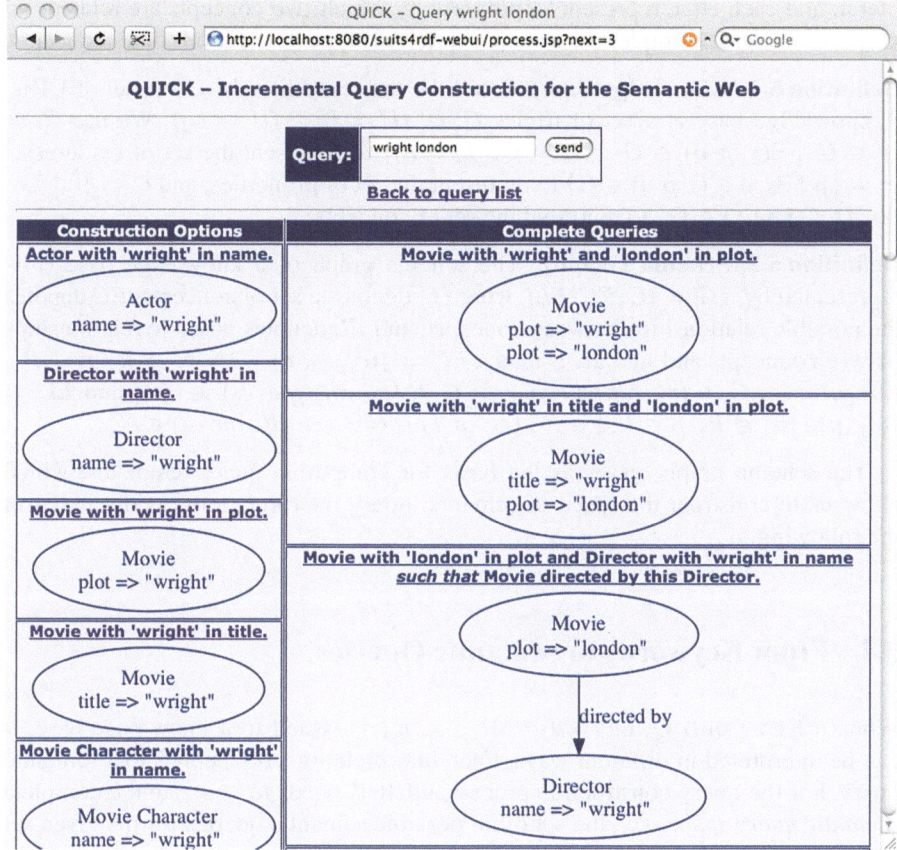

Fig. 5.1 QUICK user interface

"*london*" refers to a movie and not a person, more than half of all possible semantic queries are eliminated. After a few choices, the query space comprises only a few queries, from which the user can select the intended one easily.

In the following sections, we introduce the query construction framework and show how the interactive construction process of semantic queries is supported in QUICK.

5.3 Preliminaries

QUICK works on any RDF knowledge base with an associated schema in RDFS; this schema is the basis for generating semantic queries. We model schema information as a *schema graph*, where each node represents either a concept or a free literal, and each edge represents a property by which two concepts are related. To keep Definition 5.1 simple, we assume explicit rdf:type declarations of all concepts.

Definition 5.1 (Knowledge Base). Let L be the set of literals, U the set of URIs. A knowledge base is a set of triples $G \subset (U \times U \times (U \cup L))$. We use $R = \{r \in U \mid \exists (s\ p\ o) \in G : (r = s \lor r = o)\}$ to represent the set of resources,[3] $P = \{p \mid \exists s, o : (s\ p\ o) \in G\}$ to represent the set of properties, and $C = \{c \mid \exists s : (s\ rdf : type\ c) \in G\}$ to represent the set of concepts.

Definition 5.2 (Schema Graph). The schema graph of a knowledge base G is represented by $SG = (C, EC, EL)$, where C denotes a set of concepts, EC denotes the possible relationships between concepts, and EL denotes possible relationships between concepts and literals. Namely, $EC = \{(c_1, c_2, p) \mid \exists r_1, r_2 \in R,\ p \in P : (r_1, p, r_2) \in G \land (r_1\ rdf\text{:}type\ c_1) \in G \land (r_2\ rdf\text{:}type\ c_2) \in G\}$, and $EL = \{(c_1, p) \mid \exists r_1 \in R,\ p \in P, l \in L : (r_1,\ p, l) \in G \land (r_1\ rdf\text{:}type\ c_1) \in G\}$

The schema graph serves as the basis for computing query templates, which allow us to construct the space of semantic query interpretations, as discussed in the following.

5.4 From Keywords to Semantic Queries

When a KEYWORD QUERY $kq = \{t_1, \ldots, t_n\}$ is issued to a knowledge base, it can be interpreted in different ways. Each interpretation corresponds to a semantic query. For the query construction process, QUICK needs to generate the complete *semantic query space*, i.e., the set of all possible semantic queries for the given set of keywords.

The query generation process consists of two steps. First, possible query patterns for a given schema graph are identified, not taking into account actual keywords. We call these patterns *query templates*. Templates corresponding to the example queries from Sect. 5.2 are: "retrieve movies directed by a director" or "retrieve actors who have played a character."

Formally, a query template is defined as composition of schema elements. To allow multiple occurrences of concepts or properties, they are mapped to unique names. On query execution, they are mapped back to the corresponding source concept/property names of the schema graph.

Definition 5.3 (Query Template). Given a schema graph $SG = (C_{SG}, EC_{SG}, EL_{SG})$, $T = (C_T, EC_T, EL_T)$ is a query template of SG, iff (1) there is a function $\tau : C_T \rightarrow C_{SG}$ mapping the concepts in C_T to the source concepts in C_{SG}, such that $(c_1, c_2, p) \in EC_T \Rightarrow (\tau(c_1), \tau(c_2), p) \in EC_{SG}$ and $(c_1, L, p) \in EL_T \Rightarrow$

---

[3]To keep the presentation clear we do not consider blank nodes; adding them to the model is straightforward.

$(\tau(c_1), L, p) \in EL_{SG}$, and (2) the graph defined by T is connected and acyclic. We call a concept that is connected to exactly one other concept in T *leaf concept.*

Figure 5.2 shows three query templates with sample variable bindings. QUICK automatically derives all possible templates off-line from the schema graph (up to a configurable maximum size), according to Definition 5.3. This is done by enumerating all templates having only one edge, and then recursively extending the produced ones by an additional edge, until the maximum template size is reached.

Currently, we limit the expressivity of templates to acyclic conjunctions of triple patterns. Further operators (e.g., disjunction) could be added, however, at the expense of an increased query space size. Investigation of this trade-off is part of future work.

In the second step, *semantic queries* are generated by binding keywords to query templates. A keyword can be bound to a literal if an instance of the underlying knowledge base supports it. Alternatively, it can be bound to a concept or property, if the keyword is a synonym (or homonym) of the concept or property name. A full-text index on the knowledge base is used to efficiently identify such bindings. Figure 5.2 shows some semantic queries for the keyword set *"wright london,"* which bind the keywords to the literals of three different query templates. The left one searches for a movie with *"wright"* and *"london"* in its title. The middle one searches for a movie with *"london"* in its title directed by a director *"wright."* The right one searches for an actor *"wright"* playing a character in a movie with *"london"* in its title. Furthermore, keywords can also be matched to properties and classes, such as *"name"* or *"Movie."*

Definition 5.4 (Semantic Query). Given a keyword query kq, a semantic query is a triple $sq = (kq, T, \theta)$, where $T = (C_T, EC_T, EL_T)$ is a query template, and θ is a function which maps kq to the literals, concepts, and properties in T. $sq = (kq, T, \theta)$ is a valid semantic query, iff for any leaf concept $c_i \in C_T$, there exists a keyword $k_i \in kq$ that is mapped by θ to c_i itself, or a property or a literal connected to c_i.

The SEMANTIC QUERY SPACE for a given query kq and schema graph SG is the set of all queries $SQ = \{sq | \exists \theta, T : (kq, T, \theta)$ is a query template$\}$.

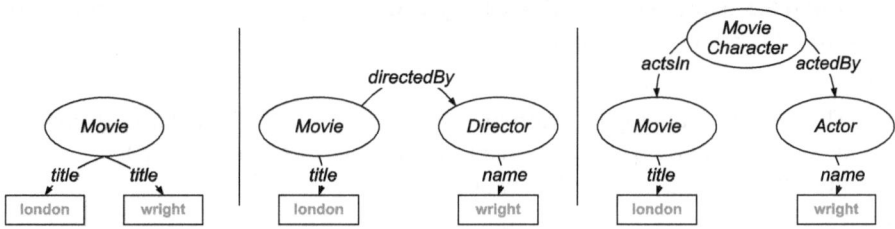

Fig. 5.2 Sample query templates for the IMDB schema; the terms in *gray* represent instantiations of these templates to semantic queries for *"wright london"*

In our model, each term is bound separately to a node of a template. Phrases can be expressed by binding all corresponding terms to the same property, cf. the left-hand example in Fig. 5.2. Additionally, linguistic phrase detection could be performed as a separate analysis step; in this case, a phrase consisting of several keywords would be treated as one term when guiding the user through the construction process.

The QUICK user interface prototype shows the queries as graphs as well as in textual form. The query text is created by converting graph edges to phrases. For each edge connecting a concept with a bound property, we create the phrase "*<concept>* **with** *<keyword>* **in** *<property>*," using the respective concept and property labels. If an edge connects two concepts, the relation is translated to the phrase "**this** *<concept1>* *<property>* **this** *<concept2>*." For the second query in Fig. 5.2, the following text is be generated: "*Movie* **with** "london" **in** *title* **and** *Director* **with** "wright" **in** *name* **such that** *Movie directed by* **this** *Director*."

As shown in Sect. 5.7, a semantic query corresponds to a combination of SPARQL triple pattern expressions, which can be directly executed on an RDF store.

5.5 Construction Guides for Semantic Queries

QUICK presents the user with query construction options in each step. By selecting an option, the user restricts the query space accordingly.

These options are similar to semantic queries, except they do not bind all query terms. Therefore, the construction process can be seen as the stepwise process of selecting partial queries that subsume the intended semantic query.

To describe precisely how a query guide is built, we introduce the notions of partial query and of subquery relationship. Our notion of query subsumption relies on the RDF Schema definition of concept and property subsumption. Note that our algorithms are not dependent on a specific definition of query subsumption, it would work equally well with more complex approaches, e.g., concept subsumption in OWL.

Definition 5.5 (subquery, Partial Query). $sa = (q_a, T_a, \theta_a)$ is a subquery of $sb = (q_b, T_b, \theta_b)$, or sa subsumes sb, iff:

1.1 $q_a \subset q_b$.
2.1 There exists a subgraph isomorphism ϕ between T_a and T_b, so that each concept $a_1 \in T_a$ subsumes $\phi(a_1)$ and each property $p \in T_a$ subsumes $\phi(p)$.
3.1 For any $k_1 \in q_a$, $\phi(\theta_a(k_1)) = \theta_b(k_1)$.

A partial query is a subquery of a semantic query.

For example, in Fig. 5.3, the partial queries pq_1, pq_2, and pq_3 are subqueries of sq_1, sq_2, and sq_3, respectively.

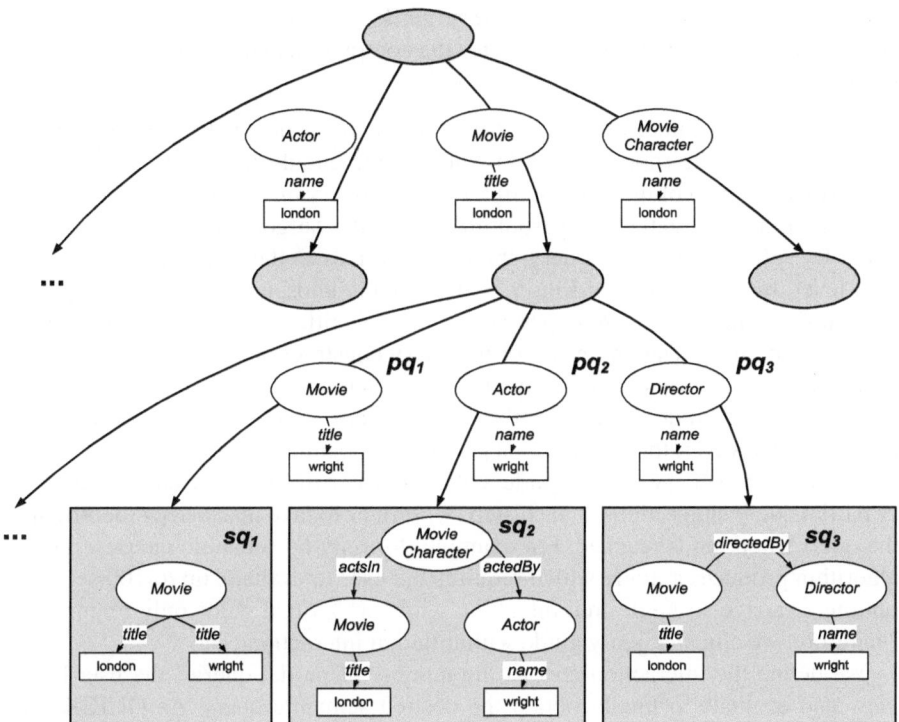

Fig. 5.3 Part of a query guide for "*wright london*"

The construction options of QUICK are modeled as a *query construction graph* (QCG) , as illustrated in Fig. 5.3. While the example shown is a tree, in general, the QCG can be any directed acyclic graph with exactly one root node. Given a set of semantic queries SQ, a QCG of SQ satisfies:

1.1 The root of QCG represents the complete set of queries in SQ.
2.1 Each leaf node represents a single semantic query in SQ.
3.1 Each non-leaf node represents the union of the semantic queries of its children.
4.1 Each edge represents a partial query.
5.1 The partial query on an incoming edge of a node subsumes all the semantic queries represented by that node.

Definition 5.6 (Query Construction Graph). Given a set of semantic query SQ and its partial queries PQ, a query construction graph is a graph $QCG = (V, E)$, where $V \subset SQ^*$, $E \subset \{(v_1, v_2, p) | v_1, v_2 \in V, v_2 \subset v_1, p \in PQ, p$ subsumes $v_2\}$ and $\forall v \in V, |v| > 1 : v = \{\bigcup v_i | \exists p : (v, v_i, p) \in E\}$.

If SQ is the complete query space of a keyword query, a QCG of SQ is a *Query Guide* of the keyword query.

Definition 5.7 (Query Guide). A *query guide* for a keyword query is a query construction graph whose root represents the complete semantic query space of that keyword query.

With a query guide, query construction can be conducted. The construction process starts at the root of the guide, and incrementally refines the user's intent by traversing a path of the graph until a semantic query on a leaf is reached. In each step, the user is presented the partial queries on the outgoing edges of the current node. By selecting a partial query, the user traverses to the respective node of the next level. In the example of Fig. 5.3, after having chosen that "*wright*" is part of the actor's name and "*london*" part of the movie's title, QUICK can already infer the intended query. The properties of the query construction graph guarantee that a user can construct every semantic query in the query space.

Every query guide comprises the whole query space, i.e., covers all query intentions. However, these guides vary widely in features such as branching factor and depth. A naïvely generated guide will either force the user to evaluate a huge list of partial query suggestions at each step (width), or to take many steps (depth) until the query intention is reached. For example, for only 64 semantic queries, a naïve algorithm produces a guide which requires the user to evaluate up to 100 selection options to arrive at the desired intention, while an optimal guide only requires 17. Therefore, we aim at a query guide with minimal interaction cost.

We define the interaction cost as the number of partial queries the user has to view and evaluate to finally obtain the desired semantic query. As QUICK does not know the intention when generating the guide, the worst case is assumed: the interaction cost is the cost of the path through the guide incurring most evaluations of partial queries. This leads to the following cost function definition.

Definition 5.8 (Interaction Cost of a Query Construction Graph). Let $cp = (V', E')$ be a path of a query construction graph $QCG = (V, E)$, i.e., $V' = \{v_1, ..., v_n\} \subset V$ and $E' = \{(v_1, v_2, p_1), (v_2, v_3, p_2), ..., (v_{n-1}, v_n, p_{n-1})\} \subset E$. Then: $cost(cp) = \sum_{v \in V'} |\{p : (v, v_1, p) \in E\}|$ and $cost(QCG) = \max(cost(cp) : cp)$.

Definition 5.9 (Minimum Query Construction Graph). Given a set of semantic queries SQ, a query construction graph QCG is a *minimum query construction graph* of SQ, iff there does not exist another query construction graph QCG' of SQ such that $cost(QCG) > cost(QCG')$.

A query guide which satisfies Definition 5.9 leads the user to the intended query with minimal interactions. In the following section, we show how to compute such guides efficiently.

5.6   Query Guide Generation

For a given keyword query, multiple possible query guides exist. While every guide allows the user to obtain the wanted semantic query, they differ significantly in effectiveness as pointed out in Sect. 5.5. It is thus essential to find a guide that imposes as little effort on the user as possible, i.e., a minimum query guide. Query construction graphs have several helpful properties for constructing query guides:

Lemma 5.1 (Query Construction Graph Properties)

  (i) *Given a node in a query construction graph, the complete subgraph with this node as root is also a query construction graph.*

 (ii) *Suppose QCG is a query construction graph, and A is the set of children of its root. The cost of QCG is the sum of the number of nodes in A and the maximum cost of the subgraphs with root in A, i.e., $Cost(T) = |A| + MAX(Cost(a) : a \in A)$.*

(iii) *Suppose QCG is a minimum query construction graph and A is the set of children of its root. If g is the most expensive subgraph with root in A, then g is also a minimum query construction graph.*

5.6.1   Straightforward Guide Generation

Lemma 5.1 can be exploited to construct a query construction guide recursively. Based on property (ii), to minimize the cost of a query construction graph, we need to minimize the sum of (1) the number of children of the root, i.e., $|A|$ and (2) the cost of the most expensive subgraph having one of these children as root, i.e., $MAX(Cost(a) : a \in A)$. Therefore, to find a minimum construction graph, we can first compute all its possible minimum subgraphs. Using these subgraphs, we find a subset A with the minimum $|A| + MAX(Cost(a) : a \in A)$. The method is outlined in Algorithm 10.

Algorithm 10: Straightforward query guide generation

Simple_QGuide()
Input: Partial queries P, semantic queries S
Output: Query guide G.
if $|S| = 1$ **then**
  ⌊ **return** S ;
for *each* $p \in P$ **do**
  | $p.sg :=$ **Simple_QGuide**$(P - \{p\}, S \cap p.SQ)$;
  ⌊ // p.SQ denotes the semantic queries subsumed by p
$G.cost := \infty$;
for *each* $p \in P$ **do**
  | $Q(p) := \{(p' \in P) : p'.sg.cost \leq p.sg.cost\}$;
  | $min\_set :=$ MINSETCOVER$(S - p.SQ, Q(p))$;
  | **if** $G.cost > |min\_set| + p.sg.cost + 1$ **then**
  | | $G := min\_set \cup \{p\}$;
  | ⌊ $G.cost := |min\_set| + p.sg.cost$;
return G;

According to Lemma 5.1, this algorithm always finds a minimum query guide. However, it relies on the solution of the SETCOVER problem, which is NP complete [12]. Although there are polynomial approximation algorithms for MINSETCOVER with logarithmic approximation ratio, our straightforward algorithm still incurs prohibitive costs. Using a greedy MINSETCOVER, the complexity is still $O(|P|! \cdot |P|^2 \cdot |S|)$. In fact, we can prove that the problem of finding a minimum query guide is NP hard.

Definition 5.10 (minSetCover). Given a universe U and a family S of subsets of U, find the smallest subfamily $C \subset S$ of sets whose union is U.

Theorem 5.1. *The* MINCONSTRUCTIONGRAPH *problem is NP hard.*

Proof. We reduce MINSETCOVER to MINCONSTRUCTIONGRAPH:
$M_S : U \leftrightarrow U_S$ is a bipartite mapping between U and a set of semantic queries U_S. $M_P : S \leftrightarrow S_P$ is a bipartite mapping between S and a set of partial queries S_P, such that each partial query $p \in S_P$ subsumes the semantic queries $M_S(M_P^{-1}(p))$. Create another set of semantic queries A_S and a set of partial queries A_P. Let $|A_S| = 2 \times |M_S|$. Let A_P contain two partial queries, each covering half of A_S. Therefore, the cost of the minimum query construction graph of A_S is $|M_S| + 1$, which is larger than any query construction graph of M_S. Based on Lemma 5.1, if we solve MINCONSTRUCTIONGRAPH($U_S \cup A_S, U_P \cup A_P$), we solve MINSETCOVER($U, S$).

5.6.2 Incremental Greedy Query Guide Generation

As shown, the straightforward algorithm is too expensive. In this section, we propose a greedy algorithm, which computes the query construction graph in a top-down incremental fashion.

Algorithm 11 starts from the root node and estimates the optimal set of partial queries that cover all semantic queries. These form the second level of the query construction graph. In the same fashion, it recurses through the descendants of the root to expand the graph. Thereby, we can avoid constructing the complete query construction graph; as the user refines the query step by step, it is sufficient to compute only the partial queries of the node the user has just reached.

The algorithm selects partial queries one by one. Then, it enumerates all remaining partial queries and chooses the one incurring minimal *total estimated cost*. It stops when all semantic queries are covered. The complexity of the algorithm is $O(|P| \cdot |S|)$.

The formula for the *total estimated cost* of a query construction graph is given in Definition 5.11.

Definition 5.11 (Total Estimated Cost). Let S be the semantic queries to cover, SP, the set of already selected partial queries, and p, the partial query to evaluate, the estimated cost of the cheapest query construction graph is

---

Algorithm 11: Incremental greedy query guide generation

Input: partial queries P, semantic queries S
Output: query guide G
if $|S| = 1$ **then**
  └ **return** S ;
$G := \emptyset$
while $|S| \neq 0$ **do**
  │ select $p \in P$ with min. $TotalEstCost(S, G \cup \{p\})$
  │ **if** *no such p exists* **then**
  │   └ break ;
  │ $G := G \cup \{p\}$;
  │ $S := S - p.SQ$;
  └ // p.SQ denotes the semantic queries subsumed by p
if $|S| \neq 0$ **then**
  └ $G := G \cup S$;
return G

$$TotalEstCost(S, SP) = |S| \frac{|SP|}{|S \cap \bigcup SP|} + \max(minGraphCost(|p|) : p \in SP),$$

where

$$minGraphCost(n) = \begin{cases} n = 1 : & 0 \\ n = 2 : & 2 \\ n > 2 : & e \cdot \ln(n) \end{cases}$$

Here, $minGraphCost(|p|)$ estimates the minimum cost of the query construction graph of p. Suppose f is the average fan-out for n queries, then the cost is approximately $f \cdot \log_f(n)$, which is minimal for $f = e$. The first addend of *TotalEstCost* estimates the expected number of partial queries that will be used to cover all semantic queries. This assumes the average number of semantic queries covered by each partial query does not vary.

As discussed above, the algorithm runs in polynomial time with respect to the number of partial and semantic queries. Although the greedy algorithm can still be costly when keyword queries are very long, our experimental results of Sect. 5.8.4 show that it performs very well if the number of keywords is within realistic limits.

5.7   Query Evaluation

When the user finally selects a query that reflects the actual intention, it will be converted to a SPARQL query and evaluated against an RDF store to retrieve the results. The conversion process is straightforward: for each concept node in the query or edge between nodes, a triple pattern expression of SPARQL is generated. In the first case, it specifies the node type; in the second case, it specifies the relation

```
SELECT * WHERE { ?movie rdf:type imdb:Movie.
    ?movie rdf:type imdb:Director.
    ?movie imdb:directedBy ?director.
    ?movie imdb:title ?term1 FILTER regex(?term1, ".*london.*").
    ?director imdb:name ?term2 FILTER regex(?term2, ".*wright.*"). }
```

Fig. 5.4 SPARQL query for the right-hand sample in Fig. 5.2

between the nodes. Finally, for each search term, a filter expression is added. See Fig. 5.4 for an example.[4]

To make QUICK work, these SPARQL queries need to be processed efficiently. Recent research in the area of SPARQL query evaluation has made significant progress [23, 25, 28, 30], mainly based on dynamic programming, histograms, and statistical methods for estimating cardinality and selectivity. However, available mature SPAQL engines either do not employ these techniques or do not offer them in combination with the full-text querying capabilities QUICK requires. In [20], we evaluated the performance of the most popular RDF engines with respect to these features, using an extended Lehigh University Benchmark (LUBM). The results show that the evaluated engines do not perform well on the type of hybrid queries needed by QUICK, as they still use rather simple heuristics to optimize the order of join operations.

Statistics of join cardinality can be employed to optimize the join order effectively. We adopted this approach in QUICK to improve the semantic query execution performance. In the following, we show how to estimate the cardinality of each triple pattern, and explain how to exploit these estimates for join ordering.

5.7.1 Cardinality Estimation

Triple patterns in SPARQL queries can be categorized into four types. For each type, we use a different method to estimate the cardinality. Let s p o be a triple pattern, where p is always a constant. For patterns of type s p ?o, where !s is a constant and ?o is a free variable, we exploit the BTree subject index, which is employed in most RDF stores [4, 9, 23]. We estimate the cardinality as the distance between the leftmost and rightmost matching element in the BTree. For patterns of type ?s p o, the BTree object index is used. For patterns of type !s p ?o, where s is a variable already bound in the query plan, and o is a free variable, the cardinality can—assuming uniform distribution of values—be estimated as $card(s, p) = |triples(p)| / |subjects(p)|$, where $triples(p)$ are the triples containing p, and $subjects(p)$ are the distinct subjects occurring in these triples. The same

---

[4]In our actual implementation, we use the custom language extension of LuceneSail to express full-text filters.

technique is applied to the pattern ?s p !o. These statistics can be precomputed and only need to be updated on significant knowledge base changes.

5.7.2 Join Order Optimization

Among the set of SPARQL algebra operators, i.e., *select*, *join*, and *triple pattern*, query execution costs are dominated by *join* in most cases. This makes join ordering crucial for efficient query processing. For a query containing n join operators, they cannot be exhaustively checked, as the number of possible join orders is factorial. Dynamic programming is thus used to identify a near-optimal join order [27]. Our implementation works as follows: It starts with a pool of (distinct) join sequence candidates, where each one initially contains only one join. Then, the join sequence with the minimum cost is chosen, and the join with smallest cardinality that is not yet in this sequence is added to the pool. The plan generation is complete as soon as the join sequence contains all joins.

To compute the join operator cost, we rely on the fact that RDF stores use the *Index Nested Loop Join* (INLJ) (e.g., [4, 10]). Let *INLJ* be an index nested loop join. Let *INLJ.left* (*INLJ.right*) represent the left (right) child of the join. Then the join's cost can be calculated as $cost(INLJ) = cost(INLJ.left) + (card(INLJ) * cost(INLJ.right))$, where $card(INLJ)$ represents the cardinality estimation of the join. The join cardinality is estimated as $card(join) = card(join.left) * card(join.right)$, where $card(join.left)$ and $card(join.right)$ are obtained using our statistics.

As shown in Sect. 5.8.4.1, this approach ensures efficient evaluation of semantic queries.

5.8 Experimental Evaluation

We implemented the QUICK system using Java. The implementation uses Sesame2 [4] as RDF store and the inverted index provided by LuceneSail [19] to facilitate semantic query generation. Parts of the described query optimization approaches have been integrated to Sesame2 version 2.2. We have used this implementation to conduct a set of experiments to evaluate the effectiveness and efficiency of the QUICK system and present our results in this section.

5.8.1 Experiment Setup

Our experiments use two real-world datasets. The first one is the Internet Movie Database (IMDB). It contains 5 concepts, 10 properties, more than 10 million instances, and 40 million facts. The second dataset (Lyrics, [6]) contains songs and artists, and consists of 3 concepts, 6 properties, 200,000 instances, and 750,000 facts. Although the vocabulary of the datasets is rather small, they still enable us to show the effectiveness of QUICK in constructing domain-specific semantic queries.

To estimate the performance of QUICK in real-world settings, we used a query log of the AOL search engine. We pruned the queries by their visited URLs to obtain 3,000 sample keyword queries for IMDB and 3,000 sample keyword queries for Lyrics Web pages. Most of these queries are rather simple, i.e., only referring to a single concept, such as a movie title or an artist's name, and thus cannot fully reflect the advantages of semantic queries. We therefore manually went through these queries and selected the ones referring to more than two concepts. This yielded 100 queries for IMDB and 75 queries for Lyrics, consisting of two to five keywords. We assume that every user has had a clear intent of the keyword query, implying that each one can be interpreted as a unique semantic query for the knowledge base. We manually assessed the intent and chose the corresponding semantic query as its interpretation. It turned out that most keyword queries had a very clear semantics. These interpretations served as the ground truth for our evaluation.

The experiments were conducted on a 3.60 GHz Intel Xeon server. Throughout the evaluation, QUICK used less than 1 GB memory.

5.8.2 Effectiveness of Query Construction

Our first set of experiments is intended to assess the effectiveness of QUICK in constructing semantic queries, i.e., how fast a user can turn a keyword query into the corresponding semantic query. At each round of the experiment, we issued a keyword query to QUICK and followed its guidance to construct the corresponding semantic query. We measured the effectiveness using the following two metrics:

1. The interaction cost of each query construction process, i.e., the total number of options a user had evaluated to construct each semantic query
2. The number of selections a user performed to construct each semantic query, i.e., the number of clicks a user had to make

The results of the experiments are presented in Table 5.1 and Figs. 5.5 and 5.6.

Table 5.1 shows that the size of the semantic query space grows very fast with the number of terms in a keyword query. Because the datasets are large, a term usually occurs in more than one place of the schema graph. As the size of the query space is usually proportional to the occurrences of each term in the schema graph, it grows exponentially with the number of terms. Furthermore, even for less than five terms, the size of the query space can be up to 9,000 for IMDB and up to 12,000 for Lyrics—such a huge query space makes it difficult for any ranking function to work effectively. For comparison purposes, we applied the SPARK [35] ranking scheme to the semantic queries generated by QUICK, but experiments showed that SPARK could not handle it in a satisfactory manner. In most cases, a user needed to

Table 5.1 Effectiveness of QUICK for IMDB (left) and Lyrics (right)

No. of terms	Avg. query space size	Cost		No. of terms	Avg. query space size	Cost	
		Avg.	Max			Avg	Max
2	60.5	5.08	7	2	23.9	3.21	7
3	741	8.69	15	3	235	7.96	13
4	7,365	10.17	32	4	1,882	12.30	19
>4	9,449	14.88	33	>4	12,896	14.44	22
All	4,535	9.46	33	all	2,649	7.50	22

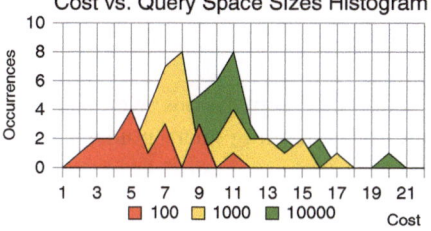
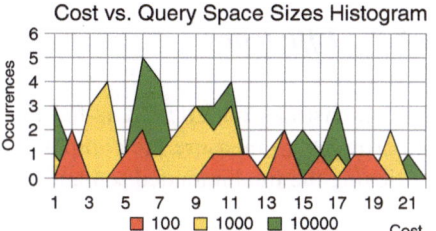

Fig. 5.5 Query construction cost histograms for IMDB (*left*) and Lyrics (*right*) for three different query space sizes

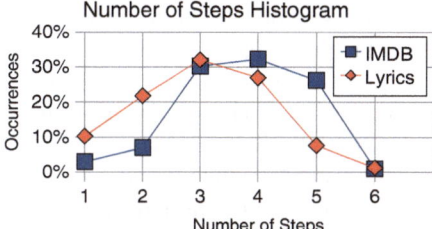
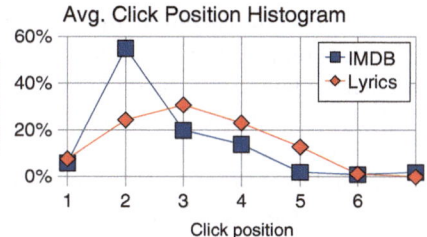

Fig. 5.6 Histograms of the number of interactions and average click position

go through hundreds or thousands of queries to obtain the desired one. In contrast, QUICK displays steady performance when confronted with such big query spaces. As shown in Table 5.1, the maximum number of options a user needs to examine until obtaining the desired semantic query is always low (33 for IMDB respectively 22 for Lyrics). On average, only 9 respectively 7 options have to be examined by the user. The cost of the query construction process grows only linearly with the size of the keyword queries. This verifies our expectation that QUICK helps users in reducing the query space exponentially, enabling them to quickly construct the desired query.

Figure 5.5 shows the cost distribution of the query construction for different query space sizes. We can see that for most queries, the user only has to inspect between 4 and 11 queries. Only in rare cases, more than 20 queries had to be checked. The cost of the query construction process shows a similar trend, growing only logarithmically with the size of the query space. As shown on the left-hand side of Fig. 5.6, in most cases, only two to five user interactions were needed. On the right, we show the average position of the selected partial queries. These were almost always among the first five presented options.

To summarize, this set of experiments shows that QUICK effectively helps users to construct semantic queries. In particular, the query construction process enables users to reduce the semantic query space exponentially. This indicates the potential of QUICK in handling large-scale knowledge bases.

5.8.3 Efficiency

To demonstrate that QUICK is feasible for real-world applications, we conducted experiments to measure the computation time for generating query guides and for retrieving the final intended semantic queries.

5.8.3.1 Query Guide Generation

We recorded the response times for each interaction of the query construction process. The initialization time as shown in the second and third columns of Table 5.2 comprises (1) the creation of the semantic query space, (2) computation of subquery relationships, and (3) keyword lookup in the full-text index. These tasks are fully dependent on the RDF store. The response times to user interactions were very short (fourth and fifth columns), enabling a smooth construction process.

In implementing QUICK, we focused on efficient algorithms for query guide generation and query evaluation. We are confident that for the initialization tasks, the performance can be improved significantly, too, e.g., by adapting techniques from [17] and by introducing special indexes.

5.8.4 Quality of the Greedy Approach

To evaluate the quality of the query guides generated by the greedy algorithm discussed in Sect. 5.6.2, we compared it against the straightforward algorithm

Table 5.2 QUICK response time for IMDB (left) and lyrics (right)	No. of terms	Init time (ms)		Response time (ms)	
		IMDB	Lyrics	IMDB	Lyrics
	2	98	664	2	0.5
	3	993	384	19	4
	4	16,797	4,313	1,035	107
	>4	31,838	120,780	3,290	7,895
	All	3,659	17,277	314	1,099

of Sect. 5.6.1. As the latter is too expensive to be applied to a real dataset, we restricted the experiments to simulation. We generated artificial semantic queries, partial queries, and subquery relationships. The semantic queries subsumed by each partial query were randomly picked, while the number of these was fixed. Therefore, three parameters are tunable when generating the queries, *n_complete*—the number of semantic queries; *n_partial*—the number of partial queries; and *coverage*—the number of semantic queries subsumed by each partial query.

In the first set of experiments, we fixed *n_complete* to 128 and *coverage* to 48, and varied *n_partial* between 4 and 64. We run both algorithms on the generated queries, and recorded the cost of the resulting query guides and their computation time. To achieve consistent results, we repeatedly executed the simulation and calculated the average.

As shown in the left-hand side of Fig. 5.7, the chance to generate cheaper query guides increases with the number of partial queries. Guides generated by the greedy algorithm are only slightly worse (by around 10%) than those generated by the straightforward algorithm, independent of the number of partial queries. The computation time of the straightforward algorithm increases exponentially with the number of partial queries, while that of the greedy algorithm remains almost linear. This is consistent with the complexity analysis of Sect. 5.6.

In the second set of experiments, we varied *n_complete* between 32 and 256, fixed *n_partial* to 32, and set *coverage* to ¼ of *n_complete*. The results are shown in Fig. 5.8.

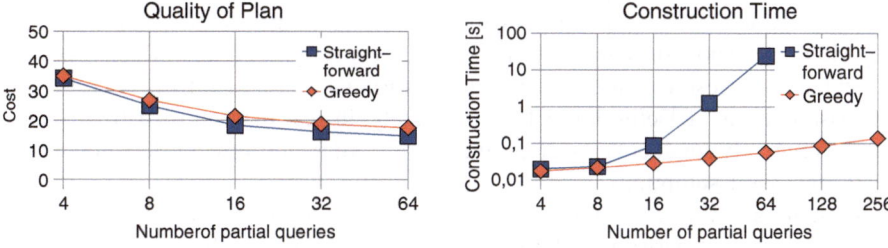

Fig. 5.7 Varying number of partial queries

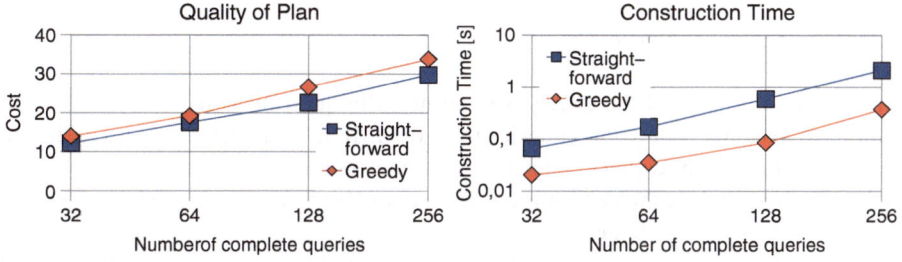

Fig. 5.8 Varying number of semantic queries

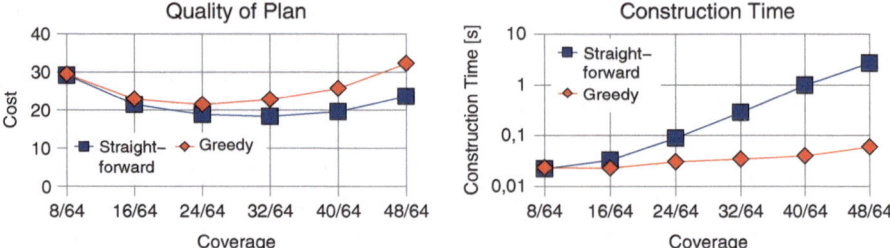

Fig. 5.9 Varying coverage of partial queries

As expected, as the number of semantic queries increases exponentially, the cost of query construction increases only linearly. The guides generated by the greedy algorithm are still only slightly worse (by around 10%) than those generated by the straightforward algorithm. This difference does not change significantly with the number of semantic queries. The performance conforms to the complexity analysis of Sect. 5.6.

In the third set of experiments, we fixed *n_complete* to 64 and *n_partial* to 16, and varied *coverage* between 8 and 48.

Figure 5.9 shows that as the *coverage* increases, the cost of resulting query guides first decreases and then increases again. This confirms that partial queries with an intermediate coverage are more suitable for creating query construction graphs, as they tend to minimize the fan-out and the cost of the most expensive subgraph simultaneously. The difference between the greedy algorithm and the straightforward algorithm increases with the *coverage*. This indicates that the greedy algorithm has a nonconstant performance with respect to *coverage*, which was to be expected, as a result of the logarithmic performance rate of MINSETCOVER and the assumptions of Definition 5.11. Fortunately, in real data, most partial queries have a relatively small coverage (less than 20%), where this effect is less noticeable, justifying our assumptions.

In summary, the experiments showed the greedy algorithm to have the desired properties. In comparison to the straightforward algorithm, the generated guides are just slightly more costly for the user, but are generated much faster, thereby demonstrating the applicability of the QUICK approach.

5.8.4.1 Query Evaluation

To assess the impact of the query evaluation techniques discussed in Sect. 5.7, we randomly selected 14 keyword queries from the IMDB query set. Using QUICK, we generated the semantic query space for these queries with a maximum size of 7. The 5,305 semantic queries which returned more than 100 results were used to assess the query evaluation performance.

We computed the improvement factor in terms of query acceleration. Figure 5.10 shows the distribution of this factor. In comparison with the unoptimized RDF store,

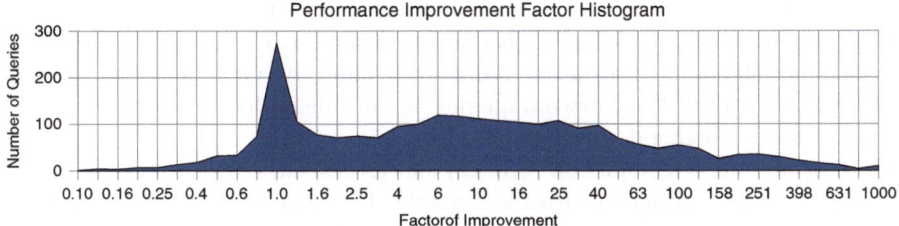

Fig. 5.10 Histogram of performance improvements

some queries did not run faster or even took slightly longer. However, the majority of the queries improved significantly (factor 4–40), demonstrating the benefits of our join order optimizations.

5.9 Related Work

In recent years, a number of user interfaces have been proposed to facilitate construction of semantic queries. These interfaces can be mainly classified into visual graphic interfaces [21, 26] and natural language interfaces [3, 14, 18]. Natural language interfaces are potentially more convenient for end users [13], as they require little prior knowledge of the data schema or a query language. However, the state-of-the-art natural language interfaces still require users to use a terminology that is compatible with the data schema and form grammatically well-formed sentences [13]. To overcome this limitation, a number of techniques have been used to help users construct valid natural language queries. For instance, the interface of [14] provides a dialog for users to align natural language terms to the ontology. The interface of [3] utilizes autocompletion to guide users to create meaningful sentences. In comparison with these methods, QUICK offers more flexibility in issuing queries. It accepts arbitrary keyword queries and allows users to incrementally structure the query through an optimized process.

Extensive investigations have recently been conducted on how to perform keyword search on the semantic Web [16, 32, 33, 35] and databases [1, 31]. The majority of work treats each dataset as a graph, and regards the query results as subgraphs, e.g., Steiner trees [15], which contain the query terms. They have in common that relevance ranking of these graphs is performed. As identifying the top-k query results would incur prohibitive I/O and computational cost, most of the approaches have been focusing on improving the performance of query processing. In contrast, QUICK is designed to help users to construct semantic queries. As the query results are retrieved after the semantic query is constructed, query processing is not a critical issue for QUICK. Work that is closest to QUICK includes [31,32,35]. Instead of retrieving search results directly, these approaches attempt to translate a keyword query into a set of semantic queries that are most likely to be intended by users. However, these approaches can at best rank the most popular query intentions on top. As the number of semantic query interpretations is very high, it is impossible to take the intentions of all users into consideration. As QUICK allows users to clarify the intent of their keyword queries, it can satisfy diverse user information needs to a much higher degree.

Automatic query completion [2, 8, 22] and refinement [29] are techniques that help users form appropriate structured queries by suggesting possible structures, terms, or refinement options based on the partial queries the user has already entered. By using these suggestions, the user constructs correct database queries without completely knowing the schema. However, as this technique still requires users to form complete structured queries, it is less flexible than QUICK, which allows users to start with arbitrary keyword queries. Moreover, they do not tackle the issue of minimizing the users' interaction effort.

A main advantage of QUICK is its ability to allow users to clarify the intent of their keyword queries through a sequence of steps. In the area of information retrieval, document clustering and classification have been used for similar purposes, especially in connection with faceted search interfaces. For example, Broughton and Heather [5] classify document sets based on predefined categories and let users disambiguate their search intent by selecting the most preferred categories. However, information retrieval approaches do not work on complex structured data, because joins over different concepts are not supported.

In [7], the idea of interactive query construction was combined with a probabilistic model for the possible informational needs behind an entered keyword query to make the incremental construction process faster.

5.10 Conclusion

In this chapter, we introduced QUICK, a system for guiding users in constructing semantic queries from keywords. QUICK allows users to query semantic data without any prior knowledge of its ontology. A user starts with an arbitrary keyword query and incrementally transforms it into the intended semantic query. In this way, QUICK integrates the ease of use of keyword search with the expressiveness of semantic queries.

The presented algorithms optimize this process such that the user can construct the intended query with near-minimal interactions. The greedy version of the algorithm exhibits a polynomial runtime behavior, ensuring its applicability on large-scale real-world scenarios. To our knowledge, QUICK is the first approach that allows users to incrementally express the intent of their keyword query. We presented the design of the complete QUICK system and demonstrated its effectiveness and practicality through an extensive experimental evaluation.

As shown in our study, QUICK can be further improved and extended in the following directions. (1) While QUICK currently works well on focused domain schemas, large ontologies pose additional challenges with respect to usability as well as efficiency. To improve usability, we plan to make use of concept hierarchies to aggregate query construction options. In that way, we keep their number manageable and prevent the user from being overwhelmed by overly detailed options. To improve further on efficiency, we are working on an algorithm that streamlines the generation of the semantic query space. (2) A further field of improvement is making the user interface more intuitive, especially for users without expertise in semantic Web or databases. (3) Based on the improved user interface, we will conduct a user study to verify its suitability for nonexpert users and its effectiveness on a larger scale.

References

1. Agrawal, S., Chaudhuri, S., Das, G.: DBXplorer: a system for keyword-based search over relational databases. ICDE (2002). DOI 10.1109/ICDE.2002.994693
2. Bast, H., Weber, I.: The CompleteSearch engine: interactive, efficient, and towards IR& DB integration. CIDR (2007)
3. Bernstein, A., Kaufmann, E.: Gino – a guided input natural language ontology editor. ISWC, pp. 144–157 (2006)
4. Broekstra, J., Kampman, A., van Harmelen, F.: Sesame: a generic architecture for storing and querying RDF and RDF Schema. ISWC (2002)
5. Broughton, V., Heather, L.: Classification schemes revisited: applications to web indexing and searching. J. Inter. Catalog. 2(3/4), 143–155 (2000)
6. Fang, L., Clement, T.Y., Weiyi, M., Abdur, C.: Effective keyword search in relational databases. Proceedings of the ACM SIGMOD International Conference on Management of Data, pp. 563–574. Chicago, Illinois, USA (2006)
7. Demidova, E., Zhou, X., Nejdl, W.: IqP: incremental query construction, a probabilistic approach. ICDE 2010, pp. 349–352 (2010)
8. Haller, H.: QuiKey – the smart semantic commandline (a concept). Poster and extended abstract presented at ESWC2008 (2008)
9. Harth, A., Decker, S.: Optimized index structures for querying RDF from the Web. Proceedings of the 3rd Latin American Web Congress (2005)
10. Harth, A., Umbrich, J., Hogan, A., Decker, S.: YARS2: a federated repository for querying graph structured data from the Web. ISWC/ASWC (2007)
11. Jagadish, H.V., Chapman, A., Elkiss, A., Jayapandian, M., Li, Y., Nandi, A., Yu, C.: Making database systems usable. SIGMOD (2007)
12. Karp, R.M.: Reducibility among combinatorial problems. In: Miller, R.E., Thatcher, J.W. (eds.) Complexity of Computer Computations. Plenum Press, NY, USA (1972)
13. Kaufmann, E., Bernstein, A.: How useful are natural language interfaces to the semantic web for casual end-users. ISWC/ASWC, pp. 281–294 (2007)
14. Kaufmann, E., Bernstein, A., Zumstein, R.: Querix: a natural language interface to query ontologies based on clarification dialogs. ISWC, pp. 980–981 (2006)
15. Kimelfeld, B., Sagiv, Y.: Finding and approximating top-k answers in keyword proximity search. PODS (2006). DOI http://doi.acm.org/10.1145/1142351.1142377
16. Lei, Y., Uren, V.S., Motta, E.: Semsearch: a search engine for the semantic web. EKAW (2006)
17. Li, G., Ooi, B.C., Feng, J., Wang, J., Zhou, L.: Ease: an effective 3-in-1 keyword search method for unstructured, semi-structured and structured data. SIGMOD Conference (2008)
18. Lopez, V., Uren, V., Motta, E., Pasin, M.: Aqualog: an ontology-driven question answering system for organizational semantic intranets. J. Web Semant. 5(2), 72–105 (2007)

19. Minack, E., Sauermann, L., Grimnes, G., Fluit, C., Broekstra, J.: The Sesame LuceneSail: RDF queries with full-text search. Tech. Rep. 2008-1, NEPOMUK (2008)
20. Minack, E., Siberski, W., Nejdl, W.: Benchmarking fulltext search performance of RDF stores. Proceedings of the 6th European Semantic Web Conference (ESWC 2009), pp. 81–95. Heraklion, Greece (2009)
21. Möller, K., Ambrus, O., Josan, L., Handschuh, S.: A visual interface for building SPARQL queries in Konduit. International semantic web conference (posters & demos) (2008)
22. Nandi, A., Jagadish, H.V.: Assisted querying using instant-response interfaces. SIGMOD (2007). DOI http://doi.acm.org/10.1145/1247480.1247640
23. Neumann, T., Weikum, G.: RDF-3X: a RISC-style engine for RDF. Proc. VLDB Endowment 1(1), 647–659 (2008)
24. Reichert, M., Linckels, S., Meinel, C., Engel, T.: Student's perception of a semantic search engine. IADIS CELDA, pp. 139–147. Porto, Portugal (2005)
25. Ruckhaus, E., Vidal, M.E., Ruiz, E.: OnEQL: an ontology efficient query language engine for the semantic web. ALPSWS (2007)
26. Russell, A., Smart, P.R.: NITELIGHT: a graphical editor for SPARQL queries. International semantic web conference (posters & demos) (2008)
27. Selinger, P.G., Astrahan, M.M., Chamberlin, D.D., Lorie, R.A., Price, T.G.: Access path selection in a relational database management system. SIGMOD (1979)
28. Stocker, M., Seaborne, A., Bernstein, A., Kiefer, C., Reynolds, D.: Sparql basic graph pattern optimization using selectivity estimation. Proceedings of the 17th International Conference on World Wide Web, pp. 595–604. Beijing, China (2008)
29. Stojanovic, N., Stojanovic, L.: A logic-based approach for query refinement in ontology-based information retrieval systems. ICTAI 2004. 16th IEEE International Conference on Tools with Artificial Intelligence, pp. 450–457 (2004). DOI 10.1109/ICTAI.2004.13
30. Stuckenschmidt, H., Vdovjak, R., Houben, G.J., Broekstra, J.: Index structures and algorithms for querying distributed RDF repositories. WWW, pp. 631–639 (2004)
31. Tata, S., Lohman, G.M.: SQAK: doing more with keywords. SIGMOD (2008). DOI http://doi.acm.org/10.1145/1376616.1376705
32. Tran, T., Cimiano, P., Rudolph, S., Studer, R.: Ontology-based interpretation of keywords for semantic search. ISWC (2007)
33. Wang, H., Zhang, K., Liu, Q., Tran, T., Yu, Y.: Q2semantic: a lightweight keyword interface to semantic search. ESWC, pp. 584–598 (2008)
34. Zenz, G., Zhou, X., Minack, E., Siberski, W., Nejdl, W.: From keywords to semantic queries – incremental query construction on the semantic web. J. Web Semat. 7(3), 166–176 (2009)
35. Zhou, Q., Wang, C., Xiong, M., Wang, H., Yu, Y.: SPARK: adapting keyword query to semantic search. ISWC (2007)

Chapter 6
Understanding the Semantics of Keyword Queries on Relational Data Without Accessing the Instance

Sonia Bergamaschi, Elton Domnori, Francesco Guerra, Silvia Rota, Raquel Trillo Lado, and Yannis Velegrakis

6.1 Introduction

The birth of the Web has brought an exponential growth to the amount of the information that is freely available to the Internet population, overloading users and entangling their efforts to satisfy their information needs. Web search engines such as Google, Yahoo, or Bing have become popular mainly due to the fact that they offer an easy-to-use query interface (i.e., based on keywords) and an effective and efficient query execution mechanism.

The majority of these search engines do not consider information stored on the *deep* or *hidden Web* [9,28], despite the fact that the size of the deep Web is estimated to be much bigger than the surface Web [9,47]. There have been a number of systems that record interactions with the deep Web sources or automatically submit queries to them (mainly through their Web form interfaces) in order to index their context. Unfortunately, this technique is only partially indexing the data instance. Moreover, it is not possible to take advantage of the query capabilities of data sources, for example, of the relational query features, because their interface is often restricted from the Web form. Besides, Web search engines focus on retrieving documents and

S. Bergamaschi · E. Domnori · S. Rota
DII-UNIMORE, via Vignolese 905 Modena, Italy
e-mail: sonia.bergamaschi@unimore.it; elton.domnori@unimore.it; silvia.rota@unimore.it

F. Guerra
DEA-UNIMORE, v.le Berengario 51, Modena, Italy
e-mail: francesco.guerra@unimore.it

R. Trillo Lado
Informática e Ing. Sistemas, c/ María de Luna 50018 Zaragoza, Spain
e-mail: raqueltl@unizar.es

Y. Velegrakis (✉)
University of Trento, Trento, Italy
e-mail: velgias@disi.unitn.eu

R. De Virgilio et al. (eds.), *Semantic Search over the Web*,
Data-Centric Systems and Applications, DOI 10.1007/978-3-642-25008-8_6,
© Springer-Verlag Berlin Heidelberg 2012

not on querying structured sources, so they are unable to access information based on concepts [31].

There are, on the other hand, numerous companies and organizations that have lots of data, so far in their own private (structured) data sources, and are willing to make them public on the Web. These data will remain unexploited unless they can be queried through keyword-based interfaces which is the de facto standard on the Web. There are already various studies on how to offer such a service [18, 41, 44, 48, 50], but they all require prior access to the instance in order to build an index that will allow them at runtime to understand what part of the database that a keyword in the query is referring to. This is not always feasible since companies and organizations may have their own restrictions and concerns about allowing an external service getting full access to the data.

A recent initiative that has attracted considerable attention is the notion of the *semantic Web*.[1] The idea of the semantic Web is to extend the data of the current Web with more structured data (typically expressed in RDF) that will allow them to be used by machines as well as by people. The success of the semantic Web depends on the existence of such kind of information and on the ability to query it. The semantic Web community has so far focused on ways to model this information. Allowing relational databases to be published on the semantic Web will provide the community with large amounts of data. However, it will also require the design and development of techniques and tools for querying that information in a way similar to the way it is currently done on the Web, i.e., through keyword queries. This means that any effort toward supporting keyword queries for structural data is of major importance for the specific community.

This chapter deals exactly with the problem of answering a keyword query over a relational database. To do so, one needs to understand the meaning of the keywords in the query, "guess" its possible semantics, and materialize them as SQL queries that can be executed directly on the relational database. The focus of the chapter is on techniques that do not require any prior access to the instance data, making them suitable for sources behind wrappers or Web interfaces or, in general, for sources that disallow prior access to their data in order to construct an index. The chapter describes two techniques that use semantic information and metadata from the sources, alongside the query itself, in order to achieve that. Apart from understanding the semantics of the keywords themselves, the techniques are also exploiting the order and the proximity of the keywords in the query to make a more educated guess. The first approach is based on an extension of the Hungarian algorithm [11] for identifying the data structures having the maximum likelihood to contain the user keywords. In the second approach, the problem of associating keywords into data structures of the relational source is modeled by means of a hidden Markov model, and the Viterbi algorithm is exploited for computing the mappings. Both techniques have been implemented in two systems called KEYMANTIC [5, 6] and KEYRY [7], respectively.

---

[1] http://www.w3.org/standards/semanticweb/

The chapter is structured as follows. First, a motivating example is presented to introduce the reader to the problem and the challenges. Then the problem statement is formally formulated (Sect. 6.3). Sections 6.4 and 6.5 describe the two approaches in detail. Section 6.6 provides an overview of the related works and how they differ from the two approaches presented in this chapter.

6.2   Motivating Example

Let us assume that a virtual tourism district composed of a set of companies (travel agencies, hotels, local public administrations, tourism promotion agencies) wants to publish an integrated view of their tourism data about a location (see Fig. 6.1). Keymantic allows users to query that data source with a two-step process: firstly, the keyword query is analyzed for discovering its intended meaning then a ranked set of SQL queries, expressing the discovered meaning according to the database structure, is formulated.

Each keyword represents some piece of information that has been modeled in the database, but, depending on the design requirements of the data source, this piece might have been modeled as data or metadata. Thus, the first task is to discover what each keyword models in the specific data source and to which metadata/data may be associated to. The association between keywords and database needs to be approximate: the synonymous and polysemous terms might allow the discovery of multiple intended meanings, each one with a rank expressing its relevance. Let us consider, e.g., a query consisting of the keywords "Restaurant Naples." For instance, a possible meaning of the query might be "find information about the restaurant called Naples." In this case, the former keyword should be mapped into a metadata (the table Restaurant and the other one into a value of the attribute Name of the same table Restaurant). A user might have in mind other meanings for the same

Person

Name	Phone	City	Email
Saah	4631234	London	saah@aaa.bb
Sevi	6987654	Auckland	eevi@bbb.cc
Edihb	1937842	Santiago	edibh@ccc.dd

Reserved

Person	Hotel	Date
Saah	x123	6/10/2009
Sevi	cs34	4/3/2009
Edihb	cs34	7/6/2009

Hotel

id	Name	Address	Service	City
x123	Galaxy	25 Blicker	restaurant	Shanghai
cs34	Krystal	15 Tribeca	parking	Cancun
ee67	Hilton	5 West Ocean	air cond.	Long Beach

City

Name	Country	Description
Shanghai	China	...
Cancun	Mexico	...
Long Beach	USA	...
New York	USA	...

Booked

Person	Rest	Date
Saah	Rx1	5/4/2009
Sevi	Rx1	9/3/2009

Restaurant

id	Name	Address	Specialty	City
Rx1	Best Lobster	25, Margaritas	Seafood	Cancun
Rt1	Naples	200 Park Av.	Italian	New York

Fig. 6.1 A fraction of a database schema with its data

keywords, e.g., "find the restaurants that are located in the Naples Avenue," or "in the Naples city," or "that cook Naples specialties." All these intended meanings give rise to different associations of the keyword Naples; attributes Address, City, or Specialty of the table Restaurant. This example shows also that keywords in a query are not independent: we expect that the keywords express different features of what the user is looking for. For this reason, we expect that in our example, "Naples" is a value referring to an element of the Restaurant table. If the user had formulated the keyword query "Restaurant name Naples," the number of possible intended meanings would have been reduced, since the keywords name forces the mappings of Naples into the attribute Name of the table Restaurant. Notice that different intended meanings may generate a mapping from the same keyword both into metadata and into data values. For example, in our database, restaurant is the name of a table, but it is also one of the possible values of the attribute Service in the table Hotel. Finally, the order of the keywords in a query is also another element to be taken into account since related elements are usually close. If a user asks for "Person London restaurant New York," one possible meaning of the query is that the user is looking for the restaurant in New York visited by people from London. Other permutations of the keywords in the query may generate other possible interpretations.

The second step in answering a keyword query concerns the formulation of an SQL query expressing one of the discovered intended meanings. In a database, semantic relationships between values are modeled either through the inclusion of different attributes under the same table or through join paths across different tables. Different join paths can lead to different interpretations. Consider, for instance, the keyword query "Person USA." One logical mapping is to have the word Person corresponding to the table Person and the word USA to a value of the attribute Country of the table City. Even when this mapping is decided, there are different interpretations of the keywords based on the different join paths that exist between the tables Person and City. For instance, one can notice that a person and a city are related through a join path that goes through the City attribute referring to the attribute Name in the table City (determining which people in the database are from USA), through another path that is based on the table Hotel (determining which people reserved rooms of hotels in USA), and also through another path that is based on the table Restaurant (determining which people reserved a table in an American restaurant).

Finding the different semantic interpretations of a keyword query is a combinatorial problem which can be solved by an exhaustive enumeration of the different mappings to database structures and values. The large number of different interpretations can be brought down by using internal and external knowledge that helps in eliminating mappings that are not likely to lead to meanings intended by the user. For instance, if one of the provided keywords in a query is "320-463-1463," it is very unlikely that this keyword refers to an attribute or table name. It most probably represents a value and, in particular, due to its format, a phone number. Similarly, the keyword "Bistro" in a query does not correspond to a table or an attribute in the specific database. Some auxiliary information, such as a thesaurus, can provide the information that the word "bistro" is typically used to represent a restaurant; thus, the keyword can be associated to the Restaurant table.

6.3   Problem Statement

Definition 6.1. A database D is a collection V_t of relational tables $R_1, R_2, \ldots, R_n$. Each table R is a collection of attributes $A_1, A_2, \ldots, A_{m_R}$, and each attribute A has a domain, denoted as $\text{dom}(A)$. Let $V_a = \{A \mid A \in R \wedge R \in V_t\}$ represent the set of all the attributes of all the tables in the database and $V_d = \{d \mid d = \text{dom}(A) \wedge A \in V_a\}$ represent the set of all their respective domains. The *database vocabulary* of D, denoted as V_D, is the set $V_D = V_t \cup V_a \cup V_d$. Each element of the set V_D is referred to as a *database term*.

We distinguish two subsets of the database vocabulary: the *schema vocabulary* $V_{SC} = V_t \cup V_a$ and the *domain vocabulary* $V_{DO} = V_d$ that concerns the instance information. We also assume that a keyword query KQ is an ordered l-tuple of keywords $(k_1, k_2, \ldots, k_l)$.

Definition 6.2. A *configuration* $f_c(KQ)$ of a keyword query KQ on a database D is an injective function from the keywords in KQ to database terms in V_D. In other words, a configuration is a mapping that describes each keyword in the original query in terms of database terms.

The reason we consider a configuration to be an injective function is because we assume that (1) each keyword cannot have more than one meaning in the same configuration, i.e., it is mapped into only one database term; (2) two keywords cannot be mapped to the same database term in a configuration since overspecified queries are only a small fraction of the queries that are typically met in practice [22]; and (3) every keyword is relevant to the database content, i.e., keywords always have a correspondent database term. Furthermore, while modeling the keyword-to-database term mappings, we also assume that every keyword denotes an element of interest to the user, i.e., there are no stop words or unjustified keywords in a query. In this chapter, we do not address query cleaning issues. We assume that the keyword queries have already been preprocessed using well-known cleansing techniques.

Answering a keyword query over a database D means finding the SQL queries that describe its possible semantics in terms of the database vocabulary. Each such SQL query is referred to as an *interpretation* of the keyword query in database terms. An interpretation is based on a configuration and includes in its clauses all the database terms that are part of the image[2] of the query keywords through the configuration. In the current work, we consider only select-project-join (SPJ)

---

[2]Since a configuration is a function, we use the term image to refer to its output.

interpretations that are typically the queries of interest in similar works [2, 19], but interpretations involving aggregations [42] are part of our future work.

Definition 6.3. An *interpretation* of a keyword query $KQ = (k_1, k_2, \ldots, k_l)$ on a database D using a configuration $f_c^*(KQ)$ is an SQL query in the form select $A_1, A_2, \ldots, A_o$ from R_1 JOIN R_2 JOIN $\ldots$ JOIN R_p where $A_1' = v_1$ AND $A_2' = v_2$ AND $\ldots$ AND $A_q' = v_q$ such that the following holds:

- $\forall A \in \{A_1, A_2, \ldots, A_o\} : \exists k \in KQ$ such that $f_c^*(k) = A$
- $\forall R \in \{R_1, R_2, \ldots, R_p\}$: (i) $\exists k \in KQ : f_c^*(k) = R$ or (ii) $\exists k_i, k_j \in KQ :$ $f_c^*(k_i) = R_i \wedge f_c^*(k_j) = R_j \wedge$ exists a join path from R_i to R_j that involves R
- $\forall$ "$A' = v$" $\in \{A_1' = v_1, A_2' = v_2, \ldots, A_o' = v_o\}$: $\exists k \in KQ$ such that $f_c^*(k) = \text{dom}(A') \wedge k = v$
- $\forall k \in KQ : f_c^*(k) \in \{A_1, A_2, \ldots, A_o, R_1, R_2, \ldots, R_p, \text{dom}(A_1'), \ldots, \text{dom}(A_q')\}$

The existence of a database term in an interpretation is justified either by belonging to the image of the respective configuration or by participating in a join path connecting two database terms that belong to the image of the configuration. Note that even with this restriction, due to the multiple join paths in a database D, it is still possible to have multiple interpretations of a keyword query KQ given a certain configuration $f_c^*(KQ)$. We use the notation $\mathcal{I}(KQ, f_c^*(KQ), D)$ to refer to the set of these interpretations and $\mathcal{I}(KQ, D)$ for the union of all these sets for a query KQ.

Since each keyword in a query can be mapped into a table name, an attribute name, or an attribute domain, there are $2\Sigma_{i=1}^n |R_i| + n$ different mappings for each keyword, with $|R_i|$ denoting the *arity* of the relation R_i and n the number of tables in the database. Based on this, and on the fact that no two keywords can be mapped to the same database term, for a query containing l keywords, there are $\frac{|V_D|!}{(|V_D|-l)!}$ possible configurations. Of course, not all the interpretations generated by these configurations are equally *meaningful*. Some are more likely to represent the intended keyword query semantics. In the following sections, we will show how different kinds of metainformation and interdependencies between the mappings of keywords into database terms can be exploited in order to effectively and efficiently identify these meaningful interpretations and rank them higher.

6.4 The Hungarian Algorithm Approach

The generation of interpretations that most likely describe the intended semantics of a keyword query is based on semantically meaningful configurations, i.e., sets of mappings between each keyword and a database term. We introduce the notion of *weight* that offers a quantitative measure of the relativeness of a keyword to a database term, i.e., the likelihood that the semantics of the database term are the intended semantics of the keyword in the query. The sum of the weights of the keyword–database term pairs can form a score serving as a quantitative measure of the likelihood of the configuration to lead to an interpretation that accurately describes the intended keyword query semantics. The range and full semantics of the score cannot be fully specified in advance. They depend on the method used to compute the similarity. This is not a problem as long as the same method is used to compute the scores for all the keywords. This is the same approach followed in schema matching [37] where a score is used to measure the likelihood that an element of a schema corresponds to an element of another.

The naive approach for selecting the best configurations, and as a consequence, generating the most prominent interpretations of a keyword query, is the computation of the score of each possible configuration and then selecting those that have the highest scores. Of course, we would like to avoid an exhaustive enumeration of all the possible configurations and compute only those that give high scores. The problem of computing the mapping with the maximum score without an exhaustive computation of the scores of all the possible mappings is known in the literature as the problem of *bipartite weighted assignments* [13]. Unfortunately, solutions to this problem suffer from two main limitations. First, apart from the mutual exclusiveness, they do not consider any other interdependencies that may exist between the mappings. Second, they typically provide only the best mapping instead of a ranked list based on the scores.

To cope with the first limitation, we introduce two different kinds of weights: the *intrinsic* and the *contextual* weights. Given a mapping of a keyword to a database term, its intrinsic weight measures the likelihood that the semantics of the keyword is that of the database term if considered in isolation from the mappings of all the other keywords in the query. The computation of an intrinsic weight is bed on syntactic, semantic, and structural factors, such as attribute and relation names, or other auxiliary external sources, such as vocabularies, ontologies, domains, common syntactic patterns. On the other hand, a contextual weight is used to measure the same likelihood but considering the mappings of the remaining query keywords. This is motivated by the fact that the assignment of a keyword to a database term may increase or decrease the likelihood that another keyword corresponds to a certain database term. This is again bed on observations that humans tend to write queries in which related keywords are close to each other [22]. A similar idea has already been exploited in the context of schema matching [30] with many interesting results. To cope with the second limitation, we have developed a novel algorithm for computing the best mappings. The algorithm is based on and extends the Hungarian (a.k.a. Munkres) algorithm [11] and will be described in detail in Sect. 6.4.3.

A visual illustration of the individual steps in the keyword query translation task is depicted in Fig. 6.2. A special data structure, called *weight matrix*, plays a central role in these steps. The *weight matrix* is a two-dimensional array with a row for each keyword in the keyword query and a column for each database term. The value of a cell $[i, j]$ represents the weight associated to the mapping between the keyword i and the database term j. Figure 6.3 provides an abstract illustration of a weight matrix. R_i and $A_j^{R_i}$ columns correspond to the relation R_i and the attribute A_j of R_i, respectively, while a column with an underlined attribute name $\underline{A_j^{R_i}}$ represents

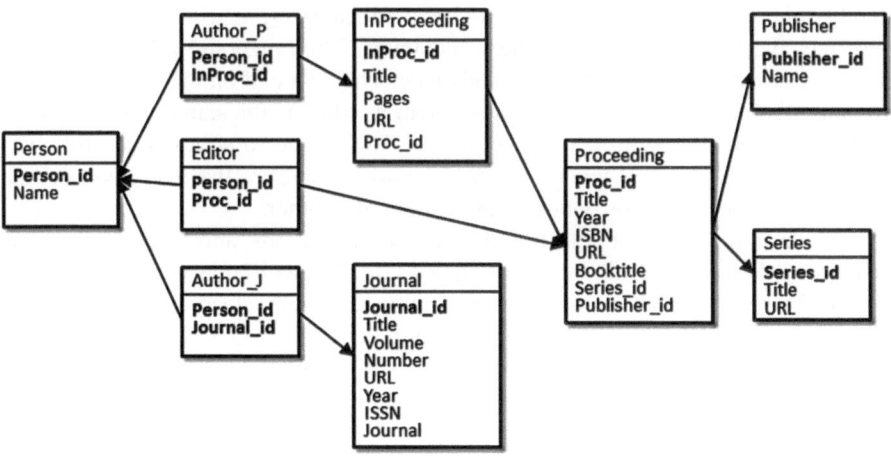

Fig. 6.2 Overview of the keyword query translation process

	R_1	...	R_n	$A_1^{R_1}$	...	$A_{n_1}^{R_1}$	...	$A_{n_n}^{R_n}$	$A_1^{R_1}$	...	$A_{n_1}^{R_1}$	...	$A_{n_n}^{R_n}$
$keyword_1$													
$keyword_2$													
...													
$keyword_k$													

Fig. 6.3 Weight table with its SW (*light*) and VW (*dark*) parts

the data values in the column A_j of table R_i may have, i.e., its domain. Two parts (i.e., submatrices) can be distinguished in the weight matrix. One corresponds to the database terms related to schema elements, i.e., relational tables and attributes, and the other one corresponds to attribute values, i.e., the domains of the attributes. We refer to database terms related to schema elements *schema databe terms* and to those related to domains of the attributes *value database terms*. In Fig. 6.3, these two submatrices are illustrated with different shades of gray. We refer to the weights in the first submatrix *schema weights* and to those of the second *value weights*. We also use the notation SW and VW to refer either to the respective submatrix or to their values. The details of the individual steps of Fig. 6.2 are provided next.

Intrinsic Weight Computation. The first step of the process is the intrinsic weight computation. The output is the populated SW and VW submatrices. The computation is achieved by the exploitation and combination of a number of similarity techniques based on structural and lexical knowledge extracted from the data source and on external knowledge, such ontologies, vocabularies, domain terminologies, etc. Note that the knowledge extracted from the data source is basically the meta-information that the source makes public, typically, the schema structure and constraints. In the absence of any other external information, a simple string comparison based on tree-edit distance can be used for populating the SW submatrix. For the VW submatrix, the notion of *semantic distance* [15] can always be used in the absence of anything else. As it happens in similar situations [37], measuring the success of such a task is not easy since there is no single correct answer. In general, the more metainformation has been used, the better. However, even in the case that the current step is skipped, the process can continue with the weight matrix where all the intrinsic values have the same default value. The computation of the intrinsic weights is detailed in Sect. 6.4.1.

Selection of the Best Mappings to Schema Terms. The intrinsic weights provide a first indication of the similarities of the keywords to database terms. To generate the prominent mappings, we need on top of that to take into consideration the interdependencies between the mappings of the different keywords. We consider first the prominent mappings of keywords to schema terms. For that, we work on the SW submatrix. Based on the intrinsic weights, a series of mappings, M_1^S, M_2^S, ..., M_n^S, of keywords to schema terms are generated. The mappings are those that achieve the highest overall score, i.e., the sum of the weights of the individual keyword mappings. The mappings are partial, i.e., not all the keywords are mapped to some schema term. Those that remain unmapped will play the role of an actual data value and will be considered in a subsequent step for mapping to value database terms. The selection of the keywords to remain unmapped is bed on the weight matrix and some cutoff threshold. Those with a similarity below the threshold remain unmapped. For each of the mappings M_i^S, the weights of its SW matrix are adjusted to take into consideration the context generated by the mapping of the neighboring keywords. It is based on the observation that users form queries in which keywords referring to the same or related concepts are adjacent [22, 45]. The generation of the mappings and the adjustment of the weights in SW are performed by our extension of the Hungarian algorithm that is described in detail in Sect. 6.4.3. The output of such a step is an updated weight matrix SW_i and, naturally, an updated score for each mapping M_i^S. Given the updated scores, some mappings may be rejected. The selection is based on a threshold. There is no golden value to set the threshold value. It depends on the expectations from the keyword query answering systems. The higher its value, the less the interpretations generated at the end, but with higher confidence. In contrast, the lower the threshold value, the more the mappings with lower confidence.

Contextualization of VW and Selection of the Best Mappings to Value Terms. For each partial mapping M_i^S of keywords to schema terms generated in the previous step, the mappings of the remaining unmapped keywords to value terms need to be decided. This is done in two phases. First, the intrinsic weights of the VW submatrix that were generated in Step 1 are updated to reflect the added value provided by the mappings in M_i^S of some of the keywords to schema database terms. This is called the process of contextualization of the VW submatrix. It is based on the documented observation that users form queries in which keywords specifying metadata information about a concept are adjacent or at let neighboring [22, 45]. Thus, when a keyword is mapped to a schema term, it becomes more likely that an adjacent keyword should be mapped to a value in the domain of that schema term. The contextualization process increases the weights of the respective value terms to reflect exactly that. For example, in the keyword query ``Name Alexandria'' assume that the keyword Alexandria was found during the first step to be equally likely the name of a person or of a city. If in Step 2 the keyword Name has been mapped to the attribute Name of the table Person, the confidence that Alexandria is actually the name of a person is increased; thus, the weight between that keyword and the value database term representing the domain of attribute Name should be increased, accordingly. In the second phase, given an updated VW_i submatrix, the most prominent mappings of the remaining unmapped keywords to value database terms are generated. The mappings are generated by using again the adapted technique of the Hungarian algorithm (ref. Sect. 6.4.3). The result is a series of partial mappings M_{ik}^V, with $k = 1 \cdots m_i$, where i identifies the mapping M_i^S on which the computation of the updated matrix VW_i was based. Given one such mapping M_{ik}^V, the value weights are further updated to reflect the mappings of the adjacent keywords to value database terms, in a way similar to the one done in Step 2 for the SW submatrix. The outcome modifies the total score of each mapping M_{ik}^V, and based on that score, the mappings are ranked.

Generation of the Configurations. As a fourth step, each pair of a mapping M_{ik}^V together with its associated mapping M_i^S is a total mapping of the keywords to database terms, forming a configuration C_{ik}. The score of the configuration is the sum of the scores of the two mappings, or alternatively the sum of the weights in the weight matrix of the elements $[i, j]$ where i is a keyword and j is the database term to which it is mapped through M_{ik}^V or M_i^S.

Generation of the Interpretations. Having computed the best configurations, the interpretations of the keyword query, i.e., the SQL queries, can be generated. The score of each such query is the score of the respective configuration. Recall, however, that a configuration is simply a mapping of the keywords to database terms. The presence of different join paths among these terms results in multiple interpretations. Different strategies can be used to further rank the selections. One popular option is the length of the join path [21], but other heuristics found in the literature [19] can also be used. It is also possible that a same interpretation be obtained with different configurations. A postprocessing analysis and the application of data-fusion techniques [10] can be used to deal with this issue. However, this is not the main focus of the current work, and we will not elaborate further on it. We adopt a greedy approach that computes a query for every alternative join path. In particular, we construct a graph in which each node corresponds to a database term. An edge connects two terms if they are structurally related, i.e., through a table-attribute-domain value relationship, or semantically, i.e., through a referential integrity constraint. Given a configuration, we mark all terms that are part of the range of the configuration "marked." Then we run a breath-first traversal (that favors shorter paths) to find paths that connect the disconnected components of the graph (if possible). The final SQL query is then constructed using the "marked" database terms and, in particular, the tables for its from clause, the conditions modeled by the edges for its where clause, and the remaining attributes for its select clause. Then the process is repeated to find a different interpretation that will be based on a different join path. The final order of the generated interpretations is determined by the way the different paths are discovered and the cost of the configuration on which each interpretation is based.

It is important to note here that if the thresholds used in the above steps are all brought down to zero, then our technique is able to generate all the possible interpretations that can be defined on a databe, even the most unlikely. In that sense, our technique is complete. The thresholds serve only to exclude from the results any interpretation that is not likely to represent the semantics of the keyword query, while the weights are used to provide the basis for a ranking metric.

6.4.1   Intrinsic Weight Computation

To compute the intrinsic weights, we need to compute the relevance between every query keyword and every database term. Some fundamental information that can be used toward this direction, and that is typically available, is the schema information. It may include the table and attribute names, the domains of the attributes, and very often, referential and integrity constraints, such as keys and foreign keys. Syntactic descriptions of the contents of an attribute (e.g., regular expressions) can also lead to a better matching of keywords to database terms since they offer indications on whether a keyword can serve as a value for an attribute or not. There are already many works that offer typical syntax for common attributes such as phone numbers, addresses, etc. [37], and have been used extensively and successfully in other areas. If access to the catalog tables is possible, assertion statements can offer an alternative source of syntactic information. In the same spirit, relevant values [8], i.e., clusters of the attribute domains, are also valuable auxiliary information. Furthermore, there is today a large volume of grammatical and semantic information that is publicly available on the Internet and can be used as a service. Examples include the popular WordNet and the many community-specific ontologies.

6.4.1.1   Weights for Schema Database Terms

Finding matches between the flat list of keywords and the schema terms looks like the situation of schema matching [37] in which one of the schemas is the flat universal relation [29]. We follow a similar approach in which we employ a number of different similarity, measurement techniques and consider the one that offers the best result. One of these techniques is the string similarity [16]. For the string similarity, we further employ a number of different similarity metrics such as the Jaccard, the Hamming, the Levenshtein, etc., in order to cover a broad

---

Algorithm 12: Intrinsic SW matrix computation

Data: Q: Keyword Query, T: Schema Database Terms
Result: SW matrix
begin
    $SW \leftarrow [0, 0, \ldots, 0]$;
    $\Sigma \leftarrow \{$ Synonyms(w,t), Hyponyms(w,t), Hypernyms(w,t), StringSimilarity(w,t) $\ldots \}$;
    for $w \in Q$ **do**
        for $e \in T$ **do**
            $sim \leftarrow 0$;
            for $m \in \Sigma$ **do**
                if $m(w, e) > sim$ **then**
                    $sim \leftarrow m(w, e)$;
            if $ssim \leq threshold$ **then**
                $sim \leftarrow 0$;
        $SW[w, c] = ssim * 100$;
end

---

spectrum of situations that may occur. Since string similarity may fail in cases of highly heterogeneous schemas that lack a common vocabulary, we also measure the relativeness of a keyword to schema database term based on their semantic relationship. For that we employ public ontologies, such as SUMO,[3] or semantic dictionaries such as WordNet, which can provide synonyms, hypernyms, hyponyms, or other terms related to a given word.

Algorithm 12 describes the computation procedure of the intrinsic schema weight matrix SW. The set Σ represents the similarity methods we employ. We have a number of default methods that represent the state of the art in the area, but additional methods can be included. Each such method takes as input two strings and returns their respective similarity in a range between 0 and 1. We trust the method that gives the highest similarity. If a similarity between a keyword and a schema term is found below a specific threshold (that is set by the application), then the similarity is set explicitly to 0. As a result, at the end of the procedure, there might be rows in the matrix SW containing only zeros. These rows represent keywords that are not similar enough to any of the schema database terms; thus, they will be considered later as candidates for mapping to value database terms, i.e., domains of the schema attributes. The fact that their rows in the SW matrix are 0 instead of some low value makes the similarities of the keyword to the value database terms that will be computed in a later step to be the dominating factor determining the guess on the role a specific keyword can play.

Example 6.1. Consider the keyword query "people restaurant Naples" posed on the database of Fig. 6.1. Figure 6.4 illustrates a fraction of the weight matrix containing the intrinsic weights for the database terms derived from the tables Person and

---

[3]www.ontologyportal.org

	P	R	P.Na	P.Ph	P.Ci	P.Em	R.Id	R.Na	R.Ad	R.Sp	R.Ci	P.Na	P.Ph	P.Ci	P.Em	R.Id	R.Na	R.Ad	R.Sp	R.Ci
people	75	0	0	0	0	0	0	0	0	0	0	1	0	1	0	0	1	1	1	1
restaurant	0	100	0	0	0	0	0	0	0	0	0	1	0	1	0	0	1	1	1	1
Naples	0	0	0	0	0	0	0	0	0	0	0	1	0	1	0	0	1	1	1	1

Fig. 6.4 Intrinsic weight SW (*light gray*) and VW (*dark gray*) matrix

Restaurant. Instead of the full names of tables and attributes, only the first letter of the tables and the first two letters of the attributes are used. The schema weights SW are the light gray-colored part of the matrix. Note that the keyword `Naples` has not been mapped to any of the schema terms since all the values of its row in SW are 0.

6.4.1.2 Weights for Value Database Terms

For computing the intrinsic value weights, we mainly exploit domain information and base our decision on whether a keyword belongs to the domain of an attribute or not. Furthermore, we have adapted the notion of *semantic distance* [15] that is based on results retrieved by a search engine in order to evaluate the relatedness of two concepts. In particular, we define the *semantic relatedness* $SR(x, y)$ of two terms x and y as

$$SR(x, y) = e^{-2\text{NXD}(x,y)}, \quad \text{where}$$

$$\text{NXD}(x, y) = \{\max\{\log f(x), \log f(y)\} - \log f(x, y)\}/$$

$$\{\log N - \min\{\log f(x), \log f(y)\}\}$$

with $f(x)$ denoting the number of Web documents containing x and $f(x, y)$ the number of documents containing both x and y, as these numbers are reported by specific search engines such as Google, Yahoo!, Cuil, Excite!, etc. The number N represents the number of documents indexed by the corresponding search engine. For our purpose, we compute the semantic relatedness of every keyword–attribute domain pair and this gives us an indication of the similarity degree between the keyword and the attribute domain. Information about possible values that an attribute can accept is also an important factor. The information is based on the explicit enumeration of values, as in the *relevant values* approach [8]. When a keyword is found among (or is similar to) the valid values that an attribute can get, the keyword receives a high weight. Additional comparison techniques include semantic measures based on external knowledge bases.

Example 6.2. For the keyword query introduced in Example 6.1, the intrinsic value weights are indicated in the VW part of Fig. 6.4, i.e., the dark gray-colored part. These weights have been computed by using domain knowledge and regular expressions. Note that these are the value weights; thus, the similarity is not between the keyword and the name of the attribute but concerns the compatibility of the keyword with the attribute domain.

6.4.2 Contextualization

The process of contextualization, as previously explained, exploits the interdependencies across mappings of different keywords. There are three different forms of contextualization that we consider. The first one increases the confidence of a keyword corresponding to an attribute (respectively, relation), if an adjacent keyword is mapped to the relation it belongs (respectively, one of the attributes of the relation). This is based on the generally observed behavior that users may sometimes provide more than one specification for a concept in a keyword query. For instance, they may use the keyword `Person` before the keyword `Name` to specify that they refer to the name of a person. The second form of contextualization is similar to the first, but applies on the value weights instead of the schema weights. The third and most important contextualization form is the one that updates the confidence of certain keywords corresponding to value database terms based on the mappings of other keywords to schema terms. The process consists of three phases and takes as input the value weight matrix VW and a partial mapping of keywords to schema database terms and returns an updated matrix VW. Let K be the ordered list of keywords in a query, M_i^S a partial mapping of keywords in K to schema terms, and K^S the subset of K containing the keywords for which M_i^S is defined, i.e., those that are mapped to some schema terms. We define the notion of *free trailing keywords* of a keyword k, denoted as $T(k)$, to be the maximum set $k_1, k_2, \ldots, k_m$ of consecutive keywords in K that are between two keywords k_s and k_e in the query and for which $k_s = k$, M_i^S is defined for k_s and k_e and undefined for every k_i with $i = 1 \cdots m$. The notion of *free preceding keywords* of a keyword k, denoted as $P(k)$, is defined accordingly, with k playing the role of k_e.

As an initialization step, all the weights in the rows of VW corresponding to keywords already mapped to database terms are set to zero. This is done to guarantee that in the three phases that are described next, none of these keywords will be mapped to a value term. In the first phase of the contextualization, for every keyword k mapped to a relation R through M_i^S, the weights of the trailing and preceding keywords $T(k)$ and $P(k)$ for terms representing the domains of the attributes of the relation R are increased by a constant value Δw. The rational of this action is that queries typically contain keywords that are generic descriptions for the values they provide. For instance, "`Person Bill`," "`Restaurant Naples`," etc., which means that consecutive keywords may correspond to a relation and a value of one of that relation's attributes. During the second phase, for every keyword k mapped to an attribute A through M_i^S, the weights of the trailing and preceding keywords $T(k)$ and $P(k)$ with the database terms representing domains of attributes in the same relation as A are also increased by a constant value Δw. The rational of this rule is that consecutive keywords may represent value specifications and related values. An example is the query "`Restaurant Vesuvio Pizza`" intended to ask about the restaurant "Vesuvio" that has the "Pizza" as specialty. In the third phase, if a keyword k is mapped to an attribute A, the weights of the trailing and preceding keywords related to domains of attributes related to A through some join path are increased by the constant value Δw. The rational is that users use keywords referring to concepts that are semantically related, even if these concepts have been modeled in the database in different tables. An example of this situation is the keyword query "`Phone Tribeca`." If `phone` is mapped to the attribute Phone of the relation Person, then the keyword `Tribeca` most likely represents the address of the department, which is stored in a separate table, and then the keyword query is about finding the phone number of the department that is on Tribeca. Note that the weight increase Δw can also be a percentage, instead of a constant, but our experimentations have shown no significant differences.

6.4.3   Selecting the Best Mappings

Given a weight matrix, computing the best possible mapping of keywords to database terms is known as the *assignment problem* [13]. Unfortunately, the traditional solutions return the first best mapping while we would like them all in descending order, or at least the top-k. Furthermore, we need a solution that, during the computation of the best mappings, takes into consideration interdependencies of the different assignments, i.e., the contextualization process. For this reason, we have adapted the popular systematic Hungarian, a.k.a. Munkres, algorithm [11] in order not to stop after the generation of the best mapping but to continue to the generation of the second best, the third, etc. Furthermore, some of its internal steps have been modified so that the weight matrix is dynamically updated every time that a mapping of a keyword to a database term is decided during the computation.

The execution of the algorithm consists of a series of iterative steps that generate a mapping with a maximum score. Once done, the weight matrix is modified accordingly to exclude the mapping that was generated and the process continues to compute the mapping with the second largest score, etc. More specifically, the maximum weight of each row is first identified and characterized as *maximum*. If the characterized-as-maximum weights are all located in different columns, then a mapping is generated by associating for each of the characterized-as-maximum weights the keyword and the database term that correspond to its respective row and column. On the other hand, if there is a column containing more than one weight characterized as maximum, all maximums in the column except the one with the maximum value lose their characterization as maximum. This last action means that some of the rows are left without some characterized weight. The values of the weights in these rows are then updated according to a number of contextual rules mentioned in Sect. 6.4. This is the effect of the mapped keywords to those that have remained unmapped.

In the sequel, for each row with no characterized weight, the one with the maximum value that belongs to a column corresponding to a database term different from the previous one is selected and characterized as *maximum*. If this leads to a matrix that has each characterized weight in a different column, then a mapping

---

Algorithm 13: Keyword to db term mapping selection

Data: $I(i_{ij})$ where $I \equiv SW$ or $I \equiv VW$
Result: $M^I = \{M^I_1, \ldots, M^I_z\}$: Mappings generated by I

MAPPING(I, W_{MAX});
begin

    $tempM = \bigcup i_{pt} \leftarrow HUNGARIAN_{Ext} * (I)$;
    $W \leftarrow \sum i_{pt}$;
    $M^I \leftarrow tempM$;
    if ($W > c * W_{MAX}$) **then**
        $W_{MAX} \leftarrow W$;
    while ($W > c * W_{MAX}$) **do**
        for $i_{pt} \in tempM$ **do**
            $i_{pt} \in I \leftarrow -100$;
            $Mapping(I, W_{MAX})$;

end

---

is generated as above or the process of uncharacterizing some of the values as previously described is repeated.

Once a mapping of all the keywords has been formed, it is included in the set of mappings that will be returned by the algorithm. Then, the algorithm needs to be repeated to generate additional mappings. To avoid recomputing the same assignments, the algorithm is reexecuted cyclically with a new matrix as input. The new matrix is the old one modified to exclude mappings that have already been considered in previous runs of the algorithm. This is done by setting the values of the respective weights to a large negative number, forcing the algorithm to never select them again. This whole process is repeated until the scores of the mappings that the algorithm generates fall below some specific threshold. By construction, the most prominent mapping is the one that is first reported by this task.

The original Hungarian algorithm for rectangular matrices has an $O(n^2 * m)$ complexity [11], where n is the number of keywords and m is the number of database terms. Extending the algorithm to consider dynamic weights as described above brings the complexity to $O(n^3 * m^2)$ which is due to the fact that a mapping may affect any other mapping; thus, in the worst case, $(n - 1) * (m - 1)$ weight updates may take place. Nevertheless, this worst case rarely happens since only a subset of the matrix is updated in each iteration and, due to the threshold, not all the possible updates are evaluated.

Algorithm 13 depicts the overall process of computing the set of most prominent mappings of a set of keywords to database terms, given a weight matrix. The expression $HUNGARIAN_{ext}$ refers to our extended version of the Hungarian algorithm.

Example 6.3. Figure 6.5 illustrates a VW matrix similar to the one of Fig. 6.4, but with additional keywords to better demonstrate the steps described in this section. The initial version of the matrix is the one composed of the first five lines. The lines of the keywords people and restaurant will remain unchanged since

	P.Na	P.Ph	P.Ci	P.Em	R.Id	R.Na	R.Ad	R.Sp	R.Ci
people	0	0	0	0	0	0	0	0	0
restaurant	0	0	0	0	0	0	0	0	0
Vesuvio	50	0	50	0	0	75	50	50	50
pizza	35	0	10	0	0	32	40	55	45
Naples	30	0	40	0	0	20	25	50	45

	P.Na	P.Ph	P.Ci	P.Em	R.Id	R.Na	R.Ad	R.Sp	R.Ci
Vesuvio	50	0	50	0	0	75	50	50	50
pizza	35	0	10	0	0	32	40	55	45
Naples	30	0	40	0	0	20	25	50	45

	P.Na	P.Ph	P.Ci	P.Em	R.Id	R.Na	R.Ad	R.Sp	R.Ci
Vesuvio	45	0	45	0	0	75	55	55	55
pizza	30	0	5	0	0	37	45	55	50
Naples	30	0	40	0	0	20	25	55	50

	P.Na	P.Ph	P.Ci	P.Em	R.Id	R.Na	R.Ad	R.Sp	R.Ci
Vesuvio	50	0	50	0	0	75	50	50	50
pizza	35	0	10	0	0	32	40	55	45
Naples	30	0	40	0	0	20	25	50	45

Fig. 6.5 Weight matrix during best mapping computation

the keywords are mapped to schema terms, and for this reason, they are omitted
from the subsequent versions. The weights in white cells are those characterized
as maximum. Each one is the largest weight in its row. Note that for column R.Sp,
there are more than one weight characterized as maximum. From those, only the
largest one is kept, in our case, 55. This leaves the row of keyword Naples
with no weight characterized as maximum. The result is the second VW matrix
illustrated in Fig. 6.5. The three characterized weights suggest a mapping for the
keywords Vesuvio and pizza. Given these mappings, the weights are adjusted
to reflect the interdependencies according to the contextual rules. For instance,
the mapping of Vesuvio to the database term R.Na triggers an increase in the
weights of the database terms on the attributes in the same table. The result of
firing the contextual rules is the third matrix in Fig. 6.5. In the updated matrix,
the highest value is 49, which is in the column R.Sp, but cannot be chosen since
the keyword pizza is already mapped to it. The second largest weight, 45, is in
a column of a database term that no keyword is mapped to, and it is becoming
characterized as maximum. The final outcome is the fourth matrix of Fig. 6.5 and,
based on this, the mappings of keywords Vesuvio,pizza, and Naples to the
database terms R.Na, R.Sp, and R.Ci, respectively, which is added to the mapping
results generated by the algorithm. After that, the mapping is again considered
for generating a new input for the algorithm. Four new matrices are derived
from it, each one having one of the weights that was in a white cell in the last
matrix reduced. For each obtained matrix, the whole process starts again from the
beginning.

6.5 The Viterbi Approach

In an effort to define the configuration function, we can divide the problem of matching a whole query to database terms into smaller subtasks. In each subtask the best match between a single keyword and a database term is found. Then the final solution to the global problem is the union of the matches found in the subtasks. This approach works well when the keywords in a query are independent of each other, meaning that they do not influence the match of the other keywords to database terms. Unfortunately, this assumption does not hold in real cases. On the contrary, interdependencies among keyword meanings are of fundamental importance in disambiguating the keyword semantics.

In order to take into account these interdependencies, we model the matching function as a sequential process where the order is determined by the keyword ordering in the query. In each step of the process, a single keyword is matched against a database term, taking into account the result of the previous keyword match in the sequence. This process has a finite number of steps, equal to the query length, and is stochastic since the matching between a keyword and a database term is not deterministic: the same keyword can have different meanings in different queries and hence being matched with different database terms; vice versa, different database terms may match the same keyword in different queries. This type of process can be modeled, effectively, by using a hidden Markov model (HMM for short), which is a stochastic finite state machine where the states are hidden variables.

An HMM models a stochastic process that is not observable directly (it is hidden), but it can be observed indirectly through the observable symbols produced by another stochastic process. The model is composed of a finite number N of states. Assuming a time-discrete model, at each time step a new state is entered based on a *transition probability distribution*, and an observation is produced according to an *emission probability distribution* that depends on the current state, where both these distributions are time independent. Moreover, the process starts from an initial state based on an *initial state probability distribution*. We will consider first-order HMMs with discrete observations. In these models, the *Markov property* is respected, i.e., the transition probability distribution of the states at time $t + 1$ depends only on the current state at time t and it does not depend on the past states at time $1, 2, \ldots, t - 1$. Moreover, the observations are discrete: there exists a finite number, M, of observable symbols; hence, the emission probability distributions can be effectively represented using *multinomial distributions* dependent on the states. More formally, the model consists of the following: (1) a set os states $S = \{s_i\}$, $1 \leq i \leq N$; (2) a set of observation symbols $V = \{v_j\}$, $1 \leq j \leq M$; (3) a transition probability distribution $A = \{a_{ij}\}$, $1 \leq i \leq N$, $1 \leq j \leq N$ where

$$a_{ij} = P(q_{t+1} = s_j | q_t = s_i) \quad \text{and} \quad \sum_{0 < j < N} a_{ij} = 1$$

(4) an emission probability distribution $B = \{b_i(m)\}$, $1 \le i \le N$, $1 \le m \le M$ where

$$b_i(m) = P(o_t = v_m | q_t = s_i) \quad \text{and} \quad \sum_{0 < m < M} b_i(m) = 1$$

and (5) an initial state probability distribution $\Pi = \{\pi_i\}$, $1 \le i \le N$ where

$$\pi_i = P(q_1 = s_i) \quad \text{and} \quad \sum_{0 < i < N} \pi_i = 1$$

Based on the above, the notation $\lambda = (A, B, \Pi)$ will be used to indicate an HMM. In our context, the keywords inserted by the user are the observable part of the process, while the correspondent database terms are the unknown variables that have to be inferred. For this reason, we model the keywords as observations and each term in the database vocabulary as a state.

6.5.1 Setting HMM Parameters

In order to define an HMM, its parameters have to be identified. This is usually done using a training algorithm that, after many iterations, converges to a good solution for the parameter values. In our approach, we introduce some heuristic rules that allow the definition of the parameter values even when no training data are available. The HMM parameter values are set by exploiting the semantics collected from the data source metadata. In particular:

The transition probabilities are computed using heuristic rules that take into account the semantic relationships that exist between the database terms (aggregation, generalization, and inclusion relationships). The goal of the rules is to foster the transition between database terms belonging to the same table and belonging to tables connected through foreign keys. The transition probability values decrease with the distance of the states, e.g., transitions between terms in the same table have higher probability than transitions between terms in tables directly connected through foreign keys, which, in turn, have higher probability than transitions between terms in tables connected through a third table.

The emission probabilities are computed on the basis of similarity measures. In particular, two different techniques are adopted for the database terms in V_{SC} and V_{DO}. We use the well-known *edit distance* for computing the lexical similarity between the keywords and each term (and its synonyms extracted from WordNet[4]) in the

---

[4]http://wordnet.princeton.edu

schema vocabulary V_{SC}. On the other side, the similarity between keywords and the terms in the domain vocabulary V_{DO} is based on domain compatibilities and regular expressions. We use the calculated similarity as an estimate for the conditional probability $P(q_t = s_i | o_t = v_m)$, then, using the Bayes theorem, we calculate the emission probability $P(o_t = v_m | q_t = s_i)$. Note that the model is independent of the similarity measure adopted. Other more complex measures that take into account external knowledge sources (i.e., public ontologies and thesauri) can be applied without modifying the model.

The initial state probabilities are estimated by means of the scores provided by the HITS algorithm [25]. The HITS algorithm is a link analysis algorithm that calculates two different scores for each page: *authority* and *hub*. A high authority score indicates that the page contains valuable information with respect to the user query, while a high hub score suggests that the page contains useful links toward authoritative pages. This algorithm has been adapted to our context in order to rank the tables in a database based on their authority scores. The higher the rank, the more valuable is the information stored in the tables. For this reason, the authority score is used as an estimate of the initial state probabilities.

6.5.1.1 Adapted HITS Algorithm

In order to employ the HITS algorithm, we build the database graph $G_D = (V_t, E_{fk})$ which is a directed graph where the nodes are the database tables in V_t and the edges are connections between tables through foreign keys, i.e., given two tables R_i, R_j, there exists an edge in E_{fk} from R_i to R_j, denoted as $R_i \rightarrow R_j$, if an attribe in R_j is referred by a foreign key defined in R_i. Let A be the $n \times n$ adjacency matrix of the graph G_D

$$A = [a_{ij}], a_{ij} = 1 \text{ iff } e_{ij} \in E_{fk}, a_{ij} = 0 \text{ iff } e_{ij} \notin E_{fk}$$

In our approach, we use the modified matrix B that takes into account the number of attributes minus the number of foreign keys in a table (foreign keys are considered as links):

$$B = [b_{ij}], b_{ij} = a_{ij} \cdot (|R_i| - \|\{R_i \rightarrow R_j, 1 \le j \le n\}\|)$$

Let us define the authority weight vector $auth$ and the hub weight vector hub

$$auth^T = [u_1, u_2, \ldots, u_n] \text{ and } hub^T = [v_1, v_2, \ldots, v_n]$$

The algorithm initializes these vectors with uniform values, e.g., $\frac{1}{n}$, then the vectors are updated in successive iterations as follows:

$$\begin{cases} auth = B^T \cdot hub \\ hub = B \cdot auth \end{cases}$$

At each iteration, a normalization step is performed to obtain authority and hub scores in the range $[0, 1]$. After few iterations, the algorithm converges and the authority scores are used as estimate for the initial state probabilities.

Example 6.4. Let us consider the database in Fig. 6.1. This database generates 52 states, one for each database term. Concerning the transition probability distribution, the heuristic rules foster transitions between database terms of the same table or in tables connected via foreign key. According to this, the most probable states subsequent to the state associated to the table *People* are the states associated to the names and the domains of the attributes *Name*, *Phone*, *City*, etc., then, the state associated to the tables *Booked*, *Reserved*, and *City*, subsequently, the states associated to the tables *Hotel* and *Restaurant*. We use different similarity measures for computing the emission probability distribution. Domain compatibility and regular expressions are used for measuring the probabilities of the values associated to states of terms in the V_{DO}. The probabilities of values associated to states of terms in the V_{SC} are computed on the basis of lexical similarity computed on the term and on its synonyms, hypernyms, and hyponyms. For example, we consider "Brasserie" as synonym of restaurant.

6.5.2 Decoding the HMM

By applying the Viterbi algorithm to an HMM, we find the state sequence which has the highest probability of generating the observation sequence. If we consider the user keyword query as an observation sequence, the algorithm retrieves the states (i.e., the data source elements) that more likely represent the intended meaning of the user query. Note that, in general, the N best sequences, each one terminating in a different state, found by the Viterbi algorithm during the recursion are not the top-N best sequences. The Viterbi algorithm divides the solution space (the number of configurations between l keywords and d database terms is $P(l, d) = \frac{l!}{(l-d)!}$) into N subspaces, where each subspace contains all the sequences that end in state S_i, $1 \le i \le N$. The algorithm finds the best solution in each subspace, then orders them to find the best overall solution. This process guarantees to find only the single best solution.

The Viterbi algorithm is not a good choice for facing the general problem of finding the top-K solutions. The algorithm finds all K solutions only in the particular case where $K \le N$ and each subspace contains 0 or 1 of the top-K solutions. In the worst scenario, when all the top-K solutions are concentrated in a single subspace, the algorithm finds just the single best one. Moreover, we do not know in advance how the K solutions are distributed in the N subspaces. In order to solve the general problem of finding the overall best K sequences, we implemented a generalization of the Viterbi algorithm, called f, which keeps track of the best K solutions in each subspace and guarantees to find the top-K sequences even in the worst scenario.

Our implementation of List Viterbi is presented in pseudocode in Algorithm 14. The algorithm is a generalization of the Viterbi algorithm because for $K = 1$, it finds the same solution as the original algorithm, and for $K = \frac{l!}{(l-d)!}$, it finds all the existing solutions and orders them globally. The algorithm is based on a tree structure that memorizes the sequences found (each sequence starts from the root and ends in one of the leaves). Each node at distance t from the root represents a state q_t traversed in a particular sequence at step t. The tree structure is built iteratively by the List Viterbi algorithm. In the first step, the tree height is 1 and the leaves represent all possible initial states given the observation sequence $O = (o_1, o_2, \ldots, o_T)$, i.e., there are at maximum N leaves at this step. In all other

---

Algorithm 14: List Viterbi

Data: $\lambda = (A, B, \Pi)$: HMM, $KQ = (k_1, k_2, \ldots, k_l)$: a keyword query, K : top-K
Result: $Q[K][l]$: top-K state sequences, $P[K][l]$: top-K state sequences probabilities

Compute_Tree(A,B,Π,KQ,k);
begin
    $Tree \leftarrow newnode(root)$;
    for $state\ S_i$ **do**
        $\delta_0 \leftarrow b_i \cdot \pi_i$;
        $appendNode((S_i, \delta_0), Tree)$;
    $L[\ ] \leftarrow leaves(Tree)$;
    for $k_i \in KQ$ **do**
        $array\ Tmp[N][K]$;
        for $state\ S_i$ **do**
            for $j \in L$ **do**
                $\delta_k \leftarrow a_{ij} \cdot b_i \cdot \delta_{k-1}$;
                $appendNode((S_i, \delta_k), Tmp[S_i][\ ])$;
            $insert(Tmp[S_i][], Tree)$;
            $L[\ ] \leftarrow L[\ ] + Tmp[S_i][\ ]$;
            $orderLeafs(L[\ ])$;
end

Backtracking(Tree);
begin
    $t \leftarrow l$;
    for $j \in L$ **do**
        $Q[j][t] \leftarrow state(L[j])$;
        $P[j][t] \leftarrow probability(L[j])$;
        for $t = l - 1, l - 2, 1$ **do**
            $Q[j][t] \leftarrow state(parent(Q[j][t + 1], Tree))$;
            $P[j][t] \leftarrow probability(parent(Q[j][t + 1], Tree))$;
end

steps t, where $2 \leq t \leq T$, a maximum of K leaves representing a state q_t are added to the tree, i.e., the tree memorizes up to K best paths that end in state q_t. A maximum of $K \cdot N$ leaves are added to the tree at each step. After the tree is built, the $K \cdot N$ leaves are ordered based on their probability and the first K are the top-K solutions we were looking for. The complete sequences are then extracted from the tree by backtracking the paths from the leaves to the root.

Example 6.5. The top-3 results of the keyword query "people restaurant Naples" are the ones mapping the keyword people into the table *People*, restaurant into the table *Restaurant*, and Naples into the domains of the attributes *Name*, *Specialty*, and *City*, respectively. Both the solutions have the same transition probabilities but different emission probabilities since the likelihood of the mapping of Naples into the attribute *City* is higher than the one into *Restaurant* and *Specialty*.

6.6   Related Work

The popularity of keyword searching is constantly increasing. For more than a decade, it has been the successful model in IR for text databases [40] and the Web [12]. It has also been adopted by the data management community in the context of XML [17, 26, 43]. To answer a keyword query over XML data, the appearances of the query keywords are first identified within the documents (possibly through some free-text search) and then combined together into meaningful lowest common ancestor structures (MLCAS). A score is computed based on this structure, and according to this score, the respective XML documents containing the MLCAS are ranked and returned to the user. XML benefits from the fact that its basic information model is the "document," which is the same as in IR; thus, many IR techniques can be easily employed in the XML context. On the other hand, keyword search in relational databases is particularly challenging [42], first because the database instances are way larger and second because the basic model is fundamentally different, making hard the identification of the information units that are to be returned. Nevertheless, keyword search over relational data is particularly appealing, and there are already many interesting proposals in the scientific literature [14, 49]. DISCOVER [19] and DBXplorer [2] have been among the first such systems. The typical approach is to build a special index on the contents of the database and then to use that index to identify the appearances of the query keywords in the attribute values. Many approaches use inverted indexes [1, 19, 39] for that purpose, while others, like DBXplore, use symbol tables. A symbol table is an index consisting of a set of triples ⟨*value, attribute, relation*⟩, used to map every value to its schema information. Once the keywords are located, the different ways by which their respective tuples are connected are discovered, forming the so-called "joining network" of tuples or tuple trees that often become the information unit returned to the user. The joining networks are constructed either directly from the instances or by building query expressions and evaluating them [19]. DISCOVER is interested in finding total and minimal joining networks. A joining network is total if each keyword query is contained in at least one tuple of the network, and minimal if the removal of any tuple makes the network no longer total. More recent approaches [36] are oriented toward reducing the number of tuples that need to be considered in order to improve previous techniques. BANKS [1] follows a similar approach but employs the Steiner tree algorithm to discover how the tuples are associated. SQAK [42] is another system that is based on the same generic principles but focuses on the discovery of aggregate SQL expressions that describe the intended keyword query semantics. Since the set of possible answers may be large, and since the results are already ranked, the above systems typically return the top-k results.

As have happened in all the above approaches, the two methods that we presented in this chapter are also trying to identify the possible semantics (i.e., expected answers) to the ambiguous keywords queries and rank the results. The fundamental difference is that they do not assume any a priori access to the database instance. Unavoidably, the approaches are based on schema and metadata, i.e., the intensional information, which makes them applicable to scenarios where the other techniques cannot work. Nevertheless, presented approaches should not be seen as an alternative to the above methods. Since they operate on different information, i.e., the metadata, they can be used to enhance these techniques by providing a better exploitation of the metainformation and the relationships among the keywords. The idea of using schema information and keyword semantics has been considered in one of the approaches [27], but this is only limited to word semantics based on WordNet. The presented two approaches go further by combining not only additional semantic similarity techniques, similar to those used in schema matching [37], but also on syntactic and structural information. Data behavior has also been considered [42]. All these works are complementary.

Another distinction is on the relationship among the keywords. Existing approaches compute the relationship among the keywords by considering the relationships of the data values in the database instance. It is believed by many that the keyword query should be the one driving the translation and not the data. The presented approaches take into consideration in a systematic way the position of the keywords in the query itself and the interdependencies between the matchings of the keywords to the database structure. Furthermore, they map the keywords to schema elements that will form the SQL query, instead of mapping them to the tuples themselves [42]. This allows them, without performing any query evaluation, to present these queries to the user and communicate the considered semantics. Of course, this is an optional step, but in highly heterogeneous environments, this is the norm for matching and mapping techniques [33].

A related field is keyword disambiguation where several approaches have been developed. For example, in [4] an incremental technique based on WordNet and description logics is proposed, in [46] context and ontologies are exploited for removing ambiguity, and in [34] attribute disambiguation enables faceted searches.

With specific reference to the KEYRY approach, a large number of techniques based on HMM that have been proposed typically address the following three basic problems [3]: (1) *finding the MLSS,* i.e., given an HMM model λ and a sequence of observations O_l, find the correspondent state sequence Q_l that has the highest probability of generating O_l; (2) *evaluation problem,* i.e., given an model λ and a sequence of observations O_l, evaluate the probability that the model λ has generated the observations O_l; and (3) *learning the parameters,* i.e., given a training dataset of observation sequences O, learn the model λ that maximizes the probability of generating O. To the best of our knowledge, HMMs have been applied in fields related to the keyword search in databases only in [35], where a HMM has been exploited for performing keyword query cleaning. Nevertheless, the approaches differ in several aspects: in particular, [35] requires to access the database instance for setting the HMM parameters and its training is based on a gradient based optimization algorithm. This chapter described a way to apply the List Viterbi algorithm for addressing the first problem, i.e., decoding the HMM by computing the top-K answers to a keyword query. Other interesting applications of List Viterbi have been proposed especially in the data transmission field, where it has been exploited for detecting the correct message in cases of transmission errors [38] and for source-channel coding of images [20].

In [23], the Baum-Welch, the Viterbi training, and the Monte Carlo EM training are described, and an extension of the latter two approaches is proposed in order to make them more efficient. Since these algorithms can in practice be slow and computationally expensive, several techniques have been proposed for improving the learning under particular conditions: Lember and Koloydenko [24] propose an "adjusted Viterbi training" with the same complexity level as the Viterbi training algorithm, but computing more accurate results. Differently from these proposals, the presented scenario requires an online training approach in order to take into account the user's feedback as soon as it is received.

Finally, the presented methods can also find applications in the field of graphical tools that assist the user in formulating queries [32]. By finding the different interpretations of a keyword query, one could detect related schema structures, make suggestions, and guide the user in the query formulation. Furthermore, in cases of exploratory searches, the user can use the generated interpretations as a way to explore an (unknown) data source and understand better its semantics.

6.7   Conclusion

The chapter presented an overview of two methods for translating keyword queries over a relational database into SQL so that they can be executed. The main focus was in a situation in which the contents of the database are unknown and the only information available is the metainformation, i.e., schema and constraints. In both cases, the idea was to understand the semantics of the keywords in order to correctly map them to database structures and then use this mapping to guide the query generation process. The first method was an extension of the Hungarian algorithm and the second of the Viterbi algorithms. Preliminary experiments have shown that both approaches work equally well; however, a clear understanding on when each one performs better is still not clear.

References

1. Aditya, B., Bhalotia, G., Chakrabarti, S., Hulgeri, A., Nakhe, C., Parag, Sudarshan, S.: Banks: browsing and keyword searching in relational databases. VLDB, pp. 1083–1086. Morgan Kaufmann, New York (2002)
2. Agrawal, S., Chaudhuri, S., Das, G.: Dbxplorer: a system for keyword-based search over relational databases. ICDE, pp. 5–16. IEEE Computer Society, Silver Spring, MD (2002)
3. Alpaydin, E.: Introduction to Machine Learning, 2nd edn. MIT, Cambridge, MA (2010)
4. Bergamaschi, S., Bouquet, P., Giacomuzzi, D., Guerra, F., Po, L., Vincini, M.: An incremental method for the lexical annotation of domain ontologies. Int. J. Semant. Web Inf. Syst. 3(3), 57–80 (2007)
5. Bergamaschi, S., Domnori, E., Guerra, F., Lado, R.T., Velegrakis, Y.: Keyword search over relational databases: a metadata approach. In: Sellis T.K., Miller R.J., Kementsietsidis A., Velegrakis Y. (eds.) SIGMOD Conference, pp. 565–576. ACM, New York (2011)
6. Bergamaschi, S., Domnori, E., Guerra, F., Orsini, M., Lado, R.T., Velegrakis, Y.: Keymantic: semantic keyword-based searching in data integration systems. PVLDB 3(2), 1637–1640 (2010)
7. Bergamaschi, S., Guerra, F., Rota, S., Velegrakis, Y.: A hidden markov model approach to keyword-based search over relational databases. In: to appear in ER. Springer (LNCS) (2011)
8. Bergamaschi, S., Sartori, C., Guerra, F., Orsini, M.: Extracting relevant attribute values for improved search. IEEE Inter. Comput. 11(5), 26–35 (2007)
9. Bergman, M.K.: The deep web: surfacing hidden value. J. Electron. Publ. 7(1) (2001). URL http://dx.doi.org/10.3998/3336451.0007.104
10. Bleiholder, J., Naumann, F.: Data fusion. ACM Comput. Surv. 41(1) (2008)
11. Bourgeois, F., Lassalle, J.C.: An extension of the Munkres algorithm for the assignment problem to rectangular matrices. Commun. ACM 14(12), 802–804 (1971)
12. Brin, S., Page, L.: The anatomy of a large-scale hypertextual web search engine. Comput. Networks 30(1–7), 107–117 (1998)
13. Burkard, R., Dell'Amico, M., Martello, S.: Assignment problems. SIAM society for industrial and applied mathematics, Philadelphia (2009)
14. Chakrabarti, S., Sarawagi, S., Sudarshan, S.: Enhancing search with structure. IEEE Data Eng. Bull. 33(1), 3–24 (2010)
15. Cilibrasi, R., Vitányi, P.M.B.: The google similarity distance. IEEE Trans. Knowl. Data Eng. 19(3), 370–383 (2007)
16. Cohen, W.W., Ravikumar, P.D., Fienberg, S.E.: A comparison of string distance metrics for name-matching tasks. IIWeb, pp. 73–78 (2003)
17. Florescu, D., Kossmann, D., Manolescu, I.: Integrating keyword search into xml query processing. BDA (2000)
18. Haofen, W., Kang Zhang, Q.L., Tran, D.T., Yu, Y.: Q2semantic: a lightweight keyword interface to semantic search. Proceedings of the 5th European Semantic Web Conference, LNCS, pp. 584–598. Tenerife, Spain (2008)
19. Hristidis, V., Papakonstantinou, Y.: Discover: keyword search in relational databases. VLDB, pp. 670–681 (2002)
20. Konstanz, U., Roder, M., Hamzaoui, R.: Fast list viterbi decoding and application for source-channel coding of images. Konstanzer schriften in mathematik und informatik, http://www.inf.uni-konstanz.de/Preprints/preprints-all.html, pp. 801–804 (2002)
21. Kotidis, Y., Marian, A., Srivastava, D.: Circumventing data quality problems using multiple join paths. CleanDB (2006)

22. Kumar, R., Tomkins, A.: A characterization of online search behavior. IEEE Data Eng. Bull. **32**(2), 3–11 (2009)
23. Lam, T.Y., Meyer, I.M.: Efficient algorithms for training the parameters of hidden markov models using stochastic expectation maximization (em) training and viterbi training. Algorithms Mol. Biol. **5**(38) (2010). DOI 10.1186/1748-7188-5-38
24. Lember, J., Koloydenko, A.: Adjusted viterbi training. Probab. Eng. Inf. Sci. **21**, 451–475 (2007). DOI 10.1017/S0269964807000083. URL http://portal.acm.org/citation.cfm?id=1291117.1291125
25. Li, L., Shang, Y., Shi, H., Zhang, W.: Performance evaluation of hits-based algorithms. Communications, internet, and information technology, pp. 171–176 (2002)
26. Li, Y., Yu, C., Jagadish, H.V.: Schema-free XQuery. VLDB, pp. 72–83 (2004)
27. Liu, F., Yu, C.T., Meng, W., Chowdhury, A.: Effective keyword search in relational databases. SIGMOD, pp. 563–574. ACM, New York (2006)
28. Madhavan, J., Ko, D., Kot, L., Ganapathy, V., Rasmussen, A., Halevy, A.: Google's deep web crawl. Proc. Very Large Databases (VLDB) Endow. **1**(2), 1241–1252 (2008). DOI http://doi.acm.org/10.1145/1454159.1454163. URL http://portal.acm.org/citation.cfm?id=1454163
29. Maier, D., Ullman, J.D., Vardi, M.Y.: On the foundations of the universal relation model. ACM Trans. Database Syst. **9**(2), 283–308 (1984)
30. Melnik, S., Garcia-Molina, H., Rahm, E.: Similarity flooding: a versatile graph matching algorithm and its application to schema matching. ICDE, pp. 117–128. IEEE Computer Society, Silver Spring, MD (2002)
31. Mena, E.: OBSERVER: an approach for query processing in global information systems based on interoperation across pre-exisiting ontologies, University of Zaragoza, 1998
32. Nandi, A., Jagadish, H.V.: Assisted querying using instant-response interfaces. SIGMOD, pp. 1156–1158. ACM, New York (2007)
33. Popa, L., Velegrakis, Y., Miller, R.J., Hernandez, M.A., Fagin, R.: Translating web data. VLDB, pp. 598–609 (2002)
34. Pound, J., Paparizos, S., Tsaparas, P.: Facet discovery for structured web search: a query-log mining approach. SIGMOD conference, pp. 169–180. ACM, New York (2011)
35. Pu, K.Q.: Keyword query cleaning using hidden markov models. In: Özsu, M.T., Chen, Y., 0002, L.C. (eds.) KEYS, pp. 27–32. ACM, New York (2009)
36. Qin, L., Yu, J.X., Chang, L.: Keyword search in databases: the power of rdbms. SIGMOD, pp. 681–694. ACM, New York (2009)
37. Rahm, E., Bernstein, P.A.: A survey of approaches to automatic schema matching. VLDB J. **10**(4), 334–350 (2001)
38. Seshadri, N., Sundberg, C.E.: List Viterbi decoding algorithms with applications. IEEE Trans. Commun. **42**(234), 313–323 (1994). DOI 10.1109/TCOMM.1994.577040
39. Simitsis, A., Koutrika, G., Ioannidis, Y.E.: Précis: from unstructured keywords as queries to structured databases as answers. VLDB J. **17**(1), 117–149 (2008)
40. Singhal, A., Buckley, C., Mitra, M.: Pivoted document length normalization. SIGIR, pp. 21–29 (1996)
41. Tata, S., Lohman, G.M.: Sqak: doing more with keywords. In: Wang J.T.L. (ed.) Proceedings of the ACM SIGMOD International Conference on Management of data, SIGMOD 2008, Vancouver, BC, Canada, pp. 889–902. ACM, New York (2008)
42. Tata, S., Lohman, G.M.: SQAK: doing more with keywords. SIGMOD, pp. 889–902. ACM, New York (2008)
43. Theobald, M., Bast, H., Majumdar, D., Schenkel, R., Weikum, G.: TopX: efficient and versatile top-k query processing for semistructured data. VLDB J. **17**(1), 81–115 (2008)
44. Tran, T., Mathäß, T., Haase, P.: Usability of keyword-driven schema-agnostic search. 7th extended semantic web conference (ESWC'10), Greece. Springer, Berlin, Heidelberg, New York (2010)
45. Tran, T., Wang, H., Rudolph, S., Cimiano, P.: Top-k exploration of query candidates for efficient keyword search on graph-shaped (rdf) data. ICDE, pp. 405–416. IEEE Computer Society, Silver Spring, MD (2009). DOI http://dx.doi.org/10.1109/ICDE.2009.119

46. Trillo, R., Gracia, J., Espinoza, M., Mena, E.: Discovering the semantics of user keywords. J. UCS **13**(12) (2007)
47. Wright, A.: Searching the deep web. Commun. ACM **51**, 14–15 (2008). DOI 10.1145/1400181. 1400187
48. Yu, J.X., Qin, L., Chang, L.: Keyword Search in Databases. Morgan and Claypool, San Francisco (2010)
49. Yu, J.X., Qin, L., Chang, L.: Keyword search in databases. Synthesis Lectures on Data Management. Morgan and Claypool, San Francisco (2010)
50. Zenz, G., Zhou, X., Minack, E., Siberski, W., Nejdl, W.: From keywords to semantic queries-incremental query construction on the semantic web. J. Web Semant. **7**(3), 166–176 (2009). DOI http://dx.doi.org/10.1016/j.websem.2009.07.005

Chapter 7
Keyword-Based Search over Semantic Data

Klara Weiand, Andreas Hartl, Steffen Hausmann,
Tim Furche, and François Bry

7.1 Introduction

For a long while, the creation of Web content required at least basic knowledge of Web technologies, meaning that for many Web users, the Web was de facto a read-only medium. This changed with the arrival of the "social Web," when Web applications started to allow users to publish Web content without technological expertise. Here, content creation is often an inclusive, iterative, and interactive process. Examples of social Web applications include blogs, social networking sites, as well as many specialized applications, for example, for saving and sharing bookmarks and publishing photos.

Social *semantic* Web applications are social Web applications in which knowledge is expressed not only in the form of text and multimedia but also through informal to formal annotations that describe, reflect, and enhance the content. These annotations often take the shape of RDF graphs backed by ontologies, but less formal annotations such as free-form tags or tags from a controlled vocabulary may also be available.

Wikis [29] are one example of social Web applications for collecting and sharing knowledge. They allow users to easily create and edit documents, so-called wiki pages, using a Web browser. The pages in a wiki are often heavily interlinked, which makes it easy to find related information and browse the content.

K. Weiand (✉) · A. Hartl · S. Hausmann · F. Bry
Ludwig-Maximilians-Universität München, Oettingenstr. 67, 80538 München, Germany
e-mail: klara.weiand@ifi.lmu.de; andreas-hartl@gmx.de; steffen.hausmann@ifi.lmu.de;
bry@lmu.de

T. Furche
Department of Computer Science and Institute for the Future of Computing,
Oxford University, Wolfson Building, Parks Road, Oxford OX1 3QD, UK
e-mail: tim@furche.net

R. De Virgilio et al. (eds.), *Semantic Search over the Web*,
Data-Centric Systems and Applications, DOI 10.1007/978-3-642-25008-8_7,
© Springer-Verlag Berlin Heidelberg 2012

Semantic wikis [43] are wikis that also offer—more or less sophisticated—formal languages for expressing knowledge as machine-processable annotations to wiki pages. In traditional wikis, knowledge is given in the form of text in natural language, and is not directly amenable to automated semantic processing. Information can therefore only be located through full-text keyword search or via simple, mostly user-generated, structures like tables of content and links between pages. More sophisticated functionalities such as querying, reasoning, and semantic browsing are not available. The goal behind semantic wikis is to provide at least some of these enhancements by relying on semantic technologies, that is, knowledge representation formalisms and methods for automated reasoning.

To be able to leverage the knowledge contained in rich data repositories such as semantic wikis and other social semantic applications, a query language for social semantic Web applications should be expressive enough to allow for precise selections using complex criteria and to enable the aggregation and combination of data, and thus the derivation of new data through a simple form of reasoning. Automation in the form of embedded queries (queries that are contained in a piece of content and are evaluated when this content is retrieved) and continuous queries (queries that are evaluated repeatedly at set intervals or when the data change) further requires query evaluation to operate without the need for human intervention.

Making it easy for nonexperts to publish data on the Web is an important achievement of the social Web and a primary goal of the social semantic Web. The goal of making the data thus produced easily accessible in turn has received relatively little attention. This is problematic because users are likely to be less motivated to participate in the creation of content if they cannot leverage the data that they and others have contributed and the exploitation of the data is reserved to expert users. The success of a social semantic Web application crucially depends on the active participation and the contributions of its users, most of which cannot and should not be expected to have much experience with query languages.

Data retrieval in semantic wikis and other social (semantic) Web applications is currently realized through keyword search or Web query languages. Keyword search is the prevalent paradigm for search on the Web. Its strength, and presumably the main reason for its success, is that it is very accessible: there is no syntax that has to be learned before queries can be issued, and relevant information can be found without any knowledge of the structure of the underlying data. On the downside, keyword search is inherently imprecise and inexpressive. It does not allow for the specification of structure-based selection criteria, and often not even for logical operations. As a consequence, queries remain vague. Even when users know precisely which data they are interested in, they may not be able to express the corresponding selection criteria merely through keywords.

Web query languages are in many respects the exact opposite of keyword search: similar to queries on relational databases, Web queries are highly specific and select individual data items which can then be processed further to reformat the data or deduce and display new knowledge. Once defined, these tasks can be performed automatically and without human intervention. Web query languages are comparable to programming languages both in their expressive power and their complexity of use. A high cognitive investment is required before a user can employ a Web query language to retrieve data from a given dataset: in addition to the schema, the user has to know and understand the data types involved as well as the query language itself. Especially for casual or beginning Web users, acquiring this knowledge can be a hard and laborious process, and many may lack the time, dedication, motivation, or confidence to tackle it.

In summary, keyword search is generally more appropriate for search over weakly structured or unstructured text, while Web query languages are well suited for querying structured data. In a social semantic Web application, one typically finds both types of data. None of the methods currently available provides both a sufficient level of expressiveness and ease of use.

This article describes the design and implementation of KWQL, a query language for the semantic wiki KiWi. KWQL allows for rich combined queries over textual content, metadata, document structure, and informal to formal semantic annotations. The language combines keyword search and Web querying to enable a form of querying that adapts to the user's information need and knowledge and accommodates simple search and complex selections alike. A novel aspect of KWQL is that it combines both paradigms, keyword search and Web queries, in a bottom-up fashion. It treats neither of the two as an extension to the other, but instead integrates both in one framework. Depending on the user's knowledge and query intent, the language can behave more like keyword search or more like Web querying.

While querying the semantic wiki KiWi [44] is the main focus of this chapter, the underlying ideas apply more generally to querying and search on the social and social semantic Web. As such, the concepts of KWQL could be transferred to derive similar languages targeting other social semantic applications, and we consider KWQL to be exemplary of a novel family of query languages.

The remainder of this chapter is structured as follows: Sect. 7.2 introduces wikis and semantic wikis and gives an overview over the state of the art in querying in semantic wikis and keyword querying of semistructured data. The next section, Sect. 7.3, describes the KiWi wiki and its conceptual model. Section 7.4 then introduces KWQL and its syntax, and Sect. 7.5 gives a relational semantics for the language. visKWQL, KWQL's visual rending, is described in Sect. 7.6. A first user evaluation of KWQL and visKWQL is described in Sect. 7.7. The following section, Sect. 7.8, describes KWilt, KWQL's patchwork-based implementation, and gives the results of a performance evaluation.

7.2 State of the Art

This section introduces wikis and semantic wikis and gives an overview of the search and querying functionalities provided by current semantic wiki engines. We further summarize recent research on keyword search over semistructured data.

7.2.1   Wikis: Collaborative Content Creation

In many respects, wikis are a prototypical social Web application, and their success is tightly connected to the proliferation of the social Web: wikis are conceptually simple, easy to use, and support users in the content creation process.

Apart from the original WikiWikiWeb[1] wiki engine, there exist a large number of wiki engines differing in their features, implementation, and application area, for example, MediaWiki,[2] Atlassian Confluence,[3] and PhpWiki.[4]

The basic elements of the conceptual model of a wiki are wiki pages and links between them. Creating or editing a wiki page is no harder than using a word-processing application, and content can be formatted using WYSIWYG editors or wiki markup. Wikis are particularly well suited for the collaborative, gradual creation of content, and they live from user participation: a wiki page may start out as a short outline and grow and evolve as more people participate or more details become known. A typical wiki page is edited and enhanced repeatedly, meaning that a final, definite version does not necessarily exist, but that each wiki page is a perpetual work in progress.

At the same time, wikis as knowledge management applications could profit from improved methods for structuring knowledge, making it more accessible and amenable to automatic processing. As mentioned above, wiki pages, on the one hand, are often heavily interlinked, meaning that related concepts are often connected. In terms of structuring knowledge, this is a valuable contribution. Individual wiki pages, on the other hand, are often weakly structured and only express knowledge as free text or multimedia.

The term "semantic wiki" is used to refer to two different types of systems [28, 43]: semantic wikis of the first type ("wikitology" [24] or "wikis for semantics") use wiki technology as a means for the collaborative authoring of ontologies. The main focus here is on creating semantic Web data, and human-readable wiki content is only needed to support the editing process. When used in the second sense, "semantic wiki" refers to a wiki that uses (social) semantic Web technologies to enhance the functionality of the wiki and support the process of collaborative content creation ("semantics for wikis"). Here, the focus is not (only) on metadata but (also) on text and multimedia content. Some semantic wiki engines fall clearly into one of these two categories, while others can be used for both purposes [43]. In the following, we use "semantic wiki" in the second meaning.

Semantic wikis extend conventional wikis by providing functionalities for expressing knowledge in a structured form. This is realized mainly by adding support for annotations to data items, most frequently wiki pages and tags, but also

---

[1]http://c2.com/cgi/wiki/

[2]http://www.mediawiki.org/

[3]http://www.atlassian.com/software/confluence/

[4]http://phpwiki.sourceforge.net/

smaller portions of text [23]. The annotations may be freely chosen tags [12], but sometimes, more formal mechanisms such as RDF backed by (imported) RDFS or OWL ontologies are offered as well. In particular, several semantic wikis support limited RDF annotations where the subject is always the URI of the annotated resource, and predicate and object are provided by the user [3,4,47].

The annotations, whether they have been assigned manually or extracted (semi) automatically, may be used for realizing functionalities like consistency checking, improved navigation, search, querying, personalization, context-dependent presentation, and reasoning. Annotations are often represented in RDF. They can thus be exported and integrated with data from other sources and are compatible with standard RDF technologies such as SPARQL.

The annotation of wiki content is optional, and semantic wikis do not require users to add annotations. While in particular only some of the users may actually annotate content, this can still enable all users of the semantic wiki to benefit from the functionalities that semantic wikis offer over conventional wikis, for example, an automatically generated table of contents [43]. Furthermore, the semantic wiki data may be formalized in a collaborative fashion over time, with different users providing the textual content and informal and formal annotations. This holds especially when different modes of annotations are available, for example, free-form tags and RDF. Semantic wikis thus maintain, at least to some extent, the ease of use of conventional wikis.

7.2.2   Searching and Querying in Semantic Wikis

Better search and querying is one of the main ways in which semantic wikis intend to improve upon conventional wikis. The need for simple yet powerful data retrieval [2,40] and for combined queries over content and annotations [3] has been pointed out in particular. So far, however, all semantic wikis that we are aware of treat the querying of content and annotations separately [40,43], while other sources of data such as content structure and system metadata cannot be queried at all.

In many cases, semantic wikis provide simple full-text search for the querying of textual content or RDF literals [23, 39, 47]. In addition, a standard RDF query language such as SPARQL or RDQL can often be used for querying the annotations [1, 2, 12, 42]. A number of semantic wikis also come with their own language for querying annotations that can be used in addition to or instead of a conventional RDF query language:

- KAON, the query language of COW [13], can make use of simple reasoning to find query answers.
- Rhizome [46] and its query language RxPath aim at making RDF querying easy for users who are already familiar with XML. To this end, RDF triples are mapped to a virtual, possibly infinitely recursive tree which can then be queried with XPath expressions.

- WikSAR [4] uses queries consisting of a series of predicate–object pairs. The answer to such a query then consists of all wiki pages whose annotations match all predicate–object conditions. Predicate and object can be connected by operators for equality, ranges, and regular expressions.
- Two different query languages have been suggested for Semantic MediaWiki. The first, referred to as "SMW-QL" by Bao et al. [6], has a syntax similar to that used to express annotations in SMW. SMW-QL supports subqueries, (implicit) conjunction, disjunction, negation, and comparison operators, but not variables. By default, queries return wiki pages, but so-called print requests can be used to display specific property values in the query answers. Krötzsch and Vrandecic [25] provide a semantics for SMW-QL through a translation to DL queries; Bao et al. [6] define a semantics that is based on the translation of SMW-QL queries into logic programs. The second query language [17] employs keyword search over RDF data (see Section 7.2.3). Users express their query intent using a number of keywords which are matched in the data using a fuzzy scheme that considers semantic and syntactic similarity and translated into SPARQL queries which are displayed to the user in a visual, table-based form. The user can then select the query that corresponds to his or her query intent and the matching entity tuples are returned.

AceWiki [26] differs from all approaches discussed above in that it employs a controlled natural language, Attempto Controlled English [15] (or ACE), to represent information in the wiki. The language is a subset of English but can be translated into a variant of first-order logic, meaning that it can be understood by humans and machines alike. Consequently, there is no distinction between content and annotations in AceWiki. The authors suggest that using ACE, queries can simply be represented as questions.

Usability and expressiveness of the above query languages vary widely; however, none of the existing languages fulfills all criteria outlined in Section 7.1, namely, that it can be used without prior training, is expressive enough to allow complex selections and can be used to query not only annotations, but also content, content structure, and metadata.

7.2.3 Keyword Querying over Semistructured Data

When we talk about Web queries, we subsume two distinct areas of research and technology: Web search as provided, for example, by Google or Yahoo!, and database-style queries on Web data (mostly in the form of XML or RDF) as provided through languages such as XQuery or SPARQL.

Where Web search allows us to operate on (nearly) all the Web, database-style Web queries operate only on a small fraction. Where Web search is limited to filtering relevant documents for human consumption, Web queries allow for the precise selection of data items in Web documents as well as their formatting, reorganization, aggregation, and the generation of new data. Where Web search can operate on all kinds of Web documents, Web queries are usually restricted to a more homogeneous collection of documents (e.g., XHTML documents or DocBook documents). Where Web search requires a human in the loop to ultimately judge the relevance of a search result, Web queries allow automated processing, aggregation, and deduction of data. Where Web search can be used by untrained users, Web queries usually require significant training to be employed effectively.

In the context of social semantic software, both aspects of Web queries play an essential role: we want to be able to precisely specify selection criteria for data items and automatically derive new information, operations that squarely fall into the domain of database-style Web queries. On the other hand, the essential premise of the social semantic Web is accessibility to untrained users. In this sense, a mechanism closer to Web search is needed. Web search and Web queries have mostly been treated separately in the past, but recently, this has started to change in more than one way.

The most significant efforts toward combining some of the virtues of Web search, viz. being accessible to untrained users and being able to cope with vastly heterogeneous data, are keyword-based Web query languages for XML and RDF documents. These languages operate in the same setting as XQuery or SPARQL, but with an interface suitable for untrained or barely trained users instead of a complex query language. The interface is often (in label-keyword query languages) enhanced to allow not only bag-of-word queries but also some annotations to each word, most notably a context (e.g., that a term must occur as the author or title of an article). Results are excerpts of the queried documents, though the precise extent is often determined automatically rather than by the user. Thus, keyword-based query languages trade some of the precision of languages like XQuery for a more accessible interface. The yardstick for these languages becomes an easily accessible interface (or query language) that does not sacrifice the essential premise of database-style Web queries, namely, that selection and construction are precise enough to allow for automated processing of data.

We can distinguish three types of keyword-based query languages for structured data according to the extent to which structure can be used as a selection criterion:

- In keyword-only query languages, queries consist of a number of terms which are matched to the textual content of nodes in an XML or RDF document, and in some cases to node or (in the case of RDF) edge labels. Queries make no reference to the structure of the data. This category includes most keyword query languages, like XKeyword [5, 20], XRank [16], Spark [54], and XKSearch [53].
- In label-keyword query languages such as XSearch [10] and XBridge [33], a query term is a label-keyword pair of the form l:k. The term matches data where a node with the label l contains, either directly or through a descendant node, text matching the associated keyword k. It is thus possible to indicate the context in which the keyword should occur.
- Keyword-enhanced query languages [14, 35, 45] extend traditional Web query languages with simple keyword querying. They allow for the specification of

structure to the extent to which it is known, but also include constructs for the use of keyword querying where it is not. Keyword-enhanced query languages constitute an extension of traditional query languages and therefore provide their full expressive power.

Given that (some) Web query languages also offer ways to specify queries when the user lacks knowledge about the schema, for example, through regular path expressions in XPath, one might wonder what distinguishes traditional query languages and keyword-enhanced query languages. As pointed out by Florescu et al. [14] and Schmidt et al. [45], regular path expressions are useful when the schema is not completely known to the user, but not when the user has no knowledge of the schema at all. The reason for this is that query evaluation in Web query languages is not optimized for evaluating vague queries. Furthermore, while the schema of the data may not have to be known, knowledge of the query language itself is still necessary, making Web query languages unsuitable for casual users.

A second, orthogonal characteristic of keyword query languages is the way they are implemented:

- Most keyword query languages are implemented as stand-alone systems that handle all steps of the query evaluation.
- Another group of keyword query languages translate the keyword queries into another query language and thus outsource the query evaluation. This category includes many RDF keyword query languages [48, 50, 54] but, to the best of our knowledge, only one XML language, XBridge [33], which translates keyword queries into XQuery. The approach of Ladwig and Tran [27] takes an exceptional position in that it tightly integrates query translation and query evaluation, and generates queries and candidate answers at the same time.
- Keyword-enhanced query languages finally build on existing systems by combining conventional query languages like XPath or XML-QL with keyword-querying techniques.

The majority of keyword query languages for semistructured data in the literature are concerned with keyword-only querying of XML data. Fewer proposals exist for querying RDF data, and a majority of them translate keyword queries into traditional query languages. Most XML keyword query languages, on the other hand, evaluate queries without mapping them to another query language.

At the same time, keyword query languages for XML usually limit themselves to the processing of tree-shaped data, that is, roughly to XML without hyperlinks. Those languages that do work on graph-shaped XML, like XRank, ignore hyperlinks during the matching and grouping process and only use them for ranking. A notable exception is SAILER [31], which models XML and HTML documents as graphs. As Schmidt et al. [45] point out, one reason for the relative lack of keyword querying for graph-shaped XML is the expected increase in complexity and thus processing time, which would be very problematic in an application area dealing with large amounts of data.

Similarly, the lack of RDF keyword query languages that evaluate queries directly can be attributed to the fact that RDF is graph shaped and cannot be converted into tree-shaped data as easily as XML. In addition, querying RDF poses additional challenges because of labeled edges and blank nodes. A possible way to overcome these challenges is to summarize the RDF graph into a different structure [41,50], but this comes at the cost of partially ignoring the structure of the data and thus reducing the granularity of the query result.

For XML querying, on the other hand, the grouping of matches is of great importance, and it is a central aspect of many approaches. The reason why determining these semantic entities in structured data is so important to keyword querying is that, in contrast to traditional query languages, queries are never fully specified, and in fact often cannot be fully specified by the user. The inferred semantics are what is used to determine what constitutes a relevant result.

Various heuristics for grouping have been proposed, a large majority of which are refinements of the established concept of the lowest common ancestor (LCA) [18], the most specific element that is an ancestor to at least one match instance of each keyword. These include, for example, SLCA [53], MLCA [35], CVLCA [30], and interconnection semantics [10]. All of these approaches add constraints to LCA in order to remedy the problem of false positives in LCA and improve the grouping of matched nodes according to their semantic entities. The approaches differ in the filter that they apply to remove undesirable results from the set of LCA nodes; each of them produces a set of results that is a subset of the results obtained by applying LCA.

On the one hand, the different heuristics for grouping aim at being universal or at least versatile; on the other hand, they are data driven and make assumptions about the relations between structure and semantics that may not be universal. Consequently, all LCA-based grouping strategies are not universally applicable and, under certain circumstances, may lead to both false positives and false negatives [49]. This raises the question to what extent it is possible to reliably deduce semantics from structural characteristics of data alone.

While most of the approaches determine the LCA or a variant thereof automatically based on keyword match instances, an alternative approach that was used in XKeyword [5,20] but also mentioned in connection with XRank [16] and employed in keyword querying databases [8, 11] is to manually group the data into concepts and thus predefine the possible query answer components. This method uses an extra level of processing where parts of query answers are defined a priori and therefore independent of a specific query. An obvious disadvantage is that it requires users or administrators to invest time and effort to define the groupings.

A small number of very recent approaches not only group keyword matches not just based on structure, but also take the distribution of keyword matches and node types in the data into account [7,34]. Whether these methods will solve the problems associated with LCA-based grouping remains to be seen.

An important characteristic of traditional query languages, namely, the targeted and flexible retrieval of elements, can be found only in two of the presented stand-alone keyword query languages, in that of Cohen et al. [10] and in XSeek [36,37].

Both of these languages return the content of a node whose label is matched. However, neither of them allows for the binding of specific values to variables. Query results thus cannot be used further in construction terms. Furthermore, it is not possible in XSeek to specify explicitly that the content of a node with a specific label should be retrieved. Rather, the necessary information is inferred from the keyword query and is therefore relatively hard to control by the user, even if he or she knows exactly which nodes he or she would like to have returned.

Keyword-enhanced query languages, on the other hand, allow for a more targeted selection and enable construction to varying degrees. Schmidt et al. [45] only retrieve the label of the LCA node, the approach of Florescu et al. [14] makes the granularity of the return value dependent on the specificity of the query, and schema-free XQuery allows for the binding of variables to specific nodes in an entity subtree.

Flexibility with respect to the data type, that is, the ability to query data in different formats, has received relatively little attention. XRank and Sailer can be used to query both XML and HTML documents, but do so mainly by treating HTML documents as unstructured text. The combined querying of XML and RDF is particularly desirable in the context on the semantic Web, where not all content of the (XML) data is necessarily represented in (e.g., RDF) metadata, or vice versa [9]. If both could be queried using a single query language, recall would be increased, and users would only have to familiarize themselves with one query language.

While to the best of our knowledge there are currently no systems for the combined keyword querying of XML and RDF data, a number of approaches to keyword querying are explicitly concerned with queries over HTML and XML data and relational databases [22, 32], thereby realizing data type flexibility to a certain extent.

7.3   The KiWi Wiki

KiWi[5] is a semantic wiki with extended functionality in the areas of information extraction, personalization, reasoning, and querying. KiWi relies on a simple, modular conceptual model consisting of the following building blocks:

Content items   are the primary units of information in KiWi; they correspond roughly to wiki pages in other wikis, but they can be nested: a content item can include other content items. The nesting of content items then forms a tree structure. Each content item has a URI through which it is accessible and uniquely identifiable. Content items can contain fragments, links, and tags. A content item consists of text or multimedia and an optional sequence of *contained* content items. Thus, content item nesting provides a conventional structuring of documents, for example, a chapter may consist of a sequence of

---

[5]http://www.kiwi-project.eu

sections. For reasons of simplicity, content item containment precludes any form of overlapping or of cycles, and thus, a content item can be seen as a directed acyclic graph (of content items).

Text fragments are user-defined continuous portions of text within contents items. They can consist of a word, a sentence, or any other section of text, and can be annotated. Text fragments are useful for—especially collaborative—document editing for adding annotations like "improve transition," "style to be polished," or "is this correct?" While content item expresses the structure of written text, text fragments convey narratives. Fragments can be nested but do not overlap and do not span over content items. Fragments of this kind are generally desirable, but are problematic with respect to query evaluation. While content items allow the authors to create and organize their documents in a modular and structured way, the idea behind fragments is to enable the annotation of pieces of content independently of the canonical structure given through content item nestings. If content items are like chapters and sections in a book, then fragments can be seen as passages that readers mark; they are individual and linear and in that transcend the structure of the document, possibly spanning, fragment across paragraphs or sections.

Links are simple hypertext links and can be used for relating content items to each other or to external Web sites. Links have a single origin, which is a content item, an anchor in this origin, and a single target, which is also a content item. Links can be annotated.

Tags are metadata that can be attached to content items, fragments, and links, describing their content or properties. They can be added by users, but can also be created by the system through automatic reasoning. Two kinds of annotations are available: tags and RDF triples. Tags allow to express knowledge informally, that is, without having to use a predefined vocabulary, while RDF triples are used for formal knowledge representation, possibly using an ontology or some other application-dependent predefined vocabulary. KWQL as presented here only supports the querying of tags, but the integration of RDF query facilities is discussed in Weiand [51].

Structure, within as well as between resources, plays an important role for expressing knowledge in the wiki, ranging from tags to complex graphs of links or content item containment.

In the following, *resources* refer to the basic concepts in the data model—content items, links, fragments, and tag assignments (in the following referred to as "tag") and *qualifiers* refer to properties of resources like metadata and content. *Qualifier values*, that is, the content associated with qualifiers, are of different types depending on the type of the qualifier. Qualifiers referring to data and metadata are associated with data in the form of dates, integers, URIs, or text. Structural qualifiers, on the other hand, describe nesting and linking relationships among pairs of content items or fragments. When used in a query, they take as a value a subquery describing the linked or nested resource.

7.4   KWQL: Principles and Syntax

KWQL, pronounced "quickel," is a rule-based query language that combines the
characteristics of keyword search with those of Web querying in order to enable
versatile querying in the KiWi wiki. The language allows for rich combined queries
of textual content, metadata, document structure, and informal to formal semantic
annotations. KWQL queries range from elementary and relatively unspecific to
complex and fully specified (meta)data selections.

The key principle of KWQL is that the complexity of queries increases with
their expressiveness, enabling a gradual learning of the language where required.
Beginning users can immediately profit from using KWQL by posing basic keyword
queries. As users learn more about the system and the data contained in it, their
information needs might begin to become more complex. KWQL allows users to
learn the advanced features of the language bit by bit as required to realize their
query intents.

KWQL does not require a specific amount of learning from the user—it is likely
that some users will never venture past basic keyword queries, while others may
only learn to use some slightly advanced constructs but not the full language. A third
group may invest more time, study the full syntax, and use it to write complex rules.
The goal for KWQL is to equally accommodate all of these users, letting them use
as much or as little of the language as suits their needs.

KWQL queries may be vague and amount to simple full-text search or take the
shape of selections of individual data items using precise constraints. The language
is designed to support both types of queries, one similar in functionality to Web
search and the other similar to web querying, as well as the range of queries in
between.

Full KWQL rules consist of a query body which specifies the data to be selected,
and an optional head indicating how this data should be processed further. In the
following, we will focus on query bodies, that is, pure selection queries, and exclude
the discussion of construction and reasoning in KWQL.

Query bodies can express selections of varying levels of complexity using any
combination of data sources in the wiki. For example, a content item selection
can refer not only to the textual content of the content item to be selected, but
also to the structuring of its contained content items, to the links from or to the
content item, and to its annotations. In short, KWQL is fully aware of the underlying
conceptual model.

To improve the user experience, and simplify the mental transfer of the query
intent into a query, query bodies take the shape of abstracted descriptions of the data
to be matched. This query-by-example-like syntactic style is further substantiated by
the fact that KWQL query terms are injective, meaning that no two query terms may
match the same data item. For example, when a query body describes a content item
with two tags, one with name "wiki" and one created by the user Mary, the query
will retrieve only content items where the two conditions hold for two distinct tags,
but not those where a single tag satisfies both criteria but no other tag meets either of
them. Apart from enhancing the expressive power of KWQL, injectivity also more

tightly couples the user experience—what the user sees and perceives when he or she uses the wiki—to the way in which queries are expressed in KWQL.

Each query body evaluates to a set of content items, namely, those that are compatible with the given description. Compatibility here means that the content item has all the properties specified in the query body and may in addition have any number of other properties not in contradiction with the selection criteria.

KWQL's scaling with user experience and the specificity of the query intent is realized through far-reaching and comprehensive support for the underspecification of queries. The simplest—and at the same time most vague—description of content items to be matched consists of one or several keywords that the content items must contain. When the context in which the keywords may occur is not restricted further, all content items that contain the given keywords in their text, title, fragments, links, tags, or associated metadata—but not in linked or nested content items—are compatible with the query and returned as results. Basic keyword queries in KWQL therefore constitute a true full-text search over all parts of the individual content items.

To make queries more selective and precise, the structural context in which the keywords should occur can be specified fully or in part. In addition to conjunction, which is implicitly assumed when no operator is given, operators for disjunction and negation may be used. KWQL bodies thus amount to descriptions of the data to be retrieved that, depending on the users' knowledge and information need, can be more or less specific.

This approach lends itself particularly well to stepwise querying, the gradual refinement of queries: starting with explorative queries using a small set of keywords, users can go through several iterations of evaluating a query, examining the results, and then further substantiating the query until the desired information is found.

KWQL allows for the selection of data based on the structure of content items and fragments through the `child` and `descendant` qualifiers. To keep the language simple, navigational queries are avoided and no qualifiers are offered for parents and ancestors. Olteanu et al. [38] have shown that adding these *backward axes* does not increase the expressiveness of a query language.

KWQL's structural qualifiers give rise to recursive data retrieval through a wiki page structure. These qualifiers take subqueries as a value, that is, arbitrary KWQL queries specifying selection constraints on a linked or nested content item or fragment. Structure qualifiers can thus be seen as edges to other content items or fragments, and recursive querying as traversal of the resulting graph.

Link traversal can be expressed similarly. It should be noted that, despite the fact that structural queries and link traversals can be nested, no infinite loops can occur. This is due to the fact that queries are always finite and KWQL does not support Kleene closure.

Query bodies may also contain variables. In the query evaluation process, these are bound to specific values of the matching content items, for example, their authors or the titles of the content items that they link to. Variables can serve three purposes:

Table 7.1 KWQL qualifier types

Qualifier	Resource type(s)	Value type	Arity
	Data		
Title	Content item	String	1
Text	Content item; fragment	String	1
Anchortext	Link	String	1
Name	Tag	String	1
	Metadata		
URI	Content item; fragment; tag	URI	1
Author	Content item; fragment; tag	String	+
Created	Content item; fragment; tag	Date	1
lastEdited	Content item	Date	1
numberEdits	Content item	Integer	1
	Structure		
Child	Content item	Content item	*
Child	Fragment	Fragment	*
Descendant	Content item	Content item	*
Descendant	Fragment	Fragment	*
Target	Link	Content item	1

- To bind values for further use in the construction part of a rule.
- As a wildcard or existential quantifier.
- To enforce that two qualifiers have identical values. In KWQL, all occurrences of a variable in a query body must have the same value; using the same variable several times therefore amounts to imposing equality constraints on the values of the respective qualifiers.

KWQL supports two types of queries: regular queries, evaluated only once, and embedded queries. Embedded queries are part of a content item and are evaluated every time the content is loaded. They enable predefined views that always display the latest information without the need for manual updating.

7.4.1 Syntax

Table 7.1 lists all qualifier types together with the resources in which they can appear, the data type of their value, and the arity of the qualifier term. $*$ and $+$ here are used as in regular expressions, indicating that the qualifier can appear any number of times ($*$) or, arbitrarily, often but at least once ($+$).

Nonstructural qualifiers and subresources describe the *intracontent item* structure. Structural qualifiers impose constraints on the *intercontent item* structure and the *interfragment* structure in the case of `child` and `descendant`.

```
⟨kwql-query⟩      ::=  ⟨resource-term⟩
⟨resource-term⟩   ::=  ⟨value-term⟩ | ⟨qualifier-term⟩
                   |   ⟨structure-term⟩
                   |   ⟨resource-term⟩ (‘OR’ | ‘AND’)? ⟨resource-term⟩
                   |   ‘ (’ ⟨resource-term⟩ ‘) ’
                   |   ‘NOT’ ⟨resource-term⟩
                   |   ⟨resource⟩ ‘ (’ ⟨resource-term⟩ ‘) ’
⟨resource⟩        ::=  ‘link’ | ‘ci’ | ‘fragment’ | ‘tag’
⟨structure-term⟩  ::=  (‘child’ | ‘descendant’ | ‘target’) ‘:’
                       ⟨resource-term⟩
⟨value-term⟩      ::=  ⟨STRING⟩
⟨qualifier-term⟩  ::=  ⟨qualifier⟩ ‘:’ ( ⟨value-term⟩ | ⟨variable⟩)
⟨qualifier⟩       ::=  ‘text’ | ‘title’ | ‘name’ | ‘URI’ | ‘agree’
                   |   ‘disagree’ | ‘lastEdited’ | ‘numberEd’
                   |   ‘author’ | ‘created’ | ‘anchorText’
⟨variable⟩        ::=  ‘$’⟨IDENTIFIER⟩
```

Fig. 7.1 KWQL syntax

Table 7.2 KWQL example queries

Java	Content items containing *"Java"* directly or in any of its tags or other metadata
ci(author:Mary)	Content items authored by Mary
ci(Java OR (tag(XML) AND author:Mary))	Content items that either contain *"Java"* or have a tag containing *"XML"* and are authored by Mary
ci(tag(name:$x author:Mary) tag(name:$x author:John))	Content items that are tagged with the same tag by both John and Mary
ci(tag(episode) tag(name:like author:Mary) tag(name:like author:John))	*"Episode"* content items that both Mary and John like
ci(tag(Java) link(target:ci(Lucene)))	Content items with a tag containing *"Java"* that contain a link to a content item containing *"Lucene"*
ci(URI:$a tag(character) link(target:ci(tag(location) link(target:ci(URI: $a)))))	Character content items that link to a location content item that links back to them

A (somewhat simplified) grammar for KWQL query bodies is given in Figure 7.1. Examples of KWQL queries together with their natural language translations are shown in Table 7.2.

7.5 Semantics

For defining a formal semantics of KWQL, we introduce an abstraction of the data model of KWQL, called KWQL graphs.

Definition 7.1 (KWQL Graph). Let $\mathcal{Q} = \{text, title, \ldots\}$ be the set of all n KWQL qualifiers and $\mathcal{V}$ the set of all qualifier values. Then, a *KWQL graph* is an $(n + 6)$-tuple $G = (\mathcal{C}, \mathcal{F}, \mathcal{L}, \mathcal{T}, S, C, Q_{\lambda_1}, \ldots, Q_{\lambda_n})$, where

- $\mathcal{C}$ is the set of all content items (wiki pages)
- $\mathcal{F}$ is the set of all fragments
- $\mathcal{L}$ is the set of all links
- $\mathcal{T}$ is the set of all tags
- $\mathcal{R} := \mathcal{C} \uplus \mathcal{L} \uplus \mathcal{T} \uplus \mathcal{F}$ is the set of all resources
- $S \subset (\mathcal{C} \times \mathcal{C}_<) \cup (\mathcal{F} \cup \mathcal{F}_<) \cup (\mathcal{L} \cup \mathcal{L}_<)$ is the association relation between resources where $\mathcal{C}_< = \mathcal{F} \cup \mathcal{L} \cup \mathcal{T}, \mathcal{F}_< = \mathcal{L} \cup \mathcal{T}, \mathcal{L}_< = \mathcal{T} \cup \mathcal{C} \cup \mathcal{F}$
- $C \subset \mathcal{C} \times (\mathcal{C} \cup \mathcal{F})$ is the containment relation between wiki pages and fragments and $C^+ = \bigcup_{n \geq 1} C^n$ is the transitive closure of C
- For each qualifier $\lambda \in \mathcal{Q}, Q_\lambda \subset \mathcal{R} \times \mathcal{V}$ associates the values for λ to a KWQL resource

The KWQL semantics is defined based on KWQL graphs and given in Table 7.3 in terms of three functions, $[\![]\!]_{\text{ci}}$, $[\![]\!]$, and $[\![]\!]_{\text{dir}}$. A KWQL query is constrained by $[\![]\!]_{\text{ci}}$ to return only content items (i.e., elements of $\mathcal{C}$). Most expressions can occur in two contexts, represented by the semantic functions $[\![]\!]$ and $[\![]\!]_{\text{dir}}$: In the first context, a query such as Java returns all resources that contain "Java" directly in any of their qualifiers or indirectly in the qualifiers of any of their fragments, tags, and links. In the second context, only resources that contain "Java" directly are returned. The exception to this rule are keyword queries which are always interpreted in the first manner.

The semantics in Table 7.3 handles variables, but omits the injectivity constraints for readability reasons. To handle variables, we introduce the set $\mathcal{I}$ of KWQL variables and the set $\mathcal{B} = 2^{\mathcal{I} \times \mathcal{V}}$ of possible variable assignments (pairs of variables and value). We further extend the set operators $\cup$ and $\cap$ to pairs of resources and variable assignments as follows: Let $A, B \in 2^{\mathcal{R} \times \mathcal{B}}$.

Then $A \sqcap B = \{(r, \beta) \in \mathcal{R} \times \mathcal{B} : (r, \beta') \in A \wedge (r, \beta'') \in B \wedge \beta = \beta' \cap \beta'' \wedge \beta \neq \emptyset\}$, $A \sqcup B = \{(r, \beta' \cup \beta'') \in \mathcal{R} \times \mathcal{B} : (r, \beta') \in A \wedge (r, \beta'') \in B\} \cup \{(r, \beta') \in \mathcal{R} \times \mathcal{B} : (r, \beta') \in A \wedge \nexists \beta'' : (r, \beta'') \in B\} \cup \{(r, \beta') \in \mathcal{R} \times \mathcal{B} : (r, \beta') \in B \wedge \nexists \beta'' : (r, \beta'') \in A\}$.

7.6 visKWQL

This chapter describes visKWQL (Hartl et al. [19]), a visual rendering of KWQL that allows to expressing queries using a visual formalism.

visKWQL fully supports KWQL in the sense that every KWQL query can be expressed as an equivalent visKWQL query and vice versa. In order to avoid introducing additional constructs and thus additional complexity, the rendering stays close to the textual language in its visual representation: visKWQL uses a form-based approach. All KWQL elements, including resources, qualifiers, and operators, are represented as boxes. Resource-value or qualifier-value associations

Table 7.3 Semantics for KWQL

$[\![\langle \textit{kwql-query}\rangle]\!]_{\mathrm{ci}}$	$= \pi_1([\![\langle \textit{kwql-query}\rangle]\!](\emptyset)) \cap C$
$[\![\langle STR\rangle]\!]_{\mathrm{dir}}(\beta) = [\![\langle STR\rangle]\!](\beta)$	$= \{(r,\beta) \in \mathcal{R} \times \mathcal{B} : \exists\lambda, v : Q_\lambda(r,v) \wedge \mathrm{contains}(v,\langle STR\rangle)\} \cup$ $\{(r,\beta) : \exists r' \in \mathcal{R} : S(r,r') \wedge (r',\beta) \in [\![\langle STR\rangle]\!])(\beta)\}$
$[\![\langle \textit{qualifier}\rangle\text{':'}\langle STRING\rangle]\!]_{\mathrm{dir}}(\beta)$	$= \{(r,\beta) \in \mathcal{R} \times \mathcal{B} : Q_{\langle \textit{qualifier}\rangle}(r,v) \wedge \mathrm{contains}(v,\langle STRING\rangle)\}$
$[\![\langle \textit{qualifier}\rangle\text{':'}\langle STRING\rangle]\!](\beta)$	$= [\![\langle \textit{qualifier}\rangle\text{':'}\langle STRING\rangle]\!]_{\mathrm{dir}}(\beta) \cup$ $\{(r,\beta) : \exists r' \in \mathcal{R} : S(r,r') \wedge (r',\beta) \in [\![\langle \textit{qualifier}\rangle\text{':'}\langle STRING\rangle]\!](\beta)\}$
$[\![\langle \textit{qualifier}\rangle\text{':'}\text{'}\$\text{'}\langle IDENT\rangle]\!]_{\mathrm{dir}}(\beta)$	$= \{(r,\beta \cup \{(\langle IDENT\rangle, v)\}) \in \mathcal{R} \times \mathcal{B} : Q_{\langle \textit{qualifier}\rangle}(r,v) \wedge$ $(\nexists v' : (\langle IDENT\rangle, v') \in \beta \vee (\langle IDENT\rangle, v) \in \beta)\}$
$[\![\langle \textit{qualifier}\rangle\text{':'}\text{'}\$\text{'}\langle IDENT\rangle]\!](\beta)$	$= [\![\langle \textit{qualifier}\rangle\text{':'}\langle STRING\rangle]\!]_{\mathrm{dir}}(\beta) \cup$ $\{(r,\beta) : \exists r' \in \mathcal{R} : S(r,r') \wedge (r',\beta) \in [\![\langle \textit{qualifier}\rangle\text{':'}\text{'}\$\text{'}\langle IDENT\rangle]\!](\beta)\}$
$[\![\langle \textit{resource}\rangle\text{':'}\langle \textit{res-term}\rangle]\!]_{\mathrm{dir}}(\beta)$	$= \{(r,\beta') \in \mathcal{R} \times \mathcal{B} : \mathrm{type}(r,\langle \textit{resource}\rangle) \wedge (r,\beta') \in [\![\langle \textit{res-term}\rangle]\!]_{\mathrm{dir}}\}$
$[\![\langle \textit{resource}\rangle\text{':'}\langle \textit{res-term}\rangle]\!](\beta)$	$= [\![\langle \textit{resource}\rangle\text{':'}\langle \textit{res-term}\rangle]\!]_{\mathrm{dir}}(\beta) \cup$ $\{(r,\beta) : \exists r' \in \mathcal{R} : S(r,r') \wedge (r',\beta) \in [\![\langle \textit{resource}\rangle\text{':'}\langle \textit{res-term}\rangle]\!](\beta)\}$
$[\![\text{'child'':'}\langle \textit{kwql-query}\rangle]\!](\beta)$	$= \{(r,\beta') \in (\mathcal{C} \cup \mathcal{F}) \times \mathcal{B} : \exists r' \in \mathcal{R} : C(r,r') \wedge (r',\beta') \in [\![\langle \textit{kwql-query}\rangle]\!]\}$
$[\![\text{'descendant'':'}\langle \textit{kwql-query}\rangle]\!](\beta)$	$= \{(r,\beta') \in (\mathcal{C} \cup \mathcal{F}) \times \mathcal{B} : \exists r' \in \mathcal{R} : C^+(r,r') \wedge (r',\beta') \in [\![\langle \textit{kwql-query}\rangle]\!]\}$
$[\![\text{'target'':'}\langle \textit{kwql-query}\rangle]\!](\beta)$	$= \{(r,\beta') \in \mathcal{L} \times \mathcal{B} : \exists r' \in \mathcal{R} : S(r,r') \wedge (r',\beta') \in [\![\langle \textit{kaw-query}\rangle]\!]\}$
$[\![\langle \textit{res-term}\rangle_1 \, \langle \textit{res-term}\rangle_2]\!](\beta)$	$= [\![\langle \textit{res-term}\rangle_1]\!](\beta) \sqcap [\![\langle \textit{res-term}\rangle_2]\!](\beta)$
$[\![\langle \textit{res-term}\rangle_1 \,\text{'AND'}\,\langle \textit{res-term}\rangle_2]\!](\beta)$	$= [\![\langle \textit{res-term}\rangle_1]\!](\beta) \sqcap [\![\langle \textit{res-term}\rangle_2]\!](\beta)$
$[\![\langle \textit{res-term}\rangle_1 \,\text{'OR'}\,\langle \textit{res-term}\rangle_2]\!](\beta)$	$= [\![\langle \textit{res-term}\rangle_1]\!](\beta) \sqcup [\![\langle \textit{res-term}\rangle_2]\!](\beta)$
$[\![\text{'('}\langle \textit{res-term}\rangle\text{')'}]\!](\beta)$	$= [\![\langle \textit{res-term}\rangle]\!](\beta)$
$[\![\text{'NOT'}\text{'('}\langle \textit{res-term}\rangle\text{')'}]\!](\beta)$	$= \mathcal{R} \setminus \pi_1([\![\langle \textit{res-term}\rangle]\!](\beta)) \times \{\beta\}$
$[\![\langle \textit{res-term}\rangle_1 \, \langle \textit{res-term}\rangle_2]\!]_{\mathrm{dir}}(\beta)$	$= [\![\langle \textit{res-term}\rangle_1]\!]_{\mathrm{dir}}(\beta) \sqcap [\![\langle \textit{res-term}\rangle_2]\!]_{\mathrm{dir}}(\beta)$
$[\![\langle \textit{res-term}\rangle_1 \,\text{'AND'}\,\langle \textit{res-term}\rangle_2]\!]_{\mathrm{dir}}(\beta)$	$= [\![\langle \textit{res-term}\rangle_1]\!]_{\mathrm{dir}}(\beta) \sqcap [\![\langle \textit{res-term}\rangle_2]\!]_{\mathrm{dir}}(\beta)$
$[\![\langle \textit{res-term}\rangle_1 \,\text{'OR'}\,\langle \textit{res-term}\rangle_2]\!]_{\mathrm{dir}}(\beta)$	$= [\![\langle \textit{res-term}\rangle_1]\!]_{\mathrm{dir}}(\beta) \sqcup [\![\langle \textit{res-term}\rangle_2]\!]_{\mathrm{dir}}(\beta)$
$[\![\text{'('}\langle \textit{res-term}\rangle\text{')'}]\!]_{\mathrm{dir}}(\beta)$	$= [\![\langle \textit{res-term}\rangle]\!]_{\mathrm{dir}}(\beta)$
$[\![\text{'NOT'}\text{'('}\langle \textit{res-term}\rangle\text{')'}]\!]_{\mathrm{dir}}(\beta)$	$= \mathcal{R} \setminus \pi_1([\![\langle \textit{res-term}\rangle]\!]_{\mathrm{dir}}(\beta)) \times \{\beta\}$

are represented as box nestings. Boxes consist of a label, the name of the represented KWQL element, and a body, which can hold one or more child boxes. This approach has several advantages: it stays close to KWQLs textual structure, keeping visKWQL simple and making it easy to translate between the two representations; it also lends itself well to rendering in HTML. Figure 7.2 shows an example of a visKWQL query corresponding to the textual KWQL query tag(author:Mary AND name:wiki), which retrieves content item that Mary has tagged with "wiki" or that contain a fragment or link with such a tag.

An accompanying editor, the KWQL query builder (KQB, see Figure 7.3), allows for the easy and straightforward construction of queries using drag-and-drop and, in addition, supports the user during query construction by displaying tooltips, preventing syntactic errors where possible, and by pointing the user to syntactically incorrect parts of a query. All actions in the editor apart from entering text into text

Fig. 7.2 A visKWQL query

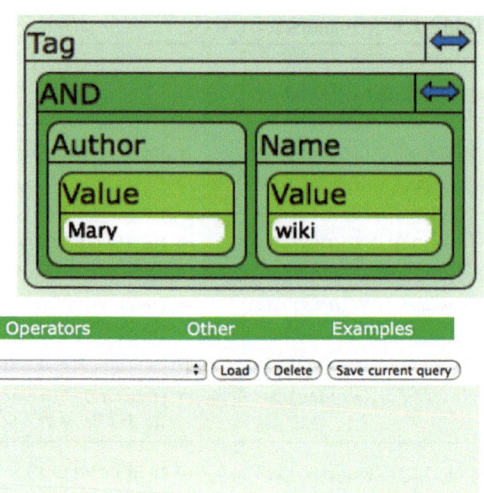

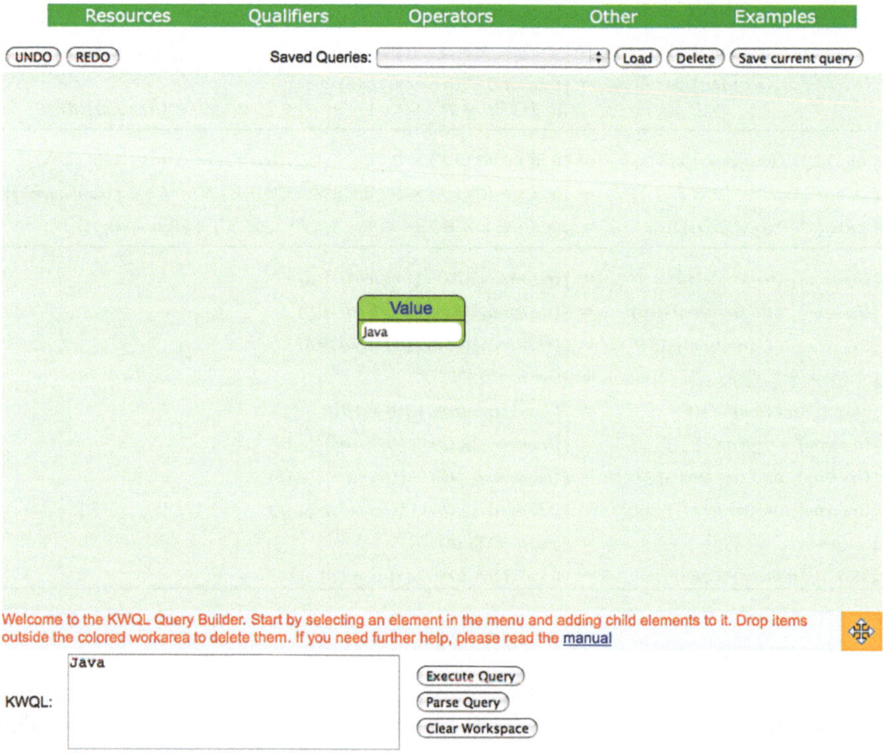

Fig. 7.3 The KiWi query builder

fields consist of drag-and-drop or left-click operations. There are no context menus or other interaction modes that might confuse users.

The KQB further provides features like information hiding to only display parts of larger queries and the highlighting of all occurrences of a variable when the mouse pointer is positioned over a variable in a query.

One particularly important feature of KQB is round tripping, which allows users to edit a query in both representations, visual and textual, at the same time, and see any changes made to one representation reflected in the other. The side-by-side display of both representations offers the additional advantage of helping users to learn KWQL by creating queries in visKWQL. Users do not have to decide in advance which formalism, textual or visual, they use to create a query, but should be able to switch between both at any time. For example, the user can start with a simple textual query, add an element to it in the visual representation, and finally edit a value in the textual representation before evaluating the query.

The visual KWQL query editor does not require the installation of special software or browser plug-ins, but instead is implemented using DHTML, with HTML and CSS for the presentation and Javascript for the program logic and user interaction. As a consequence, the system runs completely on the client side, within the users' Web browser, and the translation from visKWQL to KWQL can be seen as a serialization of the visual query.

7.7   User Evaluation

This section describes the setup and results of a user study performed to evaluate the suitability of KWQL and visKWQL for querying tasks in the KiWi wiki. A question of particular interest is whether the results differ (1) between users with varying amounts of previous experience in the area of query languages and social semantic software and (2) between participants using textual KWQL and those using its visual rendering.

The evaluation discussed here was performed as a single-session experiment where participants were given a short introduction into the KiWi wiki and, depending on the group they had been assigned to, KWQL or visKWQL was then asked to formulate queries ranging from simple and vague to precise and expressive. In a second task, participants were confronted with KWQL or visKWQL queries which they then translated into natural language descriptions of the data selected by the queries. Throughout the process, participants were encouraged to write down their thoughts and opinions on KiWi, the query language, and individual tasks.

However, to limit the scope of the experiment and focus on the aspects outlined above, several factors are intentionally not treated in this first evaluation. These include the gradual, self-paced learning process, user's individual query intents, long-distance effects and individual preferences for either KWQL or visKWQL.

7.7.1   Experimental Setup and Execution

To reflect the collaborative process of content creation and annotation, several user accounts were created in an installation of the KiWi wiki. Each account was used to compose a number of content items containing text from a wiki on the TV show The

Simpsons.[6] These content items were then annotated with tags. The final dataset, used in this study, consisted of 653 content items.

Twenty-one participants were recruited via an Internet forum aimed at LMU Munich computer science students and via announcements in several computer science lectures at the university. Sixteen of the participants were students of computer science or media computer science, one was a researcher in a nonrelated area of computer science, and four participants were students of subjects other than computer science.

Before the experiment, participants were asked to fill out a questionnaire about their previous experience in areas relevant to semantic wikis and KWQL such as the semantic Web, tagging, and XML; participants were also asked which programming and query languages they knew. Each participant was then randomly assigned to either the KWQL or the visKWQL group.

In an introductory phase, participants were allowed to familiarize themselves with the KiWi wiki and KWQL or visKWQL for 30 min. This was followed by a query creation task and a query understanding task, which, respectively, lasted 45 and 15 min. The objective of the query creation task was to use KWQL or visKWQL to answer questions, given in natural language, about the data in the wiki. In total, the task consisted of ten assignments of increasing difficulty. In the query understanding task, participants were given six KWQL or visKWQL queries of intermediate to advanced complexity, and were asked to describe the underlying query intent, that is, the common characteristics of the content items selected by each query, using natural language.

7.7.2 Results

Participants' self-assessed average knowledge of various areas relevant to KWQL and visKWQL was very similar for the two groups. The only concepts participants were familiar with to some extent were wikis, XML, and tags.

For the analysis, participants were divided into two groups based on their previous knowledge of query languages, social software, and semantic Web technologies. In the following, participants will often be referred to as "novice participants" or "advanced participants" based on the group they were assigned to. Depending on previous knowledge and the query language used, each participant thus belonged to one of four groups. The number of participants in each group was between four and six.

---

[6]http://simpsons.wikia.com/wiki/Simpsons_Wiki

Task 1: Query Creation

Table 7.4 shows the average number of questions, out of a total of ten, answered by the participants in each group (ignoring whether the solution was correct or not). The number is higher for advanced participants (8.34) compared to novice participants (8.02), and slightly higher for KWQL users (8.20) than for visKWQL users (8.12). Furthermore, KWQL and visKWQL show reversed effects with respect to how the amount of questions answered differs with proficiency: while advanced KWQL participants on average answered 0.8 questions more than their less experienced counterparts, advanced visKWQL users answered 0.2 questions less than visKWQL novices.

Table 7.5 shows the average percentage of the given answers that were correct. Among all participants, almost two thirds of all answers given, 62.24%, were correct. The visKWQL group was responsible for both the best and the worst results, with 93.33% correct answers for advanced visKWQL users and 35.66% correct answers for novice visKWQL. This result is particularly noteworthy since both groups answered a very similar amount of questions, as shown in Table 7.4. While novice visKWQL users answered more questions on average than novice KWQL users, a smaller percentage of those answers were correct, leading to a higher absolute number of correct answers for the KWQL group. Among the advanced groups, the situation is different: visKWQL users answered fewer questions but did so at a very high rate of correctness. As a consequence, the average absolute number of correct answers is higher for advanced visKWQL users.

Out of the total of 171 queries given as answers to questions in the query creation task, only seven, four KWQL queries and three visKWQL queries, were invalid in the sense that they could not be parsed or violated a validity constraint.[7] Consequently, 95% of all KWQL queries and 97% of all visKWQL queries given as answers were valid. The majority of incorrect answers therefore consisted of queries that were valid but did not correspond to the assignment.

Table 7.4 Average number of questions (out of ten) answered

	KWQL	visKWQL	Overall
Novice	7.8	8.2	8.02
Advanced	8.6	8.0	8.34
Overall	8.20	8.12	8.16

Table 7.5 Average percentage of given answers that are correct

	KWQL	visKWQL	Overall
Novice	53.33	35.66	43.70
Advanced	78.17	93.33	84.91
Overall	65.75	58.73	62.24

---

[7] In addition, six queries were bracketed incorrectly, but since participants had to write down their answers by hand, this is likely due to clerical errors and was ignored.

Table 7.6 Average number of questions (out of six) answered in task 2

	KWQL	visKWQL	Overall
Novice	5.5	5.5	5.5
Advanced	6	6	6
Overall	5.75	5.7	5.72

Table 7.7 Average number of questions (out of six) answered correctly

	KWQL	visKWQL	Overall
Novice	4.75	4.0	4.34
Advanced	5.5	5.5	5.5
Overall	5.13	4.6	4.89

Task 2: Query Understanding

In the query understanding task, all advanced participants provided answers to all six questions, while the novice participants answered 5.5 questions on average (see Table 7.6). Overall, participants answered 4.89 of the questions correctly. There was no difference in the number of correct answers between advanced participants who used KWQL and those who used visKWQL: both gave 5.5 correct answers on average. The situation is different for the novice users: here, those using KWQL had 4.75 correct answers on average, while participants in the visKWQL group only answered 4.0 questions correctly on average. Overall, this means that KWQL users gave more correct answers than visKWQL users by 0.53 questions, while advanced users on average answered 1.16 more questions correctly than novice users did (Table 7.7).

User Judgments

After completing the two tasks, participants were asked about their opinion on KWQL or visKWQL. Most participants, 13 out of 20, said that they felt they had understood how to use the respective query language. Six participants stated that they had understood the language to some extent, but had trouble with specific concepts or needed more time to understand it fully. Only one participant claimed to not have understood visKWQL at all.

With respect to the question whether KWQL or visKWQL was easy to use, a majority of participants answered that it was. However, many qualified their response and listed particular aspects they found hard to understand. Specifically, participants experienced problems with variables, URIs, injectivity, nesting of content items, and links. In several cases, participants did not understand the question or were unsure how to translate it into a query.

Finally, participants were asked what they considered to be advantages and disadvantages of KWQL and visKWQL. All participants thought that KWQL and visKWQL are powerful and allow for precise queries, while some remarked that they are harder to use than Web search and take some time to learn.

7.7.3   Discussion

All in all, the results of the experimental evaluation are very positive: KWQL and visKWQL were well perceived by the participants. Given only a very short introduction and a small amount of time to solve the assignments, participants overall could provide correct answers to more than half the questions in the query writing task and over 80% of the questions in the query understanding task.

The amount of learning required could explain why visKWQL novices performed worse than the participants in the novice KWQL group: apart from having to learn all the new concepts, they also had to acquaint themselves with visual querying, which likely was unfamiliar to them. The novice KWQL users, on the other hand, had to write textual queries, which, given that all participants can be assumed to have used Web search engines before, was more familiar to them.

Another contributing factor to the comparatively bad performance of novice visKWQL users could be that visKWQL is not ideally suited for creating vastly underspecified queries. visKWQL makes it easy to understand the structure of queries and to create structured queries, but offers no advantage when then queries involved are very simple. Indeed, novice visKWQL participants performed particularly badly compared to novice KWQL participants on questions that require underspecified queries, and the difference in the percentage of correct answers was smaller when the answer queries contained more structure.

This result indicates that it might be better to introduce beginning users whose queries exclusively consist of keywords to textual KWQL, and to only add visKWQL once the queries become more complex. On the other hand, given the round-tripping capabilities of visKWQL, it is possible that users could achieve equivalent or better results when textual and visual query editing are introduced simultaneously; a follow-up study could investigate which of the three methods yields the best results.

Advanced participants achieved good results regardless of the query language: on average, they answered 71% of the questions in the query creation task and over 90% of the questions in the query understanding task correctly. Their results also showed that visKWQL can help to improve the performance: advanced visKWQL participants gave fewer answers overall than advanced KWQL participants, but nearly all of their answers were correct. These findings indicate that participants who are familiar with querying and structured data and to whom the information in the introductions is less novel can make effective use of visKWQL and the advantages it offers over textual KWQL. This result gives further weight to the explanation that the comparatively bad performance of novice visKWQL participants is due to them being confronted with an overwhelming amount of new information that makes it hard for them to additionally absorb the concepts of visual querying and visKWQL.

Across all groups, participants had more success understanding queries than writing them. In the query understanding task, novice KWQL users again outperformed novice visKWQL users, both of which had a lower percentage of correct answers than either advanced group. Both advanced groups on average answered more than

90% of the questions correctly, indicating that this task was very easy for them overall. The fact that participants performed better at understanding queries than at writing them indicates that users could benefit from the addition of query templates that users can modify according to their needs.

7.8   KWilt: Patchwork Knowledge Management

KWilt is the implementation of KWQL in KiWi. It provides an easily extensible, high-performance implementation of the KWQL features over the wide range of data available in KiWi. Previous approaches have often tried to engineer a knowledge information systems for such diverse information and user needs from the start. By contrast, KWilt uses a "patchwork" approach, combining performance and mature technologies where available. For example, KWilt uses a scalable and well-established information retrieval engine to evaluate keyword queries. The patchwork approach has three main advantages:

- Many queries can be evaluated at the speed of search engines, yet all the power of first-order logic is available if needed. The three steps use increasingly more expressive, but at the same time less scalable technologies. Thus, even for queries that involve full first-order constraints, we can in many cases substantially reduce the number of candidates in the information retrieval engine. This property is particularly relevant in the context of KWQL, as (novice) users who use KWQL like a search engine also expect the speed of a search engine, unaware of the additional expressiveness provided by KWQL.
- Each part is implemented using proven technologies and algorithms with minimal "glue" between the employed tools.
- The separation makes it easy to adapt each of the parts, for example, to reflect additional data sources. If KiWi would introduce data with different structural properties, for example, strictly hierarchical taxonomies in addition to RDF ontologies, only the part of KWilt that evaluates structural constraints needs to be modified. Similarly, if KWQL would introduce other content primitives other than keywords (e.g., for image retrieval), only the first (retrieval) part of KWilt would be affected.

7.8.1   Architecture and Evaluation Phases

Despite the unique combination of features found in KWQL, KWilt does not try to "reinvent the wheel." Instead, we used a *patchwork*, or integration, approach to combine off-the-shelf state-of-the-art tools in a single framework. To this end, the evaluation is split into three different evaluation phases, which are dedicated to certain aspects of the query, see Figure 7.4. Each step makes use of a tool that is

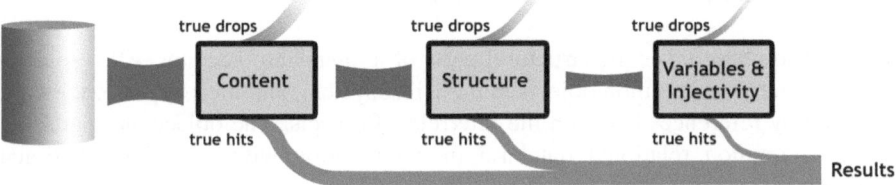

Fig. 7.4 The evaluation pipeline of the framework

particularly suitable for evaluating the query constraints covered by that aspect of the entire evaluation. Thus, efficient and mature algorithms form the basis of our framework.

7.8.1.1 Evaluation of Keyword Queries

Most KWQL queries, in particular by novice users, mainly or exclusively regard the content of the pages. Therefore, the first evaluation phase regards the keyword parts of a query in order to evaluate them in an early phase of the evaluation with as little overhead as possible. If all constraints of the query can be validated in this phase, the two subsequent phases can be skipped.

The information retrieval engine Solr provides a highly optimized inverted list index structure to carry out keyword queries on a set of documents. Each document consists of an arbitrary number of named fields, which are most commonly used to store the text of a document and its metadata.

In order to use Solr for the evaluation of KWQL queries, the metadata of wiki pages and further the metadata of its tags, fragments, and links are stored in a Solr document. The main principle of the translation is to materialize joins between content items and the directly connected resources.

The transformation of the resources connected to a content item to fields in the Solr index is lossy, since the value of multiple resources is stored in a single field. Thus, if multiple properties of a resource are queried, it cannot be guaranteed that hits in the index belong to the same resource.

To keep the index small, only dependencies to flat resources are materialized, which omits, in particular, nesting and linking of content items. Therefore, only queries that access content items together with their content, metadata, and directly related flat resources can be evaluated entirely in Solr. As soon as nesting and linking of content items come into play, however, we use Solr only to generate a set of candidates which match those parts of the query for which all necessary information is stored in the Solr index.

In order to evaluate a KWQL query through Solr, a portion of the KWQL query (that can be evaluated by Solr) is converted to the query language of Solr. Information which is not covered by the materialized joins and variables is either disregarded or at least converted to an existential quantification in order to reduce the number of false positives.

7.8.1.2   Evaluation of Structural Constraints

The second phase takes the structural parts of a query into account. All resources
are represented as common objects in the KiWi system, and their dependencies are
modeled by references between the interrelated objects. The objects are persisted
using a common relational database in combination with an object-relational
mapping.

In the current prototype, we validate the structural properties of a query for each
candidate item individually. That means, nested resources (tags, fragments, links,
and contained content items) which are specified in the query are considered by
traversing the references of the currently investigated object.

We choose this approach, as structural constraints are often validated fairly
quickly and far less selective than the keyword portions of KWQL queries. However,
for future work, we envision an extension of KWilt that improves on the current
implementation in two aspects: (a) It estimates whether the structural part is
selective enough to warrant its execution without considering the candidates from
the previous phase, followed by a join between the candidate sets from the two
phases. (b) If structural constraints become more complex, specialized evaluation
engines for hierarchical (XML-style) data, for example, a high-performance XPath
engine, for link data, e.g., various graph reachability indexes, and for RDF data
might be advantages.

In addition to the verification of the structural constrains, the structural dependencies of the contributing resources and the required values of their qualifiers are
stored in relations which are needed during the last evaluation phase.

7.8.1.3   Evaluation of First-Order Constraints over Wiki Resources

In the final evaluation phase, first-order constraints over wiki resources are considered, as induced by the KWQL variables (and some advanced features of KWQL
such as injectivity).

Following constraint programming notation, we consider a first-order constraint
a formula over logical relation on several variables. In order to use these constraints
to express a KWQL query, every expression of a query that is involved in constraints
not yet fully validated is represented by some variables. These variables are
then connected using relations which reflect the structural constraints between
the resources from the query and their metadata. These relations are constructed
during the prior evaluation phase since all required values and dependencies of the
resources are regarded in this phase anyhow.

Thus, the relations are used to connect the formal representation of the query and
the candidate matches. The first-order constraints are evaluated using the constraint
solver choco [21].

Any content item that fulfills the constraints validated in all three phases is a
match for the entire query. In fact, since we only feed candidate matches from

the prior phase to each subsequent phase, the content item (identifiers) returned by choco immediately gives us the KWQL answers.

7.8.2   Skipping Evaluation Phases: KWQL's Sublanguages

The evaluation of a general KWQL query in KWilt is performed in three phases as described in the previous section. However, not all evaluation phases are required for every KWQL query. In the following, we give a characterization of KWQL queries that can be evaluated using only the first phase (and skipping the remaining ones), or only the first and second.

7.8.2.1   Keyword KWQL or $KWQL_K$

$KWQL_K$ is the restriction of KWQL to mostly flat queries where *resource terms* may not occur nested inside other resource terms and *structure terms* are not allowed at all.

Since tags and fragments itself cannot be nested more than one level, we can also materialize all tags and fragments for each content item. However, in contrast to (string-valued) qualifiers, a content item can have multiple tags or fragments. To allow evaluation with an information retrieval engine such as Solr, we have to ensure that multiple tag or fragment expressions always match with different tags or fragments of the surrounding content item. This avoids that we have to enforce the injectivity of these items in a later evaluation phase.

To ensure this, we allow tag and fragment queries but disallow

- Two keyword queries as sibling expressions in tag or fragment queries
- Two tag or fragment queries as sibling expressions

$KWQL_K$ expressions can be evaluated entirely by the information retrieval engine, here Solr.

7.8.2.2   Tree-Shaped KWQL or $KWQL_T$

$KWQL_T$ allows only queries corresponding to tree-shaped constraints, thus, no multiple occurrences of the same variable, and no potentially overlapping expression siblings.

We define an equivalence relation on expressions, called *potential overlap*, as a conservative approximation of overlapping. It holds between two expressions if they have the same return type in the KWQL semantics (see Section 7.5) or if the return type of one is a subset of that of the other one.

KWQL$_T$ expressions can be evaluated by using only Solr and checking the remaining structural conditions in the second evaluation phase. Full first-order constraints are not needed, and the third (choco) phase can be skipped.

Proposition 7.1. *Given an arbitrary KWQL query, we can decide in linear time and space in the size of the query if that query is a KWQL$_K$ query and in quadratic time if it is a KWQL$_T$ query.*

Proof. From the definitions of KWQL$_K$ and KWQL$_T$, it is easy to see that testing membership of a general KWQL expression can be done by a single traversal of the expression tree. In the case of KWQL$_T$, we also have to test each (of the potentially quadratic) pair of siblings for overlap and store already visited variables.   □

Whether a given query is a KWQL$_T$ query can actually be determined when transforming the query into first-order constraints in the third evaluation phase. During this transformation, we need to execute the constraint solver in any case. In practice, this is often cheaper than a separate test, as the generation of first-order constraints is fairly cheap and polynomial, except for queries with many potentially overlapping expression siblings.

7.8.3   Performance Evaluation

To analyze the performance of the KWilt prototype, the evaluation times of various queries of all three types were measured. For the experiment, the KiWi system was executed on a virtual server with a dual core 2.5 GHz processor and 4 GB of RAM running Ubuntu Linux.

In a first experiment, a number of queries, among them our example query from the introduction, were evaluated on a dataset consisting of 339 content items on the KiWi project. For all queries, preprocessing, that is, parsing, verification, and determining whether the query can be fully processed using only phase 1, was found to take between 27 and 42 ms. Table 7.8 further shows the processing times and number of results per query and processing phase. The first part of the table gives the numbers for queries that are covered by KWQL$_K$. As the results show, these queries can overall be evaluated fairly quickly.

The second group of queries displayed in the table are those that can be evaluated using KWQL$_T$. As the table illustrates, those queries can be evaluated quickly, but only if the first evaluation step has sufficiently reduced the candidate set. One underlying assumption behind KWilt is that most queries exclusively or predominantly use value-based selection criteria, that is, selection criteria that can be covered by the information retrieval engine in the first phase of the evaluation. When this assumption does not hold, the candidate set still contains a considerable amount of content items after the first evaluation phase. As the second evaluation phase is considerably slower than the first, evaluation times in such a situation can become very high. Correspondingly, the evaluation times for all four KWQL$_T$

Table 7.8 Evaluation times in the KiWi dataset (339 content items)

Query						
Phase 1		Phase 2		Phase 3		Total time [ms]
Time [ms]	Results	Time [ms]	Results	Time [ms]	Results	
KiWi						
31	14	–	–	–	–	31
ci(text:KWQL title:KiWi)						
6	1	–	–	–	–	6
KiWi tag(name:$t)						
42	9	–	–	–	–	42
ci(tag(name:KWQL) child:ci(tag(Example)))						
10	5	44	1	–	–	54
ci(Munich link(target:ci(KiWi)))						
33	4	52	4	–	–	85
ci(KiWi link(target:ci(KiWi)))						
60	10	206	4	–	–	266
ci(tag(name:r)text :r)						
149	9	53	9	103	9	305
ci(tag(author:admin) tag(name:KWQL))						
9	5	55	5	67	4	131
ci(KiWi tag(name:$t) link(target:ci(URI:$u tag(name:$t))))						
44	9	181	4	194	3	419

queries are roughly inversely proportional to the size of the candidate set after the first evaluation phase (Table 7.9).

Finally, the lower three queries in the table make use of the full power of KWQL and require all three evaluation phases.

Overall, the results of this first experiment show that $KWQL_T$ queries can be evaluated using Solr with only little overhead for preprocessing the query. However, Solr queries involving wildcards are evaluated comparatively slowly. More critically, the second evaluation phase constitutes a bottleneck in the query evaluation process, particularly when the first phase does not sufficiently decrease the size of the candidate set.

In summary, this first small-scale evaluation of KWilt shows that the approach overall is viable and delivers good results as long as the underlying assumption holds true, namely, that most selection criteria used in queries are value based. As long as this is true, KWilt can employ Solr which quickly evaluates the query, either in total or by reducing the candidate set to a size that is manageable for the following evaluation phases.

Table 7.9 Evaluation times in the RSS dataset (2049 content items)

Query						
Phase 1		Phase 2		Phase 3		Total time [ms]
Time [ms]	Results	Time [ms]	Results	Time [ms]	Results	
tag(author:Mary)						
48	35	–	–	–	–	48
semantic web						
51	22	–	–	–	–	51
tag(name:web author:Peter)						
99	34	1769	34	–	–	1868
ci(example title:*rtext* :r)						
105	38	21	38	15	1	141
ci(title:*rtext* :r)						
679	505	15	505	75	58	769
ci(tag(name:web) tag(author:Peter))						
92	34	863	34	3246	34	4201

These, in particular the second evaluation phase, constitute the weak point of KWilt as it is currently implemented: the simple traversal of all candidate content items that constitutes the second phase in the current implementation performs very slowly. When a query does not use mainly value-based selection criteria or when the dataset is big, the size of the candidate set is not sufficiently decreased in the first evaluation phase and the second evaluation phase can take several seconds or longer.

Overall, the system delivers good results, but changes to the system are required to improve the performance of the second evaluation phase. The following section discusses possible steps that could be taken.

Despite the two possibilities for improving the second evaluation phase discussed above, namely, an evaluation strategy more closely tailored to the individual queries and their keyword and structure constraints and a reimplementation of the second evaluation phase using Web querying technology, two further changes could be employed to improve query performance:

- While saving all information about structurally connected content items in the index representation of a content item is clearly not practicable, some basic structural information could be represented. For example, the index could indicate whether a content item has any children or links to any other content items. Depending on how frequently nesting and linking relations are used in the wiki, this information could then help narrow down the candidate set, meaning that fewer content items have to be processed in the second evaluation phase.

- Queries that cannot be fully evaluated using Solr could be handled through a translation into SQL that treats both the second and third evaluation phases. The relational semantics given in Section 7.5 can serve as a basis for such a translation of KWQL into SQL. The resulting alternative implementation of KWQL would not be based on the principle of gradually refining the query results like KWilt, but rather on choosing the best-suited tool before query evaluation begins. An evaluation of the resulting system could also show whether the use of Solr is justified, or whether translating fully translating KWQL into SQL is preferable.

7.9   Outlook

At least two extensions to KWQL as described here are desirable: to add two important features of keyword search to the language, fuzzy matching, and ranking should be provided. Toward this end, we suggest PEST [52], a PageRank-like approach to approximate querying of structured data that exploits the structure to propagate term weights between related data items and uses the resulting modified index for ranking as well as fuzzy matching over data structure. Secondly, one issue that has not been addressed so far is that of querying RDF with KWQL. While dealing with complex RDF graphs may indeed overburden many users, simple RDF triples are intuitive and easy to understand. KWQL should therefore allow users to query at least these simple RDF annotations that they and others have created. Weiand [51] discussed three solutions for adding support for RDF queries, one native and two based on the integration of existing RDF query languages.

7.10   Conclusion

The work presented in this chapter addresses the question how ease of use and rich functionality, two seemingly conflicting characteristics, can be consolidated in the context of the social semantic Web, and more specifically in the semantic wiki KiWi. We feel that this issue is crucial to the success of the social semantic Web: social semantic Web applications live from user participation and the adoption by a broad user base, but often fail to provide annotation and querying formalisms that allow casual and expert users alike to formalize knowledge and compose expressive queries to fully leverage the functionality of the application at hand. We presented KWQL, a query language for the KiWi wiki based on the label-keyword query paradigm that allows for rich combined queries of textual content, metadata, document structure, and annotations.

We described the underlying principles and the syntax of KWQL, provided a formal semantics for the language, and discussed KWilt, an implementation of KWQL query evaluation based on a patchwork approach. We then distinguished three sublanguages of increasing complexity and showed that it is possible to efficiently recognize the sublanguage a given KWQL query belongs to and to adapt the evaluation process accordingly. The power of full first-order queries can be leveraged where needed, but at the same time, KWilt can evaluate basic queries at almost the speed of the underlying search engine, as we showed in a performance evaluation. Participants in a user study reacted positively to KWQL and visKWQL. They found the languages useful, expressive, and easy to use, at least given some time and practice. Even after a short introduction and a minimal amount of time to solve the assignments, participants overall were able to provide correct answers to more than half of the questions in a query writing task and over 80% of the questions in a query understanding task.

References

1. Auer, S., Dietzold, S., Lehmann, J., Riechert, T.: OntoWiki: a tool for social, semantic collaboration. Proceedings of the Workshop on Social and Collaborative Construction of Structured Knowledge (2007)
2. Aumueller, D.: Semantic authoring and retrieval within a wiki. Proceedings of the 2nd European Semantic Web Conference (2005a)
3. Aumueller, D.: SHAWN: structure helps a wiki navigate. Proceedings of the BTW-Workshop WebDB Meets IR (2005b)
4. Aumueller, D.: Towards a semantic wiki experience – desktop integration and interactivity in WikSAR. Proceedings of the 1st Workshop on the Semantic Desktop (2005c)
5. Balmin, A., Hristidis, V., Koudas, N., Papakonstantinou, Y., Srivastava, D., Wang, T.: A system for keyword proximity search on XML databases. Proceedings of 29th International Conference on very Large Data Bases, pp. 1069–1072 (2003)
6. Bao, J., Ding, L., Hendler, J.: Knowledge representation and query in semantic MediaWiki: a formal study. Technical Report TW-2008-42, Tetherless World Constellation (RPI) (2008)
7. Bao, Z., Ling, T.W., Chen, B., Lu, J.: Effective XML keyword search with relevance oriented ranking. Proceedings of the 25th International Conference on Data Engineering, pp. 517–528 (2009)
8. Bhalotia, G., Hulgeri, A., Nakhe, C., Chakrabarti, S., Sudarshan, S.: Keyword searching and browsing in databases using BANKS. Proceedings of the 18th International Conference on Data Engineering, pp. 431–440 (2002)
9. Bischoff, K., Firan, C.S., Nejdl, W., Paiu, R.: Can all tags be used for search? Proceedings of the 17th ACM Conference on Information and Knowledge Management, pp. 193–202 (2008)
10. Cohen, S., Mamou, J., Kanza, Y., Sagiv, Y.: XSearch: a semantic search engine for XML. Proceedings of 29th International Conference on very Large Data Bases, pp. 45–56 (2003)
11. Dar, S., Entin, G., Geva, S., Palmon, E.: DTL's DataSpot: database exploration using plain language. Proceedings of 24rd International Conference on very Large Data Bases, pp. 645–649 (1998)
12. El Ghali, A., Tifous, A., Buffa, M., Giboin, A., Dieng-Kuntz, R.: Using a semantic wiki in communities of practice. Proceedings of the 2nd International Workshop on Building Technology Enhanced Learning Solutions for Communities of Practice (2007)
13. Fischer, J., Gantner, Z., Rendle, S., Stritt, M., Schmidt-Thieme, L.: Ideas and improvements for semantic wikis. Proceedings of the 3rd European Semantic Web Conference, pp. 650–663 (2006)
14. Florescu, D., Kossmann, D., Manolescu, I.: Integrating keyword search into XML query processing. Comput. Networks 33(1–6), 119–135 (2000)

15. Fuchs, N.E., Kaljurand, K., Schneider, G.: Attempto Controlled English meets the challenges of knowledge representation, reasoning, interoperability and user interfaces. Proceedings of the 19th International Florida Artificial Intelligence Research Society Conference, pp. 664–669 (2006)
16. Guo, L., Shao, F., Botev, C., Shanmugasundaram, J.: XRANK: ranked keyword search over XML documents. Proceedings of the ACM SIGMOD International Conference on Management of Data, pp. 16–27 (2003)
17. Haase, P., Herzig, D., Musen, M.A., Tran, T.: Semantic wiki search. Proceedings of the 6th European Semantic Web Conference, pp. 445–460 (2009)
18. Harel, D., Tarjan, R.E.: Fast algorithms for finding nearest common ancestors. SIAM J. Comput. **13**, 338–355 (1984)
19. Hartl, A., Weiand, K., Bry, F.: visKQWL, a visual renderer for a semantic web query language. Proceedings of the 19th International Conference on World Wide Web, pp. 1253–1256 (2010)
20. Hristidis, V., Papakonstantinou, Y., Balmin, A.: Keyword proximity search on XML graphs. Proceedings of the 19th International Conference on Data Engineering, pp. 367–378 (2003)
21. Jussien, N., Prud'homme, C., Cambazard, H., Rochart, G., Laburthe, F.: choco: an open source java constraint programming library. Proceedings of the Workshop on Open-source Software for Integer and Constraint Programming (2008)
22. Kacholia, V., Pandit, S., Chakrabarti, S., Sudarshan, S., Desai, R., Karambelkar, H.: Bidirectional expansion for keyword search on graph databases. Proceedings of the 31st International Conference on very Large Data Bases, pp. 505–516 (2005)
23. Kiesel, M.: Kaukolu: hub of the semantic corporate intranet. Proceedings of the 1st Workshop on Semantic Wikis (2006)
24. Klein, B., Höcht, C., Decker, B.: Beyond capturing and maintaining software engineering knowledge – "Wikitologies" as shared semantics. Proceedings of the Workshop on Knowledge Engineering and Software Engineering (2005)
25. Krötzsch, M., Vrandecic, D.: Semantic Wikipedia. In: Blumauer, A., Pellegrini, T. (eds.) Social Semantic Web, pp. 393–421. Springer, Berlin, Heidelberg, New York (2009)
26. Kuhn, T.: AceWiki: a natural and expressive semantic wiki. CoRR abs/0807.4618 (2008)
27. Ladwig, G., Tran, T.: Combining query translation with query answering for efficient keyword search. Proceedings of the 7th Extended Semantic Web Conference, pp. 288–303 (2010)
28. Landefeld, R., Sack, H.: Collaborative web-publishing with a semantic wiki. Proceedings of the 1st Conference on Social Semantic Web, pp. 23–34 (2007)
29. Leuf, B., Cunningham, W.: The Wiki Way: Quick Collaboration on the Web. Addison-Wesley, Reading, MA, USA (2001)
30. Li, G., Feng, J., Wang, J., Zhou, L.: Effective keyword search for valuable LCAs over XML documents. Proceedings of the 16th ACM Conference on Information and Knowledge Management, pp. 31–40 (2007)
31. Li, G., Feng, J., Wang, J., Song, X., Zhou, L.: SAILER: an effective search engine for unified retrieval of heterogeneous XML and web documents. Proceedings of the 17th International Conference on World Wide Web, pp. 1061–1062 (2008)
32. Li, G., Ooi, B.C., Feng, J., Wang, J., Zhou, L.: EASE: an effective 3-in-1 keyword search method for unstructured, semi-structured and structured data. Proceedings of the ACM SIGMOD International Conference on Management of Data, pp. 903–914 (2008)
33. Li, J., Liu, C., Zhou, R.: XBridge: answering XML keyword search with structured queries (2008)
34. Li, J., Liu, C., Zhou, R., Wang, W.: Suggestion of promising result types for XML keyword search. Proceedings of the 13th International Conference on Extending Database Technology, pp. 561–572 (2010)
35. Li, Y., Yu, C., Jagadish, H.V.: Schema-free XQuery. Proceedings of the 13th International Conference on very Large Data Bases, pp. 72–83 (2004)
36. Liu, Z., Chen, Y.: Identifying meaningful return information for XML keyword search. Proceedings of the ACM SIGMOD International Conference on Management of Data, pp. 329–340 (2007)

37. Liu, Z., Walker, J., Chen, Y.: XSeek: a semantic XML search engine using keywords. Proceedings of the 33rd International Conference on very Large Data Bases, pp. 1330–1333 (2007)
38. Olteanu, D., Meuss, H., Furche, T., Bry, F.: XPath: looking forward. Proceedings of the EDBT Workshop on XML-based Data Management, pp. 109–127 (2002)
39. Oren, E.: SemperWiki: a semantic personal wiki. Proceedings of the 1st Workshop on the Semantic Desktop (2005)
40. Panagiotou, D., Mentzas, G.: A comparison of semantic wiki engines. Proceedings of the 22nd European Conference on Operational Research (2007)
41. Qu, Y.: Q2RDF: ranked keyword query on RDF data. Technical Report, Southeast University, China (2008)
42. Schaffert, S.: IkeWiki: a semantic wiki for collaborative knowledge management. Proceedings of the 15th IEEE International Workshops on Enabling Technologies: Infrastructures for Collaborative Enterprises, pp. 388–396 (2006)
43. Schaffert, S., Bry, F., Baumeister, J., Kiesel, M.: Semantic wikis. IEEE Software **25**(4), 8–11 (2008)
44. Schaffert, S., Eder, J., Grünwald, S., Kurz, T., Radulescu, M.: Kiwi – a platform for semantic social software. Proceedings of the 6th European Semantic Web Conference, pp. 888–892 (2009)
45. Schmidt, A., Kersten, M.L., Windhouwer, M.: Querying XML documents made easy: nearest concept queries. Proceedings of the 17th International Conference on Data Engineering, pp. 321–329 (2001)
46. Souzis, A.: Building a semantic wiki. IEEE Intel. Syst. **20**(5), 87–91 (2005)
47. Tazzoli, R., Castagna, P., Campanini, S.: Towards a semantic wiki wiki web. Proceedings of the 3rd International Semantic Web Conference (2004)
48. Tran, T., Wang, H., Rudolph, S., Cimiano, P.: Top-k exploration of query candidates for efficient keyword search on graph-shaped (RDF) data. Proceedings of the 25th International Conference on Data Engineering, pp. 405–416 (2009)
49. Vagena, Z., Colby, L.S., Özcan, F., Balmin, A., Li, Q.: On the effectiveness of flexible querying heuristics for XML data. Proceedings of the 5th International XML Database Symposium, pp. 77–91 (2007)
50. Wang, H., Zhang, K., Liu, Q., Tran, T., Yu, Y.: Q2Semantic: a lightweight keyword interface to semantic search. Proceedings of the 5th European Semantic Web Conference, pp. 584–598 (2008)
51. Weiand, K.: Keyword-based querying for the social semantic web – the kwql language: concept, algorithm and system. PhD Thesis, University of Munich, Germany (2011)
52. Weiand, K., Kneißl, F., Lobacza, W., Furche, T., Bry, F.: PEST: Fast approximate keyword search in semantic data using eignevector-based term propagation. Information Systems **37**(4), 372–390 (2012)
53. Xu, Y., Papakonstantinou, Y.: Efficient keyword search for smallest LCAs in XML databases. Proceedings of the ACM SIGMOD International Conference on Management of Data, pp. 537–538 (2005)
54. Zhou, Q., Wang, C., Xiong, M., Wang, H., Yu, Y.: SPARK: adapting keyword query to semantic search. Proceedings of the 6th International Semantic Web Conference and 2nd Asian Semantic Web Conference, pp. 694–707 (2007)

Chapter 8
Semantic Link Discovery over Relational Data

Oktie Hassanzadeh, Anastasios Kementsietsidis, Lipyeow Lim,
Renée J. Miller, and Min Wang

8.1 Introduction

From small research groups to large organizations, there has been tremendous effort
in the last few years in publishing data online so that it is widely accessible to a
large community. These efforts have been successful across a number of domains
and have resulted in a proliferation of online sources. In the field of biology, there
were 1, 330 major online molecular databases at the beginning of 2011, which is 96
more than a year earlier [14]. In the Linking Open Data (LOD) community project
at the W3C, the number of published RDF triples has grown from 500 million in
May 2007 to over 28 billion triples in March 2011 [29].

Fueling this data publishing explosion are tools for translating relational and
semistructured data into RDF. Translation tools try to faithfully translate the

Part of this work has appeared in Proceedings of the 18th ACM Conference on Information and
Knowledge Management [17]. ©2009 Association for Computing Machinery, Inc. Reprinted by
permission.

O. Hassanzadeh (✉) · R.J. Miller
University of Toronto, Toronto, Ontario, M5S 3G4, Canada
e-mail: oktie@cs.toronto.edu; miller@cs.toronto.edu

A. Kementsietsidis
IBM T.J. Watson Research Center, 19 Skyline Drive, Hawthorne, NY 10532, USA
e-mail: akement@us.ibm.com

L. Lim
University of Hawaii at Manoa, 1680 East West Road, POST 303E, Honolulu, HI 96822, USA
e-mail: lipyeow@hawaii.edu

M. Wang
HP Labs China, Beijing, China
e-mail: min.wang6@hp.com

R. De Virgilio et al. (eds.), *Semantic Search over the Web*,
Data-Centric Systems and Applications, DOI 10.1007/978-3-642-25008-8_ 8,
© Springer-Verlag Berlin Heidelberg 2012

structure and semantics of data. Relational data are often designed to ensure the data remain consistent by minimizing redundancy. Warehouse data may be designed to facilitate aggregation on specific dimensions of interest to a business. Semistructured data are often designed to facilitate data exchange. No matter what the *source* model, data translations typically result in data that are dirty (e.g., from duplicate, incorrect, or invented values due to partial/missing mappings), and RDF translation is no exception. To make matters worse, it is rare that organizational data are designed to facilitate Web-scale data sharing. Hence, many of these data sources, when published as RDF, may be missing internal semantics (links between data values) that would assist in using them effectively as part of the Semantic Web. And rarely do these data sources contain sufficient semantics to connect them with other Semantic Web resources.

To enhance the usability of published data, we need to be able to create referential links between data both within a data source and between different sources. These links should have a known and specified semantics. Of course, discovering such links requires the use of both approximate matching (to overcome syntactic representational differences and errors) and semantic matching (to find specific semantic relationships). These two types of matching must be used in concert to accommodate the tremendous heterogeneity found in Web data and to accommodate for errors or missing semantics within a data source.

In spite of their importance, research in discovering such semantic links has mainly focused on a more restricted version of the problem, namely, on *entity resolution* [11, 23], i.e., the identification of entities that represent the same *real-world* entity. Techniques for finding more general semantic relationships may make use of natural language semantics to improve the precision of information extraction [1], but tend not to apply robustly to structured data on the Web. The importance of discovering such links is also highlighted by the LOD project, where a number of tools and frameworks have been developed that allow the generation and publication of linked data from relational databases. Examples of such frameworks include D2RQ [7], Triplify [3], and OpenLink's Virtuoso [12]. Although these frameworks simplify the process of translating and publishing linked data, they do not provide a link discovery mechanism so that data publishers can establish links to external sources (or find implicit internal links). For typical users, this means they must manually experiment with a myriad of different link discovery methods to find one that suits their needs.

In this chapter, we present LinQuer, a generic and extensible framework for integrating link discovery methods over relational data. The goal of this framework is to facilitate experimentation and help users find and combine the link discovery methods that will work best for their application domain. To ease experimentation, the framework is declarative and permits the interleaving of standard data manipulation operators with link discovery.

The LinQuer framework permits the discovery of links within and between relational sources using LinQL, an extension of SQL that integrates querying with link discovery. LinQL includes a variety of native link discovery methods and is extensible to additional methods, written in SQL or as user-defined functions (UDF).

This permits users to interleave declarative queries with interesting combinations of link discovery requests. The link discovery methods may be syntactic (approximate match or similarity functions), semantic (using ontologies or dictionaries to find specific semantic relationships), or a combination of both.

In this chapter, we show that by integrating ad hoc querying and a rich collection of link discovery methods, the LinQuer framework supports rapid prototyping, testing and comparison of link discovery methods. A common way to use this framework would be to declaratively specify a portion of the data of interest (over which accuracy can be assessed) and to invoke one or more link discovery methods. The accuracy of the results can be evaluated by a user or an automated technique, and the specification of the link method can be interactively refined to produce better results.

Often, link discovery algorithms are implemented using general programming languages by third-party developers, and are automatically invoked with arguments defined through the declarative specification. For data publishers, these programs act as *black-boxes* that sit outside the data publishing framework and whose modification requires the help of their developers. The LinQuer framework addresses these shortcomings by leveraging native SQL implementations for a number of link discovery algorithms. This approach has several advantages: (a) this framework can be easily implemented on existing relational data sources with minimum effort and without any need for externally written program code; (b) we can take advantage of the underlying DBMS query engine optimizations while evaluating the SQL implementations of the linkage methods; and (c) we can support efficiency and functionality enhancements (e.g., a link index) to improve the efficiency and accuracy of linking algorithms.

We also show how the declarative invocation of linkage methods permits users to tune linkage methods and their performance. The native support for methods permits customization where domain knowledge is available. We give examples where domain knowledge can be specified in the database and used to greatly enhance the performance of the discovery process. Finally, we describe a case study of how this framework can be used to discover links over real clinical trial data drawn from a number of disparate Web sources.

The rest of the chapter is organized as follows. Section 8.2 introduces our running example, while Sect. 8.3 describes how links between data sources can be specified declaratively and Sect. 8.4 describes the linkage methods that LinQuer provides natively. Section 8.5 presents the algorithms for translating the link specifications into SQL queries. Our experimental study is described in Sect. 8.6. Section 8.7 highlights related work and we conclude in Sect. 8.8.

8.2 Motivating Example

In this chapter (and in our case study in Sect. 8.6), we use an example from the health care domain drawn from a set of real-world data sources. One such source is a clinical trials database which includes the sample relation in Fig. 8.1a. For each trial, the *CT* relation stores its identifier *trialid*, the *cond*ition considered, the suggested *inter*vention, as well as the *loc*ation, *city*, and a related *pub*lication. Another source stores patient electronic medical records (EMR) and includes a patient visit relation *PV* (Fig. 8.1b), which stores for each patient visit its identifier *visitid*, the *diag*nosis, recommended *prescr*iption, and *location*. Finally, we consider a Web source extracted from DBpedia [6], which stores information about drugs and diseases and includes the *DBPD* and *DBPG* relations (Fig. 8.1c, d) that store the *name* in DBpedia of diseases and drugs, respectively.

We now describe briefly some types of links users and data publishers may like to discover between these sources. For the *CT* and *PV* relations, we note that the *cond*ition column in the *CT* relation is semantically related and can be linked to the *diag*nosis column in the *PV* relation. Such links may be useful to clinicians since they associate a patient's condition with related clinical trials, and might be used to suggest alternative drugs or interventions. In Fig. 8.1, patient visit "VID770" with diagnosis "Thalassaemia" in the *PV* relation may be linked to the trial "NCT00579111" with condition "Hematologic Diseases" since "Thalass*a*emia" is a different representation of "Thalassemia" and according to the NCI medical thesaurus [24] "Thalassemia" *is a type of* "Hematologic Diseases." As this example illustrates, a clinician may be interested in not only *same-as* relationships, but also hyponym relationships such as *type-of*. Similarly, note that the *inter*vention column in the *CT* relation can be linked to the *prescr*iption column in the *PV* relation. Such links can provide evidence for the relevance and effectiveness of a drug for a particular condition. For example, both patient visits in Fig. 8.1b may link to trial "NCT00336362" (Fig. 8.1a) based on the fact that "hydroxycarbamide," "Hydroxyura," and "Hydroxyurea" all refer to the same drug.

Additional links are possible if one considers the existence of links between the locations of patients and the presence of clinical trials in these locations. As an example, "Westchester Med. Ctr" from visit "VID777" could link to "Columbia University" based on geographic proximity. Another interesting link discovery scenario arises when a user who is interested in a particular trial, wants to find other related trials based on certain criteria, for example, the similarity of the title and

trialid	cond	inter	loc	city	pub
NCT00336362	Beta-Thalassemia	Hydroxyurea	Columbia University	New York	14988152
NCT00579111	Hematologic Diseases	Campath	Texas Children's Hospital	Austin	3058228

(a) Clinical trials (*CT*)

visitid	diag	prescr	location
VID770	Thalassaemia	Hydroxyura	Texas Hospital
VID777	PCV	Hydroxycarbamide	Westchester Med. Ctr

(b) Patient visit (*PV*)

name
Thalassemia
Blood_Disorders

name
Alemtuzumab
Hydroxyurea

(c) DBpedia Disease   (d) DBpedia Drug
      (*DBPD*)   (*DBPG*)

Fig. 8.1 Sample relations

authors of the trials' corresponding publications. Obviously, to be effective, links should be tolerant of errors and differences in the data, such as typos or abbreviation differences.

Data publishers often build online Web-accessible views of their data. In such settings, they often want to provide links between their data and those in other online Web sources. As an example, a Web source of clinical trials requires links to other Web sources related to the trials like, say, the DBpedia or YAGO [25] sources. In our sample relations, the above example translates into finding links between the *cond* and *inter* columns of *CT* and the *name* column of the *DBPD* and *DBPG* relations, respectively. The online trials data source can link the condition "Hematologic Diseases" to DBpedia resource (or Wikipedia page) on "Blood_Disorders," and link the intervention "Campath" to DBpedia resource "Alemtuzumab" using the semantic knowledge that "Campath" is the brand name for the chemical name "Alemtuzumab." In our work, we will focus on the implementation, evaluation, and testing of link discovery methods. We will be agnostic as to how the discovered links are published. A user can create his or her own identifiers for a specific semantic relationship (e.g., brandNameOf) or reuse identifiers for common relationships (e.g., owl:sameAs).

8.3   The LinQL Language

In this section, we introduce the LinQL language. LinQL extends SQL with constructs that allow declarative specification of methods and requirements for linking values or records in an RDBMS. We show several features of LinQL, how it can be used to define linkage methods, how the methods can be used inside an SQL statement for link discovery, and how indices can be defined to speed up linkage discovery.

Figure 8.2 shows the main constructs of the LinQL grammar (the full grammar can be found elsewhere [30]). A *link specification*, or *linkspec* for short, defines the conditions that two given values must satisfy before a link can be established between them. As shown in Fig. 8.2, a CREATE LINKSPEC statement defines a new linkspec and accepts as parameters the name of the linkspec, the linkage method, and its parameters. LinQL provides several *native* (or *built-in*) linkage methods including semantic (synonym and hyponym), and a variety of syntactic (string matching) similarity measures. See more details on the native methods in the following section. Native methods can be used as such, or they can be customized through parameters.

Example 8.1. A common string similarity measure that has been shown to have good accuracy and efficiency is the token-based weighted Jaccard measure [16]. Like all our methods based on similarity, this method takes a similarity threshold θ as input. Only pairs of values with similarity over θ will be output as a link. The weighted Jaccard is a measure of set similarity over the set of tokens in two strings. A token is either a substring of length q (an input parameter to the method) or a word (when $q = 0$). This measure is supported by LinQL as a native linkage method

```
linkspec_stmt:= CREATE LINKSPEC linkspec_name
                AS link_method opt_limit;

linkindex_stmt:= CREATE LINKINDEX opt_idx_args
                 linkindex_name ON table(col)
                 USING native_method;

link_method:= native_method | link_clause_expr | UDF;

native_method:= ( synonym | hyponym | string_method ) opt_args;

string_method:= jaccard | weightedJaccard | cosine | bm25 | hmm | ··· ;

link_clause_expr:= link_clause AND link_clause_expr
                 | link_clause OR link_clause_expr
                 | link_clause;

link_clause:= LINK source WITH target
              USING link_terminal opt_limit;

link_terminal:= native_method | UDF opt_args | linkspec_name;

opt_limit:= LINKLIMIT number;
```

Fig. 8.2 The LinQL grammar (Version 1.1)

called `weightedJaccard`. A user can create a link specification using this measure by setting the parameters used in the similarity computation. For example, he or she may set the threshold parameter to 0.5, tokenize using q-grams of size 2, and set the maximum string length to 50, creating the following link specification:

```
CREATE LINKSPEC myJaccard1
AS weightedJaccard (0.5, 2, 50);
```

Now this link specification can be used as a join predicate in queries by any user. Notice that this specification does not indicate processing constraints.

A link specification can also be defined in terms of *link clause expressions*. These are Boolean combinations of link clauses, where each link clause is semantically a Boolean condition on two columns and is specified using either (a) a native method; (b) a user-defined function (UDF); or (c) a previously defined linkspec.

Example 8.2. Consider a setting in which a link between two values is established if a semantic relationship (e.g., synonymy or hyponymy) exists between these values in an ontology. This scenario commonly occurs in a number of domains, including health care, where sources are free to use their own local vocabularies (e.g., diagnosis and drug names) as long as these vocabularies can eventually be matched through a commonly accepted ontology (e.g., the NCI thesaurus [24]). Assume that the ontology is stored in table *ont* with concept IDs in column *cid* and terms in *term*.

The following linkspec illustrates the power of link clauses. It creates a link between two values *src* and *tgt* if their corresponding terms in an ontology are synonyms of each other. In the linkspec, the `weightedJaccard` native method (customized as in the previous example) is used to match the values to corresponding terms in the ontology (accounting this way for possible syntactic errors in the values). Then, the corresponding terms are tested for synonymy through the `synonym` native method.

```
CREATE LINKSPEC mixmatch
AS LINK src WITH tgt
   USING synonym(ont,cid,term) LINKLIMIT 10
   AND
   LINK src WITH ont.term
   USING myJaccard1 LINKLIMIT 10
   AND
   LINK ont.term WITH tgt
   USING myJaccard2 LINKLIMIT 10;
```

Clearly, semantic links are not necessarily one-to-one and, in general, a value from one relation can be linked to more than one value from a second relation. For example, it is common for drugs to have more than one name. Therefore, while a drug appears as *"aspirin"* in one relation it might appear as *"acetylsalicylic acid"* or *"ASA"* in another. When multiple such links are possible, users may (optionally) limit the number of such links and only consider k results, or the *top-k* where ordering is possible. The LINKLIMIT essentially specifies the value of this k parameter.

Example 8.3. In the previous example, while defining the mixmatch linkspec, LINKLIMIT is set equal to 10, for all three link clauses. Hence, only the top 10 links are considered in each method.

The previous examples consider the *local* version of the LINKLIMIT construct that is associated with a particular clause. The LinQL grammar also includes a *global* LINKLIMIT construct that is associated with the whole CREATE LINKSPEC statement. This can be thought of as a postprocessing filter of the links returned by the linkspec methods used in the statement.

Another feature of LinQL is supporting Boolean valued user-defined functions (UDFs). In the next section, we discuss in detail the differences and advantages of native linkage methods over UDFs. Here, we just mention that a distinguishing characteristic of the two is that the former are implemented in SQL, while the latter are not. UDFs essentially provide (desirable) extensibility to the LinQuer framework since the framework can incorporate new or existing linkage methods that either have not been implemented yet in SQL or cannot be implemented in SQL at all.

Example 8.4. Suppose a user writes a UDF that implements his or her own similarity function. This UDF, `myLinkUDF(thr, delC, insC, subC)`, returns true only

if the value of edit similarity (a popular string similarity measure [11]) of the values
on which it is applied is above the threshold value `thr` (where `delC`, `insC`, and
`subC` are the costs of delete, insert, and substitute operations, respectively). Then,
the following linkspec can use that UDF as follows:

```
CREATE LINKSPEC myLink
AS myLinkUDF(0.5, 1, 1, 1);
```

So far, we have only looked at how linkspecs are defined. We now show how
linkspecs are used inside queries.

Example 8.5. In the sample relations of Fig. 8.1, suppose we want to find links
between the diagnosis of patient visit with id 1234 and the condition of a trial in
the clinical trials relation *CT* that is located in New York city, using the native
`weightedJaccard` method with default parameter values as the linkspec. Then, the
following query can be used:

```
SELECT PV.*, CT.*
FROM    visit PV, trial CT
WHERE   PV.visitid = 1234 AND
        CT.city='New York' AND
        LINK PV.diag WITH CT.cond
        USING weightedJaccard LINKLIMIT 10;
```

Notice that the linkspec here is essentially defined *inline*. For more complex
linkspecs, or for situations where the same linkspec is used multiple times by one or
more users, the query can refer to a previously defined linkspec in a similar fashion.
This is a way for a DBA to provide a set of specifications for methods using the *best*
parameter settings for different domains, making these methods more accessible to
less expert users who may not know how to set the parameters. For example, in the
query above, we can use the `mixmatch` linkspec instead of the weightedJaccard, as
follows:

```
SELECT PV.*, CT.*
FROM    visit PV, trial CT
WHERE   PV.visitid = 1234 AND
        CT.city='New York' AND
        LINK PV.diag WITH CT.cond
        USING mixmatch LINKLIMIT 10;
```

For cases where a linkspec is used many times over a possibly large set of records,
LinQL allows definition of an index (or linkindex) over columns for specific linkage
methods. These indices can significantly lower query execution times.

Example 8.6. Consider the previous example, and assume that we would like to improve the performance of the `weightedJaccard`-based linking. We can do that by issuing the following LINKINDEX statements which create indices appropriate for the particular linking method:

```
CREATE LINKINDEX FOR visit.diag USING weightedJaccard;
CREATE LINKINDEX FOR trial.cond USING weightedJaccard;
```

8.4   Native Linkage Methods

In what follows, we discuss the generic link finding primitives that are *necessary* to effectively discover links in *real-world scenarios*. We show that LinQL not only can accommodate these primitives, but also supports them in the form of *native* linkage methods. We show how these native methods are translated into standard SQL queries in the next section.

8.4.1   Similarity Functions as Linkage Methods

Over many domains, there is a natural notion of similarity. Any similarity function $sim(v1, v2)$ that quantifies how close two values within a domain are can form the basis of a linkage method. Some similarity functions are asymmetric, in which case we will refer to the first argument as the *base* and the second as the *target*. Any similarity function together with a similarity threshold θ can be used as a linkage method. In such a method, there is a link between two input values if their similarity score, returned by function $sim()$, is above θ. The right value of the threshold depends on the characteristics of the dataset, the similarity function, and the application. The user can find a good value for the threshold for each application by trying different thresholds and evaluating the accuracy of (a subset of) the links that result.

8.4.2   String Similarity Functions

In publishing data on the Web, string data have a special prominence. String data are prone to several types of inconsistencies and errors including typos, spelling mistakes, use of abbreviations or different conventions. Therefore, finding similar strings, often referred to as approximate (or fuzzy) string matching (or approximate join) [8], is an important feature of a link discovery framework.

There exist a variety of similarity functions for string data in the literature. The performance of a similarity function usually depends on the characteristics of data, such as length of the strings, and the type of errors and inconsistencies present in the data. As stated earlier, in LinQuer we are interested in algorithms that are fully expressible in SQL (the benefits of which are well known [15, 16]). There are additional benefits of this choice for this framework. Specifically, the use of SQL as an implementation language for linkage methods permits on-the-fly calculations of the similarity scores that can be enhanced dynamically to increase the functionality of the matching algorithm by relying on characteristics of the domain of the source and target relations. Moreover, custom indexing techniques can be used to speed up the query execution time.

A popular class of string similarity functions is based on tokenization of the strings into q-grams, i.e., substrings of length q of the strings. By using q-gram tokens, we can treat strings as sets of tokens, and use a set similarity measure as the measure of similarity between the two strings. Furthermore, q-gram generation, storage and set similarity computation can all be done in SQL. This makes the following class of functions suitable for this framework:

- Size of the *intersection* of the two sets of q-grams, i.e., the number of common q-grams in the two strings.
- *Jaccard similarity* of the two sets of q-grams which is the size of the intersection divided by the size of the union, i.e., the percentage of common q-gram tokens between the two strings.
- Weighted version of the above measures. The weight of each q-gram is associated with its *commonality* in the base (or target or both) data sources. The higher the weight of a q-gram, the more important the q-gram is. For example, when matching diagnosis across medical sources, q-grams for commonly occurring strings like "Carcinoma" or "Cancer" should have low weights so that the value of the similarity function for the strings "Renal cell carcinoma" and "Squamous cell carcinoma" is small, compared to that for the strings "Renal cell carcinoma" and "Renal cell cancer."

The other string similarity measures suitable for this framework include methods derived from relevance functions developed for documents in information retrieval, namely Cosine with tf-idf, Okapi-BM25, Language Modeling and Hidden Markov Models [16]. There are several other string similarity measures including but not limited to edit similarity, Jaro, Jaro-Winkler, SoftTFIDF, and Generalized Edit similarity [9, 16]. These functions can be implemented using a UDF. In this chapter, we only focus on the above q-gram-based set-similarity measures and refer the readers to the project's online documentation page for a list of all supported linkage methods [30].

8.4.2.1 Token Weight Assignment

To assign weights to q-gram tokens, we use an approach inspired by the Inverse Document Frequency (IDF) metric in information retrieval. IDF weights reflect the commonality of tokens in documents with tokens that occur more frequently in the documents having less weight. So, by analyzing (offline) the q-gram token frequency, we assign less weight to common tokens like "Disorder" or "Cancer" in a medical source. As a functionality enhancement, we also let the user manually specify or adjust the weights of some tokens in a user-defined table. These weights override the automatically assigned (IDF-based) weights for these tokens. Manual weight adjustment is useful in applications where the user has prior knowledge about the importance of some tokens. For example, when matching diagnosis across sources, the user knows that often the use of numbers plays a more important role in the diagnosis than the name of the disease itself. So, by assigning a very low (or negative) weight to numbers, wrong matches between highly similar strings like "Type 1 Diabetes" and "Type 2 Diabetes" can be avoided. Similarly, when matching conditions (e.g., "Diabetes", "Cancer") from an online source such as WebMD to their corresponding entries in, say, Wikipedia, the conditions in Wikipedia might include the term "(disease)" to disambiguate the disease from other terms with the same name (e.g., "Choreia" is a medical disorder, but also an ancient Greek dance), although "disease" may not occur very frequently over all disease names (since most disease names are unique). Knowing this, the user can adjust the weight of the token "disease" to increase the likelihood of a correct link.

8.4.3   Semantic Matching Methods

Link discovery between values often requires the use of domain knowledge. In a number of domains, there are existing, commonly accepted, semantic knowledge bases that can be used to this end. In domains where such semantic knowledge is not available, users often manually define and maintain their own knowledge bases.

A common type of such semantic knowledge is an ontology. In the health care domain, well-known ontologies such as the NCI thesaurus [24] are widely used and encapsulate a number of diverse relationship types between their recorded medical terms, including, synonymy, hyponymy/hypernymy, etc. Such relationship types can be conveniently represented in the relational model and (recursive) SQL queries can be used to test whether two values are associated with a relationship of a certain type [21]. Therefore, semantic knowledge in the form of ontologies can be seamlessly incorporated in LinQuer and used for the discovery of links. So, while considering links between two sources, semantic knowledge can be used to link a diagnosis on "Pineoblastoma" to one on "PNET of the Pineal Gland," since the two terms are synonyms of each other. Similarly, a diagnosis on "Brain Neoplasm" can be potentially linked with both of the previous diagnoses, since the latter term is a hypernym of the former terms. Semantic matching is an important complement to string matching and both can enhance the recall of link discovery.

8.4.4 Indexing for Native Linkage Methods

As mentioned earlier, the main goal of the LinQuer framework is to provide genericity, extensibility, and ease of use for linkage methods. To achieve scalability without sacrificing these goals, LinQuer provides a set of indexing techniques for native linkage methods within the framework that depending on the linkage method and application can be used during query evaluation to improve performance. These techniques rely on preprocessing strategies based on the specific linkage methods that will be used on specific columns. A basic strategy is materialization and indexing of parts of the similarity score calculation algorithms to avoid repetition. For string matching, additional indexing and hashing techniques can be used for the above-mentioned string similarity predicates. Examples of such techniques include the all-pairs indexing algorithms of Bayardo et al. [4], the *Weighted Enumeration* (WTENUM) signature generation algorithm [2], and *Locality Sensitive Hashing* [20].

8.5 From LinQL to SQL

In what follows, we describe the main algorithm for translating a LinQL query to an SQL query, and then describe the algorithm for implementing each native linkage method. At the end, we discuss the effect of LINKINDEX definitions on the implementation of the linkage methods.

Algorithm LINQL2SQL translates a single LinQL query to an SQL query (or script) by first splitting the LinQL query into a base query Q_{base} (which is in SQL) and a link clause expression which is a Boolean expression in disjunctive normal form (DNF) over a set of link clauses. The algorithm LINKCLAUSEEXPR2SQL considers each disjunction in the link expression creating an SQL query for each and then returns the SQL UNION ALL of these queries. Within a disjunct, the link clauses are applied in order by calling LINKCLAUSEEXPR2SQL for each conjunct. Note that the rewritings applied by LINKCLAUSEEXPR2SQL are specific to the type of link clause used (native or UDF) and these rewriting may not be commutative. In Example 8.2, instead of applying the mixmatch linkspec, a developer could have directly used an approximate string link specification (via weightedJaccard or another method) and then applied a semantic ontology linking. This may yield different results than a query that applies the ontology linking first followed by approximate string linking over the ontology terms. In the former case, data terms must match the ontology exactly, in the latter case the linking with the ontology will be tolerant of string errors.

Note that we assume that before running the LinQL query statement, the linkspec and linkindex statements are processed and loaded into a system definitions repository. LINKCLAUSE2SQL parses a link clause to determine what type of link terminal is used. If the link terminal is a UDF, we simply add an invocation of the

UDF (and its parameters if any) in the where clause of the SQL base query. If the link terminal is a native method, we rewrite the SQL base query using the rewrite rules associated with that particular native method. If the link terminal is a reference to a named linkspec, we retrieve the associated linkspec statement from the system definitions repository and parse the associated link method. The link method can be a UDF, native method or link clause expression. UDFs and native methods are translated as described previously. Link clause expressions are translated by a recursive call to the LINKCLAUSEEXPR2SQL sub-routine. The recursion stops when either a UDF or a native method is encountered.

The main translation logic is in the rewriting rules associated with the native methods. A native method's rewriting rules are specified in two parts: view definitions and link conditions. For example, the rewriting rules for the weightedJaccard native method on column *col1* of table *tab1* and column *col2* of table *tab2* consist of the view definitions *tab1col1tokens*, *tab1col1tokenweights*, *tab1col1weights*, *tab1col1sumweights*, *tab2col2tokens* that are needed for similarity score calculation, view definition *scores* for score calculation, and the link conditions *scores.col1=tab1.col1 AND scores.col2=tab2.col2* and additional conditions depending on the similarity threshold, the value of LINKLIMIT and those given by the user. The use of the view definition syntax here is purely for readability. In practice, the SQL queries associated with the view definitions can be inlined into the actual query itself (resulting in a possibly hard to read query). The WITH statement supported by some DBMS (including the DMBS we used, IBM DB2) is another means for inlining some of the view definitions. Depending on the application, one

---

Algorithm 15: The LINQL2SQL Algorithm

---

input : LinQL query L
output: SQL query Q

$lce \leftarrow$ extract link clause expression in DNF from L;
$Q_{base} \leftarrow L - lce$;
$Q \leftarrow$ LINKCLAUSEEXPR2SQL(Q_{base}, lce);
return Q;

Algorithm 16: The LINKCLAUSEEXPR2SQL Algorithm

---

input : An SQL base query Q_{base}, a link clause expression lce
output: SQL query Q

$i \leftarrow 0$;
forall *disjuncts D in lce* **do**
   $Q_i \leftarrow Q_{base}$;
   foreach *next link clause l in D* **do**
      $Q_i \leftarrow$ LINKCLAUSE2SQL(Q_i, l);
   $i \leftarrow i + 1$;
% final query is the SQL 'UNION ALL' of all Q_i ;
$Q \leftarrow \cup_i Q_i$;
return Q;

Algorithm 17: The LINKCLAUSE2SQL Algorithm

---

input : A SQL base query Q_{base}, a link clause l
output: SQL query Q

$Q \leftarrow Q_{base}$;
if *link_terminal(l) = UDF* **then**
  | add UDF invocation to where clause in Q;
else if *link_terminal(l) = native_method* **then**
  | rewrite Q using native_method's rewriting rules;
else if *link_terminal(l) = linkspec_name* **then**
  | get link_method from associated linkspec_stmt in system definitions repository;
  | **if** *link_method = UDF* **then**
  | | add UDF invocation (with the optional parameters) to where clause in Q;
  | **else if** *link_method = native_method* **then**
  | | rewrite Q using native_method's rewriting rules;
  | **else if** *link_method = link_clause_expr* **then**
  | | $lce \leftarrow$ get associated link_clause_expr;
  | | $Q \leftarrow$ LINKCLAUSEEXPR2SQL(Q_{base}, lce);

return Q;

---

may choose to materialize all or part of these views using LINKINDEX statements in order to speed up the query time. The rest of this section describes the rewriting rules used to implement some of the native linkage methods. We first present the SQL queries based on view definitions and then discuss the effect of linkindex definitions.

8.5.1 Approximate String Matching Implementation

The SQL rewriting of the native link specification for approximate string matching consists of three steps, namely, (1) the (creation of views for) tokenization of strings into q-grams or word tokens; (2) the gathering of statistics and calculation of token weights; and (3) the calculation of link scores based on the weights. In more detail:

Step 1: This step can be done fully in SQL using standard string functions present in almost every DBMS, or with the addition of small (efficient) UDFs. Assume a table *integers* exists that stores integers 1 to N (maximum allowable length of a string). The main idea is to use basic string functions SUBSTR and LENGTH along with the sequence of integers in table *integers* to create substrings of length q from the strings in column *col1* of table *table1* with primary key *tid1*. The following SQL code shows this idea for $q = 3$:

```
SELECT tid1 as tid, SUBSTR(col1,integers.i,3) as token
FROM   integers INNER JOIN table1
       ON integers.i <= LENGTH(col1) - 2
```

In practice, the string in *col1* is used along with UPPER() (or LOWER()) functions to make the search case insensitive. Also, the string is padded with $q-1$ occurrences of a special character not in any word (e.g., "$") at the beginning and end using the CONCAT() function. Similarly, the spaces in the string are replaced by $q-1$ special characters. In case of tokenization using word tokens a similar SQL-based approach can be used. At the end of this process, the token generation queries are declared as views to be used in the following steps.

Steps 2 and 3: These steps are partly native-method specific, so we present them through an example. In what follows, we use the weightedJaccard native method as an example.

*Example 8.7 (*weightedJaccard *native method).* The following LinQL query considers patient visit 1234 and finds (through weightedJaccard) the clinical trial records in New York City that match the visit condition:

```
SELECT  PV.visitid, CT.trialid
FROM    visit AS PV, trial AS CT
WHERE   PV.visitid = 1234 AND CT.city='NEW YORK' AND
        LINK PV.diag WITH CT.cond
        USING weightedJaccard
```

This specification is translated into the following SQL queries. Initially, three queries calculate the IDF weights for the tokens and the auxiliary views needed for the final score calculation:

```
CREATE VIEW visit_diagnosis_tokenweights AS
SELECT token, LOG(size - df + 0.5) - LOG(df+0.5) as weight
FROM   ( SELECT token, count(*) as df
         FROM     (SELECT * FROM visit_diagnosis_tokens
                   GROUP BY tid, token) f
         GROUP BY token ) D,
       ( SELECT count(*) as size
         FROM visit_diagnosis_tokens ) S

CREATE VIEW visit_diagnosis_weights AS
SELECT tid, B.token, weight
FROM   visit_diagnosis_tokenweights idf,
       (SELECT DISTINCT tid, token
        FROM visit_diagnosis_tokens B) B
WHERE  B.token = idf.token

CREATE VIEW visit_diagnosis_sumweights AS
SELECT      tid, sum(weight) as sumw
FROM        visit_diagnosis_weights
GROUP BY    tid
```

Then, the next query returns the links along with their final scores:

```
WITH    scores(tid1, tid2, score) AS (
        SELECT tid1, tid2,
               (SI.sinter/(BSUMW.sumw+QSUMW.sumw-SI.sinter))
               AS score
        FROM   (SELECT  BTW.tid AS tid1,QT.tid AS tid2,
                        SUM(BTW.weight) AS sinter
                FROM    (SELECT * FROM visit_diagnosis_
                        weights
                        WHERE visitid = 1234) AS BTW,
                        trial_condition_tokens AS QT
                WHERE   BTW.token = QT.token
                GROUP BY BTW.tid, QT.tid) AS SI,
               (SELECT  *
                FROM    visit_diagnosis_sumweights
                WHERE   visitid = 1234 ) AS BSUMW,
               (SELECT  Q.tid, SUM(BTW.weight) AS sumw
                FROM    trial_condition_tokens Q,
                        visit_diagnosis_tokenweights AS BTW
                WHERE   Q.token = BTW.token
                GROUP BY Q.tid ) AS QSUMW
        WHERE  BSUMW.tid=SI.tid1 and SI.tid2 = QSUMW.tid )
SELECT PV.visitid, CT.trialid, s.score
FROM   visit AS PV, trial AS CT, scores AS S
WHERE  PV.visitid = 1234 AND CT.city='NEW YORK' AND
       S.tid1=PV.visitid AND S.tid2=CT.trialid AND
       S.score>0.5
```

8.5.2 Semantic Matching Implementation

Assume that the synonym and hyponym data are stored in two tables *synonym* and *hyponym* with columns *src* and *tgt*. The column *src* contains *concept IDs* of the terms, and the column *tgt* contains the terms. This is a common approach in storing semantic knowledge, used in NCI thesaurus [24] and Wordnet's synonym sets (*synsets*) [22], for example. Alternatively, these data could be stored in a table *thesaurus* with an additional column *rel* that stores the type of the relationship, or it could even be stored in XML. In the case of XML, *synonym* and *hyponym* can be views defined in a hybrid XML relational DBMS such as DB2. For brevity, we limit our discussion to semantic knowledge stored as relational data, although the framework is easily extensible to other formats. We show the details of the SQL implementation of the synonym and hyponym native linkage methods in the following two examples.

Example 8.8 (synonym *Native Method).* The following LinQL query considers again patient visit 1234 but now uses synonyms to find matching clinical trials.

```
SELECT  PV.visitid, CT.trialid
FROM    visit AS PV, trial AS CT
WHERE   PV.visitid = 1234 AND CT.city='NEW YORK' AND
        LINK PV.diag WITH CT.cond
        USING synonym
```

This query is rewritten to:

```
SELECT  DISTINCT PV.visitid, CT.trialid
FROM    trial AS CT, visit AS PV, synonym AS syn
WHERE   PV.visitid = 1234 AND CT.city='NEW YORK' AND
        (src in (SELECT src
                 FROM synonym s
                 WHERE s.tgt = CT.cond))
        AND PV.diag = syn.tgt
UNION
SELECT  PV.visitid, CT.trialid
FROM    trial AS CT, visit AS PV
WHERE   PV.visitid = 1234 AND CT.city='NEW YORK' AND
        CT.cond = PV.diag
```

Example 8.9 (hyponym *Native Method*). The following LinQL query considers again patient visit 1234, but now uses hyponyms for the matching:

```
SELECT  PV.visitid, CT.trialid
FROM    visit AS PV, trial AS CT
WHERE   PV.visitid = 1234 AND CT.city ='NEW YORK' AND
        LINK PV.diag WITH CT.cond
        USING hyponym
```

This query is rewritten to:

```
WITH    traversed(src, tgt, depth) AS
        (SELECT src,tgt,1
        FROM    hyponym AS ths
        UNION ALL
        (SELECT ch.src, pr.tgt, pr.depth+1
        FROM    hyponym AS ch, traversed AS pr
        WHERE   pr.src=ch.tgt AND
                pr.depth<2 AND ch.src!='root_node'))
SELECT  distinct PV.visitid, CT.trialid
FROM    trial AS CT, visit AS PV, hyponym AS ths
WHERE   PV.id = 1234 AND CT.city ='NEW YORK' AND
        (src in (SELECT distinct src
                 FROM traversed tr
                 WHERE tr.tgt = CT.cond)) AND
        PV.diag = ths.tgt
```

Note that the hyponym depth is set to 2, but can be customized to any value.

8.5.3   Effect of Link Index Definitions

When a linkindex is defined for a column using a specific linkage method, the above rewriting algorithms will be modified with the goal of speeding up the query execution time at the expense of an extra (offline) preprocessing step. A common indexing strategy for all the native methods is basically materializing parts or all of the view definitions required in their implementation. For example, in the weightedJaccard implementation of Example 8.7, if a LINKINDEX is defined for *visit.diagnosis* (using the statement shown in Example 8.6), the following views are materialized: *visit_diagnosis_tokens*, *visit_diagnosis_weights*, *visit_diagnosis_tokenweights*, and *visit_diagnosis_sumweights*. Note that our initial translation algorithms create views in a way that allows effective materialization. For example, the view *visit_diagnosis_sumweights* is defined as an SQL query that simply calculates the sum of the weight of the tokens on-the-fly, only so that this calculation is avoided at run time when the views are materialized.

Depending on the DBMS, the views can be materialized manually by creating a table for each view definition, caching the results as a preprocessing step and keeping them fresh (possibly using triggers), or automatically using DBMS support for materialized views. For example, the views can be defined as materialized query tables (MQT) in DB2. Using the optional FULL argument, appropriate database indices are also defined over the target columns and their related (manually) materialized views (tables). Other more specific linkindex definitions are also possible depending on the linkage method, such as specific hash tables as discussed in Sect. 8.4.4. Refer to LinQuer's documentation page for a detailed description of the possible index definitions and their parameters for each native method [30] .

8.5.4   Other Enhancements

So far we have only discussed the core algorithms for translation of a simple LinQL query with no additional arguments. As discussed in previous section, LinQL allows definition of several *optional* arguments. Most of these arguments are link method-specific, and used for setting parameters such as the value of q for q-gram-based methods, the maximum length of the string, the similarity threshold, and the name of the ontology table and its columns. Another link method-specific argument is the name of a (manually created) weight adjustment table as described in Sect. 8.4.2.

Another type of optional argument is the linklimit argument. Although each native linkage method results in a distinct query which can be evaluated independently, when the user sets a global linklimit value, the queries of different native methods can *cooperate* to optimize performance by avoiding running potentially expensive linkage queries when there are already enough links returned to the user. To achieve such a cooperation, the LINKCLAUSEEXPR2SQL algorithm needs to be modified. A key assumption we make here is that the sequence of the specifications reflects their importance, i.e., the specification that appears first must be evaluated first. Therefore, a condition will be added at the end of each SQL code to limit the number of results returned (using, e.g., MySQL's LIMIT). Then, in Algorithm LINKCLAUSEEXPR2SQL, in addition to using UNION, another condition should be added at the end of each query (in the WHERE clause) to check for the number of links returned by the previous query. Note that this may result in performance gain if one subquery is not evaluated more than once, which is the case in most DBMSs.

8.6   Case Study

In this section, we illustrate the flexibility of the LinQuer framework by applying it in a variety of linkage scenarios. We use these scenarios to justify the choices we have made in developing LinQuer. These scenarios are built around an online database of clinical trials published on ClinicalTrials.gov [28]. This database is a registry of federally and privately supported clinical trials conducted in research centers all around the world. It contains detailed information about the trials, including information about the medical conditions associated with the trials, their eligibility criteria, and locations.

8.6.1   Datasets

The clinical trials database used in our experiments contains 111,227 trials. We retrieved the data in XML format, and transformed the data into relational (and RDF) using the xCurator framework [27], as a part of the LinkedCT project [18]. Other datasets that we used in our experiments include a database of patient visits or Electronic Medical Records (EMR), and a database of DBpedia [6] objects of type *disease* and *drug*. We also used the National Cancer Institute's (NCI) thesaurus [24] as a source of semantic information about medical terms. Detailed statistics on these datasets is shown in Table 8.1.[1]

Due to privacy issues associated with EMR data, our patient visits database is synthetic, generated using an extension of the UIS database generator [19] that picks diagnosis and prescription values from the NCI terms to fill the patient visits

---

[1]To make our example queries simple, we assume that the databases are denormalized and we have a single table for clinical trials (*trial*), a table storing patient visits (*visit*), and tables storing DBpedia disease (*dbpedia_disease*) and drug (*dbpedia_drug*) data. In reality, the database is normalized and these relations are decomposed into multiple relations.

Table 8.1 Dataset statistics

Dataset	Entity (*table.attribute*)	Count
Clinical trials	Trial (*trial.trialid*)	111,227
	Condition (*trial.condition*)	25,935
	Intervention (*trial.intervention*)	149,958
	Drug (*trial.drug_intervention*)	87,231
	Reference (*trial.reference*)	86,214
Patient visits	Visit (*visit.visitid*)	10,000
	Diagnosis (*visit.diagnosis*)	9,319
	Prescription (*visit.prescription*)	8,289
DBpedia	Disease (*dbpedia_disease.label*)	5,154
	Drug (*dbpedia_drug.label*)	4,658
NCI thesaurus	Concept (*ontology.conceptid*)	89,129
	Term (*ontology.term*)	246,511
	Synonym Relationship	244,192
	(*synonym.conceptid, synonym.term*)	
	Hyponym Relationship	99,553
	(*hyponym.conceptid, hyponym.term*)	

table. Our data generator also randomly injects a small amount of string error in the diagnosis field to resemble real EMR records. The error injected in the string resembles real errors and typos occurring in string databases, for example, replacing a character with an adjacent character on a keyboard, or swapping two characters or word tokens.

8.6.2 Effectiveness and Accuracy Results

In what follows, we describe several link discovery scenarios involving clinical trials. While the first scenario is described in more detail (including its intermediate steps and corresponding linkage specifications), for the other scenarios we only show the final results and only mention changes to preceding LinQL statements.

Case 1 (Linking patient visits to trial conditions) The objective here is to discover links to clinical trials that are related to the conditions of certain patients. For this study, we consider 1,000 random patients from table *visit*, where column *diagnosis* stores the condition associated with a patient's visit. The *trial* table stores the trial condition in its column *condition*. The records linked by a simple exact matching are obtained by the SQL query:

```
SELECT DISTINCT PV.visitid, CT.trialid
FROM    visit PV, trial CT
WHERE   PV.diagnosis = CT.condition
```

The query links only 46 out of the 1,000 patient visits records, each to an average of 90 trial records, resulting in 4,127 visit-trial links. The reason why only 5% of the patient visits are linked is that very different (string) representations of the same entities (conditions) are used in the two sources, while string errors in *diagnosis* values make the situation worse. As a next step, we try a string matching linkage method starting with a low similarity threshold (expecting this to give a high recall) using the following linkspec and query:

```
CREATE LINKSPEC weightedJaccard04
AS weightedJaccard (0.4, 2, 50)
```

```
SELECT PV.*, CT.*
FROM    visit PV, trial CT
WHERE   LINK PV.diagnosis WITH CT.condition
        USING weightedJaccard04
```

The user can now go through a small subset of the results obtained from the above query to estimate the precision of the returned links with respect to the similarity score. The accuracy of the links is subjective and depends on the application. In our scenario, for example, links from a visit record with diagnosis "Alpa Thalassemia" (misspelled record of "Alpha Thalassemia") to trials with conditions "Alpha Tha-lassemia," "α-Thalassemia," and "Thalassemia" should be considered correct and we would like to find them. However, linking to a trial with condition "Beta Tha-lassemia" is not a correct link for "Alpha Thalassemia" diagnosis. We obtained the following accuracy results for this scenario by investigating the results of the above query for 100 random distinct *diagnosis* values matched with *condition* values:

Threshold	Number of links	Accuracy (Precision)
0.70	22	91%
0.65	36	86%
0.60	63	84%
0.55	104	77%
0.50	182	66%
0.45	303	54%
0.40	579	40%

By choosing a high threshold of 0.70, 22 links are returned out of which 20 (91%) are correct. However, by choosing a threshold of 0.4, 579 links are returned (more than five links per diagnosis value in the 100 results), but only 231 (40%) of them are correct. Given these observations, a user can choose the appropriate threshold that works best for the specific linkage needs. For our example, we choose a threshold of 0.55 that returns on average almost one link per diagnosis value, and has a reasonable accuracy. Overall, we get 32,919 links for 421 (out of 1,000) distinct patient visits. Based on the above evaluation, we can estimate that around 324 (77%) of the visits will link correctly to a trial's condition.

The next step is to use the semantic information in NCI to improve the linkage using the LinQL query below:

```
SELECT DISTINCT PV.visitid, CT.trialid
FROM    visit PV, trial CT
WHERE   LINK PV.diagnosis WITH CT.condition
        USING synonym
```

Linking using semantic matching based only on synonyms results in 12,343 links from 130 distinct visits. Note that these links are all correct links since they are derived using accurate synonyms provided by the NCI thesaurus, and no further approximate string matching is performed at this stage. From these, 2,453 links from 15 distinct visits could not be found using exact or string matching.

Repeating the above query with hyponym linkage method for semantic matching based on hyponyms of depth 2 from NCI, results in 15,464 links from 60 visit records, out of which 14,571 links from 14 visit records could not be found in previous steps. Note that the number of discovered links per visit is much higher for the hyponym method when compared to the synonym or string matching methods. This not only shows the importance of the hyponym method but also illustrates its usefulness in situations like the current setup where trials refer to broad disease categories instead of specific disease names (e.g., "Blood Disorder" instead of "Beta-Thalassemia").

One reason for the relatively low total number of discovered links by the synonym and hyponym methods (linking only 173 out of the 1,000 visit records) is the errors present in the *diagnosis* values of the *visit* table. This calls for using a linkspec that combines semantic matching (e.g., synonym method) with string matching (e.g., weightedJaccard method). The LinQL code to do this is:

```
CREATE LINKSPEC mixmatch
AS LINK source WITH target
   USING synonym(synonym,conceptid,term)
   AND
   LINK source WITH synonym.term
   USING weightedJaccard (0.7, 2, 50)

SELECT DISTINCT PV.visitid, CT.trialid
FROM    visit PV, trial CT
WHERE   LINK PV.diagnosis WITH CT.condition
        USING mixmatch
```

Using a combined string and semantic matching results in 49,931 links from 363 distinct visits, 28,444 more links from 33 more visit records when compared with matching based on synonyms or string matching. In the above linkspec, we have chosen a higher similarity threshold for string matching which results in highly accurate links based on our manual verification of the results. Depending on the results of the above steps, the user can write a single query for the linkage needs specific to the application. Here, we choose to combine exact matching, string matching, semantic matching based on synonyms and hyponyms, and mixed semantic matching allowing string errors. This can all be expressed using the query below:

```
SELECT DISTINCT PV.visitid, CT.trialid
FROM    visit PV, trial CT
WHERE   LINK PV.diagnosis WITH CT.condition
        USING weightedJaccard
        OR
        LINK PV.diagnosis WITH CT.condition
        USING synonym
        OR
        LINK PV.diagnosis WITH CT.condition
        USING hyponym
        OR
        LINK PV.diagnosis WITH CT.condition
        USING mixmatch
```

The combined approach results in 73,387 links from 482 visit records to the related clinical trials. Overall, we have:

Method	Links #	Visits #
1. Exact match	4,127	46
2. String match	32,919	421
3. Synonym match	12,343	130
4. Hyponym match	15,464	60
5. Mixed match	49,931	363
Total (combined)	73,387	482

The above clearly illustrates that the LinQuer framework facilitates the fast development and testing of linkage methods. Since LinQuer is fully integrated with declarative querying, the accuracy (precision and recall) of linkage methods can easily be tested over small portions of the data, or over portions where a user knows what links he or she desires.

Case 2 (Linking prescriptions to trial interventions) Now consider a user who wishes to link patients who were prescribed a drug with *all* clinical trials that use that drug. To collect all these trials, the user will again need the results produced from a variety of algorithms. As in the previous case, we start with exact matching, try string matching and tune its threshold, and then use synonym, hyponym and the mixmatch linkspec defined above. For string matching using weightedJaccard method, we choose threshold 0.6 based on a similar manual inspection of a subset of the results. The table below summarizes the results obtained for linking 1,000 visit records to trials by matching prescription values of the visits to drug intervention values of trial records:

Method	Links #	Visits #
1. Exact match	1,323	93
2. String match	7,200	270
3. Synonym match	16,804	349
4. Hyponym match	145	12
5. Mixed match	20,730	399
Total (combined)	23,528	470

Notice that the synonym method is much more effective here (when compared to Case 1), in terms of both the number of records linked and the number of links per record. This is mainly due to the fact that the same drug can be listed under a variety of different names (brand names and scientific names), depending on the institution that performs the trial. Also notice that (like in Case 1) multiple methods do find the same links (the total number of links is less than the sum of the links returned by each method). However, each of the five methods is effective in finding links that cannot be found using any of the other methods. This is highly desirable since the goal is to link as many potential visit records as possible.

Case 3 (Linking trial conditions to DBpedia diseases) and *Case 4 (Linking trial interventions to DBpedia drugs)* In these scenarios, we are seeking links from the clinical trials' condition and interventions fields to the DBpedia disease and drug entities, respectively. Unlike the previous cases, assume here that the user only needs to link to a single DBpedia entity per each condition and drug. This makes sense since in most cases there should be a single record in DBpedia for a single disease (condition) or drug intervention in the trials data. Therefore, the user uses the LINKLIMIT 1 option in the LinQL query to limit the number of links. Then, when a link based on exact matching is found for a record, there is no need to look for approximate string or semantic matches for that record. This could potentially lead to a significant performance improvement.

The final linkage specification query for linking trial conditions to DBpedia diseases (table *dbpedia_disease*) is as follows. The query for trial interventions to DBpedia drugs is similar.

```
SELECT DISTINCT CT.condition, DBPD.uri
FROM   trial CT, dbpedia_disease DBPD
WHERE  LINK CT.condition WITH DBPD.label
       USING weightedJaccard
       OR
       LINK CT.condition WITH DBPD.label
       USING synonym
       OR
       LINK CT.condition WITH DBPD.label
       USING hyponym
       OR
       LINK CT.condition WITH DBPD.label
       USING mixmatch
       LINKLIMIT 1
```

Again we choose threshold 0.6 for `weightedJaccard` method based on investigation of the accuracy of the links for a random subset of the conditions. The table below summarizes the results for different steps of the linkage from 1,000 condition and drug interventions:

Method	Disease links#	Drugs links#
2. Exact match	22	239
3. String match	239	393
4. Synonym match	26	333
5. Hyponym match	46	0
5. Mixed match	101	347
Total	292	422

Notice the obvious need for allowing mixed string and semantic matching in these two cases. The trials source, NCI thesaurus and DBpedia/Wikipedia names all use different conventions and therefore there are cases where strings do not exactly match. For example, "Adenocarcinoma of Esophagus" in trials matches with "Carcinoma of Esophagus," synonym of "Esophageal Cancer" in the thesaurus which matches with "Esophageal_cancer" in DBpedia. Notice that though we are combining many methods, the LinQL LINKLIMIT 1 option allows us to (efficiently) return the best match for each record.

Case 5 (Finding related trials) To show the flexibility of the LinQuer framework, we investigate its effectiveness in a rather different scenario. In this case, the goal is linking trials that are related to each other. Different attributes and measures can be used to identify trials that are related. In this experiment, we use the *reference* attribute of the trials and consider two trials related if the title and authors of their associated references (publications) are similar. Our trials database stores references in a single long text record that includes the names of the authors, title of the paper, the conference or journal and the date of the publication. Therefore, in order to find similarity we do not have any relevant semantic information to exploit. Furthermore, we are not interested in typos and different representations of the same string here. Instead, the similarity function should measure the amount of co-occurrence of (important) words in the two strings. The following weightedJaccard linkspec performs linkage based on word tokens:

```
CREATE LINKSPEC wordTokenJaccard
AS weightedJaccard (0.7, 0, 100)
```

Using the linkspec over 10,000 random trials results in 667 links between these trials, whereas exact matching results in only seven links. Note that here we assume that similarity score above 0.7 between the reference strings indicates correlation between the trials, and we have verified that this assumption is reasonably accurate by manually going through a subset of the links.

8.6.3   Effectiveness of Weight Tables

In what follows, we briefly show the effectiveness of the functionality enhancement we proposed based on manual definition of a weight-adjustment table by the user. Assume that the user defines the following simple weight table:

String	Weight
"Syndrome"	0.4
"The"	0.1
"Disorder"	0.2
"Disease"	0.2

We repeat the experiment for Case 1 (linking to trial conditions from a database of patient visits) with updated weight tables based on the above input weight adjustment table. This results in lower weights for the tokens of the above strings in the weight tables (views) of *visit.diagnosis* and *trial.condition* columns. String matching with the same settings, i.e., using `weightedJaccard` similarity function with threshold 0.55 on 1,000 random base records, results in 121 additional links out of which 91 are correct (accuracy 75%) and drops 63 of the links found with no weight adjustments out of which 15 were wrong links. This means that overall, the linkage has resulted in 58 more links with roughly the same accuracy as the case with no adjustments.

Note that we obtained these results by choosing the weight adjustment values in the above simple table based only on our domain knowledge, and we have not varied the values to obtain the best results. What is more important is that we can use this extensible technique and leverage weight values to improve the accuracy of the link discovery, as a result of the SQL-based implementation method. The implementation of the weighted Jaccard similarity function and the above customization of weights using a UDF, rather than a native method, could be quite complex and inefficient.

8.6.4   Performance Results

Here, we report running times of the above examples to show the performance of the system. Note that since our focus in this chapter has been on the functionality of the framework, we have not applied specific hashing techniques (some of which we discussed briefly in Sect. 8.4) to improve efficiency. We also do not compare the benefits of possible indexing and hashing strategies. We ran the experiments on a Dell PowerEdge R310 Server with 24 GB memory and Intel X3470 Xeon Processor 2.93 GHz (8MB Cache, Turbo HT), running Ubuntu 10.04.3 LTS (64-bit), and IBM DB2 9.7 Data Server Trial Edition. To obtain statistical significance, we report the average time from several runs of each experiment.

We first report the running times for LINKINDEX statements over the attributes and linkage methods used in all the cases described in this section. For Case 1 (linking visits to trial conditions), for example, we define LINKINDEX over *visit.diagnosis*, *trial.condition* and *synonym.term* columns using weightedJaccard method as follows:

```
CREATE LINKINDEX FULL FOR visit.diagnosis USING weightedJaccard;
CREATE LINKINDEX FULL FOR trial.condition USING weightedJaccard;
CREATE LINKINDEX FULL FOR synonym.term USING weightedJaccard;
```

As stated earlier, the above statements translate into a set of preprocessing queries that materialize the views for tokenization and token weight calculation required for the final linkage queries. With the FULL argument, database indices are also built over the result tables. It is also possible to use the HALF option that will result only in materialization of the tokenization views. This is useful for more dynamic tables, and when the attribute is used only as target (and not source) in the LinQL queries, where token weights are not needed. Figure 8.3 shows the running time for tokenization queries (that materialize token views), weight table queries (that materialize token weight views), and the time for building database indices for token and weight tables, for all the attributes and linkage methods used in our study.

Notice that the overall preprocessing times are less than a minute for small tables, and a few minutes for larger ones. Word tokenization for references (case 5) takes the longest time due to the more expensive tokenization query and longer average string size (the average *reference* string length is 226, whereas as the average length of ontology terms is 25 characters).

	Tokenization Queries	Tokenization Indexing	Weight Table Queries	Weight Table Indexing	Total
trial.condition	3.4	66.1	9.0	69.5	148.0
trial.drug_intervention	9.7	146.1	113.1	119.0	387.9
visit.diagnosis	1.2	21.1	3.6	21.8	47.7
visit.prescription	0.7	12.8	4.5	12.2	30.2
dbpedia_drug.label	0.4	8.4	3.0	7.8	19.6
dbpedia_disease.label	3.6	21.5	6.2	15.6	46.9
trial.reference	58.7	547.7	43.6	696.7	1346.7
synonym.term	84.6	171.3	64.6	227.0	547.5

Fig. 8.3 Preprocessing (indexing) time (in seconds)

Other linkage methods can also take advantage of LINKINDEX definitions. For the hyponym method and a given depth, for example, the view for traversing the ontology tree can be materialized in advance. For our ontology table and for our cases (using depth 2), this can be done using the statement below, which takes just below 53 min to run. For the custom link method mixmatch over *visit.diagnosis*, for example, defining LINKINDEX FULL as shown below will result in materializing the scores view between the ontology terms and diagnosis values using the weightedJaccard method with the given parameters, which takes around 42 min in this case. Note that these are expensive preprocessing queries but can speed up running time significantly when the query needs to be repeated many times, and when the indexed relations do not change frequently. In our scenario, NCI thesaurus is updated monthly, and the clinical trials are updated once every night, which will allow enough time to repeat the preprocessing. Of course, better index update strategies can be used, and depending on the DBMS, the view materialization can be automated, using materialized query tables (MQTs) in DB2, for example.

```
CREATE LINKINDEX USING hyponym(hyponym,term,2);
CREATE LINKINDEX FULL FOR visit.diagnosis USING mixmatch;
```

The table below shows the running time (in seconds) for all the cases and linkage methods described in this section. Note that these are running times for batch processing of 1,000 base records in each case. The average running time of each method for linking a single record is under a second (a few milliseconds in most cases), which shows the suitability of the methods for online link discovery scenarios. Also note that due to the above LINKINDEX statements, hyponym and mixmatch methods take only slightly longer than the synonym method. The string matching, however, is the most expensive step. This calls for more advanced hashing and indexing strategies for larger databases (see Sect. 8.4 for a brief discussion).

	Case 1	Case 2	Case 3	Case 4	Case 5
Exact match	0.01	0.02	<0.01	<0.01	0.27
String match	187.10	240.20	38.32	16.97	672.23
Synonym match	0.12	0.22	0.13	0.11	N/A
Hyponym match	0.21	0.22	0.19	0.19	N/A
Mixed match	0.21	0.31	0.11	0.11	N/A

8.7   Related Work

In terms of the overall framework, the work described in this chapter is closely related to the work on declarative data quality and cleaning [5, 13, 16]. When compared with all the existing techniques in this area, a distinctive feature of the LinQuer framework is its focus on enabling the discovery of any type of semantic link, not just the *same-as* link that is the result of entity resolution or duplicate detection. Another closely related framework is the work of Das et al. [10], in which a set of SQL operators are proposed to support ontology-based semantic linking over relational data. A key advantage of the LinQuer framework is allowing string matching along with semantic matching which is crucial in many real-world scenarios. Moreover, the LinQL specification language allows the definition of new operators, which could be a mix of several semantic and string matching operators. Overall, LinQuer complements and extends the above-mentioned frameworks by providing a framework for fast prototyping and testing of semantic and syntactic matching for link discovery. LinQuer can clearly be used in combination with a nonrelational framework for link discovery such as SILK [26]. Whereas LinQuer discovers links over relational data *before* these are published as RDF, SILK focuses on the discovery of semantic links *after* the RDF publication occurs. Another key difference between the two systems is that while LinQuer is an extensible framework that employs several semantic and syntactic methods particularly suitable for string data, SILK offers a limited set of attribute-similarity measures that can be combined in various ways for link discovery.

As stated earlier, one of the main applications of the LinQuer framework is to enhance Web data publishing. There are many methodologies for generating RDF views over relational data. These methodologies are often based on declarative specification of the mapping between relational tables and RDF triples. These frameworks include, but are not limited to, D2RQ and D2R Server [7], Openlink Virtuoso [12], and Triplify [3]. The success of these tools motivates a similarly declarative framework for link discovery such as LinQuer so that the published data sources can be enriched internally and linked to other data sources to enhance data sharing.

8.8 Conclusion

In this chapter, we presented a declarative extensible framework for link discovery from relational data. We presented LinQL, an extension of SQL for specification of linkage requirements for linking relational records, along with the details of its implementation. We showed how this framework adopts and extends existing syntactic and semantic matching techniques, and described a few functionality enhancements specifically designed for this framework. We showed the effectiveness of this approach in several link discovery scenarios in a real-world health care application. Our focus in this chapter has been on efficient techniques that can handle large datasets, but also on usability. We showed how a user can interactively experiment with and customize different linkage methods to better understand what are the most effective methods for his or her domain. We believe that this framework can significantly simplify and enhance the process of publishing a high-quality data source with links to other data sources on the Web. A user/data publisher can use this framework to easily find the appropriate linkage algorithms for the specific domain, as well as the optimal value of the required parameters. Combined with an existing popular declarative approach for generating linked data on the Web such as D2R Server [7], this can lead to a quick and simple way of publishing an online data source with high-quality links. This will in turn enable or enhance effective semantic search over the data source and the Web of Data.

Acknowledgements This work has been partially supported by the NSERC Business Intelligence Network. Hassanzadeh has been supported by an IBM Graduate Fellowship. We thank Reynold S. Xin for implementation of the LinQuer API and Web interface, and improving the overall design of the system and the LinQL grammar.

References

1. Appelt, D.E.: Introduction to information extraction. AI Commun. **12**(3), 161–172 (1999)
2. Arasu, A., Ganti, V., Kaushik, R.: Efficient exact set-similarity joins. Proceedings of the International Conference on very Large Data Bases (VLDB), pp. 918–929 (2006)
3. Auer, S., Dietzold, S., Lehmann, J., Hellmann, S., Aumueller, D.: Triplify: light-weight linked data publication from relational databases. International World Wide Web Conference (WWW), pp. 621–630 (2009)
4. Bayardo, R.J., Ma, Y., Srikant, R.: Scaling up all pairs similarity search. International World Wide Web Conference (WWW), pp. 131–140. Banff, Canada (2007)
5. Bilke, A., Bleiholder, J., Böhm, C., Draba, K., Naumann, F., Weis, M.: Automatic data fusion with HumMer. Proceedings of the International Conference on very Large Data Bases (VLDB), pp. 1251–1254 (2005)
6. Bizer, C., Lehmann, J., Kobilarov, G., Auer, S., Becker, C., Cyganiak, R., Hellmann, S.: DBpedia – a crystallization point for the web of data. J. Web Semant. **7**(3), 154–165 (2009)
7. Bizer, C., Seaborne, A.: D2RQ – treating non-RDF databases as virtual RDF graphs. Proceedings of the International Semantic Web Conference (ISWC) (2004)
8. Cohen, W.W.: Data integration using similarity joins and a word-based information representation language. ACM Trans. Inf. Syst. **18**(3), 288–321 (2000)

9. Cohen, W.W., Ravikumar, P., Fienberg, S.E.: A comparison of string distance metrics for name-matching tasks. Proceedings of IJCAI-03 Workshop on Information Integration on the Web (IIWeb-03), pp. 73–78. Acapulco, Mexico (2003)
10. Das, S., Chong, E.I., Eadon, G., Srinivasan, J.: Supporting ontology-based semantic matching in RDBMS. Proceedings of the International Conference on very Large Data Bases (VLDB), pp. 1054–1065 (2004)
11. Elmagarmid, A.K., Ipeirotis, P.G., Verykios, V.S.: Duplicate record detection: a survey. IEEE Trans. Knowl. Data Eng. **19**(1), 1–16 (2007)
12. Erling, O., Mikhailov, I.: Virtuoso: RDF support in a native RDBMS. Semantic Web Information Management, pp. 501–519. Springer, Berlin, Heidelberg, New York (2009)
13. Galhardas, H., Florescu, D., Shasha, D., Simon, E., Saita, C.A.: Declarative data cleaning: language, model, and algorithms. Proceedings of the International Conference on very Large Data Bases (VLDB), pp. 371–380 (2001)
14. Galperin, M.Y., Cochrane, G.: The 2011 nucleic acids research database issue and the online molecular biology database collection. Nucleic Acids Res. **39**(Database-Issue), 1–6 (2011)
15. Gravano, L., Ipeirotis, P.G., Jagadish, H.V., Koudas, N., Muthukrishnan, S., Srivastava, D.: Approximate string joins in a database (almost) for free. Proceedings of the International Conference on very Large Data Bases (VLDB), pp. 491–500 (2001)
16. Hassanzadeh, O.: Benchmarking declarative approximate selection predicates. Master's Thesis, University of Toronto, Toronto, Ontario, Canada (2007)
17. Hassanzadeh, O., Kementsietsidis, A., Lim, L., Miller, R.J., Wang, M.: A framework for semantic link discovery over relational data. Proceedings of the Conference on Information and Knowledge Management (CIKM), pp. 1027–1036 (2009). URL http://dx.doi.org/10.1145/1645953.1646084
18. Hassanzadeh, O., Kementsietsidis, A., Lim, L., Miller, R.J., Wang, M.: LinkedCT: a linked data space for clinical trials. CoRR **abs/0908.0567** (2009)
19. Hernández, M.A., Stolfo, S.J.: The merge/purge problem for large databases. ACM SIGMOD international conference on the management of data, pp. 127–138 (1995)
20. Indyk, P., Motwani, R., Raghavan, P., Vempala, S.: Locality-preserving hashing in multidimensional spaces. ACM Symposym on Theory of Computing (STOC), pp. 618–625 (1997)
21. Kementsietsidis, A., Lim, L., Wang, M.: Supporting ontology-based keyword search over medical databases. Proceedings of the AMIA 2008 Symposium, pp. 409–13. American Medical Informatics Association (2008)
22. Miller, G.A.: WordNet: a lexical database for English. Commun. ACM **38**(11), 39–41 (1995)
23. Naumann, F., Herschel, M.: An introduction to duplicate detection. Synthesis Lectures on Data Management. Morgan and Claypool Publishers, Seattle, WA USA (2010)
24. Sioutos, N., de Coronado, S., Haber, M.W., Hartel, F.W., Shaiu, W., Wright, L.W.: NCI thesaurus: a semantic model integrating cancer-related clinical and molecular information. J. Biomed. Inform. **40**(1), 30–43 (2007)
25. Suchanek, F.M., Kasneci, G., Weikum, G.: YAGO: a large ontology from Wikipedia and WordNet. J. Web Semant. **6**(3), 203–217 (2008)
26. Volz, J., Bizer, C., Gaedke, M., Kobilarov, G.: Discovering and maintaining links on the web of data. Proceedings of the International Semantic Web Conference (ISWC), pp. 650–665 (2009)
27. Yeganeh, S.H., Hassanzadeh, O., Miller, R.J.: Linking semistructured data on the web. Proceedings of the International Workshop on the Web and Databases (WebDB) (2011)
28. ClinicalTrials.gov, A Service of the US National Institutes of Health – http://clinicaltrials.gov/ (2011). Accessed 28 July 2011
29. State of the LOD Cloud. Version 0.2. http://www4.wiwiss.fu-berlin.de/lodcloud/state/ (2011). Accessed 28 July 2011
30. The LinQuer Project - http://purl.org/linquer (Accessed 28 July 2011).

Chapter 9
Embracing Uncertainty in Entity Linking

Ekaterini Ioannou, Wolfgang Nejdl, Claudia Niederée, and Yannis Velegrakis

9.1 Introduction

The modern Web has grown from a publishing place of well-structured data and HTML pages for companies and experienced users into a vivid publishing and data exchange community in which everyone can participate, both as a data consumer and as a data producer. Unavoidably, the data available on the Web became highly heterogeneous, ranging from highly structured and semistructured to highly unstructured user-generated content, reflecting different perspectives and structuring principles. The full potential of such data can only be realized by combining information from multiple sources. For instance, the knowledge that is typically embedded in monolithic applications can be outsourced and, thus, used also in other applications [10]. Numerous systems nowadays are already actively utilizing existing content from various sources such as WordNet or Wikipedia. Some well-known examples of such systems include DBpedia, Freebase, Spock, and DBLife.

A major challenge during combining and querying information from multiple heterogeneous sources is *entity linkage*, i.e., the ability to detect whether two pieces of information correspond to the same real-world object [19, 28]. The task is also important in data cleaning applications [13] and can be found in the literature under different names, such as merge-purge [23], entity identification [29], deduplication [33], data matching [8,15], reference reconciliation [17], or resolution [5]. This topic

E. Ioannou (✉)
Technical University of Crete, University Campus – Kounoupidiana, 73100 Chania, Greece
e-mail: ioannou@softnet.tuc.gr

W. Nejdl · C. Niederée
L3S Research Center, Appelstr. 9a, 30167 Hannover, Germany
e-mail: nejdl@L3S.de; niederee@L3S.de

Y. Velegrakis
University of Trento, Via Sommarive 14, 38123 Trento, Italy
e-mail: velgias@disi.unitn.eu

R. De Virgilio et al. (eds.), *Semantic Search over the Web*,   225
Data-Centric Systems and Applications, DOI 10.1007/978-3-642-25008-8_9,
© Springer-Verlag Berlin Heidelberg 2012

has received considerable research attention with many interesting results relying on different methodologies, such as string similarity metrics [8, 9], entity inner-relationships [17, 27], and clustering [7].

Unfortunately, existing approaches for entity linkage assume that data are relatively static. Thus, they typically perform data processing off-line in order to have the results readily available at query time. To achieve this, existing approaches first collect matching evidence, such as similarities between the entity strings or inner-relationships between entities, and based on them, generate information to link the entities, then use predefined thresholds or human intervention to merge the entities. Queries are processed over the resulted merged entities. In modern Web applications, where data may at any time change not only their syntax or structure but also their semantics [35], these techniques are so effective or efficient [19]. This calls for entity linkage techniques that consider and deal with the special characteristics of such data.

This chapter introduces a novel approach for addressing the entity linkage problem for heterogeneous, uncertain, and volatile data. In the following paragraphs, we present the motivation for this work (Sect. 9.1.1), followed by a discussion of the related challenges (Sect. 9.1.2). We then provide an overview of the approach introduced in this chapter (Sect. 9.4), summarize its contributions (Sect. 9.1.4), and finally present the structure of the chapter (Sect. 9.1.5).

9.1.1 Motivation

Consider a system created for monitoring and integrating data from multiple heterogeneous data sources on the Web. The basic data exchange unit of the system is an entity, composed of an identifier and a number of attribute name–value pairs describing the properties of the real-world object the entity represents.

The first part of Fig. 9.1 illustrates three entities existing in the system. The top two entities are referring to the story of Harry Potter and the Chamber of Secrets. The first entity has been extracted through text analysis of Wikipedia articles. Since entity extraction from text is not always accurate, the extracted entity attributes are accompanied with some probabilities reflecting the amount of confidence on the existence of these attributes. In the figure, this confidence is illustrated by the numbers next to the attribute values. The second entity has been extracted from a set of online bookstore databases. A number of these databases contain outdated or inconsistent data; thus, the attributes of the entity are also probabilistic. Finally, the third entity has been extracted by a corpus of news archives. For reasons similar to those of the first entity, its attributes have also some confidence associated with them.

Since the system needs to handle volatile data, we expect continuous appearance of new entities and these entities that need to be integrated with the data already present in the system. The second part of Fig. 9.1 illustrates two additional entities, which the system needs to integrate. Similar to the entities already existing in the

title:	Harry Potter and the Chamber of Secrets	0.6
starring:	Daniel Radcliffe	0.7
starring:	Emma Watson	0.4
writer:	J.K. Rowling	0.6
genre:	Fantasy	0.6

title:	Harry Potter and the Chamber of Secrets	0.8
genre:	Fantasy	0.8
writer:	J.K. Rowling	0.7

name:	International Business Machines	0.9
base:	New York	0.7
date:	2002	0.7

....existing entities

title:	Harry Potter and the Chamber of Secrets	0.7
date:	2002	0.8
starring:	Daniel Radcliffe	0.5
starring:	Emma Watson	0.9

codename:	The Big Blue	0.8
location:	California	0.5

new entities

Fig. 9.1 A small fraction of new entities that should be integrated with the entities already existing in the system. Entities are modeled as a set of attributes, i.e., name–value pairs, each with some confidence value that indicates our belief that this attribute describes the specific entity

system, these two entities are also modeled as a set of attribute name–value pairs, each with some confidence value.

A traditional entity linkage methodology [19] would simply use a predefined threshold and accept the merging of these entities when their computed similarity is above this threshold. For the entities of Fig. 9.1, this might mean merging the first two entities. In this situation, a new entity would be created using the data from both entities, which might also involve the removal of some name–value pairs when these are considered as redundant, conflicting, or replicas.

There are two main issues with the traditional entity linkage methodologies. The first is that the system will return no results if asked to return an entity described using some of the attributes that were removed during the merging. The second is that the arrival of a new entity might cause the system to get into a stage that does not accurately reflect reality, since the system is now limited to two options: either decide that the new entity describes the same real-world object as one of those that already exist in the system or that the new entity is not among the already existing entities. This unfortunately ignores the possible options that would arise from reviewing any of the previous merging decisions. As an example, consider a system that has previously performed a merging between entities e_a and e_b, and that it now needs to process the new entity e_c. Merging entity e_c with e_a might provide a better solution than merging it with the previously merging of e_a with e_b. An alternative methodology for considering all possible options would of course be to maintain the original entities and, at each addition, reexecute an entity linkage technique over the original entities, ignoring the results from previous executions. Unfortunately, this approach has a prohibitively high computational cost, which means that it cannot be applied.

9.1.2 Challenges

To create an effective and efficient solution for the entity linkage problem, we need to consider the characteristics as well as the resulting challenges that appear in the scenarios we are focusing on (Sect. 9.1.1). This can be summarized as follows:

Challenge 1—Volatile Data. Collections created by combining data from various Web applications or extracted data describing resources may constantly change and evolve through interactions with users or external applications. Therefore, the knowledge available to the entity linkage techniques is subject to data reduction, addition, and modification. This implies the need for supporting an incremental computation and adaptation of the linkage information.

Challenge 2—Heterogeneous Information. Effectively addressing the entity linkage problem implies the ability to handle highly heterogeneous data. Dealing with heterogeneity is a task that touches a number of aspects. For instance, the data model for the entities should be able to also capture the possible data heterogeneity. In addition, we need to consider that we are using an entity linkage technique that handles heterogeneous information. The most common methodology to detect entity linkages is based on observing similarities between the attribute values from the entities. However, this assumes that entities describing the same real-world objects would have the same, or at least similar, attribute values. Another methodology relies on identifying and facilitating semantic information, such as relationships between the entities. For example, coauthoring relationship in publications increases the belief that two authors describe the same object. Our solution should therefore allow the combination of results generated by various entity linkage techniques, as a way to capture different linkage methodologies.

Challenge 3—Data Uncertainty. Apart from the uncertainty in the linkage information, data uncertainty also appears for other reasons. One example is data uncertainty that comes directly from the extraction process due to the very low quality that typically accompanies the unstructured data of such applications [21]. Another example is the uncertainty introduced when building structures for processing the data, e.g., social network analysis [1]. These approaches typically affect the quality of data, which is then reflected through probabilities. Unfortunately, incorporating uncertainty in a system may break a number of assumptions that many entity linkage techniques rely upon. Thus, performing entity linkage over uncertain data is a major challenge.

9.1.3 Summary of the Approach

The methodology we follow takes into consideration heterogeneity, uncertainty, and the volatile nature of the data. It is based on maintaining the linkage information among the entities. As an example, let us consider the entities in Fig. 9.1. It is easy to see that the first two entities may represent the same real-world object, for instance, the first entity may represent the actual movie, whereas the second entity is a DVD with the respective movie. Given that we do not have enough evidence to support a definite decision on whether these entities represent the same real-world object or not, we do not perform a merging between them. We compute and store a probabilistic linkage connecting the two entities. The addition of the new entities requires only the computation of the linkages or (in some cases) the recomputation of the probability of existing linkages.

Figure 9.2 illustrates the computed linkages through the interconnecting dotted lines and alongside their probabilities. As depicted in the figure, these entities have three probabilistic linkages, two among the movie entities that are labeled e_1-e_3, and one among the company entities that are labeled as e_4 and e_5. Once we reach a final decision that two or more entities are linked, we can replace them by an equivalent entity consisting of the union of their attributes.

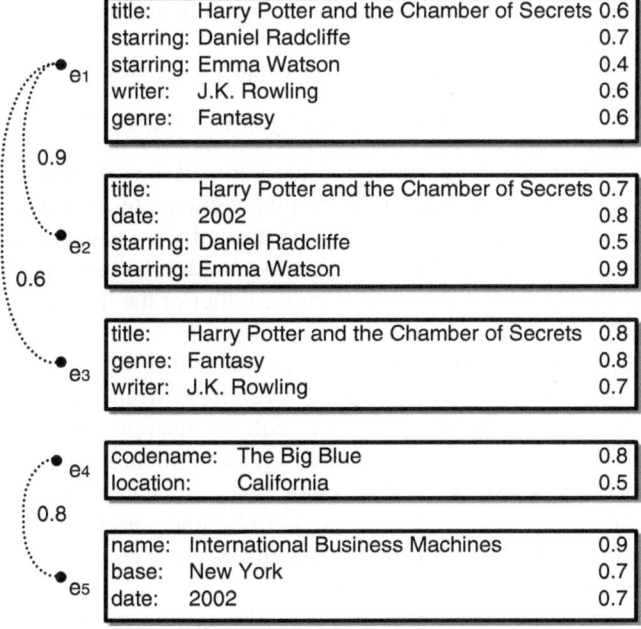

Fig. 9.2 Entities and their probabilistic linkage information, which is shown with the *dotted lines*

Consider now a user looking for the IBM consulting corporation. As is typically the case in dataspaces [22], queries are expressed as a series of attribute name–value pairs. Thus, the user sends the following query to the system:

$$\langle name = \text{``International Business Machines''}, base = \text{``New York''}\rangle$$

Clearly among the five entities e_1, e_2, e_3, e_4, and e_5, only the fourth satisfies these two conditions. Of course, since the attributes of the specific entity exist with some uncertainty, specified by the respective probabilities, the existence of the entity in the query answers should also be probabilistic. A significant amount of research has been carried out in the area of the probabilistic databases [12] on specifying the semantics and on the development of efficient query answering techniques for this kind of scenarios.

Assume now that a user is interested in the works of J.K. Rowling in the year 2002. He sends to the system the following query:

$$\langle writer = \text{``J.K. Rowling''}, year = \text{``2002''}\rangle$$

None of the three entities in Fig. 9.2 contain both attribute name–value pairs as specified in the query; thus, any probabilistic database approach will return an empty set as an answer. However, the linkage information between entity e_1 and e_2 indicates that they may represent the same real-world object. If they do, then they can be both merged into one entity, say e_{12} that contains as attributes the union of the attributes e_1 and e_2. That entity will satisfy both the conditions of the last query and should be part of the answer set, even though it is not one of the three entities that are actually stored in the repository.

In a similar situation, assume that the user sends the query:

$$\langle writer = \text{``J.K. Rowling''}, genre = \text{``Fantasy''}\rangle$$

Answer to the query should take into consideration all the different cases that may exist based on the entity linkages. In particular, a complete answer should contain three entities, namely, entity e_1, entity e_3, and the entity e_{13} which is the merging of entities e_1 and e_3. Each of these entities should of course be in the answer set of the query with some degree of belief, based on the belief of the linkages and the belief of the attributes *writer* and *genre*.

The answer set for this query could also contain entities e_{12} and e_{123}, which are created by the merging of entity e_2 with e_1, and entity e_2 with e_1 and e_3, respectively. Included in the merging, the attributes of e_2 will create entities that have additional attributes, such as *date = 2002*. We consider such additional attributes as redundant, since the user did not request them through the query. Our basic principle is that we do not want to produce results that are not required, and therefore, no merging should take place unless it is justified by the query given by the user, the linkages, and the attributes composing the entities.

Our approach creates the entity mergings by using available entity linkages. Since the linkages are probabilistic, for an effective query mechanism, we need to take into consideration all the different combinations that may occur. Each such combination will partially contribute to the answer set. However, materialization of all combination will lead to exponential increase of the data, which is inefficient to generate and store. Instead, query processing at runtime takes into consideration the related probabilistic linkages; computes the different combinations, along with their respective probability of existence; and then generates the answer set by merging the data produced from each combination.

9.1.4 Contributions

The main focus of this chapter is to efficiently and effectively address the entity linkage problem as this appears in heterogeneous, uncertain, and volatile data. This is achieved by allowing data integration systems to maintain probabilistic linkage information and perform entity-aware query processing over the data and thus retrieve answers to queries that reflect the corresponding real-world objects. This methodology avoids pitfalls that may result from the one-time a priori merging decisions, as performed by traditional entity linkage techniques. Furthermore, it can support highly volatile data more efficiently. The reason is that since no merging decisions have taken place, the only updates required are on the linkages related to new data incorporated in the system, or modified data.

In an effort to address the entity linkage problem for volatile data, we introduce a model for representing entities and linkages that aims at bringing together two worlds: the world of entity linkage and the world of probabilistic databases. The novelty of this data model is that it uses a generic entity-based representation model for highly heterogeneous data that support the simultaneous representation of possible linkages between entities alongside the original data, as generated by a number of the existing entity linkage techniques. This means that no data merging is performed in advance, but the outcome of the entity linkage algorithms, i.e., the pairs of entities possibly representing the same real-world object with the belief of that being true, is stored in the data. The outcome is a database that contains uncertainty not only on the attributes of the entities but also on their linkages.

Relying on the introduced model that contains a set of probabilistic linkages, we introduce a methodology to efficiently compute the answers for entity queries . Query answers reflect the entity linkage and entity representation information, with special emphasis given to the computation of the probabilities of the possible worlds based on the data and the matching uncertainty.

Generating entities by combining probabilistic linkages has several benefits. First, it produces additional valid query answering results compared to those of entity linkage and probabilistic databases, which cannot be simulated with previous techniques. An interesting feature is that reasoning about the entity linkages is done on the fly, meaning that some query results may not be explicitly represented in the database but might be a product of the reasoning which is based on the data as well as on the query conditions, i.e., by considering the union of all the attributes of the structures to be merged with corresponding probabilities [36].

9.1.5   Organization

The remaining of this chapter is structured as follows. Section 9.2 presents and discusses existing approaches that are related to the techniques presented in this chapter. Section 9.3 introduces and explains the data model, which includes the representation of entities and linkages, as well as the mechanism for dealing with data uncertainty. Section 9.4 explains the mechanism for dealing with probabilistic linkage information through on-the-fly entity-aware query processing. Section 9.5 reports on our experimental evaluation performed on two real-world datasets. Finally, Sect. 9.6 provides conclusions and provides an overview of current and future work.

9.2   Related Work

Most existing techniques for entity linkage focus on the off-line detection and linkage of data referring to the same real-world objects [14,19,20]. These techniques deploy a variety of different methodologies and directions. These includes string similarity metrics [8, 9] for computing the matching being the given textual representations of entities, the use of the available inner-relationships between the entities [17, 27], clustering [7], and blocking techniques [30, 31] for reducing the required execution time. However, as already explained in Sect. 9.1, these techniques have major limitations in addressing the entity linkage problem as this appears in current data [19], e.g., data evolution, uncertainty, and incompleteness.

Few existing data integration proposals focus on dealing with uncertain linkage information during query processing. More specifically, Dong et al. [18] investigate the use of the probabilistic mappings between the attributes of the contributing sources with a mediated schema. Applying this method on the data from Sect. 9.1.1 would have considered the possible mappings between the attribute names as given by contributing sources with a mediated schema S. This means that "title" attribute of e_1, e_2, and e_3 is mapped to a "Title" attribute from S with a probability to show the uncertainty of each mapping. Querying the mediated schema S will be based on these mappings. For example, query "title = Harry Potter..." returns e_1, e_2, and e_3. However, it does not really reflect the expected answer, since we know that some of the entities are the same, and thus they should be merged accordantly. In fact, the probabilistic schema mappings described in this approach could actually become an input to our approach.

The approach presented in [3] is more similar to ours, since their focus is not on the schema information but on the actual data. The authors assume that the duplicate tuples for each entity are given. In our motivating example (Sect. 9.1.1), this means that all tuples which describe the same entity should have the same identifier, e.g.,:

Identifier	Entity	Probability
5	e_1	p_1
5	e_2	p_2
5	e_3	p_3

The tuples that represent different entities are considered as independent and the tuples representing the same entity (having the same identifier) as conditionally dependent. The latter means that only one tuple for each identifier can be part of the results. Our proposal does not require this. We explain how entity linkages can contain correlations and provide an appropriate solution.

Other related approaches are dataspaces [22] and Trio [2]. The main focus of these approaches is to create database systems that support uncertainty along with inconsistency and lineage. At some extent, these systems also deal with duplicate tuples and uncertain data. Our approach addresses more challenges of heterogeneous data, mainly by considering linkage/matching on the data (not only on schema information), and also correlations between entities.

Another important aspect of our approach is the efficient management of uncertainty in data; a topic that has received a lot of attention recently. Dalvis and Suciu [11] used the notion of possible worlds to introduce query semantics for independent probabilistic data and presented how to efficiently evaluate queries. The approach by Sen et al. [34] moved towards defining and using different correlations, e.g., that existence of one tuple implies or disallows the existence of another tuple.

9.3 Data Model

To effectively model highly heterogeneous information, we need a simple and flexible model that will be able to represent relational, XML, RDF, and object-oriented data without significant loss of information. We have chosen to go with a graph-based model that is typically used in dataspaces [22]. The main component of the model is an entity which consists of a number of attributes describing its characteristics and a set of associations between the entities. In particular, we assume the existence of an infinite set of entity identifiers $\mathcal{O}$, names $\mathcal{N}$, and atomic values $\mathcal{V}$. An entity is a design artifact used to model a real-world object. It consists of a unique entity identifier and a set of attributes. An *attribute* is a pair $\langle n, v \rangle$ of a name and a value and describes some characteristic of the entity. The set $\mathcal{A} = \mathcal{N} \times \mathcal{V}$ represents the infinite set of all the possible attributes.

Definition 9.1. An *entity e* is a tuple $\langle id, A \rangle$ called the *entity identifier* of the entity and $A \subseteq \mathcal{A}$ is a finite set called the set of *entity attributes*. ∎

Since each entity is distinguished by its unique identifier, for the rest of the document, the term entity and entity identifier will be used interchangeably.

Entity identifiers can be considered a special type of atomic values, allowing identifiers to serve as the value of an attribute. Through this mechanism, the data model is able to support not only entities and their characteristics but also relationships among them.

A database is a set of entities. Among these entities, there may be groups modeling the same real-world object but using a different or overlapping set of attributes. Such entities are said to be *linked*.

Definition 9.2. A *database* is a tuple $\langle \mathcal{E}, \mathcal{L} \rangle$, where $\mathcal{E}$ is a finite set of entities and $\mathcal{L}$ is a linkage assignment on $\mathcal{E}$. A *linkage assignment* over a set E is a binary relation $L \subseteq E \times E$ that is commutative, symmetric, and reflexive. Two entities $e_1, e_2 \in \mathcal{E}$ of a database $\langle \mathcal{E}, \mathcal{L} \rangle$ are said to be *linked* and is denoted as $e_1 \equiv e_2$ if $(e_1, e_2) \in \mathcal{L}$. A maximal group of entities that are pairwise linked forms a *factor*. ∎

It is important to note that a linkage assignment can be equivalently expressed either through an explicit statement of the binary relationships or through a set of groups of entities, with each such group representing a factor. For instance, given six entities $e_1, e_2, \ldots, e_6$, the set $\{\{e_1, e_2, e_3\}, \{e_4, e_5\}, \{e_6\}\}$ describes a linkage assignment with three factors. The first factor consists of entities e_1, e_2, and e_3; the second contains e_4 and e_5; and the third contains only e_6. The set of linkages are the set of all the pairwise links in each factor.

Since linked entities in a database represent the same real-world object, they can be replaced by a new entity that combines the information described by them. (Note that linked entities may have different, or even disjoint, sets of attributes) This process is referred to as *entity merge* and leads to more compact database representations without losing any information. A database in which no merge can be performed is said to be *minimal*.

Definition 9.3. The *merge* of a set of entities $e_i = \langle id_i, A_i \rangle$ for $1 \leq i \leq n$, denoted as $merge(e_1, e_2, \ldots, e_n)$, is a new entity $\langle id, A \rangle$ such that id is a new identifier and $A = \cup_{i=1}^{n} A_i$. The *minimal* form of a database $\langle \mathcal{E}, \mathcal{L} \rangle$ is a database $\langle \mathcal{E}', \mathcal{L}' \rangle$, where $\mathcal{L}' = \emptyset$ and $\mathcal{E}' = \{e | e = merge(e_1, e_2, \ldots, e_n) \wedge \{e_1, e_2, \ldots, e_n\}$ is a factor in $\langle \mathcal{E}, \mathcal{L} \rangle\}$. ∎

To capture the uncertainty that may exist on the data, every attribute of an entity is associated with a value between 0 and 1, which indicates a likelihood that the information described by the attribute is among the characteristics of the real-world object that the entity models. Uncertainty exists also on the linkage information among the entities. Thus, we extend the definition of the database to include this uncertainty.

Definition 9.4. A *probabilistic linkage database* is a tuple $\langle \mathcal{E}, \mathcal{L}, p^a, p^l \rangle$, where $\mathcal{E}$ is a set of entities and $\mathcal{L}$ is a linkage assignment on $\mathcal{E}$. p^a is a function that assigns a probability weight to the attributes of the entities, i.e., $p^a | B \mapsto [0, 1]$ with $B = \{a | a \in A \wedge \langle id, A \rangle \in \mathcal{E}\}$. p^l is also a function that assigns a probability weight to the entity linkages, i.e., $p^l | \mathcal{L} \mapsto [0, 1]$. ∎

Note, that our notion of a probabilistic database goes beyond the traditional probabilistic database [12] that simply associates probabilities with attributes, by assigning probabilities also to linkage relationships that exist among the entities.

Example 9.1. Figure 9.2 illustrates a small fraction of a probabilistic linkage database. It contains a total of five entities; therefore, $\mathcal{E} = \{e_1, e_2, e_3, e_4, e_5\}$. The entity linkage techniques we executed on these five entities generated three entity linkages, and thus, $\mathcal{L} = \{l_{e_1, e_2}, l_{e_1, e_3}, l_{e_4, e_5}\}$. From the figure, we can also see the attributes composing the entities. For example, entity e_1 has five attributes, with the first attribute having a value "Harry Potter and the Chamber of Secrets" for the name "title". The probability for the specific attribute is 0.6, which corresponds to the belief we have that the specific attribute describes e_1. These probabilities are provided by function p^a. Similarly, function p^l provides the probabilities for the entity linkages, shown in the figure with the line between the entities. ∎

Having the right probabilities on the attributes of a probabilistic entity is a critical issue. One of the challenges is to understand the semantics of these probability numbers and to adequately use them to perform the merge. This task is challenging since very often, different algorithms may have been used to compute the probabilities for the attributes of different entities, or the employed algorithms may not be known. In certain cases, these numbers may not even be probabilities in the strict mathematical sense but rather numbers that are meant to provide a relative ranking of the likelihood of the respective attributes in the entity. This can make the computation of the query results even harder. The same issues arise on the linkage information. There is a large amount of literature on the topic of computing entity linkage [19], with most methods analyzing the structural similarity of the data and returning some numbers measuring the likelihood that two data structures represent the same real-world entity. All these issues are outside of the scope of the current paper. We assume that this information is explicitly provided or computed in advance using some data analysis tools [6].

A probabilistic linkage database models multiple different real-world situations, i.e., possible databases, depending on what entity linkages actually exist among the entities and on what attributes each entity actually has. To differentiate between the situations that arise from the different linkages, the notion of *possible l-worlds* is introduced (short for possible linkage worlds).

Definition 9.5. Given a probabilistic linkage database $\langle \mathcal{E}, \mathcal{L}, p^a, p^l \rangle$, a *consistent* linkage specification is a linkage assignment $\mathcal{L}^{sp}$ such that $\forall x, y \in \mathcal{L}^{sp}: x, y \in \mathcal{L} \wedge p^l(x, y)! = 0$. The probabilistic database with linkages $\langle \mathcal{E}, \mathcal{L}^{sp}, p^a, p^l_{sp} \rangle$, where $p^l_{sp}(x, y) = 1$, $\forall (x, y) \in \mathcal{L}^{sp}$, is called a *possible l-world*. The set of all the possible l-worlds of probabilistic database with linkages $\langle \mathcal{E}, \mathcal{L}, p^a, p^l \rangle$ is denoted as $plw(\langle \mathcal{E}, \mathcal{L}, p^a, p^l \rangle)$. ∎

Since a linkage specification uniquely defines a possible l-world (Definition 9.5), the terms "consistent linkage specification" and "possible l-world" will be used equivalently. Furthermore, we will consider only consistent linkage specifications; thus, we will not mention the word "consistent" any more.

Fig. 9.3 An illustration of
the linkage specification
$\mathcal{L}^{sp} = \{l_{e_1,e_2}, l_{e_4,e_5}\}$ for the
probabilistic linkage database
shown in Fig. 9.2

$\bullet e_{12}$

title:	Harry Potter and the Chamber of Secrets	0.6
starring:	Daniel Radcliffe	0.7
starring:	Emma Watson	0.4
writer:	J.K. Rowling	0.6
genre:	Fantasy	0.6
title:	Harry Potter and the Chamber of Secrets	0.7
date:	2002	0.8
starring:	Daniel Radcliffe	0.5
starring:	Emma Watson	0.9

$\bullet e_3$

title:	Harry Potter and the Chamber of Secrets	0.8
genre:	Fantasy	0.8
writer:	J.K. Rowling	0.7

$\bullet e_{45}$

codename:	The Big Blue	0.8
location:	California	0.5
name:	International Business Machines	0.9
base:	New York	0.7
date:	2002	0.7

Table 9.1 A summary of the notation introduced in Sect. 9.3 and used throughout this chapter

Notation	Description
$a_i = \langle n, v \rangle$	Attribute: a pair of name n and value v
$e_i = \langle id, A \rangle$	Entity: a tuple with an identifier id and a set of attributes A
l_{e_i,e_j}	Linkage: denotes a possible match between entity e_i with entity e_j
$\langle \mathcal{E}, \mathcal{L}, p^a, p^l \rangle$	Probabilistic linkage database
$plw(\langle \mathcal{E}, \mathcal{L}, p^a, p^l \rangle)$	Possible l-worlds of a probabilistic linkage database
$\mathcal{L}^{sp}$	Linkage assignment
f_i	Factor: a set pairwise linked entities

Example 9.2. Consider again the probabilistic linkage database of Fig. 9.2. The
entity linkage set is $\mathcal{L} = \{l_{e_1,e_2}, l_{e_1,e_3}, l_{e_4,e_5}\}$. One of the possible linkage specifications $\mathcal{L}^{sp} = \{l_{e_1,e_2}, l_{e_4,e_5}\}$, which means accepting the two out of the three
linkages of this original entity linkage set $\mathcal{L}$. As explained, each linkage we accept
implies a merge between the entities of the linkages. Therefore, the specific linkage
specification means we need to merge e_1 with e_2 and e_4 with e_5. The result is a
probabilistic database with linkages, as shown in Fig. 9.3.   ∎

In the remaining chapter, we will use the notation l_{e_1,e_2} as a shorthand for
$(e_1, e_2) \in \mathcal{L}$. A summary of the introduced notation, which is used throughout this
chapter, is listed in Table 9.1.

Note that a possible l-world still has probabilities assigned to the attributes of its
elements. The possible worlds of each possible l-world describe a number of nonprobabilistic databases, depending on whether each probabilistic attribute is present
or not. These nonprobabilistic databases are referred to as *regular database*, or a
solution. A solution actually corresponds to what is referred to as a possible world
in the probabilistic database literature [12].

For queries, a simple, but flexible, query language is adopted. A query is a series of attributes, i.e., a list of name–value pairs. Intuitively, the semantics of the query is to discover entities that contain the attributes described in its attribute list. An entity e is included in the answer of a query q if it contains all the requested attributes. Evaluating the query on a probabilistic linkage database can be performed on the basis of the traditional query answering approaches.

Using entity linkage, it is possible to go beyond this expressiveness and be able to retrieve new entities that may not be explicitly represented in the database. These entities result from the merge of two or more entities as specified by their linkage information. In particular, the results of evaluating a query q over a probabilistic linkage database with a linkage $\mathcal{L}$ is equal to the results of the evaluation of the query q over the minimal form of the database, as specified by the linkage assignment $\mathcal{L}$.

If the database is probabilistic, and a specific linkage assignment $\mathcal{L}$ has been decided, then its minimal form can be computed but will also be probabilistic, since the entity attributes will have probabilities. Evaluation of a query over such a database can be performed based on various techniques proposed for probabilistic databases [12]. However, if the linkage assignment is also probabilistic, as in the general case of a probabilistic database, then a query is evaluated over the database by computing all its possible worlds, i.e., all the possible linkage assignments, and then evaluating the query on the minimal form of each such worlds. The final result of the query will by the union of the results of the evaluations on the individual worlds. However, since the linkage information is probabilistic in the first place, so is the linkage assignment, and as a consequence, the results of each evaluation on the individual worlds should also be coming with some probability.

A fundamental property that differentiates our work from other work related to querying probabilistic data is that the query results are computed from entities that are compiled on the fly at query execution time from the available linkage information. The entities used in query evaluation thus consider entities that are not materialized in the repository in this form. In particular, traditional approaches evaluate the queries on the extensional data that can be found in the database. In our work, we view the probabilistic entity linkage as an intensional description of a number of possible entities that can result from the merge of those linked. We compute these entities through the possible worlds on the fly and offer additional query results.

Example 9.3. Consider again the probabilistic linkage dataset illustrated in Fig. 9.2 and the query:

$$\langle \text{starring:``Emma Watson'', starring: ``Radcliffe, Daniel''} \rangle$$

In can be observed that there is no entity with both the attributes requested by the query. Traditional query answering techniques would have failed to return results or would have returned with a low confidence, those having at least one of the two requested attributes. However, in the possible world described by the entity linkage $\{\{e_1, e_2, e_3, e_4, e_6\}, \{e_8, e_9\}\}$, the merge of the entities of the first of the two factors represents an entity with both the attributes requested in the query. Thus, such an entity can be returned with a much higher confidence. ∎

The following sections deal with the challenge of computing the right probabilities of the possible l-worlds and possible worlds, and performing query answering on the fly without having to materialize all them.

9.4   Efficient Query Evaluation

In this section, we present how query evaluation can be performed efficiently over a probabilistic linkage database. A more detailed description of the algorithm and experimental evaluation is available in [24] and [25].

Our query evaluation approach is based on an idea similar to the one incorporated in probabilistic databases for dealing with datasets of large sizes. In particular, the probability values on the linkages are interpreted as the probability distribution over the set of all the possible l-worlds $plw(\langle \mathcal{E}, \mathcal{L}, p^a, p^l \rangle)$. Given a linkage specification, i.e., a possible l-world, the probability values of the attributes are interpreted as the probability distribution over all the possible solutions (ref. Sect. 9.3) within one possible world leading to a two-level approach. The answer of a query on a probabilistic linkage database, thus, is the union of the answers over all the possible worlds of all the l-worlds fulfilling the query conditions. Each element in the answer set, however, is accompanied by an aggregated probability value which reflects the probability of existence of the specific possible world, which contains the answer element, as well as the probability of the possible l-world, which contains the respective solution.

This description of semantics for query answering is indirectly suggesting a query evaluation strategy: compute all possible worlds of all possible l-worlds, compute their probability of existence, evaluate the query in each one of them, and return the results along with computed probability. Unfortunately, following this approach is prohibitively expensive.

Here, we propose an alternative evaluation strategy that avoids the high computational cost without any loss of accuracy. The basic idea is to restrict the computation to only those possible l-worlds that are meaningful for the query at hand. Since there is a one-to-one correspondence between possible l-worlds and linkage specifications, and between linkage specifications and entity merges, we start from the entity merges that are required in order to generate an answer to the given query. From the merges, we can find the linkage specifications, and from these assignments, the possible l-worlds. The probability of each possible l-world is computed based on the probabilities of the linkages included or not included when generating the specific l-world. Finally, the possible worlds of each l-world are generated along with their own probability, which is combined with the probability of the respective world and then included in the answer set of the query. An overview of the proposed query evaluation is given by Algorithm 18, while the following subsections describe these steps of the algorithm in more detail.

Algorithm 18: Query evaluation

Input: Q: a query describing an entity
Output: R: a set of entities satisfying query conditions
$LS \leftarrow$ findRequiredLinkageSpefications(Q);
$PLW \leftarrow \emptyset$;
$R \leftarrow \emptyset$;
foreach $ls \in LS$ **do**
    $W \leftarrow$ findPossibleLWorlds(ls);
    foreach $w \in W$ **do**
        $w.prob \leftarrow$ calculateWorldLProbability(ls);
        $PLW \leftarrow PLW \cup \{w\}$;
    foreach $plw \in PLW$ **do**
        $E \leftarrow$ evaluateQuery(plw, Q);
        foreach $e \in E$ **do**
            $e.prob \leftarrow$ combineProb($e.prob$, $plw.prob$);
            $R \leftarrow R \cup \{e\}$;

9.4.1 Indexing Structure

A commonly used approach in answering queries over probabilistic data is to partition the data into a series of disjoint/independent groups [4, 12, 32, 34]. These groups can be found in the literature under the name factors [34] or components [4]. The set of the possible combinations between the data of these groups produces all the possible worlds.

This idea is not directly applicable to our case. The reason is that the existing approaches operate under the assumption that the data within one factor or component are independent. This assumption does not hold in our case. The transitive property of the linkages may generate additional correlation, i.e., dependencies, that are equally important for the correct identification of the possible worlds. For instance, entity linkages l_{e_1,e_2} and l_{e_1,e_3} without linkage l_{e_2,e_3} cannot be considered, since the first two linkages imply the information encoded in the third linkage.

We follow an idea similar to the management of uncertain data with correlations [34]. As a first step, we divide the set of entities into sets of connected components, i.e., factors (Definition 9.2). For example, given $\mathcal{L} = \{l_{e_1,e_2}, l_{e_1,e_3}, l_{e_2,e_3}, l_{e_8,e_9}\}$, two independent factors can be identified. The first factor contains entities e_1, e_2, and e_3 with linkages $L_1 = \{l_{e_1,e_2}, l_{e_1,e_3}, l_{e_2,e_3}\}$, while the second factor contains simply e_8 and e_9 with one linkage $L_2 = \{l_{e_8,e_9}\}$.

To compute all possible l-worlds of a probabilistic linkage database $\langle \mathcal{E}, \mathcal{L}, p^a, p^l \rangle$, we need to consider all the possible valid linkage specifications of $\mathcal{L}$. This number can easily get large enough to make the computation intractable. Based on the fact that no linkage exists between entities in different factors, we can improve the situation by considering each factor independently. We will use notation $\mathcal{L}_{f_i}^{sp}$ to denote all the possible valid linkage specifications between entities of the ith factor and $\mathcal{L}_{f_i}^{sp}(k)$ one of the possible assignments.

Each possible l-world is using a specific specification within each factor. Thus, the set of possible l-worlds can be derived by combining all the alternative valid linkage specifications within each factor as follows:

$$\mathrm{plw}(\langle \mathcal{E}, \mathcal{L}, p^a, p^l \rangle) = \mathcal{L}_{f_1}^{\mathrm{sp}} \times \mathcal{L}_{f_2}^{\mathrm{sp}} \times \cdots \times \mathcal{L}_{f_n}^{\mathrm{sp}}$$

Example 9.4. Consider a probabilistic linkage database with entity linkages $\mathcal{L} = \{l_{e_1,e_2}, l_{e_1,e_3}, l_{e_4,e_5}\}$. For the specific set of entity linkages, we have two factors. Factor f_1 with entities $\{e_1, e_2, e_3\}$ and factor f_2 with entities $\{e_4, e_5\}$. The corresponding linkage specifications are $\mathcal{L}_{f_1}^{\mathrm{sp}} = \{l_{e_1,e_2}, l_{e_1,e_3}\}$ and $\mathcal{L}_{f_2}^{\mathrm{sp}} = \{l_{e_4,e_5}\}$, and thus, the possible l-worlds can be retrieved as follows:

$$
\begin{array}{ll}
\mathcal{L}_{f_1}^{\mathrm{sp}}(1) = \{l_{e_1,e_2}, l_{e_1,e_3}\} & \mathcal{L}_{f_2}^{\mathrm{sp}}(1) = \{l_{e_4,e_5}\} \\
\mathcal{L}_{f_1}^{\mathrm{sp}}(2) = \{l_{e_1,e_2}\} \qquad \times & \mathcal{L}_{f_2}^{\mathrm{sp}}(2) = \{\} \\
\mathcal{L}_{f_1}^{\mathrm{sp}}(3) = \{l_{e_1,e_3}\} & \\
\mathcal{L}_{f_1}^{\mathrm{sp}}(4) = \{\} &
\end{array}
$$

The cartesian product of these linkage assignments results into the number of possible l-worlds for the whole database. The next table illustrates these l-worlds (through the specifications) along with the entity merges for each of these possible l-world.

Possible worlds	Entity merges
$D_1 = \{l_{e_1,e_2}, l_{e_1,e_3}, l_{e_4,e_5}\}$	$e_1 \equiv e_2 \equiv e_3,\quad e_8 \equiv e_9$
$D_2 = \{l_{e_1,e_2}, l_{e_1,e_3}\}$	$e_1 \equiv e_2 \equiv e_3,\quad e_8,\quad e_9$
$D_3 = \{l_{e_1,e_2}, l_{e_4,e_5}\}$	$e_1 \equiv e_2,\quad e_3,\quad e_8 \equiv e_9$
$D_4 = \{l_{e_1,e_2}\}$	$e_1 \equiv e_2,\quad e_3,\quad e_4,\quad e_5$
$D_5 = \{l_{e_1,e_3}, l_{e_4,e_5}\}$	$e_2,\quad e_1 \equiv e_3,\quad e_4 \equiv e_5$
$D_6 = \{l_{e_1,e_3}\}$	$e_2,\quad e_1 \equiv e_3,\quad e_4,\quad e_5$
$D_7 = \{l_{e_4,e_5}\}$	$e_1,\quad e_2,\quad e_3,\quad e_4 \equiv e_5$
$D_8 = \{\}$	$e_1,\quad e_2,\quad e_3,\quad e_4,\quad e_5$

■

To avoid recomputing the factors every time, we maintain an index structure which is dynamically maintained. The index structure is based on the idea of equivalence classes. In reality, each factor is actually an equivalence class. When data are modified and new linkages are introduced or old ones are eliminated, changes should occur in the equivalence class memberships, thus on the factors. Algorithm 19 illustrates how the factor index is maintained under new linkage insertions.

Once the various l-worlds have been constructed, the second important step is to compute the probability of each possible l-world. Since the factors are independent of each other, the probability of an l-world can be computed as the product of the probabilities of the involved factors (Sect. 9.4.3). It is thus given by:

Algorithm 19: Updating factor indexing

Input: (a) $l_{\alpha,\beta} := (e_\alpha, e_\beta, p)$: a new linkage
                 (b) $F := F_1, F_2, \ldots, F_n$: the factors
Output: Updated factors F
$F_\alpha \leftarrow$ getFactorOf(e_α);
$F_\beta \leftarrow$ getFactorOf(e_β);
if $F_\alpha \notin F$ **then**
 | $F \leftarrow F \cup F_\alpha$;
if $F_\beta \notin F$ **then**
 | $F \leftarrow F \cup F_\beta$;
if $F_\alpha == F_\beta$ **then**
 | // already in the same factor ;
 | **return** F;
else if $F_\alpha \mathrel{!=} F_\beta$ **then**
 | $F_\gamma \leftarrow F_\alpha \cup F_\beta$;
 | $F \leftarrow F \setminus F_\alpha \setminus F_\beta \cup F_\gamma$;

$$\Pr(1 - \text{world}) = \prod_{i=1}^{n} \Pr(\mathcal{L}_{f_i}^{\text{sp}}(.)) \tag{9.1}$$

Example 9.5. Assume that the possible worlds that satisfy condition $e_1 \equiv e_2$ and $e_4 \equiv e_5$ needs to be retrieved. Based on Example 9.4, it can be easily seen that the left part of the condition is satisfied by factors $\mathcal{L}_{f_1}^{\text{sp}}(1)$ and $\mathcal{L}_{f_1}^{\text{sp}}(3)$, while the right part by factor $\mathcal{L}_{f_2}^{\text{sp}}(1)$. Therefore, only the possible 1-worlds given by the product of these factors needs to be considered. These are:

$$\mathcal{L}_{f_1}^{\text{sp}}(1) = \{l_{e_1,e_2}, l_{e_1,e_3}\} \quad \times \quad \mathcal{L}_{f_2}^{\text{sp}}(1) = \{l_{e_4,e_5}\}$$
$$\mathcal{L}_{f_1}^{\text{sp}}(3) = \{l_{e_1,e_3}\}$$

This results in two possible 1-worlds. The first 1-world is given by

$$\text{plw}_1 = \mathcal{L}_{f_1}^{\text{sp}}(1) \times \mathcal{L}_{f_2}^{\text{sp}}(1) \text{ with probability } \Pr(\mathcal{L}_{f_1}^{\text{sp}}(1)) \cdot \Pr(\mathcal{L}_{f_2}^{\text{sp}}(1)) \tag{9.2}$$

and the second 1-world is given by

$$\text{plw}_2 = \mathcal{L}_{f_1}^{\text{sp}}(3) \times \mathcal{L}_{f_2}^{\text{sp}}(1) \text{ with probability } \Pr(\mathcal{L}_{f_1}^{\text{sp}}(3)) \cdot \Pr(\mathcal{L}_{f_2}^{\text{sp}}(1))$$

∎

9.4.2 Retrieving Possible 1-Worlds

In order to avoid the creation of all possible 1-worlds when a query is issued, we exploit the list of factors we are maintaining, as mentioned in the previous section, and the attributes in the query. We do so in order to restrict the creation of only those possible 1-worlds that are necessary, i.e., those that will lead to the generation of some query results. We achieve this by first detecting the entity merges that are required in order to satisfy the conditions of the query. In particular, for every attribute specification a_i in the query, a list E_{a_i} is constructed with all the entities having attribute a_i. Clearly an entity satisfies all the query conditions, that is, contains all the attributes set by the query, if it appears in each one of the lists E_{a_i}, for $i = 1..n$. It is not always the case that such an entity exists. However, by merging two or more entities, it is possible to create a new one (the result of the merge) whose attributes contain all the attributes in the query. Let S be a set of such entities. For the set S to serve the required purpose, two main properties need to be satisfied. First, all its members have to belong to the same factor (it is not possible to talk about merge of entities that belong to different factors), and second, there must be at least one entity $e \in S$ from every list E_{a_i}, with $i = 1...n$. Of course, one can always create "super entities" by merging all the entities in every factor. However, this may generate merges that are not necessary. To avoid this form or redundancy, we require that each set E_{a_i} contributes at most one entity. This means that the number of entities to merge can never be more than the number of attributes in the query.

To compute all the possible merge combinations, we generate the cartesian product of the sets E_{a_i} with the extra requirement that they should belong to the same factor. Algorithm 20 provides a brief description of the described steps.

Example 9.6. For example, assume that a query q contains attributes a_1, a_2, and a_3, and each one is satisfied by the entity sets $E_{a_1} = \{f_1 - e_a, f_1 - e_b, f_2 - e_c\}$, $E_{a_2} = \{f_1 - e_b, f_2 - e_d\}$, and $E_{a_3} = \{f_1 - e_g, f_1 - e_h, f_2 - e_i\}$, respectively. For each entity in the sets, we also indicate the factor in which the entity belongs to. We first compute all the possible combinations:

E_{a_1}		E_{a_2}		E_{a_3}
$f_1 - e_a$	$\times_{(E_{a_1} \cdot f_i = E_{a_2} \cdot f)_j}$	$f_1 - e_b$	$\times_{(E_{a_2} \cdot f_i = E_{a_3} \cdot f_j)}$	$f_1 - e_g$
$f_1 - e_b$		$f_2 - e_d$		$f_1 - e_h$
$f_2 - e_c$				$f_2 - e_i$

which lead to the following merges: $merge(e_a, e_b, e_g), merge(e_a, e_b, e_h)$, $merge(e_b, e_g), merge(e_b, e_h)$, and $merge(e_c, e_d, e_i)$. Note that e_b belongs to both sets E_{a_1} and E_{a_2}, which means that the entity e_b has both attributes a_1 and a_2; thus, being merged with e_g or e_h is enough to create an entity that satisfies the query conditions. ∎

Consider now a merge of entities e_α and e_β from a factor f_i. From all possible worlds that can be generated from the specific factor, we are only interested in those that contain the specific entity merge. The remaining can be ignored. All entities constructed from this merge will contain some common attributes, which correspond to the attributes directly coming from the entities e_α and e_β. The

---

Algorithm 20: Generate entity merges

Input: $Q := \langle a_1, a_2, \ldots, a_k \rangle$: an entity query
$\langle \mathcal{E}, \mathcal{L}, p^a, p^l \rangle$
: a probabilistic linkage database**Output:** M: a set of entity merges
foreach a_i **in** Q **do**
  $E_i \leftarrow \{e \mid e = \langle id, A \rangle \wedge e \in \mathcal{E} \wedge a_i \in A\}$;
  $N \leftarrow \{(e_1, \ldots e_n) \mid \forall i = 1..n : e_i \in E_i \wedge \forall i = 2..n : factor(e_{i-1}) = factor(e_i)\}$;
  $M \leftarrow \{eliminateDuplicates(m) \mid m \in N\}$;

---

remaining attributes in the possible l-worlds will come from entities participating in other linkages which exist in the specific possible l-world. To further optimize our framework, we exploit this behavior and instead of returning all the entities for each factor, we return only one *partial entity*. The partial entity contains the minimum set of attributes required by the specific merge since this is commonly found in all entities generated by this factor.

9.4.3 Computing Probabilities of Possible l-Worlds

The next step in the query answering process is to decide the probability of a merge, i.e., a partial match as mentioned in the previous section. Recall that a partial match may be true in many possible worlds. There are two alternatives that one can follow. The first is to assign as the probability of the partial match the sum of the probabilities of these worlds. The second is to compute and consider only the maximum of these probabilities. The latter requires significantly less computation time, since it only needs to identify the world with the highest probability. For systems that simply use the match probability as a ranking mechanism for the entities before displaying them to the user, this second option is typically sufficient.

The algorithm for computing the match probability is based on the algorithm for finding shortest paths on graphs. In particular, provided the entity linkages L_i in a factor, we generate a weighted undirected graph G as follows: every entity participating in the linkages of L_i becomes a node of the graph. Each linkage l_{e_α, e_β} becomes an edge that connects the nodes representing entities e_α and e_β. The weight of such an edge is given by the probability of the respective linkage.

An entity merging $merge(e_1, e_2, \ldots, e_n)$ corresponds to a spanning tree that connects all entities $e_1, e_2, \ldots, e_n$. Computing the merge that maximizes the probability is similar to computing the maximum connected component of the graph that has the highest total probability (i.e., multiplication of the probabilities of its edges). Since the nodes of the graph correspond to the entities of a factor, they are all connected; thus, the maximum connected component will include all the nodes of the graph. To compute it, we rank the edges in decreasing order of their linkage probability. Initially, all the entities (i.e., nodes) are marked as not visited. The highest ranked edge is first selected and the two nodes it connects are marked as visited. Then a list of edges is considered the subset of the edges that have one endpoint marked visited and one nonvisited. The one with the highest probability is selected and its nonvisited endpoint is marked as visited. The same step is repeatedly executed until all the nodes in the graph have been marked as visited. The probability of the merge is the multiplication of the probabilities of the edges that have been used in this process, and this probability is actually the maximum.

9.4.4 Retrieving and Computing Probabilities of Possible Worlds

The previous sections have dealt with the problem of processing a query by efficiently deriving the possible 1-worlds $\text{plw}((\mathcal{E}, \mathcal{L}_c, p^a, p^l))$ along with the corresponding entity merges. However, this is not all. Recall that entity attributes themselves have probabilities; thus, even a possible 1-world may be describing multiple different (nonprobabilistic) databases. These different databases are what we call solutions.

Each solution essentially represents a different combination over the attributes of the entities participating in a specific merge. For instance, consider the data in Fig. 9.3 and, in particular, the attributes involved in $merge(e_1, e_2)$. The entity $merge(e_1, e_2)$ needs to include all attributes from entities e_1 and e_2, as shown in Fig. 9.4. Two issues need to be taken into consideration. One is the probabilities of the attributes, specifically in the case of duplication, and the other is the dependencies that may exist among them.

The simplest approach regarding attribute dependencies is to consider the attributes as independent and include them all as attributes in the merge result entity. However, the attributes that appear in real-world datasets are not always independent. The correlations (i.e., dependencies) between attributes that need to be considered in attribute merge highly depend on the nature of the sources and their datasets. Our framework is able to handle such correlations in a uniform manner. A simple method is to cluster the exclusive attributes from each entity, i.e.,

aid.	name	value	p		Solutions		
		Attributes for $merge(e_1 \equiv e_2)$					
• a_{10}	starring	Daniel Radcliffe	0.7	(1)	(2)	(3)	(4)
◇ a_{11}	starring	Emma Watson	0.4	a_{10}	a_{20}	a_{10}	a_{20}
a_{12}	writer	J.K. Rowling	0.6	a_{11}	a_{11}	a_{21}	a_{21}
a_{13}	genre	Fantasy	0.6	a_{12}	a_{12}	a_{12}	a_{12}
• a_{20}	starring	Radcliffe, Daniel	0.5	a_{13}	a_{13}	a_{13}	a_{13}
◇ a_{21}	starring	Watson, Emma (II)	0.9				

Fig. 9.4 The attributes involved in $merge(e_1, e_2)$ along with the solutions when we deal with exclusive attributes (same name and similar values)

$M = \{\{e_1.\alpha_i, e_1.\alpha_j, \ldots\}\}$. We can then use this set to generate the solutions and compute their probability. The following paragraphs provide more details for generating solutions.

9.4.4.1 Independent Attributes

One option is to assume no correlation between the attributes and thus no restrictions on which attributes to include in the merge result entity. In this case, there is only one solution which is given by the union of all entity attributes.

$$\text{merge}(e_1, e_2, \ldots, e_n) = \langle id', \cup_{i=1}^n e_i.A \rangle$$

9.4.4.2 Exclusive Attributes

In certain cases, the attributes originating from different entities participating in the entity merge are exclusive. This requires that only one occurrence of such an attribute to be in the entity resulted by the merge. A typical example of such an attribute is the distinct attribute names, e.g., a person can have only one name. Other examples are the attributes with the same name but similar (semantically or syntactically) values, e.g., attributes a_{11} and a_{21} from Fig. 9.4. A simple method is to cluster the exclusive attributes from each entity, i.e., $M = \{\{e_1.\alpha_i, e_1.\alpha_j, \ldots\}\}$. We can then use this set to generate worlds with these correlations:

$$\text{merge}(e_1, \ldots, e_n) = \langle \text{id}', A \rangle, \text{ where}$$

$$A \subseteq (M_1 \times M_2 \times \cdots \times M_m) \cup \{\alpha \mid \alpha \notin \cup_{i=1}^m M_i.\alpha\}.$$

The overall probability of a possible world depends on the probability of the attributes included or not included in the world. It is computed as the product of probability p^α when attribute α is part of the world and $(1 - p^\alpha)$ when attribute α is not part of it:

$$\Pr(e' \mid \text{merge}(e_1, \ldots, e_n)) = \Pr(l - \text{world}) \times \prod_{\alpha \in e'.A} p^\alpha$$

$$\times \prod_{\alpha \notin e'.A \,\&\, \alpha \in e_i.A} (1 - p^\alpha).$$

Example 9.7. Figure 9.4 shows the attributes involved in *merge*(e_1, e_2). The exclusive attributes are given by set $M = \{\{\alpha_{10}, \alpha_{20}\}, \{\alpha_{11}, \alpha_{21}\}\}$. Figure 9.4 shows the four generated possible worlds, and their probability is computed according to above formula.

9.5 Evaluation

This section presents the results of the experimental evaluation for the suggested entity linkage methodology. The goal was twofold: (1) to study the effectiveness of our approach and identify its advantages over traditional techniques for entity linkage and (2) to investigate the efficiency of query processing and the overhead it introduces. We implemented our approach using Java 1.6 and performed all experiments on a computer with 5,400 rpm hard disk, a core 2 duo processor of 1.8 Ghz, and 2 GB RAM. For storing entities, we used MySQL 5, on the same computer. The following paragraphs present our datasets.

Movie Dataset. For evaluating the efficiency, we needed a sufficiently large dataset. Also, to investigate effectiveness, we needed linkages generated from different linkage techniques. We generated such a dataset by integrating data describing movies coming from two real-world systems, *IMDb* and *DBpedia*. *IMDb* data were stored in relational format, and *DBpedia* data were stored in RDF format. We converted both datasets to our data model and stored them in a relational database. To find the true matches (i.e., ground truth), we have used the *imdb_id* field from the *DBpedia* dataset, which contains the id of the movie in the *IMDb* dataset. The table in Fig. 9.5 shows the details for the movie dataset.

For generating the entity linkages, we compared the movie titles using two standard string similarity methods [9], *Jaccard* and *Jaro*. Figure 9.5 plots the precision-recall plot resulting when using these techniques to link entities, with *Jaccard* being more successful in linking *IMDb* to *DBpedia* movies than *Jaro*. As expected, for both techniques, we see the clear dependency between precision and recall. While recall increases, precision decreases, and vice versa. The linkage techniques always have to decide the trade-off between precision and recall. In our experiments, we investigate how our approach addresses this issue.

IMDb		DBpedia		Real-world objects
Entities:	23.182	Entities:	28.040	13.435
Attributes:	820.999	Attributes:	186.655	

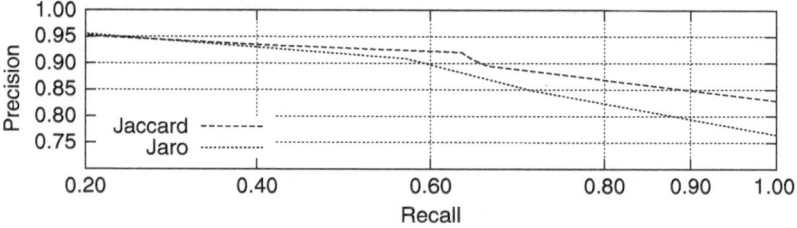

Fig. 9.5 Information about the movie datasets: the data composing the dataset (*top*) and the precision-recall plot for two entity linkage techniques (*bottom*)

Attributes	Entities	Real-world objects	Entity linkages (under threshold t)					
5764	2882	9774	$t = 0.52$	$t = 0.58$	$t = 0.62$	$t = 0.68$	$t = 0.72$	$t = 0.78$
			12440	12012	10775	6394	5985	4184

Fig. 9.6 Information about the Cora datasets: the data composing the dataset (*left*) and the number of linkages for various thresholds (*right*)

Cora Dataset. Our second dataset was a collection of publications and authors from CiteSeer.[1] Cora dataset is typically used to evaluate entity linkage techniques [3, 16, 17]. Its data comes from CiteSeer, a real-world application, and it contains various author descriptions that refer to the same real-world object (maximum is 88 author instances describing the same real-world object).

We generated entity linkages between authors (i.e., entities) using the probabilistic entity linkage [26]. Entity linkage techniques typically select a linkage threshold and incorporate in the original data all entities with corresponding linkages above this threshold. Figure 9.6 provides the details for this dataset along with the number of linkages under different thresholds. Precision and recall of the generated entity linkages are similar to the ones generated by other algorithms such as [16, 17]. For our approach, we did not apply such a threshold but also used the linkages with low probabilities.

Entity Queries. The evaluations for both datasets were performed with 800 queries. Each query was generated by randomly selecting attributes of entities belonging to the same real-world object. We generated queries for real-world objects which contained at least two entities in our dataset. All reported results are computed on the average of 800 queries.

9.5.1 Effectiveness of Query Processing

We evaluate effectiveness of entity-aware query processing in a twofold manner. First, we examine the quality of entities returned when querying with our approach. Second, we compare entities returned from entity-aware query processing (EAQP) with entities returned when we use directly the results of the entity linkage techniques (ELA), i.e., applying the threshold on the entity linkages. We performed both evaluations using the Cora Dataset.

Our first experiment was as follows. We used the entity linkage technique to link all authors in the Cora dataset and stored the proposed linkages in the database. Then we processed the 800 queries and compared the results returned with EAQP and with ELA. As we already explained, entity linkage techniques select a threshold and accept linkages that have a higher probability than this threshold.

---

[1]http://www.cs.umass.edu/˜mccallum/data/cora-refs.tar.gz

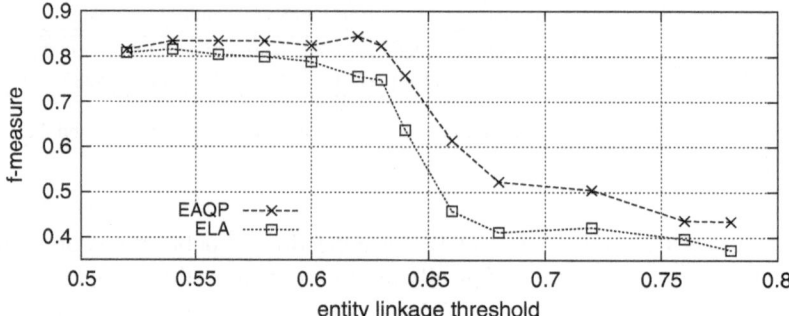

Fig. 9.7 F-measure with entity-aware query processing (EAQP) and entity linkage algorithm (ELA) over various thresholds for the accepted linkages

Selecting a low threshold ($t = 0.6$) will provide linkages with a high recall but low precision, whereas selecting a higher threshold ($t = 0.8$) will provide linkages with significantly higher precision but also with lower recall. One can easily see that when the selected threshold increases, the number of linkages is reduced since we then accept only the entities with high probabilities (see Fig. 9.6 for the exact numbers). We examine the behavior of the entity-aware query processing as well as the entity linkage algorithm when the value of the threshold is increased.

To measure quality of query results, we computed F-measure, which is a weighted harmonic mean of precision and recall. We consider a query as correct when it returns the real-world object by merging the information found in the various corresponding entities.

Figure 9.7 shows the average F-measure of the 800 queries for various entity linkage thresholds. As expected, when moving toward higher thresholds, the entity linkage technique accepts less and less linkages. This makes the technique unable to find the entities described by the queries. On the contrary, even for high thresholds, EAQP is able to identify the entities. For example, for $t = 0.66$, EAQP returned the correct entity for around 10% more queries than ELA. This is because EAQP can find connected linkages to construct the entity described in the query. ELA had to reject these linkages because of their low threshold. The exact precision and recall values for some of these thresholds are shown in the following table:

t	EAQP		ELA	
	Precision	Recall	Precision	Recall
0.62	1.00	0.73	1.00	0.61
0.63	0.99	0.71	1.00	0.60
0.64	0.91	0.65	1.00	0.47

Figure 9.8 shows the numbers of queries that were correctly answered for different linkage thresholds. As shown, query processing with our approach returns the correct results to more queries than ELA.

We further analyzed the results of this evaluation and identified two situations in which EAQP performs better than ELA. The first is that our approach has less failures, i.e., empty result set for queries. For instance, for $t = 0.6$, EAQP was able to return the correct answers for the 150 queries in which ELA did not return anything. The second situation is that there are cases in which the entities returned by EAQP were with higher confidence (i.e., with higher probability) than the entities returned by ELA. As shown in Fig. 9.8, for $t = 0.6$, EAQP returned 421 correct answers, whereas ELA returned 238 correct answers. For 91 answers, EAQP had higher probability than ELA. Figure 9.9 presents the numbers for these two situations.

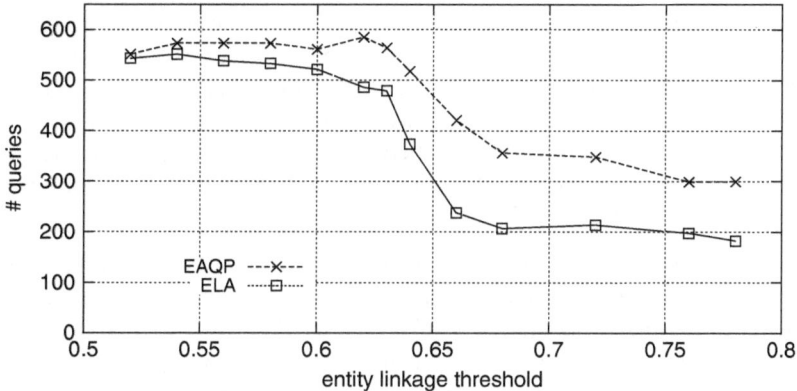

Fig. 9.8 Number of queries correctly returned with EAQP and ELA over various thresholds for the accepted linkages

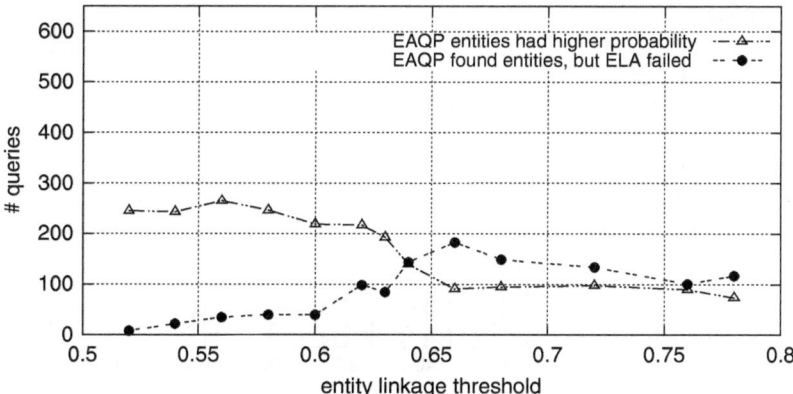

Fig. 9.9 Number of queries from the ones shown in Fig. 9.8 in which EAQP returned answers with higher probability and identified requested entities, whereas the ELA failed

9.5.2   Efficiency of Query Processing

We now report the results for the efficiency evaluation of our approach.

Size of Generated Factors. The core of our approach is based on generating factors by grouping linkages which are pairwise linked (Sect. 9.4.1). During query processing, we select the related factors and process them to construct the entities. The sizes of the factors influence the execution time of our approach.

We computed the size of the generated factors as the number of entity linkages contained in the factors. We then constructed the histogram of factor sizes. Figure 9.10 shows appearances per factor sizes as generated by both entity linkage techniques, *Jaro* and *Jaccard*. As shown, most of the factors have a small size and few factors are of bigger size. In addition, we see that for the entity linkage technique generated with *Jaro*, we have more factors of bigger sizes. Considering again the characteristics of the linkages generated by the *Jaro* and *Jaccard* (cf. Fig. 9.5), precision and recall results of *Jaccard* were better than *Jaro*. Clearly, *Jaro* is less capable to identify the correct linkages between entities, and thus, it generates more linkages which are less certain. This generates more pairwise-linked entities which are now reflected in the size of factors.

Time to Retrieve Possible Worlds. Given that factors have different sizes, we measured the time needed to identify the possible world with the highest probability in respect to the factor size (Sect. 9.4.3). Figure 9.11 shows the required time for different factor sizes. As expected, for small factor sizes (i.e., 20–40 entity linkages) which is the dominating majority among the factors, the algorithm requires around 1 millisecond. For larger factor sizes, the algorithm requires more time, which however still remains below 4 ms.

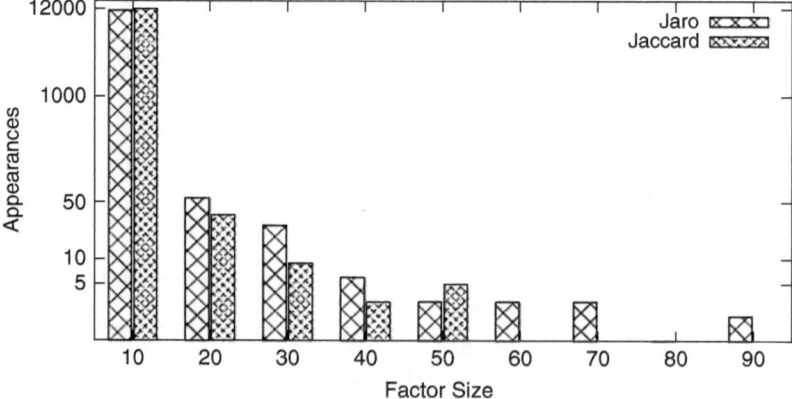

Fig. 9.10 Appearance numbers for the factor sizes generated for our two movie datasets

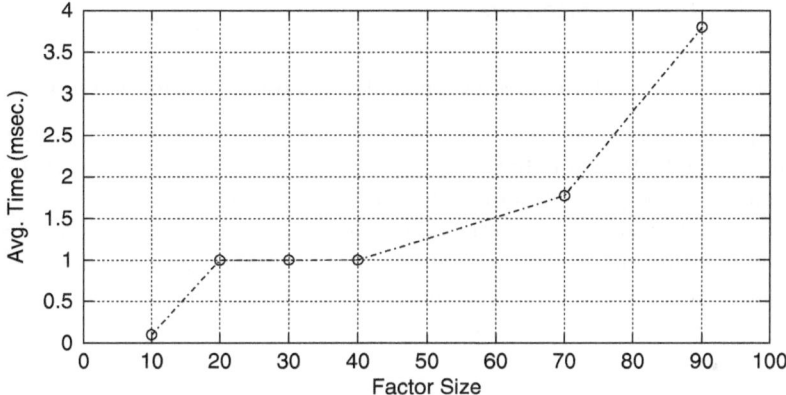

Fig. 9.11 Average time for computing the possible world with the maximum probability over factor sizes

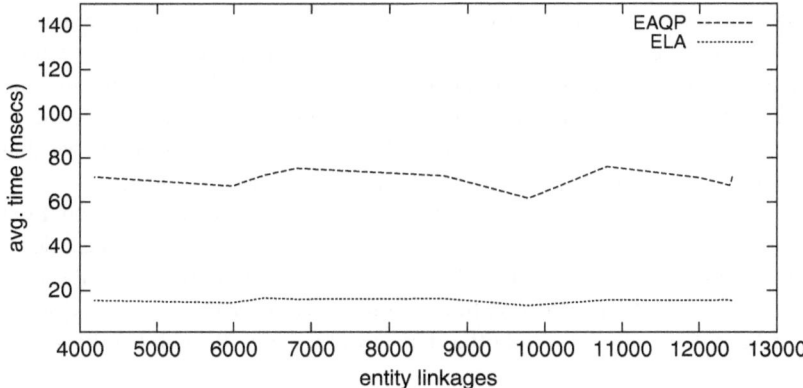

Fig. 9.12 Total time for processing queries over different numbers of entity linkages in dataset

Execution Time. Our final evaluation was to measure the time required for entity-aware query processing and also to compute the overhead that a system will have for offering this additional functionality. Figure 9.12 shows the average time taken to answer queries with and without our approach. We show time over different numbers of entity linkages in dataset. As expected, there is an increase in the time required with our approach, but this is relatively small and it remains under 70 ms. Furthermore, time does not increase as the dataset gets larger. On the contrary, query time remains stable even when the dataset is double the size. This behavior results from the effective grouping of linkages into factors which allows the algorithm to easily detect and use only a small subset of the linkages during query processing.

9.5.3   Evaluation Summary

Summarizing, the result of our experimental evaluation confirms the following:

- Incorporating entity-aware query processing in a system makes the system able to better handle the entity linkage problem and especially provide query answers which reflect the possible entity solutions for the current data.
- Our approach has a small overhead in time required for processing queries, but due to our efficient processing strategy, this cost remains low and constant even for large datasets with a large amount of entity linkages.

9.6   Conclusions

We have introduced a novel approach that allows on-the-fly entity-aware query processing in the presence of linkage information. Our approach can be applied on various data formats and structures using a generic entity representation. We explained how query processing can be performed efficiently over the entities and their possible linkages as these are generated by existing entity linkage techniques. Special focus was given on handling the uncertainty that appears in the entity linkage information as well as in the entity data. Our evaluation shows that the approach is both efficient and effective in answering entity queries.

We are currently investigating several directions to extend our approach. First, we would like to cover provenance information related to the possible linkage decisions and answers returned by querying. Also, we would like to investigate the implications of having conflicting information for the entity descriptions, as is typically the case for Web data, and to try out effective ways to deal with such conflicts.

References

1. Adar, E., Re, C.: Managing uncertainty in social networks. IEEE Data Eng. Bull. 15–22 (2007)
2. Agrawal, P., Benjelloun, O., Sarma, A., Hayworth, C., Nabar, S., Sugihara, T., Widom, J.: Trio: a system for data, uncertainty, and lineage. VLDB, pp. 1151–1154 (2006)
3. Andritsos, P., Fuxman, A., Miller, R.: Clean answers over dirty databases: a probabilistic approach. ICDE (2006)
4. Antova, L., Koch, C., Olteanu, D.: $10^{(10)^6}$ worlds and beyond: efficient representation and processing of incomplete information. VLDB J. **18**(5), 1021–1040 (2009)
5. Benjelloun, O., Garcia-Molina, H., Menestrina, D., Su, Q., Whang, S., Widomr, J., Jonas, J.: Swoosh: a generic approach to entity resolution. VLDB J. **18**(1), 255–276 (2009)
6. Bex, G., Neven, F., Vansummeren, S.: Inferring xml schema definitions from xml data. VLDB, pp. 998–1009 (2007)
7. Bhattacharya, I., Getoor, L.: Iterative record linkage for cleaning and integration. DMKD, pp. 11–18 (2004)

8. Bilenko, M., Mooney, R., Cohen, W., Ravikumar, P., Fienberg, S.: Adaptive name matching in information integration. IEEE Intel. Syst. **18**(5), 16–23 (2003)
9. Cohen, W., Ravikumar, P., Fienberg, S.: A comparison of string distance metrics for name-matching tasks. IIWeb, pp. 73–78 (2003)
10. Dalvi, N., Kumar, R., Pang, B., Ramakrishnan, R., Tomkins, A., Bohannon, P., Keerthi, S., Merugu, S.: A web of concepts. PODS, pp. 1–12 (2009)
11. Dalvi, N., Suciu, D.: Efficient query evaluation on probabilistic databases. VLDB J. **16**(4), 523–544 (2007)
12. Dalvi, N., Suciu, D.: Management of probabilistic data: foundations and challenges. PODS, pp. 1–12 (2007)
13. Dasu, T., Johnson, T.: Exploratory Data Mining and Data Cleaning. Wiley, NY, USA (2003)
14. Doan, A., Halevy, A.Y.: Semantic integration research in the database community: a brief survey. AI Mag. **26**(1), 83–94 (2005)
15. Doan, A., Lu, Y., Lee, Y., Han, J.: Object matching for information integration: a profiler-based approach. IIWeb, pp. 53–58 (2003)
16. Domingos, P.: Multi-relational record linkage. Multi-relational data mining workshop co-located with KDD, pp. 31–48 (2004)
17. Dong, X., Halevy, A., Madhavan, J.: Reference reconciliation in complex information spaces. SIGMOD conference, pp. 85–96 (2005)
18. Dong, X., Halevy, A., Yu, C.: Data integration with uncertainty. VLDB, pp. 687–698 (2007)
19. Elmagarmid, A., Ipeirotis, P., Verykios, V.: Duplicate record detection: a survey. IEEE Trans. Knowl. Data Eng. **19**(1), 1–16 (2007)
20. Getoor, L., Diehl, C.: Link mining: a survey. SIGKDD explorations (2005)
21. Gupta, R., Sarawagi, S.: Creating probabilistic databases from information extraction models. VLDB, pp. 965–976 (2006)
22. Halevy, A., Franklin, M., Maier, D.: Principles of dataspace systems. PODS, pp. 1–9 (2006)
23. Hernández, M., Stolfo, S.: Real-world data is dirty: data cleansing and the merge/purge problem. Data Mining Knowledge Dis. **2**(1), 9–37 (1998)
24. Ioannou, E., Nejdl, W., Niederée, C., Velegrakis, Y.: On-the-fly entity-aware query processing in the presence of linkage. PVLDB **3**(1), 429–438 (2010)
25. Ioannou, E., Nejdl, W., Niederée, C., Velegrakis, Y.: LinkDB: a probabilistic linkage database system. SIGMOD conference, pp. 1307–1310 (2011)
26. Ioannou, E., Niederée, C., Nejdl, W.: Probabilistic entity linkage for heterogeneous information spaces. CAiSE, pp. 302–316 (2008)
27. Kalashnikov, D., Mehrotra, S.: Domain-independent data cleaning via analysis of entity-relationship graph. ACM Trans. Database Syst. **31**(2), 716–767 (2006)
28. Lenzerini, M.: Data integration: a theoretical perspective. PODS, pp. 233–246 (2002)
29. Morris, A., Velegrakis, Y., Bouquet, P.: Entity identification on the semantic web. SWAP (2008)
30. Papadakis, G., Ioannou, E., Niederée, C., Fankhauser, P.: Efficient entity resolution for large heterogeneous information spaces. WSDM, pp. 535–544 (2011)
31. Rastogi, V., Dalvi, N., Garofalakis, M.: Large-scale collective entity matching. PVLDB **4**(4), 208–218 (2011)
32. Re, C., Suciu, D.: Managing probabilistic data with MystiQ: the can-do, the could-do, and the can't-do. SUM, pp. 5–18 (2008)
33. Sarawagi, S., Bhamidipaty, A.: Interactive deduplication using active learning. KDD, pp. 269–278 (2002)
34. Sen, P., Deshpande, A.: Representing and querying correlated tuples in probabilistic databases. ICDE, pp. 596–605 (2007)
35. Velegrakis, Y.: On the importance of updates in information integration and data exchange systems. DBISP2P (2008)
36. Whang, S., Menestrina, D., Koutrika, G., Theobald, M., Garcia-Molina, H.: Entity resolution with iterative blocking. SIGMOD Conference, pp. 219–232 (2009)

Chapter 10
The Return of the Entity-Relationship Model: Ontological Query Answering

Andrea Calì, Georg Gottlob, and Andreas Pieris

10.1 Introduction

The Entity-Relationship (ER) model is a fundamental formalism for conceptual modeling in database design; it was introduced by Chen in his milestone paper [18], and it is now widely used, being flexible and easily understood by practitioners. With the rise of the Semantic Web, conceptual modeling formalisms have gained importance again as *ontology formalisms*, in the Semantic Web parlance. Ontologies and conceptual models are aimed at representing, rather than the structure of data, the domain of interest, that is, the fragment of the real world that is being represented by the data and the schema. A prominent formalism for modeling ontologies are *Description Logics (DLs)* [14], which are decidable fragments of first-order logic, particularly suitable for ontological modeling and querying. In particular, DL ontologies are sets of assertions describing sets of objects and (usually binary) relations among such sets, exactly in the same fashion as the ER model.

Recently, research on DLs has been focusing on the problem of *answering queries* under ontologies, that is, given a query q, an instance B, and an ontology $\mathcal{K}$, answering q under B and $\mathcal{K}$ amounts to compute the answers that are *logically entailed* from B by using the assertions of $\mathcal{K}$. In this context, where data size is usually large, a central issue the *data complexity* of query answering, i.e., the computational complexity with respect to the data set B only, while the ontology $\mathcal{K}$ and the query q are fixed.

A. Calì (✉)
Department of Computer Science and Information Systems, Birkbeck University of London, London, UK
e-mail: andrea@dcs.bbk.ac.uk

G. Gottlob · A. Pieris
Department of Computer Science, University of Oxford, Oxford, UK
e-mail: georg.gottlob@cs.ox.ac.uk; andreas.pieris@cs.ox.ac.uk

R. De Virgilio et al. (eds.), *Semantic Search over the Web*,
Data-Centric Systems and Applications, DOI 10.1007/978-3-642-25008-8_10,
© Springer-Verlag Berlin Heidelberg 2012

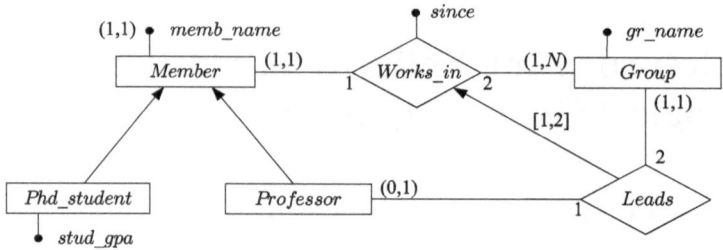

Fig. 10.1 An ER$^+$ schema

For this reason the tractable *DL-Lite* family [16, 26], for instance, has become a prominent family of DL languages. More precisely, DL-Lite languages are *first-order rewritable*, i.e., for every conjunctive query q, for every initial instance B, and for every DL-Lite knowledge base $\mathcal{K}$, it is possible to construct a first-order query $q_{\mathcal{K}}$ (which, in particular, is a union of conjunctive queries), such that directly evaluating $q_{\mathcal{K}}$ over B (without resorting to the knowledge base $\mathcal{K}$ any more) returns the correct answers to q under B and $\mathcal{K}$. The first-order rewritability implies two desirable properties: (a) the data complexity of conjunctive query answering is very low, namely, in the highly tractable class AC_0 (which is the complexity class of recognizing words in languages defined by constant-depth Boolean circuits with (unlimited fan-in) AND and OR gates), and (b) query answering can be performed efficiently by translating the rewritten query $q_{\mathcal{K}}$ into SQL, thus taking advantage of the optimization capabilities of the underlying relational DBMS.

In this chapter we consider the problem of conjunctive query answering under an extended version of the ER model, which we call ER$^+$. Our model is obtained from the original ER model by adding is-a relations among entities and relationships, functional and mandatory participation constraints on the participation of entities to relationships, and functional and mandatory constraints on attributes of entities and relationships. Figure 10.1 shows an ER$^+$ schema, where the reader will recognize the familiar graphical notation of Chen's ER model. The schema describes members of a university department working in research groups. Ph.D. students and professors are both members. For instance, the constraint $(1, 1)$ (min. 1, max. 1) on the participation of *Member* in *Works_in* imposes that every instance of *Member* participates at least once (mandatory participation) and at most once (functional participation) in *Works_in*. The constraint $(0, 1)$ (min. 0, max. 1) on the participation of *Professor* in *Leads* imposes that every instance of *Professor* participates at most once (functional participation) in *Leads*. The constraint $(1, N)$ (min. 1, max. arbitrary) on the participation of *Group* in *Works_in* imposes that every instance of *Group* participates at least once (mandatory participation) in *Works_in*. The constraint $(1, 1)$ on the attribute *memb_name* states that such an attribute is mandatory (at least one value) and functional (at most one value). The is-a constraint among the relationships states that each professor works in the same group that (s)he leads, considering the components in the same order; components of relationships are ordered and marked by the integers 1 and 2. The notation $[1, 2]$ indicates the permutation of the components involved in the containment.

In our setting we admit arbitrary *permutations* of objects in an is-a between two relationships. For example, we can assert that each instance $\langle a, b, c \rangle$ of a ternary relationship R_1 is also an instance of another ternary relationship R_2, but the three objects (instances of the participating entities) appear in R_2 in the order $\langle c, a, b \rangle$; this would be indicated by the annotation $[3, 1, 2]$ in the corresponding diagram. The addition of the permutation feature increases the complexity of query answering. The permutation is a common feature in DL-Lite and other Semantic Web languages, where it is usually in the form of *inverse roles*, where roles are binary relations among *concepts* (sets). With this feature we can express, for instance, the reflexive property of a relation; for example (in first-order logic) $\forall X \forall Y \ brother(X, Y) \rightarrow brother(Y, X)$.

Similar to what is found in the literature on DL-Lite, we are interested in query answering under ontologies, and in particular in the data complexity of (the decision version of) such problem in the presence of ER^+ ontologies. We identify and study sub-languages of ER^+ which are tractable in data complexity, and we also provide a complete complexity study (data and combined complexity) of query answering under such sub-languages.

10.1.1   Summary of the Chapter

We first introduce, in Sect. 10.3, the ER^+ model, and provide a formal semantics for it in terms of a relational representation; that is, each ER^+ schema is encoded in a relational schema, plus a set of relational constraints—belonging to the well-known classes of *inclusion dependencies* and *key dependencies*. A set of inclusion and key dependencies in such a form that it can represent an ER^+ schema is called a set of *conceptual dependencies (CDs)*. We study different variants of the ER^+ model in terms of the corresponding (sub)classes of CDs. Our central algorithmic tool is the *chase* [22, 25], widely adopted in the literature in the context of query containment and answering under relational constraints.

It turns out that ER^+ is *not* first-order rewritable. The chief reason for this is the interaction between inclusion dependencies and key dependencies in a set of CDs, which mirrors the interaction between functional participation constraints and the other kinds of constraints in the corresponding ER^+ schema. The central (semantic) notion here is then *separability*, which guarantees a decoupling between inclusion and key dependencies in a set of CDs: under a set Σ of separable CDs, answering a query q on an instance D is equivalent to answering q on D under the inclusion dependencies of Σ only. We provide a *syntactic* condition, in Sect. 10.4, which implies separability of CDs; we do this by defining *non-conflicting CDs* (and, consequently, non-conflicting ER^+ schemata). We show that the aforementioned condition is not only sufficient, but also necessary; this way, we do precisely characterize the class of separable ER^+ schemata.

Table 10.1 Summary of complexity results

Language	Arity	Perm.	Combined	Data
Non-conflicting ER^+	Any	Yes	PSPACE-complete	AC_0
			UB: [22]	UB: [5]
Non-conflicting $ER_{\mathscr{I}}^+$	Any	No	NP-complete	AC_0
			LB: [17]	UB: [5]
Non-conflicting $ER_{\mathscr{B}}^+$	Bounded	Yes	NP-complete	AC_0
			UB: [22] LB: [17]	UB: [5]

We provide, in Sect. 10.5, a complexity analysis of the query answering problem for the following three cases: (a) non-conflicting ER^+ schemata, (b) non-conflicting ER^+ schemata with *identity permutations*, i.e., schemata where every is-a among relationships has the identity permutation associated to it (non-conflicting $ER_{\mathscr{I}}^+$), and (c) non-conflicting ER^+ schemata with the arity of relationships bounded by a constant (non-conflicting $ER_{\mathscr{B}}^+$). Observe that ER^+ properly generalizes both $ER_{\mathscr{I}}^+$ and $ER_{\mathscr{B}}^+$. The complexity results shown in this chapter are summarized in Table 10.1. When results in the table are already known from the literature, this is indicated (UB and LB stand for upper and lower bound, respectively). Notice that *all* non-conflicting variants of ER^+ enjoy first-order rewritability, which in turn guarantees AC_0 data complexity.

We then turn our attention, in Sect. 10.6, to *negative constraints*, which allows us to express, for instance, non-participation of an entity to a relationship, but also more general assertions. We show that the addition of negative constraints does not increase the complexity of query answering.

Last but not least, in Sect. 10.7, we mention that the tractable ER^+ languages we present here have most DL-Lite languages as special cases. This confirms the usefulness of ER^+ in ontology modeling and ontology-based query answering.

10.1.2 Related Work

Our model is based on Chen's ER model [18]. The extended model considered in [28] includes the generalization and full aggregation constructs, while the one in [21] allows for arbitrary data types, optional and multivalued attributes, a concept for specialization and generalization, and complex structured entity types. Markowitz and Makowsky [29] considers relational schemata with referential integrity constraints that can be associated with an extended ER schema.

The paper [3] gives a formal first-order semantics to the ER model. Reasoning tasks under theories expressed in different variants of the ER model, whose constructs are given a formal semantics, are studied in [2].

Query answering under ER ontologies is tackled in [4], where the proposed ER language is strictly less expressive than the ones presented in this chapter;

the problem is studied in the context of data integration systems, and a first-order rewriting technique is proposed, later extended in [5]. The notion of separability was first introduced in [6]. Sufficient conditions for separability appear, for instance, in [8, 9].

The formalism of [31], which is also studied with respect to query answering, is more expressive than ER^+, and it does not offer the same tractability of query answering.

Other works [13, 22] consider query containment, which is tightly related to the query answering problem in the case of incomplete information. Calvanese et al. [13] considers query containment in a formalism similar to ER^+, but with less expressive negative constraints, and eventually incomparable to ER^+; the combined complexity is higher than the one under non-conflicting ER^+, and data complexity is not studied.

Our work is tightly related to the Semantic Web and, in general, to web data management. The World Wide Web Consortium (W3C) defines several standards, including the *Resource Description Framework (RDF)* for the data layer, the *Web Ontology Language (OWL)*, based on DLs, for the ontology layer, and the *Rule Interchange Format (RIF)*, currently being defined as a standard, for the rule layer. Several ontology languages have been proposed, many of which are more expressive than ER^+, while being less efficient in terms of query answering. The ER^+ model is intended to be a viable alternative to the most prominent *tractable* OWL sublanguages. Our ER^+ variants offer the same, desirable tractability properties (first-order rewritability, in particular), while in addition avoiding the description logic syntax, which could turn out to be slightly awkward to database practitioners. Due to the popularity of the ER model in the industry, and to its intuitive graphical representation, the ER^+ formalism is likely to be adopted as ontology language, especially when employed in visual design tools. More specifically, the languages of the DL-Lite family [16, 26], as already explained, enjoy the desirable property of tractable conjunctive query answering, in particular in AC_0 in data complexity, again ensured by their first-order rewritability. Both our formalisms non-conflicting ER^+ and non-conflicting $ER^+_{\mathscr{B}}$, with the addition of negative constraints, which do not increase the complexity of query answering, properly generalize the languages DL-Lite$_{\mathscr{F}}$ and DL-Lite$_{\mathscr{R}}$; at the same time, the data complexity of query answering is the same as that of the DL-Lite languages.

The notion of *chase* [6, 22, 25] of a database against a set of inclusion dependencies is crucial in ontological query answering; such notion has been extended to expressive rules called *tuple-generating dependencies (TGDs)* [19, 20]. In particular [20], considers the *data exchange* problem, where a target database is materialized starting from a source database and a mapping expressed as a set of TGDs; in this setting the chase procedure needs to terminate [19, 30]. However, this is not appropriate for ontological databases. The first work to tackle the problem of a non-terminating chase was [22].

Recent works [7–10] deal with so-called *TGDs*, rules that constitute the *Datalog$^\pm$* family of languages, some of which are first-order rewritable. Datalog$^\pm$ languages (enriched with non-conflicting key dependencies as in [8] or [9]) are not capable of capturing non-conflicting ER^+ schemata. For an overview of some Datalog$^\pm$ languages we refer the reader to [11].

Finally, the work [12] deals with general (non-separable) ER^+ schemata: a technique for query rewriting into recursive Datalog is presented, and complexity bounds are significantly higher than those shown here.

10.2 Preliminaries

In this section we recall some basics on databases, queries, dependencies, and the chase procedure.

10.2.1 General

We define the following pairwise disjoint (infinite) sets of symbols: (a) a set Γ of *constants* (constitute the "normal" domain of a database), (b) a set Γ_N of *labeled nulls* (used as placeholders for unknown values, and thus can be also seen as variables), and (c) a set Γ_V of *variables* (used in queries and dependencies). Different constants represent different objects (*unique name assumption*), while different nulls may represent the same object. A lexicographic order is defined on $\Gamma \cup \Gamma_N$, such that every value in Γ_N follows all those in Γ. We denote by **X** sequences (or sets) of variables and constants $X_1, \ldots, X_k$, where $k > 0$; it will be clear from the context when we regard **X** as a sequence of symbols, and when as a set of symbols. For an integer $n > 1$, we denote by $[n]$ the set $\{1, \ldots, n\}$.

A *relational schema* $\mathcal{R}$ (or simply *schema*) is a set of *relational symbols* (or *predicates*), each with its associated arity. We write r/n to denote that the predicate r has arity n and we refer to the integer n by $arity(r)$. A *position* $r[i]$, in a schema $\mathcal{R}$, is identified by a predicate $r \in \mathcal{R}$ and its ith argument (or attribute). A *term* t is either a constant or a null or a variable. An *atomic formula* (or simply *atom*) has the form $r(t_1, \ldots, t_n)$, where r/n is a relation, and $t_1, \ldots, t_n$ are terms. For an atom **a**, we denote as $dom(\mathbf{a})$ and $pred(\mathbf{a})$ the set of its terms and its predicate, respectively. These notations naturally extends to sets and conjunctions of atoms. Conjunctions of atoms will be often identified with the sets of their atoms.

A *substitution* from a set $S_1 \subset \Gamma \cup \Gamma_N \cup \Gamma_V$ to a set $S_2 \subset \Gamma \cup \Gamma_N \cup \Gamma_V$ is a function $h : S_1 \rightarrow S_2$ defined as follows: (a) $\varnothing$ is a substitution, and (b) if h is a substitution, then $h \cup \{X \rightarrow Y\}$ is a substitution, where $X \in S_1$ and $Y \in S_2$. A *homomorphism* from a set of atoms A_1 to a set of atoms A_2 is a substitution $h : dom(A_1) \rightarrow dom(A_2)$ such that: (a) if $t \in \Gamma$, then $h(t) = t$, and (b) if $r(t_1, \ldots, t_n) \in A_1$, then $h(r(t_1, \ldots, t_n)) = r(h(t_1), \ldots, h(t_n)) \in A_2$. If there exists a homomorphism from A_1 to A_2 and vice-versa, then A_1 and A_2 are *homomorphically equivalent.* The notion of homomorphism naturally extends to conjunctions of atoms.

10.2.2 Databases and Queries

A *relational instance* (or simply *instance*) I for a schema $\mathscr{R}$ is a (possibly infinite) set of atoms of the form $r(\mathbf{t})$, where $r/n \in \mathscr{R}$ and $\mathbf{t} \in (\Gamma \cup \Gamma_N)^n$. We denote as $r(I)$ the set $\{\mathbf{t} \mid r(\mathbf{t}) \in I\}$. A database D for $\mathscr{R}$ is a finite instance for $\mathscr{R}$ such that $dom(D) \subset \Gamma$. For simplicity, we assume source databases which contain only ground atoms, i.e., atoms whose arguments are constants of Γ. However, it is not difficult to show that the results of this paper hold even if we allow incomplete source databases which may include labeled nulls.

A *conjunctive query (CQ)* q of arity n over a schema $\mathscr{R}$, written as q/n, is an assertion the form $p(\mathbf{X}) \leftarrow \varphi(\mathbf{X}, \mathbf{Y})$, where $\varphi(\mathbf{X}, \mathbf{Y})$ is a conjunction of atoms over $\mathscr{R}$, and p is an n-ary predicate not occurring in $\mathscr{R}$. $\varphi(\mathbf{X}, \mathbf{Y})$ is called the *body* of q, denoted as $body(q)$. The *answer* to a CQ q/n of the above form over an instance I, denoted as $q(I)$, is the set of all n-tuples $\mathbf{t} \in \Gamma^n$ for which there exists a homomorphism $h : \mathbf{X} \cup \mathbf{Y} \to \Gamma \cup \Gamma_N$ such that $h(\varphi(\mathbf{X}, \mathbf{Y})) \subseteq I$ and $h(\mathbf{X}) = \mathbf{t}$.

10.2.3 Dependencies

A *TGD* σ over $\mathscr{R}$ is a first-order formula of the form $\forall \mathbf{X} \forall \mathbf{Y} \, \varphi(\mathbf{X}, \mathbf{Y}) \to \exists \mathbf{Z} \, \psi(\mathbf{X}, \mathbf{Z})$, where $\varphi(\mathbf{X}, \mathbf{Y})$ and $\psi(\mathbf{X}, \mathbf{Z})$ are conjunctions of atoms over $\mathscr{R}$, called the *body* and the *head* of σ, denoted as $body(\sigma)$ and $head(\sigma)$, respectively. Henceforth, for notational convenience, we will omit the universal quantifiers in front of TGDs. Such σ is satisfied by an instance I for $\mathscr{R}$ if whenever there exists a homomorphism h such that $h(\varphi(\mathbf{X}, \mathbf{Y})) \subseteq I$, then there exists an extension h' of h, i.e., $h' \supseteq h$, such that $h'(\psi(\mathbf{X}, \mathbf{Z})) \subseteq I$.

A *key dependency (KD)* κ over $\mathscr{R}$ is an assertion of the form $key(r) = \mathbf{A}$, where $r \in \mathscr{R}$ and $\mathbf{A}$ is a set of attributes of r. Such κ is satisfied by an instance I for $\mathscr{R}$ if for each pair of distinct tuples $\mathbf{t}_1, \mathbf{t}_2 \in r(I)$, $\mathbf{t}_1[\mathbf{A}] \neq \mathbf{t}_2[\mathbf{A}]$, where $\mathbf{t}[\mathbf{A}]$ is the projection of tuple $\mathbf{t}$ over $\mathbf{A}$.

A *negative constraint (NC)* ν over $\mathscr{R}$ is a first-order formula $\forall \mathbf{X} \, \varphi(\mathbf{X}) \to \bot$, where $\varphi(\mathbf{X})$ is a conjunction of atoms over $\mathscr{R}$, called the *body* of ν and denoted as $body(\nu)$, and $\bot$ is the truth constant *false*. For brevity, we will omit the universal quantifiers in front of NCs, and assume such a quantification implicitly. Such ν is satisfied by an instance I if there is *no* homomorphism h such that $h(\varphi(\mathbf{X})) \subseteq I$.

Given an instance I and a dependency δ, we write $I \models \delta$ (resp., $I \not\models \delta$) if I satisfies (resp., violates) δ. Given a set of dependencies Σ, we say that I satisfies Σ, written as $I \models \Sigma$, if for each $\delta \in \Sigma$ it holds that $I \models \delta$. Conversely, we say that I violates Σ, written as $I \not\models \Sigma$, if there exists $\delta \in \Sigma$ such that $I \not\models \delta$.

10.2.4 Query Answering Under Dependencies

Let us now introduce the problem of query answering under dependencies. Given a database D and a set of dependencies Σ, the answers we consider are those that are true in *all* models of D with respect to Σ, i.e., all instances that contain D and satisfy the dependencies of Σ. Formally, the *models* of D with respect to Σ, denoted as $mods(D, \Sigma)$, is the set of all instances I such that $I \models D \cup \Sigma$. The *answer* to a CQ q/n with respect to D and Σ is the set of n-tuples $ans(q, D, \Sigma) = \{\mathbf{t} \mid \mathbf{t} \in q(I), \text{ for each } I \in mods(D, \Sigma)\}$.

The *decision problem* associated to conjunctive query answering under dependencies, dubbed *CQ-Ans*, is defined as follows: given a CQ q/n over a schema $\mathscr{R}$, a database D for $\mathscr{R}$, a set Σ of dependencies over $\mathscr{R}$, and an n-tuple $\mathbf{t} \in \Gamma^n$, decide whether $\mathbf{t} \in ans(q, D, \Sigma)$. Following Vardi's taxonomy [33], the *data complexity* of the above problem is the complexity calculated taking only the database as input, while the query and the set of dependencies are considered fixed. The *combined complexity* is the complexity calculated considering as input, together with the database, also the query and the set of dependencies.

For the moment we put NCs aside and deal only with TGDs and KDs; we shall return to consider also NCs in Sect. 10.6.

10.2.5 The Chase Procedure

The *chase procedure* (or simply *chase*) is a fundamental algorithmic tool introduced for checking implication of dependencies [25], and later for checking query containment [22]. The chase is a process of repairing a database with respect to a set of dependencies so that the resulting instance satisfies the dependencies. We shall use the term chase interchangeably for both the procedure and its result. The chase works on an instance through the so-called TGD and KD *chase rules*.

TGD Chase Rule. Consider an instance I for a schema $\mathscr{R}$, and a TGD $\sigma = \varphi(\mathbf{X}, \mathbf{Y}) \rightarrow \exists \mathbf{Z} \, \psi(\mathbf{X}, \mathbf{Z})$ over $\mathscr{R}$. If σ is *applicable* to I, i.e., there exists a homomorphism h such that $h(\varphi(\mathbf{X}, \mathbf{Y})) \subseteq I$, then: (a) define $h' \supseteq h$ such that $h'(Z_i) = z_i$ for each $Z_i \in \mathbf{Z}$, where $z_i \in \Gamma_N$ is a "fresh" labeled null not introduced before, and following lexicographically all those introduced so far, and (b) add to I the set of atoms in $h'(\psi(\mathbf{X}, \mathbf{Z}))$, if not already in I.

KD Chase Rule. Consider an instance I for a schema $\mathscr{R}$, and a KD κ of the form $key(r) = \mathbf{A}$ over $\mathscr{R}$. If κ is *applicable* to I, i.e., there are two (distinct) tuples $\mathbf{t}_1, \mathbf{t}_2 \in r(I)$ such that $\mathbf{t}_1[\mathbf{A}] = \mathbf{t}_2[\mathbf{A}]$, then (a) if there exists $i \notin \mathbf{A}$ such that both $\mathbf{t}_1[i]$ and $\mathbf{t}_2[i]$ are constants of Γ, then there is a *hard violation* of κ and the chase *fails*, otherwise (b) for each $i \notin \mathbf{A}$, either replace each occurrence of $\mathbf{t}_1[i]$ with $\mathbf{t}_2[i]$, if the former follows lexicographically the latter, or vice-versa otherwise.

Given a database D for a schema $\mathscr{R}$ and set $\Sigma = \Sigma_T \cup \Sigma_K$ over $\mathscr{R}$, where Σ_T are TGDs and Σ_K are KDs, the chase algorithm for D with respect to Σ consists of an exhaustive application of the chase rules, which leads to a (possibly infinite) instance, denoted as $chase(D, \Sigma)$. In particular, $chase(D, \Sigma)$ is the instance constructed by applying (a) the TGD chase rule once, and (b) the KD chase rule as long as it is applicable (i.e., until a fixpoint is reached). We assume that the chase algorithm is *fair*, i.e., each TGD that must be applied during the construction of $chase(D, \Sigma)$ is eventually applied. We denote as $chase^{[k]}(D, \Sigma)$ the *initial segment* of the chase of D with respect to Σ obtained by applying k times the (TGD or KD) chase rule during the construction of the chase.

Example 10.1. Let $\mathscr{R} = \{r, s\}$. Consider the set Σ of TGDs and KDs over $\mathscr{R}$ constituted by the TGDs $\sigma_1 = r(X, Y) \rightarrow \exists Z\, r(Z, X), s(Z)$ and $\sigma_2 = r(X, Y) \rightarrow r(Y, X)$, and the KD κ of the form $key(r) = \{2\}$. Let $D = \{r(a, b)\}$. During the construction of $chase(D, \Sigma)$ we first apply σ_1, and we add the atoms $r(z_1, a), s(z_1)$, where z_1 is a "fresh" null of Γ_N. Moreover, σ_2 is applicable and we add the atom $r(b, a)$. Now, the KD κ is applicable and we replace each occurrence of z_1 with the constant b; thus, we get the atom $s(b)$.   ∎

The fairness assumption allows us to show that the chase of D with respect to Σ is a *universal model* of D with respect to Σ, i.e., for each $I \in mods(D, \Sigma)$, there exists a homomorphism from $chase(D, \Sigma)$ to I (see, e.g., [19, 20]). Thus, the answer to a CQ q with respect to D and Σ, if the chase does not fail, can be obtained by evaluating q over $chase(D, \Sigma)$, and discarding tuples containing at least one null [20]. If the chase fails, then $mods(D, \Sigma) = \varnothing$ and $ans(q, D, \Sigma) = \Gamma^n$.

Theorem 10.1. *Consider a CQ q/n over a schema $\mathscr{R}$, a database D for $\mathscr{R}$, a set Σ of TGDs and KDs over $\mathscr{R}$, and an n-tuple $\mathbf{t} \in \Gamma^n$. It holds that $\mathbf{t} \in ans(q, D, \Sigma)$ if and only if $\mathbf{t} \in q(chase(D, \Sigma))$ or $chase(D, \Sigma)$ fails.*

10.3   The Conceptual Model ER$^+$

In this section we present the conceptual model we shall deal with in this paper, and we give its semantics in terms of relational schemata with dependencies. This model, which is called ER$^+$, incorporates the basic features of the Entity-Relationship model [18] and OO models, including subset (or is-a) constraints on both entities and relationships. It is an extension of the one presented in [4], and we use a notation analogous to that of [4].

10.3.1   Syntax of ER$^+$

The schemata expressed in the ER$^+$ model are called ER$^+$ *schemata*. An ER$^+$ schema consists of a collection of entity, relationship, and attribute definitions over an alphabet of symbols partitioned into a set of entity symbols *Ent*, a set of relationship symbols *Rel*, and a set of attribute symbols *Att*.

An *entity definition* has the form

> entity E
> isa: $E_1, \ldots, E_k$
> participates($\geqslant$ 1): $R_1 : c_1, \ldots, R_\ell : c_\ell$
> participates($\leqslant$ 1): $R'_1 : c'_1, \ldots, R'_m : c'_m$,

where (a) $E \in Ent$ is the entity to be defined, (b) the isa clause specifies the set of entities to which E is related via is-a, i.e., the set of entities that are supersets of E, (c) the participates($\geqslant$ 1) clause specifies that an instance of the entity E must necessarily participate in relationship $R_i \in Rel$ as the c_ith component, and (d) the participates($\leqslant$ 1) clause specifies that an instance of the entity E cannot participate in relationship $R'_i \in Rel$ as the c'_ith component more than once. The isa, participates($\geqslant$ 1) and participates($\leqslant$ 1) clauses are optional.

A *relationship definition* has the form

> relationship R among $E_1, \ldots, E_n$
> isa: $R_1[j_{1_1}, \ldots, j_{1_n}], \ldots, R_\ell[j_{\ell_1}, \ldots, j_{\ell_n}]$,

where (a) $R \in Rel$ is the relationship to be defined, (b) the entities of *Ent* listed in the among clause are those among which the relationship R is defined (n is the *arity* of R), i.e., the ith component of R is an instance of the entity E_i, and (c) the isa clause specifies the set of relationships to which R is related via is-a, i.e., the set of relationships that are supersets of R; for each relationship R_i, we specify in square brackets how the components of R are related to those of R_i, by giving a permutation $[j_{i_1}, \ldots, j_{i_n}]$ of the set $[n]$. The isa clause is optional.

An *attribute definition* has the form

> attribute A of X
> *qualification*,

where (a) $A \in Att$ is the attribute to be defined, (b) $X \in (Ent \cup Rel)$ is either the entity or the relationship to which the attribute is associated, and (c) *qualification* consists of none, one, or both of the keywords mandatory and functional, specifying respectively that each instance of X needs to have at least one value for attribute A, and that each instance of X has a unique value for A. If both mandatory and functional are missing, the attribute is assumed by default to be optional and multivalued, respectively.

We assume that each attribute is associated to a unique entity or relationship, i.e., different entities and relationships have disjoint sets of attributes. Also, for simplicity, we assume that attributes have atomic values.

Example 10.2. Consider the ER$^+$ schema $\mathscr{C}$ defined as follows:

> entity *Member*
> participates($\geqslant$ 1): *Works_in* : 1
> participates($\leqslant$ 1): *Works_in* : 1

> entity *Phd_student*
>   isa: *Member*
> entity *Professor*
>   isa: *Member*
>   participates($\leqslant 1$): *Leads* : 1
> entity *Group*
>   participates($\geqslant 1$): *Works_in* : 2, *Leads* : 2
>   participates($\leqslant 1$): *Leads* : 2
> relationship *Works_in* among *Member, Group*
> relationship *Leads* among *Professor, Group*
>   isa: *Works_in*[1,2]
> attribute *memb_name* of *Member*
>   mandatory, functional
> attribute *stud_gpa* of *Phd_student*
> attribute *gr_name* of *Group*
> attribute *since* of *Works_in*.

It is easy to verify that $\mathscr{C}$ is actually the schema depicted in Fig. 10.1. ■

10.3.2 Semantics of ER⁺

The semantics of an ER^+ schema $\mathscr{C}$ is defined by associating a relational schema $\mathscr{R}$ to it, and then specifying when a database for $\mathscr{R}$ satisfies all the constraints imposed by the constructs of $\mathscr{C}$. We first define the relational schema that represents the so-called *concepts*, i.e., entities, relationships and attributes, of an ER^+ schema $\mathscr{C}$ as follows: (a) each entity E in $\mathscr{C}$ has an associated predicate $e/1$; intuitively, $e(c)$ asserts that c is an instance of entity E, (b) each attribute A of an entity E in $\mathscr{C}$ has an associated predicate $a/2$; intuitively, $a(c, d)$ asserts that d is the value of attribute A (of some entity E) associated to c, where c is an instance of E, (c) each relationship R of arity n in $\mathscr{C}$ has an associated predicate r/n; intuitively, $r(c_1, \ldots, c_n)$ asserts that $\langle c_1, \ldots, c_n \rangle$ is an instance of relationship R (among entities $E_1, \ldots, E_n$), where $c_1, \ldots, c_n$ are instances of $E_1, \ldots, E_n$, respectively, and (d) each attribute A of a relationship R of arity n in $\mathscr{C}$ has an associated predicate $a/(n + 1)$; intuitively, $a(c_1, \ldots, c_n, d)$ asserts that d is the value of attribute A (of some relationship R of arity n) associated to the instance $\langle c_1, \ldots, c_n \rangle$ of R.

Example 10.3. Consider the ER^+ schema $\mathscr{C}$ given in Example 10.2. The relational schema $\mathscr{R}$ associated to $\mathscr{C}$ consists of the predicates *member*/1, *phd_student*/1, *professor*/1, *group*/1, *works_in*/2, *leads*/2, *memb_name*/2, *stud_gpa*/2, *gr_name*/2, *since*/3. Note that queries over an ER^+ schema are queries over the relational schema associated to it. The CQ $p(B) \leftarrow phd\_student(A), memb\_name(A, B), works\_in(A, C), since(A, C, 2006), gr\_name(C, db)$ asks for the names of the students who work in the "db" group since 2006. ■

Table 10.2 Derivation of relational constraints from an ER^+ schema

ER^+ construct	Relational constraint
Attribute A for an entity E	$a(X, Y) \rightarrow e(X)$
Attribute A for a relationship R	$a(X_1, \ldots, X_n, Y) \rightarrow r(X_1, \ldots, X_n)$
Rel. R with entity E as ith component	$r(X_1, \ldots, X_n) \rightarrow e(X_i)$
Mandatory attribute A of entity E	$e(X) \rightarrow \exists Y\, a(X, Y)$
v Mandatory attribute A of relationship R	$r(X_1, \ldots, X_n) \rightarrow \exists Y\, a(X_1, \ldots, X_n, Y)$
Functional attribute A of an entity	$key(a) = \{1\}$ (a has arity 2)
Functional attribute A of a relationship	$key(a) = \{1, \ldots, n\}$ (a has arity $n + 1$)
is-a between entities E_1 and E_2	$e_1(X) \rightarrow e_2(X)$
is-a between relationships R_1 and R_2 where components $1, \ldots, n$ of R_1 correspond to components $i_1, \ldots, i_n$ of R_2	$r_1(X_1, \ldots, X_n) \rightarrow r_2(X_{i_1}, \ldots, X_{i_n})$
Mandatory part. of E in R (ith comp.)	$e(X_i) \rightarrow \exists \mathbf{X} r(X_1, \ldots, X_n)$
Functional part. of E in R (ith comp.)	$key(r) = \{i\}$

Once we have defined the relational schema $\mathscr{R}$ for an ER^+ schema $\mathscr{C}$, we give the semantics of each construct of $\mathscr{C}$. We do that by using the dependencies introduced in Sect. 10.2.3, as shown in Table 10.2 (the relationships have arity n).

Definition 10.1. Consider an ER^+ schema $\mathscr{C}$, and let $\mathscr{R}$ be the relational schema associated to it. The set of TGDs and KDs over $\mathscr{R}$ obtained from $\mathscr{C}$ as described in Table 10.2 is called the set of *conceptual dependencies (CDs)* associated to $\mathscr{C}$.

Example 10.4. Consider the ER^+ schema $\mathscr{C}$ given in Example 10.2. The relational schema $\mathscr{R}$ associated to $\mathscr{C}$ is given in Example 10.3. The set Σ of CDs over $\mathscr{R}$ associated to $\mathscr{C}$ is the following:

$$member(X) \rightarrow \exists Y\, works\_in(X, Y) \quad leads(X, Y) \rightarrow professor(X)$$
$$key(works\_in) = \{1\} \quad leads(X, Y) \rightarrow group(Y)$$
$$phd\_student(X) \rightarrow member(X) \quad leads(X, Y) \rightarrow works\_in(X, Y)$$
$$professor(X) \rightarrow member(X) \quad memb\_name(X, Y) \rightarrow member(X)$$
$$key(leads) = \{1\} \quad member(X) \rightarrow \exists Y\, memb\_name(X, Y)$$
$$group(X) \rightarrow \exists Y\, works\_in(Y, X) \quad key(memb\_name) = \{1\},$$
$$group(X) \rightarrow \exists Y\, leads(Y, X) \quad stud\_gpa(X, Y) \rightarrow phd\_student(X)$$
$$key(leads) = \{2\} \quad gr\_name(X, Y) \rightarrow group(X)$$
$$works\_in(X, Y) \rightarrow member(X), \quad since(X, Y, Z) \rightarrow works\_in(X, Y)$$
$$works\_in(X, Y) \rightarrow group(Y)$$

In general, a set of CDs associated to an ER^+ schema consists of *key* and *inclusion dependencies*, where the latter are a special case of TGDs [1].   ∎

Notice that it is possible to characterize the form of relational dependencies resulting from the translation of ER^+ schemata into relational schemata. This characterization appears in [12]. Relational dependencies (key and inclusion dependencies) which are derived from ER^+ schemata are said to be in *conceptual dependency form* (abbreviated as *CD-form*). It is also possible to show that a set of key and inclusion dependencies is associated to some ER^+ schema if and only if it is in CD-form.

A relational schema $\mathscr{R}$ which represents an ER^+ schema can be partitioned into four sets $\mathscr{R}_e$, $\mathscr{R}_r$, $\mathscr{R}_{ae}$ and $\mathscr{R}_{ar}$, where $\mathscr{R}_e$ are predicates associated to entities, $\mathscr{R}_r$ are predicates associated to relationships, $\mathscr{R}_{ae}$ are predicates associated to attributes of entities, and $\mathscr{R}_{ar}$ are predicates associated to attributes of relationships. We define the function $\mathsf{f}_{\mathscr{R},x} : \mathscr{R} \to 2^{\mathscr{R}}$ such that $\mathsf{f}_{\mathscr{R},x}(\mathscr{R}) = \mathscr{R}_x$, where $x \in \{e, r, ae, ar\}$; when $\mathscr{R}$ is obvious from the context, we shall denote the above function as f_x.

10.3.3   Relevant Sublanguages

Two subclasses of ER^+ schemata that are of special interest are schemata where only the identity permutation can be used in is-a constraints between relationships, and where only relationships of bounded arity are allowed.

Definition 10.2. Consider a set Σ of CDs over a schema $\mathscr{R}$. Σ is a set of *identity permutation CDs (IPCDs)* if for each TGD of Σ of the form $r_1(X_1, \dots, X_n) \to r_2(X_{i_1}, \dots, X_{i_n})$, where $\{r_1, r_2\} \subseteq \mathsf{f}_r(\mathscr{R})$, it holds that $[i_1, \dots, i_n] = \mathsf{id}_n$, where id_n is the identity permutation $[1, \dots, n]$ of the set $[n]$. Σ is a set of *bounded arity CDs (BACDs)* if all the predicates of f_r are of bounded arity.

Being able to encode ER^+ schemata into relational ones with dependencies, in our study we will exploit techniques used in the case of relational schemata with dependencies. Henceforth, when using the term TGD (resp., KD), unless stated otherwise, we shall refer to TGDs (resp., KDs) that are part of a set of CDs (the results of this paper do not hold in general).

10.4   Separable Conceptual Dependencies

In this section we introduce the novel class of *non-conflicting CDs*. This class ensures that the TGDs and the KDs do not interact, so that answers to queries over an ER^+ schema can be computed by considering the TGDs only, and ignoring the KDs, once it is known that the initial data are consistent with respect to the schema. This semantic property is known as *separability* [6, 8].

Definition 10.3. Consider a set $\Sigma = \Sigma_T \cup \Sigma_K$ of CDs over a schema $\mathscr{R}$, where Σ_T are TGDs and Σ_K are KDs. Σ is *separable* if for every database D for $\mathscr{R}$, either $chase(D, \Sigma)$ fails or, for every CQ q over $\mathscr{R}$, $ans(q, D, \Sigma) = ans(q, D, \Sigma_T)$.

10.4.1 Definition of Non-Conflicting CDs

Before syntactically defining non-conflicting CDs, we need some preliminary technical definitions.

Consider a set $\Sigma = \Sigma_T \cup \Sigma_K$ of CDs over a schema $\mathscr{R}$, where Σ_T and Σ_K are TGDs and KDs, respectively. The *CD-graph* of Σ is a multigraph $\langle V, E, \lambda \rangle$, where V is the node set, E is the edge set, and λ is a labeling function $E \rightarrow \Sigma_T$. The node set V is the set of positions of $(f_e(\mathscr{R}) \cup f_r(\mathscr{R}))$. For each TGD $\sigma \in \Sigma_T$ such that $\{pred(body(\sigma)), pred(head(\sigma))\} \subseteq V$, and for each universally quantified variable X that occurs in $body(\sigma)$ at position π and in $head(\sigma)$ at position π', there exist: (a) an edge e from π to π' with $\lambda(e) = \sigma$, and (b) for each existentially quantified variable Y in $head(\sigma)$ at position π'', a *special* edge e' from π to π'' with $\lambda(e') = \sigma$. A node $v = p[i] \in V$ is called *e-node* (resp., *r-node*) if $p \in f_e(\mathscr{R})$ (resp., $p \in f_r(\mathscr{R})$). Moreover, if v is an r-node and the KD $key(p) = \{i\}$ occurs in Σ_K, then v is called *k-node*.

Let G be the CD-graph of Σ. Consider an edge $u \frown v$ in G which is labeled by the TGD $r_1(X_1, \ldots, X_n) \rightarrow r_2(X_{j_1}, \ldots, X_{j_n})$, where $\{r_1, r_2\} \subseteq f_r(\mathscr{R})$ and $[j_1, \ldots, j_n]$ is a permutation of the set $[n]$. Intuitively, the permutation $[j_1, \ldots, j_n]$ indicates that the j_ith component of the relationship R_1 is the ith component of the relationship R_2. This fact can be represented by the bijective function $f_{u \frown v} : [n] \rightarrow [n]$, where for each $i \in [n]$, $f_{u \frown v}(j_i) = i$. Now, consider a cycle $C = v_1^{\frown} v_2^{\frown} \ldots^{\frown} v_m^{\frown} v_1$ of only r-nodes in G. The permutation associated to C, denoted as $\pi_G(C)$, is defined as the permutation $g([1, \ldots, n]) = [g(1), \ldots, g(n)]$, where $g = f_{v_m \frown v_1} \circ \cdots \circ f_{v_2 \frown v_3} \circ f_{v_1 \frown v_2}$.

We are now ready to give the formal definition of non-conflicting CDs, which is based on the notion of the CD-graph.

Definition 10.4. Consider a set Σ of CDs over a schema $\mathscr{R}$, and let G be the CD-graph of Σ. Σ is *non-conflicting* if for each path $v_1^{\frown} v_2^{\frown} \ldots^{\frown} v_m$, for $m \geqslant 2$, in G such that v_1 is an e-node, $v_2, \ldots, v_{m-1}$ are r-nodes, and v_m is a k-node, the following two conditions are satisfied: (a) for each cycle C of only r-nodes in G going through v_m, $\pi_G(C) = \text{id}_n$, where n is the arity of the predicate of v_m, and (b) if $m \geqslant 3$ and the edge $v_1^{\frown} v_2$ is non-special, then there exists a path of only r-nodes from v_m to v_2.

Observe that if only the identity permutation is allowed on is-a among relationships, then the first condition stated above is satisfied trivially. Thus, given a set of IPCDs, to decide whether is non-conflicting it suffices to check only the validity of the second condition.

Example 10.5. Consider the ER^+ schema $\mathscr{C}$ given in Example 10.2; for simplicity we ignore the attributes. The set Σ of CDs associated to $\mathscr{C}$ is given in Example 10.4. The CD-graph of Σ is depicted in Fig. 10.2 (edge labels are omitted for brevity). It is immediate to see that Σ is non-conflicting.   ∎

In what follows we give a more involved example of non-conflicting CDs, where a cycle of only r-nodes going through a k-node occurs in the underlying

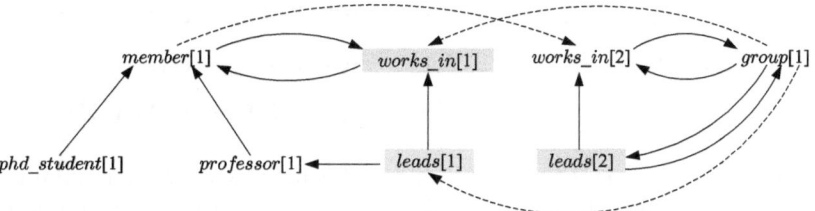

Fig. 10.2 CD-graph for Example 10.5; k-nodes are shaded and special edges are represented using *dashed lines*

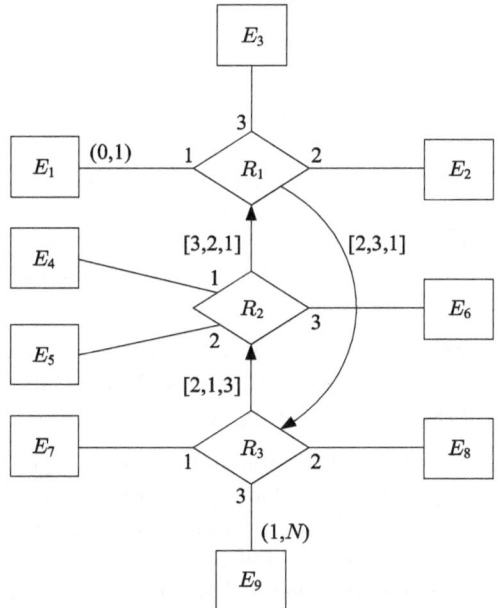

Fig. 10.3 ER$^+$ schema for Example 10.6

CD-graph, and also arbitrary permutations (other than the identity one) are used in is-a constraints among relationships.

Example 10.6. Consider the ER$^+$ schema $\mathscr{C}$ depicted in Fig. 10.3; the formal definition of $\mathscr{C}$ is omitted. The set Σ of CDs over $\mathscr{R} = \{e_1, \ldots, e_9, r_1, r_2, r_3\}$ associated to $\mathscr{C}$ is the following:

$$key(r_1) = \{1\}, \quad r_2(X, Y, Z) \rightarrow e_5(Y),$$
$$e_9(X) \rightarrow \exists Y \exists Z \, r_3(Y, Z, X), \quad r_2(X, Y, Z) \rightarrow e_6(Z),$$
$$r_1(X, Y, Z) \rightarrow e_1(X), \quad r_2(X, Y, Z) \rightarrow r_1(Z, Y, X),$$
$$r_1(X, Y, Z) \rightarrow e_2(Y), \quad r_3(X, Y, Z) \rightarrow e_7(X),$$

$$r_1(X, Y, Z) \rightarrow e_3(Z), \quad r_3(X, Y, Z) \rightarrow e_8(Y),$$

$$r_1(X, Y, Z) \rightarrow r_3(Y, Z, X), \quad r_3(X, Y, Z) \rightarrow e_9(Z),$$

$$r_2(X, Y, Z) \rightarrow e_4(X), \quad r_3(X, Y, Z) \rightarrow r_2(Y, X, Z).$$

Observe that the path $e_9[1]^\frown r_3[3]^\frown r_2[3]^\frown r_1[1]$, where the edge $e_9[1]^\frown r_3[3]$ is non-special, occurs in the CD-graph G of Σ. Moreover, the edge $r_1[1]^\frown r_3[3]$ occurs in G, and thus the cycle $C = r_1[1]^\frown r_3[3]^\frown r_2[3]^\frown r_1[1]$ occurs in G; in fact, C is the only cycle of r-nodes in G going through the k-node $r_1[1]$. Clearly,

$$f_{e_1} = \begin{cases} 3 & \text{if } x = 1, \\ 1 & \text{if } x = 2, \\ 2 & \text{if } x = 3, \end{cases} \quad f_{e_2} = \begin{cases} 2 & \text{if } x = 1, \\ 1 & \text{if } x = 2, \\ 3 & \text{if } x = 3, \end{cases} \quad f_{e_3} = \begin{cases} 3 & \text{if } x = 1, \\ 2 & \text{if } x = 2, \\ 1 & \text{if } x = 3, \end{cases}$$

where $e_1 = r_1[1]^\frown r_3[3]$, $e_2 = r_3[3]^\frown r_2[3]$ and $e_3 = r_2[3]^\frown r_1[1]$. By defining g to be the composition $f_{e_3} \circ f_{e_2} \circ f_{e_1}$, we get that the permutation associated to C is $\pi_G(C) = [g(1), g(2), g(3)] = [1, 2, 3] = \text{id}_3$. Hence, the first condition of the Definition 10.4 is satisfied. Due to the edge $r_1[1]^\frown r_3[3]$, the second condition is also satisfied. Thus, Σ is non-conflicting. ∎

The following example shows that during the construction of the chase of a database with respect to a set of non-conflicting CDs, a KD may be violated which implies that the KD chase rule must be applied.

Example 10.7. Consider the set Σ of non-conflicting CDs given in Example 10.4. Let $D = \{professor(p), leads(p, g)\}$. During the construction of $chase(D, \Sigma)$, we add the atoms $member(p)$, $works\_in(p, g)$ and $works\_in(p, z_1)$, where $z_1 \in \Gamma_N$. The KD $key(works\_in) = \{1\}$ of Σ implies that p cannot participates more than once in $Works\_in$ as the first component. Thus, we deduce that $z_1 = g$. We must therefore replace each occurrence of z_1 with g in the part of the $chase(D, \Sigma)$ constructed so far. ∎

10.4.2 Separable CDs Vs. Non-Conflicting CDs

In this subsection we show that the non-conflicting condition is a sufficient and necessary condition for separability. We first establish that every set of non-conflicting CDs is separable. To this aim we need an auxiliary technical lemma.

Lemma 10.1. *Consider a database D for a schema $\mathcal{R}$, and a set $\Sigma = \Sigma_T \cup \Sigma_K$ of non-conflicting CDs over $\mathcal{R}$, where Σ_T are TGDs and Σ_K are KDs. If $chase(D, \Sigma)$ does not fail, then there exists a homomorphism h that maps $chase(D, \Sigma)$ to $chase(D, \Sigma_T)$.*

Proof. We proceed by induction on the number of applications of the (TGD or KD) chase rules in the construction of $chase(D, \Sigma)$. We need to show that, for each $k \geq 0$, there exists a homomorphism h_k that maps $chase^{[k]}(D, \Sigma)$ to a set of atoms of $chase(D, \Sigma_T)$.

BASE STEP. Clearly, for $k = 0$, $chase^{[0]}(D, \Sigma) = D \subseteq chase(D, \Sigma_T)$. Therefore, the claim holds trivially with h_0 be the identity homomorphism on $dom(D)$.

INDUCTIVE STEP. By induction hypothesis there exists a homomorphism h_{k-1} such that $h_{k-1}(chase^{[k-1]}(D, \Sigma)) \subseteq chase(D, \Sigma_T)$. We proceed by considering the two cases where the applied rule is either the TGD or the KD chase rule.

Suppose that we apply the TGD chase rule because the TGD $\sigma = r(\mathbf{X}, \mathbf{Y}) \rightarrow \exists \mathbf{Z}\, s(\mathbf{X}, \mathbf{Z})$ of Σ_T is violated. This implies that there exists a homomorphism μ that maps $r(\mathbf{X}, \mathbf{Y})$ to a set of atoms of $chase^{[k-1]}(D, \Sigma)$, and the atom $\mathbf{a} = \mu'(s(\mathbf{X}, \mathbf{Z}))$ is obtained, where μ' is an extension of μ as in the TGD chase rule. Clearly, $chase^{[k]}(D, \Sigma) = chase^{[k-1]}(D, \Sigma) \cup \{\mathbf{a}\}$. Observe that the homomorphism $\lambda = h_{k-1} \circ \mu$ maps $r(\mathbf{X}, \mathbf{Y})$ to a set of atoms of $chase(D, \Sigma_T)$. Since $chase(D, \Sigma_T) \models \Sigma_T$ it follows that there exists $\lambda' \supseteq \lambda$ such that $\lambda'(s(\mathbf{X}, \mathbf{Z})) \in chase(D, \Sigma_T)$. Denoting $\mathbf{Z} = Z_1, \ldots, Z_m$, for $m \geq 0$, we define the substitution $h_k = h_{k-1} \cup \{\mu'(Z_i) \rightarrow \lambda'(Z_i)\}_{i \in [m]}$. Since none of the $\mu'(Z_i)$ occurs in h_{k-1}, it follows that h_k is a well-defined substitution. Clearly, $h_k(\mathbf{a}) = h_k(\mu'(s(\mathbf{X}, \mathbf{Z}))) = s(h_{k-1}(\mu(\mathbf{X})), h_k(\mu'(\mathbf{Z}))) = s(\lambda(\mathbf{X}), \lambda'(\mathbf{Z})) = \lambda'(s(\mathbf{X}, \mathbf{Z})) \in chase(D, \Sigma_T)$. Thus, $h_k(chase^{[k]}(D, \Sigma)) \subseteq chase(D, \Sigma_T)$, as needed.

Now, suppose that we apply the KD chase rule because the KD $\kappa \in \Sigma_K$ is violated. We proceed by case analysis on the type of κ.

Assume first that κ is of the form $key(a) = \{1\}$, where $a \in f_{ae}(\mathcal{R})$. This implies that in $chase^{[k-1]}(D, \Sigma)$ there exist two atoms $\mathbf{a} = a(c_1, c_2)$ and $\mathbf{b} = a(c_1, c_2')$. If $\{c_1, c_2, c_2'\} \subset \Gamma$, then $chase(D, \Sigma)$ fails and the claim holds trivially. The case where $\{c_1, c_2, c_2'\} \subset \Gamma_N$, and also the case where $c_1 \in \Gamma$ and $\{c_2, c_2'\} \subset \Gamma_N$ are excluded since, by definition of CDs, $\mathbf{a}$ and $\mathbf{b}$ must be the same atom which is a contradiction. Now, consider the case where $\{c_1, c_2\} \subset \Gamma$ and $c_2' \in \Gamma_N$ (the case where $\{c_1, c_2'\} \subset \Gamma$ and $c_2 \in \Gamma_N$ is symmetric). Observe that, by definition of CDs, c_2' does not occur elsewhere in $chase^{[k-1]}(D, \Sigma)$. This implies that by applying κ we just eliminate atom $\mathbf{b}$, and thus $chase^{[k]}(D, \Sigma) \subset chase^{[k-1]}(D, \Sigma)$. Consequently, $h_k = h_{k-1}$.

Assume now that κ is of the form $key(a) = [n]$, where $a \in f_{ar}(\mathcal{R})$. This implies that in $chase^{[k-1]}(D, \Sigma)$ there exist two atoms $\mathbf{a} = a(c_1, \ldots, c_n, c_{n+1})$ and $\mathbf{b} = a(c_1, \ldots, c_n, c_{n+1}')$. If $\{c_1, \ldots, c_{n+1}, c_{n+1}'\} \subset \Gamma$, then $chase(D, \Sigma)$ fails and the claim holds trivially. The cases where $\{c_1, \ldots, c_{n+1}, c_{n+1}'\} \subset \Gamma_N$, or $\{c_1, \ldots, c_n\} \subset \Gamma$ and $\{c_{n+1}, c_{n+1}'\} \subset \Gamma_N$, or for some $i \in [n]$, $c_i \in \Gamma$ and $\{c_1, \ldots, c_{i-1}, c_{i+1}, \ldots, c_{n+1}, c_{n+1}'\} \subset \Gamma_N$, are excluded since, by definition of CDs, $\mathbf{a}$ and $\mathbf{b}$ must be the same atom which is a contradiction. Now, consider the case where $\{c_1, \ldots, c_{n+1}\} \subset \Gamma$ and $c_{n+1}' \in \Gamma_N$ (the case where $\{c_1, \ldots, c_n, c_{n+1}'\} \subset \Gamma$ and $c_{n+1} \in \Gamma_N$ is symmetric). By definition of CDs, c_{n+1}' does not occur elsewhere in $chase^{[k-1]}(D, \Sigma)$. By applying κ we just eliminate atom $\mathbf{b}$, and hence $chase^{[k]}(D, \Sigma) \subset chase^{[k-1]}(D, \Sigma)$. Therefore, $h_k = h_{k-1}$.

We continue to consider the case where κ is of the form $key(r) = \{1\}$ (without loss of generality we assume the first attribute to form the key). This implies that in $chase^{[k-1]}(D, \Sigma)$ we have the atoms $\mathbf{a} = r(c_1, c_2, \ldots, c_n)$ and $\mathbf{b} = a(c_1, c_2', \ldots, c_n')$. If $\{c_1, \ldots, c_n, c_2', \ldots, c_n'\} \subset \Gamma$, then $chase(D, \Sigma)$ fails and the claim holds trivially. The case where $\{c_1, \ldots, c_{i-1}, c_{i+1}, \ldots, c_n, c_2', \ldots, c_{j-1}', c_{j+1}', \ldots, c_n'\} \subset \Gamma_N$ and $\{c_i, c_j'\} \subset \Gamma$, for some $i, j \in \{2, \ldots, n\}$, is excluded since, by definition of CDs, $\mathbf{a}$ and $\mathbf{b}$ must be the same atom which is a contradiction. We define $\mu = \{c_i' \to c_i\}_{2 \leqslant i \leqslant n}$. During the application of the violated KD we apply μ to $chase^{[k-1]}(D, \Sigma)$ and the atom $\mathbf{b}$ is eliminated (the case where $\mu = \{c_i \to c_i'\}_{2 \leqslant i \leqslant n}$ and $\mathbf{a}$ is eliminated is symmetric). Consider an arbitrary atom $\mathbf{c} \in chase^{[k-1]}(D, \Sigma)$, where $dom(\mathbf{c}) \cap \{c_2', \ldots, c_n'\}$ is not empty. We are going to show that $h_{k-1}(\mu(\mathbf{c})) \in chase(D, \Sigma_T)$. Suppose that the atom $\mathbf{b}$ is obtained during the chase due to the application of the TGD $\sigma \in \Sigma_T$. We proceed by case analysis on the type of σ.

Let $\sigma = a(X_1, \ldots, X_n, Y) \to r(X_1, \ldots, X_n)$, where $a \in \mathfrak{f}_{ar}(\mathscr{R})$. Observe that, by definition of CDs, the atoms generated during the chase due to the application of σ are necessarily of the form $r(d_1, \ldots, d_n)$, where $\{d_1, \ldots, d_n\} \subset \Gamma$. Therefore, this case is not possible since $\{c_2', \ldots, c_n'\} \subset \Gamma_N$.

Assume now that $\sigma = e(X) \to \exists X_2 \ldots \exists X_n \, r(X, X_2, \ldots, X_n)$, where $e \in \mathfrak{f}_e(\mathscr{R})$. Clearly, the labeled nulls $c_2', \ldots, c_n'$ are created during the application of σ, i.e., $\mathbf{b}$ is the atom at which $c_2', \ldots, c_n'$ are invented during the construction of the chase. Therefore, the atom $\mathbf{c}$ is obtained starting from $\mathbf{b}$. Since, by induction hypothesis, $h_{k-1}(\mu(\mathbf{b})) \in chase(D, \Sigma_T)$, it follows that $h_{k-1}(\mu(\mathbf{c})) \in chase(D, \Sigma_T)$, as needed.

Suppose now that $\sigma = r'(X_1, \ldots, X_n) \to r(X_{i_1}, \ldots, X_{i_n})$, where $r' \in \mathfrak{f}_r(\mathscr{R})$ and $[i_1, \ldots, i_n]$ is a permutation of $[n]$. Assume first that $\mathbf{c}$ is such that $pred(\mathbf{c}) \in \mathfrak{f}_r(\mathscr{R})$ and $dom(\mathbf{c}) = \{c_1, c_2', \ldots, c_n'\}$. By definition of non-conflicting CDs, the only way to obtain $\mathbf{b}$ during the chase is due to a path P of the form $e[1] {\frown} s_1[j_1] {\frown} \ldots {\frown} s_m[j_m] {\frown} r'[j_{m+1}] {\frown} r[1]$, where $m \geqslant 0$, $\{j_1, \ldots, j_{m+1}\} \subseteq [n]$, $e \in \mathfrak{f}_e(\mathscr{R})$ and $\{s_1, \ldots, s_m\} \subset \mathfrak{f}_r(\mathscr{R})$, in the CD-graph G of Σ. Note that $e[1]$ is an e-node, and all the other nodes in P are r-nodes. Moreover, due to the existence of κ in Σ_K, $r[1]$ is a k-node. In case that $\mathbf{c}$ is obtained starting from $\mathbf{b}$, then $h_{k-1}(\mu(\mathbf{c})) \in chase(D, \Sigma_T)$ since, by induction hypothesis, $h_{k-1}(\mu(\mathbf{b})) \in chase(D, \Sigma_T)$. The interesting case is when $\mathbf{c}$ is generated before $\mathbf{b}$ due to the existence of the path P. By definition of non-conflicting CDs, in G we have a path P' of only r-nodes from $r[1]$ to $s_1[j_1]$. Furthermore, the permutation $\pi_G(C)$, where C is the cycle $r[1] {\frown} \ldots {\frown} s_1[j_1] {\frown} \ldots {\frown} s_m[j_m] {\frown} r'[j_{m+1}] {\frown} r[1]$ in G, is equal to id_n. Since, by induction hypothesis, $h_{k-1}(\mu(\mathbf{b})) \in chase(D, \Sigma_T)$, we get that $h_{k-1}(\mu(\mathbf{c})) \in chase(D, \Sigma_T)$. Finally, suppose that $\mathbf{c}$ is such that $pred(\mathbf{c}) \in \mathfrak{f}_e(\mathscr{R}) \cup \mathfrak{f}_{ae}(\mathscr{R}) \cup \mathfrak{f}_{ar}(\mathscr{R})$. It is clear that $\mathbf{c}$ is obtained starting from some atom $\mathbf{d} \in chase^{[k-1]}(D, \Sigma)$ such that $pred(\mathbf{d}) \in \mathfrak{f}_r(\mathscr{R})$ and $dom(\mathbf{d}) = \{c_1, c_2', \ldots, c_n'\}$. Since $h_{k-1}(\mu(\mathbf{d})) \in chase(D, \Sigma_T)$, then $h_{k-1}(\mu(\mathbf{c})) \in chase(D, \Sigma_T)$, as needed.

The desired homomorphism from $chase(D, \Sigma)$ to $chase(D, \Sigma_T)$ is eventually $h = \bigcup_{k=0}^{\infty} h_k$. □

By using Lemma 10.1, it is easy to establish separability of non-conflicting CDs.

Theorem 10.2. *Consider a set Σ of CDs over a schema $\mathscr{R}$. If Σ is non-conflicting, then it is separable.*

Proof. Let $\Sigma = \Sigma_T \cup \Sigma_K$, where Σ_T are TGDs and Σ_K are KDs, and let D be a database for $\mathscr{R}$. Suppose that $chase(D, \Sigma)$ does not fail (otherwise the claim holds trivially). By Lemma 10.1, we get that there exists a homomorphism that maps $chase(D, \Sigma)$ to $chase(D, \Sigma_T)$. Moreover, since $chase(D, \Sigma_T)$ is a universal model of D with respect to Σ_T, and $chase(D, \Sigma) \in mods(D, \Sigma_T)$, there exists a homomorphism that maps $chase(D, \Sigma_T)$ to $chase(D, \Sigma)$. Therefore, $chase(D, \Sigma)$ and $chase(D, \Sigma_T)$ are homomorphically equivalent, which implies that for each CQ q over $\mathscr{R}$, $q(chase(D, \Sigma)) = q(chase(D, \Sigma_T))$. The claim follows by Theorem 10.1. □

Interestingly, for CDs the property of being non-conflicting, it is not only sufficient for separability, but it is also necessary. This way we precisely characterize the class of separable CDs by means of a graph-based syntactic condition.

Theorem 10.3. *Consider a set Σ of CDs over a schema $\mathscr{R}$. If Σ is not non-conflicting, then it is not separable.*

Proof. Let $\Sigma = \Sigma_T \cup \Sigma_K$, where Σ_T are TGDs and Σ_K are KDs. We prove this result by exhibiting a database D such that $chase(D, \Sigma)$ does not fail, and show that there exists a Boolean CQ q such that $\langle \rangle \in ans(q, D, \Sigma)$ but $\langle \rangle \notin ans(q, D, \Sigma_T)$. Let G be the CD-graph for $\mathscr{R}$ and Σ. We proceed by considering the following two cases.

Suppose that the first condition of the Definition 10.4 is violated. Thus, there exists a path $v_1^{\frown} v_2^{\frown} \ldots^{\frown} v_m$, for $m \geqslant 2$, in G as in the Definition 10.4 for which the following holds. Let $v_1 = e_1[1]$ and $v_i = r_i[j_i]$, for each $i \in \{2, \ldots, m\}$. Assume that r_m is a predicate of arity n. There exists a cycle C of only r-nodes in G going through $r_m[j_m]$ such that $\pi_G(C) \neq id_n$. Consider the database $D = \{e_1(c)\}$. The arc $e_1[1]^{\frown} r_2[j_2]$ is necessarily labeled by the TGD

$$e(X) \rightarrow \exists X_1 \ldots \exists X_{j_2-1} \exists X_{j_2+1} \ldots \exists X_n \, r_2(X_1, \ldots, X_{j_2-1}, X, X_{j_2+1}, X_n).$$

Thus, eventually the atom $r_m(z_1, \ldots, z_{j_m-1}, c, z_{j_m+1}, \ldots, z_n)$ is obtained during the chase, where, for each $i \in \{1, \ldots, j_m - 1, j_m + 1, \ldots, n\}$, $z_i \in \Gamma_N$. Since the cycle C exists in G, $r_m(w_1, \ldots, w_{j_m-1}, c, w_{j_m+1}, \ldots, w_n)$ is generated, where $\{w_1, \ldots, w_{j_m-1}, w_{j_m+1}, \ldots, w_n\} = \{z_1, \ldots, z_{j_m-1}, z_{j_m+1}, \ldots, z_n\}$. Clearly, after the application of the KD $key(r_m) = \{j_m\}$, we get an atom **a** such that at least two attributes of **a** have the same null. Note that it is not possible to get such an atom during the construction of $chase(D, \Sigma_T)$. Therefore, we can construct an atomic Boolean CQ q, i.e., with just one atom in its body, for which there exists a homomorphism h such that $h(body(q)) = \mathbf{a}$, and thus $h(body(q)) \in chase(D, \Sigma)$, but there is no a homomorphism h' such that $h'(body(q)) \in chase(D, \Sigma_T)$. Hence, $\langle\rangle \in ans(q, D, \Sigma)$ but $\langle\rangle \notin ans(q, D, \Sigma_T)$. Obviously, since in $dom(D)$ we have just one constant of Γ, the chase does not fail.

Now, suppose that the second condition of the Definition 10.4 is violated. This implies that there exists a path $v_1^{\curvearrowright} v_2^{\curvearrowright} \ldots^{\curvearrowright} v_m$, for $m \geq 3$, in G as in the Definition 10.4, but there is no path of only r-nodes from v_m to v_2. Assume that $v_1 = e_1[1]$ and $v_i = r_i[j_i]$, for each $i \in \{2, \ldots, m\}$. Consider the database $D = \{e_1(c), r_m(c, \ldots, c)\}$. The arc $e[1]^{\curvearrowright} r_2[j_2]$ is necessarily labeled by the TGD

$$e(X) \rightarrow \exists X_1 \ldots \exists X_{j_2-1} \exists X_{j_2+1} \ldots \exists X_n \, r_2(X_1, \ldots, X_{j_2-1}, X, X_{j_2+1}, X_n).$$

Hence, $r_2(z_1, \ldots, z_{j_2-1}, c, z_{j_2+1}, \ldots, z_n)$ is obtained during the chase, where, for each $i \in \{1, \ldots, j_2 - 1, j_2 + 1, \ldots, n\}$, $z_i \in \Gamma_N$. Eventually, due to the path $v_2^{\curvearrowright} \ldots^{\curvearrowright} v_m$, the atom $r_m(w_1, \ldots, w_{j_m-1}, c, w_{j_m+1}, \ldots, w_n)$ is generated, where $\{w_1, \ldots, w_{j_m-1}, w_{j_m+1}, \ldots, w_n\} = \{z_1, \ldots, z_{j_2-1}, z_{j_2+1}, \ldots, z_n\}$. Since v_m is a k-node, we replace w_k with c, for each $k \in \{1, \ldots, j_m - 1, j_m + 1, \ldots, n\}$. Thus, we get (among others) the atom $r_2(c, \ldots, c)$. Instead, in $chase(D, \Sigma_T)$ the atom $r_2(z_1, \ldots, z_{j_2-1}, c, z_{j_2+1}, \ldots, z_n)$ remains in place, and there is no way to obtain the atom $r_2(c, \ldots, c)$ due to the absence of a path of only r-nodes from v_m to v_2 in G. Now, let us define the atomic Boolean CQ $q = p \leftarrow r_2(c, \ldots, c)$. It is easy to see that $\langle\rangle \in ans(q, D, \Sigma)$ but $\langle\rangle \notin ans(q, D, \Sigma_T)$. Finally, since we have just one constant of Γ in $dom(D)$, there is no chase failure. □

It is straightforward to see that Theorem 10.2 holds for IPCDs and BACDs, since these two classes are special cases of CDs. Moreover, for both IPCDs and BACDs the property of being non-conflicting it is necessary for separability; the proof of this result is similar to that of Theorem 10.3. The following corollary follows immediately.

Corollary 10.1. *Consider a set Σ of IPCDs or BACDs over a schema $\mathscr{R}$. Σ is separable if and only if is non-conflicting.*

10.5   Query Answering Under Non-Conflicting CDs

Let us now investigate the data and combined complexity of the (decision) problem of conjunctive query answering under non-conflicting CDs.

10.5.1   Data Complexity

As we shall see, once we know that the chase does not fail, the problem under consideration is in the highly tractable class AC_0 in data complexity. Before we proceed further, let us recall the semantic notion of *first-order rewritability* introduced in the context of description logics [16].

A class $\mathfrak{C}$ of dependencies is *first-order rewritable*, henceforth abbreviated as *FO-rewritable*, if for every CQ q/n, and for every set Σ of dependencies in $\mathfrak{C}$, it is possible to construct a (finite) first-order query q_Σ such that, for every database D and an n-tuple $\mathbf{t} \in \Gamma^n$, $\mathbf{t} \in ans(q, D, \Sigma)$ if and only if $\mathbf{t} \in q_\Sigma(D)$. It is well-known that evaluating first-order queries is in the highly tractable class AC_0 in data complexity [34]. Recall that AC_0 is the complexity class of recognizing words in languages defined by constant-depth Boolean circuits with an (unlimited fan-in) AND and OR gates (see, e.g., [32]).

Theorem 10.4. *Consider a CQ q/n over a schema $\mathcal{R}$, a database D for $\mathcal{R}$, a set Σ of non-conflicting CDs over $\mathcal{R}$, and an n-tuple $\mathbf{t} \in \Gamma^n$. If chase(D, Σ) does not fail, then deciding whether $\mathbf{t} \in ans(q, D, \Sigma)$ is in AC_0 in data complexity.*

Proof. Let $\Sigma = \Sigma_T \cup \Sigma_K$, where Σ_T are TGDs and Σ_K are KDs. Theorem 10.2 implies that $ans(q, D, \Sigma)$ and $ans(q, D, \Sigma_T)$ coincide. Thus, the problem whether $\mathbf{t} \in ans(q, D, \Sigma)$ is equivalent to the problem whether $\mathbf{t} \in ans(q, D, \Sigma_T)$. Recall that Σ_T is a set of inclusion dependencies. It is well-known that the class of inclusion dependencies is FO-rewritable [6], and the claim follows.   □

Since IPCDs and BACDs are special cases of CDs, it is obvious that the above result holds also for non-conflicting IPCDs and non-conflicting BACDs. Notice that Theorem 10.4 does not give the exact upper bound for the data complexity of the problem under consideration. This is because we assume that the chase does not fail. The data complexity of the problem of deciding whether the chase fails will be studied in Sect. 10.5.3.

Interestingly, general CDs are not FO-rewritable; the proof of this result is similar to a non-FO-rewritability proof given in [15].

Theorem 10.5. *The class of CDs is not FO-rewritable.*

Proof. This result can be established by exhibiting a Boolean CQ q over a schema $\mathcal{R}$, a database D for $\mathcal{R}$, and a set Σ of CDs over $\mathcal{R}$ for which there is no a (finite) first-order query q_Σ such that $\langle\rangle \in ans(q, D, \Sigma)$ if and only if $\langle\rangle \in q_\Sigma(D)$.   □

10.5.2   Combined Complexity

We now focus on the combined complexity of the CQ answering problem under non-conflicting CDs. First we show that, providing that the chase does not fail, the problem is in PSPACE in general, and is in NP in the case of IPCDs and BACDs.

Theorem 10.6. *Consider a CQ q/n over a schema $\mathcal{R}$, a database D for $\mathcal{R}$, a set Σ of non-conflicting CDs (resp., IPCDs or BACDs) over $\mathcal{R}$, and an n-tuple $\mathbf{t} \in \Gamma^n$. If chase(D, Σ) does not fail, then the problem of deciding whether $\mathbf{t} \in ans(q, D, \Sigma)$ is in PSPACE (resp., NP) in combined complexity.*

Proof. Let $\Sigma = \Sigma_T \cup \Sigma_K$, where Σ_T are TGDs and Σ_K are KDs. Since *chase*(D, Σ) does not fail, Theorem 10.2 implies that our problem is equivalent to the problem whether $\mathbf{t} \in ans(q, D, \Sigma_T)$. Recall that Σ_T is a set of inclusion dependencies. Moreover, observe that if Σ is a set of BACDs, then the maximum arity over all predicates of $\mathscr{R}$ is bounded by a constant. The claim for non-conflicting CDs and non-conflicting BACDs follows from the fact that CQ answering under inclusion dependencies is in PSPACE in general, and in NP in the case of bounded arity [22].

The NP upper bound in the case of non-conflicting IPCDs does not follow immediately from the fact that CQ answering under inclusion dependencies, in the case of bounded arity, is in NP since we have to deal with predicates of unbounded arity. It is possible to show that under non-conflicting IPCDs, for query answering purposes, it suffices to consider an initial finite part of the chase whose depth is polynomial with respect to q and $\mathscr{R}$. This fact allows us to exhibit a non-deterministic PTIME algorithm which decides whether $\mathbf{t} \in chase(D, \Sigma_T)$. For the formal proof we refer the reader to (Calì et al., 2011, Ontological query answering under expressive Entity-Relationship schemata, Unpublished). $\square$

As for Theorem 10.4, it is important to say that Theorem 10.6 does not provide the exact upper bound for the combined complexity of the problem under consideration, since we assume that the chase does not fail. The combined complexity of the problem of deciding whether the chase fails will be studied in the next subsection.

Let us now establish the desired lower bounds for CQ answering under non-conflicting CDs (resp., BACDs, IPCDs). A useful decision problem that we are going to employ in the proof of the following result is the *finite function generation (FFG)* problem introduced and studied by Kozen in [23]. Consider a finite set of functions $F \cup \{f\}$ from a set S to itself. The question is whether we can obtain f by composing functions of F. This problem is PSPACE-hard, even in the case of bijective functions.

Theorem 10.7. *CQ-Ans under non-conflicting CDs is* PSPACE-*hard in combined complexity.*

Proof. The proof is by reduction from FFG. Consider a set $F \cup \{f\}$ of bijective functions from a set S to itself. Suppose that $F = \{f_1, \ldots, f_m\}$, for $m \geqslant 1$. Moreover, without loss of generality, assume that $S = [n]$, for some integer $n \geqslant 2$.

Let q be the Boolean CQ $p \leftarrow r(c_{f(1)}, \ldots, c_{f(n)})$, $D = \{r(c_1, \ldots, c_n)\}$, where $\langle c_1, \ldots, c_n \rangle \in \Gamma^n$, and Σ be the set of CDs associated to the schema

> entity E
> relationship R among $\underbrace{E, \ldots, E}_{n}$
>
> isa: $R[f_1(1), \ldots, f_1(n)], \ldots, R[f_m(1), \ldots, f_m(n)]$.

Clearly, Σ is a set of non-conflicting CDs since in the CD-graph of Σ there is no k-node. It is straightforward to see that $\langle \rangle \in ans(q, D, \Sigma)$ if and only if f can be obtained by composing functions of F. This completes the proof. $\square$

We conclude this subsection by showing that in the case of non-conflicting IPCDs and non-conflicting BACDs CQ answering is NP-hard.

Theorem 10.8. *CQ-Ans under non-conflicting IPCDs and non-conflicting BACDs is* NP-*hard in combined complexity.*

Proof. It is well-known that the problem of CQ answering under no dependencies, even for a relational schema with fixed arity, is NP-hard in combined complexity [17]. The desired lower bounds can be easily established by providing a reduction from the above problem. □

10.5.3   Chase Failure

In this subsection we show, by exploiting a technique proposed in [8], that the problem whether the chase fails is tantamount to the CQ answering problem (providing that the chase does not fail). In what follows we are going to use the notion of union of CQs. A *union of conjunctive queries* Q of arity n is a set of CQs, where each $q \in Q$ has the same arity n and uses the same predicate symbol in the head. The answer to Q over a database D is defined as the set $Q(D) = \{\mathbf{t} \mid \text{there exists } q \in Q \text{ such that } \mathbf{t} \in q(D)\}$.

Lemma 10.2. *Consider a database D for $\mathscr{R}$, and a set $\Sigma = \Sigma_T \cup \Sigma_K$ over $\mathscr{R}$, where Σ_T are TGDs and Σ_K are KDs. If both $\mathscr{R}$ and Σ are arbitrary (resp., fixed), then we can construct in* PTIME *(resp., in* AC_0*) a database D' and a union of Boolean CQs Q such that chase(D, Σ) fails if and only if $\langle\rangle \in Q(\text{chase}(D', \Sigma_T))$.*

Proof. Let D' be the database obtained from D by adding a fact $neq(c_1, c_2)$, for each pair of distinct constants c_1 and c_2 that appear in $dom(D)$, where neq is an auxiliary predicate symbol not occurring in $\mathscr{R}$. The union of Boolean CQs Q is constructed as follows: for every KD $key(r) = [m] \in \Sigma_K$, where $r/n \in \mathscr{R}$ (without loss of generality we assume the first $m < n$ attributes to form the key), and for each $j \in \{m + 1, \ldots, n\}$, we add to Q the Boolean CQ $p \leftarrow r(\mathbf{X}, Y_{m+1}, \ldots, Y_n), r(\mathbf{X}, Z_{m+1}, \ldots, Z_n), neq(Y_j, Z_j)$, where $\mathbf{X} = X_1, \ldots, X_m$.

In the case where both $\mathscr{R}$ and Σ are arbitrary, then D' and Q can be constructed in polynomial time. In particular, the number of atoms that we add in D is less than $(|dom(D)|)^2$, while the number of Boolean CQs that we construct is $|\Sigma_K|$. Now, in the case where both $\mathscr{R}$ and Σ are fixed, the required atoms can be obtained by evaluating the first-order query

$$const(X_i) \leftarrow \bigvee_{r/n \in \mathscr{R}} \bigvee_{i \in [n]} \exists X_1 \ldots \exists X_{i-1} \exists X_{i+1} \ldots \exists X_n \, r(X_1, \ldots, X_n),$$
$$neq(X, Y) \leftarrow const(X) \wedge const(Y) \wedge X \neq Y,$$

over the database D, which is feasible in AC_0 in data complexity [34]. The above first-order query depends only on the schema $\mathscr{R}$, and thus can be constructed in constant time. Obviously Q can be constructed in constant time. It is not difficult to show that $chase(D, \Sigma)$ fails if and only if $\langle\rangle \in Q(chase(D', \Sigma_T))$.   □

By exploiting Lemma 10.2 and Theorems 10.4 and 10.6–10.8, it is not difficult to establish the exact data and combined complexity of CQ answering.

Corollary 10.2. *CQ-Ans under non-conflicting CDs is in* AC$_0$ *in data complexity, and* PSPACE-*complete in combined complexity. Also, CQ-Ans under non-conflicting IPCDs and BACDs is* NP-*complete in combined complexity.*

10.6 Adding Negative Constraints

Negative constraints (NCs) of the form $\varphi(\mathbf{X}) \to \bot$ (see Sect. 10.2.3) can be used in order to express several relevant constructs in ER$^+$ schemata, e.g., disjointness between entities and relationships, and non-participation of entities to relationships, but also more general ones. The new conceptual model which arises is called ER$_\bot^+$. In fact, an ER$_\bot^+$ schema $\mathscr{C}$ is an ER$^+$ schema with an additional set $\Sigma_\bot$ of NCs over $\mathscr{R}$, where $\mathscr{R}$ is the relational schema associated to $\mathscr{C}$.

Example 10.8. Consider the ER$^+$ schema $\mathscr{C}$ obtained from the one in Example 10.2 (see Fig. 10.1) by adding the entity *Pension_scheme* and a relationship *Enrolled* among *Member* and *Pension_scheme*, without any cardinality constraints. The fact that students and professors are disjoint sets can be represented with the NC $phd\_student(X), professor(X) \to \bot$ (entity disjointness). Moreover, the fact that a student cannot be enrolled in a pension scheme (i.e., it does not participate to *Enrolled* as the first component) can be represented by the NC $phd\_student(X)$, $enrolled(X, Y) \to \bot$ (non-participation of an entity to a relationship).   ■

A set of CDs and NCs is separable if the answers to queries can be computed by considering the TGDs only, and ignoring the KDs and the NCs, once it is known that the chase does not fail, and also that the chase satisfies the set of NCs.

Definition 10.5. Consider a set $\Sigma = \Sigma_T \cup \Sigma_K$ of CDs over a schema $\mathscr{R}$, where Σ_T are TGDs and Σ_K are KDs, and a set $\Sigma_\bot$ of NCs over $\mathscr{R}$. $\Sigma \cup \Sigma_\bot$ is *separable* if for every database D for $\mathscr{R}$, we have that either $chase(D, \Sigma)$ fails or $chase(D, \Sigma) \not\models \Sigma_\bot$ or, for every CQ q over $\mathscr{R}$, $ans(q, D, \Sigma) = ans(q, D, \Sigma_T)$.

It is straightforward to see that given a set Σ of CDs and a set $\Sigma_\bot$ of NCs, the fact that Σ is non-conflicting is sufficient for separability of $\Sigma \cup \Sigma_\bot$; this follows immediately from Theorem 10.2. The question that comes up is whether the non-conflicting property is also necessary for separability. It is not difficult to show that there exists a set Σ of CDs and a set $\Sigma_\bot$ of NCs such that Σ is not non-conflicting, but $\Sigma \cup \Sigma_\bot$ is separable.

Interestingly, if we consider only *strongly consistent* schemata [2], then the non-conflicting property is also necessary for separability. An ER$_\bot^+$ schema $\mathscr{C}$, where Σ is the of CDs over $\mathscr{R}$ associated to $\mathscr{C}$ and $\Sigma_\bot$ is the of NCs over $\mathscr{R}$ associated to $\mathscr{C}$, is strongly consistent if there exists a (possibly infinite) instance I for $\mathscr{R}$ such that $I \models \Sigma \cup \Sigma_\perp$, and for each $e \in f_e(\mathscr{R})$ and $r \in f_r(\mathscr{R})$, $e(I) \neq \varnothing$ and $r(I) \neq \varnothing$. It is possible to show that the problem of deciding whether an $\mathsf{ER}_\perp^+$ schema $\mathscr{C}$, where the set of CDs associated to $\mathscr{C}$ is non-conflicting, is strongly consistent is PSPACE-complete. The formal proofs are omitted and can be found in (Calì et al., 2011, Ontological query answering under expressive Entity-Relationship schemata, Unpublished).

We conclude this section by showing that the addition of NCs does not alter the complexity of CQ answering under non-conflicting CDs.

Theorem 10.9. *CQ-Ans under non-conflicting CDs and NCs is in* AC$_0$ *in data complexity, and* PSPACE-*complete in combined complexity. Also, CQ-Ans under non-conflicting IPCDs and BACDs is* NP-*complete in combined complexity.*

Proof. Consider a CQ q/n over a schema $\mathscr{R}$, a database D for $\mathscr{R}$, a set $\Sigma = \Sigma_T \cup \Sigma_K$ of non-conflicting CDs (resp., IPCDs, BACDs) over $\mathscr{R}$, where Σ_T are TGDs and Σ_K are KDs, a set $\Sigma_\perp$ of NCs over $\mathscr{R}$, and an n-tuple $\mathbf{t} \in \Gamma^n$. It holds that $\mathbf{t} \in ans(q, D, \Sigma \cup \Sigma_\perp)$ if and only if $chase(D, \Sigma)$ fails or $chase(D, \Sigma) \not\models \Sigma_\perp$ or $\mathbf{t} \in ans(q, D, \Sigma)$. Therefore, we can decide whether $\mathbf{t} \in ans(q, D, \Sigma \cup \Sigma_\perp)$ by applying the following simple algorithm; given a NC $\nu = \varphi(\mathbf{X}) \to \perp$, we denote by q_ν the Boolean CQ $p \leftarrow \varphi(\mathbf{X})$:

1. Construct the database D' from D and the union of Boolean CQs Q from Σ_K, as described in the proof of Lemma 10.2.
2. If $\langle\rangle \in Q(chase(D', \Sigma_T))$, then *accept*.
3. If there exists $\nu \in \Sigma_\perp$ such that $\langle\rangle \in ans(q_\nu, D, \Sigma)$, then *accept*.
4. If $\mathbf{t} \in ans(q, D, \Sigma)$, then *accept*; otherwise, *reject*.

Soundness and completeness of the above algorithm follows immediately from Lemma 10.2. Step 1 can be carried out in PTIME in general, and in AC$_0$ in case both $\mathscr{R}$ and Σ are fixed (see Lemma 10.2). Since Σ is a set of non-conflicting CDs (resp., IPCDs, BACDs), the claim follows immediately from Corollary 10.2. $\square$

10.7   Discussion

In this chapter we have introduced an extension of Chen's Entity Relationship model, that is, the ER^+ family. ER^+ is a very natural formalism for modeling data, as it builds upon the ER model, which has been used for decades in database design. We argue that the ER model is a powerful tool for ontological query answering, which at the same time is not awkward to understand and use; in particular, practitioners and even persons without any technical knowledge can profitably use ER (and its extensions) to express ontologies.

We have presented three ER^+ languages which, by means of mild restrictions specified by efficiently-testable syntactic conditions, enjoy the separability property and first-order rewritability. The latter ensures not only that query answering under our languages is in the low complexity class AC_0, but that answering can be done by evaluating a suitable SQL query over the initial data. This opens the possibility of efficient implementation of query answering under non-conflicting ER^+ schemata on large data sets. Our study also pinpoints the complexity of query answering under our three non-conflicting ER^+ languages with respect to both data and combined complexity.

It is worth noticing that the problem we deal with in this chapter has several other applications. It is tightly related to the analogous problem of query answering on incomplete data under constraints [6, 27] and to semantic data integration [24]. Moreover, our problem of query answering is mutually reducible to the query containment problem (see, e.g., [7]), therefore all our results carry on to the latter.

Finally, we remind the reader that the complexity results for most DL-Lite languages come, in fact, as special cases of our results on ER^+. For instance, non-conflicting $ER^+_{\mathscr{B}}$ with negative constraints is strictly more expressive than the languages $DL\text{-}Lite_{\mathscr{F}}$ and $DL\text{-}Lite_{\mathscr{R}}$ [16, 26]. This shows that, if DL-Lite languages are useful and important for modeling database schemata and ontologies, then *a fortiori* also ER^+ is.

References

1. Abiteboul, S., Hull, R., Vianu, V.: Foundations of Databases. Addison-Wesley, Reading (1995)
2. Artale, A., Calvanese, D., Kontchakov, R., Ryzhikov, V., Zakharyaschev, M.: Reasoning over extended ER models. In: Proceedings of ER, pp. 277–292 (2007)
3. Battista, G.D., Lenzerini, M.: A deductive method for entity-relationship modeling. In: Proceedings of VLDB, pp. 13–21 (1989)
4. Calì, A., Calvanese, D., Giacomo, G.D., Lenzerini, M.: Accessing data integration systems through conceptual schemas. In: Proceedings of ER, pp. 270–284 (2001)
5. Calì, A., Lembo, D., Rosati, R.: Query rewriting and answering under constraints in data integration systems. In: Proceedings of IJCAI, pp. 16–21 (2003)
6. Calì, A., Lembo, D., Rosati, R.: Decidability and complexity of query answering over incosistent and incomplete databases. In: Proceedings of PODS, pp. 260–271 (2003)
7. Calì, A., Gottlob, G., Kifer, M.: Taming the infinite chase: query answering under expressive relational constraints. In: Proceedings of KR, pp. 70–80 (2008)
8. Calì, A., Gottlob, G., Lukasiewicz, T.: A general Datalog-based framework for tractable query answering over ontologies. In: Proceedings of PODS, pp. 77–86 (2009)
9. Calì, A., Gottlob, G., Pieris, A.: Advanced processing for ontological queries. PVLDB 3, 554–565 (2010)
10. Calì, A., Gottlob, G., Pieris, A.: Query answering under non-guarded rules in Datalog+/−. In: Proceedings of RR 1–17 (2010)
11. Calì, A., Gottlob, G., Kifer, M., Lukasiewicz, T., Pieris, A.: Ontological reasoning with F-Logic Lite and its extensions. In: Proceedings of AAAI (2010)
12. Calì, A., Martinenghi, D.: Querying incomplete data over extended ER schemata. TPLP 10, 291–329 (2010)
13. Calvanese, D., Giacomo, G.D., Lenzerini, M.: On the decidability of query containment under constraints. In: Proceedings of PODS, pp. 149–158 (1998)
14. Calvanese, D., Lenzerini, M., Nardi, D.: Description logics for conceptual data modeling. In: Logics for Databases and Information Systems, pp. 229–263. Kluwer, Norwell (1998)

15. Calvanese, D., Giacomo, G.D., Lembo, D., Lenzerini, M., Rosati, R.: What to ask to a peer: ontology-based query reformulation. In: Proceedings of KR, pp. 469–478 (2004)
16. Calvanese, D., De Giacomo, G., Lembo, D., Lenzerini, M., Rosati, R.: Tractable reasoning and efficient query answering in description logics: the DL-Lite family. J. Autom. Reasoning **39**, 385–429 (2007)
17. Chandra, A.K., Merlin, P.M.: Optimal implementation of conjunctive queries in relational data bases. In: Proceedings of STOC, pp. 77–90 (1977)
18. Chen, P.P.: The Entity-Relationship model: towards a unified view of data. ACM Trans. Database Syst. **1**, 9–36 (1976)
19. Deutsch, A., Nash, A., Remmel, J.B.: The chase revisisted. In: Proceedings of PODS, pp. 149–158 (2008)
20. Fagin, R., Kolaitis, P.G., Miller, R.J., Popa, L.: Data exchange: semantics and query answering. Theor. Comput. Sci. **336**, 89–124 (2005)
21. Gogolla, M., Hohenstein, U.: Towards a semantic view of an extended Entity-Relationship model. ACM Trans. Database Syst. **16**, 369–416 (1991)
22. Johnson, D.S., Klug, A.C.: Testing containment of conjunctive queries under functional and inclusion dependencies. J. Comput. Syst. Sci. **28**, 167–189 (1984)
23. Kozen, D.: Lower bounds for natural proof systems. In: Proceedings of FOCS, pp. 254–266 (1977)
24. Lenzerini, M.: Data integration: a theoretical perspective. In: Proceedings of PODS, pp. 233–246 (2002)
25. Maier, D., Mendelzon, A.O., Sagiv, Y.: Testing implications of data dependencies. ACM Trans. Database Syst. **4**, 455–469 (1979)
26. Poggi, A., Lembo, D., Calvanese, D., De Giacomo, G., Lenzerini, M., Rosati, R.: Linking data to ontologies. J. Data Semantics **10**, 133–173 (2008)
27. van der Meyden R.: Logical approaches to incomplete information: a survey. In: Logics for Databases and Information Systems, pp. 307–356. Kluwer, Norwell (1998)
28. Markowitz, V.M., Shoshani, A.: Representing extended Entity-Relationship structures in relational databases: a modular approach. ACM Trans. Database Syst. **17**, 423–464 (1992)
29. Markowitz, V.M., Makowsky, J.A.: Identifying extended Entity-Relationship object structures in relational schemas. IEEE Trans. Software Eng. **16**, 777–790 (1990)
30. Marnette, B.: Generalized schema-mappings: from termination to tractability. In: Proceedings of PODS, pp. 13–22 (2009)
31. Ortiz, M., Calvanese, D., Eiter, T.: Characterizing data complexity for conjunctive query answering in expressive description logics. In: Proceedings of AAAI (2006)
32. Papadimitriou, C.H.: Computational Complexity. Addison-Wesley, Reading (1999)
33. Vardi, M.Y.: The complexity of relational query languages. In: Proceedings of STOC, pp. 137–146 (1982)
34. Vardi, M.Y.: On the complexity of bounded-variable queries. In: Proceedings of PODS, pp. 266–276 (1995)

Chapter 11
Linked Data Services and Semantics-Enabled Mashup

Devis Bianchini and Valeria De Antonellis

11.1 Introduction

The Web of Linked Data can be seen as a global database, where resources are identified through URIs, are self-described (by means of the URI dereferencing mechanism), and are globally connected through RDF links. According to the Linked Data perspective, research attention is progressively shifting from data organization and representation to linkage and composition of the huge amount of data available on the Web [1]. For example, at the time of this writing, the DBpedia knowledge base describes more than 3.5 million things, conceptualized through 672 million RDF triples, with 6.5 million external links into other RDF datasets. Useful applications have been provided for enabling people to browse this wealth of data, like Tabulator [7]. Other systems have been implemented to collect, index, and provide advanced searching facilities over the Web of Linked Data, such as Watson [15] and Sindice [39]. Besides these applications, domain-specific systems to gather and mash up Linked Data have been proposed, like DBpedia Mobile [4] and Revyu.com. DBpedia Mobile is a location-aware client for the semantic Web that can be used on an iPhone and other mobile devices. Based on the current GPS position of a mobile device, DBpedia Mobile renders a map indicating nearby locations from the DBpedia dataset. Starting from this map, the user can explore background information about his or her surroundings. Revyu.com is a Web site where you can review and rate whatever is possible to identify (through a URI) on the Web. Nevertheless, the potential advantages implicit in the Web of Linked Data are far from being fully exploited. Current applications hardly go beyond presenting together data gathered from different sources [10]. Recently, research on the Web

D. Bianchini (✉) · V. De Antonellis
Department of Information Engineering, University of Brescia, via Branze 38,
25123 – Brescia, Italy
e-mail: bianchin@ing.unibs.it; deantone@ing.unibs.it

R. De Virgilio et al. (eds.), *Semantic Search over the Web*,
Data-Centric Systems and Applications, DOI 10.1007/978-3-642-25008-8_11,
© Springer-Verlag Berlin Heidelberg 2012

of Linked Data has been devoted to the study of models and languages to add functionalities to the Web of Linked Data by means of *Linked Data services*. As it is known, Web services and semantic Web technologies have been widely addressed and studied to bring into reality the principles of software reuse and interoperability, although their uptake on a Web scale has been significantly less prominent than initially foreseen [16]. This is due to several reasons: first of all, service-oriented architectures have been mainly suited for enterprises and for the most part targeted WSDL/SOAP-based Web services [21]. The world around services on the Web has significantly evolved toward a proliferation of Web APIs, also called RESTful services [45] when they conform to the REST architectural style [24], and of RSS/Atom feeds. On the other hand, the complexity of semantic Web service modeling solutions like OWL-S [36] and WSMO [11] requires the use of rich semantic languages and complex reasoners, which hampered their significant uptake. For the Web of Linked Data, different lightweight solutions have been proposed like the WSMO-Lite language [47] for the semantic annotation of WSDL/SOAP-based Web services and the combined use of MicroWSMO/hRESTS languages [32] for annotating Web APIs, which do not present any structure and in most cases are mainly described through Web pages in plain HTML for human consumption.

Tools have been created to specifically support users in the annotation of services by leveraging the Web of Linked Data as a source of background knowledge. Such applications, such as SWEET [35], which assist users in annotating HTML descriptions of Web APIs, and SOWER,[1] for supporting the semantic annotation of WSDL/SOAP-based Web services, rely on solutions like Watson [15] for browsing the Web of Linked Data so that it is possible to identify suitable vocabularies (e.g., eCl@ass, Good Relations [29], and FOAF) and use them for the annotation. So-called Linked Data services can be used for processing the Web of Linked Data and for producing Linked Data from the large body of information behind RESTful services and WSDL services in legacy systems. The aim is to build a serving system on top of Linked Data whereby people are enabled to collaboratively develop and deploy applications by reusing existing components.

When the selection from the shelf of available components and their aggregation are performed to build value-added, short-living, situational Web applications, the term *mashup* is often used [5]. Mashup can be performed both for domain-independent actions such as transforming data between different schemas or determining how trustworthy is a portion of data and for domain-dependent applications such as sending an SMS or booking a hotel online. Actually, users are overwhelmed by the growing number of existing components, and this phenomenon is also described as lost in hyperspace [18]. To facilitate mashup of components, an information retrieval perspective, where the mashup designer has a specific query in mind which he/she tries to answer, is often assumed. Approaches of this kind are inspired or by Yahoo! Pipes, as, for example, semantic Web pipes [42], or by the query-by-example paradigm, such as MashQL [30]. Note that these kinds of

[1]http://technologies.kmi.open.ac.uk/soa4all-studio/provisioning-platform/sower/.

approaches hold the perspective of "data" mashup, while the vision of Linked Data services aims at extending the Web of Linked Data with "functionalities" that should be properly combined. According to this vision, we consider Web APIs on top of the Web of Linked Data and their composition or mashup.

In this chapter, we address the above-mentioned issues by proposing a new approach for "serving up" Linked Data by semantics-enabled mashup of existing Web APIs. A basic semantics-enabled model of Web APIs is proposed. The model has been designed (1) to support providers who publish new Web APIs used to access the Web of Linked Data, (2) to support the Web designer who aims at exploring and selecting available Web APIs to build or maintain a Web mashup, and (3) to make it available on top of the Web of Linked Data. Based on the proposed model, we define automated matching techniques apt to establish *semantic links* among Linked Web APIs according to properly defined criteria: (1) *functional similarity links*, set between APIs that provide similar functionalities and enable access to similar Linked Data, and (2) *functional coupling links*, set between APIs that can be wired to realize new, value-added Web mashups. Finally, we identify recurrent use cases to support the construction of Web mashups by means of Linked Web API composition. The analyzed use cases enable a proactive suggestion and interactive selection of available Linked Web APIs in order to support the browsing of available resources according to an exploratory perspective, that is, a step-by-step construction of the final mashup, which evolves depending on the available APIs and the associated links. The model and the techniques we propose adhere to the Linked Data principles for publishing resources on the Web in a meaningful way: (1) HTTP URIs are used to identify published resources (i.e., Web APIs); (2) useful (RDF) information are provided on the Web API description when someone looks up a Web API through its URI; and (3) functional similarity links and functional coupling links are set to relate Web APIs to each other, thus enabling easy development and sharing of new Web applications. Moreover, we rely on the Web of Linked Data for Web API semantic annotation, following the lesson learned for Linked Data services in [41], where Linked Data are used as source of knowledge.

The chapter is organized as follows. After describing a motivating example, we will discuss the state of the art on semantic Web services and Web of Linked Data and on existing mashup approaches. Therefore, we present the proposed approach for Linked Data services, the techniques, and the use cases to support the mashup construction. Finally, we close the chapter with the architecture of a system which implements the proposed metrics and use cases.

11.2 Motivating Example

Just consider Veruschka, a Web designer who has been charged by the organizers of a Michelangelo Antonioni's movie festival to design a Web application which collects all the services related to the festival, such as search services to find movie theaters which host the showing of the films, services to buy the tickets online, or services to reserve hotels in order to spend several days at the festival. This is an example of situational application, that is, an application targeted on the organizers' specific requirements and potentially useful for short periods of time (i.e., the interval of days in which the movie festival is held). The Web of Linked Data can be useful to collect knowledge on the considered topic and to expand this knowledge by means of RDF links. In a nutshell, this is the tenet of explorative search. For instance, the Web designer starts with a particular query in mind (e.g., Michelangelo Antonioni's movies) and linked metadata and knowledge can be suggested, such as information about Antonioni's preferred actress or a gallery of famous Antonioni's movie location, like Zabriskie Point, that were not in the Web designer's mind when he submitted the original query. Similarly, we rely on the same concepts to suggest Linked Data services used to access, manage, and transform the relevant information. Available services can be found among (1) Web APIs that enable to access contents coming from existing databases and legacy systems, such as Web APIs that provide information about reviews on movies (`Screerat.com` or `Rottentomatoes.com`) or to obtain the addresses of movie theaters where a selected movie is shown, and (2) Web APIs and services that provide functionalities to process Linked Data, for example, to locate points on a map (`GoogleMaps` APIs) or to buy tickets online (e.g., `eBay` APIs). The Web designer decides to build his own Web application starting from available Web APIs instead of designing the application from scratch (that could be a nontrivial and time-consuming task, for instance, for what concerns displaying features on a map). On the other hand, browsing and selection of the right functionalities from a huge list of heterogeneous Web APIs is not an easy task if manually performed. See, for example, the scenario shown in Fig. 11.1. Firstly, the Web designer performs a generic search of available Web APIs by specifying some keywords, such as "movies." A list of available APIs whose descriptions match the specified keywords are proposed to him. Suggested Web APIs present the specified keywords in the API inputs/outputs, or have been associated with them as a related topic. By exploiting the Web of Linked Data, additional APIs can be suggested, annotated with related concepts, such as "movie theaters" or "film review." The Web designer keeps building the new Web application by adding new Linked Web APIs (e.g., the `GoogleMap` APIs to display the location of movie theaters) or by substituting already selected ones with new solutions found in the list. This procedure continues incrementally until the Web mashup is completed.

11.3   State of the Art

In this section, we will present the current background on Web services and Web API technologies and how they meet the semantic Web and the Web of Linked Data. Moreover, we will review the main efforts concerning support systems and technologies for data and service mashup in the context of Linked Data.

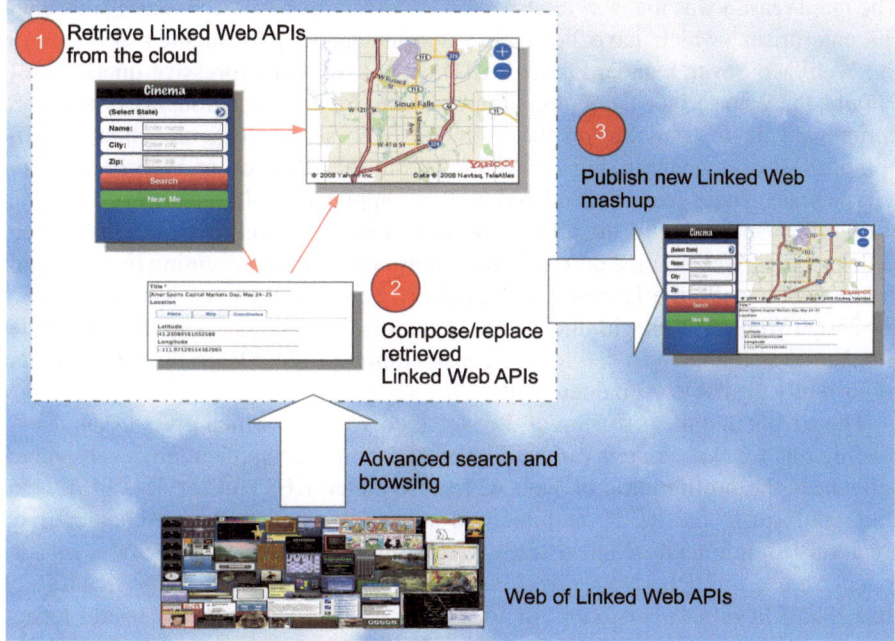

Fig. 11.1 The Linked Web mashup vision

11.3.1   Web Services and Web APIs

Web services have been proposed as a technology to increase software reuse and interoperability across the Web. Web services are defined as loosely coupled software components provided on the Web via open, platform-independent standards like XML, SOAP, and WSDL [21]. Web services can be composed to build more complex, value-added distributed applications. Besides SOAP and WSDL, several languages have been defined on the service-oriented architectures, such as BPEL4WS [3] to model process-oriented service orchestration, WS-Security [37] to apply security policies, WS-Interoperability [13] to improve interoperability between vendor implementations, and so on. The stack of WS-* specifications is characterized by high complexity and is purely syntactic; therefore, service discovery, composition, and monitoring are still a manual task. First attempts to create a public registry of Web services, with limited, keyword-based searching capabilities, proposed the Universal Business Registry within the Universal Description Discovery and Integration (UDDI) standard [28] and, more recently, the ebXML Registry Information Model.[2] These proposals were discontinued in 2006.

---

[2]http://www.ebxml.org/.

The main reason was that service-oriented architectures have been mainly designed for enterprises, which have been always reluctant to publish their services on the Web. Moreover, standards like UDDI do not support expressive queries [43]. Finally, the Web service technology imposes that, for each functionality or software component made available on the Web, the Web service provider must specify complex WS-* standards, thus preventing from the adoption of Web services on a large scale. These features hindered the large application of Web services over the Web. OPOSSum,[3] one of the most important Web service repositories on the Web, lists few, toys Web service descriptions that are far from representing real software components, while the largest list of publicly available Web services, accounting for 25000 Web services with their documentation, is Seekda.com. Therefore, the number of available Web services is considerably different from the huge amount of currently available Web documents.

The advent and the diffusion of the so-called Web 2.0, which gives to the user a leading role for Web content publication and for new Web application development, influenced the proliferation of Web APIs, also called RESTful services [45] when they conform to the REST architectural style [24]. Web APIs are characterized by a very simple technological stack, based on HTTP, XML, and JSON, and the extensive use of URIs. Nowadays, Web APIs are used to access large quantity of data, like Flickr and Facebook, or to expose on the Web contents inside legacy systems. In Programmableweb.com,[4] an online registry of mashups and APIs, nearly 3,500 Web APIs and 5,900 mashups are listed at the time of this writing, while Yahoo! Pipes contains over 20,000 user-defined components. Web APIs are usually described using plain, unstructured HTML, although some efforts such as WADL (Web application description language) [27] are being developed to be the counterpart of the WSDL standard for WSDL/SOAP-based Web services. The unstructured nature of Web API descriptions makes their automatic discovery a difficult task, that is, currently mainly performed manually. In [25], a faceted classification of unstructured Web APIs and a ranking algorithm to improve their retrieval are proposed. The classification and searching solution is based on IR techniques.

11.3.2 Semantic Web Services

Semantic Web services have been proposed to apply the semantic Web vision [6] to the world of Web services. We can define a semantic Web service as a Web service whose functionality is further specified through a semantic annotation over a well-defined ontology or semantic model.

Definition 11.1 (Semantic Web Service). We define a semantic Web service as a pair $\langle S, A \rangle$, where S is the Web service description and A is the corresponding semantic annotation expressed by an ontology or semantic model.

---

[3]OPOSSum - Online Portal for Semantic Services, http://hnsp.inf-bb.uni-jena.de/opossum/.
[4]http://www.programmableweb.com/.

This definition has been meant for WSDL/SOAP-based Web services and in this context, a number of conceptual models have been proposed. Considering existing languages and service discovery infrastructures based on them, S mainly coincides with the Web service abstract interface contained in the WSDL specification. The semantic annotation A ranges from complex, top-down solutions like the OWL-S [36] or the WSMO [11] ones to the bottom-up perspective of the SAWSDL [22] proposal. In particular, OWL-S defines an upper level service ontology, where a semantic Web service has three properties: it *presents* a *Service-Profile*, describing what the service does (i.e., the Web service interface), exploited for discovery purposes; it is *describedBy* a *ServiceModel*, describing how the service works; and it *supports* a *ServiceGrounding* for its invocation. WSMO proposes a semantic Web service model based on four core elements: (1) *ontologies*, to provide the terminology used by other WSMO elements in terms of machine-processable formal definitions; (2) *Web services*, to describe all the aspects of Web Services, including their *nonfunctional properties*, their *capabilities*, and their *interfaces*; (3) *goals*, to represent the user's requirements in terms of expected outputs and effects; and (4) *mediators*, to deal with interoperability problems between different WSMO elements. The Web service interfaces and goals are the elements involved in the discovery process. The SAWSDL proposal distinguished between the WSDL specification and the semantic model, introducing special extension attributes for semantic annotation of interface elements (e.g., operations, input/output messages). SAWSDL supports semantic annotation of WSDL and XML documents by means of three kinds of annotations, namely, *model reference, lifting schema mapping*, and *lowering schema mapping*, which allow pointing to semantic elements on the Web and specify data transformation from a syntactical representation to the semantic counterpart and vice versa. With respect to OWL-S/WSMO, by externalizing the semantic model, an agnostic perspective on the ontology representation language is taken, without constraining to a particular semantic model. Recently, efforts to ground OWL-S to SAWSDL and several tools and APIs to facilitate the use of these languages, hiding representation details, have been developed, and SAWSDL is gaining more and more popularity as semantic Web service description language. Such models are essentially incompatible to each other due to the adopted representation language and expressivity of the semantic model, thus raising interoperability issues. The World Wide Web Consortium (W3C) proposed a WSDL RDF mapping [31] to add WSDL data to the semantic Web. This mapping specification has two main parts: a WSDL ontology and a formal mapping from WSDL documents to RDF data. Since this representation is independent from the WSDL one, it is extensible and supports any mechanism to annotate Web services. Moreover, interoperability is achieved by merging different semantic Web data and allowing to read WSDL documents as RDF inputs. Nevertheless, the inefficiency of this representation presents relevant issues of scalability and management capabilities [17].

As stated above, the most part of semantic Web service approaches are focused on WSDL/SOAP-based Web services, while the attention is shifting toward Web APIs and RESTful services. Moreover, all these approaches are characterized by a considerable complexity in the conceptual model used for the semantic annotation of services and Web APIs. As wished by [40], with the advent of the Web of Linked Data and with the new role assumed by the users that are recently referred to as *prosumers* joining the characteristics of providers and consumers, lightweight semantics is yielding significant benefits that justify the investment in annotating data and services. In this context, the Web of Linked Data can be assumed as a repository of knowledge to be used for supporting the annotation of Linked Data services. Tools such as SWEET [35] work in this direction. In particular, SWEET guides the providers to give a structured representation of their Web APIs (by using the hRESTS formalism) and add semantics by referencing concepts in publicly available domain ontologies through the MicroWSMO language [32]. Another related effort is the SA-REST language [33] that allows semantic annotation of RESTful service descriptions, and it is proposed in the context of semantic mashups. Data mediation between heterogeneous services is addressed by means of lowering and lifting schema mappings. In SA-REST, semantic annotation of RESTful services should be supplied by their providers. Similarly, for what concerns WSDL/SOAP-based services, WSMO-Lite [47] has been proposed to overcome some of the SAWSDL limitations that do not commit any semantic model. Basically, WSMO-Lite includes a lightweight RDFS ontology together with a methodology to express functional and nonfunctional semantics and an information model for WSDL services based on the SAWSDL model reference.

In order to provide a common vocabulary based on existing Web standards to semantically describe services and to enable their publication on the Web of Linked Data, [40] proposed the minimal service model (MSM), originally introduced together with hRESTS and WSMO-Lite. In a nutshell, the MSM is a simple RDFS built upon existing vocabularies, namely, SAWSDL, WSMO-Lite, and hRESTS, and captures the maximum common denominator between existing conceptual models for services. On top of the MSM, the iServe architecture is implemented [41], to publish semantic annotations of services as Linked Data and provide a SPARQL endpoint for executing advanced querying over the service annotations.

11.3.3   Computer-Aided Web API Mashup

Recent efforts to provide mashup platforms underline the importance of mitigating the burden of mashup composition that requires programming skills, the in-depth knowledge of inputs/outputs formats for manually implementing data mediation in the final composition, and the integration of different kinds of components (e.g., components with their own UI, WSDL/SOAP-based Web services, RESTful services, RSS/Atom feeds).

To better support mashup development, it is crucial to abstract from underlying heterogeneity. In [14], an abstract component model and a composition model are proposed, expressed by means of an XML-based language. In particular, components are defined as stateful elements, with events for state changes notification and operations for querying and modifying the state. A composition model is also proposed, where components are coupled according to a publish/subscribe mechanism, where events raised from a component are associated with operations of other components in the final mashup application. Both the component model and the composition model are not based on any semantic characterization. In [2], a formal model based on datalog rules is proposed to capture all the aspects of a mashup component. Mashups are combined into patterns, and a notion of inheritance relationship between components is introduced. Nevertheless, the proposed formal model is quite complex, and it is difficult to adapt it to the Linked Data perspective, where the adoption of lightweight semantics techniques is of paramount importance.

Works [2, 14] do not provide environments with on-the-fly support for mashup composition. Mashup composition is manual, and no component selection strategies or metrics to support it is proposed. In [38], authors propose a novel application of semantic annotation together with a matching algorithm for finding sets of functionally equivalent components out of a large set of available non-Web-service-based components. The approach described in [26] addresses the problem of proactive suggestion of components to be combined in a mashup. The MATCHUP system is proposed to support a rapid, on-demand, and intuitive mashup development. This approach is based on the notion of autocompletion: when the designer selects a component (called *mashlet*), the system suggests other components to be connected on the basis of recurrent patterns of components in the repository. The MATCHUP system is based on the formal component model described in [2], therefore suffers from the limitations we underlined above. A tag-based navigation technique for composing data mashups to integrate data sources is proposed in [44]. MashMaker [20] suggests widgets that might assist in handling data currently managed by the mashup designer. For example, the tool might suggest adding "map" location or "distance" widgets if the designer currently views a list of addresses. The MashupAdvisor [19] system recommends a set of possible outputs for a specific mashup. Each specific output corresponds to some transformation of the data being manipulated by the mashup. After the user has selected one output, MashupAdvisor computes an extension of the mashup in order to achieve the selected output. A Web-based interface which supports mashup of semantic-enriched Web APIs is proposed in sMash [34]. Possible mashups are shown as a graph, where each vertex represents an API, and an edge between two APIs means that they are mashupable, that is, they can be used together in a mashup.

11.4 Linked Web APIs Model

A fundamental step for bridging Web APIs closer to the Web of Linked Data is their publication based on current best practices. Following the lesson learnt by the iServe platform [41], which proposes the use of Linked Data publication principles [10] to enrich the Web of Data with functionalities provided as OWL-S, SAWSDL, and RESTful services, we propose a conceptual model for semantically annotated

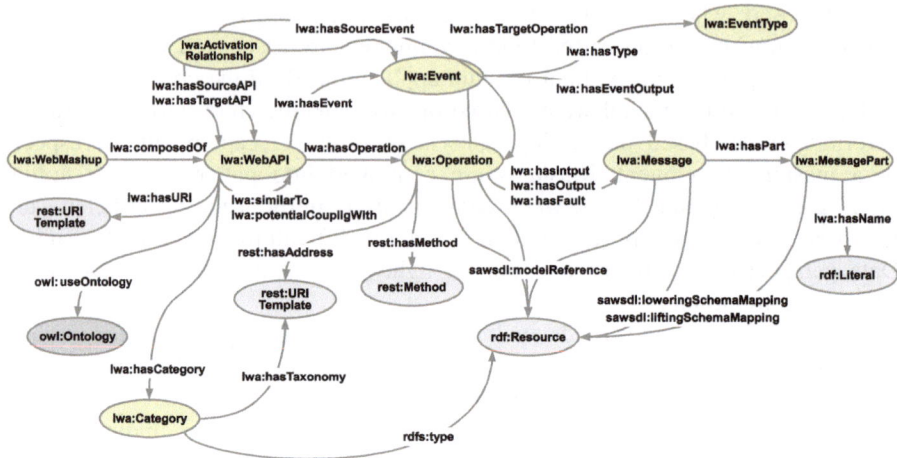

Fig. 11.2 The semantics-enabled Web API conceptual model

Web APIs and Web mashups in order to link them to the Web of Data through the use of lightweight semantics. The conceptual model abstracts from implementation aspects and guides the publication of Web APIs within the Web of Linked Data through the application of matching techniques introduced in [9], which are based on the semantic annotations of model elements. Matching techniques support the identification of semantic links between APIs in the Web of Linked Data. We distinguish between two kinds of semantic links: *functional similarity links* between APIs which provide similar functionalities and *functional coupling links* between APIs which can be wired together in a Web mashup.

Basic elements of the semantics-enabled Web API model are shown in Fig. 11.2 and have been defined in the lwa namespace. We rely on existing vocabularies, namely SAWSDL, RDF(S), and hRESTS, identified with the sawsdl, rdf/rdfs, rest namespace prefixes, respectively. A Web API is uniquely identified by a URI. Moreover, a set of common elements can be identified in Web API descriptions: (1) *inputs* and *outputs*, represented through the Message construct, which in turn can be composed of several MessageParts; (2) *operations*, usually associated with buttons or links on the Web API graphical interface; and (3) *events*, to model user's interactions with the Web API interface. Operations are described by an address, which is built by concatenating the API URI with the operation name and is used to invoke the operation itself, and a method (e.g., classical POST and GET HTTP methods) for its invocation. Events are described by an event type (e.g., onmouseover, onmouseclick) and the outputs or arguments which are raised on event occurrence (for instance, a click on a map raises an event which contains the coordinates of the points which the mouse is positioned on). Message parts have a name that is modeled as an RDF literal. To add semantics to the Linked Web API model, we used the *model reference, lifting schema mapping*, and *lowering schema mapping* constructs proposed in the SAWSDL specification. Schema mappings are used to provide grounding from the conceptual model to the concrete message formats (lowering schema mapping) and vice versa (lifting schema mapping). Model reference construct is used to associate operation names, inputs and outputs, and event outputs to concepts taken from the Web of Linked Data. Concepts are also identified by means of URIs as usual in the Web of Linked Data. Finally, APIs are classified with respect to categories (hasCategory construct) that are taken from standard taxonomies available on the Web (identified by a taxonomy URI). We do not commit a particular ontology formalism, but the wide range of ontologies and semantic data available on the Web of Linked Data is used as a source of knowledge. To this aim, techniques, formats, and tools for semantic annotation of Web APIs based on lightweight semantic models, like the SWEET tool proposed in [35], have been adapted to the proposed Web API model. The SWEET tool provides support in the identification of elements that characterize a Web API, which typically relies on nonstructured HTML documentation that makes difficult machine processing, to produce a description according to the hRESTS language. Annotation and classification of the Web APIs is performed according to the MicroWSMO [32] notation extended with semantically annotated events.

An event of a Web API can be connected to an operation of another Web API in a publish/subscribe-like mechanism. An event-operation pair is represented in the model through an activation relationship. For example, in Fig. 11.1, an activation relationship is shown from the cinema API to the map API: once a movie title is specified in the former, the locations of the projection rooms for the selected movie are shown on the map. An activation relationship is modeled with reference to the source and target Web APIs (hasSourceAPI and hasTargetAPI constructs), to the source event (hasSourceEvent construct), and to the target operation (hasTargetOperation construct).

Finally, Web APIs published on the Web of Linked Data are linked toward other APIs that provide similar functionalities (similarTo construct, which models the functional similarity link) or other APIs that could be coupled with the current one and included in the same Web mashup (potentialCouplingWith construct, which models the functional coupling link). Exploitation of these links will be shown in Sect. 11.6. Functional similarity links and functional coupling links aim at being the counterpart of RDF links of the Web of Linked Data. They could be set during Web API publication. In this way, the model we propose relies on the Linked Data principles [10] for Web API publication: (1) HTTP URIs are used to identify published resources (i.e., Web APIs); (2) useful (RDF) information are provided on the Web API description when someone looks up a Web API through its URI; (3) RDF statements (similarTo and potentialCouplingWith constructs) are used that link to other Web APIs that are related to each other (through functional similarity and functional coupling links).

Activation relationships, functional similarity links, and functional coupling links are based on the identification of IO correspondences across different Web APIs. In the next section, we describe matching techniques built on top of Linked Data to support the Web API provider and Web mashup designer during the identification of such correspondences.

11.5 Linked Web API Publication

As stated above, semantic characterization of Web API descriptions is performed by relying on existing tools and techniques, such as SWEET. Nevertheless, publication of new Web APIs and new Web mashups on the Web of Linked Data must be properly supported to help providers in identifying relationships with existing resources. We distinguish among two situations: (a) publication of a new semantically described Web API by a Web API provider and (b) publication of a new Web mashup by a Web designer.

Publication of a new semantically annotated Web API. The Web API provider has to identify related Web APIs that could be linked to the current one through `similarTo` or `potentialCouplingWith` constructs.

Publication of a new Web mashup. The Web designer has to select available Web APIs and properly set activation relationships between them.

We provide a set of matching techniques to support the Web API provider and the Web designer to perform their tasks. These techniques are based on the computation of a concept affinity $CAff() \in [0..1]$ between pairs of concepts, used in the semantic annotation of, respectively, (1) operations, (2) I/Os parameters, and (3) event outputs and operation inputs. To this purpose, we rely on techniques such as those extensively defined in [8]. Here, we simply state that $CAff$ is based on both a terminological (domain-independent) matching based on the use of WordNet [23] and a semantic (domain dependent) matching based on the ontologies on the Web of Linked Data, used as source of knowledge.

Given a new semantically annotated Web API description $\mathcal{W}_i$, another Web API $\mathcal{W}_j$ is *functionally similar* to $\mathcal{W}_i$ if (1) the $\mathcal{W}_i$ and $\mathcal{W}_j$ categories are compatible, that is, at least one $\mathcal{W}_j$ category is the same or less specific than one $\mathcal{W}_i$ category, and (2) the *functional similarity degree* $Sim_{IO}(\mathcal{W}_i, \mathcal{W}_j)$ is equal to or greater than a threshold $\delta \in [0, 1]$ experimentally set. The functional similarity degree is defined as follows.

Definition 11.2 (Functional Similarity Degree). The Functional Similarity Degree $Sim_{IO}(\mathcal{W}_i, \mathcal{W}_j) \in [0, 1]$ between two semantically annotated Web APIs $\mathcal{W}_i$ and $\mathcal{W}_j$ is evaluated as:

$$Sim_{IO}(\mathcal{W}_i, \mathcal{W}_j) = \frac{1}{3} \left[\frac{\sum_{s,t} CAff(in_s, in_t)}{|IN(\mathcal{W}_j)|} + \frac{\sum_{h,k} CAff(out_h, out_k)}{|OUT(\mathcal{W}_i)|} \right.$$
$$\left. + \frac{\sum_{l,m} CAff(op_l, op_m)}{|OP(\mathcal{W}_i)|} \right] \tag{11.1}$$

where $IN(\mathcal{W}_j)$ (resp., $OUT(\mathcal{W}_i)$) is the set of concepts used to annotate the operation inputs of the $\mathcal{W}_j$ Web API description (resp., the operation outputs of the $\mathcal{W}_i$ Web API description); $OP(\mathcal{W}_i)$ is the set of concepts used to annotate the operations of the $\mathcal{W}_i$ Web API description; $in_s \in IN(\mathcal{W}_i)$, $in_t \in IN(\mathcal{W}_j)$, $out_h \in OUT(\mathcal{W}_i)$, $out_k \in OUT(\mathcal{W}_j)$, $op_l \in OP(\mathcal{W}_i)$, $op_m \in OP(\mathcal{W}_j)$.

The $Sim_{IO}(\mathcal{W}_i, \mathcal{W}_j)$ formula measures how much $\mathcal{W}_j$ provides at least the operations and outputs required in $\mathcal{W}_i$, no matter if $\mathcal{W}_j$ provides additional operations and outputs. The building block of this expression is the Dice coefficient [46], used in information retrieval. When the provider publishes a new semantically annotated Web API description, a preliminary search of the available Web APIs on the Web of Linked Data is performed on the basis of Web API categories, and the functional similarity degree is computed. Those Web APIs which present a functional similarity degree value equal to or greater than the threshold δ are proposed to the provider to set the similarTo link between them.

Similarly, we defined a procedure to assist the Web API provider for finding potentially coupled Web APIs on the Web of Linked Data. Given a new semantically annotated Web API description $\mathcal{W}_i$, another Web API $\mathcal{W}_j$ can be *functionally coupled* with $\mathcal{W}_i$ if the *functional coupling degree* $Coupl_{IO}(\mathcal{W}_i, \mathcal{W}_j)$ is equal to or greater than a threshold $\theta \in [0, 1]$ experimentally set. The functional coupling degree is based on the *event-operation coupling coefficient* $CouplEvOp(ev_i, op_j)$, evaluated as the average $CAff()$ value between the event outputs of $ev_i \in EV(\mathcal{W}_i)$ and the inputs of $op_j \in OP_j$, where $EV(\mathcal{W}_i)$ is the set of events of the $\mathcal{W}_i$ Web API description.

Definition 11.3 (Event-Operation Coupling Degree). The Event-Operation Coupling Degree $CouplEvOp(ev_i, op_j) \in [0, 1]$ between an event ev_i of a semantically annotated Web API $\mathcal{W}_i$ and an operation op_j of a semantically annotated Web API $\mathcal{W}_j$ is evaluated as:

$$CouplEvOp(ev_i, op_j) = \frac{\sum_{h,k} CAff(out_h, in_k)}{|OUT_{ev}(ev_i)|} \tag{11.2}$$

where $OUT_{ev}(ev_i)$ is the set of concepts used to annotate the event outputs of the ev_i event, $out_h \in OUT_{ev}(ev_i)$, in_k is a concept used to annotate the kth input of the op_j operation.

The $CouplEvOp(ev_i, op_j)$ formula measures how many outputs of the ev_i event are catched by an input of the op_j operation. This formula is used to compute the *functional coupling degree* as follows.

Definition 11.4 (Functional Coupling Degree). The Functional Coupling Degree $Coupl_{IO}(\mathcal{W}_i, \mathcal{W}_j) \in [0, 1]$ between two semantically annotated Web APIs $\mathcal{W}_i$ and $\mathcal{W}_j$ is evaluated as:

$$Coupl_{IO}(\mathcal{W}_i, \mathcal{W}_j) = \frac{\sum_{i,j} Coupl_{EvOp}(ev_i, op_j)}{|EV(\mathcal{W}_i)|} \tag{11.3}$$

where $ev_i \in EV(\mathcal{W}_i)$ and $op_j \in OP(\mathcal{W}_j)$.

The $Coupl_{IO}(\mathcal{W}_i, \mathcal{W}_j)$ formula measures how much the events raised on the $\mathcal{W}_i$ Web API interface can be coupled with operations provided by the $\mathcal{W}_j$ Web API. When the provider publishes a new semantically annotated Web API description, a preliminary search of the available Web APIs on the Web of Linked Data is performed to find those Web APIs whose operation inputs are annotated with concepts related to the ones used to annotate the event outputs of the Web API to be published. Among these Web APIs, the ones which present a functional coupling degree value equal to or greater than the threshold θ are proposed to the provider to set the potentialCouplingWith link between them.

The main task to be performed by a Web designer when he/she is creating and linking a new Web mashup is to find relevant Web APIs on the Web of Linked Data. To this purpose, he/she exploits the network of similarTo and potentialCouplingWith links, as we will show in the next section. After selecting the Web APIs to be included in the new Web mashup, the Web designer must provide activation relationships between pairs of coupled APIs. To this purpose, the Web designer is supported for the identification of IO correspondences between event outputs and operation inputs. Also in this case, the $CAff()$ evaluation is used to suggest potential couplings. Finally, IO correspondence is manually confirmed by the Web designer and relies on the lowering and lifting schema mappings provided together with the semantically annotated Web APIs (see Fig. 11.2).

11.6 Selection Strategies for Linked Web API Mashup

We distinguish two Web mashup development scenarios that could take benefits from the organization of semantically annotated Web APIs on top of the Web of Linked Data. We analyze the scenarios in the following and then we formalize a solution to support the Web designer in completing his/her task.

Building a mashup from the scratch. Let us consider Veruschka who needs to build from scratch the mashup application described in Sect. 11.2 and to link it to the Web of Linked Data. The designer proceeds step by step by selecting a Web API and setting activation relationships between events and operations, according to the model presented in the Sect. 11.4. The designer specifies a request for a Web API in terms of desired categories, operations, and/or I/Os. A ranked list of available Web APIs should be proposed. Once the designer selected one of the proposed APIs from the list, say $\mathcal{W}_s$, and placed it in the Web mashup under development, two additional lists of Web APIs can be suggested: (1) APIs that are similar to the selected one, that is, are related to $\mathcal{W}_s$ through a similarTo link (Veruschka can use one of them in the Web mashup as an alternative to $\mathcal{W}_s$), and (2) APIs that can be coupled with the selected one to implement additional functionalities in the mashup, that is, are related to $\mathcal{W}_s$ through a potentialCouplingWith link (e.g., Veruschka, after selecting a Web API that provides the addresses of movie theaters, could add a GoogleMaps API to locate addresses on a map). For each additional coupled API, IO correspondences among inputs of its operations and outputs of $\mathcal{W}_s$ events are suggested on demand to the designer to model activation relationships. Exploration of these suggestions allows the designer to gain better insight into the interpretation of the Web API descriptions within the Web mashup under development.

Modifying an existing application. Let us now consider Veruschka who needs to modify the Web mashup by replacing one or more descriptors. Similarly, we could consider another Web designer, Caecilius, who finds Veruschka's Web mashup on the Web of Linked Data and desires to replace one of the component Web APIs. Web APIs can be substituted because of (1) they become unavailable, (2) application requirements have been changed, and (3) the designer needs to improve the QoS of the Web mashup [12]. Once the designer selects a Web API to be substituted, say $\mathcal{W}_s$, a ranked list of alternative APIs are suggested as candidates for replacing $\mathcal{W}_s$. In this case, a good alternative to $\mathcal{W}_s$ is an API that is highly similar to $\mathcal{W}_s$ and highly coupled with other APIs which were connected to $\mathcal{W}_s$ in the original mashup. The designer compares the features of candidate descriptors to decide the most suitable alternatives.

The analysis of the above development scenarios raised the need of implementing different kinds of *selection patterns* that rely on the semantic organization of Web APIs and mashups built upon the Web of Linked Data. In the following, we better formalize the patterns and we present the I-MASH platform which implements them.

11.6.1   Linked Web API Selection Patterns

Formally, a *selection pattern* is defined as follows.

Definition 11.5 (Selection Pattern). A selection pattern σ is a quadruple:

$$\sigma_\tau = \langle \mathcal{W}_\tau, m_\tau, \delta_\tau, \prec_\tau \rangle \tag{11.4}$$

where τ is the goal of the selection pattern. If τ = 'search,' the aim is to suggest a set of Web APIs that match a Web API specification $\mathcal{W}_\tau$. If τ = 'completion,' or τ = 'substitution,' then the aim is to suggest a list of Web APIs that can be coupled or substituted to the Web API $\mathcal{W}_\tau$, respectively. The metric m_τ is used to evaluate the degree of matching (if τ = 'search'), the degree of coupling (if τ = 'completion') or the degree of similarity (if τ = 'substitution') between each suggested Web API and $\mathcal{W}_\tau$. The threshold δ_τ is used to filter out not relevant Web APIs. A Web API $\mathcal{W}_j$ is proposed to the designer if $m_\tau(\mathcal{W}_\tau, \mathcal{W}_j) > \delta_\tau$. Finally, $\prec_\tau$ is a ranking function to present the suggested Web APIs. In particular, $\mathcal{W}_i \prec_\tau \mathcal{W}_j$, that is, $\mathcal{W}_i$ is ranked higher than $\mathcal{W}_j$, if $m_\tau(\mathcal{W}_\tau, \mathcal{W}_i) \geq m_\tau(\mathcal{W}_\tau, \mathcal{W}_j)$.

We distinguish two kinds of selection patterns: (1) a selection pattern that requires the formulation of a query on the Web of Linked APIs, as formulated by Veruschka, to find Web APIs that satisfy some search criteria (*search* selection pattern) and (2) selection patterns which start from the selection of a Web API previously included in the Web mashup under development (*completion* and *substitution* selection patterns). In the latter case, the selected Web API is one of the APIs available in the Web of Linked Data, and the net of `similarTo` and `potentialCouplingWith` links is browsed to evaluate alternative APIs or Web APIs that can be added to the mashup. In the former case, the requested Web API is defined as the following query:

$$\mathcal{W}_r = \langle CAT(\mathcal{W}_r), opt(\mathcal{W}_r) \rangle \qquad (11.5)$$

$CAT(\mathcal{W}_r)$ are the required categories, and $opt(\mathcal{W}_r) = \langle OP(\mathcal{W}_r), IN(\mathcal{W}_r), OUT(\mathcal{W}_r) \rangle$ represent the optional sets of required operation names, input names, and output names. With respect to the Web API model in Sect. 11.4, the query $\mathcal{W}_r$ has a flattened structure, since the sets $IN(\mathcal{W}_r)$ and $OUT(\mathcal{W}_r)$ are specified independently from the operation in $OP(\mathcal{W}_r)$ they belong to. In fact, according to an exploratory search perspective, Veruschka does not have a very precise idea about the structure of the Web APIs to search. Veruschka specifies the categories and, optionally, the inputs, the outputs, and the functionalities (i.e., the operations) expected from the API.

Metrics are based on the `similarTo` and `potentialCouplingWith` links between Web API URIs on the Web of Linked Data and on the evaluation of similarity and coupling degree.

Let $\tau = $ `completion,` $\mathcal{W}_c$ a selected Web API already included in the Web mashup under development (identified through a URI `Wc_uri`) and cat_c a desired category. The goal is now to find Web APIs $\mathcal{W}_j$ classified in the cat_c category that can be coupled to $\mathcal{W}_c = \mathcal{W}_\tau$. The metric m_τ used to suggest candidate Web APIs $\mathcal{W}_j$ is defined as

$$m_\tau = \begin{cases} Coupl_{IO}(\mathcal{W}_c, \mathcal{W}_j) & if\ \mathcal{W}_j \in Q^1(\mathcal{W}_j) \\ 0 & otherwise \end{cases} \qquad (11.6)$$

where $Q^1(\mathcal{W}_j)$ is a SPARQL query that retrieves those Web APIs that have a category equivalent to or less specific than cat_c and are related to $\mathcal{W}_c$ through a `potentialCouplingWith` link.

```
PREFIX lwa: ...
...
SELECT ?uri
WHERE {
 ?api lwa:hasURI ?uri ;
    lwa:hasCategory ?cat .
 Wc_uri lwa:potentialCouplingWith ?api .
 {
     {?cat owl:equivalentTo cat_c .} UNION
     {cat_c rdfs:subClassOf ?cat .}
 }
}
```

Similarly, let $\tau =$ 'substitution', $\mathcal{W}_s$ a selected Web API already included in the Web mashup under development (identified through a URI Ws_uri), $\{\mathcal{W}_k\}$ a set of Web APIs in the Web mashup (identified through URIs $\{$Wk_uri$\}$) such that there exists an activation relationship between $\mathcal{W}_s$ and each $\mathcal{W}_k$, and $\{\mathcal{W}_h\}$ a set of Web APIs in the mashup (identified through URIs $\{$Wh_uri$\}$) such that there exists an activation relationship between each $\mathcal{W}_h$ and $\mathcal{W}_s$. The goal is now to find Web APIs $\mathcal{W}_j$ that substitute $\mathcal{W}_s$ and can be coupled with $\{\mathcal{W}_k\}$ and $\{\mathcal{W}_h\}$. The function m_τ is made up of three parts:

- The functional similarity degree between $\mathcal{W}_s$ and $\mathcal{W}_j$, that is, $Sim_{IO}(\mathcal{W}_s, \mathcal{W}_j)$
- The sum of the functional coupling degree between $\mathcal{W}_j$ and each $\mathcal{W}_k$
- The sum of the functional coupling degree between $\mathcal{W}_h$ and $\mathcal{W}_j$

That is,

$$
m_\tau = \begin{cases} Sim_{IO}(\mathcal{W}_s, \mathcal{W}_j) + \sum_k Coupl_{IO}(\mathcal{W}_j, \mathcal{W}_k) + \sum_h Coupl_{IO}(\mathcal{W}_h, \mathcal{W}_j) & \text{if } \mathcal{W}_j \in Q^2(\mathcal{W}_j) \\ 0 & \text{otherwise} \end{cases}
$$

$$(11.7)$$

where $Q^2(\mathcal{W}_j)$ is a SPARQL query that retrieves those Web APIs that have a category equivalent to or less specific than at least a category of $\mathcal{W}_s$, is related to $\mathcal{W}_s$ through a similarTo link, and is related to each $\mathcal{W}_k$ and each $\mathcal{W}_h$ through a potentialCouplingWith link.

```
PREFIX lwa: ...
...
SELECT ?uri
WHERE {
  ?api lwa:hasURI ?uri ;
    lwa:hasCategory ?cat ;
    lwa:similarTo Ws_uri ;
    lwa:potentialCouplingWith ?Wk_uri ;   ## for each Wk_uri
    ...
  Wh_uri lwa:potentialCouplingWith ?api .  ## for each Wh_uri
  ...
  Ws_uri lwa:hasCategory ?cat_s .
  {
    {?cat owl:equivalentTo ?cat_s .} UNION
    {?cat_s rdfs:subClassOf ?cat .}
  }
}
```

Finally, let be $\tau =$ 'search' and let be $\mathcal{W}_r$ the requested Web API (i.e., $\mathcal{W}_\tau = \mathcal{W}_r$). The metric m_τ used to suggest candidate Web APIs $\mathcal{W}_j$ that match the request $\mathcal{W}_r$ is defined as:

$$m_\tau = \begin{cases} Sim_{IO}(\mathcal{W}_r, \mathcal{W}_j) & \text{if } \mathcal{W}_j \in Q^3(\mathcal{W}_j) \text{ AND } opt(\mathcal{W}_r) \neq \langle \emptyset, \emptyset, \emptyset \rangle \\ 1 & \text{if } \mathcal{W}_j \in Q^3(\mathcal{W}_j) \text{ AND } opt(\mathcal{W}_r) = \langle \emptyset, \emptyset, \emptyset \rangle \quad (11.8) \\ 0 & \text{otherwise} \end{cases}$$

In this m_τ evaluation of the $Sim_{IO}()$ expression (see (11.1)), the terms corresponding to optional parts of the request are set to 0. $Q^3(\mathcal{W}_j)$ is a SPARQL query that retrieves those Web APIs that have a category equivalent to or less specific than at least a category of $\mathcal{W}_r$.

```
PREFIX lwa: ...
...
SELECT ?uri
WHERE {
 ?api lwa:hasURI ?uri ;
   lwa:hasCategory ?cat .
  {
    {?cat owl:equivalentTo cat_r .} UNION
    {cat_r rdfs:subClassOf ?cat .}
  }
}
```

11.7   The I-MASH Platform

Figure 11.3 shows the architecture of the I-MASH platform, which implements the Linked Web APIs publication and selection procedures. In the following, we present the main modules which compose the platform.

Mashup Engine. This is the core module of the I-MASH platform. The *Mashup Engine* implements the selection patterns detailed in Sect. 11.6 and includes the modules for functional similarity and functional coupling evaluation. The *Mashup Engine* also presents a series of methods for the evaluation of the *CAff* coefficient (see Sect. 11.5). To this aim, the *Mashup Engine* relies on the terminological knowledge provided by WordNet lexical system [23] and on the domain-specific knowledge from the Web of Linked Data that is accessed through the *Linked Web API Repository*.

Functional Similarity Evaluator. Computes the functional similarity degree according to the Definition 11.2. To this aim, this module relies on the methods for *CAff* coefficient computation provided in the *Mashup Engine*. Similarly, the *functional coupling evaluator* computes the functional coupling degree according to the Definitions 11.3 and 11.4.

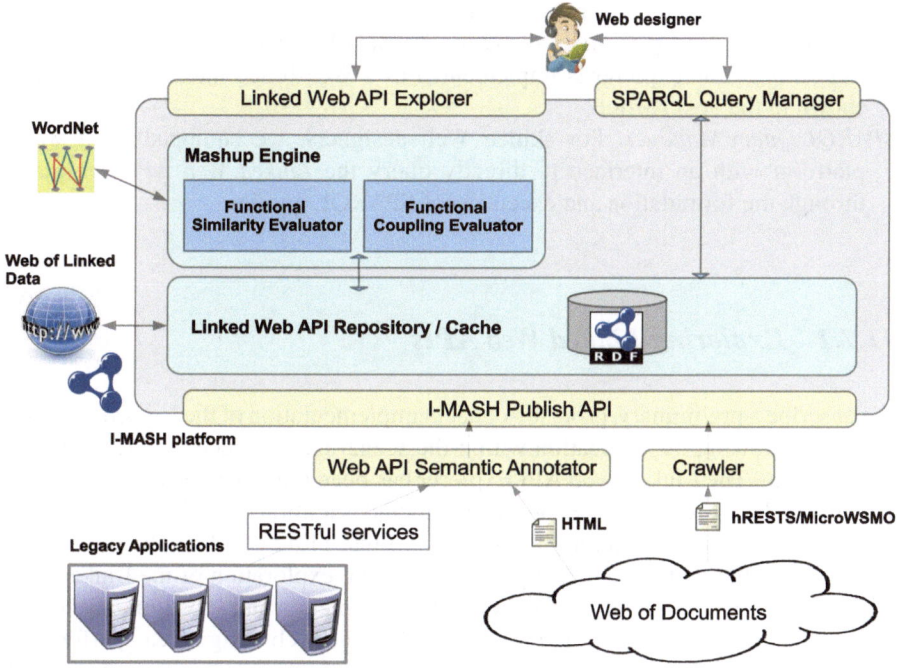

Fig. 11.3 The I-MASH platform architecture

Linked Web API Repository. Maintains the representation of Linked Web APIs published according to the model presented in Sect. 11.4. According to that model, the Linked Web API descriptions refer to things (i.e., URIs of ontological concepts) taken from the Web of Linked Data, which the *Linked Web API Repository* is built upon. Other I-MASH modules, such as the *Mashup Engine* and the I-MASH *Publish API*, exploit the *Linked Web API Repository* to access the Web of Linked Data.

I-MASH *Publish API.* Implements the publication procedures described in Sect. 11.5. To this aim, this module interacts with all the other modules of the I-MASH platform. The I-MASH *Publish API* module is the entry point for the external modules, such as crawlers or Web API semantic annotators, to populate the *Linked Web API Repository* with semantically annotated Web APIs extracted from RESTful services (e.g., used to access legacy application [41]) or plain HTML documents used to access the wealth of data on the Web which remain largely unexploited. Currently, we are developing an extension of the SWEET tool [35] for taking into account also Web API events, thus enabling UI integration as explained in Sect. 11.4.

Linked Web API Explorer. This module supports the Web designer to find Web API descriptions and compose them in a Web mashup. The module relies on the Web

API selection patterns implemented in the *Mashup Engine* and on the net of
`similarTo` and `potentialCouplingWith` links in the *Linked Web API
Repository*. The explorer is implemented as a Web-based interface and will be
shown in the next section.

SPARQL Query Manager. For skilled Web designers, we equipped the I-MASH
platform with an interface to directly query the *Linked Web API Repository*
through the formulation and execution of SPARQL queries.

11.7.1 Exploring Linked Web APIs

We describe a preliminary, proof-of-concept implementation of the Linked Web API
Explorer, showing its application within the scenarios introduced at the beginning
of Sect. 11.6. The Linked Web API Explorer has been implemented as a Web-based
GUI using the ZK open framework, which includes a library of AJAX components.
Two screenshots of the explorer are shown in Figs. 11.4 and 11.5. The screenshots
are based on the motivation example and show the exploration of the Linked Web
API Repository through the application of the completion and substitution selection
patterns. In the upper part of the Web-based GUI, the Web designer can perform the
search for available Web APIs by specifying their category (`Search for Web
APIs` fields) and, optionally, operation, input, and output names. On the right, the
explorer provides a canvas where the Web mashup can be incrementally built. The
Web designer can drag-and-drop component Web APIs from the panels on the left,

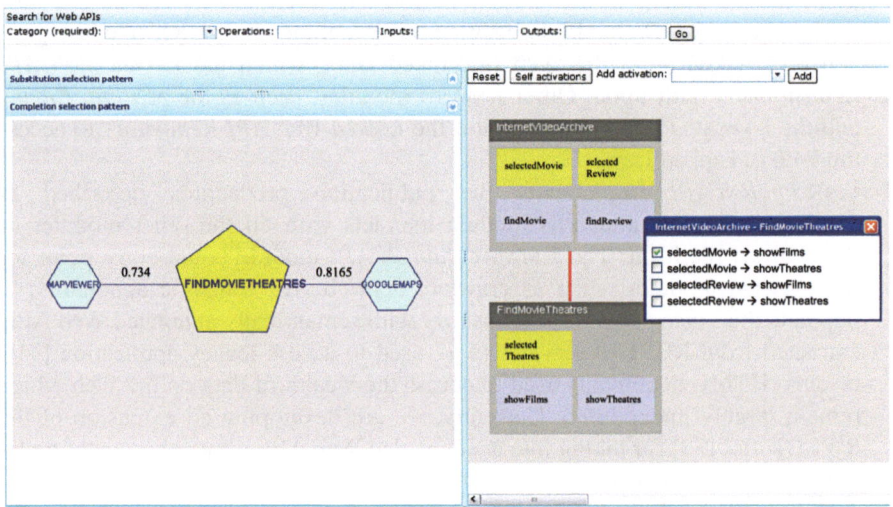

Fig. 11.4 Linked Web API Explorer: application of the completion selection pattern

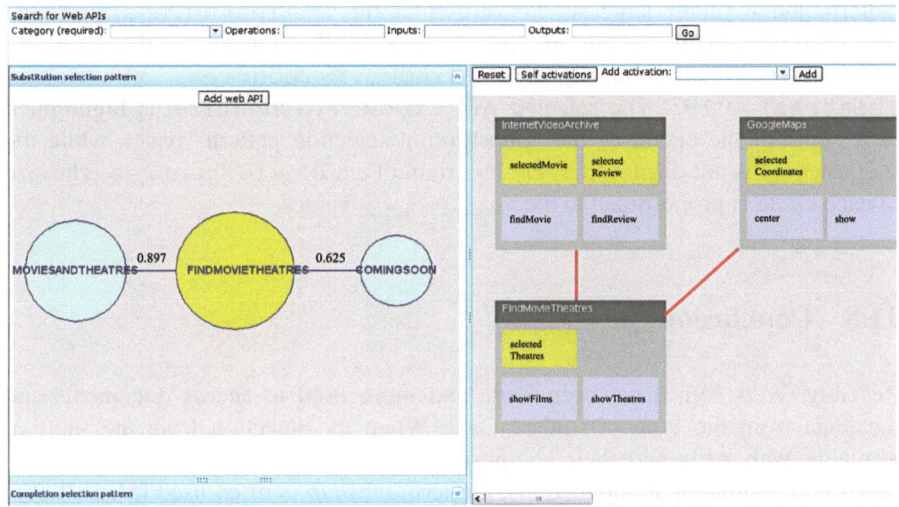

Fig. 11.5 Linked Web API Explorer: application of the substitution selection pattern

where APIs are shown following `similarTo` and `potentialCouplingWith` links in the *Linked Web API Repository*.

Let us assume that Veruschka has already selected the `InternetVideo Archive` and the `FindMovieTheatres` Web APIs and put them on the canvas as shown in Fig. 11.4. Lines connecting the rectangles in the canvas represent event-operation activations between Web APIs in the Web mashup. In this example, when a movie is selected on the `InternetVideoArchive` API (`selectedMovie` event), theaters showing the selected movie are displayed on the `FindMovieTheatres` API (`showFilms` operation). By pushing the "Self activations" button, the explorer suggests IO correspondences and event-operation mappings between Web APIs in the canvas. The mappings between events and operations are shown by double-clicking the activation relationship between the APIs. According to the completion selection pattern, if Veruschka selects the `FindMovieTheatres` API in the canvas, the explorer suggests him the `GoogleMaps` and `MapViewer` APIs, where the $m_{\text{completion}}$(FindMovieTheatres, GoogleMaps) $= 0.8165$ and $m_{\text{completion}}$(FindMovieTheatres, MapViewer) $= 0.734$. The suggested Web APIs are shown on the left within the "completion selection pattern" panel. The selected API `FindMovieTheatres` is highlighted as a pentagon in the center of the panel, while the suggested Web APIs are shown as hexagons around the pentagon; the size of each hexagon is proportional to the $m_{\text{completion}}$ values.

Let us now assume that Veruschka has added the `GoogleMaps` API in the canvas and aims at substituting the `FindMovieTheatres` API in the Web application under development (see Fig. 11.5). According to the substitution selection pattern, the explorer suggests to Veruschka the `MoviesAndTheatres` and `ComingSoon` APIs, where $m_{substitution}$(`FindMovieTheatres`, `Coming Soon`) $= 0.625$ and $m_{substitution}$(`FindMovieTheatres`, `MoviesAnd Theatres`) $= 0.897$. The selected API `FindMovieTheatres` is highlighted as a circle in the center of the "Substitution selection pattern" panel, while the suggested APIs are displayed as circles around `FindMovieTheatres`. The size of each circle is proportional to the $m_{substitution}$ values.

11.8 Conclusion

Recently, Web APIs have been more and more used to access documents and metadata from the Web of Linked Data. When the selection from the shelf of available Web APIs and their composition are performed to build value-added, short-living, situational applications, the term *mashup* is often used [5]. Different lightweight solutions have been proposed for the semantic annotation of Web APIs, like the combined use of MicroWSMO/hRESTS languages [32]. However, given the growing number of available APIs, users are overwhelmed by the quantity of data that are available to be composed. Moreover, semantic mashup of Linked Data (services) often assumes an information retrieval perspective, where the mashup designer has a specific query in mind which he/she tries to answer. Finally, mashup of Web APIs often involves the integration of UIs (also called widgets or gadgets) that is often event driven [14]. In this chapter, we addressed the above-mentioned issues by proposing a new approach for "serving up" Linked Data by semantics-enabled mashup of existing Web APIs. A basic semantics-enabled model of Web APIs is proposed. The model has been designed (a) to support providers who publish new Web APIs used to access the Web of Linked Data, (b) to support the Web designer who aims at exploring and selecting available Web APIs to build or maintain a Web mashup, and (c) to make it available on top of the Web of Linked Data. Based on the proposed model, we describe automated matching techniques apt to establish *semantic links* among Linked Web APIs according to properly defined criteria: (1) *functional similarity links*, set between APIs that provide similar functionalities and enable access to similar Linked Data, and (2) *functional coupling links*, set between APIs that can be wired to realize new, value-added Web mashups. Finally, we identified recurrent use cases to support the construction of Web mashups by means of Linked Web API composition. The analyzed use cases enable a proactive suggestion and interactive selection of available Linked Web APIs in order to support the browsing of available resources according to an exploratory perspective, that is, a step-by-step construction of the final mashup, which evolves depending on the available APIs and the associated links. The model and the techniques we propose adhere to the Linked Data principles for publishing resources on the Web in a meaningful way: (1) HTTP URIs are used to identify published resources (i.e., Web APIs), (2) useful (RDF) information are provided on the Web API description when someone looks up a Web API through its URI, and (3) functional similarity links and functional coupling links are set to relate Web APIs to each other, thus enabling easy development and sharing of new Web applications. Moreover, we rely on the Web of Linked Data for Web API semantic annotation, where Linked Data are used as source of knowledge. A preliminary, proof-of-concept implementation of the Linked Web API Explorer has also been presented.

An extensive experimentation of the proposed platform in several real-case application scenarios is being studied. Moreover, an extension of the proposed model to include also nonfunctional aspects (see, e.g., the application of quality issues to the mashup of components [12]) will be studied. Finally, the proposed selection patterns will be enriched to consider QoS aspects, context-aware Web mashup development, and complementary perspectives, like the one presented in [26].

References

1. W3C SWEO Community, Linking Open Data project (2012). Http://esw.w3.org/topic/SweoIG/TaskForces/CommunityProjects/LinkingOpenData
2. Abiteboul, S., Greenshpan, O., Milo, T.: Modeling the mashup space. Proceedings of the workshop on web information and data management, pp. 87–94 (2008)
3. Andrews, T., Curbera, F., Dholakia, H., Goland, Y., Klein, J., Leymann, F., Liu, K., Roller, D., Smith, D., Thatte, S., Trickovic, I., Weerawarana, S.: Business process execution language for web services version 1.1 (2003). http://www-128.ibm.com/developerworks/library/specification/wsbpel/
4. Becker, C., Bizer, C.: DBPedia mobile: a location-enabled linked data browser. Proceedings of WWW the International Workshop on Linked Data on the Web (LDOW08) (2008)
5. Benslimane, D., Dustdar, S., Sheth, A.: Service mashups: the new generation of web applications. IEEE Inter. Comput. **12**(5), 13–15 (2008)
6. Berners-Lee, T., Hendler, J.A., Lassila, O.: The semantic web. Sci. Am. **284**(5), 34–43 (2001)
7. Berners-Lee, T., Hollenbach, J., Lu, K., Presbrey, J., d'ommeaux, E.P., Schraefel, M.: Tabulator redux: writing into the semantic web. Technical report, ECSIAMeprint14773, Electronics and Computer Science, University of Southampton (2007)
8. Bianchini, D., Antonellis, V.D., Melchiori, M.: Flexible semantic-based service matchmaking and discovery. World Wide Web J. **11**(2), 227–251 (2008)
9. Bianchini, D., Antonellis, V.D., Melchiori, M.: Semantic-driven mashup design. Proceedings of the 12th International Conference on Information Integration and Web-based Applications and Services (iiWAS'10), pp. 245–252 (2010)
10. Bizer, C., Heath, T., Berners-Lee, T.: Linked data - the story so far. Int. J. Semant. Web Inform. Syst. **5**(3), 1–22 (2009)
11. Bussler, C., de Bruijn, J., Feier, C., Fensel, D., Keller, U., Lara, R., Lausen, H., Polleres, A., Roman, D., Stollberg, M.: Web service modeling ontology. Appl. Ontol. **1**(1), 77–106 (2005) IOS Press
12. Cappiello, C., Daniel, F., Matera, M., Pautasso, C.: Information quality in mashups. Inter. Comput. **14**(4), 14–22 (2010)
13. Chumbley, R., Durand, J., Pilz, F., Rutt, T.: WS-interoperability basic profile version 2.0. Technical report, Organization for the Advancement of Structured Information Standards (OASIS) (2010). URL http://www.ws-i.org/

14. Daniel, F., Casati, F., Benatallah, B., Shan, M.: Hosted universal composition: models, languages and infrastructure in mashart. Proceedings of the 28th International Conference on Conceptual Modeling (ER'09) (2009)
15. d'Aquin, M., Motta, E., Sabou, M., Angeletou, S., Gridinoc, L., Lopez, V., Guidi, D.: Toward a new generation of semantic web applications. IEEE Intel. 23(3), 20–28 (2008)
16. Davies, J., Domingue, J., Pedrinaci, C., Fensel, D., Gonzalez-Cabero, R., Potter, M., Richardson, M., Stincic, S.: Towards the open service web. British Telecommun. Technol. J. 26(2) (2009)
17. De Virgilio, R., Orsi, G., Tanca, L., Torlone, R.: Reasoning over large semantic datasets. Proceedings of the 17th Italian Symposium on Advanced Database Systems. Camogli (Genova), Italy (2009)
18. Edwards, D., Hardman, L.: Hypertext: theory into practice, chap. Lost in Hyperspace: cognitive mapping and navigation in a hypertext environment, pp. 90–105. Exeter, UK (1999)
19. Elmeleegy, H., Ivan, A., Akkiraju, R., Goodwin, R.: MashupAdvisor: a recommendation tool for mashup development. Proceedings of the 6th International Conference on Web Services (ICWS'08), pp. 337–344. Beijin, China (2008)
20. Ennals, R., Garofalakis, M.: MashMaker: mashups for the masses. Proceedings of the 27th ACM SIGMOD International Conference on Management of Data, pp. 1116–1118 (2007)
21. Erl, T.: SOA Principles of Service Design. Prentice Hall, Englewood, Cliffs, NJ (2007)
22. Farrell, J., Lausen, H.: Semantic annotations for WSDL and XML schema. Recommendation, W3C (2007)
23. Fellbaum, C.: Wordnet: An Electronic Lexical Database. MIT, Cambridge, MA (1998)
24. Fielding, R.: Architectural styles and the design of network-based software architectures. Ph.D. Thesis, University of California, Irvine (2000)
25. Gomadam, K., Ranabahu, A., Nagarajan, M., Sheth, A.P., Verma, K.: A faceted classification based approach to search and rank web APIs. ICWS, pp. 177–184 (2008)
26. Greenshpan, O., Milo, T., Polyzotis, N.: Autocompletion for mashups. Proceedings of the 35th International Conference on very Large Databases (VLDB'09), pp. 538–549. Lyon, France (2009)
27. Hadley, M.: Web application description language. Technical report, W3C (2009)
28. Hately, L., von Riegen, C., Rogers, T.: UDDI specification version 3.0.2. Technical report, organization for the advancement of structured information standards (OASIS) (2004)
29. Hepp, M.: Products and services ontologies: a methodology for deriving owl ontologies from industrial categorization standards. Int. J. Semant. Web Inform. Syst. 2(1), 72–99 (2006)
30. Jarrar, M., Dikaiakos, M.: A data mashup language for the data web. Proceedings of the 2nd Workshop on Linked Data on the Web (LDOW09). Madrid, Spain (2009)
31. Kopecky, J.: WSDL RDF mapping: developing ontologies from standardized XML languages. Proceedings of the 1st International ER Workshop on Ontologizing Industrial Standards (OIS'06). Tucson, Arizona, USA (2006)
32. Kopecky, J., Vitvar, T., Fensel, D.: hRESTS & MicroWSMO. Tech. rep., SOA4ALL Project, Deliverable D3.4.3 (2009)
33. Lathem, J., Gomadam, K., Sheth, A.: SA-REST and (s)mashups: adding semantics to RESTful services. Proceedings of the IEEE International Conference on Semantic Computing, pp. 469–476. IEEE CS Press (2007)
34. Lu, B., Wu, Z., Ni, Y., Xie, G., Zhou, C., Chen, H.: sMash: semantic-based mashup navigation for data API network. Proceedings of the 18th International World Wide Web Conference, pp. 1133–1134 (2009)
35. Maleshkova, M., Pedrinaci, C., Domingue, J.: Semantic annotation of Web APIs with SWEET. Proceedings of the 6th Workshop on Scripting and Development for the Semantic Web (2010)
36. Martin, D., Burstein, M., Hobbs, J., Lassila, O., McDermott, D., McIlraith, S., Narayanan, S., Paolucci, M., Parsia, B., Payne, T., Sirin, E., Srinivasan, N., Sycara, K.: OWL-S: semantic markup for web services, v1.1. Technical report, World Wide Web Consortium (W3C) (2004)
37. Nadalin, A., Kaler, C., Monzillo, R., Hallam-Backer, P.: Web services security: SOAP message security 1.1. Technical report, Organization for the Advancement of Structured Information Standards (OASIS) (2006). URL http://docs.oasis-open.org/wss/v1.1

38. Ngu, A.H.H., Carlson, M.P., Sheng, Q.Z., Paik, H.: Semantic-based mashup of composite applications. IEEE T. Serv. Comput. **3**(1), 2–15 (2010)
39. Oren, E., Delbru, R., Catasta, M., Cyganiak, R., Stenzhorn, H., Tummarello, G.: Sindice.com: a document-oriented lookup index for open linked data. Int. J. Metadata Semant. Ontol. **3**(1), 37–52 (2008)
40. Pedrinaci, C., Domingue, J., Krummenacher, R.: Services and the web of data: an unexploited symbiosis. Linked AI: AAAI spring symposium on linked data meets artificial intelligence (2010)
41. Pedrinaci, C., Liu, D., Maleshkova, M., Lambert, D., Kopecky, J., Domingue, J.: iServe: a linked services publishing platform. Proceedings of ESWC Ontology Repositories and Editors for the Semantic Web (2010)
42. Phuoc, D.L., Polleres, A., Morbidoni, C., Hauswirth, M., Tummarello, G.: Rapid prototyping of semantic mash-ups through semantic web pipes. Proceedings of the 18th World Wide Web Conference (WWW09), pp. 581–590. Madrid, Spain (2009)
43. Pilioura, T., Tsalgatidou, A.: Unified publication and discovery of semantic web services. ACM Trans. Web **3**(3), 1–44 (2009)
44. Riabov, A., Boillet, E., Feblowitz, M., Liu, Z., Ranganathan, A.: Wishful search: interactive composition of data mashups. Proceedings of the 19th International World Wide Web Conference (WWW'08), pp. 775–784. Beijin, China (2008)
45. Richardson, L., Ruby, S.: RESTful web services. O'Reilly (2007)
46. van Rijsbergen, C.J.: Information Retrieval. Butterworth, London (1979)
47. Vitvar, T., Kopecky, J., Viskova, J., Fensel, D.: WSMO-lite annotations for Web Services. Proceedings of the 5th European Semantic Web Conference (2008)

Part III
Linked Data Search Engines

Chapter 12
A Recommender System for Linked Data

Roberto Mirizzi, Azzurra Ragone, Tommaso Di Noia,
and Eugenio Di Sciascio

12.1 Introduction

Peter and Alice are at home, it is a calm winter night, snow is falling, and it is too cold to go outside. *"Why don't we just order a pizza and watch a movie?"* says Alice wrapped in her favorite blanket. *"Why not?"*—Peter replies—*"Which movie do you wanna watch?"* *"Well, what about some comedy, romance-like one? Com'on Pete, look on Facebook, there is that nice application Kara suggested me some days ago!"* answers Alice. *"Oh yes, MORE, here we go, tell me a movie you like a lot,"* says Peter excited. *"Uhm, I wanna see something like the Bridget Jones's Diary or Four Weddings and a Funeral, humour, romance, good actors..."* replies his beloved, rubbing her hands. Peter is a bit concerned, he is more into fantasy genre, but he wants to please Alice, so he looks on MORE for movies similar to the Bridget Jones's Diary and Four Weddings and a Funeral: *"Here we are my dear, MORE suggests the sequel or, if you prefer, Love Actually,"* I would prefer the second." *"Great! Let's rent it!"* nods Peter in agreement.

The scenario just presented highlights an interesting and useful feature of a modern Web application. There are tasks where the users look for items similar to the ones they already know. Hence, we need systems that recommend items based on user preferences. In other words, systems should allow an easy and friendly exploration of the information/data related to a particular domain of interest. Such characteristics are well known in the literature and in common applications such as recommender systems [23]. Nevertheless, new challenges in this field arise when

R. Mirizzi (✉) · T. Di Noia · E. Di Sciascio
Politecnico di Bari, via Orabona 4 – 70125 Bari, Italy
e-mail: mirizzi@deemail.poliba.it; t.dinoia@poliba.it; disciascio@poliba.it

A. Ragone
Politecnico di Bari, via Orabona 4 – 70125 Bari, Italy
Exprivia S.p.A., viale A. Olivetti 11/A – 70056 Molfetta, BA, Italy
e-mail: a.ragone@poliba.it; azzurra.ragone@exprivia.it

R. De Virgilio et al. (eds.), *Semantic Search over the Web*,
Data-Centric Systems and Applications, DOI 10.1007/978-3-642-25008-8_ 12,
© Springer-Verlag Berlin Heidelberg 2012

the information used by these systems exploits the huge amount of interlinked data coming from the semantic Web.

Thanks to the Linked Data initiative, the foundations of the semantic Web have been built [4]. Shared, open, and linked RDF datasets give us the possibility to exploit both the strong theoretical results and the robust technologies and tools developed since the semantic Web appearance in 2001 [3]. In a simplistic way, we may think at the semantic Web as a huge distributed database we can query to get information coming from different sources. Usually, datasets expose a SPARQL [22] endpoint to make the data accessible through exact queries. If we know the URI of the actress *Keira Knightley* in DBpedia[1] [5], we may retrieve all the movies she acted with a simple SPARQL query such as the following:

```
SELECT ?movie WHERE {
    ?movie <http://www.w3.org/1999/02/22-rdf-syntax-ns#type>
               <http://dbpedia.org/ontology/Film> .
    ?movie <http://dbpedia.org/ontology/starring>
               <http://dbpedia.org/resource/Keira_Knightley>
}
```

Although these are very exciting results and applications, there is much more behind the curtains. Datasets come with the description of their schema structured in an ontological way. Resources refer to classes which are in turn organized in well-structured and rich ontologies. Exploiting this feature further, we go beyond the notion of a distributed database and we can refer to the semantic Web as a distributed social knowledge base. Its social characteristic is inherited by the social nature of the information sources they are extracted from. This is a strong point in favor of such semantic datasets since there is no need to manually maintain and update the knowledge bases themselves, as they are automatically extracted from user-contributed contents. As an example, consider DBpedia which is the RDF version of Wikipedia.

In this chapter, we present MORE, a system for *movie recommendation* in the Web of Data. Currently, the system relies on one of the most relevant datasets in the Linked Data project, DBpedia, and on the semantic-enabled version of the *Internet Movie Database* (IMDB): LinkedMDB[2] [13]. Hence, the movie exploration and recommendation exploit semantic information embedded in social knowledge bases (see Sect. 12.2) belonging to the Linked Data cloud.

Main contributions of this chapter are:

- A semantic-based vector space model for recommendation of items in Linked Data datasets
- Presentation of a Facebook application for movie recommendation exploiting semantic datasets
- Evaluation and validation of the approach with real users

---

[1]http://dbpedia.org/resource/Keira_ Knightley

[2]http://www.imdb.com, http://www.linkedmdb.org

The remainder of the chapter is structured as follows: in Sect. 12.2, we illustrate how we exploit semantic information contained in RDF datasets to compute semantic similarities between movies, then in Sect. 12.3, we describe the interface and possible uses of MORE. In Sect. 12.4, we show how to compute similarities between movies using a semantic-adaptation of the vector space model (VSM). Section 12.5 shows the results of our evaluation, and Sect. 12.6 reviews relevant related work. Conclusion closes the chapter.

12.2   Social Knowledge Bases for Similarity Detection

MORE exploits information coming from different knowledge bases in the Linked Data cloud to provide a recommendation based on the semantic similarities between movie descriptions. Since MORE has been implemented as a Facebook application, in order to avoid the *cold start* problem typical of content-based recommender systems, when the user starts using it, we may retrieve information about the movies she likes by grabbing them from her Facebook profile.

We exploit semantic information contained in the RDF datasets to compute a semantic similarity between movies the user could like. To this extent, DBpedia can be viewed as a social knowledge base since it harvests automatically information provided by the community in Wikipedia. The DBpedia knowledge base has several advantages over existing knowledge bases: it is multidomain, it is based on a community agreement, it follows the Wikipedia changes (it is always updated), and it is multilingual. Thanks to its SPARQL endpoint, it is possible to ask sophisticated queries against the knowledge base, achieving a complexity that would not be possible just crawling Wikipedia. The current DBpedia release (3.6) contains about 54,000 movies; 53,000 actors; 18,000 directors; and 12,000 categories directly related to movies, just to cite a few. All these resources are related with each other by several ontology properties belonging to the DBpedia ontology. Each property has its own semantics, domain, and range. For instance, the ontology object property dbpedia-owl:starring has domain dbpedia-owl:Work and range dbpedia-owl:Person (see Sect. 12.5.1 for further information about movie-related dataset extraction).

The main benefit of using the ontology is that the corresponding data are clean and well structured. It is possible to ask complex queries to the DBpedia SPARQL endpoint[3] with high precision in the results. For example, suppose we were interested in knowing which are the movies where *Hugh Grant* and *Colin Firth* starred together, we could ask DBpedia the following SPARQL query:

---

[3]http://dbpedia.org/sparql

```
SELECT ?movie WHERE {
    ?movie <http://www.w3.org/1999/02/22-rdf-syntax-ns#type>
            <http://dbpedia.org/ontology/Film> .
    ?movie <http://dbpedia.org/ontology/starring>
            <http://dbpedia.org/resource/Hugh_Grant> .
    ?movie <http://dbpedia.org/ontology/starring>
            <http://dbpedia.org/resource/Colin_Firth>
}
```

and obtain the following result set:

```
http://dbpedia.org/resource/Bridget_Jones%27s_Diary_%28film%29
http://dbpedia.org/resource/Bridget_Jones:_The_Edge_of_Reason_%28film%29
http://dbpedia.org/resource/Love_Actually
```

Intuitively, it is logical to suppose that, e.g., *Bridget Jones's Diary*[4] and *Love Actually*[5] are somehow similar to each other, since they share part of the cast. However, this is not the unique similarity between the two movies. In order to obtain all the information shared between the two movies, we may pose the following SPARQL query:

```
SELECT * WHERE {
    <http://dbpedia.org/resource/Bridget_Jones%27s_Diary_%28film%29> ?p ?o .
    <http://dbpedia.org/resource/Love_Actually> ?p ?o
}
```

If we wanted to find the movies that are most related to *Bridget Jones's Diary* using DBpedia, probably one of the very first places should be occupied just by *Love Actually*. In fact, the two movies share part of the cast as seen before, have the same producer, the same writer, and some categories in common (e.g., *2000s romantic comedy films* and *Films set in London*). Roughly speaking, the more features two movies have in common, the more they are similar. In a few words, a similarity between two movies (or two resources in general) can be detected if in the RDF graph:

- They are directly related: this happens if a movie is the sequel of another movie, as, for example, with *Bridget Jones: The Edge of Reason*[6] and *Bridget Jones's Diary*. In DBpedia, this state is handled by the ontological properties `dbpedia-owl:subsequentWork` and `dbpedia-owl:previousWork` (see Fig. 12.1a).
- They are the subject of two RDF triples having the same property and the same object (see Fig. 12.1b). Referring to the previous example, *Bridget Jones's Diary* and *Love Actually* have two actors in common. In the movie domain, we take into account about 20 properties, such as `dbpedia-owl:starring`, `dbpedia-owl:director`, `dbpedia-owl:producer`, `dbpedia-owl:musicComposer`. They have been automatically extracted via SPARQL

---

[4]http://en.wikipedia.org/wiki/Bridget_Jones's_Diary_(film)

[5]http://en.wikipedia.org/wiki/Love_Actually

[6]http://en.wikipedia.org/wiki/Bridget_Jones:_The_Edge_of_Reason_(film)

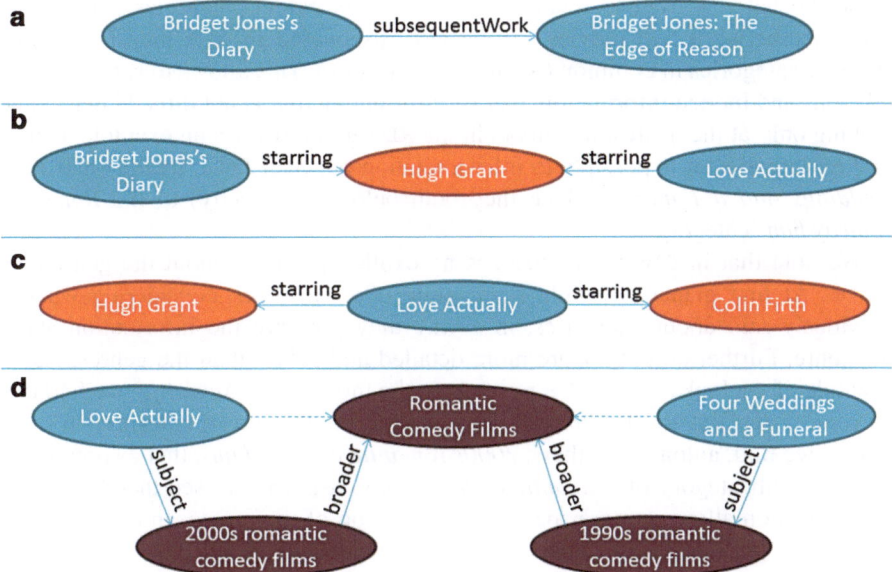

Fig. 12.1 The four types of graph matching involved in the similarity detection process

queries (see Sect. 12.5.1). The property `dcterms:subject` needs a dedicated discussion, as we will see in the following.

• They are the object of two RDF triples having the same property and the same subject. This usually does not happen for movies in DBpedia. Anyway, supposing we were interested in finding the similarities between actors, referring to the previous example, we could find that *Hugh Grant* and *Colin Firth* are related, since they acted in several movies together, i.e., they are the object of two triples where the property is `dbpedia-owl:starring` and the subject is, e.g., `dbpedia-res:Love_Actually` (Fig. 12.1c).

12.2.1   Categories and Genres

When `Wikipedia` contributors create a new article or edit an existing one, among the other things, they assign one or more categories to this article. Categories are used to organize the entire project, and help to give a structure to the whole `Wikipedia` project by grouping together pages on the same subject. The subcategorization feature makes it possible to organize categories into tree-like structures to help navigation. For example, the movie *Love Actually* belongs to the category *2000s romantic comedy films*, which in turn is a subcategory of *Romantic comedy films* (see Fig. 12.1d). In `DBpedia`, the hierarchical structure of the categories is maintained through two distinct properties, `dcterms:subject` and `skos:broader`. The former relates a resource (e.g., a movie) to its categories, while the latter is used to relate a category to its parent categories. Hence, the similarity between two movies can be also discovered in case they have some ancestor categories in common (within the hierarchy). This allows to catch implicit relations and hidden information, that is, information that is not directly detectable looking only at the nearest neighbors in the RDF graph [6]. As an example, thanks to the categories, it is possible to infer a relation between *Love Actually* and *Four Weddings and a Funeral*,[7] since they both belong (indirectly) to the *Romantic comedy films* category.

We note that in DBpedia, there is no explicit property about the genre of a movie. At first glance, it might seem quite odd. However, considering what is previously said about categories, in a way they preserve the information about the genre. Furthermore, they are more detailed and subtle than the genres. As an example, if we look at the IMDB page about the movie *Love Actually*,[8] we find that its genres are *Comedy* and *Romance*. Looking at the DBpedia categories for this movie, we find, among the others, *2000s romantic comedy films*, that as previously seen is a subcategory of *Romantic comedy films*. It is easy to see that DBpedia categorization allows a more specific classification of the movie. In order to have both a fine-grained and a standard movie classification, in our approach we also consider the IMDB genres. In fact, DBpedia is not the unique dataset we use for movie similarity detection. We exploit also LinkedMDB [13], that is the RDF version of IMDB, the popular Internet Movie Database, in order to have more robust results. For example, the LinkedMDB URI for the resource referring to the movie *Love Actually* is http://data.linkedmdb.org/resource/film/39279. According to the Linked Data principles, resources belonging to this dataset are linked to external datasets, such as DBpedia, by owl:sameAs property.

Figure 12.2 shows a sample of the RDF graph containing properties and resources coming both from DBpedia and from LinkedMDB/IMDB. For simplicity, in the picture, we omitted the rdf:type of each node.

12.3   MORE: More than Movie Recommendation

In this section, we describe MORE (*MORE* than *Movie Recommendation*), a Facebook application available online at: http://apps.facebook.com/movie-recommendation/. A screenshot of the application is depicted in Fig. 12.3.

Although the application exploits semantic datasets, the complex semantic nature of the underlying information is hidden to the end user. She does not interact directly with semantic Web languages and technologies such as RDF and SPARQL. The main goals we had in mind during the development of MORE were to build an application (1) intuitive and usable for end users, (2) rich in information taken from different

---

[7]http://en.wikipedia.org/wiki/Four_Weddings_and_a_Funeral
[8]http://www.imdb.com/title/tt0314331/

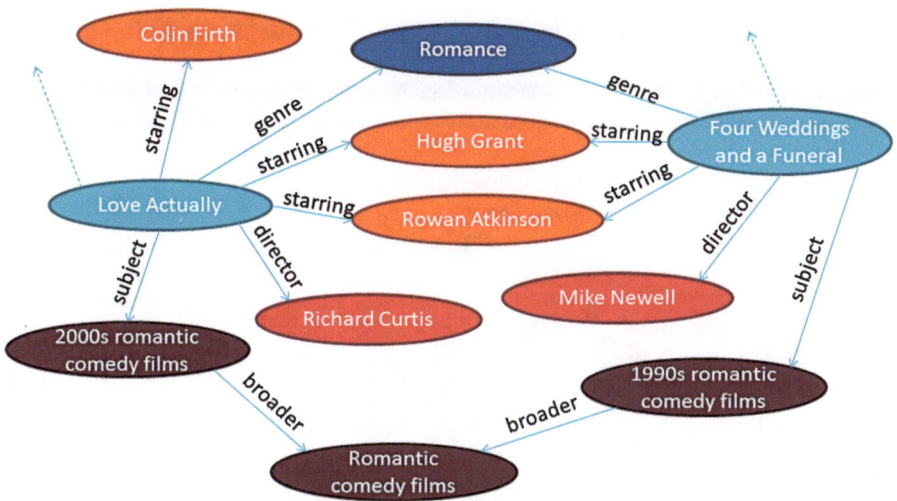

Fig. 12.2 Sample of RDF graph related to the movie domain

sources (i.e., we wanted to create an original mashup), (3) fast in providing results, and (4) fully integrated with Web 2.0 social applications as Facebook.

We chose the movie domain mainly for two reasons: (1) movies easily attract many people that can be considered "domain-expert," so it is easier to invite people to use a system and evaluate it, and (2) the resources belonging to the chosen domain are classified in a consistent DBpedia ontology. Despite the choice of the movie domain, we stress that, since our system relies on social semantic knowledge bases, it is potentially able to generate recommendations for any areas covered by DBpedia.

We decided to develop MORE as a Facebook application mainly for the following three reasons:

- Try to minimize the *cold start problem* [23] while recommending new items to the user. When the user accesses MORE for the first time, the list of movies she likes is extracted from her Facebook profile. Hence, since the first time MORE is used, it may already suggest relevant movies to the user by comparing the ones in her profile with those found in DBpedia.
- Improve the quality of recommendations by adopting also a collaborative-filtering approach. A social network, by its nature, is the best place to implement a recommender system based on collaborative filtering.[9]
- Promote quite easily a new initiative and allow a big part of Internet users to benefit of the semantic Web innovations [17].

---

[9]This feature is currently not implemented in the online version of the application, and is part of our future work.

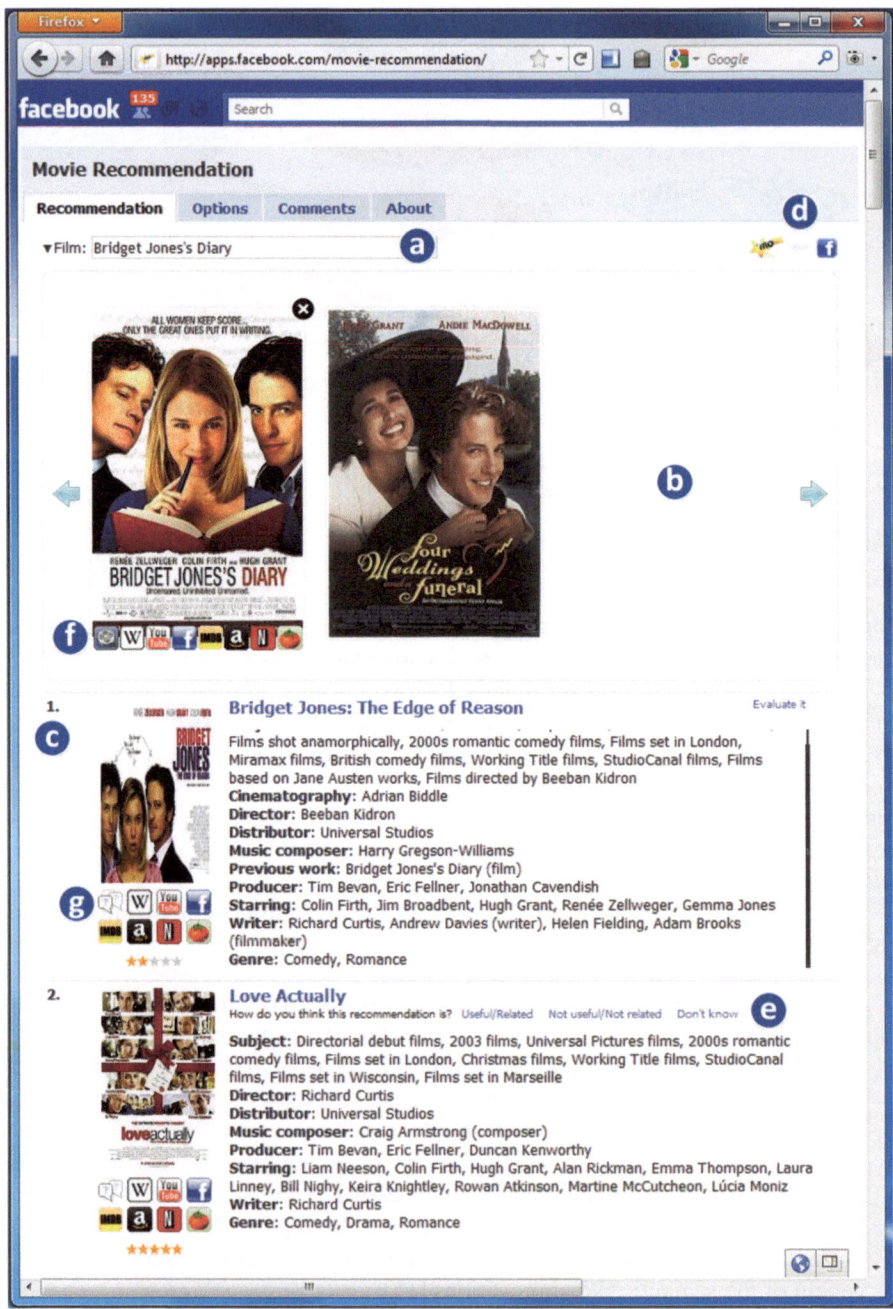

Fig. 12.3 A screenshot of MORE, available online as a Facebook app at http://apps.
facebook.com/movie-recommendation/

MORE has been designed to be multilingual, exploiting the multilingual nature of the DBpedia dataset. The language is automatically determined according to the user language set on Facebook.

After the application is loaded, the user may search for a *movie* by typing some characters in the corresponding text field, as indicated by (a) in Fig. 12.3. The system returns an *autocomplete list* of suggested movies, ranked by popularity. In order to rank the movies in the *auto-complete list*, we adapted the PageRank formula [18] to the DBpedia subgraph related to movies. To this aim, we consider only the property dbpedia-owl:wikiPageWikiLink, which corresponds to links between Wikipedia pages. In other words, this is equivalent to applying the PageRank algorithm limited to Wikipedia domain. The idea is that if a Wikipedia article (i.e., a DBpedia resource) has many incoming links (i.e., many incoming dbpedia-owl:wikiPageWikiLink relations) from other important Wikipedia articles, then it is correct to suppose that this article/resource is also important. In ranking the results shown to the user, we consider also nontopological information by weighting the results coming from the previous computation with votes on movies from IMDB users.

Once the list has been populated, the user can select one of the suggested movies. Then, the chosen movie is placed in the user's favorite movies area (see (b) in Fig. 12.3) and (a) *recommendation* of the top-40 movies related to the selected one is presented to the user (see *c* in Fig. 12.3). The relevance rankings for the movies are computed (off-line) as detailed in Sect. 12.4. The user can add more movies to her favorite list, just clicking either on its poster or on its title appearing in the recommendation list. Then, the movie is moved in the favorite area and the recommendation list is updated, taking into account also the items just added.

Another way to add a movie to the favorite list is to exploit the functionalities offered by the Facebook platform and the Graph API.[10] Facebook users can add favorite movies to their own Facebook profile. In MORE, the user can obtain her preferred Facebook movies by clicking on the icon indicated with (d) in Fig. 12.3. Then, the user can select a movie from the returned list, in order to add it to the favorite area and to obtain the related recommendation.

Each of these actions is tracked by the system. In fact, our goal is to collect relevant information about user preferences in order to provide a personalized recommendation that exploits both the knowledge bases such as DBpedia or LinkedMDB (*content-based* approach) and the similarities among users (*collaborative-filtering* approach).

The properties involved in the similarity detection process do not have the same importance. For example, the music composer of a movie is *usually* less important than the actors who played in that movie. Nevertheless, there may be cases where a user is a fan of a particular music composer and for this reason is interested to all the movies whose soundtrack is composed by that music composer. Therefore, each

---

[10]http://developers.facebook.com/docs/reference/api/

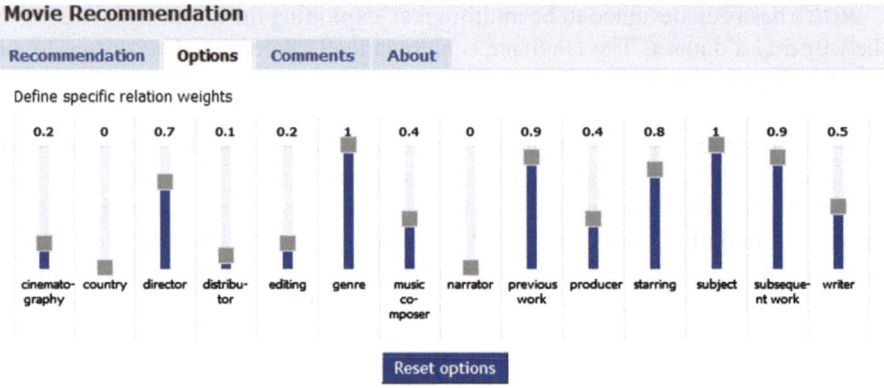

Fig. 12.4 Personalization of the user preferences

property can have a different importance for the user that can be specified through a weight (see Fig. 12.4). In Sect. 12.4, we will detail how we automatically compute the weights associated with each property. However, the user is allowed to set her personal preferences about such properties using the sliders in the *Options* tab, as shown in Fig. 12.4.

If the user moves the mouse over the poster in the favorite movies area, a list of icons fades in (see (f) in Fig. 12.3). Clicking on the first icon on the left (i.e., the one representing a reel), it is possible to obtain *information* about the selected movie, e.g., *starring, director, subject*. Each of these facets corresponds to a DBpedia property associated with the movie. Each facet can be used to further explore the knowledge associated with the selected movie. The other icons allow to retrieve information related to the selected movie from Wikipedia, YouTube, Facebook, Amazon, IMDB, RottenTomatoes, and Netflix.

For each movie that appears in the recommendation list, in addition to the just mentioned icons, an icon for *explanation* is also available (see (g) in Fig. 12.3). Clicking on it, the user may discover which features the movie shares with the other movies in the favorite area, as shown in Fig. 12.5. In particular, the common values are displayed for each facet (i.e., *subject, starring*, etc.).

12.4 Semantic Vector Space Model

In order to compute the similarities between movies, we propose a semantic-adaptation of one of the most popular models in classical information retrieval [1]: the vector space model (VSM) [24]. In VSM, nonbinary weights are assigned to index terms in queries and in documents (represented as sets of terms), and are used to compute the degree of similarity between each document in the collection and the query. In our approach, we semanticized the classical VSM, usually used for text retrieval, to deal with RDF graphs.

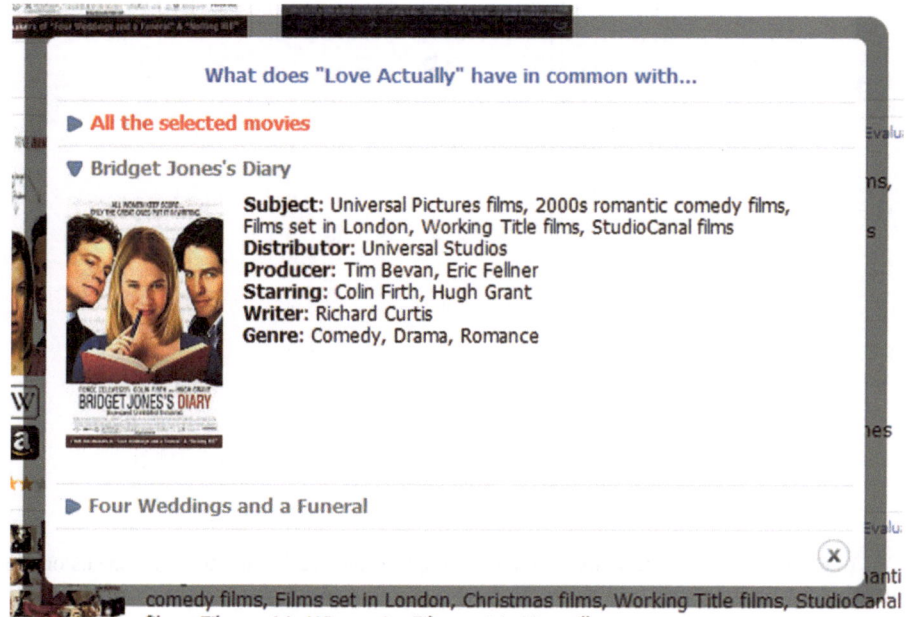

Fig. 12.5 The explanation for the recommended movie

In a nutshell, we represent the whole RDF graph as a three-dimensional tensor where each slice refers to an ontology property. Given a property, each movie is seen as a vector, whose components refer to the *term frequency-inverse document frequency* TF-IDF (or better, in this case, *resource frequency-inverse movie frequency*). For a given slice (i.e., a particular property), the similarity degree between two movies is represented by the correlation between the two vectors, and it is quantified by the cosine of the angle between them. Then, in order to obtain the global correlation between two movies, a weighted sum is calculated considering the similarity values previously computed for each property.

An RDF graph can be viewed as a labeled graph $G = (V, E)$, where V is the set of RDF nodes and E is the set of predicates (or properties) between nodes in V. In other words, given the set of triples in an RDF dataset, V represents the set of all the *subjects* and *objects*. Figure 12.2 shows a sketch of our RDF graph on movies. It contains 2 movies, 3 actors, 2 directors, 3 categories, 1 genre, and 5 different predicates.

In our model, an RDF graph is then a three-dimensional tensor **T** where each slice identifies an adjacency matrix for an RDF property (see Fig. 12.6a). All the nodes in V are represented both on the rows and on the columns. A component (i.e., a cell in the tensor) is not *null* if there is a property that relates a subject (on the rows) to an object (on the columns).

Looking at the model, we may observe and remember that:

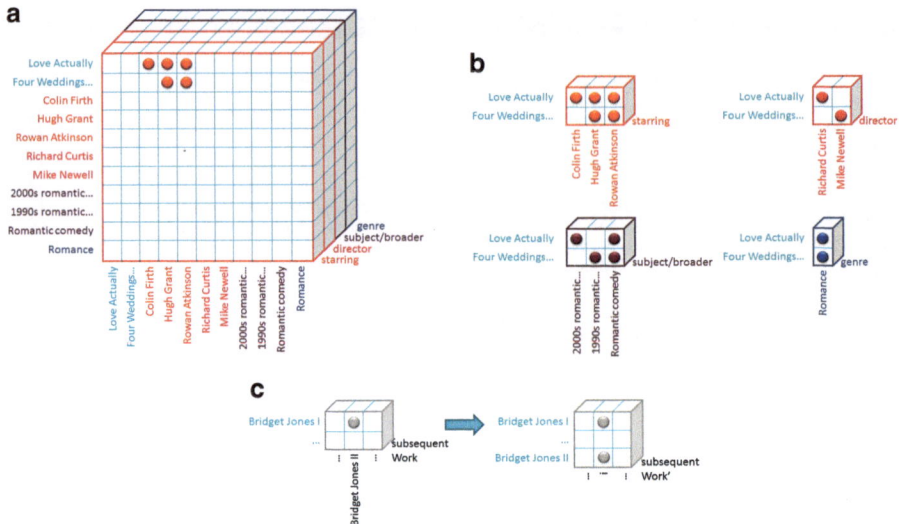

Fig. 12.6 (**a**) Tensor representation of the RDF graph of Fig. 12.2. Only the components on the first slice (i.e., *starring*) are visible. (**b**) Slices decomposition. (**c**) Property transformation

1. The tensor is very sparse.
2. Properties are independent with each other (there is no `rdfs:subPropertyOf` relation).
3. We are interested in discovering the similarities between movies (or in general between resources of the same `rdf:type` and not between each pair of resources).

Based on the above observations, we can decompose the tensor slices into smaller matrices. Each matrix of Fig. 12.6b refers to a specific RDF property, and corresponds to a slice in the tensor. In the matrices represented in Fig. 12.6b, movies of the collection are arranged on the rows and represent the *subjects* of RDF triples, while the *objects* of these triples are placed on the columns. In other words, for each matrix, the rows represent the *intensional domain* of the considered property, while the columns its *range*. For a given property, the components of each row represent the contribution of a resource (i.e., an actor, a director, etc.) to the corresponding movie. With respect to a selected property p, a movie m is then represented by a vector containing all the terms/nodes related to m via p. As for classical information retrieval, the index terms $k_{n,p}$, that is, all the nodes n linked to a movie by a specific property p, are assumed to be all mutually independent and are represented as unit vectors of a t-dimensional space, where t is the total number of index terms. Referring to Fig. 12.6b, the index terms for the *starring* property are *Colin Firth*, *Hugh Grant*, and *Rowan Aktinson*, while $t = 3$ is the number of all the actors that are objects of a triple involving *starring*.

The representation of a movie m_i, according to the property p, is a t-dimensional vector given by:

$$\overrightarrow{m_{i,p}} = (w_{1,i,p}, w_{2,i,p}, \ldots, w_{t,i,p})$$

where $w_{n,i,p}$ is a nonnegative and nonbinary value representing the weight associated with a term-movie pair $(k_{n,p}, \overrightarrow{m_{i,p}})$. The weights $w_{n,i,p}$ we adopt in our model are TF-IDF weights. More precisely, they are computed as:

$$w_{n,i,p} = f_{n,i,p} * \log\left(\frac{M}{a_{n,p}}\right)$$

where $f_{n,i,p}$ represents the TF, i.e., the frequency of the node n, as the object of an RDF triple having p as property and the node i as subject (the movie). Actually, this term can be at most 1, since two identical triples cannot coexist in an RDF graph. Then, in case there is a triple that links a node i to a node n via the property p, the frequency $f_{n,i,p}$ is 1; otherwise, $f_{n,i,p} = 0$, and the corresponding weight $w_{n,i,p}$ is set to 0.

M is the total number of movies in the collection, and $a_{n,p}$ is the number of movies that are linked to the resource n, by means of the predicate p. As an example, referring to Fig. 12.6b, for the *starring* property, and considering $n = Hugh\,Grant$, then $a_{\text{HughGrant, starring}}$ is equal to 2, and it represents the number of movies where *Hugh Grant* acted. The logarithm of the fraction in the formula represents the inverse movie frequency IDF, and as for canonical VSM, it is a global parameter that does not depend on the particular movie m_i.

Considering all the properties involved in the representation, a movie vector $\overrightarrow{m_i}$ is defined as:

$$\overrightarrow{m_i} = \frac{1}{P} \sum_p \alpha_p * \overrightarrow{m_{i,p}}$$

where P is the number of all properties we consider in our model and $0 \leq \alpha_p \leq 1$ is the importance assigned to each property p. α_p can be set by the user or elicited by the system as we will explain at the end of this section. Therefore, each movie can be represented as a $t \times P$ matrix (it corresponds to a horizontal slice in Fig. 12.6a). If we consider a projection on a property p, each pair of movies, m_i and m_j, is represented as t-dimensional vector. As for classical VSM, here we evaluate the degree of similarity of m_i with respect to m_j, as the correlation between the vectors $\overrightarrow{m_i}$ and $\overrightarrow{m_j}$. More precisely, we calculate the cosine of the angle between the two vectors as:

$$\text{sim}(m_i, m_j, p) = \frac{\overrightarrow{m_{i,p}} \bullet \overrightarrow{m_{j,p}}}{\left|\overrightarrow{m_{i,p}}\right| \times \left|\overrightarrow{m_{j,p}}\right|}$$

$$= \frac{\sum_{n=1}^{t} w_{n,i,p} * w_{n,j,p}}{\sqrt{\sum_{n=1}^{t} w_{n,i,p}^2} * \sqrt{\sum_{n=1}^{t} w_{n,j,p}^2}}$$

and finally, in order to find the global similarity between m_i and m_j, we sum each partial similarity on each property p:

$$\mathrm{sim}(m_i, m_j) = \frac{1}{P} \sum_p \alpha_p * sim(m_i, m_j, p)$$

where, again, α_p is the weight associated with each property p. Thanks to the normalization factor P, the similarity varies from 0 to 1, where higher values mean higher degree of similarity.

Summing up, in the similarity computation process, we firstly compute the similarity for each pair of movies for any property p, and then we sum all the similarities so obtained for each pair, weighted according to α_p coefficients. In this way, it is possible to ask the system questions like *"Which are the most similar movies to movie m_i according to the specific property p^*?"*, and also *"Which are the most similar movies to movie m_i according to the whole knowledge base?"*, and in case *"Which are the most similar movies to movie m_i according to the user profile?"* The first question is answered by setting $\alpha_p = 0, p \neq p^*$. The second question takes into account the coefficients as computed by the system. The last question considers the user's preferred movies.

If we go back to Fig. 12.1, we see that the method described so far to compute the similarity between two movies can be applied to case (b) and (d), i.e., when the similarity has to be found between resources that appear as subjects of RDF triples. Concerning case (c), it is simply a matter of swapping the rows with the columns in the matrices of Fig. 12.6b and applying again the same algorithm. Anyway, we point out this case is not frequent in the movie domain.

Concerning case (a) of Fig. 12.1, this allows the system to discover a similarity between resources that are directly related by some specific properties. In the considered movie domain, this situation happens, for example, with the *subsequentWork* property. In our approach, we operate a matrix transformation to revert this situation to case b) of Fig. 12.1. The transformation is illustrated in Fig. 12.6c. In order to use the VSM with two resources directly linked, the property p is transformed into the property p' and its domain remains unchanged. The object of the original RDF triple for the new property p' is mapped into a unique index associated with the original object (in Fig. 12.6c, index i is associated with *Bridget Jones II*), and a new RDF triple is created having as subject the original object and as object the index just created. Referring to Fig. 12.6c, *Bridget Jones II* becomes the subject of a new triple, where the predicate is *subsequentWork'* and the object is the index i. Now our semantic VSM can be applied straight.

In our implementation, the coefficients α_p can be set by the user. Anyway, we automatically computed their default values based on a statistical analysis on Amazon's collaborative recommender system. We collected a set of 1,000 randomly selected movies and we checked *why* users that has bought a movie m_i also bought movie m_j, analyzing the first items in the recommendation list. For example, for the movie *Bridget Jones's Diary*, the first movie suggested by Amazon is *Bridget Jones:*

The Edge of Reason. Then, looking into our semantic dataset, we checked which properties these two movies have in common. In particular, since these movies share part of the cast and some categories and one is the sequel of the other, we assign an initial score to α_{starring}, $\alpha_{\text{subject/broader}}$, and $\alpha_{\text{subsequentWork}}$. The main idea behind this assignment is that a user likes a movie m_i, given another movie m_j, because the two movies are similar according to some properties $p_1, \ldots, p_P$. More precisely, each time there is a property p that relates two movies to each other (through any of the configurations in Fig. 12.1), a counter associated with p is incremented. We iterate the process on the training movie set, and we normalize the counters to the highest one, to finally obtain the coefficients α_p in the range $[0, 1]$.

12.5 Evaluation

In order to assess the performance and the quality of our recommendation algorithm, we have analyzed the amount of time required to compute the rankings for the whole dataset and we have conducted several experiments with real users to evaluate the proposed recommendation.

12.5.1 Dataset and Performance Analysis

In order to identify the subset of DBpedia resources related to movie domain, we executed some SPARQL queries useful to evaluate its size. More in detail, in the current DBpedia release (3.6), there are 53,619 movies. They appear as the subject of 2,919,686 RDF triples (with 867,966 distinct objects), and as the object of 127,440 RDF triples (with 120,703 distinct subjects). The distinct properties whose domain is a movie are 1,338, while the distinct properties whose object is a movie are 125.

Among the almost 3 million of triples having a movie as subject, a little more than half of them (1,592,611) link a movie to a resource (e.g., an *actor* URI, a *director* URI, and not a literal). More precisely, there are 188 distinct properties of such type whose domain is a movie.

Concerning DBpedia categories, there are 316,483 RDF triples that link a movie to one of the 11,565 distinct categories (via the dcterms:subject property). Exploring the dataset one step more, there are 728,796 triples that link each of these categories to a broader category (via the skos:broader property).

In our analysis, we considered only *object properties* (i.e., properties whose type is owl:ObjectProperty), dcterms:subject and skos:broader, while we discarded both *datatype properties* (i.e., properties whose type is owl:DatatypeProperty) and properties that are not mapped in the DBpedia ontology.[11] In particular, we consider `dcterms:subject` and `skos:broader` very relevant to our approach since they encode most of the ontological knowledge in the DBpedia dataset.

We agree that considering also literals may improve the recommendation results, but in this work, our focus was just on resources. Nevertheless, we point out that our approach (cf. Sect. 12.4) works also with literals. We use only the properties belonging to the DBpedia ontology, because they allow users to deal with high-quality, clean, and well-structured data. A list of all the properties related to the *Film* class in the DBpedia ontology is available at http://mappings.dbpedia.org/server/ontology/classes/Film.

Focusing on the object properties, DBpedia contains 536,970 triples that link a movie resource to another resource via one of the 16 distinct object properties as defined in the DBpedia ontology. In the movie dataset extraction, we considered all these properties, except for the properties `dbpedia-owl:wikiPage ExternalLink` and `dbpedia-owl:thumbnail`, since they clearly do not give any useful semantic contribution to our computation. Just to summarize some of the most relevant characteristics of the extracted movie subgraph, there are 166,844 triples involving 52,949 distinct *actors*; 49,538 triples referring to 17,535 different *directors*; and 64,090 triples concerning 28,935 distinct *writers*.

Concerning the object properties that link a resource to a movie, the most popular are `dbpedia-owl:subsequentWork` and `dbpedia-owl:previousWork`.

After the movie subgraph has been extracted, we have measured the runtime performance of the ranking process executed by our semantic vector space model algorithm. The data collection and filtering steps have been excluded as they depend on the network bandwidth and the availability of the service providing the data. The program is written in Java and makes extensive use of multithreading, with 150 concurrent threads. The computation time for the recommendation of the whole extracted dataset has lasted 29 min and 3 s on a dedicated server machine with four Xeon quad-core 2.93GHz processors and 32GB RAM.

12.5.2 User Evaluation

We evaluated our semantic vector space model in two separate rounds with 85 different Facebook users per round. We asked them to express a judgment about the recommendation provided by MORE. In the second round, we made some improvements to the algorithm. More precisely, we filtered out some noninformative Wikipedia categories and the categories whose information is already implied by other properties. *English language films* is an example of noninformative category for our application: obviously, two movies do not have to be considered similar just because of the language. Another example of such type of category is *Films*

---

[11]http://wiki.dbpedia.org/Downloads36#ontologyinfoboxproperties

whose director won the Best Director Golden Globe: if the directors of two different movies won a prize, this does not imply that the two movies are similar. We filtered out such noninformative categories using regular expressions and identifying string patterns. We wiped out also another class of categories, such as, for example, the category *Films directed by Jon Avnet*: in this case, the information about the director is already contained within the specific *director* property. If we did not remove it, the information on the director would have been considered twice in the similarity computation. Another example of this type of category is the category *20th Century Fox films*: the distributor is already present as a specific property and has a very low importance. If this category was not eliminated, the discovery of the similarity between movies would have been affected. In order to remove this class of categories, at first we collected the labels associated with directors and distributors, and then we discarded the categories whose label contained the unwanted ones. As shown in Table 12.1, the improved recommendation achieves a precision that is on the average 7.7 percentage points above the baseline (unfiltered) recommendation.

Concerning the evaluation, after users added one or more movies in their favorite movie set, they have been asked to evaluate the proposed movie list. For each of these, the user could vote it as *"useful/related," "not useful/not related,"* or *"don't know"* (cf. (e) in Fig. 12.3). We collected 11,775 votes (on 4,849 distinct movies) in the first round and 11,486 votes (on 4,781 distinct movies) in the second round, meaning that on the average, each user voted 138 times in the first round and 135 times in the second one. The average time spent by each user to express a vote was 9.2 s. The user's favorite movie list contained 1.33 films on the average. From these votes, we calculated the precision in terms of the $P@n$ [1], with $n = 1, 3, 5, 10, 40$, where 40 is the maximum number of recommended movies. This measure provides an assessment of what is the user judgment of the results. The higher the concentration of relevant results at the top of the recommendation list, the more positive the judgment of the users. As noted by Cleverdon in [7], the majority of searches do not require high recall, but just a few relevant answers at the top. The results of the evaluation are shown in Table 12.1. In the evaluation of the precision, we considered as *nonnegative* both the votes marked as *"useful/related"* and the ones marked as *"don't know."* In our approach, the *"don't know"* vote is very useful and important: it contributes to indicate the novelty of the proposed recommendation. In other words, it can be seen as a kind of serendipitous recommendation, i.e., something new and nonobvious that the user

Table 12.1 Result of the evaluation: Precision@n

n	Useful		Not useful		Don't know		$P@n$	
	Baseline	Improved	Baseline	Improved	Baseline	Improved	Baseline	Improved
1	64.4%	76.3%	18.6%	10.2%	17.0%	13.6%	81.4%	89.8%
3	57.5%	68.4%	19.7%	12.73%	22.8%	18.8%	80.3%	87.3%
5	49.8%	60.6%	24.0%	17.8%	26.3%	21.6%	76.0%	82.2%
10	38.0%	49.8%	31.3%	24.7%	30.7%	25.6%	68.7%	75.3%
40	34.3%	48.0%	36.5%	26.2%	29.2%	25.7%	63.5%	73.7%

would likely not have discovered on her own [25] but she could be interested in. As shown in Table 12.1, the precision decreases when the number of considered results increases. For the first three rows of the table ($P@1$, $P@3$ and $P@5$), the precision (improved version) is always greater than 80% (considering *non-negative* results). It is quite high even for the next rows of the table ($P@10$ and $P40$), as it is always greater than 70%.

Then, we calculated the agreement among testers using the *index raw agreement* [29]. It represents the proportion between the measured interrater agreement and the best possible agreement. The value can vary in the range [0, 1], where 1 corresponds to the maximal agreement, while 0 corresponds to no agreement. The results from the evaluation point out a high interrater agreement. In fact, considering the specific agreement, the agreement ratio is 0.87. For the overall agreement, the interrater agreement ratio is even higher, equal to 0.91. The calculated ratios are statistically significant at the 0.05 level (1-tailed).

12.6 Related Work

Several systems have been proposed in the literature that address the problem of movie recommendations [12, 14, 16, 21, 25], even if there are very few approaches that exploit the Linked Data initiative to provide semantic recommendation. In the following, we give a brief overview of semantic-based approaches to (movie) recommendation.

Szomszor et al. [27] investigate the use of folksonomies to generate tag clouds that can be used to build better user profiles to enhance the movie recommendation. They use an ontology to integrate both IMDB and Netflix data. However, they compute similarities among movies taking into account just similarities between movie tags and keywords in the tag cloud, without considering other information like actors, directors, and writers as we do in MORE.

Filmtrust [12] integrates semantic Web-based social networking into a movie recommender system. Trust has been encoded using the FOAF trust module and is exploited to provide predictive movie recommendation. *FilmTrust* uses a collaborative filtering approaches as many other recommender systems, as *MovieLens* [14], *Recommendz* [11], and *Film-Consei* [21].

Our RDF graph representation as a three-dimensional tensor has been inspired by [10]. Here, the authors extend the paradigm of two-dimensional graph representation to obtain information on resources and predicates of the analyzed graph. In the preprocessing phase, they just prune dominant predicates, while we automatically extract, through SPARQL queries, relevant ones according to the chosen domain. Moreover, in [10], the authors consider only the objects of the RDF triples, while we look also at subject of the statements to compute similarities.

Tous and Delgado [28] use the vector space model to compute similarities between entities for ontology alignment; however, with their approach, it is possible to handle only a subset of the cases we consider, specifically only the case where resources are directly linked (see Fig. 12.1a). Eidon et al. [8] represent each concept in an RDF graph as a vector containing nonzero weights. However, they take into account only the distance from concepts and the subclass relation to compute such weights.

Effective user interfaces play a crucial role in order to provide a satisfactory user experience for content recommendation. Nowadays, there are some initiatives that exploit the Linked Data cloud to provide effective recommendations. One of these is *dbrec* [19], a music content-based recommender system that adopts an algorithm for *Linked data semantic distance* [20]. It uses only DBpedia as knowledge base in the Linked Data cloud. The recommendation is link-based, since the "semantics" of relations is not exploited and each relation has the same importance, and it does not take into account the links hierarchy, expressed in DBpedia through the SKOS vocabulary.

12.7   Conclusion and Future Work

The huge amount of Linked Data freely available in the so-called Web of Data are for sure an interesting opportunity to build new and smarter knowledge-based applications. In this chapter, we have presented MORE, a Facebook application that works as a recommender system in the movie domain. The background knowledge adopted by MORE comes exclusively from semantic datasets. In particular, in this version of the tool, we use DBpedia and LinkedMDB to collect information about movies, actors, directors, etc. The recommender algorithm relies on a semantic version of the classical vector space model adopted in information retrieval. Currently, we are working on the next version of the tool to include both technological and methodological improvements. From a technological point of view, we are testing the performances of the recommendation algorithm when using NoSQL databases [26]. In particular, due to the graph-based nature of the information we manage, we are working on an implementation based on the graph database Neo4j.[12] Moreover, we are willing to better integrate MORE in the Linked Data cloud by publishing our recommendation using the *recommendation ontology* [9]. Following the idea of Tim Berners-Lee et al. in [2]: "*one of the goals of a semantic browser is serendipitous re-use*," we want to investigate how exploratory browsing [30] might be helpful when combined with a recommender system for serendipitous recommendations [15]. We are also developing a mobile version of the system which exploits location-based information both for the exploratory search task and for the recommendation process. From a methodological perspective, we are collecting information from MORE users to implement also a collaborative-filtering approach to recommendation. This is particularly relevant and challenging since the application is integrated with Facebook.

---

[12]http://neo4j.org

References

1. Baeza-Yates, R.A., Ribeiro-Neto, B.: Modern Information Retrieval: The Concepts and Technology Behind Search. Addison-Wesley Professional, Reading, MA (2011)
2. Berners-Lee, T., Chen, Y., Chilton, L., Connolly, D., Dhanaraj, R., Hollenbach, J., Lerer, A., Sheets, D.: Tabulator: exploring and analyzing linked data on the semantic web. In Procedings of the 3rd international semantic web user interaction workshop (SWUI06) (2006)
3. Berners-Lee, T., Hendler, J., Lassila, O.: The semantic web: scientific American. Scientific American (2001)
4. Bizer, C., Heath, T., Berners-Lee, T.: Linked data – the story so far. Int. J. Semant. Web Inf. Syst. **5**(3), 1–22 (2009)
5. Bizer, C., Lehmann, J., Kobilarov, G., Auer, S., Becker, C., Cyganiak, R., Hellmann, S.: Dbpedia – a crystallization point for the web of data. Web Semant. **7**, 154–165 (2009)
6. Chernov, S., Iofciu, T., Nejdl, W., Zhou, X.: Extracting semantics relationships between wikipedia categories. In: Volkel M., Schaffert S. (eds.) Proceedings of the 1st Workshop on Semantic Wikis – from Wiki to Semantics, Workshop on Semantic Wikis. ESWC2006 (2006)
7. Cleverdon, C.W.: The significance of the cranfield tests on index languages. Proceedings of the 14th Annual International ACM SIGIR, pp. 3–12 (1991)
8. Eidoon, Z., Yazdani, N., Oroumchian, F.: A vector based method of ontology matching. Proceedings of 3rd International Conference on Semantics, Knowledge and Grid, pp. 378–381 (2007)
9. Ferris, B., Jacobson, K.: The Recommendation Ontology 0.3. http://purl.org/ ontology/rec/-core# (2010)
10. Franz, T., Schultz, A., Sizov, S., Staab, S.: Triplerank: ranking semantic web data by tensor decomposition. Proceedings of the 8th ISWC, ISWC '09, pp. 213–228 (2009)
11. Garden, M., Dudek, G.: Semantic feedback for hybrid recommendations in recommendz. IEEE international conference EEE'05, pp. 754–759 (2005)
12. Golbeck, J., Hendler, J.: Filmtrust: movie recommendations using trust in web-based social networks. Proceedings of the IEEE CCNC (2006)
13. Hassanzadeh, O., Consens, M.P.: Linked movie data base. Proceedings of the WWW2009 Workshop on Linked Data on the Web (LDOW2009) (2009)
14. Herlocker, J., Konstan, J.A., Riedl, J.: Explaining collaborative filtering recommendations. Proceeding on the ACM 2000 Conference on Computer Supported Cooperative Work, pp. 241–250 (2000)
15. Herlocker, J.L., Konstan, J.A., Terveen, L.G., Riedl, J.T.: Evaluating collaborative filtering recommender systems. ACM Trans. Inf. Syst. **22**, 5–53 (2004)
16. Mukherjee, R., Sajja, N., Sen, S.: A movie recommendation system – an application of voting theory in user modeling. User Model. User-Adapt. Interact. **13**(1–2), 5–33 (2003)
17. Nazir, A., Raza, S., Chuah, C.N.: Unveiling facebook: a measurement study of social network based applications. Proceedings of the 8th ACM SIGCOMM Conference on Internet Measurement, IMC '08, pp. 43–56. ACM, New York, NY, USA (2008)
18. Page, L., Brin, S., Motwani, R., Winograd, T.: The pagerank citation ranking: bringing order to the web. Technical Report 1999-66, Stanford InfoLab (1999)
19. Passant, A.: dbrec: music recommendations using dbpedia. Proceedings of the 9th International Sematic Web Conference, ISWC'10, pp. 209–224 (2010)
20. Passant, A.: Measuring semantic distance on linking data and using it for resources recommendations. Proceedings of the AAAI Spring Symposium "Linked Data Meets Artificial Intelligence" (2010)
21. Perny, P., Zucker, J.: Preference-based search and machine learning for collaborative filtering: the film-consei recommender system. Inform. Interac. Intel. **1**, 9–48 (2001)
22. Prud'hommeaux, E., Seaborne, A.: SPARQL query language for RDF. W3C Recommendation (2008)

23. Ricci, F., Rokach, L., Shapira, B., Kantor, P.B. (eds.): Recommender Systems Handbook. Springer, Berlin, Heidelberg, New York (2011)
24. Salton, G., Wong, A., Yang, C.S.: A vector space model for automatic indexing. Commun. ACM **18**, 613–620 (1975)
25. Schafer, J.B., Konstan, J.A., Riedl, J.: E-commerce recommendation applications. Data Mining Knowledge Dis. **5**, 115–153 (2001)
26. Stonebraker, M.: Sql databases v. nosql databases. Commun. ACM **53**, 10–11 (2010)
27. Szomszor, M., Cattuto, C., Alani, H., O'Hara, K., Baldassarri, A., Loreto, V., Servedio, V.D.: Folksonomies, the semantic web, and movie recommendation. 4th European semantic web conference (2007)
28. Tous, R., Delgado, J.: A vector space model for semantic similarity calculation and owl ontology alignment. DEXA, pp. 307–316 (2006)
29. Von Eye, A., Mun, E.Y.: Analyzing Rater Agreement: Manifest Variable Methods. Lawrence Erlbaum Associates, Mahwah, NJ, USA (2004)
30. White, R.W., Roth, R.A.: Exploratory search: beyond the query-response paradigm. Syn. Lect. Inform. Concepts Retriev. Serv. **1**(1), 1–98 (2009)

Chapter 13
Flint: From Web Pages to Probabilistic Semantic Data

Lorenzo Blanco, Mirko Bronzi, Valter Crescenzi, Paolo Merialdo,
and Paolo Papotti

13.1 Introduction

The Web is a surprisingly extensive source of information: it offers a huge number
of sites containing data about a disparate range of topics. Although Web pages are
built for human fruition, not for automatic processing of the data, we observe that
an increasing number of Web sites deliver pages containing structured information
about recognizable concepts, relevant to specific application domains, such as
movies, finance, sport, products, etc.

The development of scalable techniques to *discover*, *extract*, and *integrate* data
from fairly structured large corpora available on the Web is a challenging issue,
because to face the Web scale, these activities should be accomplished automatically
by domain-independent techniques.

To cope with the complexity and the heterogeneity of Web data, state-of-
the-art approaches focus on information organized according to specific patterns
that frequently occur on the Web. Meaningful examples are WebTables [19],
which focuses on data published in HTML tables, and information extraction
systems, such as TextRunner [4], which exploits lexical-syntactic patterns. As
noticed by Cafarella et al. [19], even if a small fraction of the Web is organized
according to these patterns, due to the Web scale, the amount of data involved is
impressive.

In this chapter, we focus on methods and techniques to wring out value from the
data delivered by large data-intensive Web sites. These sources are characterized by

L. Blanco · M. Bronzi · V. Crescenzi · P. Merialdo (✉) · P. Papotti
Dipartimento di Informatica e Automazione, Università degli Studi Roma Tre, via della Vasca
Navale 79, Rome, Italy
e-mail: blanco@dia.uniroma3.it; bronzi@dia.uniroma3.it; crescenz@dia.uniroma3.it;
merialdo@dia.uniroma3.it; papotti@dia.uniroma3.it

R. De Virgilio et al. (eds.), *Semantic Search over the Web*,   333
Data-Centric Systems and Applications, DOI 10.1007/978-3-642-25008-8_13,
© Springer-Verlag Berlin Heidelberg 2012

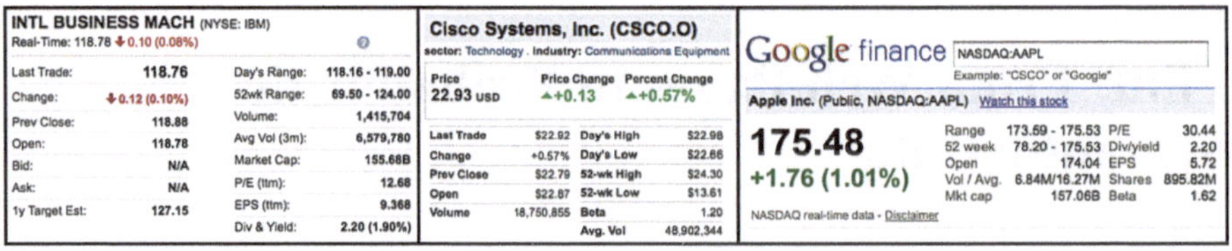

INTL BUSINESS MACH (NYSE: IBM)			Cisco Systems, Inc. (CSCO.O)			Google finance	NASDAQ:AAPL
Real-Time: 118.78 ↓0.10 (0.08%)			sector: Technology . Industry: Communications Equipment				Example: "CSCO" or "Google"
Last Trade:	118.76	Day's Range: 118.16 - 119.00	Price	Price Change	Percent Change	Apple Inc. (Public, NASDAQ:AAPL) Watch this stock	
Change:	↓0.12 (0.10%)	52wk Range: 69.50 - 124.00	22.93 USD	▲+0.13	▲+0.57%	**175.48**	Range 173.59 - 175.53 P/E 30.44
Prev Close:	118.88	Volume: 1,415,704	Last Trade	$22.92 Day's High	$22.98		52 week 78.20 - 175.53 Div/yield 2.20
Open:	118.78	Avg Vol (3m): 6,579,780	Change	+0.57% Day's Low	$22.86	**+1.76 (1.01%)**	Open 174.04 EPS 5.72
Bid:	N/A	Market Cap: 155.66B	Prev Close	$22.79 52-wk High	$24.30		Vol / Avg. 6.84M/16.27M Shares 895.82M
Ask:	N/A	P/E (ttm): 12.68	Open	$22.87 52-wk Low	$13.61	NASDAQ real-time data - Disclaimer	Mkt cap 157.06B Beta 1.62
1y Target Est:	127.15	EPS (ttm): 9.368	Volume	18,750,855 Beta	1.20		
		Div & Yield: 2.20 (1.90%)		Avg. Vol	48,902,344		

Fig. 13.1 Three Web pages containing data about stock quotes from Yahoo!, Reuters, and Google

two important features that suggest new opportunities for the automatic discovery, extraction, and integration of Web data.

- On the one hand, we observe *local regularities*: in these sites, large amounts of data are usually offered by hundreds of pages, each encoding one tuple in a local HTML template. For example, pages shown in Fig. 13.1 (which are from three different Web sites) publish information about one company stock. If we abstract this representation, we may say that each Web page displays a tuple, and that, in a given Web site, the collection of pages containing data about the same entity corresponds to a relation. According to this abstraction, the web sites for pages in Fig. 13.1 expose their own "StockQuote" relation. Local regularities also involve the access paths to reach pages offering data from the same relation. In our example, within each site, the navigation paths to reach stock quote pages from, say, the home page are similar.
- On the other hand, we notice *global information redundancy*: many sources provide similar information. For example, there are dozens of Web sites that publish pages containing stock quote data. Global information redundancy occurs both at the schema level (the same attributes are published by more than one source) and at the extensional level (some objects are published by more than one source). In our example, at the schema level, many attributes are present in all the sources (e.g., the company name, last trade price, volume); while others are published by a subset of the sources (e.g., the "Beta" indicator). At the extensional level, there is a set of stock quotes that are published by more sources. It is worth observing that, as web information is inherently imprecise, redundancy also implies inconsistencies; that is, sources can provide conflicting information for the same object (e.g., a different value for the volume of a given stock).

The above observations lead us to abstract that underlying sources of the same domain there is a *hidden conceptual relation* from which collections of pages from different Web sites are generated. According to this model, each collection can be seen as a source of data created by a generative process applied over the hidden relation. Each source publishes information about a subset of the tuples from the hidden relation, and different sources may publish different subsets of its attributes. Sources may introduce errors and imprecisions, or they may publish values by adopting different formats (e.g., miles vs. kilometers). Finally, each source encodes

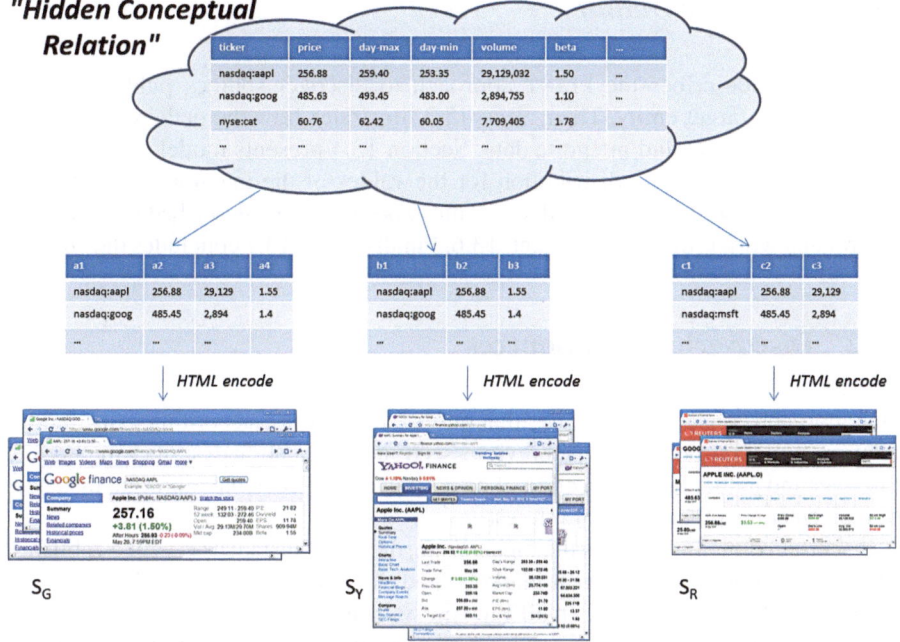

Fig. 13.2 The generative process applied to the publication of stock quote pages by GoogleFinance, YahooFinance, and Reuters

data in a local HTML template, giving rise to the published collection of pages. Figure 13.2 depicts this process applied to three finance Web sources that publish their own views of the *hidden* relation.

13.1.1   Inverting the Publishing Process

This chapter describes the main results of a research project, called FLINT, that aims at developing methods, tools, and techniques to support the construction of repositories from Web data by leveraging local regularities and global information redundancy. Given an entity of interest (such as, stock quote, book, soccer player), we have studied how to automatically *discover* sites that offer large collections of pages publishing data about that entity. Based on the hidden relation model, we have developed techniques to automatically *extract and integrate* the data offered by these pages. Finally, since Web data are inherently imprecise, and conflicting values usually arise from different sources, we have applied a Bayesian framework to *assess the quality* of the integrated data and to evaluate the accuracy of the sources.

13.1.2 Chapter Outline

Section 13.2 describes the FLINT approach to discover sources publishing data about a given target entity. Then, Sect. 13.3 illustrates how the gathered pages are processed to extract and integrate data. Section 13.4 presents models and methods to compute a probability distribution for the values of the integrated data and the accuracy of the sources. The results of some experiments are described in Sect. 13.5, and related work is discussed in Sect. 13.6. Finally, Sect. 13.7 concludes the chapter.

13.2 Discovering New Sources

Our approach concentrates on sites that publish information according to the hidden relation model introduced in the previous section. This section describes methods to discover and gather large collection of pages containing data that represent instances of a given conceptual entity of interest.

In certain domains, such as the finance one, the set of instances is well established (the stocks quoted in the largest markets) and the many authoritative Web sources are known. In these cases, a small repository of identifiers for the relevant entity can be already available or easily built (the set of the stock quote tickers can be easily obtained), and then the collection of pages can be effectively retrieved by automatically filling a search Web form within the sites with the already known identifiers (sites that offer financial information usually provide a form that accepts as input the stock ticker and that returns as output a page containing the details about the corresponding stock).

In other domains, the set of instances and their identifiers, as well as the set of sites and the methods to access the collection of relevant pages that they offer, are not known a priori. To overcome these issues, we have developed a method to discover large collections of pages that publish data about an entity of interest.

Our method leverages both global information redundancy and local regularities. On the one hand, it relies on the redundancy of information to discover and select new sources [11]; on the other hand, it exploits the local regularities of pages and navigational paths to collect the target pages delivered by the selected sites [10].

Our method takes as input a bunch of sample pages, each containing data about one instance of an entity of interest, and returns collections of pages that publish data about instances of that entity. For example, pages such as those in Fig. 13.1 can be used as input to harvest collections of pages containing company stock quote data. The overall approach can be summarized by the following three main steps:

- *Local crawling*: we crawl the Web sites of the input sample pages to collect pages with data about other instances of the entity of interest.
- *Description extraction*: from the collected pages, we automatically extract a set of keywords that represent an intensional description of the entity exemplified by the sample pages.

- *Search expansion*: using the information computed in the previous steps, we launch Web searches to discover new sources. The results of these searches are analyzed using the entity description. Pages representing valid instances of the target entity are collected and used to recursively trigger the process.

Before giving more details about the three steps, observe that our technique has a different semantics with respect to the "similar pages" facility offered by search engines. Given as input two Web pages from two different Web sites describing the basketball players "Kobe Bryant" and "Bill Bradley," our method aims at retrieving many Web pages that are similar at the intensional level, e.g., pages about other basketball players, not necessarily the same two sample players.

13.2.1 Local Crawling: Searching Entity Pages Within One Site

The first step of our method aims at searching the target pages within the Web sites that publish the input sample pages. To achieve this goal, one could cluster the pages of the whole Web sites (e.g., by means of techniques such as those proposed in [15]) and then select the clusters containing the sample pages. However, since the target pages may represent a small subset of the whole site, in order to avoid the costs of downloading a large number of pages, we have developed a structure-driven crawler, specifically tailored to accomplish this goal.

Our structure-driven crawler relies on the observation that, for the sake of scalability of the publishing process, data-intensive Web sites publish pages where the structure and the navigation paths are fairly regular. Within each site, pages containing the same *intensional* information, i.e., instances of the same entity, organize data according to a common template, and the access paths (e.g., from the home page) to these pages obey to a common pattern. Therefore, given a seed page containing data of interest, the goal of the structure-driven crawler is to navigate the seed page's site in order to pick out the largest number of pages similar in structure to the seed pages.

To model the structure of a Web page, we rely on few features that nicely abstract the template of a Web page. Our model considers that pages from large Web sites usually contain a large number of links, and pages generated by the same template have links that share the same layout and presentation properties. Therefore, whenever a large majority of the links of two pages have the same layout and presentation properties, it is likely that the two pages have been generated by the same template, that is they are similar in structure. Then, the structure of a Web page is described by means of the presentation and layout properties of the links that it offers, and the structural similarity between pages is measured with respect to these features.

Another important characteristic of data-intensive Web sites is that collections of links that share the same layout properties (consider, e.g., a list of links in one table column) usually lead to pages that contain similar information.

Based on these observations, the crawler explores the Web site to find out which pages contain lists of links toward pages which are structurally similar to the seed pages. Following these access paths, it gathers all the site's pages that are structurally similar to the seed pages.

Beside collecting these pages, the crawler also extracts the anchors of the links leading to them. As we will describe later in the chapter, the role of these anchors is very important in our methods, since they are used as identifiers for the conceptual instances published in the referenced pages. In our context, in which pages contain data about one entity of interest, it is likely that the anchor identifies the target object. In our financial example, the anchor of the links to each stock quote page usually corresponds to the name of the company stock quote. It is worth observing that, for the sake of usability, this feature has a general validity on the Web. For example, the anchor to a book page usually corresponds to the book title, the anchor to a football player page usually is the player name, and so on.

13.2.2   Learning a Description of the Entity

During the second step, our approach computes a description for the target entity. The description of an entity is expressed as a set of *weighted intensional keywords*. For instance, a possible description for the stock quote entity is the set of keywords: *price*, *volume*, *high*, and *low*, all with equal weights.

Given a set of structurally similar pages from the same site as returned by the structure-driven crawler, our method relies on the observation that pages containing data about instances of the same entity share a common set of characterizing terms among those appearing in the page template.

Therefore, the entity description is computed as the set of terms that more frequently occurs in the pages returned by the structure-driven crawler for a given Web site. However, not all these terms can be used to characterize the entity, because there is significant amount of noise due to the presence of template terms that do not describe the underlying entity. These are terms that usually belong to a site-scope template, not specific of the pages collected by the crawler; e.g., footers and headers are shared by all the pages in the site.

Noisy terms are filtered by considering multiple Web sites at once: terms shared in several templates of different Web sites are selected as keywords of the entity description and weighted according to the frequency of appearance.

13.2.3   Search Expansion

The results produced in the first two steps are used to propagate the search on the Web. This step is done by issuing a set of queries against a search engine and elaborating the results in order to select only those pages that can be considered as instances of the target entity. The selected pages are then used as seeds to trigger a new execution of the structure-driven crawler, which gathers new collections of pages. If the discovered collections contain new instances, these are used to launch new searches, and the whole process is repeated until new pages can be found at a reasonable pace.

To feed the search engine with suitable keywords, we use the identifiers associated with the pages returned by the structure-driven crawler. That is, we pose a number of queries against a search engine, where each query is composed by the anchor of a link to one of the pages retrieved by the previous structure-driven crawler execution.

Search results can include also pages that are not suitable for our purposes. Typical examples are pages from forums, blogs, or news where the keywords occur by chance, or because they are in a free-text description. To control this aspect, our method requires that the keywords of the entity description appear in the template of the retrieved page.

Then, for each page returned by the search engine, an instance of the structure-driven crawler is run to obtain a set of structurally similar pages, and their template is computed. If the computed template contains the keywords of the entity description, the page is considered valid; otherwise, it is discarded.

Valid pages are finally used as seeds for new structure-driven crawler scans, thus contributing to further discover new pages.

13.3   Extracting and Integrating Web Data

We now describe our approach to extract and integrate data from the sources. In our context, sources consist of collections of pages, where each page contains data about one instance of a given entity. Also, as we have discussed in Sect. 13.2, our source discovery method associates every page with a string that works as an identifier for the underlying instance.

According to the hidden relation model introduced in Sect. 13.1, the issue of extracting and integrating data from the sources corresponds to invert the page generation process, i.e., to build the hidden relation starting from the collections of pages.

A natural solution to the problem is a two-step "waterfall" approach. Figure 13.3 depicts the process. First, a wrapper generation tool produces wrappers to extract data from the pages; the application of the wrappers over the collections of pages returns a set of relations. Then, a schema matching algorithm integrates the relations by creating mappings among attributes with the same semantics. However, such an approach does not scale when a large number of sources are involved, and a high level of automation is required. In fact, to face the Web scale, wrappers should be generated automatically by an unsupervised process. But automatic wrapper generators can produce imprecise extraction rules (e.g., rules that extract irrelevant or wrong data), and to obtain correct rules, the wrappers should be evaluated and

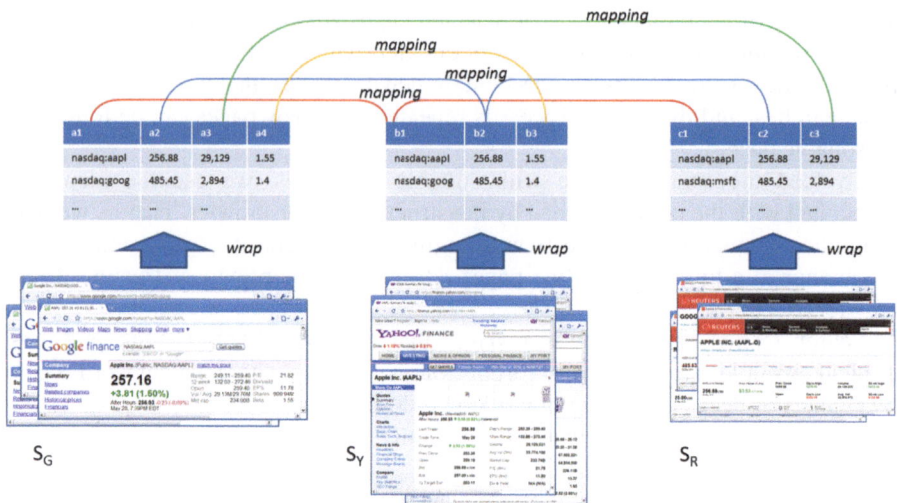

Fig. 13.3 Inverting the page generation process: automatically generated wrappers extract relations from the pages; a schema matcher creates mappings that group semantically homogeneous mappings

refined manually. Moreover, the relations extracted by automatically generated wrappers are opaque, i.e., their attributes are not associated with any (reliable) semantic label. Therefore, the matching algorithm should rely on instance-based approaches, which consider only attribute values to match schemas. Unfortunately, instance-based matching is challenging because the sources may provide conflicting values (due to the errors introduced by the publishing process), and imprecise extraction rules may return wrong, and thus inconsistent, data.

To overcome these issues, we have developed an automatic, domain-independent approach that exploits the redundancy of data among the sources to support both the extraction and the matching steps. In a bootstrapping phase, an unsupervised wrapper inference algorithm generates a set of extraction rules for each source. A domain-independent, instance-based matching algorithm compares data returned by the generated extraction rules among different sources and infers mappings. The abundance of redundancy among Web sources allows us to acquire knowledge about the domain and triggers an evaluation of the mappings. Based on the quality of the inferred mappings, the matching process provides a feedback to the wrapper generation process, which is thus driven to refine the bootstrapping wrappers in order to correct imprecise extraction rules. Better extraction rules generate better mappings, thus improving the overall quality of the solution. At the end of the process, we also rely on the evidence accumulated in order to extract from the page templates suitable semantic labels for the mappings, thus associating a semantic label with the integrated data.

In the following, we provide a description of the approach. The interested reader can find technical details in [8, 13].

13.3.1   Contextual Data Extraction and Integration

In our context, a wrapper is an ordered set of extraction rules that apply over a Web page. Each rule extracts a (possibly empty) string from the HTML of the page. Therefore, the application of a wrapper over a page returns a tuple, and the application of a wrapper over the collection of pages of a source returns a relation, whose schema has as many attributes as the number of extraction rules of the corresponding wrapper.

In a bootstrapping phase, for each source an automatic wrapper inference system (such as RoadRunner [24] or ExAlg [3]) generates a wrapper. As the process is unsupervised, the wrappers can contain *weak* rules, i.e., rules that do not correctly extract data for all the source pages, and *useless rules*, i.e., rules that extract irrelevant data. As we shall discuss later, weak rules are refined, and useless rules are identified (and discarded) contextually with the integration process, leveraging the redundancy of information.

The attributes of the relations produced by the wrappers are processed in order to produce *mappings*, i.e., sets of attributes with the same semantics. Since wrappers produce anonymous relations, mappings are computed by means of a *distance function* among the values of a small sample set of *aligned* tuple pairs. Two tuples are aligned if they refer to the same real-world object. In our framework, the task of aligning tuples is simplified by the presence of the identifiers returned by the structure-driven crawler: we align tuples that are extracted from pages having the same identifiers. The distance function returns a score between 0 and 1: the more similar are two attributes, the lower is the distance.

A simple method to infer the mappings consists in applying a variant of standard hierarchical agglomerative clustering [38] approaches. Starting from a pivot source, we build one singleton mapping for every attribute. Then, we iterate over the other relations: for each attribute of the current relation, we determine the mapping with lowest distance.[1] If such a distance is lower than a given threshold, the attribute is added to the mapping. Whenever an attribute is not added to an existing mapping, it gives rise to a new singleton mapping: it might represent an attribute that was not present in the sources processed so far.

At the end of the iteration, singleton mappings are discarded. Assuming that relevant attributes are published by at least two sources, singleton mappings represent information extracted by useless rules.

The described method is limited by the strong dependence on the matching threshold, which is statically assigned to every comparison. Low values of the threshold tend to generate many small mappings, because small imprecisions are not tolerated. Conversely, high values produce large heterogeneous mappings, composed of attributes with different semantics. The choice of a threshold that represents a nice trade-off between precision and recall is not trivial. The financial

---

[1]The distance between an attribute and a mapping is from the centroid of the mapping.

scenario introduced in the previous examples represents an interesting example
that clearly explains the problem. Observe that several attributes exhibit values
that are very close to one another: this is the case for the minimum, average,
and maximum price of a stock quote. For these attributes, low threshold values
are needed. Conversely, for other attributes, such as the volume or the market
capitalization, higher threshold values are preferable since for these values, sources
are less precise.

To address these issues, we have developed a clever approach, called SplitAnd-
Merge, that dynamically computes the matching threshold for every mapping.

13.3.1.1 SplitAndMerge Matching

SplitAndMerge is based on the observation that it is unlikely that a source publishes
the same attribute more than once, with different values. We therefore assume that
nonidentical attributes from the same source have always different semantics. As a
consequence, we impose the constraint, called *different semantic constraint*, that a
mapping is not allowed to include more than one attribute from the same source.

Also in *SplitAndMerge* mappings are created iterating over the source relations.
However, each mapping is associated with its own specific threshold. Whenever a
new mapping is created from scratch, it is associated with a given threshold, but the
threshold is dynamically updated during the process whenever the different semantic
constraint is violated.

As in the static threshold approach, an attribute can be added to a mapping if
its distance from the mapping is lower than the mapping threshold. Nevertheless,
before adding an attribute to a mapping, we check whether the mapping already
contains another attribute from the same source. Clearly, if two attributes from the
same source match a mapping, their distances from the mapping are lower than
the threshold. However, as such a threshold value would lead to a violation of the
different semantics constraint, we can conclude that the two attributes represent
different concepts, and that the values of these concepts are more similar than
expected by the current threshold, which is is too high for that mapping. We observe
that a suitable threshold value should keep well separated the two attributes that led
to the violation of the constraint. Thus, the threshold of the mapping assumes the
value of the distance between these attributes.

Attributes that were grouped in the mapping before the threshold update were
included by using an inappropriate threshold. Then, the mapping is dropped, and
its attributes are merged in new mappings around the two conflicting attributes.
Attributes from the original mapping that cannot be included in the newly generated
mappings (because their distance is greater than the new threshold) give rise to new
mappings. The thresholds of all the mappings created in these steps assume the
value of the distance between the attributes that have triggered the procedure.

To illustrate *SplitAndMerge*, consider the example shown in Fig. 13.4: m is a
mapping that groups the attributes $\{a, b, c, e_1\}$, with threshold $t_m = 0.5$, and e_2
is an attribute that belongs to the same source of e_1. Suppose that the distance

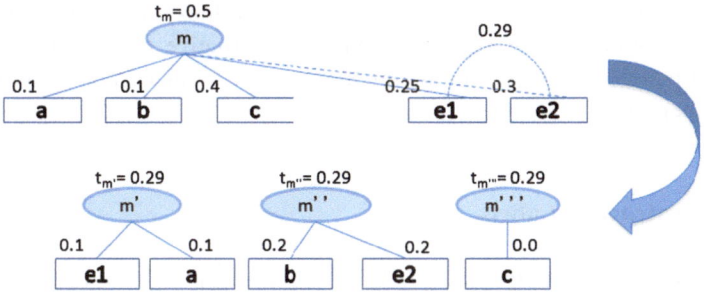

Fig. 13.4 *SplitAndMerge* over a mapping m. Labels on edges indicate distances: e_1 and e_2 belong to the same source, their distance is 0.29

between e_2 and m is 0.3: it is lower than the mapping threshold, then e_2 should be added to m. However, m already contains e_1, which comes from the same source of e_2, and thus violates the constraint. As a consequence, *SplitAndMerge* removes the initial mapping m, and creates two new mappings, m' and m''. Each of them is initialized with one of the conflicting attributes (e_1 and e_2, in the example); the threshold of these mappings is set to the value of the distance between the two conflicting attributes (0.29). The other attributes of the initial mapping are then grouped in the newly generated mapping, or they originate new mappings. In the example, assuming that a and b have lower distances from m' and m'', respectively, and that c has a distance greater than the new threshold from both m' and m'', *SplitAndMerge* would generate the mappings $m' = \{e_1, a\}$, $m'' = \{e_2, b\}$, $m''' = \{c\}$, whose thresholds assume the value of the distance between e_1 and e_2.

Note that the effects of the approach propagate for all the remaining iterations; in particular, observe that the distance between the attributes that triggered the split is assigned to the thresholds of all the mappings generated by the procedure.

13.3.2   Wrapper Refinement

Once mappings are generated, we proceed to refine the wrappers. The key idea behind the wrapper refinement process is that correct rules extract consistent information from different sources; conversely, the values returned by weak rule only partially overlap with those of other sources. Therefore, a weak rule extracts inconsistent data for some tuples, producing high but not negligible distances with the available mappings.

The refinement process corrects the wrapper by replacing a weak rule with an alternative one that extracts consistent values, thus reducing the distance from the mapping. A rule is considered weak if it produces attributes whose distance from the mapping is greater than the average distance. A weak rule usually works correctly for some pages (i.e., it extracts values that match with those extracted from other sources), but fails with other pages (the extracted values do not match with other sources). To refine the wrapper, we generate alternative rules that increase the number of matching values, minimizing the distance of the corresponding attribute from the mapping.

13.3.2.1 Extracting Labels

After all the sources have been processed (i.e., wrappers have been refined and the final mappings have been computed), in a last step, we determine the labels of the mappings. For each attribute belonging to a mapping, we process the pages of the extracted values looking for meaningful semantic labels. We leverage the observation that the labels of many attributes are part of the page template and occur close to the values.

Our technique returns as candidate labels the textual template nodes that occur closest to the extracted values. This technique may perform poorly on a single source, but it leverages the redundancy among a number of Web sites to select the best candidate labels. In other words, it is very unlikely that the same wrong label is associated with a mapping as frequently as a meaningful one. Therefore, we associate each mapping with all the labels associated with the corresponding rules, and then we rank the labels according to the number of extraction rules associated with them (higher is the number of rules, higher is the rank).

13.4 Assessing the Quality of Data

We have seen that according to our hidden relation model, Web sources provide values for the attributes of a large number of objects. For example, financial Web sites publish the values for several attributes, such as volume, open, max and min values, etc. Unfortunately, different sources can report inconsistent attribute values for the same object, making data published on the Web inherently uncertain.

The uncertainty of data can be characterized by probability distribution functions: data are associated with functions reporting the probabilities that an attribute assumes certain values for a given object.

This section describes state-of-the-art models to characterize the uncertainty of Web data. These models have a twofold goal. They aim at computing (1) the probability distributions for the data provided by the sources, and (2) the accuracy of the sources with respect to the data of interest, that is, the probability that a source provides the correct values for a set of objects. Three main factors influence the development of these models:

Object	A: authority	I: independent	IC: ind. copied	C1: copier 1	C2: copier 2	NAIVE	ACCU	DEP
	Sources					Model		
obj1	a	c	b	b	b	b	a—b	a
obj2	b	b	c	c	c	c	b	b
obj3	c	b	c	c	c	c	c	c
accuracy	1	$\frac{1}{3}$	$\frac{1}{3}$	$\frac{1}{3}$	$\frac{1}{3}$			

Fig. 13.5 Running example: *authority* always reports the correct value; *independent* and *independent copied* provide, independently from the other sources, one correct value out of three; *copier 1* and *copier 2* copy their values from *independent copied*

- *Consensus*: given an object, the larger is the number of sources that agree for the same value, the higher is the probability that the value is correct.
- *Accuracy*: the agreement of the sources' observations contributes in raising the probability that a value is correct in a measure that also depends on the accuracy of the involved sources.
- *Copiers*: the presence of copiers, that is, sources that publish data copied by other sources, can generate misleading consensus on the values proposed by the most copied sources.

As an example, consider five sources publishing the values of an attribute for the same three objects, as shown in Fig. 13.5. The first source A is an *authority* and provides the true value for each object (a, b, and c, respectively), while all the other sources (I, IC, C1, C2) provide a correct value only for one object out of three. The sources I and IC (*independent* and *independent copied*) provide their values independently from the other sources, while the remaining sources C1 and C2 merely copy the values proposed by IC. Notice that in normal settings, the role of the sources is not available as input to the models (i.e., they are not aware that A is an authority, I is independent, and so on).

13.4.1 Models Based on Consensus and Accuracy

The simplest model, called NAIVE,[2] for estimating the accuracy of sources and computing data distribution probabilities considers only the consensus: the most probable value is the one published by the largest number of sources, and the

---

[2]The names of the models presented in this chapter are inspired by those introduced by Dong et al. in [31].

probability of a value is estimated by its frequency over the given set of sources. According to NAIVE, in our running example there are two possible values for obj2 provided by the five sources considered: b is provided by sources A and I, while b is provided by three sources (IC and its copiers C1, C2). Similarly for obj1, the most likely value would erroneously be the value b. The example shows how in presence of many sources with different accuracies, a naive voting Forward could lead to incorrect conclusions. The probability distribution of the NAIVE model corresponds to the frequencies of the values. In the running example, the probability for obj1 is $a \rightarrow 1/5, b \rightarrow 3/5, c \rightarrow 1/5$.

A more involved model, called ACCU, considers at the same time the first two factors, consensus and accuracies, and produces as output an estimation of the source accuracies together with the probabilities of the values [35, 45, 46]. Indeed, consensus among sources and sources' accuracy is mutually dependent: the greater is the accuracy of the sources, the more they agree for a large number of objects and the more they will affect the general consensus. Similarly, the more the sources agree on a large number of objects, the greater is their accuracy.

The role of the accuracies consists in weighting the consensus of the sources. A voting approach similar to that used with the NAIVE model can be used to estimate the probabilities by means of the consensus: the only difference is that the votes are weighted according to the accuracies of the sources. The accuracy of a source can be estimated by comparing its observations with those of other sources for a set of objects. A source that frequently agrees with other sources is likely to be accurate, and similarly, the most accurate sources will be given the higher weights during the computation of the probabilities of the true values. In our running example, consider the accuracies given at the bottom of the table in Fig. 13.5: three sources (IC, C1, and C2) provide the wrong value c for obj2, and they will be given an overall accuracy of 1, while two sources (A,I) provide the correct value b with an overall accuracy of $\frac{4}{3}$. However, even if the accuracies are known, the model still cannot decide which value, between a and b, is the most likely value for obj1.

13.4.2 Dealing with Copying Sources

A more complex model also considers the presence of copiers, that is, sources that publish values copied by one or more other sources. The presence of copiers makes harder the problem of computing the true values and the accuracies of the sources since they can create "artificial" consensus on values. A copier, even in good faith, can propagate a wrong value originated in one of the sources from which it copies. Provided that there is enough evidence about which are the correct values, it is possible to detect which sources are copying, observing that copiers publish the same false values of the sources from which they copy. For instance, if b is considered the most likely value for obj2, the fact the IC, C1, and C2 publish the same false value attests that there are two copiers. The same argument cannot be used for obj3, for which the three sources publish the same value c: since this is a true value, it is not necessarily an evidence of copying.

DEP is a model that considers all the three factors above: consensus, accuracy, and copiers [31]. It tries to detect possible copiers by analyzing the dependencies among the sources. Once the copiers has been detected, the consensus created by their presence will be ignored during the computation of the probabilities. The dependence analysis has to consider the mutual feedbacks among consensus, accuracy, and dependencies: the accuracy of a source depends on the consensus over the values it provides; the dependencies between sources depend on source accuracy and the consensus over the values they provide; finally, the consensus should take into account both the accuracy of sources and the dependencies between sources. For instance, once that it has been detected that IC, C1, and C2 copy one another, the voting expressed by two sources will be ignored, and then it can be established that the most likely true value of obj1 is a.

Starting from the above observations, the dependence analysis has been further investigated and a more complex model M-DEP has been introduced to consider not only single attributes at a time, but whole tuples [12, 30].

13.5 Experiments

We now present some experimental results for the three main topics discussed in the chapter. We first discuss the effectiveness of the proposed solution to automatically gather sources of interest. Then we present the results obtained by the algorithms for the extraction and integration of data from these sources. Finally, we show how current state-of-the-art models for the reconciliation of conflicting values deal with such real-world Web data.

13.5.1 Discovering New Sources

We developed OUTDESIT [11], a prototype that implements the techniques described in Sect. 13.2, and we used it to perform experiments to validate the proposed techniques. Here, we focus on the results that we obtained in the *soccer* domain, as published information is easy to interpret and there are no clear authorities such as in other domains. Namely, we report some results on our experiment aimed at discovering new sources with pages publishing data about instances of the SOCCERPLAYER conceptual entity.

13.5.1.1 Entity Descriptions

We have taken three sample pages, from three different Web sites, each one publishing data about one player and we have run OUTDESIT on it. The generated entity description contains the attributes: *club*, *height*, *nationality*, and *weight*, while the keyword extracted from the sample pages is *soccer*.

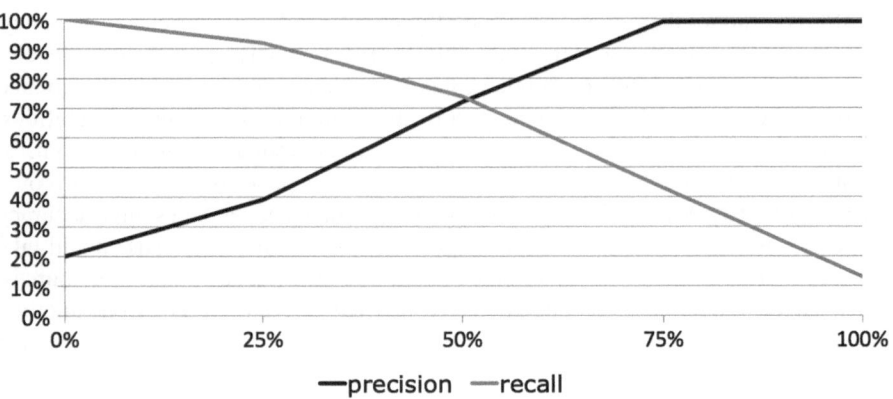

Fig. 13.6 Performance of the filtering function varying the threshold *t*

We manually analyzed the behavior of the filtering function in the search expansion step, that is, the use of the entity description to check whether a given page is valid for our purposes. We have run a single iteration of OUTDESIT with a set of identifiers pointing to 500 SOCCERPLAYER pages, selected randomly from ten soccer Web sites. The search engine returned about 15,000 pages distributed over 4,000 distinct Web sites. We then manually evaluated the Web sites to measure the precision and the recall of the function over such pages. In particular, we studied how precision and recall behave by varying the percentage of description keywords that are required in the template to accept a page (100% means that all the keywords are needed).

Figure 13.6 shows how by raising the threshold, the precision increases and the recall decreases. The system achieves 100% precision when the number of keywords from the description required to be in the template of the page is at least 75%. When only 50% of the keywords are required, the accepted pages are 74% of the total valid pages returned by the search engine, and the precision is 72%. Examples of nonvalid pages returned by the search engine results are personal pages and blogs, news, and forum pages: they are pertinent with the keywords in the queries, but they are not instance of the entity as in our definition. As these terms did not appear in the pages template, our function correctly discarded them.

13.5.1.2 Quantitative Evaluation

Figure 13.7 depicts the number of pages discovered by OUTDESIT for the target entity. The graph plots the number of new instance pages against the number of new Web sites discovered. Starting from three sample pages, for each entity the algorithm automatically discovers several thousands of pages. By a manual inspection, conducted on a representative subset of the results, we can conclude that

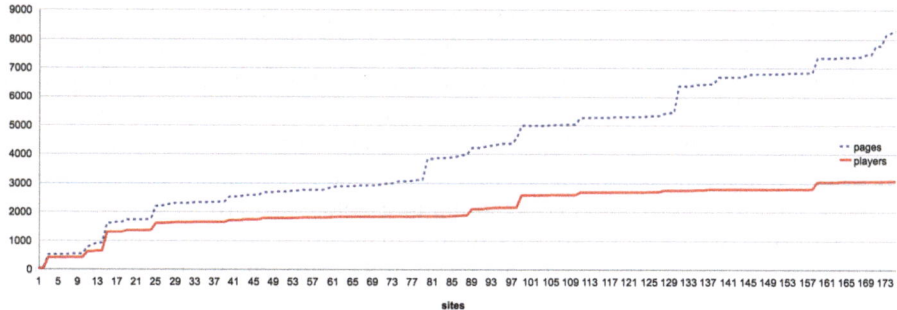

Fig. 13.7 Pages and players found by OUTDESIT

all the retrieved pages can be considered as instances of the entity exemplified by the input sample pages. The graphs also plot the number of distinct anchors (used as identifiers) that are found in each step. Somehow they can approximate the number of distinct players. As expected, it is evident that they increase less than the number of pages.

13.5.2   Extracting and Integrating Web Data

To evaluate the approach described in Sect. 13.3, we implemented in a prototype the data extraction and integration algorithms [7, 8] and run them with some collections of pages. Here we report the results concerning the *soccer* and *finance* domains. For each domain, we let OUTDESIT collect 100 sources. Each source consists of tens to thousands of pages, and each page contains detailed data about one object of the corresponding entity.

We used the standard metrics precision, recall, and F-measure to compare hand-crafted mappings with the those automatically produced by the prototype: for each mapping A generated by the prototype with respect to a golden mapping B, we computed: $P = \frac{|A \cap B|}{|A|}$; $R = \frac{|A \cap B|}{|B|}$; $F = \frac{2*P*R}{P+R}$.

13.5.2.1   Qualitative Evaluation

To evaluate the quality of the mappings, for each domain we selected 20 Web sources (the largest ones) and we manually built a golden set of mappings by inspecting ten pages per source; only the attributes that were present in at least three sources were included in the mappings. The golden schema of the stock quote entity contains 29 attributes, while that of the soccer players contains 14.

For each domain, we ran four executions to evaluate the impact of the Split-AndMerge and of the wrapper refinement on the quality of the inferred mappings. As expected, the best performances in terms of precision and F-measure are always obtained when both the *SplitAndMerge* and the wrapper refinement were activated. We report that the *NaiveMatch* (i.e., simple match without the *SplitAndMerge* technique) alone always obtains mappings with high recall but with low precision, especially in the finance domain. In fact, *NaiveMatch* gathers many valid attributes, but it aggregates several heterogeneous attributes within the same mapping, as it is not able to distinguish attributes with similar values, thus producing many false positives. The precision of the *SplitAndMerge* algorithm greatly benefits of the more advanced matching technique, especially in the finance domain. It is interesting to observe the direct correlation between the thresholds that have been dynamically increased and the improvements in the results. In the *finance* domain, which contains several similar values, an average increment of 37% for the threshold corresponds to an improvement of the precision of 250%. In the soccer domain, an increment of 32% for the threshold corresponds to a precision gain of 82%.

The wrapper refinement has always positive impacts on the performance since it increases both precision and recall: as extraction rules are improved, some attributes can reach a sufficient matching score to be added in the mapping set.

13.5.2.2 Quantitative Evaluation

Table 13.1 reports the execution of the system against the whole sets of data sources. We report for each of the eight largest output mappings, the mapping cardinality $|mapping|$ (i.e., the number of extraction rules in each of them) and the most likely label inferred by the system.

According to the model introduced in Sect. 13.1, each source provides only a partial view of the hidden relation. The mappings and the extraction rules produced by our system allow us to build an integrated view of its whole extension by accumulating information from many sources, thus obtaining more information than actually exposed by each participating source. To give an example, consider the objects and the eight attributes reported for the soccer and the finance domains in Table 13.1: the hidden relations for these entities contain at most 224 k values

Table 13.1 Top-8 results for 100 Web sources: for each mapping its most likely label and its cardinality are reported

Soccer players 45,714 pages (28,064 players)		Stock quotes 56,904 pages (576 stock quotes)	
Label	|Mapping|	Label	|Mapping|
Name	90	Stock	84
Birth	61	Price	73
Height	54	Change	73
Nationality	48	Volume	52
Club	43	Low	43
Position	43	High	41
Weight	34	Last	29
League	14	Open	24

(28 k objects × 8 attributes) and 4.6 k (5,76 × 8) values, respectively. In the finance domain, a single source covers on average about 3.2 k values (70% of the total), while the integrated view over the 100 sources reaches 4.1 k values (90% of the total). More interestingly, in the soccer domain, a single source covers on average for only 1.4 k values (1% of the total), while the integrated view reaches 134 k values (71%). As for the same object and attribute different values are provided by distinct sources, conflicting values can arise. We discuss next the experimental results for recent works that address this issue.

13.5.3 Assessing the Quality of Data

We implemented the models described in Sect. 13.4 to validate experimentally the proposed techniques on the data provided by real-life Web data sources. Here we concentrate on the results obtained in the soccer and finance domains. In particular, we report the following data extracted and integrated by our algorithms: Height, Weight, and BirthDate for soccer players; Price, Open Value, and Volume for stock quotes. For these attributes, we manually produced the correct (true) values for a set of 861 stock quotes and 100 soccer players. Stock quotes and players were selected randomly, making sure that both popular and rare objects were part of the set.

For the stock quote domain, the true values were collected by means of an authoritative source (the Nasdaq official Web site). For soccer players, since an authoritative source does not exist, the true values of the considered attributes were manually collected by inspecting the official Web site of every soccer player, whenever available, and the official Web site of his current team club, otherwise.

13.5.3.1 Accuracy of Web Data Sources

Given a truth vector $T = [t_1, \ldots, t_n]$ of correct values for an attribute, we define the *sampled accuracy* as the fraction of true values correctly reported by the site over the number of objects in the truth vector for which it publishes a value. For example, suppose we want to compute the sampled accuracy of a soccer Web site w reporting Height values for 1,000 objects. We match this set of objects with the true values for Height in T and identify 80 soccer players in the intersection of the two sets. We can now compute the sampled accuracy $\overline{a_i}$ for the source i: if, for example, the values reported by the source coincide with values in T for 40 objects, then we estimate that the source reports true values for 50% of the cases, and therefore, $\overline{a_i}=0.5$. We compute in a similar way the sampled accuracy a_i^m for every evaluated model m, the only difference is that the set of values matched with T is the one made by the most probable values computed by m.

We computed the sampled accuracy of the sources for the Height (soccer players) and the Open Value (stock quotes) attributes. The average source accuracy is 70.21% for the first and 85.78% for the latter. Sampled source accuracy is better for domains where at least an authority exists. In fact, Open Value exhibits high source accuracy (more than 78%) for every source, while in the case of the soccer players' Height and Weight, the source accuracies are sensibly lower in all the sources. Overall, results show that attributes from distinct domains may assume quite different behaviors. Conversely, the sampled accuracies of the other attributes in the same domain behave quite similarly.

13.5.3.2 Applying Different Probabilistic Models

As expected, more complex models present better results for all domains, but the best model, M-DEP, outperforms, the simplest one, NAIVE, only by 3.5% on average.

In general, for applications requiring only an estimation of the true values, even a simple approach such as the NAIVE model can be used. However, whenever a more precise characterization of the uncertainty is required, for example, to populate a probabilistic database [9], complex models exhibit significant advantages.

13.6 Related Work

The scientific literature is presented by grouping the related works in five categories related to our approach: the work related to the discovery of sources is described in Sect. 13.6.1; the data integration and information extraction related works are discussed in Sects. 13.6.2 and 13.6.3, respectively; Sect. 13.6.4 contains a description of related work in the wrapper generation field, and finally, Sect. 13.6.5 concludes this discussion considering works related to the analysis of the quality of data and sources on the Web.

13.6.1 Source Discovery

Our work is related to researches on focused crawlers (or topical crawlers) [20, 39, 43], which face the issue of efficiently fetching Web pages that are relevant to a specific topic. Focused crawlers typically rely on text classifiers to determine the relevance of the visited pages to the target topic. Page relevance and contextual information—such as, the contents around the link, the lexical content of ancestor pages—are used to estimate the benefit of following URLs contained in the most of relevant pages. Although focused crawlers present some analogy with our work, our goal is different as we aim at retrieving pages that publish the same type of information, namely, pages containing data that represent instances of the entity exemplified by means of a few sample pages.

Vidal et al. present a system, called GOGETIT! that takes as input a sample page and an entry point to a Web site and generates a sequence of *URL patterns* for the links a crawler has to follow to reach pages that are structurally similar to the input sample [44]; therefore, their approach can be used as an implementation of the step of our crawling strategy that collects within a Web site all the pages similar to an input page.

13.6.2 Information Extraction

DIPRE [16] represents a pioneering technique to extract relations from the Web. Starting from a bunch of seed pairs (e.g., author-book), it collects similar pairs by means of a process in which the research of new pages containing these pairs and the inference of patterns extracting them are interleaved. The applicability of the approach is limited, since it cannot deal with generic tuples of more than two attributes, but the paper motivated several Web information extraction projects to develop effective techniques for the extraction of facts (binary predicates, e.g., born-in⟨scientist, city⟩) from large corpora of Web pages (e.g., [1, 4]).

Web information extraction techniques mainly infer lexico-syntactic patterns from textual descriptions, but they cannot take advantage of the structures available on the Web, as they do not elaborate data that are embedded in HTML templates. For instance, Cafarella et al. developed a system to populate a probabilistic database with data extracted from the Web [17], but the data extraction task is performed by TEXTRUNNER [4], an information extraction system which is not suitable for working on data-rich Web pages that are the target of our searches.

Compared to our system, these approaches are not able to exploit the information offered by data-rich pages. In fact, they concentrate on the extraction of facts: large collections of named entities (e.g., names of scientists, politicians, cities) or simple binary predicates. Moreover, they are effective with facts that appear in well-phrased sentences, whereas they fail to elaborate data that are implied by Web page layout or markup practices, such as those typically published in Web sites containing data-rich pages.

13.6.3 Data Integration

The bootstrap of data integration architecture for structured data on the Web is the subject of [40]. However, the presented system, PAYGO, focuses on explicitly structured sources, such as Google Base, and the proposed integration techniques are based on the availability of attribute labels; on the contrary, our approach aims at integrating unlabeled data from Web sites and automatically infers the labels whenever they are encoded in the HTML templates.

The exploitation of structured Web data is the primary goal of WebTables [19], which concentrates on data published in HTML tables. Compared to information extraction approaches, WebTables extracts relations with involved relational schemas but it does not address the issue of integrating the extracted data.

Another research project that addresses issues related to ours is CIMPLE [41] whose goal is to develop a platform to support the information needs of the members of a virtual community [29]. Compared to our method, CIMPLE requires an expert to provide a set of relevant sources and to design an Entity-Relationship model describing the domain of interest. Both CIMPLE and OCTOPUS [18] systems support users in the creation of datasets from Web sites by means of a set of operators to perform search, extraction, data cleaning, and integration. Although such systems have a more general application scope than ours, they involve the user in the process, while our approach is completely automatic.

Similarly, TAP and SEMTAG by Guha et al. [26, 36] are related projects that require human intervention: TAP involves knowledge extracted from structured Web pages and encoded as entities, attributes, and relations; SEMTAG provides a semantic search capability driven by the TAP knowledge base. Contrary to our approach, TAP requires hand-crafted rules for each site that it crawls, and when the formats of those sites change, the rules need to be updated.

Also, the MetaQuerier system developed by Chang et al. has similar objectives to our proposal, as it aims at supporting exploration and integration of databases on the Web [21]. However, this approach and its methods only concentrate on the deep-web.

The idea of using duplicate instances in the matching process to deal with imprecise data and schemas has been recently studied (e.g., [6]): these proposals show how the redundancy can help in contexts where schema can be imprecise. However, these approaches are not conceived to deal with the Web scale.

Data instances and domain constraints are used also in Glue [28], which early introduced a framework for finding semantic mappings between concepts of ontologies. Although the Glue approach has a general applicability in the semantic Web context, it is not suitable in our setting, since it relies also on intensional aspects, such as element names of the ontology taxonomy and the hierarchical relationships among elements, while we make a stronger exploitation of the redundancy of information that occur at the extensional level.

Many works try to solve heterogeneity problems in duplicate detection, by composing different matching techniques [42] to deal with imprecise information, or by taking advantage from data structure, to avoid ambiguity [27]. In the schema-matching literature, there is not known an approach that considers duplicates with several kinds of errors (e.g., misspelling, misplaced characters), while in the record-linkage literature, most of the approaches developed need intensional descriptions to work.

13.6.4 Wrapper Inference and Refinement

An important issue in our solution is the automatic generation of wrappers. RoadRunner [24] and ExAlg [3] propose automatic inference techniques to create a wrapper from a collection of pages generated by the same template. These approaches are not directly suitable to our goals: they do not consider effective techniques to scale with the number of sources, and they generate complex nested schemas that can be hard to integrate when dealing with a large number of sources. However, the presented approach can be considered to further improve the level of automation these unsupervised techniques exhibit in a slightly different setting involving multiple input Web sources [14].

An approach more closely related to ours is developed in the TurboWrapper project [22], which introduces a composite architecture including several wrapper inference systems (e.g., [3, 24]). By means of an integration step of their output, it aims at improving the results of the single participating systems taken separately. Interestingly, the design of TurboWrapper is motivated by the observation that different Web sources that offer data for the same domain have a strong redundancy at the schema level. However, compared to our solution, it makes stronger domain-dependent assumptions for the integration step since it does not consider the redundancy of information that occurs at the instance level: the correlation of data in the integration step is based on the assumption that there exist distinguishable generative models for the attributes to be matched (e.g., the *isbn* in the book domain). This is a strong domain-dependent assumption that limits the application of the technique, since in several domains, such as the finance domain, distinct attributes might have a too similar underlying generative model, e.g., min and max price of a stock quote.

Our wrapper refinement phase resembles the intuitions behind the "augment method" in [37], with the remarkable difference that we automatically gather the corpus during the integration process, while in their case, the corpus is given as input. In fact, a direct application of their approach is not possible in our setting, since we do not consider a priori information about the domain (i.e., at bootstrap we do not have any corpus of schemas nor mappings).

13.6.5 Assessing the Quality of Data

Our work explores the application of probabilistic techniques to assign truth probabilities to values gathered from conflicting sources of information. Such information is then used to evaluate the quality of the Web sources in terms of their data accuracy. The problem is related to the broader context of data quality [5] and to the issue of combining probability distributions expressed by a group of experts, which has been studied in the statistics community (e.g., [23]). A related experimental comparison of authority and quality results for Web sites has been done in [2].

Many projects have recently been active in the study of imprecise databases and have achieved a solid understanding of how to represent and process uncertain data (see [25] for a survey on the topic).

The development of effective data integration solutions making use of probabilistic approaches has also been addressed by several projects in the last years. In [33], the redundancy between sources is exploited to gain knowledge, but with a different goal: given a set of text documents, they assess the quality of the extraction process. Other works propose probabilistic techniques to integrate data from overlapping sources [34].

On the contrary, only recently, there has been some focus on how to populate such databases with sound probabilistic data. Even if this problem is strongly application specific, there is a lack of solution. In [17], Cafarella et al. describe a system to populate a probabilistic database with data extracted from the Web, but they do not consider the problems of combining different probability distributions and evaluating the reliability of the sources.

TruthFinder [46] was the first project to address the problem of truth discovery in the presence of multiple Web sources providing conflicting information. TruthFinder considers both the consensus on values and the accuracy of sources, and it can be considered as the first work that realizes and exploits their mutual dependency. Based on some heuristics, an iterative algorithm computes the trustiness of values and the accuracy of the sources. A similar direction has been also explored by Wu et al. [45] and by Galland et al. [35] which present fix-point algorithms to estimate the true value of data reported by a set of sources, together with the accuracy of the sources.

Some of the intuitions behind TruthFinder were formalized in a probabilistic Bayesian framework by Dong et al. [31], who also considered how the presence of copiers (i.e., sources that copy from other sources) affects the evaluation of the source accuracy. While in TruthFinder the effects of possible copying dependencies between sources are handled by means of a simple heuristic, the authors of [31] develop a more principled approach to detect source dependencies. To achieve these results, their model (which corresponds to the DEP model illustrated in Sect. 13.4) computes the probability that a pair of sources are dependent by analyzing the co-occurrences of errors. A further variant by the same authors also considers the variations of truth values over time [32].

The model behind DEP has been extended to improve the detection of dependencies among sources. In fact, in [31], sources are seen as providers that supply data about a collection of objects, i.e., instances of a real-world entity, such as a collection of video games. However, it is assumed that objects are described by just one attribute, e.g., the publisher of a video game. On the contrary, data sources usually provide complex data, i.e., collections of tuples with many attributes, and it has been shown that by considering this information, the quality of the results can be further improved [12, 30].

13.7 Conclusions

This chapter described methods and techniques to wring out value from Web data. We concentrate on data-intensive Web sites that publish large amounts of data. Our approach builds on an abstract model that describes the generation of pages offered by these sites. The model emphasizes two important features that inspired our proposal: the redundancy of information that occurs on the Web and the presence of local regularities exhibited by data-intensive Web sites.

We described methods to discover and collect these pages. Given as input only a small set of sample pages, our method creates a description of the target entity, interacts with a search engine to locate new sources, and filters out the Web sites that do not fit the inferred description.

Then we introduced an approach to extract and integrate data from these sources. Our approach introduces an instance-based schema matching algorithm, which is adaptive to the actual data, thus presenting significant advantages in general settings where no a priori knowledge about the domain is given, and multiple sources have to be matched. Also the approach takes advantage of the coupling between the wrapper inference and the data integration tasks to improve the quality of the wrappers.

Since Web data are inherently imprecise, conflicting values usually occur among the data provided by the sources. Therefore, we presented state-of-the-art models to manage the uncertainty of Web data. These models compute the accuracy of the sources, and associate a probability distribution with the data.

To give a flavor of the effectiveness of the presented methods and techniques, we finally reported the results of some experiments conducted over real-world data from different domains.

References

1. Agichtein, E., Gravano, L.: Snowball: extracting relations from large plain-text collections. DL '00, pp. 85–94 (2000)
2. Amento, B., Terveen, L.G., Hill, W.C.: Does "authority" mean quality? predicting expert quality ratings of web documents. SIGIR, pp. 296–303 (2000)
3. Arasu, A., Garcia-Molina, H.: Extracting structured data from web pages. ACM SIGMOD international conference on management of data (SIGMOD'2003), San Diego, California, pp. 337–348 (2003)
4. Banko, M., Cafarella, M., Soderland, S., Broadhead, M., Etzioni, O.: Open information extraction from the web. IJCAI (2007)
5. Batini, C., Scannapieco, M.: Data Quality: Concepts, Methodologies, and Techniques. Springer, Berlin, Heidelberg, New York (2008)
6. Bilke, A., Naumann, F.: Schema matching using duplicates. ICDE, pp. 69–80 (2005)
7. Blanco, L., Bronzi, M., Crescenzi, V., Merialdo, P., Papotti, P.: Exploiting information redundancy to wring out structured data from the web. In: Rappa, M., Jones, P., Freire, J., Chakrabarti, S. (eds.) WWW, pp. 1063–1064. ACM, New York (2010)
8. Blanco, L., Bronzi, M., Crescenzi, V., Merialdo, P., Papotti, P.: Redundancy-driven web data extraction and integration. WebDB (2010)

9. Blanco, L., Bronzi, M., Crescenzi, V., Merialdo, P., Papotti, P.: Automatically building probabilistic databases from the web. WWW (Companion Volume), pp. 185–188 (2011)
10. Blanco, L., Crescenzi, V., Merialdo, P.: Efficiently locating collections of web pages to wrap. WEBIST (2005)
11. Blanco, L., Crescenzi, V., Merialdo, P., Papotti, P.: Supporting the automatic construction of entity aware search engines. WIDM, pp. 149–156 (2008)
12. Blanco, L., Crescenzi, V., Merialdo, P., Papotti, P.: Probabilistic models to reconcile complex data from inaccurate data sources. CAiSE, pp. 83–97 (2010)
13. Blanco, L., Crescenzi, V., Merialdo, P., Papotti, P.: Contextual data extraction and instance-based integration. International workshop on searching and integrating new web data sources (VLDS) (2011)
14. Blanco, L., Crescenzi, V., Merialdo, P., Papotti, P.: Wrapper generation for overlapping web sources. Web Intelligence (WI) (2011)
15. Blanco, L., Dalvi, N.N., Machanavajjhala, A.: Highly efficient algorithms for structural clustering of large websites. WWW, pp. 437–446 (2011)
16. Brin, S.: Extracting patterns and relations from the World Wide Web. Proceedings of the First Workshop on the Web and Databases (WebDB'98) (in conjunction with EDBT'98, pp. 102–108 (1998)
17. Cafarella, M.J., Etzioni, O., Suciu, D.: Structured queries over web text. IEEE Data Eng. Bull. 29(4), 45–51 (2006)
18. Cafarella, M.J., Halevy, A.Y., Khoussainova, N.: Data integration for the relational web. PVLDB 2(1), 1090–1101 (2009)
19. Cafarella, M.J., Halevy, A.Y., Wang, D.Z., Wu, E., Zhang, Y.: Webtables: exploring the power of tables on the web. PVLDB 1(1), 538–549 (2008)
20. Chakrabarti, S., van den Berg, M., Dom, B.: Focused crawling: a new approach to topic-specific Web resource discovery. Comput. Networks (Amsterdam, Netherlands) 31(11–16), 1623–1640 (1999)
21. Chang, K.C.C., Bin, H., Zhen, Z.: Toward large scale integration: building a metaquerier over databases on the web. CIDR 2005, pp. 44–66 (2005)
22. Chuang, S.L., Chang, K.C.C., Zhai, C.X.: Context-aware wrapping: synchronized data extraction. VLDB, pp. 699–710 (2007)
23. Clemen, R.T., Winkler, R.L.: Combining probability distributions from experts in risk analysis. Risk Anal. 19(2), 187–203 (1999)
24. Crescenzi, V., Mecca, G., Merialdo, P.: ROADRUNNER: towards automatic data extraction from large Web sites. International conference on very large data bases (VLDB 2001), Roma, Italy, 11–14 September 2001, pp. 109–118
25. Dalvi, N.N., Suciu, D.: Management of probabilistic data: foundations and challenges. PODS, pp. 1–12 (2007)
26. Dill, S., Eiron, N., Gibson, D., Gruhl, D., Guha, R., Jhingran, A., Kanungo, T., Rajagopalan, S., Tomkins, A., Tomlin, J.A., Zien, J.Y.: Semtag and seeker: bootstrapping the semantic web via automated semantic annotation. WWW '03: proceedings of the 12th International Conference on World Wide Web, pp. 178–186. ACM, New York, NY, USA (2003). http://doi.acm.org/10.1145/775152.775178
27. Do, H.H., Rahm, E.: Matching large schemas: approaches and evaluation. Inf. Syst. 32(6), 857–885 (2007)
28. Doan, A., Madhavan, J., Domingos, P., Halevy, A.: Learning to map between ontologies on the semantic web. WWW '02, pp. 662–673 (2002)
29. Doan, A., Ramakrishnan, R., Chen, F., DeRose, P., Lee, Y., McCann, R., Sayyadian, M., Shen, W.: Community information management. IEEE Data Eng. Bull. 29(1), 64–72 (2006)
30. Dong, X., Berti-Equille, L., Hu, Y., Srivastava, D.: Global detection of complex copying relationships between sources. PVLDB 3(1), 1358–1369 (2010)
31. Dong, X.L., Berti-Equille, L., Srivastava, D.: Integrating conflicting data: the role of source dependence. PVLDB 2(1), 550–561 (2009)

32. Dong, X.L., Berti-Equille, L., Srivastava, D.: Truth discovery and copying detection in a dynamic world. PVLDB **2**(1), 562–573 (2009)
33. Downey, D., Etzioni, O., Soderland, S.: A probabilistic model of redundancy in information extraction. IJCAI, pp. 1034–1041 (2005)
34. Florescu, D., Koller, D., Levy, A.Y.: Using probabilistic information in data integration. VLDB, pp. 216–225 (1997)
35. Galland, A., Abiteboul, S., Marian, A., Senellart, P.: Corroborating information from disagreeing views. Proceedings of WSDM, New York, USA (2010)
36. Guha, R., McCool, R.: Tap: a semantic web platform. Comput. Networks **42**(5), 557–577 (2003)
37. Madhavan, J., Bernstein, P.A., Doan, A., Halevy, A.Y.: Corpus-based schema matching. ICDE, pp. 57–68 (2005)
38. Manning, C.D., Raghavan, P., Schütze, H.: Introduction to Information Retrieval. Cambridge University Press, Cambridge (2008). http://www.informationretrieval.org
39. Pant, G., Srinivasan, P.: Learning to crawl: comparing classification schemes. ACM Trans. Inf. Syst. **23**(4), 430–462 (2005)
40. Sarma, A.D., Dong, X., Halevy, A.Y.: Bootstrapping pay-as-you-go data integration systems. SIGMOD conference, pp. 861–874 (2008)
41. Shen, W., DeRose, P., McCann, R., Doan, A., Ramakrishnan, R.: Toward best-effort information extraction. SIGMOD conference, pp. 1031–1042 (2008)
42. Shen, W., DeRose, P., Vu, L., Doan, A., Ramakrishnan, R.: Source-aware entity matching: a compositional approach. ICDE, pp. 196–205. IEEE Computer Society, Silver Spring, MD (2007)
43. Sizov, S., Biwer, M., Graupmann, J., Siersdorfer, S., Theobald, M., Weikum, G., Zimmer, P.: The bingo! system for information portal generation and expert web search. CIDR 2003, First Biennial conference on innovative data systems research, Asilomar, CA, USA, 2003
44. Vidal, M.L.A., da Silva, A.S., de Moura, E.S., Cavalcanti, J.M.B.: Structure-driven crawler generation by example. In: Efthimiadis, E.N., Dumais, S.T., Hawking, D., Järvelin, K. (eds.) SIGIR, pp. 292–299. ACM, New York (2006)
45. Wu, M., Marian, A.: Corroborating answers from multiple web sources. WebDB (2007)
46. Yin, X., Han, J., Yu, P.S.: Truth discovery with multiple conflicting information providers on the web. IEEE Trans. Knowl. Data Eng. **20**(6), 796–808 (2008)

Chapter 14
Searching and Browsing Linked Data with SWSE*

Andreas Harth, Aidan Hogan, Jürgen Umbrich, Sheila Kinsella, Axel Polleres, and Stefan Decker

14.1 Introduction

Web search engines such as Google, Yahoo! MSN/Bing, and Ask are far from the consummate Web search solution: they do not typically produce direct answers to queries but instead typically recommend a selection of related documents from the Web. We note that in more recent years, search engines have begun to provide direct answers to prose queries matching certain common templates—for example, "population of china" or "12 euro in dollars"—but again, such functionality is limited to a small subset of popular user queries. Furthermore, search engines now provide individual and focused search interfaces over images, videos, locations, news articles, books, research papers, blogs, and real-time social media—although these tools are inarguably powerful, they are limited to their respective domains.

In the general case, search engines are not suitable for complex information gathering tasks requiring aggregation from multiple indexed documents: for such tasks, users must manually aggregate tidbits of pertinent information from various pages. In effect, such limitations are predicated on the lack of machine-interpretable

---

*The present chapter is an abridged version of [76].

A. Harth (✉)
Karlsruhe Institute of Technology, Institute AIFB, 76128 Karlsruhe, Germany
e-mail: harth@kit.edu

A. Hogan · J. Umbrich · S. Kinsella · S. Decker
Digital Enterprise Research Institute, National University of Ireland, Galway
e-mail: aidan.hogan@deri.org; juergen.umbrich@deri.org; sheila.kinsella@deri.org; stefan.decker@deri.org

A. Polleres
Digital Enterprise Research Institute, National University of Ireland, Galway

Siemens AG Österreich, Siemensstrasse 90, 1210 Vienna, Austria
e-mail: axel@polleres.net

R. De Virgilio et al. (eds.), *Semantic Search over the Web*,
Data-Centric Systems and Applications, DOI 10.1007/978-3-642-25008-8_14,
© Springer-Verlag Berlin Heidelberg 2012

structure in HTML documents, which is often limited to generic markup tags mainly concerned with document rendering and linking. Most of the real content is contained in prose text which is inherently difficult for machines to interpret. Addressing the problem of automated interpretation of HTML documents, the Semantic Web movement provides a stack of technologies for publishing machine-readable data on the Web, the core of the stack being the Resource Description Framework (RDF).

Using URIs to name things—and not just documents—RDF offers a standardized and flexible framework for publishing structured data on the Web such that (1) data can be linked, incorporated, extended, and reused by other RDF data across the Web; (2) heterogeneous data from independent sources can be automatically integrated by software agents; and (3) the meaning of data can be well defined using ontologies described in RDF using the RDF Schema (RDFS) and Web Ontology Language (OWL) standards.

Thanks largely to the "Linking Open Data" project [14]—which has emphasized more pragmatic aspects of Semantic Web publishing—a rich lode of open RDF data now resides on the Web: this "Web of Data" includes content exported from, for example, Wikipedia, the BBC, the New York Times, Flickr, Last.fm, scientific publishing indexes, biomedical information, and governmental agencies. Assuming large-scale adoption of high-quality RDF publishing on the Web, the question is whether a search engine indexing RDF feasibly could improve upon current HTML-centric engines. Theoretically at least, such a search engine could offer advanced querying and browsing of structured data with search results automatically aggregated from multiple documents and rendered directly in a clean and consistent user interface, thus reducing the manual effort required of its users. Indeed, there has been much research devoted to this topic, with various incarnations of (mostly academic) RDF-centric Web search engines emerging—e.g., Swoogle, Falcons, Watson, Sindice—and in this chapter, we present the culmination of over 6 years of research on another such engine: the "Semantic Web Search Engine" (SWSE).[1]

Indeed, the realization of SWSE has implied two major research challenges:

1. The system must *scale* to large amounts of data.
2. The system must be *robust* in the face of heterogeneous, noisy, impudent, and possibly conflicting data collected from a large number of sources.

Semantic Web standards and methodologies are not naturally applicable in such an environment; in presenting the design and implementation of SWSE, we show how standard Semantic Web approaches can be tailored to meet these two challenging requirements.

As such, we present the core of a system which we demonstrate to provide scale, and which is distributed over a cluster of commodity hardware. Throughout, we focus on the unique challenges of applying standard Semantic Web techniques and methodologies and show why the consideration of the source of data is an integral

---

[1] http://swse.deri.org/

part of creating a system which must be tolerant to Web data—in particular, we show how Linked Data principles can be exploited for such purposes. Also, there are many research questions still very much open with respect to the direction of the overall system, as well as improvements to be made in the individual components; we discuss these as they arise, rendering a road map of past, present, and possible future research in the area of Web search over RDF data.

More specifically, we

- Present high-level related work in RDF search engines (Sect. 14.3)
- Present core preliminaries required throughout the rest of the chapter (Sect. 14.4)
- Present the architecture and modus operandi of our system for offering search and browsing over RDF Web data (Sect. 14.5)
- Detail the high-level design of the off-line index building components, including *crawling* (Sect. 14.6), *consolidation* (Sect. 14.7), *ranking* (Sect. 14.8), *reasoning* (Sect. 14.9), and *indexing* (Sect. 14.10)
- Detail the high-level design of the runtime components, including our (lightweight) query processor (Sect. 14.11) and user interface (Sect. 14.12)
- Conclude with discussion of future directions (Sect. 14.13)

14.2 Motivating Example

To put later discussion into context, we now give a brief overview of the lightweight functionality of the SWSE system; please note that although our methods and algorithms are tailored for the specific needs of SWSE, many aspects of their implementation, design, and evaluation apply to more general scenarios.

Unlike prevalent document-centric Web search engines, SWSE operates over structured data and holds an entity-centric perspective on search: in contrast to returning links to documents containing specified keywords [19], SWSE returns data representations of real-world entities. While current search engines return search results in different domain-specific categories (Web, images, videos, shopping, etc.), data on the Semantic Web is flexibly typed and does not need to follow predefined categories. Returned objects can represent people, companies, locations, proteins— anything people care to publish data about.

In a manner familiar to traditional Web search engines, SWSE allows users to specify keyword queries in an input box and responds with a ranked list of result snippets; however, the results refer to entities not documents. A user can then click on an entity snippet to derive a detailed description thereof. The descriptions of entities are automatically aggregated from arbitrarily many sources, and users can cross-check the source of particular statements presented; descriptions also include inferred data—data that have been derived from the existing data through reasoning. Users can subsequently navigate to associated entities.

Figure 14.1 shows a screenshot containing a list of entities returned as a result to the keyword search "bill clinton"—such results pages are

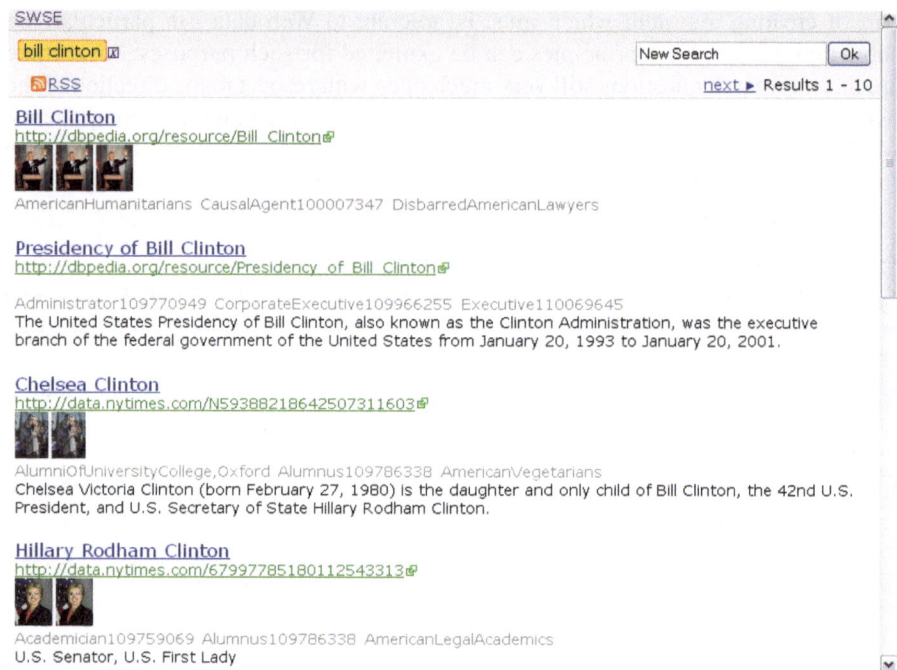

Fig. 14.1 Results view for keyword query `bill clinton`

familiar to HTML-centric engines, with the addition of result types (e.g., `DisbarredAmericanLawyers`, `AmericanVegetarians`). Results are aggregated from multiple sources. Figure 14.2 shows a screenshot of the focus (detailed) view of the `Bill Clinton` entity, with data aggregated from 54 documents spanning six domains (`bbc.co.uk`, `dbpedia.org`, `freebase.com`, `nytimes.com`, `rdfize.com`, and `soton.ac.uk`), as well as novel data found through reasoning.

14.3 State of the Art

In this section, we give an overview of the state of the art, first detailing distributed architectures for Web search (Sect. 14.3.1), then discussing related systems in the field of "Hidden Web" and "Deep Web" (Sect. 14.3.2), and finally describing current systems that offer search and browsing over RDF Web data (Sect. 14.3.3)—for a further survey of the latter, cf. [127]. Please note that we will give further detailed related work in the context of each component throughout the chapter.

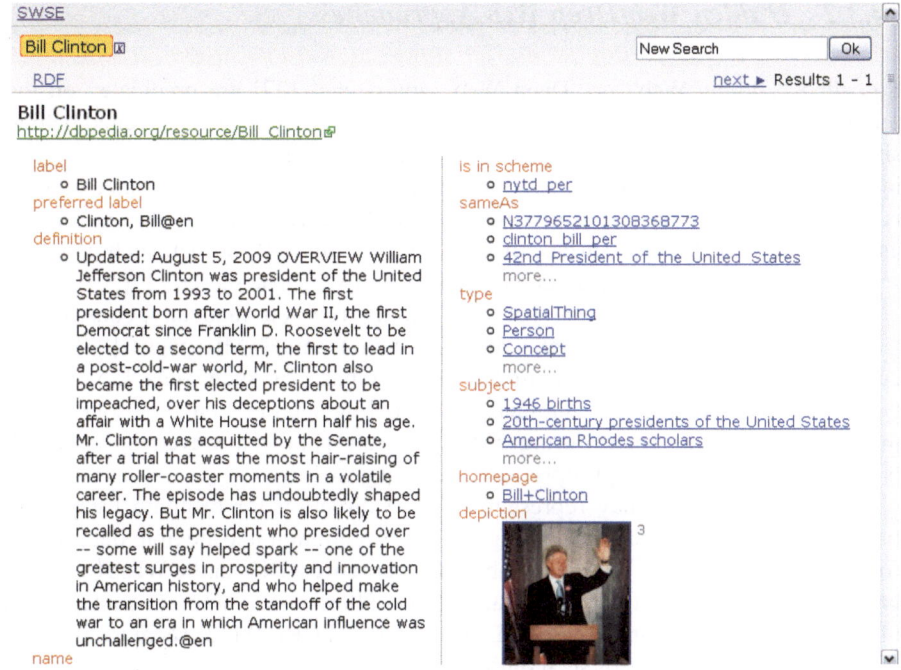

Fig. 14.2 Focus view for entity `Bill Clinton`

14.3.1   Distributed Web Search Architectures

Distributed architectures have long been common in traditional information retrieval-based Web search engines, incorporating distributed crawling, ranking, indexing, and query-processing components [18, 19]. More recent publications relate to the MapReduce framework [31] and to the underlying BigTable [24] distributed database system.

Similar system architectures have been defined in the literature, including WebBase [68] which includes an incremental crawler, storage manager, indexer, and query processor; in particular, the authors focus on hash- and log-based partitioning for storing incrementally updated vast repositories of Web documents. The authors of [97] also describe a system for building a distributed inverted index (based on an embedded database system) over a large corpus of Web pages, for subsequent analysis and query processing.

Much of the work presented herein is loosely inspired by such approaches and thus constitutes an adaptation of such works for the purposes of search over structured data. Since we consider replication, fault tolerance, incremental indexing, etc., currently out of scope, many of our techniques are more lightweight than those discussed.

14.3.2 Hidden Web/Deep Web Approaches

So-called "Hidden Web" or "Deep Web" approaches [22] are predicated on the premise that a vast amount of the information available on the Web is veiled behind sites with heavy dynamic content, usually backed by relational databases. Such information is largely impervious to traditional crawling techniques since content is usually generated by means of bespoke flexible queries; thus, traditional search engines can only skim the surface of such information [64]. In fact, such data-rich sources have lead to early speculative work on entity-centric search [29].

Approaches to exploit such sources heavily rely on manually constructed, site-specific wrappers to extract structured data from HTML pages [22] or to communicate directly with the underlying database of such sites [25]. Some works have also looked into automatically crawling such hidden-Web sources, by interacting with forms found during traditional crawls [114]; however, this approach is "task specific" and not appropriate for general crawling.

The Semantic Web may represent a future direction for bringing Deep Web information to the surface, leveraging RDF as a common and flexible data model for exporting the content of such databases, leveraging RDFS and OWL as a means of describing the respective schemata, and thus allowing for automatic integration of such data by Web search engines. Efforts such as D2R(Q) [13] seem a natural fit for enabling RDF exports of such online databases.

14.3.3 RDF-Centric Search Engines

Early prototypes using the concepts of ontologies and semantics on the Web include Ontobroker [32] and SHOE [65], which can be seen as predecessors to standardization efforts such as RDFS and OWL, describing how data on the Web can be given in structured form and subsequently crawled, stored inferenced, and queried over.

Swoogle[2] offers search over RDF documents by means of an inverted keyword index and a relational database [38]. Swoogle calculates metrics that allow ontology designers to check the popularity of certain properties and classes. In contrast to SWSE, which is mainly concerned with entity search over instance data, Swoogle is mainly concerned with more traditional document search over ontologies.

Watson[3] also provides keyword search facilities over Semantic Web documents but additionally provides search over entities [30,115]. However, they do not include components for consolidation or reasoning and instead focus on providing APIs to external services.

---

[2]http://swoogle.umbc.edu/

[3]http://watson.kmi.open.ac.uk/WatsonWUI/

Sindice[4] is a registry and lookup service for RDF files based on Lucene and a MapReduce framework [104]. Sindice originally focused on providing an API for finding documents which reference a given RDF entity or given keywords— again, document-centric search. More recently, however, Sindice has begun to offer entity search in the form of Sig.ma[5] [120]. However, Sig.ma maintains a one-to-one relationship between keyword search and results, representing a very different user-interaction model to that presented herein.

The Falcons search engine[6] offers entity-centric searching for entities (and concepts) over RDF data [28]. They map certain keyword phrases to query relations between entities and also use class hierarchies to quickly restrict initial results. Conceptually, this search engine most closely resembles our approach. However, there are significant differences in how the individual components of SWSE and Falcons are designed and implemented. For example, like us, they also rank entities, but using a logarithm of the count of documents in which they are mentioned—we employ a link-based analysis of sources. Also, Falcons supports reasoning involving class hierarchies, whereas we apply a more general rule-based approach, applying a scalable subset of OWL 2 RL/RDF rules. Such differences will be discussed further throughout the chapter.

Aside from domain-agnostic search systems, we note that other systems focus on exploiting RDF for the purposes of domain-specific querying; for example, the recent GoWeb system[7] demonstrates the benefit of searching structured data for the biomedical domain [36]. However, in catering for a specific domain, such systems do not target the same challenges and use cases as we do.

14.4   Preliminaries

Before we continue, we briefly introduce some standard notation used throughout the chapter—relating to RDF terms (constants), triples, and quadruples—and also discuss Linked Data principles. Note that we will generally use boldface to refer to infinite sets: e.g., **G** refers to the set of all triples; we will use calligraphy font to denote a subset thereof: e.g., $\mathcal{G}$ is a particular set of triples, where $\mathcal{G} \subset \mathbf{G}$.

14.4.1   Resource Description Framework

The Resource Description Framework provides a structured means of publishing information describing entities through use of RDF terms and RDF triples and

---

[4]http://sindice.com/

[5]http://sig.ma/

[6]http://iws.seu.edu.cn/services/falcons/

[7]http://gopubmed.org/goweb/

constitutes the core data model for our search engine. In particular, RDF allows for optionally defining names for entities using URIs and allows for subsequent reuse of URIs across the Web; using triples, RDF allows to group entities into named classes, allows to define named relations between entities, and allows for defining named attributes of entities using string (literal) values. We now briefly give some necessary notation.

RDF Constant. Given a set of URI references **U**, a set of blank nodes **B**, and a set of literals **L**, the set of *RDF constants* is denoted by $\mathbf{C} = \mathbf{U} \cup \mathbf{B} \cup \mathbf{L}$. The set of blank nodes **B** is a set of existensially quantified variables. The set of literals is given as $\mathbf{L} = \mathbf{L}_p \cup \mathbf{L}_d$, where $\mathbf{L}_p$ is the set of *plain literals* and $\mathbf{L}_d$ is the set of *typed literals*. A typed literal is the pair $l = (s,d)$, where s is the lexical form of the literal and $d \in \mathcal{U}$ is a datatype URI. The sets **U**, **B**, $\mathbf{L}_p$, and $\mathbf{L}_t$ are pairwise disjoint.

Please note that we treat blank nodes as their skolem versions, that is, not as existential variables, but as denoting their own syntactic form. We also ensure correct merging of RDF graphs [63] by using blank node labels unique for a given source.

For URIs, we use namespace prefixes as common in the literature—the full URIs can be retrieved from the convenient http://prefix.cc/ service. For space reasons, we sometimes denote owl: as the default namespace.

RDF Triple. A triple $t = (s, p, o) \in (\mathbf{U} \cup \mathbf{B}) \times \mathbf{U} \times (\mathbf{U} \cup \mathbf{B} \cup \mathbf{L})$ is called an *RDF triple*. In a triple (s, p, o), s is called subject, p predicate, and o object.

RDF Graph. We call a finite set of triples an *RDF graph* $\mathcal{G} \subset \mathbf{G}$ where $\mathbf{G} = (\mathbf{U} \cup \mathbf{B}) \times \mathbf{U} \times (\mathbf{U} \cup \mathbf{B} \cup \mathbf{L})$.

RDF Entity. We refer to the referent of a URI or blank-node as an *RDF entity*, or commonly just entity.

14.4.2 Linked Data

To cope with the unique challenges of handling diverse and unverified Web data, many of our components and algorithms require inclusion of a notion of provenance: consideration of the source of RDF data found on the Web. Tightly related to such notions are the Linked Data best practices (here paraphrasing [9]):

LDP1   use URIs to name things
LDP2   use HTTP URIs so that those names can be looked up
LDP3   provide useful structured information when a lookup on a URI is made— loosely, called *dereferencing*
LDP4   include links using external URIs

In particular, within SWSE, these best practices form the backbone of various algorithms designed to interact with and be tolerant to Web data.

We must thus extend RDF triples with *context* to denote the source thereof [52, 56]. We also define some relations between the identifier for a data source and the graph it contains, including a function to represent HTTP redirects prevalently used in Linked Data for **LDP3** [9].

Data Source. We define the *http-download* function $\mathsf{get} : \mathbf{U} \to 2^{\mathbf{G}}$ as the mapping from a URI to an RDF graph it may provide by means of a given HTTP lookup [46] which directly returns status code 200 OK and data in a suitable RDF format.[8] We define the set of *data sources* $\mathbf{S} \subset \mathbf{U}$ as the set of URIs $\mathbf{S} = \{s \in \mathbf{U} \mid \mathsf{get}(s) \neq \emptyset\}$. We define the *reference function* $\mathsf{refs} : \mathbf{C} \to 2^{\mathbf{S}}$ as the mapping from an RDF term to the set of data sources that mention it.

RDF Triple in Context/RDF Quadruple. A pair (t, c) with a triple $t = (s, p, o)$, $c \in \mathbf{S}$ and $t \in \mathsf{get}(c)$ is called a *triple in context c*. We may also refer to (s, p, o, c) as an *RDF quadruple* or quad q with context c.

HTTP Dereferencing. We define *dereferencing* as the function $\mathsf{deref} : \mathbf{U} \to \mathbf{U}$ which maps a given URI to the identifier of the document returned by HTTP lookup operations upon that URI following redirects (for a given finite and noncyclical path) [46] or which maps a URI to itself in the case of failure. The function involves stripping the fragment identifier of a URI [11]. Note that we do not distinguish between the different $30\mathsf{x}$ redirection schemes. All HTTP level functions $\{\mathsf{get}, \mathsf{refs}, \mathsf{deref}\}$ are set at the time of the crawl and are bounded by the knowledge of our crawl: for example, refs will only consider documents accessed by the crawl.

14.5   System Architecture

The high-level system architecture of SWSE loosely follows that of traditional HTML search engines [18, 19]. Figure 14.3 illustrates the pre-runtime architecture of our system, showing the components involved in achieving a local index of RDF Web data amenable for search. Similar to traditional search engines, SWSE contains components for crawling, ranking, and indexing data; however, there are also components specifically designed for handling RDF data, namely, the consolidation component and the reasoning component. The high-level index building process is as follows:

- The crawler accepts a set of seed URIs and retrieves a large set of RDF data from the Web.
- The consolidation component tries to find synonymous (i.e., equivalent) identifiers in the data and canonicalizes the data according to the equivalences found.
- The ranking component performs link-based analysis over the crawled data and derives scores indicating the importance of individual elements in the data (the

---

[8] $2^{\mathbf{G}}$ refers to the power set of $\mathbf{G}$.

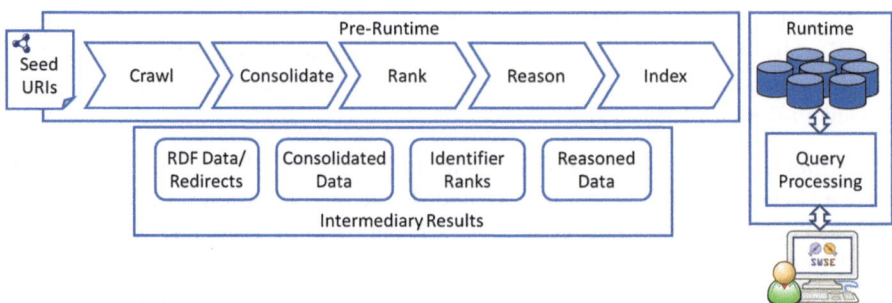

Fig. 14.3 System architecture

ranking component also considers URI redirections encountered by the crawler
when performing the link-based analysis).

- The reasoning component materializes new data which are implied by the
  inherent semantics of the input data (the reasoning component also requires URI
  redirection information to evaluate the trustworthiness of sources of data).
- The indexing component prepares an index which supports the information
  retrieval tasks required by the user interface.

Subsequently, the query-processing and user interface components service queries
over the index built in the previous steps.

Our methods follow the standards relating to RDF [95], RDFS [63], and
OWL [116] and leverage the Linked Data principles [9] which state how RDF
should be published on the Web. As such, our methods should be sound with
respect to data correctly published according to these documents, but we note that
oftentimes, the noise inherent in heterogenous RDF Web data may create unintended
results. We characterize these problems as they occur, although we know of no
method for accurately determining the amount of incorrect or unwanted results
generated by these tasks—we note that such considerations may also be subjective
(e.g., see [53]).

In order to scale, we deploy each of our components over a distributed framework, which is based on a shared nothing architecture [117] and consists of one
master machine which orchestrates the given tasks and several slave machines which
perform parts of the task in parallel. We note that our distribution framework resembles the MapReduce framework [31]. Distribution of our algorithms is facilitated
by the fact that the preprocessing algorithms are based on scan and sort operations.
We omit detailed description of the distributed versions of our algorithms due to
space constraints; see [76] for an in-depth treatment of distribution, including full-
scale evaluation of each component.

14.6 Crawling

We now begin the discussion of the first component required for building the index, and thus, for retrieving the raw RDF documents from the Web, that is, the *crawler*. Our crawler starts with a set of seed URIs, retrieves the content of URIs, parses and writes content to disk in the form of quads, and recursively extracts new URIs for crawling. We leverage Linked Data principles (see Sect. 14.4.2) to discover new sources, where following **LDP2** and **LDP3**, we consider all http: protocol URIs extracted from an RDF document as candidates for crawling.

We identify the following requirements for crawling:

- *Politeness:* The crawler must implement politeness restrictions to avoid hammering remote servers with dense HTTP GET requests and to abide by policies identified in the provided robots.txt files.[9]
- *Throughput:* The crawler should crawl as many URIs as possible in as little time as is possible within the bounds of the politeness policies.
- *Scale:* The crawler should employ scalable techniques and on-disk indexing as required.
- *Quality:* The crawler should prioritize crawling URIs it considers to be "high quality."

Thus, the design of our crawler is inspired by related work from traditional HTML crawlers. Additionally—and specific to crawling structured data—we identify the following requirement:

- *Structured Data:* The crawler should retrieve a high percentage of RDF/XML documents and avoid wasted lookups on unwanted formats, for example, HTML documents.

Currently, we crawl for RDF/XML syntax documents—RDF/XML is still the most commonly used syntax for publishing RDF on the Web, and we plan in future to extend the crawler to support other formats such as RDFa, N-Triples, and Turtle.

14.6.1 High-Level Approach

Our high-level approach is to perform breath-first crawling, following precedent set by traditional Web crawlers (cf. [15, 67]): the crawl is conducted in rounds, with each round crawling a *frontier*. On a high level, Algorithm 21 represents this round-based approach applying ROUNDS number of rounds. The frontier comprises of seed URIs for round 0 (Algorithm 21, line 21), and thereafter with novel URIs extracted from documents crawled in the previous round (Algorithm 21, line 21). Thus, the crawl emulates a breadth-first traversal of interlinked Web documents.

---

[9]http://www.robotstxt.org/orig.html

Algorithm 21: Algorithm for crawling

---

input: Seeds, Rounds, Min-Delay
$frontier \leftarrow$ Seeds ;
$pld_{0...n} \leftarrow$ new *queue*;
$stats \leftarrow$ new *stats*;
while $rounds + 1 <$ Rounds **do**
  put $frontier$ into $pld_{0...n}$;
  for $i = 0$ *to* n **do**
  ⌊ prioritise(pld_i, $stats$) ;
  $start \leftarrow$ current_time();
  for $i = 0$ *to* n **do**
      cur_i = calculate_cur(pld_i, $stats$) ;
      if $cur_i >$ *random([0,1])* **then**
          get uri from pld_i;
          $uri_{deref} = $ deref(uri);
          if $uri_{deref} = uri$ **then**
            $\mathcal{G} = $ get(uri);
            output $\mathcal{G}$;
            $U_{\mathcal{G}} \leftarrow$ URIs in $\mathcal{G}$;
            $\overline{U_{\mathcal{G}}} \leftarrow$ prune blacklisted from $U_{\mathcal{G}}$;
            add unseen URIs in $\overline{U_{\mathcal{G}}}$ to $frontier$;
          ⌊ update $stats$ wrt. $\overline{U_{\mathcal{G}}}$;
          else
              if uri_{deref} is *unseen* **then**
                  add uri_{deref} to $frontier$;
                ⌊ update $stats$ for uri_{deref};

  $elapsed \leftarrow$ current_time() - $start$;
  if $elapsed <$ Min-Delay **then**
  ⌊ wait(Min-Delay $- elapsed$) ;

As the bottleneck for a single-threaded crawler will be the response times of remote servers, our implementation of the crawling algorithm is multithreaded and performs concurrent HTTP lookups. Note that the algorithm is further tailored according to requirements we will describe as the section progresses.

14.6.1.1 Incorporating Politeness

The crawler must be careful not to bite the hands that feed it by hammering the servers of data providers or breaching policies outlined in the provided `robots.txt` file [118]. We use pay-level domains [91] (PLDs; a.k.a. "root domains"; e.g., `bbc.co.uk`) to identify individual data providers, and implement politeness on a per-PLD basis. First, when we first encounter a URI for a PLD, we cross-check the `robots.txt` file to ensure that we are permitted to crawl that site; second, we implement a "minimum PLD delay" to avoid hammering servers, viz., a minimum time period between subsequent requests to a given PLD (Min-Delay in Algorithm 21).

In order to accommodate the min-delay policy with minimal effect on performance, we must refine our crawling algorithm: large sites with a large internal branching factor (large numbers of unique intra-PLD outlinks per document) can result in the frontier of each round being dominated by URIs from a small selection of PLDs. Thus, naïve breadth-first crawling can lead to crawlers hammering such sites; conversely, given a politeness policy, a crawler may spend a lot of time idle waiting for the min-delay to pass.

One solution is to reasonably restrict the branching factor [91]—the maximum number of URIs crawled per PLD per round—which ensures that individual PLDs with large internal fan-out are not hammered; thus, in each round of the crawl, we implement a cutoff for URIs per PLD, given by PLD-LIMIT in Algorithm 21.

Second, to ensure the maximum gap between crawling successive URIs for the same PLD, we implement a per-PLD queue (given by $pld_{0...n}$ in Algorithm 21), whereby each PLD is given a dedicated queue of URIs filled from the frontier, and during the crawl, a URI is polled from each PLD queue in a round-robin fashion. If all of the PLD queues have been polled before the min-delay is satisfied, then the crawler must wait: this is given by lines 21–21 in Algorithm 21. Thus, the minimum crawl time for a round—assuming a sufficiently full queue—becomes MIN-DELAY * PLD-LIMIT.

14.6.1.2 On-Disk Queue

As the crawl continues, the in-memory capacity of the machine will eventually be exceeded by the capacity required for storing URIs [91]. Performing a stress test, we observed that with 2 GB of Java heap-space, the crawler could crawl approximately 199 k URIs (additionally storing the respective frontier URIs) before throwing an out-of-memory exception. To scale beyond the implied main-memory limitations of the crawler, we implement on-disk storage for URIs, with the additional benefit of maintaining a persistent state for the crawl and thus offering a "continuation point" useful for extension of an existing crawl, or recovery from failure.

We implement the on-disk storage of URIs using Berkeley DB which comprises of two indexes—the first provides lookups for URI strings against their status (polled/unpolled); the second offers a key-sorted map which can iterate over unpolled URIs in decreasing order of inlink count. The inlink count reflects the total number of documents from which the URI has been extracted thus far; we deem a higher count to roughly equate to a higher priority URI.

The on-disk index and in-memory queue are synchronized at the start of each round:

1. Links and respective inlink counts extracted from the previous round (or seed URIs if the first round) are added to the on-disk index.
2. URIs polled from the previous round have their status updated on-disk.
3. An in-memory PLD queue is filled using an iterator of on-disk URIs sorted by descending inlink count.

The above process ensures that only the URIs active (current PLD queue and frontier URIs) for the current round must be stored in memory. Finally, the in-memory PLD queue is filled with URIs sorted in order of inlink count, offering a cheap form of intra-PLD URI prioritization (Algorithm 21, line 21).

14.6.1.3 Crawling RDF/XML

Since our architecture is currently implemented to index RDF/XML, we would feasibly like to maximize the ratio of HTTP lookups which result in RDF/XML content; that is, given the total HTTP lookups as L and the total number of downloaded RDF/XML pages as R, we would like to maximize the *useful ratio*: $ur = R/L$.

To reduce the amount of HTTP lookups wasted on non-RDF/XML content, we implement the following heuristics:

1. First, we blacklist non-`http` protocol URIs.
2. Second, we blacklist URIs with common file extensions that are highly unlikely to return RDF/XML (e.g., `html`, `jpg`, `pdf`) following arguments we previously laid out in [121].
3. Third, we check the returned HTTP header and only retrieve the content of URIs reporting `Content-type: application/rdf+xml`.[10]
4. Finally, we use a *credible useful ratio* when polling PLDs to indicate the probability that a URI from that PLD will yield RDF/XML based on past observations.

With respect to the first two heuristics, any form of URI can be extracted from an RDF/XML document in any position, so from the set of initially extracted URIs, we blacklist those which are non-HTTP or those with common non-RDF file extensions (given in line 21 of Algorithm 21). Although blacklisting URIs with schemes such as `mailto:` or `urn:` is optional (since no HTTP lookup will be performed), pruning them early on avoids the expense of putting them through the queueing process. Note that we do not blacklist HTTP URIs which do not have an explicit file extension and whose content cannot be detected a priori (e.g., those with trailing slashes). Thus, we employ two further heuristics to improve the ratio of RDF/XML.

Our third heuristic involves rejecting content based on header information; this is perhaps arguable in that previous observations [74] indicate that 17% of RDF/XML documents are returned with a `Content-type` other than `application/rdf+xml`. Still we automatically exclude such documents from our crawl; however, here we put the onus on publishers to ensure correct reporting of `Content-type`.

---

[10]Indeed, one advantage RDF/XML has over RDFa is an unambiguous MIME-type useful in such situations.

With respect to the fourth heuristic, we implement an algorithm for selectively polling PLDs based on their observed useful ratio; since our crawler only requires RDF/XML, we use this score to access PLDs which offer a higher percentage of RDF/XML more often. Thus, we can reduce the amount of time wasted on lookups of HTML documents and save the resources of servers for non-RDF/XML data providers.

The credible useful ratio for PLD i is derived from the following credibility formula:

$$cur_i = \frac{rdf_i + \mu}{total_i + \mu}$$

where rdf_i is the total number of RDF documents returned thus far by PLD i, $total_i$ is the total number of lookups performed for PLD i excluding redirects, and μ is a "credibility factor." The purpose of the credibility formula is to dampen scores derived from few readings (where $total_i$ is small) toward the value 1 (offering the benefit of the doubt), with the justification that the credibility of a score with few readings is less than that with a greater number of readings: with a low number of readings ($total_i \ll \mu$), the cur_i score is affected more by μ than actual readings for PLD i; as the number of readings increases ($total_i \gg \mu$), the score is affected more by the observed readings than the μ factor. Note that we set μ to 10.[11]

Example 14.1. If we observe that PLD a = deri.org has returned 1/5 RDF/XML documents and PLD b = w3.org has returned 1/50 RDF/XML documents, and if we assume $\mu = 10$, then $cur_a = (1 + \mu)/(5 + \mu) = 0.7\overline{3}$ and $cur_b = (1 + \mu)/(50 + \mu) = 0.18\overline{3}$. We thus ensure that PLDs are not unreasonably punished for returning non-RDF/XML documents early on (i.e., are not immediately assigned a *cur* of 0.

To implement selective polling of PLDs according to their useful ratio, we simply use the *cur* score as a probability of polling a URI from that PLD queue in that round (Algorithm 21, lines 21–21). Thus, PLDs which return a high percentage of RDF/XML documents—or indeed PLDs for which very few URIs have been encountered—will have a higher probability of being polled, guiding the crawler away from PLDs which return a high percentage of non-RDF/XML documents.

14.6.1.4   PLD Starvation

Please note that in our experiments, we have observed the case where there are not enough unique PLDs to keep all crawler threads occupied until the MIN-DELAY has been reached. We term the state in which crawling threads cannot download content in fully parallel fashion *PLD starvation*. Given the politeness restriction

---

[11] Admittedly, a "magic number"; however, the presence of such a factor is more important than its actual value: without the credibility factor, if the first document returned by a PLD was non-RDF/XML, then that PLD would be completely ignored for the rest of the crawl.

of, for example, 500 ms per PLD, one PLD with many URIs becomes the hard limit for performance independent of system architecture and crawling hardware, instead imposed by the nature of the Web of Data itself. Also, as a crawl progresses, active PLDs (PLDs with unique content still to crawl) will become less and less, and the performance of the multithreaded crawl will approach that of a single-threaded crawl. As Linked Data publishing expands and diversifies, and as the number of servers offering RDF content increases, better performance would be observed.

14.6.2 Related Work

Parts of our architecture and some of our design decisions are influenced by work on traditional Web crawlers; e.g., the IRLBot system of Lee et al. [91] and the distributed crawler of Boldi et al. [15].

The research field of focused RDF crawling is still quite a young field, with most of the current work based on the lessons learned from the more mature area of traditional Web crawling. Related work in the area of focused crawling can be categorized [7] roughly as follows:

- *Classic focused crawling*: e.g., Chakrabarti et al. [23] uses primary link structure and anchor texts to identify pages about a topic using various text similarity of link analysis algorithms.
- *Semantic focused crawling*: a variation of classical focused crawling but uses conceptual similarity between terms found in ontologies [40, 41].
- *Learning focused crawling*: Diligenti et al. and Pant and Srinivasan [37, 108] use classification algorithms to guide crawlers to relevant Web paths and pages.

However, a major difference between these approaches and ours is that our definition of high-quality pages is not based on topics or ontologies but instead on the content type of documents.

With respect to crawling RDF, the Swoogle search engine implements a crawler which extracts links from Google and further crawls based on various—sometimes domain-specific—link extraction techniques [38]; like us, they also use file extensions to throw away non-RDF URIs. In [28], the authors provide a very brief description of the crawler used by the Falcons search engine for obtaining RDF/XML content; interestingly, they provide statistics identifying a power-law type distribution for the number of documents provided by each pay-level domain, correlating with our discussion of PLD starvation. In [115], for the purposes of the Watson engine, the authors use Heritrix[12] to retrieve ontologies using Swoogle, Google, and Protégé indexes and also crawl by interpreting rdfs:seeAlso and owl:imports as links—they do not exploit the dereferenceability of URIs popularized by Linked Data. Similarly, the Sindice crawler [104] retrieves content

---

[12]http://crawler.archive.org/

based on a *push* model, crawling documents which pinged some central service such as PingTheSemanticWeb;[13] they also discuss a PLD-level scheduler for ensuring politeness and diversity of data retrieved.

14.6.3   Future Directions and Open Research Questions

From a pragmatic perspective, we would prioritize extension of our crawler to handle arbitrary RDF formats—especially the RDFa format which is growing in popularity. Such an extension may mandate modification of the current mechanisms for ensuring a high percentage of RDF/XML documents: for example, we could no longer blacklist URIs with a .html file extension, nor could we rely on the Content-type returned by the HTTP header (unlike RDF/XML, RDFa does not have a specific MIME type).

Along these lines, we could perhaps also investigate extraction of structured data from non-RDF sources; these could include microformats, metadata embedded in documents such as PDFs and images, extraction of HTML metainformation, HTML scraping, etc. Again, such a process would require revisitation of our RDF-centric focused crawling techniques.

The other main challenge posed in this section is that of PLD starvation; although we would expect PLD starvation to become less of an issue as the Semantic Web matures, it perhaps bears further investigation. For example, we have yet to fully evaluate the trade-off between small rounds with frequent updates of URIs from fresh PLDs and large rounds which persist with a high delay rate but require less coordination. Also, given the inevitability of idle time during the crawl, it may be practical from a performance perspective to give the crawler more tasks to do in order to maximize the amount of processing done on the data and minimize idle time.

Finally, we have not discussed the possibility of incremental crawls: choosing URIs to recrawl may lead to interesting research avenues. Besides obvious solutions such as HTTP caching, URIs could be recrawled based on, e.g., detected change frequency of the document over time, some quality metric for the document, or how many times data from that document were requested in the UI. More practically, an incremental crawler could use PLD statistics derived from previous crawls and the HTTP headers for URIs—including redirections—to achieve a much higher ratio of lookups to RDF documents returned. Such considerations would largely countermand the effects of PLD starvation, by reducing the amount of lookups the crawler needs in each run.

---

[13]http://pingthesemanticweb.com/

14.7   Entity Consolidation

In theory, RDF enables excellent data integration over data sourced from arbitrarily
many sources—as is the case for our corpora collected by our crawler. However, the
integration is premised on the widespread sharing and reuse—across all sources—
of URIs for specific entities. In reality, different RDF documents on the Web
published by independent parties often speak about the same entities using different
URIs [73];[14] to make matters worse, RDF allows for the definition of anonymous
entities—entities identified by a blank node—without a prescribed URI.

As an example, in our 1.118 bn statement Linked Data corpus, we found 23
different URIs identifying the person Tim Berners-Lee—these identifiers spanned
nine different PLDs.[15] Now, given a keyword query for "tim berners lee,"
the data using each of the 23 different identifiers would be split over 23 different
results, even though they all refer to the same entity.

Offering search and querying over a raw RDF dataset collected from the Web
would thus entail many duplicate results referring to the same entity, emulating the
current situation on the HTML Web where information about different resources
is fragmented across source documents. Given a means of identifying *equivalent
entities* in RDF data—entities representing the same real-world individual but
identified incongruously—would enable the merging of information contributions
on an entity given by heterogeneous sources without the need for consistent URI
naming of entities.

In fact, OWL [116] provides some standard solutions to such problems. First,
OWL defines the owl:sameAs property which is intended to relate two equivalent
entities; the property has symmetric, transitive, and reflexive semantics as one
would expect. Many sources on the Web offer owl:sameAs links between entities
described locally and equivalent entities described remotely.

Further, OWL provides some other mechanisms for discovering implicit owl:-
sameAs relations in the absence of explicit relations: the most prominent such
example is provision of the class owl:InverseFunctionalProperty, which
defines a class of properties whose value uniquely identifies an entity. One example
of an inverse-functional property would be an ISBN property, where ISBN values
uniquely identify books. If two entities share the same ISBN value, a same-as
relation can be inferred between them. Using OWL, same-as relations can also be
detected using owl:FunctionalProperty, owl:maxCardinality, and
owl:cardinality (and now in OWL 2 RL using owl:maxQualified-
Cardinality and owl:qualifiedCardinality); however, the recall of
inferences involving the latter OWL constructs are relatively small [75] and thus
considered out of scope here.

---

[14]In fact, Linked Data principles could be seen as encouraging this practice, where dereferenceable
URIs must be made local.

[15]These equivalent identifiers were found through explicit owl:sameAs relations.

In [73], we provided a straightforward batch-processing technique for deriving `owl:sameAs` relations using inverse-functional properties defined in the data. However, the precision of such inferences is questionable. As an example, in [73] we found 85,803 equivalent individuals to be inferable from a Web dataset through the "void" values `08445a31a78661b5c746feff39a9db6e4e2cc5cf` and `da39a3ee5e6b4b0d3255bfef95601890afd80709` for the prominent inverse-functional property `foaf:mbox_sha1sum`: the former value is the sha1-sum of an empty string and the latter is the sha1-sum of the "`mailto:`" string, both of which are erroneously published by online Friend-of-a-Friend (FOAF—a very popular vocabulary used for personal descriptions) exporters.[16] Aside from obvious pathological cases—which can of course be blacklisted—publishers commonly do not respect the semantics of inverse-functional properties [74].

More recently, in [70], we showed that we could find $1.31\times$ more sets of equivalent identifiers by including reasoning over inverse-functional properties and functional properties, than when only considering explicit `owl:sameAs`. These sets contained $2.58\times$ more identifiers. However, we found that the additional equivalences found through such an approach were mainly between blank nodes on domains which do not use URIs to identify resources, common for older FOAF exporters: we found a 6% increase in URIs involved in an equivalence. We again observed that the equivalences given by such an approach tend to offer more noise than when only considering explicit `owl:sameAs` relations.

In fact, the performance of satisfactory, high-precision, high-recall entity consolidation over large-scale Linked Data corpora is still an open research question. At the moment, we rely on `owl:sameAs` relations which are directly asserted in the data to perform consolidation.

14.7.1   High-Level Approach

The overall approach involves two scans of the main body of data, with the following high-level steps:

1. `owl:sameAs` statements are extracted from the data: the main body of data is scanned once identifying `owl:sameAs` triples and buffering them to a separate location.
2. The transitive/symmetric closure of the `owl:sameAs` statements are computed, inferring new `owl:sameAs` relations.
3. For each set of equivalent entities found (each *equivalence class*), a *canonical identifier* is chosen to represent the set in the consolidated output.

---

[16]See, for example, http://blog.livedoor.jp/nkgw/foaf.rdf

4. The main body of data is again scanned and consolidated: identifiers are rewritten to their canonical form—we do not rewrite identifiers in the predicate position, objects of rdf:type triples, or literal objects.

In previous work, we have presented two approaches for performing such consolidation; in [73], we stored owl:sameAs in memory, computing the transitive/symmetric closure in memory, and performing in-memory lookups for canonical identifiers in the second scan. In [75], we presented a batch-processing technique which uses on-disk sorts and scans to execute the owl:sameAs transitive/symmetric closure, and the canonicalization of identifiers in the main body of data. The former approach is in fact much faster in that it reduces the amount of time consumed by hard-disk I/O operations; however, the latter batch-processing approach is not limited by the main-memory capacity of the system. Either approach is applicable with our consolidation component (even in the distributed case); however, since for the moment we only operate on asserted owl:sameAs statements (we found ∼12 m owl:sameAs statements in our full-scale crawl, which we tested to be within our 4GB in-memory capacity using the flyweight pattern), for now we apply the faster in-memory approach.

Standard OWL semantics mandates duplication of data for all equivalent terms by the semantics of replacement (cf. Table 4, [50]), which, however, is not a practical option at scale. First, the amount of duplication will be quadratic with respect to the size of an equivalence class. Empirically, we have found equivalence classes with 8.5 k elements from explicit owl:sameAs relations [76]. If one were to apply transitive, reflexive, and symmetric closure of equivalence over these identifiers, we would produce $8.5k^2 = 72.25m$ owl:sameAs statements alone; further assuming an average of six unique quads for each identifier—51 k unique quads in total—we would produce a further 433.5 m repetitive statements by substituting each equivalent identifier into each quad. Second, such duplication of data would result in multitudinous duplicate results being presented to end users, with obvious impact on the usability of the system.

Thus, the practical solution is to abandon standard OWL semantics and instead *consolidate* the data by choosing a canonical identifier to represent the output data for each equivalence class. Canonical identifiers are chosen with preference to URIs over blank nodes, and thereafter we arbitrarily use a lexicographical order—the canonical identifiers are only used internally to represent the given entity.[17] Along these lines, we also preserve all URIs used to identify the entity by outputting owl:sameAs relations to and from the canonical identifier (please note that we do not preserve redundant blank-node identifiers which are only intended to have a local scope, have been assigned arbitrary labels during the crawling process, and are not subject to reuse), which can subsequently be used to display all URIs originally used to identify an entity, or to act as a "redirect" from an original identifier to the canonical identifier containing the pertinent information.

---

[17]If necessary, the ranking algorithm presented in the next section could be used to choose the most popular identifier as the canonical identifier.

In the in-memory map structure, each equivalence class is assigned a canonical identifier according to the above ordering. We then perform a second scan of the data, rewriting terms according to canonical identifiers. Please note that according to OWL full semantics, terms in the predicate position and object position of rdf:type triples should be rewritten (referring to term positions occupied by properties and classes respectively in membership assertions; again, cf. Table 4, [50]). However, we do not wish to rewrite these terms: in OWL, equivalence between properties can instead be specified by means of the owl:equivalentProperty construct, and between classes as the owl:equivalentClass construct.[18] We omit rewriting class/property terms in membership assertions, handling inferences involving classes/properties by alternate means in Sect. 14.9.

Thus, in the second scan, the subject and object of non-rdf:type statements are rewritten according to the canonical identifiers stored in the in-memory map, with rewritten statements written to output. If no equivalent identifiers are found, the statement is buffered to the output. When the scan is complete, owl:sameAs relations to/from canonical URIs and their equivalent URIs are appended to the output. Consolidation is now complete.

14.7.2   Related Work

Entity consolidation has an older related stream of research relating largely to databases, with work under the names of record linkage, instance fusion, and duplicate identification; cf. [26, 98, 103] and a survey at [42]. Due to the lack of formal specification for determining equivalences, these older approaches are mostly concerned with probabilistic methods.

With respect to RDF, Bouquet et al. [17] motivate the problem of (re)using common identifiers as one of the pillars of the Semantic Web and provide a framework for mapping heterogeneous identifiers to a centralized naming scheme for reuse across the Web—some would argue that such a centralized service would not be in tune with the architecture or philosophy of the Web.

Consolidation has also been tackled in the context of applying rule-based reasoning for OWL, where choosing canonical (or "pivot") identifiers is a common optimization [73, 75, 85, 88, 122]. Algorithms for building the equivalence partition have also been proposed by these works, where, e.g., Kolovski et al. propose a similar union–find algorithm to that presented herein. In previous works [75], we have presented an algorithm which iteratively connects elements in an equivalence class toward the common, lowest-ordered element, pruning connections to elements to

---

[18]As an example of naïve usage of owl:sameAs between classes and properties on the Web, please see: http://colab.cim3.net/file/work/SICoP/DRMITIT/DRM_OWL/Categorization/TaxonomyReferenceModel.owl

higher orders; the result of this process is a canonical identifier which connects directly to all elements of the equivalence class. Urbani et al. [122] propose an algorithm which is similar in principle, but which is implemented in a distributed MapReduce setting and optimized to prevent load-balancing issues. We discuss related rule-based reasoning approaches in more detail later in Sect. 14.9.2.

The Sindice and Sig.ma search systems internally use inverse-functional properties to find equivalent identifiers [104, 120]—Sindice uses reasoning to identify a wider range of inverse-functional properties [104]. Online systems RKBExplorer [49],[19] <sameAs>,[20] and ObjectCoref[21] offer on-demand querying for owl:sameAs relations found for a given input URI, which they internally compute and store; as previously alluded to, the former publish owl:sameAs relations for authors and papers in the area of scientific publishing.

Some more recent works have looked at hybrid approaches for consolidation, combining symbolic (i.e., reasoning) methods and statistical/inductive methods [78, 80].

The authors of [124] present *Silk*: a framework for creating and maintaining interlinkage between domain-specific RDF datasets; in particular, this framework provides publishers with a means of discovering and creating owl:sameAs links between data sources using domain-specific rules and parameters. Thereafter, publishers can integrate discovered links into their exports, enabling better linkage of the data and subsequent consolidation by data consumers: this framework goes hand in hand with our approach, producing the owl:sameAs relations which we consume.

In [53], the authors discuss the semantics and current usage of owl:sameAs in Linked Data, discussing issues relating to *identity* and providing four categories of owl:sameAs usage to relate entities which are closely related, but for which the semantics of owl:sameAs—particularly substitution—do not quite hold.

14.7.3   Future Directions and Open Research Questions

In this section, we have focused on the performance of what we require to be a scalable consolidation component. We have not presented analysis of the precision or recall of such consolidation—such evaluation is difficult to achieve in practice given a lack of a gold standard, or suitable means of accurately verifying results. The analysis of the precision and recall of various scalable consolidation methods on current Web data would represent a significant boon to research in the area of querying over Linked Data.

We are currently investigating statistical consolidation methods, with particular emphasis on extracting some notion of the quality or trustworthiness of

---

[19]http://www.rkbexplorer.com/sameAs/

[20]http://sameas.org/

[21]http://ws.nju.edu.cn/objectcoref/

derived equivalences [78]. Presently, we try to identify "quasi-inverse-functional" and "quasi-functional" properties (properties which are useful for distinguishing identity) using statistical analysis of the input data. We then combine shared property/value pairs for entities and derive a fuzzy value representing the confidence of equivalence between said entities. However, this preliminary work needs further investigation—including scalability and performance testing, and integration with more traditional reasoning-centric approaches for consolidation—before being included in the SWSE pipeline.

A further avenue for research in the same vein is applying "disambiguation," or attempting to assert that two entities cannot (or are likely not to) be equivalent using statistical approaches or analysis of inconsistencies in reasoning: disambiguation would allow for increasing the precision of the consolidation component by quickly removing "obvious" false positives.

Again, such approaches would likely have a significant impact on the quality of data integration possible in an engine such as SWSE operating over RDF Web data.

14.8   Ranking

Ranking is an important mechanism in the search process with the function of prioritizing data elements. Herein, we want to quantify the importance of consolidated entities in the data for use in ordering the presentation of results returned when users pose a keyword query (e.g., see Fig. 14.1), such that the most "important" results appear higher in the list. Note that we will combine these ranking scores with relevance scores later in Sect. 14.10.

There is a significant body of related work on link-based algorithms for the Web; seminal works include [86, 107]. A principal objective when ranking on the Web is rating popular pages higher than unpopular ones—further, ranks can be used for performing top-k processing, allowing the search engine to retrieve and process small segments of results ordered by their respective rank. Since we share similar goals, we wish to leverage the benefits of link-based analysis, proven for the HTML Web, for the purposes of ranking Linked Data entities. We identify the following requirements for ranking Linked Data, which closely align with those of HTML-centric ranking schemes:

- The methods should be *scalable* and applicable in scenarios involving large corpora of RDF.
- The methods should be *automatic* and *domain agnostic*, and not inherently favoring a given domain or source of data.
- The methods should be *robust* in the face of spamming.

With respect to ranking the entities in our corpus in a manner sympathetic with our requirements, we further note the following:

- On the level of triples (data level), publishers can provide arbitrary information in arbitrary locations using arbitrary identifiers; thus, to discourage low-effort spamming, the source of information must be taken into account.
- Following traditional link-based ranking intuition, we should consider links from one source of information to another as a "positive vote" from the former to the latter.
- In the absence of sufficient source-level ranking, we should infer links between sources based on usage of identifiers on the data level and some function mapping between data-level terms and sources.
- Data providers who reuse identifiers from other sources should not be penalized: their data sources should not lose any rank value.

In particular, our methods are inspired by Google's PageRank [107] algorithm, which interprets hyperlinks to other pages as positive votes. However, PageRank is generally targeted toward hypertext documents, and adaptation to Linked Data sources is nontrival, given that the notion of a hyperlink (interpreted as a vote for a particular page) is missing: Linked Data principles mandate *implicit* links to other Web sites or data sources through reuse of dereferenceable URIs. Also, the unit of search is no longer a document, but an entity.

In previous work [59], we proposed a scalable algorithm for ranking structured data from an open, distributed environment, based on a concept we term *naming authority*. We reintroduce selected important discussion from [59] and extend here by implementing the method in a distributed way and reevaluating with respect to performance.

14.8.1   High-Level Approach

Although we wish to rank entities, our ranking algorithm must consider the source of information to avoid low-effort data-level spamming. Thus, we must first have a means of ranking source-level identifiers and thereafter can propagate such ranks to the data level.

To leverage existing link-based analysis techniques, we need to build a graph encoding the interlinkage of Linked Data sources. Although one could examine use of, for example, `owl:imports` or `rdfs:seeAlso` links, and interpret them directly as akin to a hyperlink, the former is used solely in the realm of OWL ontology descriptions and the latter is not restricted to refer to RDF documents; similarly, both ignore the data-level linkage that exists by means of **LDP4** (include links using external URIs). Thus, we aim to infer source-level links through usage of data-level URIs in the corpus.

To generalize the idea, we previously defined the notion of "naming authority" for identifiers: a naming authority is a data source with the power to define identifiers of a certain structure [59]. Naming authority is an abstract term which could be applied to a knowable provenance of a piece of information, be that a document, host, person, organization, or other entity. Data items which are denoted by unique identifiers may be reused by sources other than the naming authority.

Example 14.2. With respect to Linked Data principles (see Sect. 14.4.2), consider for example the data-level URI http://danbri.org/foaf.rdf#danbri. Clearly the owner(s) of the http://www.danbri.org/foaf.rdf document (or, on a coarser level, the danbri.org domain) can claim some notion of "authority" for this URI: following **LDP4**, the usage of the URI on other sites can be seen as a vote for the respective data source. We must also support redirects as commonly used for **LDP3**—thus we can reuse the deref function given in Sect. 14.4.2 as a function which maps an arbitrary URI identifier to the URI of its naming authority document (or to itself in the absence of a redirect).

Please note that there is no obvious function for mapping from literals to naming authority, we thus omit them from our source-level ranking (one could consider a mapping based on datatype URIs, but we currently see no utility in such an approach). Also, blank nodes may only appear in one source document and are not subject to reuse: although one could reduce the naming authority of a blank node to the source they appear in, clearly only self-links can be created.

Continuing, we must consider the granularity of naming authority: in [59], we discussed and contrasted interpretation of naming authorities on a document level (e.g., http://www.danbri.org/foaf.rdf) and on a PLD level (danbri.org). Given that the PLD-level linkage graph is significantly smaller than the document-level graph, the overhead for aggregating and analyzing the PLD-level graph is significantly reduced, and thus, we herein perform ranking at a PLD level.

Please note that for convenience, we will assume that PLDs are identified by URIs, for example, (http://danbri.org/). We also define the convenient function pld : $U \rightarrow U$ which extracts the PLD identifier for a URI (if the PLD cannot be parsed for a URI, we simply ignore the link)—we may also conveniently use the function plds : $2^U \rightarrow 2^U$ for sets of URIs.

Thus, our ranking procedure consists of the following steps:

1. Construct the *PLD-level naming authority graph*: for each URI u appearing in a triple t in the input data, create links from the PLDs of sources mentioning a particular URI to the PLD of that URI: plds(refs(u)) $\rightarrow$ pld(deref(u)).
2. From the naming authority graph, use the PageRank algorithm to derive scores for each PLD.
3. Using the PLD ranks, derive a rank value for terms in the data, particularly terms in $U \cup B$ which identify entities.

14.8.1.1 Extracting Source Links

As a first step, we derive the naming authority graph from the input dataset. That is, we construct a graph which encodes links between data source PLDs, based on the implicit connections created via identifier reuse.

Given PLD identifiers $p_i, p_j \in \mathbf{U}$, we specify the naming authority matrix A as a square matrix defined as:

$$a_{i,j} = \begin{cases} 1 & \text{if } p_i \neq p_j \text{ and } p_i \text{ uses an identifier} \\ & \quad \text{with naming authority } p_j \\ 0 & \text{otherwise} \end{cases}$$

This represents an $n \times n$ square matrix where n is the number of PLDs in the data, and where the element at (i, j) is set to 1 if $i \neq j$ and PLD i mentions a URI which leads to a document hosted by PLD j.

As such, the naming authority matrix can be arbitrarily derived through a single scan over the entire dataset. Note that we optionally can omit URIs found in the predicate position of a triple, or the object position of an `rdf:type` triple, in the derivation of the naming authority graph, such that we do not want to overly inflate scores for PLDs hosting vocabularies: we are concerned that such PLDs (e.g., `w3.org`, `xmlns.org`) would receive rankings orders of magnitude higher than their peers, overly inflating the ranks of arbitrary terms appearing in that PLD; further, users will generally not be interested in results describing the domain of knowledge itself [59].

14.8.1.2 Calculating Source Ranks

Having constructed the naming authority matrix, we now can compute scores for data sources. For computing ranking scores, we perform a standard PageRank calculation over the naming authority graph: we calculate the dominant eigenvector of the naming authority graph using the Power iteration while taking into account a damping factor (see [107] for more details).

14.8.1.3 Calculating Identifier Ranks

Based on the rank values for the data sources, we now calculate the ranks for individual identifiers. The rank value of a constant $c \in \mathbf{C}$ is given as the summation of the rank values of the PLDs for the data sources in which the term occurs:

$$idrank(c) = \sum_{pld \in plds(refs(c))} sourcerank(pld)$$

This follows the simple intuition that the more highly ranked PLDs mentioning a given term, the higher the rank of that term should be.[22] Note again—and with similar justification as for deriving the named authority graph—we do not include URIs found in the predicate position of a triple, or the object position of an `rdf:type` triple in the above summation for our evaluation. Also note that the ranking for literals may not make much sense depending on the scenario—in any case, we currently do not require ranks for literals.

14.8.1.4 User Evaluation

Herein, we summarize the details of our user evaluation, where the full details are available in [59]. We conducted a study asking 10–15 participants to rate the ordering of SWSE results given for five different input keyword queries, including the evaluator's own name. We found that our method produced preferable results (with statistical significance) for ranking entities than the baseline method of implementing PageRank on the RDF node-link graph (an approach which is similar to existing work such as ObjectRank [6]). Also, we found that use of the PLD-level graph and document-level graph as input for our PageRank calculations yielded roughly equivalent results for identifier ranks in our user evaluation.

14.8.2 Related Work

There have been numerous works dedicated to comparing hypertext-centric ranking for varying granularity of sources. Najork et al. [101] compared results of the HITS [86] ranking approach when performed on the level of document, host, and domain granularity and found that domain granularity returned the best results: in some cases, PLD-level granularity may be preferable to domain or host-level granularity because some sites like LiveJournal (which export vast amounts of user profile data in the Friend-of-a-Friend [FOAF] vocabulary) assign subdomains to each user, which would result in large tightly-knit communities if domains were used as naming authorities. Previous work has performed PageRank on levels other than the page level, for example, at the more coarse granularity of directories, hosts, and domains [83], and at a finer granularity such as logical blocks of text [21] within a page.

There have been several methods proposed to handle the task of ranking Semantic Web data.

Swoogle ranks documents using the OntoRank method, a variation on PageRank which iteratively calculates ranks for documents based on references to terms

---

[22]The generic algorithm can naturally be used to propagate PLD/source-level rankings to any form of RDF artifact, including triples, predicates, classes, etc.

(classes and properties) defined in other documents. We generalize the method described in [39] to rank entities and perform link analysis on the PLD abstraction layer.

ObjectRank [6] ranks a directed labeled graph using PageRank using "authority transfer schema graphs," which requires manual weightings for the transfer of propagation through different types of links; further, the algorithm does not include consideration of the source of data and is perhaps better suited to domain-specific ranking over verified knowledge.

We note that Falcons [28] also rank the importance of entities (what they call "objects"), but based on a logarithm of the number of documents in which the object is mentioned.

In previous work, we introduced ReConRank [72]: an initial effort to apply a PageRank-type algorithm to a graph which unifies data-level and source-level linkage. ReConRank does take data provenance into account; however, because it simultaneously operates on the object graph, it is more susceptible to spamming than the presented approach.

A recent approach for ranking Linked Data called Dataset rankING (DING) [35]—used by Sindice—holds a similar philosophy to ours: they adopt a two-layer approach consisting of an entity layer and a dataset layer. However, they also apply rankings of entities within a given dataset, using PageRank (or optionally link-counting) and unsupervised link-weighting schemes, subsequently combining dataset and local entity ranks to derive global entity ranks. Because of the local entity ranking, their approach is theoretically more expensive and less flexible than ours, but would offer better granularity of results—less entity results with the same rank. However, as we will see later, we will be combining global entity ranks with keyword query-specific relevance scores, which mitigates the granularity problem.

There are numerous other loosely related approaches, which we briefly mention: SemRank [3] ranks relations and paths on Semantic Web data using information-theoretic measures; AKTiveRank [1] ranks ontologies based on how well they cover specified search terms; Ontocopi [2] uses a spreading activation algorithm to locate instances in a knowledge base which are most closely related to a target instance; the SemSearch system [92] also includes relevance ranks for entities according to how well they match a user query.

14.8.3   Future Directions and Open Research Questions

Ranking in Web search engines depends on a multitude of factors, ranging from globally computed ranks to query-dependent ranks to location, preferences, and history of the searcher. Factoring additional signals into the ranking procedure is the area for further research, especially in the face of complex database-like queries and results beyond the simple list of objects. For example, we have already seen that we exclude predicate and class identifiers from the ranking procedure in order not to adversely affect our goal of ranking entities (individuals) in the data;

specific modes and display criteria of the UI may require different models of ranks, providing multiple contextual ranks for identifiers in different roles—e.g., creating a distinctive ranking metric for identifiers in the role of predicates, reflecting the expectations of users given various modes of browsing.

Another possibly fruitful research topic relates to the question of finding appropriate mathematical representations of directed labeled graphs and appropriate operations on them [47, 58]. Most of the current research in ranking RDF graphs is based around the directed graph models borrowed from hypertext ranking procedures. A bespoke mathematical model for RDF (directed, labeled, and named) graphs may lead to a different view on possible ranking algorithms.

Finally, the evaluation of link-based ranking as an indicator of trustworthiness would also be an interesting contribution; thus far, we have evaluated the approach according to user evaluation reflecting preference for the prioritization of entity results in the UI. However, given that we also consider the source of information in our ranking, we could see if there was a co-occurrence, for example, of poorly ranked PLDs and inconsistent data. Such a result would have impact for the reasoning component, presented next, and some discussion is provided in the respective future work section to follow.

14.9 Reasoning

Using the Web Ontology Language (OWL) and the RDF Schema language (RDFS), instance data (i.e., assertional data) describing individuals can be supplemented with structural data (i.e., terminological data) describing classes and properties, allowing to well define the domain of discourse and ultimately provide machines a more sapient understanding of the RDF data. Numerous vocabularies have been published on the Web of Data, encouraging reuse of terms for prescribed classes and properties across sources and providing formal RDFS/OWL descriptions thereof.

We have already seen that OWL semantics can be used to automatically aggregate heterogeneous data—using `owl:sameAs` relations and, for example, the `owl:InverseFunctionalProperty` to derive said—where the knowledge is fractured by the use of discordant identifiers.[23] However, RDFS and OWL descriptions in the data can be further exploited to infer new statements based on the terminological knowledge and provide a more complete dataset for query answering and to automatically translate data from one conceptual model to another (where appropriate mappings exist in the data).

Example 14.3. In our data, we find 43 properties whose memberships can be used to infer an `foaf:page` relationship between a resource and a Web page pertaining to it. These include specializations of the property within the FOAF

---

[23]Note that in this chapter, we deliberately decouple consolidation and reasoning, since in future work we hope to view the unique challenges of finding equivalent identifiers as separate from those of inferencing according to terminological data presented here.

namespace itself, such as `foaf:homepage`, `foaf:weblog`, etc., and specializations of the property outside the FOAF namespace, including `mo:wikipedia`,
`rail:arrivals`, `po:microsite`, `plink:rss`, `xfn:mePage`, etc. All such
specializations of the property are related to `foaf:page` (possibly indirectly)
through the `rdfs:subPropertyOf` relation in their respective vocabulary.
Similarly, *inverses* of `foaf:page` may also exist, where in our corpus we find that
`foaf:topic` relates a Web page to a resource it pertains to. Here, `foaf:topic`
is related to `foaf:page` using the built-in OWL property `owl:inverseOf`.
Thus, if we know that:

> ex:resource mo:wikipedia ex:wikipage .
> mo:wikipedia rdfs:subPropertyOf foaf:page .
> foaf:page owl:inverseOf foaf:topic .

we can *infer* through *reasoning* that:

> ex:resource foaf:page ex:wikipage .
> ex:wikipage foaf:topic ex:resource .

In particular, through the RDFS and OWL definitions given in the data, we
infer a new fact about the entities `ex:resource` and `ex:wikipage`. (Note that
reasoning can also apply over class memberships in a similar manner.)

We identify the following requirements for large-scale RDFS and OWL reasoning over Web data:

- *Precomputation:* the system should precompute inferences to avoid the runtime
  expense of backward chaining such that could negatively impact upon response
  times.
- *Reduced output:* the system should not produce so many inferences that it over-
  burdens the consumer application.
- *Scalability:* the system should scale near linearly with respect to the size of the
  Linked Data corpus.
- *Web tolerant:* the system should be tolerant to noisy and possibly inconsistent
  data on the Web.
- *Domain agnostic:* the system should be applicable over data from arbitrary
  domains and consider noncore Web ontologies (ontologies other than
  RDF(S)/OWL) as equals.

In previous work [75], we introduced the scalable authoritative OWL reasoner
(SAOR) system for performing large-scale materialization using a rule-based
approach over a fragment of OWL, according to the given requirements. We
subsequently generalized our approach, extended our fragment to a subset of OWL
2 RL/RDF, and demonstrated distributed execution in [77]. We now briefly reintroduce important aspects from that work, focusing on discussion relevant to the
SWSE use case.

14.9.1   High-Level Approach

First, we choose a rule-based approach which offers greater tolerance in the inevitable event of inconsistency than description logics-based approaches—indeed, consistency cannot be expected on the Web (cf. [74] for our discussion on reasoning issues in Linked Data). Second, rule-based approaches offer greater potential for scale following arguments made in [45]. Finally, many Web ontologies—although relatively lightweight and inexpressive—are not valid DL ontologies: for example, FOAF defines the data-type property `foaf:mbox_sha1sum` as inverse-functional, which is disallowed in OWL DL—in [8] and [125], the authors provided surveys of Web ontologies and showed that most are in OWL full, albeit for largely syntactic reasons.

However, there does not exist a standard ruleset suitable for application over arbitrary Web data—we must compromise and deliberately abandon complete-ness, instead striving for a more pragmatic form of reasoning tailored for the unique challenges of Web reasoning [69]. In [75], we discussed the tailoring of a nonstandard OWL ruleset—viz. pD* [79]—for application over Web data. More recently, OWL 2 has become a W3C Recommendation, and interestingly from our perspective includes a standard rule-expressible fragment of OWL, viz.: OWL 2 RL [50]. In [77], we presented discussion on the new ruleset from the perspective of application over Web data, and showed that the ruleset is not immediately amenable to the requirements outlined, and still needs amendment for our purposes. We also refer the interested reader to [70] for more detail on use cases and techniques for applying OWL reasoning over Linked Data.

First, from the OWL 2 RL/RDF ruleset, we do not apply rules which specifically infer what we term as "tautological statements," which refer to syntactic RDFS and OWL statements such as `rdf:type rdfs:Resource` statements and reflexive `owl:sameAs` statements—statements which apply to every term in the graph. Given n rules which infer such statements and t unique terms in the dataset, such rules would burden the consumer application with $t*n$ largely jejune statements—in fact, we go further and filter such statements from the output.

Second, we identified that separating terminological data (our T-Box)[24] that describes classes and properties from assertional data (our A-Box) that describes individuals could lead to certain optimizations in rule execution, leveraging the observation that only <1% of Linked Data are terminological and that the termi-nological data are the most frequently accessed segment for OWL reasoning [75]. We used such observations to justify the identification, separation, and provision of optimized access to our T-Box, storing it in memory.

Third, after initial evaluation of the system at scale encountered a puzzling deluge of inferences, we discovered that incorporating the source of data into the

---

[24]For example, we consider the triples `mo:wikipedia rdfs:subPropertyOf foaf:page` `.` and `foaf:page owl:inverseOf foaf:topic .` to be terminological.

reasoning algorithm is of utmost importance; naïvely applying reasoning over the merge of arbitrary RDF graphs can lead to unwanted inferences whereby third parties redefine classes and properties provided by popular ontologies [75]. For example, one document[25] defines `owl:Thing` to be a member of 55 union classes and another defines nine *properties* as the domain of `rdf:type`.[26] We counteract such behavior by incorporating the analysis of authoritative sources for classes and properties in the data.

We will now discuss the latter two issues in more detail, but beforehand, let us treat some preliminaries used in this section.

14.9.1.1   Reasoning Preliminaries

We briefly reintroduce some notions formalized in [75, 77]; for brevity, in this section, we aim to give an informative and informal description of terms and refer the interested reader to [75, 77] for a more formal description thereof.

Generalized Triple. A *generalized triple* is a triple where blank nodes and literals are allowed in all positions [50]. Herein, we assume generalized triples internally in the reasoning process and postfilter non-RDF statements from the output.

Metaclass. Informally, we consider a *metaclass* as a class specifically of classes or properties; i.e., the members of a metaclass are themselves either classes or properties. Herein, we restrict our notion of meta-classes to the set defined in RDF(S) and OWL specifications, where examples include `rdf:Property`, `rdfs:Class`, `owl:Class`, `owl:Restriction`, `owl:DatatypeProperty`, `owl:-FunctionalProperty`, etc.; `rdfs:Resource`, `rdfs:Literal`, e.g., are not metaclasses.

Metaproperty. A *metaproperty* is one which has a metaclass as its domain; again, we restrict our notion of metaproperties to the set defined in RDF(S) and OWL specifications, where examples include `rdfs:domain`, `rdfs:-subClassOf`, `owl:hasKey`, `owl:inverseOf`, `owl:oneOf`, `owl:onProperty`, `owl:unionOf`, etc.; `rdf:type`, `owl:sameAs`, `rdfs:label`, e.g., do *not* have a metaclass as domain.

Terminological Triple. We define the set of *terminological triples* as the union of the following sets of generalized triples:

1. Triples with `rdf:type` as predicate and a metaclass as object
2. Triples with a metaproperty as predicate
3. Triples forming a *valid* RDF list whose head is the object of a metaproperty (e.g., a list used for `owl:unionOf`, `owl:intersectionOf`)

---

[25]http://lsdis.cs.uga.edu/~oldham/ontology/wsag/wsag.owl
[26]http://www.eiao.net/rdf/1.0

Example 14.4. The triples:

> mo:wikipedia rdfs:subPropertyOf foaf:page .
> foaf:page owl:inverseOf foaf:topic .

are considered terminological, whereas the following are not:

> ex:resource mo:wikipedia ex:wikipage .
> ex:resource rdf:type rdfs:Resource .

Triple Pattern. A *triple pattern* is a generalized triple where variables from the infinite set **V** are allowed in all positions. We call a set (to be read as conjunction) of triple patterns a *basic graph pattern*. Following standard notation, we prefix variables with "?" We say that a triple is a *binding* of a triple pattern if there exists a mapping of the variables in the triple pattern to some set of RDF constants such that, subsequently, the triple pattern equals the triple; we call this mapping *variable binding*. The notion of a binding for a graph pattern follows naturally.

Terminological/Assertional Pattern. We refer to a *terminological-triple/terminbological-graph pattern* as one that can only be bound by a terminological triple or, resp., a set thereof. An *assertional pattern* is any pattern which is not terminological.

Inference Rule. We define an *inference rule r* as the pair $(\mathcal{A}nte, \mathcal{C}on)$, where the antecedent $\mathcal{A}nte$ and the *consequent* $\mathcal{C}on$ are basic graph patterns [112]; all variables in $\mathcal{C}on$ are contained in $\mathcal{A}nte$, and if $\mathcal{A}nte$ is nonempty, at least one variable must coexist in $\mathcal{A}nte$ and $\mathcal{C}on$. Every unique match—in the union of the input and inferred data—for the graph pattern $\mathcal{A}nte$ leads to the inference of $\mathcal{C}on$ with the respective variable bindings. Rules with empty $\mathcal{A}nte$ can be used to model axiomatic statements which hold for every graph. Herein, we use SPARQL-like syntax to represent graph patterns, and will typically formally write inference rules as $\mathcal{A}nte \Rightarrow \mathcal{C}on$.

Example 14.5. The OWL 2 RL/RDF rule *prp-spo1* [50] supports inferences for rdfs:subPropertyOf with the following rule:

$$?p_1 \text{ rdfs:subPropertyOf } ?p_2 . \; ?x \; ?p_1 \; ?y . \Rightarrow ?x \; ?p_2 \; ?y .$$

where the antecedent $\mathcal{A}nte$ consists of the two patterns on the left side of $\Rightarrow$ and the consequent $\mathcal{C}on$ consists of the pattern on the right side of $\Rightarrow$. This can be read as an IF–THEN condition, where if data matching the patterns on the left are found, the respective bindings are used to infer the respective pattern on the right.

14.9.1.2 Separating Terminological Data

Given the above preliminaries, we can now define our notion of a $\mathcal{T}$-*split inference rule*, whose antecedent is split into two: one part which can only be matched by terminological data and one which can be matched by assertional data.

Definition 14.1 ($\mathcal{T}$-**split inference rule**). Let r be the rule $(Ante, Con)$. We define the $\mathcal{T}$-*split* version of r as the triple $(Ante_{\mathcal{T}}, Ante_{\mathcal{G}}, Con)$, where $Ante_{\mathcal{T}}$ is the set of terminological patterns in $Ante$ and $Ante_{\mathcal{G}}$ is given as all remaining antecedent patterns: $Ante \setminus Ante_{\mathcal{T}}$.

We generally write $(Ante_{\mathcal{T}}, Ante_{\mathcal{G}}, Con)$ as $\underline{Ante_{\mathcal{T}}} Ante_{\mathcal{G}} \Rightarrow Con$, identifying terminological patterns by underlining.

Example 14.6. Take the rule *prp-dom* [50]:

$$\text{?p rdfs:domain ?c . ?x ?p ?y .} \Rightarrow \text{?y rdf:type ?c .}$$

The terminological (underlined) pattern can only be matched by triples who have `rdfs:domain`—a metaproperty—as predicate, and thus must be terminological. The second pattern can be matched by nonterminological triples and so is considered an assertional pattern.

Given the general notion of terminological data, we can constrain our *T-Box* (Terminological-Box) to be the set of terminological triples present in our input data that match a terminological pattern in our rules—intuitively, our T-Box represents the descriptions of classes and properties required in our ruleset; e.g., if our ruleset is RDFS, we do not include OWL terminological triples in our T-Box. We define our *closed T-Box*—denoted $\mathcal{T}$—as the set of terminological triples derived from the input and the result of exhaustively applying rules with no assertional patterns (axiomatic and "schema-level" rules) up to a *least fixed point* [77]. Again, our "*A-Box*" is the set of all statements, including the *T-Box* and inferred statements.

When applying a $\mathcal{T}$-*split inference rule*, $Ante_{\mathcal{T}}$ is strictly only matched by our closed T-Box. Thus, in our reasoning system, we have a well-defined distinction between T-Box and A-Box information, reflected in the definition of our rules, and the application of rules over the T-Box split data. This decoupling of T-Box and A-Box allows for incorporating the following optimizations:

1. Knowing that the T-Box is relatively small and is the most frequently accessed segment for reasoning, we can store the T-Box in an optimized index.
2. We can identify optimized $\mathcal{T}$-split rules as those with low assertional-arity— namely, rules which do not require joins over a large A-Box can be performed in an optimal and scalable manner.
3. The separation of the T-Box enables straightforward distribution over commodity hardware.

With respect to the first possible optimization, at the moment, we store the entire T-Box in memory. With respect to the second optimization, rules involving more than one assertional pattern (i.e., requiring a join operation over the large A-Box) are in practice difficult to compute at the necessary scale [75]. We thus categorize rules according to the *assertional arity* of their antecedent; i.e., the number of assertional patterns in the antecedent. In [71], we performed similar categorization of OWL 2 RL/RDF rules. We then apply a subset of OWL 2 RL/RDF rules with only one assertional pattern; these rules do not require joins to be performed within the large A-Box but rather only between the T-Box and the A-Box. With regard to the third optimization for distribution, the T-Box can be replicated on each machine, minimizing the amount of data exchange and messages sent between machines [77].

Assuming that we apply rules with only one assertional pattern, we can apply the following high-level reasoning procedure:

1. To commence, we apply rules with no antecedent, inferring axiomatic statements.
2. We then run the first scan of the data, identifying terminological knowledge found in the data and separating and indexing the data in our in-memory T-Box.
3. Using this T-Box, we apply rules which only require T-Box knowledge, deriving the closed T-Box.
4. The second scan sequentially joins individual A-Box statements with the static in-memory T-Box, including recursively inferred statements.

We call the above reasoning approach "partial indexing" in that only a subset of the data needs to be indexed for lookups. In general, the partial-indexing approach is suitable when only a small subset of the data need be indexed. In the above version, rules without A-Box joins are not supported, so we need only to index the T-Box. The approach is sound with respect to standard exhaustive rule application (e.g., seminaïve evaluation) and also complete with the condition that a rule requiring assertional knowledge does not infer terminological triples (our T-Box is static and will not be updated) [77]. In summary, by avoiding expensive intra-A-Box joins, we instead perform reasoning at roughly the cost of two sequential scans of the input data and the cost of writing the inferred statements to disk [75].

14.9.1.3   Authoritative Reasoning

In order to curtail the possible side-effects of open Web data publishing, we include the source of data in inferencing. Our methods are based on the view that a publisher instantiating a vocabulary's term (class/property) thereby accepts the inferencing mandated by that vocabulary and recursively referenced vocabularies for that term. Thus, once a publisher instantiates a class or property from a vocabulary, only that vocabulary and its references should influence what inferences are possible through that instantiation.

In order to do so, we again leverage Linked Data best practices—in this case, particularly **LDP2** and **LDP3**—use HTTP URIs, and offer an entity description at the dereferenced document. Similar to the ranking procedure, we follow the intuition that the document returned by resolving a URI is authoritative for that URI, and the prerogative of that document on that URI should have special consideration. More specifically—and recalling the dereferencing function deref and HTTP lookup function get from Sect. 14.4—we can define the authoritative function which gives the set of terms for which a graph at a given Web location (source) speaks authoritatively:

$$auth :\mathbf{S} \to 2^{\mathbf{C}}$$

$$s \mapsto \{b \in \mathbf{B} \mid b \in t \in \mathsf{get}(u)\}$$

$$\cup \{u \in \mathbf{U} \mid \mathsf{deref}(u) = s\}$$

where a Web document is authoritative for the blank nodes it contains and the URIs which dereference to it; for example, the FOAF vocabulary is authoritative for terms in its namespace. Note that no document is authoritative for literals.

Now we wish to perform reasoning over terms as mandated in the respective authoritative document. For example, we want to perform inferencing over data instantiating FOAF classes and properties as mandated by the FOAF vocabulary and not let third-party vocabularies (not recursively referenced by FOAF) affect said inferencing. To negate the effects of nonauthoritative axioms on reasoning over Web data, we apply restrictions to the $\mathcal{T}$-split application of rules with nonempty $Ante^{\mathcal{T}}$ and $Ante^{\mathcal{G}}$, whereby the document serving the T-Box data bound by $Ante^{\mathcal{T}}$ must be authoritative for at least one term bound by a variable which appears in both $Ante^{\mathcal{T}}$ and $Ante^{\mathcal{G}}$: that is to say, the document serving the terminological data must speak authoritatively for at least one term in the assertional data being reasoned over. We call the nonauthoritative redefinition of third-party terms and remote vocabularies "ontology hijacking" [75].

Example 14.7. Take the OWL 2 RL/RDF rule **cax-sco**:

$$?c1 \; \mathtt{rdfs:subClassOf} \; ?c2 \, . \; ?x \; \mathtt{a} \; ?c1 \, . \; \Rightarrow \; ?x \; \mathtt{a} \; ?c2 \, .$$

where we use a as a shortcut for $\mathtt{rdf:type}$. Here, $?c1$ is the only variable that appears in both $Ante^{\mathcal{T}}$ and $Ante^{\mathcal{G}}$. Take an A-Box triple

$$\mathtt{ex:me} \; \mathtt{a} \; \mathtt{foaf:Person} \, .$$

Here, $?c1$ is bound by $\mathtt{foaf:Person}$, and $\mathsf{deref}(\mathtt{foaf:Person}) = \mathtt{foaf:}$, the FOAF spec. Now, any document serving a binding for

$$\mathtt{foaf:Person} \; \mathtt{rdfs:subClassOf} \; ?c2 \, .$$

must be authoritative for the term $\mathtt{foaf:Person}$: the triple must come from the FOAF spec. Note that $?c2$ need not be authoritatively bound; e.g., FOAF can *extend* any classes they like.

We do not consider authority for rules with empty $Ante^{\mathcal{T}}$ or $Ante^{\mathcal{G}}$. Also, we consider reasoned T-Box triples as nonauthoritative, thus *effectively* excluding these triples from the T-Box [77].

Since authoritativeness is on a T-Box level, we can effectively prefilter terminological triples for each rule based on the source providing them. We refer the reader to [70, 75] for more detail on authoritative reasoning, including empirical analysis of the explosion of inferences encountered without the notion of authority. Note that the previous two examples from documents in footnotes 25 and 26 are ignored by the authoritative reasoning.

14.9.2 Related Work

We have extended our reasoning algorithm toward larger coverage of OWL 2 RL/RDF and parallel distribution of inference [76]. Similarly, other works have been presented that tackle large-scale reasoning through parallelization: Urbani et al. [123] presented a MapReduce approach to RDFS reasoning in a cluster of commodity hardware similar to ourselves, identifying that RDFS rules have, at most, one assertional pattern in the antecedent, discussing how this enables efficient MapReduce support. Published at the same venue, Weaver and Hendler [126] also leverage a separation of terminological data to enable distribution of RDFS reasoning. Although the above works have demonstrated scale in the order of hundreds of millions and a billion triples respectively, their experiments were focused on scalability issues and not on counteracting poor data quality on the Web. Weaver et al. [126] focus on evaluation over synthetic LUBM data; Urbani et al. [123] apply RDFS over ∼865 m Linked Data triples, but produce 30 bn inferences which is against our requirement of reduced output—they do not consider authoritative reasoning or source of data, although they note in their performance-centric paper that an algorithm similar to that in SAOR could be added.

A number of systems have tackled the distributed computation of A-Box joins. The MARVIN [106] system uses a "divide-conquer-swap" technique for performing joins in a distributed setting, avoiding hash-based data partitioning to avoid problems with data skew inherent in RDF [89]. Following on from [123], Urbani et al. introduced the WebPie system [122], applying incomplete but comprehensive pD* to 100 bn LUBM triples, discussing rule-specific optimizations for performing pD* "A-Box join rules" over MapReduce.

In more recent work [88], Kolovski et al. have presented an (Oracle) RDBMS-based OWL 2 RL/RDF materialization approach. They again use some similar optimizations to the scalable reasoning literature, including parallelization, canonicalization of `owl:sameAs` inferences, and also partial evaluation of rules based on highly selective patterns—from discussion in the chapter, these selective patterns seem to correlate with the terminological patterns of the rule. Unlike the approaches mentioned thus far, the authors tackle the issue of updates, proposing variants of seminaïve evaluation to avoid rederivations.

Although these works are certainly a large step in the right direction, we feel that applying such rules over 1 bn triples of arbitrary Linked Data is still an open research question given our previous experiences documented in [75]: for example, applying full and quadratic materialization of transitive inferences over the A-Box may become infeasible.(if not now, then almost certainly in the future).

With respect to template rules, DLEJena [96] uses the Pellet DL reasoner for T-Box level reasoning and uses the results to template rules for the Jena rule engine; they only demonstrate methods on synthetic datasets up to a scale of ∼1 m triples. We take a somewhat different approach, discussing template rules in the context of the partial indexing technique, giving a lightweight bottom-up approach to optimizations.

A viable alternative approach to Web reasoning employed by Sindice [33]—the relation to which is discussed in depth in [75]—is to consider a small "per-document" closure which quarantines reasoning to a given document and the related documents it either implicitly or explicitly imports. Although such an approach misses inferences made through the merge of documents—for example, transitivity across sources—so does ours given our current limitation of not computing A-Box joins.

Falcons employ a similar approach to our authoritative analysis to do reasoning over class hierarchies, but only include support of `rdfs:subClassOf` and `owl:equivalentClass`, as opposed to our general framework for authoritative reasoning over arbitrary $\mathcal{T}$-split rules [27].

14.9.3 Future Directions and Open Research Questions

In order to make reasoning over arbitrary Linked Data feasible—both in terms of scale and usefulness of the inferred data—we currently renounce a lot of inferences theoretically warranted by the OWL semantics. We would thus like to extend our approach to cover a more complete fragment of OWL 2 RL/RDF, while still meeting the requirements outlined. This would include, for example, a cost–benefit analysis of rules which require A-Box joins for reasoning over Web data. Similarly, since we perform partial materialization—and indeed since full OWL 2 RL/RDF materialization over Linked Data will probably not be feasible— we would like to investigate some backward-chaining (runtime) approaches which complement a partial materialization strategy. Naturally, such extensions would push the boundaries for scalability and performance even further than our current, cautious approach.

Finally, we have not considered the meaningful assignment of context to inferred triples. Currently in SWSE, each inference is assigned a placeholder context which denotes the last rule fired in its derivation. Thus, the provenance of inferences is lost. Currently, since our inferences are derived from a single assertional triple, we could consider assigning the inference the same context as that triple. If more than one document is considered responsible for an inference (be it terminological or assertional), tracking the provenance of inferences then becomes much more complicated, possibly leading to a large growth in quadruples required to store all possible provenances.

Relatedly, we do not currently consider the combination of ranking into the reasoning process, where ranking is currently applied before (and independently of) reasoning. In more exploratory works [16, 70], we have extended our approach to include some notion of ranking, incorporating the ranks of triples and their contexts (using a variation of the algorithm in Sect. 14.8) into inference, and investigating the applicability of ranking as a quantification of the trustworthiness of inferences. We use these ranks to repair detected *inconsistencies*: contradictions present in the corpus. In particular, we found ~301 k inconsistencies after reasoning, although

~294 k of these were given by invalid datatypes, with ~7 k members of disjoint classes. Along similar lines, inclusion of ranking could be used to facilitate top-k materialization: for example, only materializing triples relating to popularly instantiated classes and properties. Integration of these methods into the SWSE pipeline is the subject of future work.

14.10   Indexing

Having now reached the end of the discussion on the data acquisition, analysis, and enhancement components, we look at creating an index necessary to allow users perform top-k keyword lookups and focus lookups (see Sect. 14.2) over the Linked Data crawl which has been consolidated and includes the results of the reasoning process. Note that in previous work, we demonstrated a distributed system for allowing SPARQL querying over billions of triples [60]; however, we deem SPARQL out of scope for this work, focusing instead on a lightweight, bespoke index optimized for the requirements of the user interface.

To allow for speedy access to the RDF data, we employ a set of indexes: an inverted index for keyword lookups based on RDF literals (text) and a sparse index for lookups of structured data. Inverted indexes are standard for keyword searches in information retrieval. For structured data, we use a sparse index because it represents a good trade-off between lookup performance, scalability, and simplicity [60]. Following our previous techniques aiming at application over static datasets, our index structure does not support updates and is instead read optimized [60]; in principle, we could employ any sufficiently optimized implementation of an index structure that offers prefix lookup capabilities on keys.

14.10.1   Inverted Index

The inverted index is required to formulate the direct response to a user keyword query to be rendered by the UI (again, see Fig. 14.1). Our inverted index for keyword search is based on the Lucene [62][27] engine and is constructed in the following ways during a scan of the data:

- For each entity in the RDF graph, construct a Lucene document with the union of all string literals related by some property to the RDF subject.
- To each entity, add fields containing the identifiers (URI(s) or blank node given by the subject and/or `owl:sameAs` values), labels (`rdfs:label`, `dc:title`, etc.), descriptions (`rdfs:comment`, `dc:description`, etc.),

---

[27]http://lucene.apache.org/java/

classes (objects of rdf:type triples), and possibly other metadata such as image URIs if required to create keyword result snippets.

• For each identifier, add globally computed ranks.

For lookups, we specify a set of keyword terms for which matching identifiers should be returned and, in addition, the desired slice of the result set (e.g., result 1 to 10). Following standard information retrieval techniques, Lucene combines the globally computed ranks with query-dependent *TF*IDF* (query-relevance) ranks and selects the slice of results to be returned. We additionally associate entity labels with a fixed "boost" score, giving label-term matches higher relevance, here assuming that many keyword searches will be for entity labels (e.g., galway, dan brickley). We use Lucene's off-the-shelf similarity engine [62] which can be sketched as follows.

Let q be the query, t a keyword term, e_c the entity with the canonical identifier c, $\text{lit}_p(e_c)$ the set of literals attached to e_c by the predicate p, $\text{lit}(e_c)$ the set of all literals attached to e_c, and $r_c = idrank(c)$ the global (identifier) rank for that entity. The score of an entity e_c with respect to the query q is then computed as follows:

$$\text{score}(q, e_c) = \sum_{l \in \text{lit}_p(e_c)} \sum_{t \in q \cap l} (tf_{t \in \text{lit}(e_c)} * idf_t^2 * b_p) * r_c$$

where b_p is a weighting factor for different predicates which we use to boost label fields; where

$$tf_{t \in l} = \sqrt{\text{freq}_t(\text{lit}(e_c))}$$

represents the term frequency, given here as the square root of the number of appearances of t in all literals attached to e_c; and where

$$idf_t = 1 + \log\left(\frac{n}{n_t + 1}\right)$$

represents the inverse document frequency, where n is the total number of entities indexed and n_t is the total number of entities associated with the term t.

The additional nontextual metadata stored in Lucene allows for result snippets to be directly created from the Lucene results, without requiring access to the structured index: from the contents of the additional fields, we generate an RDF graph and return the results to higher layers for generating the results page.

14.10.2   Structured Index

The structured index is implemented to give all information relating to a given entity (e.g., focus view; again see Fig. 14.2). The structured index is implemented using "sparse indexes" [60], where a blocked and sorted ISAM file contains the RDF quads and lookups are supported by a small in-memory index which holds the first entry of each block: binary search is performed on the in-memory index to locate the on-disk blocks which can potentially contribute to the answer, where subsequently, those blocks are fetched, parsed, and answers filtered and returned. Currently, we only require lookups on the subject position of quads, and thus only require one index sorted according to the natural order (s, p, o, c).

There are two tuning parameters for such an index. The first is block size, which determines (1) the size of the chunks of data fetched from disk and (2) indirectly the size of the in-memory portion of the index. The second parameter is compression: minimizing the amount of data transferred from disk to memory should speed up lookups, provided that the time saved by smaller data transfers outweighs the time required for uncompressing data.

14.10.3   Related Work

A veritable plethora of RDF stores have been proposed in the literature, most aiming at providing SPARQL functionality, and each bringing with it its own set of priorities for performance, and its own strengths and weaknesses. A subset of these systems rely on underlying relation databases for storage, including 4store [54], Bigdata®, [28] Hexastore [128], Jena SDB,[29] Mulgara,[30] Sesame [20], Virtuoso [43], etc.; the rest rely on so-called native RDF storage schemes, including HPRD [93], Jena TDB,[31] RDF3X [102], SIREn [34], Voldemort,[32] etc.

We note that many SPARQL engines include inverted indexes—usually Lucene-based—to offer keyword search over RDF data. The authors of [99] describe full-text search benchmarking of existing RDF stores—in particular Jena, Sesame2, Virtuoso, and YARS2—testing queries of varying degrees of complexity involving full-text search. They showed that for many types of queries, the performance of YARS2 was often not as competitive as other stores, and correctly verified that certain types of queries (e.g., keyword matches for literals of a given property) are not supported by our system. With respect to performance, we have only ever implemented naïve full-SPARQL query-optimization techniques in YARS2, and have instead focused on creating scalable read-optimized indexes, demonstrating batch processing of joins in a distributed environment and focusing on efficiently supporting simple lookups which potentially return large result sets. For example, we choose not to use OIDs (internal integer representations of constants): although

---

[28] http://www.systap.com/bigdata.htm

[29] http://openjena.org/SDB/

[30] http://www.mulgara.org/

[31] http://openjena.org/TDB/

[32] http://project-voldemort.com/

OIDs are a proven avenue for optimized query processing involving large amounts of intermediate results (e.g., cf. [102]), we wish to avoid the expensive translation from internal OIDs to potentially many external constants, instead preserving the ability to stream results directly. In general, we do not currently require support for complex structured queries, and question the utility of more complex full-text functionality to lay users.

14.10.4 Future Directions and Open Research Questions

The future work of the indexing section is inextricably linked with that of the future direction of the query processing and user interface components. At the moment, our index supports simple lookups for entities matching a given keyword, data required to build a keyword snippet, and the quads for which that subject appears.

Given a relatively static query model, a custom-built structured index can be tailored to offer optimized service to the user interface, as opposed to, e.g., a generic SPARQL engine. The main directions for future work in indexing would be to identify an intersection of queries for which optimized indexes can be built in a scalable manner and queries which offer greater potential to the UI.

Further investigation of compression techniques and other low-level optimizations may further increase the base performance of our system—however, we feel that the combination of RLE encoding and GZIP compression currently demonstrates satisfactory performance.

A recent trend in data management is the emergence of so-called NoSQL databases which offer distributed indexing. A possible avenue of further research involves systems following the BigTable [24] data model such as Apache Cassandra [90] which could offer distributed indexing capability for RDF.

With regard to the combination of ranking factors in the keyword index, we currently use static boosting in the off-the-shelf Lucene similarity engine. Investigating different methodologies for combining query-dependent and query-independent rankings (and across multiple fields given by different properties) is thus an open question. For example, in recent work, Pérez-Agüera et al. have recently claimed that BM25F offers better results when combining multiple structured fields for indexing keywords in RDF [109].

14.11 Query Processing

With the distributed index built and prepared on the slave machines, we now require a query processor to accept user queries; request and orchestrate lookups over the slave machines, and aggregate, process, and stream the final results. In this section, we assume that the master machine hosts the query processor: however, we look at different configurations in Sect. 14.12. We aim to characterize the query-processing steps, and give performance for sequential lookups over the distributed index, and for the various information-retrieval tasks required by the user interface. In particular, we describe the two indexes needed for processing user keyword queries and user focus queries respectively (see Sect. 14.2).

14.11.1   Distributed Keyword-Query Processing

For a top-k keyword query, the coordinating machine requests k result identifiers and ranks from each of the slave machines. The coordinating machine then computes the aggregated top-k hits and requests the snippet result data for each of the hits from the originating machines and streams data to the initiating agent. For the purposes of pagination, given a query for page n, the originating machine requests the top $n * k$ result identifiers and associated ranks and then determines, requests, and streams the relevant result snippets.

14.11.2   Distributed Focus-Query Processing

Creating the raw data for the focus view of a given entity is somewhat complicated by the requirements of the UI. The focus view mainly renders the information encoded by quads for which the identifier of the entity appears in the subject position; however, to provide a more legible rendering, the UI requires human-readable labels for each predicate and object, as well as ranks for prioritizing elements in the rendered view (see predicate/object labels in Fig. 14.2). Thus, to provide the raw data required for the focus view of a given entity, the master machine accepts the relevant identifier, performs a hash function on the identifier, and directly requests data from the respective slave machine (which itself performs a lookup on the structured index). Subsequently, the master machine generates a unique set of predicates and objects appearing in the result set; this set is then split by hash, with each subset sent in parallel to the target slave machines. The slave machines perform lookups for the respective label and global rank, streaming results to the coordinating machine, which in turn streams the final results to the initiating agent.

Collating the raw data for the focus view is more expensive than a simple lookup on one targeted machine—although helped by the hash-placement strategy, potentially many lookups may be required. We mitigate the expense using some application-level LRU caching, where the coordinating machine caches not only keyword snippet results and focus view results but also the labels and ranks for predicates and objects: in particular, this would save repetitive lookups on commonly encountered properties and classes.

14.11.3 Related Work

Besides query-processing components for systems referenced in Sect. 14.10.3, other types of query processing have been defined in the literature which do not rely on data warehousing approaches.

The system presented in [61] leverages Linked Data principles to perform live lookups on Linked Data sources, rendering and displaying resulting data; however, such an approach suffers from low recall and inability to independently service keyword queries. In [57], we have described an approach which uses a lightweight hashing-based index structure—viz. a Q-Tree—for mapping structured queries to Linked Data sources which could possibly provide pertinent information; these sources are then retrieved and query processing performed. Such approaches suffer from poorer recall than data-warehousing approaches but enable the provision of up-to-date results to users, which is particularly expedient for query processing over highly dynamic sources. We could investigate inclusion of a live-lookup component in SWSE for a subset of queries which we identify to be best answered by means of live lookup; however, further research in this area is required to identify such queries and to investigate the performance of such a system.

Preliminary work on the DARQ [113] system provides federated query processing over a set of autonomous independent SPARQL endpoints. Such an approach may allow for increased query recall; however, the performance of such a system is still an open question; also, keyword search is still not a standard SPARQL operation, and thus, federating keyword queries would probably require manual wrappers for different SPARQL endpoints.

14.11.4 Future Directions and Open Research Question

With respect to current query-processing capabilities, our underlying index structures have proven scalable. However, the focus - view currently requires on average hundreds—but possibly tens or hundreds of thousands—of lookups for labels and ranks. Given that individual result sizes are likely to continue to grow, we will need to incorporate one of the following optimizations: (1) we can build a specialized join index which precomputes and stores focus-view results, requiring one atomic lookup for the entire focus-view result at the cost of longer indexing time, and (judging from our evaluation) a doubling of structured-index size, and/or (2) we can generate a top-k focus-view result, paginating the view of a single entity and only retrieving incremental segments of the view—possibly asynchronously.

Extending the query processing to handle more complex queries is a topic of importance when considering extension and improvement of the current spartan UI. In order to fully realize the potential benefits of querying over structured data, we need to be able to perform optimized query processing. For querying data, there is a trade-off between the scalability of the approach and the expressivity of the query language used.

In the general case, joins are expensive operations, and when attempting to perform arbitrary joins on very large datasets, the system either consumes a large amount of resources per query or becomes slow. Some systems (such as [82]) solve the scalability issue by partitioning the datasets into smaller units and have the user select a subdataset before further browsing or querying; however, such a solution impinges on the data-integration properties of RDF which provides the raison d'être of a system such as SWSE. Another solution is to precompute joins, allowing for direct lookup of results emulating the current approach; however, materializing joins can lead to quadratic growth in index sizes. Investigation of partial join materialization—perhaps based on the expense of a join operation, materialized size of join, runtime caching, etc.—may enable sufficiently optimized query processing.

Another open research question here is how to optimize for top-k querying in queries involving joins; joins at large scale can potentially lead to the access of large - volumes of intermediary data, used to compute a final small result size; thus, the question is how top-k query processing can be used to immediately retrieve the best results for joins, allowing, for example, path queries in the UI (joins on objects and subject) such that large intermediate data volumes need not be accessed, and rather than the approach of joining several attribute restrictions (e.g., facets) as done in the threshold algorithm [44].

14.12   User Interface

Having discussed data acquisition, enhancing, analysis, indexing, and query-processing components, we have now come full circle and arrived at the user-facing component. The user interface offers two basic operations: keyword search, where the user specifies a set of keywords and the system returns with a list of matching entities, and object focus, where the user can navigate to a consolidated view of all information available for one entity (see Sect. 14.2). Our user interface uses XSLT to convert the raw data returned by the query processor into result pages, offering a declarative means of specifying user interface rendering and ultimately providing greater flexibility for tweaking presentation.

14.12.1   Related Work

There has been considerable work on rendering and displaying RDF data; such systems include BrowseRDF [105], Explorator [4], gFacet [66], Haystack [84],

Longwell,[33] Piggybank [81], (Power)Magpie [51], Marbles,[34] RKBExplorer,[35] Tabulator [10], Zitgist,[36] as well as user interfaces for previously mentioned engines such as Falcons, Sig.ma, Sindice, Swoogle, Watson, etc.

Fresnel [110] has defined an interesting approach to overcome the difficultly of displaying RDF in a domain-agnostic way by providing a vocabulary for describing how RDF should be rendered, thus allowing for the declarative provision of schema-specific views over data; some user interfaces have been proposed to exploit Fresnel, including LENA [87]; however, Fresnel has not seen widespread adoption on the Web thus far.

14.12.2   Future Directions and Open Research Questions

First, we must review the performance of the UI with respect to generating result pages—we had not previously considered this issue, but under high loads, UI result generation seems to be a significant factor in deciding response times.

With respect to functionality, we currently do not fully exploit the potential offered by richly structured data. First, such data could power a large variety of visualizations: for example, to render SIMILE's timeline view[37] or a GoogleMap view.[38] Countless other visualizations are possible for a history and examples of visualizations, cf. [48]. Research into rendering and visualizing large graph-structured datasets—particularly user evaluation thereof—could lead to novel user interfaces which better suit and exploit such information.

Second, offering only keyword search and entity browsing removes the possibility of servicing more expressive queries which offer users more direct answers; however, designing a system for domain-agnostic users to formulate such queries in an intuitive manner—and one which is guided by the underlying data to avoid empty results where possible—has proven nontrivial. We have made first experiments with more expressive user interfaces for interacting with data through the VisiNav system[39] [55], which supports faceted browsing [129], path traversal [5], and data visualizations on top of the keyword search and focus operations supported by SWSE. Within VisiNav, we encourage users to incrementally create expressive queries while browsing, as opposed to having a formal query formulation step—users are offered navigation choices which lead to nonempty results. However, for such extra functionality—specifically the cost of querying associated with arbitrary

---

[33]http://simile.mit.edu/wiki/Longwell

[34]http://marbles.sourceforge.net/

[35]http://www.rkbexplorer.com/explorer/

[36]http://dataviewer.zitgist.com/

[37]http://www.simile-widgets.org/timeline/

[38]http://maps.google.com/

[39]http://visinav.deri.org/

join paths—VisiNav must make scalability trade-offs: VisiNav can currently handle in the realm of tens of millions of statements.

Efforts to provide guided construction of structured queries (e.g., cf. [100]) may be useful to so-called power-users; however, such methods again rely on some knowledge of the schema of the pertinent data and query. Other efforts to match keyword searches to structured queries (e.g., cf. [28, 94, 119]) could bring together the ease of use of Web search engines and the precise answers of structured data querying; however, again such formulations still require some knowledge of the schema(ta) of the data, and which types of entities link to which by what type of link.

For the moment, we focus on providing basic functionality as should be familiar to many Web users. Previous incarnations of SWSE offered more complex user-interaction models, allowing, e.g., filtering of results based on type, traversing inlinks for an entity, and traversing links from a collection of entities. From informal feedback received, we realized that features such as inlink traversal (and the notion of directionality) were deemed confusing by certain users—or at least by our implementation thereof.[40] We are thus more cautious about implementing additional features in the user interface, aiming for minimalistic display and interaction. One possible solution is to offer different versions of the user interface, for example, a default system offering simple keyword search for casual users and an optional system offering more complex functionality for power users. In such regards, user evaluation (currently out of scope) would be of utmost importance in making such design choices.

We also wish to investigate the feasibility of offering programmatic interfaces through SWSE.[41] The main requirements for such APIs are performance and reliability: the API has to return results fast enough to enable interactive applications and has to have high uptime to encourage adoption by external services. Full SPARQL is likely too powerful (and hence too expensive to evaluate) to provide stable, complete, *and* fast responses for. One possible workaround is to provide time-out queries, which return as many answers as can be serviced in a fixed time period; another possible solution is to offer top-k query processing, or a well-supported subset of SPARQL (e.g., DESCRIBE queries and conjunctive queries with a limited number of joins or containing highly selective patterns) such that could serve as a foundation for visualizations and other applications leveraging the integrated Web data in SWSE.

---

[40]In any case, our reasoning engine supports the `owl:inverseOf` construct which solves the problem of directionality, and we would hope that most (object) properties define a corresponding inverse property.

[41]Please note that practical limitations with respect to the availability and administration of physical machines have restricted our ability to provide such interfaces with high reliability; indeed, we used to offer time-out SPARQL queries over ~1.5 bn statements through YARS2, but for the meantime, we can no longer support such a service.

14.13   Conclusion

In this chapter, we have presented the results of research carried out as part of the SWSE project over several years. In particular, we have described how we adapted the architecture of large-scale Web search engines to the case of structured data. We have presented lightweight algorithms which demonstrate the data-integration possibilities for Linked Data and shown how such algorithms can be made scalable using batch-processing techniques such as scans and sorts and how they can be deployed over a distributed architecture. We have argued for the importance of taking the source of information into account when handling arbitrary RDF Web data, showing how Linked Data principles can be leveraged for such purposes, particularly in our ranking and reasoning algorithms.

Research on how to integrate and interact with large amounts of data from a very diverse set of independent sources is fairly recent, as many characteristics of the research questions in the field became visible after the deployment of large amounts of data by a sizable body of data publishers. The traditional application development cycle for data-intensive applications is to model the data schema and build the application on top: data modeling and application development are tightly coupled. That process is separated on the Semantic Web: data publishers just model and publish data, often with no particular application in mind. At the same time, the quality of data that a system such as SWSE operates over is perhaps as much of a factor in the system's utility as the design of the system itself.

Recently, there has been significant success with Linked Data where an active community publishes datasets in a broad range of topics and maintains and interlinks these datasets. Again, efforts such as DBpedia have lead to a much richer Web of Data than the one present when we began working on SWSE. However, data heterogeneity still poses problems—not so much for the underlying components of SWSE—but for the user-facing components and the users themselves: allowing domain-oblivious users to create flexible structured queries in a convenient and intuitive manner is still an open question. Indeed, the Web of Data still cannot compete with the vast coverage of the Web of Documents, and perhaps never will [111].

That said, making Web data available for querying and navigation has significant scientific and commercial potential. First, the Web becomes subject to scientific analysis [12]: understanding the implicit connections and structure of the Web of Data can help to reveal new understandings of collaboration patterns and the processes by which networks form and evolve. Second, aggregating and enhancing scientific data published on the Web can help scientists to more easily perform data-intensive research, in particular allowing for the arbitrary repurposing of published datasets which can subsequently be used in ways unforeseen by the original publisher. Third, making the Web of Data available for interactive querying, browsing, and navigation has applications in areas such as e-commerce and e-health, allowing data analysts in such fields to pose complex structured queries over a dataset aggregated from multitudinous relevant sources.

Acknowledgments The work presented herein was funded in part by Science Foundation Ireland
under Grant No. SFI/08/CE/I1380 (Lion-2) and by an IRCSET postgraduate scholarship.

References

1. Alani, H., Brewster, C., Shadbolt, N.: Ranking ontologies with AKTiveRank. 5th international
   semantic web conference, pp. 1–15 (2006)
2. Alani, H., Dasmahapatra, S., O'Hara, K., Shadbolt, N.: Identifying communities of practice
   through ontology network analysis. IEEE Intel. Syst. **18**(2), 18–25 (2003)
3. Anyanwu, K., Maduko, A., Sheth, A.: SemRank: ranking complex relationship search results
   on the semantic web. 14th International Conference on World Wide Web, pp. 117–127 (2005).
   DOI http://doi.acm.org/10.1145/1060745.1060766
4. de Araújo, S.F.C., Schwabe, D.: Explorator: a tool for exploring RDF data through direct
   manipulation. Linked data on the web WWW2009 workshop (LDOW2009) (2009)
5. Athanasis, N., Christophides, V., Kotzinos, D.: Generating On the fly queries for the semantic
   web: the ICS-FORTH graphical RQL interface (GRQL). 3rd international semantic web
   conference, pp. 486–501 (2004)
6. Balmin, A., Hristidis, V., Papakonstantinou, Y.: Objectrank: authority-based keyword search
   in databases. Proceedings of the 13th International Conference on very Large Data Bases,
   pp. 564–575 (2004)
7. Batsakis, S., Petrakis, E.G.M., Milios, E.: Improving the performance of focused web
   crawlers. Data Knowledge Eng. **68**(10), 1001–1013 (2009). DOI http://dx.doi.org/10.1016/
   j.datak.2009.04.002
8. Bechhofer, S., Volz, R.: Patching Syntax in OWL Ontologies. International semantic web
   conference (ISWC 2004), Lecture Notes in Computer Science, vol. 3298, pp. 668–682.
   Springer, Berlin, Heidelberg, New York (2004)
9. Berners-Lee, T.: Linked Data. Design issues for the World Wide Web, World Wide Web
   Consortium (2006). http://www.w3.org/DesignIssues/LinkedData.html
10. Berners-Lee, T., Chen, Y., Chilton, L., Connolly, D., Dhanaraj, R., Hollenbach, J., Lerer,
    A., Sheets, D.: Tabulator: exploring and analyzing linked data on the semantic web. In
    Proceedings of the 3rd International Semantic Web user Interaction Workshop (2006)
11. Berners-Lee, T., Fielding, R., Masinter, L.: Uniform resource identifier (URI): generic syntax.
    RFC 3986 (2005). http://tools.ietf.org/html/rfc3986
12. Berners-Lee, T., Hall, W., Hendler, J., Shadbolt, N., Weitzner, D.J.: Creating a science of the
    web. Science **313**(11) (2006)
13. Bizer, C., Cyganiak, R.: D2R server – publishing relational databases on the web as SPARQL
    Endpoints. ISWC (2006). (poster)
14. Bizer, C., Heath, T., Berners-Lee, T.: Linked data – the story so far. Int. J. Semant. Web Inf.
    Syst. **5**(3), 1–22 (2009)
15. Boldi, P., Codenotti, B., Santini, M., Vigna, S., Vigna, S.: UbiCrawler: a scalable fully
    distributed web crawler. Soft. Pract. Exp. **34**, 2004
16. Bonatti, P.A., Hogan, A., Polleres, A., Sauro, L.: Robust and Scalable Linked Data Reasoning
    Incorporating Provenance and trust Annotations. J. Web Semant. **9**(2), Elsevier (2011)
17. Bouquet, P., Stoermer, H., Mancioppi, M., Giacomuzzi, D.: OkkaM: towards a solution to the
    "Identity Crisis" on the semantic web. Proceedings of SWAP 2006, the 3rd Italian Semantic
    Web Workshop, CEUR Workshop Proceedings, vol. 201 (2006)
18. Brewer, E.A.: Combining Systems and Databases: A Search Engine Retrospective,
    pp. 711–724. MIT Press, Cambridge, MA (2005)
19. Brin, S., Page, L.: The anatomy of a large-scale hypertextual web search engine. Comput.
    Networks **30**(1–7), 107–117 (1998)

20. Broekstra, J., Kampman, A., van Harmelen, F.: Sesame: a generic architecture for storing and querying RDF and RDF schema. 2nd international semantic web conference, pp. 54–68. Springer, Berlin, Heidelberg, New York (2002)
21. Cai, D., He, X., Wen, J., Ma, W.: Block-level link analysis. 27th international ACM SIGIR conference on research and development in information retrieval, pp. 440–447 (2004)
22. Caverlee, J., Liu, L.: QA-Pagelet: data preparation techniques for large-scale data analysis of the deep web. IEEE Trans. Knowl. Data Eng. 17(9), 1247–1262 (2005)
23. Chakrabarti, S., van den Berg, M., Dom, B.: Focused crawling: a new approach to topic-specific web resource discovery. Comput. Networks 31(11–16), 1623–1640 (1999)
24. Chang, F., Dean, J., Ghemawat, S., Hsieh, W.C., Wallach, D.A., Burrows, M., Chandra, T., Fikes, A., Gruber, R.: Bigtable: a distributed storage system for structured data. OSDI, pp. 205–218 (2006)
25. Chang, K.C.C., He, B., Zhang, Z.: Toward large scale integration: building a MetaQuerier over databases on the web. CIDR, pp. 44–55 (2005)
26. Chen, Z., Kalashnikov, D.V., Mehrotra, S.: Exploiting relationships for object consolidation. IQIS '05: Proceedings of the 2nd International Workshop on Information Quality in Information Systems, pp. 47–58. ACM, New York, NY, USA (2005). DOI http://doi.acm.org/10.1145/1077501.1077512
27. Cheng, G., Ge, W., Wu, H., Qu, Y.: Searching semantic web objects based on class hierarchies. Proceedings of Linked Data on the Web Workshop (2008)
28. Cheng, G., Qu, Y.: Searching linked objects with falcons: approach, implementation and evaluation. Int. J. Semant. Web Inf. Syst. 5(3), 49–70 (2009)
29. Cheng, T., Chang, K.C.C.: Entity search engine: towards Agile best-effort information integration over the web. CIDR, pp. 108–113 (2007)
30. d'Aquin, M., Sabou, M., Motta, E., Angeletou, S., Gridinoc, L., Lopez, V., Zablith, F.: What can be done with the semantic web? an overview Watson-based applications. SWAP (2008)
31. Dean, J., Ghemawat, S.: MapReduce: simplified data processing on large clusters. OSDI, pp. 137–150 (2004)
32. Decker, S., Erdmann, M., Fensel, D., Studer, R.: Ontobroker: ontology based access to distributed and semi-structured information. DS-8: IFIP TC2/WG2.6 eighth working conference on database semantics, pp. 351–369. Kluwer, B.V., Deventer, The Netherlands, The Netherlands (1998)
33. Delbru, R., Polleres, A., Tummarello, G., Decker, S.: Context dependent reasoning for semantic documents in Sindice. Proceedings of the 4th International Workshop on Scalable Semantic Web Knowledge Base Systems (SSWS 2008). Karlsruhe, Germany (2008). URL http://www.polleres.net/publications/delb-etal-2008.pdf
34. Delbru, R., Toupikov, N., Catasta, M., Tummarello, G.: A node indexing scheme for web entity retrieval. Proceedings of the Extended Semantic Web Conference (ESWC 2010) (2010)
35. Delbru, R., Toupikov, N., Catasta, M., Tummarello, G., Decker, S.: Hierarchical link analysis for ranking web data. Proceedings of the Extended Semantic Web Conference (ESWC 2010) (2010)
36. Dietze, H., Schroeder, M.: Semplore: a scalable IR approach to search the web of data. BMC Bioinfor. 10 (2009)
37. Diligenti, M., Coetzee, F., Lawrence, S., Giles, C.L., Gori, M.: Focused crawling using context graphs. VLDB '00: Proceedings of the 26th International Conference on very Large Data Bases, pp. 527–534. Morgan Kaufmann Publishers Inc., San Francisco, CA, USA (2000)
38. Ding, L., Finin, T., Joshi, A., Pan, R., Cost, R.S., Peng, Y., Reddivari, P., Doshi, V.C., Sachs, J.: Swoogle: a search and metadata engine for the semantic web. 13th ACM conference on information and knowledge management. ACM, New York (2004)
39. Ding, L., Pan, R., Finin, T., Joshi, A., Peng, Y., Kolari, P.: Finding and ranking knowledge on the semantic web. 4th international semantic web conference, pp. 156–170 (2005)

40. Dong, H., Hussain, F.K., Chang, E.: State of the art in semantic focused crawlers. ICCSA '09: Proceedings of the International Conference on Computational Science and its Applications, pp. 910–924. Springer, Berlin, Heidelberg (2009). DOI http://dx.doi.org/10.1007/978-3-642-02457-3_74

41. Ehrig, M., Maedche, A.: Ontology-focused crawling of Web documents. SAC '03: Proceedings of the 2003 ACM Symposium on Applied Computing, pp. 1174–1178. ACM, New York, NY, USA (2003). DOI http://doi.acm.org/10.1145/952532.952761

42. Elmagarmid, A.K., Ipeirotis, P.G., Verykios, V.S.: Duplicate record detection: a survey. IEEE Trans. Knowl. Data Eng. **19**(1), 1–16 (2007)

43. Erling, O., Mikhailov, I.: RDF support in the Virtuoso DBMS. CSSW, pp. 59–68 (2007)

44. Fagin, R.: Combining fuzzy information from multiple systems (extended abstract). PODS '96: Proceedings of the Fifteenth ACM SIGACT-SIGMOD-SIGART Symposium on Principles of Database Systems, pp. 216–226. ACM, New York (1996). DOI http://doi.acm.org/10.1145/237661.237715

45. Fensel, D., van Harmelen, F.: Unifying reasoning and search to web scale. IEEE Inter. Comput. **11**(2), 94–96 (2007). DOI http://doi.ieeecomputersociety.org/10.1109/MIC.2007.51

46. Fielding, R., Gettys, J., Mogul, J., Nielsen, H.F., Masinter, L., Leach, P., Berners-Lee, T.: Hypertext transfer protocol – HTTP/1.1. RFC 2616 (1999). ftp://ftp.isi.edu/in-notes/rfc2616.txt

47. Franz, T., Schultz, A., Sizov, S., Staab, S.: TripleRank: ranking semantic web data by tensor decomposition. 8th international semantic web conference (ISWC2009) (2009)

48. Friendly, M.: A brief history of data visualization. In: Chen, C., Härdle, W., Unwin, A. (eds.) Handbook of Computational Statistics: Data Visualization, vol. III. Springer, Heidelberg (2006)

49. Glaser, H., Millard, I., Jaffri, A.: RKBExplorer.com: a knowledge driven infrastructure for linked data providers. ESWC Demo, Lecture Notes in Computer Science, pp. 797–801. Springer, Belin, Heidelberg, New York (2008)

50. Grau, B.C., Motik, B., Wu, Z., Fokoue, A., Lutz, C.: OWL 2 Web Ontology language: profiles. W3C Working Draft (2008). http://www.w3.org/TR/owl2-profiles/

51. Gridinoc, L., Sabou, M., d'Aquin, M., Dzbor, M., Motta, E.: Semantic browsing with PowerMagpie. ESWC, pp. 802–806 (2008)

52. Guha, R.V., McCool, R., Fikes, R.: Contexts for the Semantic Web. 3rd International Semantic Web Conference, Hiroshima (2004)

53. Halpin, H., Hayes, P.J., McCusker, J.P., McGuinness, D.L., Thompson, H.S.: When owl:sameAs isn't the same: an analysis of identity in linked data. International Semantic Web Conference (1), pp. 305–320 (2010)

54. Harris, S., Lamb, N., Shadbolt, N.: 4store: The Design and Implementation of a Clustered RDF Store. 5th International Workshop on Scalable Semantic Web Knowledge Base Systems (SSWS2009) (2009)

55. Harth, A.: Visinav: a system for visual search and navigation on web data. J. Web Semat. **8**(4), 348–354 (2010)

56. Harth, A., Decker, S.: Optimized index structures for querying RDF from the web. 3rd Latin American Web Congress, pp. 71–80. IEEE Press, New York (2005)

57. Harth, A., Hose, K., Karnstedt, M., Polleres, A., Sattler, K.U., Umbrich, J.: Data summaries for on-demand queries over linked data. WWW, pp. 411–420 (2010)

58. Harth, A., Kinsella, S.: Topdis: tensor-based ranking for data search and navigation. Technical Report, DERI (2009)

59. Harth, A., Kinsella, S., Decker, S.: Using naming authority to rank data and ontologies for web search. 8th International Semantic Web Conference (ISWC 2009) (2009)

60. Harth, A., Umbrich, J., Hogan, A., Decker, S.: YARS2: a federated repository for querying graph structured data from the web. 6th International Semantic Web Conference, 2nd Asian Semantic Web Conference, pp. 211–224 (2007)

61. Hartig, O., Bizer, C., Freytag, J.C.: Executing SPARQL queries over the web of linked data. International Semantic Web Conference, pp. 293–309 (2009)

62. Hatcher, E., Gospodnetic, O.: Lucene in Action. Manning Publications (2004)
63. Hayes, P.: RDF semantics. W3C Recommendation (2004). http://www.w3.org/TR/rdf-mt/
64. He, B., Patel, M., Zhang, Z., Chang, K.C.C.: Accessing the deep web. Commun. ACM **50**(5), 94–101 (2007)
65. Heflin, J., Hendler, J., Luke, S.: SHOE: a knowledge representation language for internet applications. Technical Report CS-TR-4078, Department of Computer Science, University of Maryland (1999)
66. Heim, P., Ziegler, J., Lohmann, S.: gFacet: a browser for the web of data. Proceedings of the International Workshop on Interacting with Multimedia Content in the Social Semantic Web (IMC-SSW'08), pp. 49–58. CEUR-WS (2008)
67. Heydon, A., Najork, M.: Mercator: a scalable, extensible web crawler. World Wide Web **2**, 219–229 (1999)
68. Hirai, J., Raghavan, S., Garcia-Molina, H., Paepcke, A.: WebBase: a repository of Web pages'. Comput. Networks **33**(1–6), 277–293 (2000)
69. Hitzler, P., van Harmelen, F.: A reasonable semantic web. Semant. Web Interop. Usabil. Appl. **1** (2010)
70. Hogan, A.: Exploiting RDFS and OWL for integrating heterogeneous, large-scale, linked data corpora. Ph.D. thesis, Digital Enterprise Research Institute, National University of Ireland, Galway (2011). Available from http://aidanhogan.com/docs/thesis/
71. Hogan, A., Decker, S.: On the ostensibly silent 'W' in OWL 2 RL. Third International Conference on Web Reasoning and Rule Systems, (RR2009), pp. 118–134 (2009)
72. Hogan, A., Harth, A., Decker, S.: ReConRank: a scalable ranking method for semantic web data with context. 2nd Workshop on Scalable Semantic Web Knowledge Base Systems (SSWS2006) (2006)
73. Hogan, A., Harth, A., Decker, S.: Performing object consolidation on the semantic web data graph. 1st I3 Workshop: Identity, Identifiers, Identification Workshop (2007)
74. Hogan, A., Harth, A., Passant, A., Decker, S., Polleres, A.: Weaving the pedantic web. Linked Data on the Web WWW2010 Workshop (LDOW2010) (2010)
75. Hogan, A., Harth, A., Polleres, A.: Scalable authoritative OWL reasoning for the web. Int. J. Semant. Web Inf. Syst. **5**(2) (2009)
76. Hogan, A., Harth, A., Umbrich, J., Kinsella, S., Polleres, A., Decker, S.: Searching and browsing Linked Data with SWSE: the semantic web search engine. J. Web Semant. (2011). DOI DOI:10.1016/j.websem.2011.06.004
77. Hogan, A., Pan, J.Z., Polleres, A., Decker, S.: SAOR: template rule optimisations for distributed reasoning over 1 billion linked data triples. International Semantic Web Conference (2010)
78. Hogan, A., Polleres, A., Umbrich, J., Zimmermann, A.: Some entities are more equal than others: statistical methods to consolidate Linked Data. 4th International Workshop on New Forms of Reasoning for the Semantic Web: Scalable and Dynamic (NeFoRS2010) (2010)
79. ter Horst, H.J.: Completeness, decidability and complexity of entailment for RDF Schema and a semantic extension involving the OWL vocabulary. J. Web Semant. **3**, 79–115 (2005)
80. Hu, W., Chen, J., Qu, Y.: A self-training approach for resolving object coreference on the Semantic Web. WWW, pp. 87–96 (2011)
81. Huynh, D., Mazzocchi, S., Karger, D.R.: Piggy bank: experience the semantic web inside your web browser. J. Web Semat. **5**(1), 16–27 (2007)
82. Huynh, D.F., Karger, D.: Parallax and companion: set-based browsing for the data web. Available online (2008-12-15) http://davidhuynh.net/media/papers/2009/www2009-parallax.pdf
83. Jiang, X.M., Xue, G.R., Song, W.G., Zeng, H.J., Chen, Z., Ma, W.Y.: Exploiting PageRank at different block level . 5th International Conference on Web Information Systems, pp. 241–252 (2004)
84. Karger, D.R., Bakshi, K., Huynh, D., Quan, D., Sinha, V.: Haystack: a general-purpose information management tool for end users based on semistructured data. CIDR, pp. 13–26 (2005)

85. Kiryakov, A., Ognyanoff, D., Velkov, R., Tashev, Z., Peikov, I.: LDSR: a reason-able view to the web of linked data. Semantic Web Challenge (ISWC2009) (2009)
86. Kleinberg, J.M.: Authoritative sources in a hyperlinked environment. J. ACM **46**(5), 604–632 (1999)
87. Koch, J., Franz, T.: LENA – browsing RDF data more complex than Foaf. International Semantic Web Conference (Posters & Demos) (2008)
88. Kolovski, V., Wu, Z., Eadon, G.: Optimizing enterprise-scale OWL 2 RL reasoning in a relational database system. International Semantic Web Conference (2010)
89. Kotoulas, S., Oren, E., van Harmelen, F.: Mind the data skew: distributed inferencing by speeddating in elastic regions. WWW, pp. 531–540 (2010)
90. Lakshman, A., Malik, P.: Cassandra: a decentralized structured storage system. Operat. Syst. Rev. **44**(2), 35–40 (2010)
91. Lee, H.T., Leonard, D., Wang, X., Loguinov, D.: IRLbot: scaling to 6 billion pages and beyond. ACM Trans. Web **3**(3), 1–34 (2009). DOI http://doi.acm.org/10.1145/1541822. 1541823
92. Lei, Y., Uren, V., Motta, E.: Semsearch: a search engine for the semantic web. 14th International Conference on Knowledge Engineering and Knowledge Management, pp. 238–245 (2006)
93. Liu, B., Hu, B.: HPRD: a high performance RDF database. NPC, pp. 364–374 (2007)
94. Lopez, V., Uren, V.S., Motta, E., Pasin, M.: AquaLog: an ontology-driven question answering system for organizational semantic intranets. J. Web Semat. **5**(2), 72–105 (2007)
95. Manola, F., Miller, E., McBride, B.: RDF Primer. W3C Recommendation (2004). http://www. w3.org/TR/rdf-primer/
96. Meditskos, G., Bassiliades, N.: DLEJena: a practical forward-chaining OWL 2 RL reasoner combining Jena and Pellet. J. Web Semat. **8**(1), 89–94 (2010)
97. Melnik, S., Raghavan, S., Yang, B., Garcia-Molina, H.: Building a distributed full-text index for the web. 10th International World Wide Web Conference, Hong Kong, pp. 396–406 (2001)
98. Michalowski, M., Thakkar, S., Knoblock, C.A.: Exploiting secondary sources for automatic object consolidation. Proceeding of 2003 KDD Workshop on Data Cleaning, Record Linkage, and Object Consolidation (2003)
99. Minack, E., Siberski, W., Nejdl, W.: Benchmarking fulltext search performance of RDF stores. ESWC, pp. 81–95 (2009)
100. Möller, K., Ambrus, O., Josan, L., Handschuh, S.: A visual interface for building SPARQL queries in Konduit. International Semantic Web Conference (Posters & Demos) (2008)
101. Najork, M., Zaragoza, H., Taylor, M.: HITS on the web: how does it compare? Proceedings of the 30th Annual International ACM SIGIR Conference on Research and Development in Information Retrieval, p. 478. ACM, New York (2007)
102. Neumann, T., Weikum, G.: The RDF-3X engine for scalable management of RDF data. VLDB J. **19**(1), 91–113 (2010)
103. Newcombe, H.B., Kennedy, J.M., Axford, S.J., James, A.P.: Automatic linkage of vital records: computers can be used to extract "follow-up" statistics of families from files of routine records. Science **130**, 954–959 (1959)
104. Oren, E., Delbru, R., Catasta, M., Cyganiak, R., Stenzhorn, H., Tummarello, G.: Sindice.com: a document-oriented lookup index for open linked data. Int. J. Metadata Semant. Ontol. **3**(1), 37–52 (2008)
105. Oren, E., Delbru, R., Decker, S.: Extending faceted navigation for RDF data. International Semantic Web Conference, pp. 559–572 (2006)
106. Oren, E., Kotoulas, S., Anadiotis, G., Siebes, R., ten Teije, A., van Harmelen, F.: Marvin: distributed reasoning over large-scale Semantic Web data. J. Web Semat. **7**(4), 305–316 (2009)
107. Page, L., Brin, S., Motwani, R., Winograd, T.: The PageRank citation ranking: bringing order to the web. Technical report, Stanford Digital Library Technologies Project (1998)

108. Pant, G., Srinivasan, P.: Learning to crawl: comparing classification schemes. ACM Trans. Inf. Syst. **23**(4), 430–462 (2005)
109. Pérez-Agüera, J.R., Arroyo, J., Greenberg, J., Iglesias, J.P., Fresno, V.: Using BM25F for semantic search. 3rd International Semantic Search Workshop (SEMSEARCH) (2010)
110. Pietriga, E., Bizer, C., Karger, D.R., Lee, R.: Fresnel: a browser-independent presentation vocabulary for RDF. International Semantic Web Conference, pp. 158–171 (2006)
111. Polleres, A., Hogan, A., Harth, A., Decker, S.: Can we ever catch up with the Web? Semant. Web Interoper. Usabil. Appl. **1** (2010)
112. Prud'hommeaux, E., (eds.), Seaborne, A.: SPARQL query language for RDF. W3C Recommendation (2008). http://www.w3.org/TR/rdf-sparql-query/
113. Quilitz, B., Leser, U.: Querying Distributed RDF Data Sources with SPARQL. ESWC, pp. 524–538 (2008)
114. Raghavan, S., Garcia-Molina, H.: Crawling the hidden web. VLDB, pp. 129–138 (2001)
115. Sabou, M., Baldassarre, C., Gridinoc, L., Angeletou, S., Motta, E., d'Aquin, M., Dzbor, M.: WATSON: a gateway for the semantic web. ESWC 2007 poster session (2007-06)
116. Smith, M.K., Welty, C., McGuinness, D.L.: OWL web ontology language guide. W3C Recommendation (2004). http://www.w3.org/TR/owl-guide/
117. Stonebraker, M.: The case for shared nothing. IEEE Database Eng. Bull. **9**(1), 4–9 (1986)
118. Thelwall, M., Stuart, D.: Web crawling ethics revisited: cost, privacy, and denial of service. J. Am. Soc. Inform. Sci. Technol. **57**, 1771–1779 (2006)
119. Tran, T., Wang, H., Rudolph, S., Cimiano, P.: Top-k exploration of query candidates for efficient keyword search on graph-shaped (RDF) data. ICDE '09: Proceedings of the 2009 IEEE International Conference on Data Engineering, pp. 405–416 (2009). DOI http://dx.doi.org/10.1109/ICDE.2009.119
120. Tummarello, G., Cyganiak, R., Catasta, M., Danielczyk, S., Decker, S.: Sig.ma: live views on the web of data. Semantic Web Challenge (2009)
121. Umbrich, J., Harth, A., Hogan, A., Decker, S.: Four heuristics to guide structured content crawling. Proceedings of the 2008 Eighth international conference on web engineering-Volume 00, pp. 196–202. IEEE Computer Society, Silver Spring, MD (2008)
122. Urbani, J., Kotoulas, S., Maassen, J., van Harmelen, F., Bal, H.E.: OWL reasoning with WebPIE: calculating the closure of 100 Billion Triples. ESWC, vol. 1, pp. 213–227 (2010)
123. Urbani, J., Kotoulas, S., Oren, E., van Harmelen, F.: Scalable distributed reasoning using MapReduce. International Semantic Web Conference (ISWC 2009), vol. 5823, pp. 634–649. Springer, Washington DC, USA (2009)
124. Volz, J., Bizer, C., Gaedke, M., Kobilarov, G.: Discovering and maintaining links on the web of data. International Semantic Web Conference, pp. 650–665 (2009)
125. Wang, T.D., Parsia, B., Hendler, J.A.: A survey of the web ontology landscape. International Semantic Web Conference, pp. 682–694 (2006)
126. Weaver, J., Hendler, J.A.: Parallel materialization of the finite RDFS closure for hundreds of millions of triples. International Semantic Web Conference (ISWC2009), pp. 682–697 (2009)
127. Wei, W., Barnaghi, P.M., Bargiela, A.: Search with meanings: an overview of semantic search systems. Int. J. Commun. SIWN **3**, 76–82 (2008)
128. Weiss, C., Karras, P., Bernstein, A.: Hexastore: sextuple indexing for semantic web data management. PVLDB **1**(1), 1008–1019 (2008)
129. Yee, K.P., Swearingen, K., Li, K., Hearst, M.: Faceted metadata for image search and browsing. SIGCHI Conference on Human factors in Computing Systems, pp. 401–408 (2003). DOI http://doi.acm.org/10.1145/642611.642681

Index

A(k)index, 52
Authoritative reasoning, 396

Bisimulation, 52
    forward and backward, 53
    localized, 52
Bitmap index, 38
BTree, 36, 37

Chase, 257, 262
Chase failure, 277
Class hierarchy, 45
Cluster, 86
Clustered index, 37
Combined complexity, 262
Conceptual dependencies, 266
Conditional entity-centric query, 44, 45
Conjunctive query, 261
Connected component, 90
Crawling, 371

Data cleaning, 221
Data complexity, 255, 262
Data extraction, 349, 353
Dataguide, 52
Data integration, 352, 353, 356, 357
Data quality, 221, 355
Dataspace, 44
Dereferencing, 369
Description logics, 255
Design pattern, 67
DHTML, 177

Dictionary, 35
Disk I/O, 39
Distance-based graph index, 50
DL-Lite, 256, 280

Entity, 43
    association, 45
    attribute, 45
    consolidation, 379
    linkage, 225
    relationship, 255
    resolution, 194
Exhaustivity, 82
Exploratory search, 63

Finite function generation, 276
First-order rewritability, 275, 279
Full-path, 85

Graph, 84
Graph database, 49
GRIN index, 50
gStore, 55

Heterogeneous information, 228
Hexastore, 37
Hidden Markov model, 148
HITS algorithm, 150
Homomorphism, 260
Horizontal representation, 39
hRESTS, 284, 290
Hungarian algorithm, 136

R. De Virgilio et al. (eds.), *Semantic Search over the Web*,
Data-Centric Systems and Applications, DOI 10.1007/978-3-642-25008-8,
© Springer-Verlag Berlin Heidelberg 2012

1-Index, 52
2-Index, 52
Inverted index, 44–47

Jena, 40
Join index, 42

Key dependency, 261
Keyword-based search, 131
Keyword query, 44, 45, 112
Keyword search, 170, 189
KQB, 175
KWilt, 182

Labeled nulls, 260
Linear building, 90
Linkage method, 201
Link discovery, 193
Linked data, 3, 63, 194, 368
Linked Data principles, 285, 293
Linked Data Services, 284, 290
Linked Open Data, 31
Linked Web API, 285
    functional coupling links, 285, 292, 296
    functional similarity links, 285, 292, 295
    I-MASH platform, 300
    Linked Web API Explorer, 301, 302
    Linked Web API model, 291
    Linked Web API Repository, 301
    selection patterns, 297
LinQL, 197
LinQuer, 194
Literal indexing, 41

MapReduce, 370
Matching, 84
Materialized view, 43
Microdata, 3
Microformats, 3
MicroWSMO, 284, 290
Monotonic building, 92
Monotonicity, 94
Munkres algorithm, 137

Negative constraints, 258, 261, 278
Non-conflicting, 268

Object consolidation, 48, 379

Ontology hijacking, 396
Overlap, 82
OWL-S, 284, 289

Parameterizable index graph, 54
Path, 85
Payload, 51
Permutations, 257
P(k) index, 53
PLD starvation, 375
Probabilistic linkage database, 234
Projection index, 37
Property table, 40
Prüfer sequences, 51

Quadruple, 369
Query construction graph, 115
Query guide, 115
Query processing, 402
Query template, 112
QUICK, 110

Ranking, 82, 383
RDF, 81
RDFa, 3
RDF-3X, 37
Reasoner, 389
Relational databases, 35
Resource description framework, 367
Resource identifier, 35
    counter-based, 36
    hash-based, 35
RESTful services, 284, 288–291, 301. *See also*
    Web API

SAWSDL, 289
Scoring function, 87
Search computing, 62, 74
Search process, 66
Semantic Link Discovery, 193
Semantic query expansion, 85
Semantic Web, 255
Semantic Web Services, 284, 288
Semantic wikis, 160
Separability, 257, 267
Set operations, 44
Sindice, 46
SOAP-based Web services, 284, 288
Social web applications, 159
Sound path, 86

Source discovery, 339
SPARQL query, 298
Sparse index, 39
Specificity, 82
Strongly consistent, 278
Structural index, 51, 408
    approximate, 52
    precise, 51
Structural summary. *See* Structural index
Structure index. *See* Structural index
Structured data, 63
Suffix array, 49
System Π, 51

τ-test, 94
Text index, 399
TF-IDF, 400
Threshold, 94
Threshold algorithm, 83
T-index, 52
Top-k, 82
Tree labeling schemes, 49
Triple store. *See* Vertical representation
Tuple-generating dependency, 261

Uncertain data, 356
Uncertainty, 228
Unclustered index, 36

Vertical partitioning, 41
Vertical representation, 36
View-based query answering. *See* Materialized
    view
Virtuoso, 38
Viterbi algorithm, 132
Volatile data, 228
VS-tree, 55

Web API, 284, 288
Web mashup, 284, 290, 300
    semantic mashup, 290
Web of Data, 3
Wrapper, 339–341, 343, 349, 350, 352, 355,
    357
Wrapper inference, 340
WSMO, 284, 289
WSMO-Lite, 284, 290